HUMAN RIGHTS
AND THE ADMINISTRATION OF JUSTICE:
INTERNATIONAL INSTRUMENTS

HUMAN RIGHTS
AND THE ADMINISTRATION OF JUSTICE:
INTERNATIONAL INSTRUMENTS

Edited by
Christopher Gane, Professor of Scots Law and Dean of the
Faculty of Law, University of Aberdeen,
and
Mark Mackarel, Lecturer in Law, University of Dundee

International Bar Association
Human Rights Institute

THE HAGUE – LONDON – BOSTON

Published by
Kluwer Law International
PO Box 85889
2508 CN The Hague
The Netherlands

Kluwer Law International incorporates
the publishing programmes of
Graham & Trotman Ltd
Kluwer Law & Taxation Publishers
and Martinus Nijhoff Publishers

International Bar Association
271 Regent Street
London W1R 7PA
England

Sold and distributed in the USA
and Canada by
Kluwer Law International
675 Massachusetts Avenue
Cambridge MA 02139
USA

In all other countries sold and distributed
by Kluwer Law International
Distribution Centre
PO Box 322
3300 AH Dordrecht
The Netherlands

ISBN 90-411-0696-6
© International Bar Association 1997
First published 1997

British Library Cataloguing in Publication Data
A catalogue record for this book is available from the British Library
Library of Congress Cataloguing-in-Publication Data is available

Typeset in Palatino by BookEns Ltd, Royston, Herts
Printed and bound in Great Britain by Hartnolls Ltd, Bodmin, Cornwall

CONTENTS

PART II

HUMAN RIGHTS AND THE ADMINISTRATION OF JUSTICE

Section One: Crime and Punishment

Chapter 1: Personnel

Chapter 2: The Treatment of Prisoners

CONTENTS

Section Three: Crimes against International Law

Section Four: International Co-operation in Criminal Matters

Chapter 1: Extradition

Chapter 2: Mutual Legal Assistance

CONTENTS

INTERNATIONAL BAR ASSOCIATION
HUMAN RIGHTS INSTITUTE

The International Bar Association (IBA) is the world's foremost international legal organisation with 173 member law societies and bar associations and over 18,000 individual members in 183 countries.

The formation of the IBA's Human Rights Institute in December 1995 was one of the most significant steps taken by the IBA in its worldwide promotion of the rule of law, and the right to live under the rule of law. In its first year of operation the HRI acquired almost 9,000 individual members.

The Human Rights Institute, via its six committees, undertakes investigations into legal systems, recommending change where necessary, and makes representations to the relevant officials when reliable information has been received that lawyers, judges, officials of lawyers' associations or persons involved in the operation of legal systems are jeopardised. The Institute arranges for members of its Trial Observer Corps to observe and report upon legal proceedings where there are grounds for concern that proper standards for the administration of justice may not be met. Regular workshops, conferences and seminars are arranged to provide a forum for the exchange of information and for the education of lawyers and others about issues concerning human rights. The Human Rights Institute maintains close links with United Nations bodies and other international, regional and national organisations with an interest in human rights. Regular newsletters and other publications are produced by the Institute. It is also carrying out a number of comparative surveys.

The HRI has as its objects:

- the promotion, protection and enforcement of human rights under a just rule of law;
- the promotion and protection of the independence of the judiciary and of the legal profession worldwide;
- the worldwide adoption and implementation of standards and instruments regarding human rights accepted and enacted by the community of nations;
- the acquisition and dissemination of information concerning issues related to human rights, judicial independence and the rule of law.

International Bar Association
271 Regent Street
London W1R 7PA
England

INTRODUCTION

INTRODUCTORY NOTE

This section of the book is intended to provide a general introduction to the international protection of human rights. It cannot provide, and is not intended to provide, a detailed analysis of either the substantive law of human rights, or the procedures whereby they are protected. It should, however, provide a general account of the range of human rights currently recognised, and emerging, under international law, and the mechanisms whereby these rights may be enforced.

I. THE LEGAL PROTECTION OF HUMAN RIGHTS

1. HISTORICAL DEVELOPMENT

The idea that people enjoy rights simply by virtue of their humanity has a long history. It may be traced back through the political and legal theories of the natural law philosophers to the *ius naturale* of Roman law and perhaps even beyond that to the philosophy of Ancient Greece.

During the century between the British and French revolutions (1688 to 1789) an important shift of emphasis occurred in relation to natural rights thought. During this period natural rights claims, which had hitherto existed principally as philosophical ideas or political slogans, were translated into propositions which were intended to have the force of law. Thus documents such as the *Bill of Rights* and the *Claim of Right* promulgated by the English and Scottish Parliaments in 1689 contain provisions which would not be out of place in modern human rights charters.[1] A similar development took place in America. The broad natural rights claims set out in the American Declaration of Independence were transformed into legally enforceable claims, through the Constitution and the Bill of Rights. Like the American revolutionaries before them, the French revolutionaries promulgated a statement of their conception of the fundamental rights of man. Known as the *Declaration of the Rights of Man and the Citizen* (1789), this document stated, among

---

[1] Wm. & Mary, Cap. 2: "An Act declaring the Rights and Liberties of the Subject and settling the Succession of the Crown". Article 10 of the Bill of Rights provides, for example, that "excessive bail ought not to be required, nor excessive fines imposed, nor cruel and unusual punishment inflicted". Cf. the Scottish "Declaration of the Estates of the Kingdom of Scotland containing the Claim of Right and the offer of the Crowne to the King and Queen of England", Acts of the Parliaments of Scotland, 1689, Cap. 13, which provides, *inter alia*, "That the Imposeing of extraordinary fynes, The exacting of exorbitant Baile and the disposeing of fynes and forefaulters are Contrary to Law" and "That the Imprisoneing persones without expressing the reason thereof and delaying to put them to tryall is contrary to law". Somewhat less emphatically, the Claim of Rights also provides "That the useing torture without evidence or in ordinary Crymes is Contrary to Law".

other things, that "the aim of every political association is the preservation of the natural and imprescriptible rights of man. These Rights are, Liberty, Property, Safety and Resistance to Oppression".

The philosophies which were influential in the revolutions of 17th- and 18th-century Europe established a number of general precepts which remain influential in modern international human rights systems, at least in relation to civil and political rights. Thus we can see that an individual enjoys rights by virtue of his or her humanity, and not because they are granted to him or her by the law of a state. Rights are regarded as fundamental and inalienable: they cannot be withdrawn or arbitrarily limited by the state.

The communities which promulgated these fine statements of human rights share another feature with many modern states which adhere to the international descendants of the American Declaration and the French Declaration that of a failure to live up to the ideals which they proclaim. The society which proclaimed "Liberty and the pursuit of Happiness" as an "unalienable" right of all men tolerated slavery for nearly a hundred years after those claims were made, and the society which proclaimed "Liberty, Safety and Resistance to Oppression" saw no inconsistency between those ideals and the guillotine.

The revolutions of the 17th and 18th centuries saw natural rights embodied in municipal law. It was not until the middle of the 20th century, however, that the need systematically to promote and protect human rights at the international level was fully recognised.

Legal and political philosophy in the 19th century was not particularly favourable to the development of internationally recognised human rights. The dominant theories of international law placed the interests of the state at centre stage. The individual was not recognised as a subject of international law, and the concept of state sovereignty, so central to traditional international law thought, was profoundly hostile to any suggestion that a state could be called to account for the manner in which it treated its subjects.

Despite this, there were some important developments during the 19th century and the first half of this century. One of the most significant of these was the development of international action against slavery, which led to the declaration in 1864 that "trading in slaves is forbidden in conformity with the principles of international law".[2] The idea of "humanitarian intervention" to prevent massive violations of human rights in the territory of another state also began to take root. Equally important for the protection of individuals from the gross violations of human rights which may arise in time of war was the creation of the International Committee of the Red Cross in 1863. That organisation has sponsored the adoption of various measures intended to mitigate the effects of war on members of the armed forces and non-combatants alike. That work culminated in the adoption in 1949 of the four Geneva Conventions (now supplemented by two additional protocols).

There were also important developments in relation to the social and economic rights of individuals. In 1919 the Treaty of Versailles created the International

---

[2] General Act of the Berlin Conference on Slavery and the Slave Trade.

Labour Organisation, which has been responsible for the development of a system of internationally agreed standards for the protection of workers and their families, the protection of vulnerable groups (such as children) in the labour market, and trade union rights.

There is no doubt, however, that it was the reaction to the grave violations of human rights which occurred during the Second World War, and in certain states prior to the outbreak of war, that brought about a fundamental change in attitude towards the international recognition and protection of human rights. The Charter of the United Nations[3] placed respect for human rights at the centre of its purposes. The preamble to the Charter confirms the determination of the Peoples of the United Nations to "reaffirm faith in fundamental human rights, in the dignity and worth of the human person, in the equal rights of men and women and of nations large and small, and to establish conditions under which justice and respect for the obligations arising from treaties and other sources of international law can be maintained, and to promote social progress and better standards of life in larger freedom".

Respect for human rights was further developed in Article 1 of the Charter, paragraph 3 of which lists, as one of the purposes of the United Nations, the achievement of "international co-operation in solving international problems of an economic, social, cultural, or humanitarian character, and in promoting and encouraging respect for human rights and for fundamental freedoms for all without distinction as to race, sex, language, or religion".

Article 68 of the Charter provided that the Economic and Social Council of the United Nations should set up commissions in economic and social fields "and for the promotion of human rights". The United Nations Human Rights Commission was the first such commission to be established. Its first task was the creation of an "international bill of rights". It was decided by the Commission that this should not, at this early stage of the United Nations, take the form of an internationally binding treaty on human rights, but rather a statement of rights, to be adopted by resolution of the General Assembly, which would provide "a common standard of achievement for all peoples and all nations".[4]

That statement of rights was adopted in 1948 by the United Nations in the form of the Universal Declaration of Human Rights. It was not until 1966 that the United Nations was to adopt two general statements of human rights in the form of international treaties intended to be binding on states which adhered to them: the International Covenant on Civil and Political Rights, and the International Covenant on Economic, Social and Cultural Rights. Since these early developments, the United Nations has gone on to promote a wide range of specialised human rights conventions, particularly in the field of non-discrimination. It has also promoted the adoption of international standards in a wide range of activities, through the adoption of resolutions which encourage states to ensure that their domestic practices, especially in the fields of justice, conform to internationally recognised standards.

---

[3] Charter of the United Nations, signed at San Francisco on 26 June 1945.
[4] Eleanor Roosevelt, Chair of the United Nations Human Rights Commission.

Running in parallel to the United Nations developments, often mirroring them and frequently overlapping with them, has been the development of three regional systems for the protection of human rights. These are systems developed by the Council of Europe, the Organisation of American States and the Organisation for African Unity. (There is currently no such "regional" system for the protection of human rights in Asia or Australasia.) These regional systems have developed in some ways similar to the United Nations, in the sense that they have initially adopted general human rights conventions, followed by a range of special conventions directed towards particular human rights issues.

2. DOMESTIC LAW

Although the documents contained in this book set out "international" standards, and many of them establish international mechanisms of the protection of human rights, it is very important to emphasise that the primary responsibility for the protection and promotion of human rights rests with each individual state, and that the most effective way to secure the protection of human rights is by ensuring that they are protected by municipal law. All of the documents which follow are directed towards that objective either by imposing upon states the obligation to secure the protection of enumerated rights at the domestic level, or by setting out international standards to which municipal law and practice should conform. Indeed, it might fairly be said that the central purpose of the system of international protection of human rights is to bring about such a level of protection of human rights under municipal law that there is no longer any need for international procedures. (There will, however, always be a need for some mechanism whereby the *standards* acceptable to the international community are identified and disseminated.)

3. INTERNATIONAL LAW

International human rights law has developed as a branch of international law, although it has departed both in theory, and in practice, from some of the principal tenets of international law. Today it may be regarded as somewhat *sui generis* in the field of international law. However, its relationship to the main body of international law requires a brief consideration of the general sources of international law, before considering the more particular sources of human rights law.

The principal sources of international law are reflected in the terms of Article 38(1) of the Statute of the International Court of Justice. According to this provision, the Court, when considering cases brought before it, is directed to apply:

(1) international treaties;
(2) international custom, as evidence of a general practice accepted as law;
(3) the general principles of law recognised by civilised nations;

(4) judicial decisions and the teachings of the most highly qualified publicists of the various countries as subsidiary means for the determination of rules of law.[5]

As a relatively recently developed branch of international law, the rules governing the protection of human rights are principally derived from multilateral treaties. This is not to say, however, that general principles of international law are not relevant to the area of human rights. Many international human rights treaties make explicit reference to such principles.[6] Others claim to be no more than the embodiment in a treaty of rules which are recognised by international custom.[7] It may also be that certain rules embodied in international human rights treaties are also recognised by customary international law. It is now widely accepted, for example, that "official" torture is contrary to customary international law (as well as being prohibited by numerous international treaties).[8]

At a much more general level, it has been argued that the Universal Declaration of Human Rights, while not in itself a binding international treaty, is itself a statement of generally recognised principles of international law, and as such is binding on all states.[9] It is unlikely that this position would be generally accepted by states or international bodies. While it is true that many of the principles embodied in the Declaration are recognised as stating internationally protected principles of human rights law, it is clear that it was never intended to be anything more than a statement of principle to which all members of the United Nations should aspire.

---

[5] For an account of the sources of international law, and their relative importance in modern practice, see *Starke's International Law*, 11th edition by I. A. Shearer, Butterworths (1994), Chapter 2, and Ian A Brownlie, *Principles of Public International Law*, 4th edition, Clarendon Press, 1990, Part I.

[6] See, for examples, Article 26 of the European Convention on Human Rights and Article 46(1)(a) of the American Convention on Human Rights both of which refer to "generally recognised rules of international law" in connection with the issue of exhaustion of domestic remedies as a prerequisite to submitting alleged violations of human rights to an international body. See also Article 1 of the First Protocol to the European Convention on Human Rights, and the decision of the European Court of Human Rights in *Lithgow and Others v United Kingdom*, European Court of Human Rights, Series A, No. 102 (1986), considering the extent of a state's obligation according to "general principles of international law" to compensate individuals for the taking of property by the state.

[7] See, for example, the Genocide Convention of 1948, Article 1 of which "confirms" the existence of the crime of genocide (as opposed to creating such a crime).

[8] See, for example, *Filartiga v Peña-Irala*, 630 F 2d 876 (1980).

[9] See, for example, the Proclamation of Teheran (1968), paragraph 2 of which states: "The Universal Declaration of Human Rights states a common understanding of the peoples of the world concerning the inalienable and inviolable rights of all members of the human family and constitutes an obligation for the members of the international community".

4. THE RELATIONSHIP BETWEEN INTERNATIONAL HUMAN RIGHTS LAW AND DOMESTIC LAW

An important consideration in the effective enforcement of international human rights standards is the relationship which exists in any given legal system between international law and domestic law. In some systems it is accepted that there is no separation of international law and domestic law. Both are part of a unified system (and it is frequently accepted in such systems that international law takes precedence over the rules of domestic law). Such systems are said to adopt the *monist* theory of international law. In others the two systems are said to be separate, so that international law is not necessarily part of domestic law. In such a system, it may be necessary to incorporate international law into domestic law, by, for example, a domestic legislative act. Such systems are said to apply the *dualist* theory.

For the effective enforcement of international human rights, it may be of great practical importance which of these two theories a state adopts. In United Kingdom practice it is accepted that a rule of *customary* international law will be applied by domestic courts, at least to the extent that it does not conflict with the terms of United Kingdom legislation or binding judicial decisions[10] and provided it is a rule that is generally accepted by the international community.[11] In contrast, however, rules embodied in an international treaty cannot, in general, be enforced by domestic courts unless and until they have been incorporated into domestic law by an Act of Parliament.[12] This latter rule means that no international human rights treaty to which the United Kingdom is a party may be directly enforced by the courts in any part of the United Kingdom, except to the extent that it has been legislatively incorporated.

Although there are important exceptions,[13] it has not been the practice of the United Kingdom to incorporate human rights treaties into domestic law. However, it has been held that where there is an ambiguity in a United Kingdom statute, a court may, in construing that statute, have regard to the terms of an international treaty as an aid to the interpretation of the treaty, even though the legislation does not incorporate, or even refer to, the treaty. Following this line of approach, the courts have been invited on numerous occasions to have regard to the European Convention on Human Rights when resolving apparent ambiguities in domestic

---

[10] *Chung Chi Cheung v R* [1939] AC 160. See especially Lord Atkin at p. 168.

[11] *Compania Naviera Vascongado v SS Cristina* [1938] AC 485. See especially Lord MacMillan at p. 497. See also *Chung How Ching v R* (1949) 77 CLR 449.

[12] For discussion of these issues, see *Blackburn v Attorney-General* [1971] 1 WLR 1037, *Salomon v Customs and Excise Commissioners* [1967] 2 QB 116, *R v Secretary of State for the Home Department, ex parte Brind* [1991] 1 AC 696.

[13] See, for example, the Genocide Act 1969 (creating the crime of genocide, as defined in the Genocide Convention 1948) and the Criminal Justice Act 1988, s 134 *et seq.* (creating, in response to the United Nations Convention Against Torture and other Cruel Inhuman or Degrading Treatment or Punishment, the offence of torture, and extending the jurisdiction of the United Kingdom courts to try officially sanctioned torture committed in the United Kingdom "or elsewhere").

legislation.[14] It is important, however to emphasise that even this limited approach can only be adopted where there is an ambiguity in the legislation or, at least so far as English practice is concerned, in the common law.[15] Where there is no such ambiguity, then there can be no reference to the international treaty. So, for example, where the United Kingdom legislation clearly conflicts with the United Kingdom's obligations under a treaty such as the European Convention on Human Rights, the courts must give effect to the domestic legislation, notwithstanding the conflict with the international treaty.[16]

So far as concerns customary international law, United States practice is similar to that of the United Kingdom. Rules of customary international law are applied as part of domestic law,[17] although this judicial policy may from time to time be constrained by governmental policy.[18] There is, however, a marked contrast with United Kingdom practice when it comes to the application of treaty-based rules in the domestic courts. Article 6 of the Constitution of the United States provides that "all Treaties made, or which shall be made under the authority of the United States" shall be "the supreme Law of the Land". The apparent breadth of language used in this article is qualified by a distinction drawn by the courts in the United States between treaties which are "self-executing" and those which are not. In American practice, a treaty is "self-executing" if, expressly, or by its nature, it does not require legislation to make it operative at the domestic level. Whether or not a treaty has this effect is to be determined by reference to the intentions of the parties when signing the treaty, and to the general circumstances surrounding the adoption of the treaty.[19] Self-executing treaties are given effect at both federal and state level,[20] even if they are in conflict with prior United States statutes.[21] A self-executing treaty provision cannot, however, prevail over a subsequent act of Congress, the intention of which was clearly to overrule such a treaty provision.

In practical terms these considerations are likely to be much less important in

---

[14] See, for examples, *Brind v Secretary of State for the Home Department, supra,* per Lord Bridge of Harwich at 722j–723a, *R v Chief Immigration Officer, Heathrow Airport, ex parte Salamat Bibi,* [1976] 1 WLR 979, *Ahmad v Inner London Education Authority* [1978] 1 All ER 576 (construing s 30 of the Education Act 1944). Until relatively recently the courts in Scotland refused to follow this approach (see *Surjit Kaur v Lord Advocate,* 1981 SLT 322; *Moore v Secretary of State for Scotland,* 1985 SLT 38) but recent judicial observations suggest a shift to the English position. See *Anderson v HM Adv.,* 1996 SLT 155, Lord Justice-General (Hope) at 159B and *T, Petitioner,* 1996 SCLR 897.

[15] See, for example, *Derbyshire County Council v Times Newspapers Ltd* [1992] QB 770 (Court of Appeal), [1993] AC 534 (House of Lords).

[16] See, for example, *Brogan and Others v UK,* European Court of Human Rights, Series A, No. 145-B (1989) (detention under anti-terrorist legislation in clear conflict with Article 5 of the European Convention on Human Rights).

[17] See, for example, *The Paquete Habana* 175 US 677 (1900).

[18] See, for example, *Pauling v McElroy* 164 Fed Supp 390 (1958). In this case the court refused to restrain the detonating of nuclear devices in the Marshall Islands despite the fact that such detonation conflicted with the customary principle of the freedom of the high seas.

[19] *Sei Fujii v The United States of America* 38 Cal 2d 718 (1952), in which it was held, *inter alia,* that the human rights provisions of the Charter of the United Nations (Articles 55–56, *infra,* document 1) were not self-executing.

[20] *Clark v Allen* 331 US 503 (1947).

[21] *Whitney v Robertson* 124 US 190 (1888).

the case of the United States since the United States has ratified only a very few human rights conventions.[22]

There is a trend among some countries towards the adoption of a rule, generally embodied at the constitutional level, to the effect that international law is to be treated as part of domestic law, and, indeed, that international law takes precedence over domestic law. In some instances it is provided that international law may create rights (and duties) enforceable before the domestic courts, and this is particularly the case in relation to treaties protecting international human rights which are frequently given "direct effect" in domestic law.

The precise effect of these provisions depends, ultimately, upon the terms of domestic constitutional law. So, for example, while Article 25 of the German Constitution provides that general rules of public international law are part of German federal law and take precedence over domestic law, it appears that *treaties* concluded by the Federal Republic do not take precedence over domestic law, nor can fundamental provisions of the Constitution (the "Basic Law") be subordinated to international treaties.[23]

II. GENERAL FEATURES OF INTERNATIONAL HUMAN RIGHTS LAW

There is a quite bewildering list of international agreements protecting and promoting human rights. In finding one's way around this complex body of law, it is useful to bear in mind the following considerations.

1. GLOBAL AND REGIONAL INSTRUMENTS

In the first place, a distinction may be drawn between "global" and "regional" human rights systems. While some human rights instruments are intended to have global application (in the sense that they are open for adoption by all states), some are more geographically limited in their application. So, for example, any member of the United Nations may adhere to the International Covenant on Civil and Political Rights, which was adopted by the United Nations in 1966. In contrast, only states which are members of the Organisation of African Unity may become parties to the African Charter on Human and Peoples' Rights, which adopted by that Organisation in 1981.

Human rights instruments which are intended to have global application are in general promoted by the United Nations, although other organisations, such as the International Committee of the Red Cross and the International Labour Organisation have also made significant contributions at this level. Instruments

---

[22] See, for example, the ratifications listed in (1996) 17 HRLJ 61.
[23] See *International Handelsgesellschaft mbH v Einfür-und Vorratsstelle für Gertreide and Futtermittel* [1972] CMLR 255.

which are regionally based have been promoted by the Council of Europe, the Organisation of African Unity and the Organisation of American States.

2. GENERAL AND SPECIALISED INSTRUMENTS

Equally important are distinctions based on subject matter. It is possible to identify on the one hand a large number of "general" human rights instruments, and on the other a growing number of "specialised" instruments.

A. GENERAL INSTRUMENTS

These documents are general in the sense that they embrace a broad range of human rights, rather than seeking to develop special protection for any particular right, or for any particular group of persons. The United Nations has not adopted a single, general human rights treaty. However, a very broad spectrum of human rights is protected by the combined texts of the International Covenant on Civil and Political Rights and the International Covenant on Economic, Social and Cultural rights, adopted by the United Nations in 1966. At the regional level, one finds the European Convention on Human Rights (1950) and its associated Protocols, the American Convention on Human Rights (1969) and its associated Protocols, and the African Charter on Human and Peoples' Rights (1981).

B. SPECIALISED INSTRUMENTS

Particularly within the framework of the United Nations, a range of human rights instruments have been promoted in order to provide special or additional protection for particular human rights, or the protection of particular categories of individuals.

(a) Slavery and Related Practices

One of the earliest examples of concerted international action to combat a particular form of human rights violation is to be found in the campaign to eliminate slavery and related practices. The Treaty of Paris of 1814, between Britain and France, was the first international instrument to condemn the practice of slavery. Progress towards the abolition of slavery during the 19th century was slow, not least because of the position of the United States, although several states such as Great Britain engaged in unilateral action against the trade. As we have already noted, in 1864 the General Act of the Berlin Conference stated that the slave trade was contrary to international law. Such a declaration did not, of course, bring an end to the trade in slaves. In 1926 the League of Nations adopted an international Convention to Suppress the Slave Trade and Slavery. In 1949 the United Nations adopted the Convention for the Suppression of the Traffic in Persons and of the Exploitation of the Prostitution of Others which was supplemented in 1953 by the Protocol Amending the Slavery Convention of 1926 and in 1956 by the Supplementary Convention on the Abolition of Slavery, the Slave Trade, and Institutions and Practices Similar to Slavery.

(b) Anti-discrimination

The development of a global anti-discrimination policy has been one of the principal achievements of the United Nations in the human rights field. Racial discrimination has been addressed in a number of measures, the most important of which is the International Convention on the Elimination of All Forms of Racial Discrimination of 1966. This was followed in 1973 by the International Convention on the Suppression and Punishment of the Crime of Apartheid. The issue of gender equality has also been addressed, most notably in the International Convention on the Elimination of All Forms of Discrimination against Women (1979).

Although the bulk of anti-discrimination provisions has been developed by the United Nations, some steps have been taken at the regional level. Thus in 1995 the Council of Europe adopted a Framework Convention for the Protection of National Minorities (1995), no doubt reflecting the increased recognition of the vulnerable position of minority groups in that region.

(c) Torture

The fight against the use of torture by states is another important example of the adoption of specialised human rights instruments. The United Nations adopted the Convention Against Torture and other Cruel, Inhuman or Degrading Treatment or Punishment in 1984. In 1985 the Organisation of American States adopted the Inter-American Convention to Prevent and Punish Torture and in 1987 the European Convention for the Prevention of Torture and Inhuman or Degrading Treatment or Punishment was adopted by the Council of Europe.

(d) The Death Penalty

The abolition of the death penalty has likewise been pursued through specialised human rights instruments. This goal has largely been pursued through the adoption of optional protocols to existing general human rights instruments. The first of these was Protocol No. 6 to the European Convention on Human Rights of 1983, which was followed in 1990 by the Second Optional Protocol to the International Covenant on Civil and Political Rights, Aiming at the Abolition of the Death Penalty and the Protocol to the American Convention on Human Rights to Abolish the Death Penalty, also in 1990.

(e) Protection of Vulnerable Groups

A significant amount of effort has been devoted to the protection of vulnerable groups. The first such group to be especially identified by the United Nations was that of refugees, which led to the adoption of the Convention Relating to the Status of Refugees in 1951 and a Protocol Relating to the Status of Refugees in 1967. Little action has been taken at the regional level to address the plight of refugees. A significant exception to this is to be found in the Convention Concerning the Specific Aspects of Refugee Problems in Africa adopted by the Organisation for African Unity in 1969.

One of the most vulnerable groups in any community are children. The need to develop an awareness of this, and to provide special protection for children are recognised in the United Nations Convention on the Rights of the Child, adopted in 1989.

The position of those made vulnerable by learning difficulties and disability has also received some attention in the Declaration on the Rights of Mentally Retarded Persons proclaimed by General Assembly resolution in 1971 and the Declaration on the Rights of Disabled Persons, proclaimed by resolution of the General Assembly in 1975.

(f) Employment and Workers' Rights

The International Labour Organisation has promoted a substantial number of treaties directed towards the protection of workers and workers' organisations, including: the Convention on Freedom of Association and Protection of the Right to Organise (1948), the Convention Concerning the Application of the Principles of the Right to Organise and to Bargain Collectively (1949), the Convention Concerning Employment Policy (1964), and the Convention Concerning Protection and Facilities to be Afforded to Workers' Representatives in the Undertaking (1971). In 1977, the Council of Europe adopted the European Convention on the Legal Status of Migrant Workers.

3. THE "GENERATIONS" OF HUMAN RIGHTS

Internationally protected human rights are sometimes divided into three "generations" of human rights, reflecting in part their historical development, but also the divisions between economic and political camps which, until recently, dominated world politics.

A. FIRST GENERATION: CIVIL AND POLITICAL RIGHTS

The so-called "first generation" human rights comprise those rights which are described as "civil and political rights" These will typically include: the right to life, the right to personal liberty, the right not to be subjected to slavery or servitude, the right not to be subjected to torture or inhuman or degrading treatment or punishment, a range of "due process" rights, including the presumption of innocence, and the right to a fair trial within a reasonable time. The "first generation" rights also include privacy and respect for family life, freedom of expression, freedom of thought, conscience and religion, the right to peaceful assembly and association, and the right to participate in the government of one's country.

B. SECOND GENERATION: ECONOMIC, SOCIAL AND CULTURAL RIGHTS

The "second generation" rights embrace social, economic and cultural rights. As such, it includes the right to social security, the right to an adequate standard of living, the right to food, clothing and housing, the right to be free from hunger,[24] the right to highest attainable standard of physical and mental health, the right to education (at least to primary standard), the right to take part in cultural life of the community and the right to enjoy the benefits of scientific progress and its applications.[25]

C. THIRD GENERATION: COLLECTIVE OR PEOPLES' RIGHTS

This category of rights is said to embrace such rights as the Right to self-determination, the right to development,[26] the right to equality of all peoples, the right to existence, the right of colonised peoples to freedom,[27] the right to all peoples to freely dispose of their wealth and natural resources, the right to international peace and security[28] and the right to a satisfactory environment.

D. COMPARING THE THREE GENERATIONS

There are some important differences between these different "generations" of rights. The most obvious of these is, of course, the content of the rights claimed, since these differ materially in what is to be protected, and, indeed, how the rights claimed are to be protected. "First generation" rights are, generally speaking, expressed in such a way as to require the state to refrain from interfering in the exercise of these rights by the individual. The right to freedom of expression, or to freedom of association, are essentially claims that the state should not limit such activities by the individual. There are occasional exceptions. In some cases rights which may appear to be couched in terms which demand non-interference by the state have been interpreted as imposing upon the state a positive obligation to act. So, for example, it has been held by the European Court of Human Rights that Article 8 of the European Convention on Human Rights (which protects the right to respect for private and family life) imposes an obligation on the state not only to refrain from interfering with the privacy of the individual, but, in certain circumstances, to take positive steps to protect the individual's right to privacy.[29]

---

[24] The United Nations Universal Declaration on the Eradication of Hunger and Malnutrition, adopted on 16 November 1974 by the World Food Conference convened under General Assembly resolution 3180 (XXVIII) of 17 December 1973, and endorsed by General Assembly resolution 3348 (XXIX) of 17 December 1974.

[25] See, for example, the United Nations Declaration on the Use of Scientific and Technological Progress in the Interests of Peace and for the Benefit of Mankind, proclaimed by General Assembly resolution 3384 (XXX) of 10 November 1975 and the United Nations Declaration of the Principles of International Cultural Co-operation, proclaimed by the General Conference of the United Nations Educational, Scientific and Cultural Organisation at its 14th session on 4 November 1966.

[26] See the United Nations Declaration on the Right to Development, adopted by General Assembly resolution 41/128 of 4 December 1986.

[27] See, for example, the United Nations Declaration on the Granting of Independence to Colonial Countries and Peoples, adopted by General Assembly 1514 (XV) on 14 December 1960.

[28] See, for example, United Nations Declaration on the Right of Peoples to Peace, approved by General Assembly resolution 39/11 of 12 November 1984.

[29] *X and Y v Netherlands*, European Court of Human Rights, Series A, No. 142 (1986).

By contrast, economic, social and cultural rights are very much demands that the state take positive action in support of the individual. Such rights seek to impose upon the state the obligation to adopt measures which will positively support the individual by securing certain basic standards of social security, education and health care. As such they are necessarily linked to the capacity of the state to make such provision, and it is not uncommon to see such rights expressly limited to the economic capacity of the country.[30] It also seems to be accepted that such claims to positive economic support by the state are less amenable to enforcement by the individual. Certainly, if one looks at the enforcement mechanisms established in the major economic, social and cultural rights conventions, the capacity of the individual to take legal action to secure the rights set out in those documents is much more limited than the opportunities for enforcement of first generation rights.

"Third generation" rights present further distinctions. In the first place, in contrast to the first and second generation rights, the concern of which is to protect the rights of the individual, third generation rights are concerned with "group" or "collective" rights. This can clearly be seen, for example, in the African Charter on Human and Peoples' Rights which, as its title indicates, seeks to protect the rights not only of individuals, but of "peoples". Article 2 of the Charter states that "Every individual shall be entitled to the enjoyment of the rights and freedoms recognised in the present Charter without distinction of any kind ..." and in line with this provision, Articles 3 to 17 set out a (fairly typical) range of rights which are to be enjoyed by the individual. Article 18 identifies certain categories of individuals who are seen to be deserving of special protection. These include women and children, the aged and the disabled. Articles 19 to 23 identify a number of rights enjoyed not by individuals, or by groups of individuals, but by "all peoples". Thus Article 21(1) provides that "All peoples shall freely dispose of their wealth and natural resources. This right shall be exercised in the exclusive interest of the people. In no case shall a people be deprived of it."

Similar language is to be found in the United Nations Declaration on Social Progress and Development proclaimed by the General Assembly in 1969.[31] Article 1 of the Declaration states:

"All peoples and all human beings, without distinction as to race, colour, sex, language, religion, nationality, ethnic origin, family or social status, or political or other conviction, shall have the right to live in dignity and freedom and to enjoy the fruits of social progress and should, on their part, contribute to it".

Two problems have been identified in relation to these "third generation" rights.

The first stems from the idea that where an individual claims a right, this will generally imply that there is a correlative duty not to interfere with the exercise of

---

[30] See, for example, Article 1 of the Additional Protocol to the American Convention on Human Rights in the Area of Economic, Social and Cultural Rights (Protocol of San Salvador).
[31] General Assembly Resolution 2542 (XXIV), 11 December 1969.

that right, or even to support the exercise of that right. In ordinary contractual terms, for example, that rights of all parties to the contract are based on corresponding duties on the part of all other parties to the contract. In human rights terms, individual rights are generally rights claimed against the state. They are claims that the state shall not interfere with the exercise of individual freedoms (this is typically the case in relation to the so-called first-generation civil and political rights), or that the state shall positively support the individual in some respect (this is typically the case with regard to second-generation economic, social and cultural rights where the claim is for the satisfaction of basic needs such as health care, housing and education).

In the case of third generation or peoples' rights, although the right is claimed by "all peoples", it is less clear who owes any correlative duty. This is particularly the case where the claim is for a right, the fulfilment of which, is not within the competence of the state of which the people in question form a part. Thus, for example, Article 23 of the African Charter states that "All peoples shall have the right to national and international peace and security". This is clearly not a claim directed at any state in particular. Rather it appears to be a claim made on behalf of all peoples, and in respect of all other peoples, or at least those who are parties to the Charter (although the obligation to maintain international peace and security is one which more broadly derives from the terms of the Charter of the United Nations). In some instances, however, the "duty" element of the equation is more explicitly set out. Thus Article 22(2) of the African Charter provides that it is "States ... individual or collectively" who have the duty of ensuring the exercise of the "right to development" provided for in Article 22(1).

The United Nations Declaration on Social Progress and Development[32] attempts a compromise between the responsibility of the state and the responsibility of other agencies in the promotion of social progress and development by providing in Article 8 that "Each government has the primary role and ultimate responsibility of ensuring the social progress and well-being of its people" while also providing in Article 9 that "social progress and development are the common concerns of the international community" which is expected to "supplement, by concerted international action, national efforts to raise the living standards of peoples".

The second significant problem identified in relation to collective rights is that there is no clear consensus about what rights are recognised by the international community. Particular difficulties have been expressed in relation to the "right to development". This is a right which is proclaimed in Article 22 of the African Charter, paragraph (1) of which provides that "All peoples shall have the right to their economic, social and cultural development with due regard to their freedom and identity and in the equal enjoyment of the common heritage of mankind". Although there is growing support for the right to development being included in an international convention, and the United Nations has adopted a "Declaration on the Right to Development",[33] critics of this notion have pointed out that the claimed right to development is without substance. Economic, social and cultural

[32] Above.
[33] Above.

development may be a vehicle by which other rights (such as education, social security and health care) are achieved, but it is not a "right" in itself. Alternatively, "development" may be an objective which can be achieved by securing other rights (especially but not exclusively economic, social and cultural rights), but it is not in itself a right, and claims for an enforceable right to development do little to advance the condition of those who would benefit from such development.

There are, however, certain "third generation" rights which are firmly established in the rhetoric of international human rights, and, indeed, in international conventions which have been widely adopted. The best-known example is the right to self-determination. This is a right which has been claimed by political leaders and national independence movements for over one hundred years, and is set out as the first of the rights enshrined by the International Covenant on Civil and Political Rights and the International Covenant on Economic, Social and Cultural Rights, Article 1(1) of which states, in both cases, that "All peoples have the right of self-determination".

The legal and political recognition given to this right does, to some degree at least, challenge the views of those who would deny the existence of a right to development. It is possible to argue that if "peoples", as opposed to individuals, have rights, then the right to development may be seen as the economic or social correlative of the right to self-determination, which is regarded as a civil or political right.

4. THE HUMAN RIGHTS PECKING ORDER

The heading of this subsection may seem flippant, but it raises three important questions: (a) the relationship of human rights law to other areas of international law, (b) the relationship of human rights norms to each other, and (c) the issue of "absolute" and "qualified" human rights.

A. RELATIONSHIP OF INTERNATIONAL HUMAN RIGHTS LAW TO OTHER AREAS OF INTERNATIONAL LAW

The central question here is whether the international human rights obligations of a state take precedence over other international law obligations. According to traditional international legal theory, there is no reason why this should be so. However, there are clear indications of an emerging doctrine that at least some human rights obligations take precedence over other international legal obligations. The clearest examples of this are to be found in cases where a person facing deportation or extradition claims that the human rights obligations of the requested state prohibit his return. Thus in the cases of *Soering v United Kingdom*[34] and *Short v Netherlands*[35] it was held, by the European Court of Human Rights and the Dutch Supreme Court respectively, that the obligations imposed on

---

[34] European Court of Human Rights, Series A, No 161; 11 EHRR 439.
[35] 29 International Legal Materials 1378 (1990).

the respondent states by the European Convention on Human Rights took precedence over the states' obligations to deliver offenders under extradition or analogous procedures. So, for example, a state (such as the Netherlands) which has ratified the Sixth Protocol to the European Convention on Human Rights, cannot extradite a fugitive to face a capital charge in another state.

B. THE RELATIONSHIP OF HUMAN RIGHTS NORMS TO EACH OTHER

One of the problems which the classification of rights discussed above reflects is that of "prioritisation" of human rights. Are some rights more important than others, or can it be said that human rights are indivisible? Can some rights be set aside or suspended in order to make sure that others (regarded as more important) are secured? If one has regard to the historical development of human rights thought, and in particular to its expression in international instruments, then it is clear that, historically at least, there has been a clear tendency to separate civil and political rights on the one hand, from social, economic and cultural rights on the other, and that this has been accompanied by a clear prioritisation of the former over the latter. To a large extent this has reflected the political differences which divided the United Nations as the world emerged from global war to cold war in the late 1940s, and which persisted until the establishment of the democracy movement in the late 1980s.

Interestingly, this division, and consequent separation, of first and second generation rights is not so clearly reflected in the Universal Declaration of Human Rights. When that Declaration was adopted by the United Nations in 1948, it contained, in addition to an extensive list of civil and political rights, whose presence is entirely predictable, the main social, economic and cultural rights, including the right to social security,[36] the right to work,[37] the right to an adequate standard of living (including the right to food, clothing, housing, medical care and necessary social services),[38] the right to education[39] and the right to participate freely in the cultural life of the community.[40] The Universal Declaration was the first international instrument to refer to the right to rest and leisure as including the right to periodical holidays with pay.[41]

The Universal Declaration is, however, unusual in its integrated approach to the establishment of human rights. This is in part explained by the political compromises which lay behind the adoption of its provisions by the General Assembly, and in part by the legal status of the Declaration. The Declaration was seen at the time as being no more than that a declaration of rights providing a "common standard of achievement for all peoples and nations".[42] It was never intended to be an enforceable charter of human rights, and consequently it was

---

[36] Article 22.
[37] Article 23.
[38] Article 25.
[39] Article 26.
[40] Article 27.
[41] Article 24.
[42] Universal Declaration of Human Rights, preamble.

easier for states to accept it as a statement of broad principle, rather than a document which they could be compelled, whether by individual action or at the instance of other states, to observe within their own territory.

When the United Nations did eventually promulgate a list of enforceable human rights standards, a very sharp distinction was drawn between first and second generation rights, both in the manner in which these rights were set out, and in the mechanisms adopted for their enforcement. In 1966 the United Nations promulgated two international human rights conventions: the International Covenant on Civil and Political Rights and the International Covenant on Economic, Social and Cultural Rights. The lack of an integrated approach to the recognition and protection of human rights can be seen not only in the fact that the rights were separated out into two different conventions, but also in the fact that there was no link made between the two. States were free to accept one set of rights with no obligation to recognise the other. Furthermore, the arrangements within the two conventions for the enforcement of the rights which they enshrined were markedly different.

The International Covenant on Civil and Political Rights provides for a triple system of enforcement of the rights which it sets out. Part IV of the Covenant established a Human Rights Committee. Under Article 40 of the Covenant, states undertake to submit to the Committee, reports on the measures they have adopted in order to give effect to the rights recognised in the Covenant, and on the progress they have made in the enjoyment of those rights. Such reports are submitted within a year of a state becoming bound by the Covenant and thereafter whenever the Committee so requests.[43] Under Article 41 of the Covenant, states may declare that they recognise the competence of the Committee to receive and consider communications from a state party to the effect that another state party is not fulfilling its obligations under the Covenant. Finally, under Article 1 of the (First) Optional Protocol to the Covenant, a state party to the Covenant which adopts the Protocol recognises the competence of the Committee to receive and consider communications for individuals claiming to be victims of a violation by that state of any of the rights set out in the Covenant. There is, therefore, a threefold system of enforcement: supervision by the Human Rights Committee, which is an obligatory feature of the Covenant; inter-state complaint to the Committee; individual complaint to the Committee. The first of these is an obligatory feature of the system, the second two are optional.

In marked contrast, the International Covenant on Economic, Social and Cultural Rights contains no system of inter-state or individual enforcement. The extent to which states are prepared to abide by their obligations under the Economic, Social and Cultural Rights Covenant is dependent entirely upon a system of state reports to the Secretary-General of the United Nations and through that office to the Economic and Social Council of the United Nations.

This separation of civil and political rights is reflected at regional level. Thus while the Council of Europe adopted the European Convention on Human Rights, which is essentially concerned with the protection of civil and political rights, in

[43] International Covenant on Civil and Political Rights, Article 40(1)(a) and (b).

1950, it was not until 1961 that the same body adopted the European Social Charter. Even when the Council included the "right to education" in the First Protocol to the Convention in 1952, this was expressed in terms which linked it closely to the exercise of other civil and political rights, and expressed it in the negative proposition that "no person shall be denied the right to education", rather than as a positive affirmation of the state's obligation to provide education. The gulf in enforcement procedures between the European Convention on Human Rights and the European Social Charter has been, until recently, at least as great as that embodied in the United Nations Covenants of 1966. However, in 1996, the Council of Europe adopted a Protocol amending the European Social Charter to provide for a system of collective complaints, which may be seen as a significant step in strengthening the system of enforcement provided for in the Charter.

The same pattern was adopted in the Americas. The Organisation of American States adopted the American Convention on Human Rights in 1969. The Convention establishes an elaborate enforcement system, including the obligatory recognition of the right of individual complaint to the Inter-American Commission on Human Rights. However, the Convention is, with one exception, entirely devoted to the protection of civil and political rights. That exception is to be found in Article 26 which imposed upon states the obligation to adopt measures directed towards the "full realisation of the rights implicit in the economic, social, educational, scientific, and cultural standards set forth in the Charter of the Organisation of American States". Those steps were not, however, enshrined in an enforceable convention until the OAS adopted the Additional Protocol to the American Convention on Human Rights in the Area of Economic, Social and Cultural Rights in 1988. In general, the enforcement of the rights set out in the Additional Protocol is left to a system of periodic reports by the states of the measures they have taken to ensure respect for the rights set out in the Protocol. However, in what may be a significant development, and one which may provide a model for other human rights systems, Article 6 of the Protocol provides that under certain conditions, state violations of the right of workers to organise trade unions and to join the union of their choice under Article 8(a) of the Protocol, and the right to education enshrined in Article 13, may be enforced through the system of individual complaint to the Inter-American Commission on Human Rights, and the Inter-American Court of Human Rights established by the American Convention on Human Rights.

C. "ABSOLUTE" AND "QUALIFIED" HUMAN RIGHTS

A very obvious feature of all general human rights instruments is that they recognise, at least implicitly, that some human rights are deserving of a higher degree of protection than others. If one looks, for example, at the terms in which the prohibition on torture and related practices is expressed in the European Convention on Human Rights (Article 3), the American Convention on Human Rights (Article 5(2)), the African Charter on Human and Peoples' Rights (Article 5) and the International Covenant on Civil and Political Rights (Article 7), it is clear that all of these documents impose an absolute prohibition on such practices. No qualifications of, or exceptions to, the prohibition are envisaged by these provisions. Similarly, the provisions of the European Convention, the American Convention and the International Covenant which permit derogation from, or suspension of, the rights protected by each of these documents do not apply to the prohibition on torture or inhuman or degrading treatment or punishment.[44] The right to life, freedom from slavery, and protection from *ex post facto* criminal laws are accorded the same degree of protection in the European Convention, the American Convention, the International Covenant and the African Charter.[45]

By way of contrast, many, if not most, of the rights set out in these conventions are subject to qualifications and general derogation in times of war or other public emergency which threatens the life of the nation.[46] Similarly, there is a pattern of qualification of many human rights. So, for example, the freedom to manifest one's religion or beliefs is made subject to "such limitations as are prescribed by law and are necessary to protect public safety, order, health or morals and the fundamental rights and freedoms of others".[47] Similarly, freedom of expression is generally made subject to restrictions necessary "for respect of the rights or reputations of others" or "for the protection of national security or *ordre public* or of public health or morals".[48]

The formulation of human rights in these terms reflects a fundamental assumption in all of the conventions under discussion, namely that, subject to certain limited exceptions, individual rights cannot be demanded in absolute terms. Many individual rights may only be recognised and protected to the extent that their exercise does not infringe the rights of others. Indeed, Article 27(2) of the African Charter on Human and Peoples' Rights expressly provides that "The rights and freedoms of each individual shall be exercised with due regard to the rights of others, collective security, morality and common interest". In other words, the rights protected may be "fundamental" but they are not, in general, "absolute".

---

[44] European Convention, Article 15(2), American Convention, Article 27(2), International Covenant, Article 4(2). The African Charter contains no such general provision.

[45] *Ibid.* The African Charter, as noted, contains no general derogation provision. The protection of the right to life, freedom from slavery and protection from *ex post facto* criminal laws are all expressed in terms which are as "absolute" as those of the other conventions. See Articles 4, 5 and 7(2) of the African Charter.

[46] International Covenant on Civil and Political Rights, Article 4(1), European Convention on Human Rights, Article 15(1), American Convention on Human Rights, Article 27(1). See also European Social Charter, Article 30. Neither the International Covenant on Social, Economic and Cultural Rights (*infra*, Document 5), nor the First Protocol to the American Convention on Human Rights in the Area of Economic, Social and Cultural Rights (*infra*, Document 21) contains any such general derogation provision.

[47] International Covenant on Civil and Political Rights, Article 18(3). Cf. European Convention on Human Rights, Article 9(2), American Convention on Human Rights, Article 12(3). The African Charter provides that "No one may, subject to law and order, be submitted to measures restricting the exercise of these freedoms".

[48] International Covenant on Civil and Political Rights, Article 19(3). Cf. European Convention on Human Rights, Article 10(2) which imposes a broader range of restrictions, and the American Convention on Human Rights, Article 13(2) and (3), which permits the censorship of public entertainments "for the moral protection of childhood and adolescence". The restrictions recognised by the African Charter are potentially very wide. Article 9(2) provides that "Every individual shall have the right to express and disseminate his opinions within the law". The Charter places no limits upon the restrictions which may be imposed "within the law".

This general structure is reinforced by provisions to the effect that nothing in the convention "may be interpreted as implying for any State, group or person any right to engage in any activity or perform any act aimed at the destruction of any of the rights and freedoms" recognised therein.[49]

5. CULTURAL DIVERSITY AND HUMAN RIGHTS

Paragraph 5 of the Vienna Declaration refers to the need for states to bear in mind "historical, cultural and religious backgrounds" when securing compliance with internationally agreed human rights standards. This raises an important issue in the process of securing such compliance. The criticism has been levelled, particularly at western politicians and lawyers, that insufficient attention is paid to the question of cultural diversity, not only when determining international human rights standards, but also when reaching judgments as to whether or not a country is complying with those standards. Practices which western opinion might regard as violations of human rights will not necessarily be so regarded in countries which adopt different religious or ethical codes. This has been a particular problem in relation to the observance of human rights in those countries which apply religiously based laws, such as the *Shariah* law applied in several Middle Eastern and African states. One particular example is the use of punishments such as flogging or the amputation of hands or feet, and stoning to death.

Punishments of this order are carried out in compliance with the religious laws of many Islamic countries. But such punishments would undoubtedly be regarded as serious violations of international human rights standards. Thus amputations undoubtedly violate the prohibition on cruel and inhuman punishments to be found in all general international human rights documents. Judicially imposed corporal punishment has been held by at least one international human rights court necessarily to violate the prohibition on inhuman and degrading punishment.[50] And while the death penalty itself is not yet generally regarded as a violation of international human rights,[51] the manner in which it is carried out may clearly violate internationally agreed standards.

Is it correct, however, to condemn such actions, based as they are on religious precepts strongly adhered to by many millions of believers? Although the view is frequently expressed that to do so is to impose upon one group the cultural norms and legal standards of another, it may equally be argued that if human rights are truly universal and indivisible, then there must be some limits to what may be carried out in the name of culture, history or religion.

---

[49] International Covenant, Article 5(1). Cf. European Convention, Article 17, American Convention, Article 29. There is no equivalent provision in the African Charter.

[50] See *Tyrer v United Kingdom*, European Court of Human Rights, Series A No. 26 (1979) (considering Article 3 of the European Convention on Human Rights).

[51] At least in the sense of violating the right to life. See, for example, *Soering v United Kingdom*, European Court of Human Rights, Series A, No. 161 (1989).

6. THE "INTEGRATED APPROACH" TO HUMAN RIGHTS

Despite these fairly marked differences in approach to the protection of different categories of rights, it has, for some time, been the received wisdom, both within the United Nations, and among academic commentators, that the effective protection of human rights requires an "integrated approach". According to this view, human rights cannot be effectively protected unless *all* human rights are protected. This view was very clearly expressed in the Proclamation of Teheran, adopted by a United Nations international conference on human rights held at Teheran in May 1968. Paragraph 13 of the Proclamation stated:

"Since human rights and fundamental freedoms are indivisible, the full realisation of civil and political rights without the enjoyment of economic, social and cultural rights is impossible. The achievement of lasting progress in the implementation of human rights is dependent upon sound and effective national and international policies of economic and social development."

It is clearly implied in this paragraph that the Conference favoured greater emphasis on the protection of economic, social and cultural rights. While it is undoubtedly the case that for many years international action directed towards the protection of human rights has prioritised the protection of civil and political rights, it is equally the case that in certain countries, and within certain political regimes, the view was put forward that in order to secure progress on the economic and social fronts, it was both necessary and acceptable to curtail the exercise of certain civil and political rights. According to this theory, there was little point in securing such rights as freedom of expression, and freedom of assembly if people were so pre-occupied with the problems of mere existence that they could not take full advantage of those rights and, indeed, the exercise of such rights, particularly in the form of political opposition to governmental policies, might well hinder economic and social progress. Such a thesis was not uncommonly put forward by African political leaders in the difficult years following the granting of independence in many African states. It is, of course, a view which can lead to the denial of basic human rights, and which can be invoked by the most authoritarian of regimes.

It is interesting to note, therefore, that in the Vienna Declaration and Programme of Action issued following the Vienna World Conference on Human Rights in 1993 that a more balanced and more genuinely integrated approach has been adopted by the United Nations. Article 5 of the Declaration states:

"All human rights are universal, indivisible and interdependent and interrelated. The international community must treat human rights globally in a fair and equal manner, on the same footing, and with the same emphasis. While the significance of national and regional particularities and various historical, cultural and religious backgrounds must be borne in mind, it is the duty of States, regardless of their political, economic and cultural systems, to promote and protect all human rights and fundamental freedoms."

III. ENFORCEMENT OF HUMAN RIGHTS: AN OVERVIEW

Although the vast number of international human rights instruments which have been adopted since 1945 differ significantly in the range of rights protected, broadly speaking there is a much greater degree of uniformity in the approach adopted towards the question of securing compliance with the standards which they lay down. These can be divided, broadly, into (a) reporting mechanisms, and (b) international adjudication. This section examines, in outline, the first approach, and then, in rather more detail, the principal systems for international adjudication, concentrating on the procedures available under the Optional Protocol to the International Covenant on Civil and Political Rights, the European Convention on Human Rights, the American Convention on Human Rights and the African Charter on Human and Peoples' Rights.

1. REPORTING MECHANISMS

All human rights documents are directed towards the establishment of minimum international standards, and it is the expectation that states which adopt these standards will abide by their obligations to ensure that that these standards are met at the domestic level. In order to ensure that these standards are being met, many international instruments establish procedures whereby states may report (generally to a body established by the relevant treaty) on the extent to which their domestic law and procedures comply with the standards laid down, what steps they are taking to ensure that necessary changes are made, and any difficulties or obstacles encountered in securing compliance with the international standard. Such reports will generally be required within a specified period of the state adhering to the convention, and thereafter on a periodic basis. In some instances *ad hoc* reports may be required of a state.[52]

Such mechanisms depend, very largely, on states accepting their obligations, and taking the appropriate initiatives. It is the universal experience of states in matters of human rights, however, that from time to time even the most conscientious of states will fail to abide by the standards to which it has submitted itself. Requiring states to report on such matters may be sufficient to ensure that steps are taken to remedy the deficiency in compliance, but many human rights instruments recognise that there will be a need for a more direct method of securing compliance. A state may reject the allegation that it is not abiding by the obligations imposed by the treaty, or it may simply hope that the problem will be ignored by the international community. In such cases it may be necessary to resort to a form of international adjudication, and, indeed, this has been one of the central features of international human rights law since the model was set by the European Convention on Human Rights in 1950.

---

[52] See, for example, the procedures established under Article 40 *et seq.* of the International Covenant on Civil and Political Rights.

2. ADJUDICATION OF HUMAN RIGHTS DISPUTES

Resort to a process of adjudication raises a number of issues, such as: Who may raise a complaint? Against whom can a complaint be directed? Which body is competent to determine the issues? What procedural rules must be satisfied before a complaint may be heard? What options are there for enforcement of international human rights decisions? The answers given to these questions necessarily vary in detail from system to system, but there is a surprising degree of consistency of approach between the systems under consideration.

A. COMPETENCE

Most of these questions are usually considered under the general head of "competence", which itself is usually divided into three sub-issues: competence with regard to the complainer and the respondent (competence *"ratione personae"*); competence with regard to the subject matter (competence *"ratione materiae"*); competence with regard to time (competence *"ratione temporis"*); and competence with regard to place (competence *"ratione loci"*).

(a) Competence *ratione personae*

(i) Who may bring a complaint?

International human rights conventions which provide for a system of adjudication will typically recognise two types of complainer: the individual and a state party to the convention.

Inter-state complaints
The International Covenant on Civil and Political Rights, and the European Convention on Human Rights, at least in principle, give a degree of primacy to inter-state complaints. This can be seen most clearly in the fact that both make the possibility of an inter-state complaint an obligatory feature of the treaty, while the individual complaint procedure is optional. Indeed, in the International Covenant on Civil and Political Rights scheme, the provision for individual complaint to the Human Rights Committee of the United Nations is not even contained in the main convention but is relegated to an optional Additional Protocol. In the case of the European Convention on Human Rights, Article 25 of the Convention provides that the European Commission on Human Rights may only receive complaints from individuals concerning a state party if the respondent state has "declared that it recognises the competence of the Commission to receive" such complaints. Article 25(2) further allows a state to recognise the right of individual complaint for a specific period.

The African Charter, while not making such an overt distinction between inter-state complaints and individual complaints, nevertheless appears to give priority to the former. Where a state brings a complaint about the conduct of another state it has the right to submit the matter to the African Commission on Human and Peoples' Rights, where the matter is not settled to the satisfaction of the two states concerned.[53] In marked contrast to this "communications" submitted to the Commission other than those of State parties will only be heard if a (simple) majority of the members of the Commission so decide,[54] and only subject to a number of conditions which do not apply to inter-state applications.[55]

The Organisation of American States takes a quite different approach, and makes individual complaint a compulsory feature of the American Convention on Human Rights, while inter-state complaint is available as an option.[56]

These differences of approach are in part a function of the historical development of human rights thinking, and in part the political environment in which the various systems operate. The European Convention on Human Rights was adopted at a time when mainstream thinking about international law barely recognised the individual as a subject of international law, and the idea of an individual brining a state before an international tribunal of any sort was a radical departure from traditional theories about the relationship between the individual and the state. To have made the procedure for individual complaint a compulsory feature of the system would have discouraged many states from adhering to the convention at all. This was particularly true for those European countries which had substantial colonial interests. The parties to the Convention undertook to secure the rights defined in the Convention to everyone within their jurisdiction, including colonial and dependent territories. To extend the right of individual complaint to those territories would have exposed states such as Belgium, France and the United Kingdom to a level of justified complaint that would have overwhelmed the Convention institutions.

In practice, the system of inter-state application has not been very much used. Not surprisingly, states are unwilling to cast stones at their neighbours from the relative insecurity of their own glass-houses. So, for example, under the European system there have been fewer than 20 inter-state complaints brought before the Commission, and of these only one *Ireland v United Kingdom*[57] has reached the European Court of Human Rights. By way of contrast, it is worth noting that since the Convention came into operation, there have been more than 28,000 individual complaints lodged with the Commission.

Individual complaint

Rather different approaches are to be found in the conventions under consideration to the question of who may initiate a complaint. Both the International Covenant on Civil and Political Rights and the European Convention on Human Rights require that a complainer must be in a position to "claim" to be a "victim of a violation" by the respondent state of the rights set out in the Convention. These terms appear at first sight to be somewhat restrictive. They appear to suggest, for example, that an individual cannot bring a complaint unless he or she, personally, has suffered a violation of their rights. In practice, such terms are rather more

---

[53] African Charter on Human and Peoples' Rights, Article 48.
[54] African Charter on Human and Peoples' Rights, Article 55.
[55] African Charter on Human and Peoples' Rights, Article 56.
[56] American Convention on Human Rights, Articles 44 and 45.
[57] European Court of Human Rights, Series A, No. 25 (1978).

expansively interpreted. So, for example, in a sequence of cases, the European Court of Human Rights has construed Article 25 so as to allow individuals to bring complaints before the European Commission on Human Rights if they can show that they, as an individual, or as a member of a group or class of individuals, are "at risk" of suffering a violation of their rights, or are "directly affected" by the national measures which are in violation of the Convention, even though they are not in a position to show that those measures have actually been applied to them.[58] So, for example, where a group of German lawyers suspected that secret measures of state surveillance had been applied to them in breach of Article 8 of the European Convention on Human Rights, the European Court of Human Rights held that they could claim to be victims of a violation within the meaning of Article 25 of the Convention without having to prove that the measures had been applied to them. To require proof that the measures had been applied in fact would, in the view of the Court, have undermined the protective effect of the Convention (since all that the respondent state would have had to do to thwart any complaint would have been to ensure the absolute secrecy of their methods of surveillance).

The requirement that the applicant be in a position to claim to be a victim does not always mean that applications on behalf of third parties are excluded. So, for example, parents may bring complaints on behalf of their children and the families of deceased persons may initiate, or continue, complaints on behalf of persons now deceased.[59]

However, the requirement that the complainer be in a position to claim to be a victim of a violation does mean that complaints cannot be brought by persons on behalf of third parties unless they have a close personal relationship with them. In particular, it means that non-governmental organisations (such as Amnesty International) cannot initiate a complaint under either the European Convention on Human Rights or the International Covenant on Civil and Political Rights unless they are complaining about an alleged violation of their *own* rights.

It is worth contrasting this position with the quite different approach adopted under the American Convention on Human Rights. Article 44 of that Convention provides:

"Any person or group of persons, or any non-governmental entity legally recognised in one or more member States of the Organisation [of American States] may lodge petitions with the [Inter-American] Commission on Human Rights containing denunciations or complaints of violation of this Convention by a State Party."

Not only does this provision make it clear that "third-party" complaints are

---

[58] *Klass and Others v FRG*, European Court of Human Rights, Series A, No. 28 (1978), *Dudgeon v United Kingdom*, European Court of Human Rights, Series A, No. 45 (1981), *Norris v Ireland*, European Court of Human Rights, Series A, No. 142 (1988).

[59] See, for example, *Enslinn, Baader and Raspe v FRG*, Applications 7572/76, 7586/76 and 7587/76, 14 D&R 64 (1979), (European Commission on Human Rights), *Amerkane v United Kingdom*, Application 5691/72, 44 CD 101 (1974), (European Commission on Human Rights).

fully competent under the American Convention, but it also makes it clear that such "denunciations or complaints" need not be initiated by individuals located within a state which is a party to the Convention. So, for example, a large number of petitions have been lodged with the Commission by human rights organisations based in the United States which, although it is a member of the Organisation of American States, is not a party to the American Convention on Human Rights.

(ii) Against whom may a complaint be taken?

In all cases, the respondent in an international human rights adjudication will be a state which has allegedly violated one or other of the protected rights. In other words, the international system is not intended to resolve disputes between individuals. So, for example, where an applicant complained to the European Commission on Human Rights that his employer's action in dismissing him from his job allegedly for his trade union activities violated, *inter alia*, Articles 9 and 11 of the European Convention on Human Rights, the Commission, noting that the applicant's employer was a private commercial undertaking, held that it was not competent to receive the complaint.[60]

However, "the state" does not violate human rights without the intervention of some human agency, and it is clear that the state must be held responsible for the actions of its own agents and organs the courts, the police, the armed services, civil servants, etc when they violate human rights. That responsibility attaches to the state in respect of the actions of any person exercising an official function on the part of the state, "even at the lowest level, without express authorisation and even outside or against instructions".[61]

In this connection, it is worth noting that a state cannot evade responsibility by arguing that it was unaware of practices within its jurisdiction which violate human rights. So, for example, in *Ireland v United Kingdom*,[62] in the context of physical and mental abuse of suspects by the police and military, the European Court of Human Rights was at pains to point out that that it was "inconceivable that the higher authorities of a State should be, or at least should be entitled to be, unaware of the existence" of such practices. In the same case it was stated that the state authorities are "strictly liable" for the conduct of the subordinates, in the sense that they are "under a duty to impose their will on subordinates, and cannot shelter behind their inability to ensure that it is respected".[63]

---

[60] *Application 10182/82 v Spain*, (1984) 6 EHRR 145. But see, also, *Young, James and Webster v United Kingdom*, European Court of Human Rights, Series A, No. 44 (1981). In that case the Court held that the United Kingdom could be held responsible for a violation of Article 11 by permitting dismissal from employment for refusing to join a trade union.

[61] *Ireland v United Kingdom*, Report of the European Commission on Human Rights, 1976 YB, 512 at 758.

[62] Above.

[63] *Judgment*, para. 159.

(b) Competence *ratione materiae*

Not every allegation of a violation of human rights may be brought under these international procedures. The conventions mentioned above only provide remedies where a right guaranteed by the Convention itself has been violated, or the terms of the Convention have otherwise been breached.[64] This may at first sight seem obvious, but it can give rise to difficult questions of whether or not an alleged right is actually protected by the convention. There is, for example, a substantial case-law of the European Commission on Human Rights discussing whether or not alleged violations of human rights do indeed concern violations of the Convention. So, for example, the Commission has examined the question whether the Convention guarantees, as such, the right to asylum, the right to work, or the right to social assistance from the state.[65] Whether or not a right is protected will, necessarily, depend upon the terms of each individual convention and the interpretation placed upon those terms by the bodies charged with the enforcement of the convention rights.

(c) Competence *ratione temporis*

A state cannot be held responsible for violations of human rights occurring before the relevant treaty has entered into force, or before the state has ratified the treaty. An interesting question arises where a state ratifies the relevant convention, but, where this is permitted, does not contemporaneously recognise the right of individual application (as is possible, for example, in the case of the European Convention on Human Rights). Generally the state will make clear in any declaration it makes recognising the right of individual application that this right applies only to cases arising after the declaration is made. If, however, the declaration is silent on this point, then it has been held that the state may be held responsible for any violation occurring after the date of ratification.[66]

(d) Competence *ratione loci*

The majority of the general conventions, when determining the extent of the states obligations make reference to persons within or subject to the "jurisdiction" of the state.[67] It is important to understand, however, that the "jurisdiction" of a state in this context refers not so much to the place where the violation occurs, "but rather to the relationship between the individual and the State" in relation to

---

[64] International Covenant on Civil and Political Rights, Article 41, Protocol, Article 1; European Convention on Human Rights, Articles 24, 25; American Convention on Human Rights, Article 44; African Charter on Human and Peoples' Rights, Articles 47, 49.

[65] See, respectively, *K and W v Netherlands*, Application 11278/84, 43 D&R 216 (1985), *X v Denmark*, Application 6907/75, 3 D&R 153 (1975) and *Andersson and Kullman v Sweden*, Application 11776/85, 46 D&R 251 (1986).

[66] See, for example, *X v France*, Application 9587/81, 29 D&R 228 (1982).

[67] European Convention on Human Rights, Article 1; American Convention on Human Rights, Article 1, International Covenant on Civil and Political Rights, Article 2. There is no equivalent limitation in the African Charter.

the alleged violation of human rights.[68] The term "jurisdiction" is not restricted to the national territory of a contracting state. The responsibility of the state can be involved because of the acts of their authorities, whether performed within or outside national boundaries, which produce effects outside their own territory.[69]

B. PROCEDURAL CONSIDERATIONS

Applications to international tribunals are generally subjected to a number of procedural conditions. These are designed in part to ensure that the system is not abused, to ensure that the applications are timely, and to ensure that the possibilities of securing a remedy at the domestic level have been properly explored before there is recourse to the international system of adjudication.

(a) Time Limits

The European Convention on Human Rights and the American Convention on Human Rights all contain a six-month time limit. Article 24 of the European Convention on Human Rights provides that the Commission may only deal with a complaint if it is submitted within a period of six months from the date on which the final decision was taken at the domestic level. Article 46(1)(c) of the American Convention is couched in very similar terms. The time limit in both cases applies to both individual and inter-state complaints. The African Charter on Human and Peoples' Rights is rather more generous. The Charter contains no time limit in respect of inter-state complaints, although it does subject "other communications" under Article 55 of the Charter to a requirement of submission "within a reasonable period from the time when local remedies are exhausted or from the date the Commission is seized of the matter". There is no time limit for complaints under the Optional Protocol to the International Covenant on Civil and Political Rights. Although a suggestion was raised that such a time limit be inserted in the Committee's Rules of Procedure, this was not done. The advantage that this presents is that where a complaint could be brought either before the Committee or one of the regional systems, for example, the complaint may be pursued before the Human Rights Committee, even although it would be time-barred under the European Convention on Human Rights or the American Convention on Human Rights.

(b) Exhaustion of Domestic Remedies

All systems of international adjudication contain a requirement that the international body can only deal with the complaint after all domestic remedies have been exhausted.[70] The rule is based upon the principle that, before being

---

[68] *Celiberti de Casariego v Uruguay* United Nations Human Rights Committee, Communication No. 56/1979, para 10.2.

[69] *Loizidou v Turkey*, European Court of Human Rights, Series A No 310 (1995).

[70] International Covenant on Civil and Political Rights, Article 41(1)(c) (inter-state procedure), Optional Protocol, Article 5(2)(b) (individual complaint), European Convention on Human Rights, Article 26, American Convention on Human Rights, Article 46(1)(a), African Charter on Human and Peoples' Rights, Article 50 (inter-state complaint) and Article 55(5).

subject to a process of international investigation and adjudication, the respondent state must have an opportunity to redress the wrong alleged to have been done to the individual, within the framework of its own domestic legal system.[71] The rule requires the exhaustion of all legal remedies available under domestic law, provided that these are capable of providing an effective and sufficient means of redressing the alleged wrongs which are the subject of the complaint. Remedies which do not in reality offer any chance of redress need not be pursued, but the mere fact that success at the domestic level is doubtful does not mean that an applicant need not pursue a given remedy. If, on the other hand, it is clear that the supposed domestic remedy offers no reasonable prospect of success, then it need not be pursued. Since the rule requiring exhaustion of domestic remedies is one which operates in favour of the respondent state, there would appear to be no objection to its being waived by that state.[72] But since the objection that domestic remedies have not been exhausted is one which can only be taken by the respondent state, the United Nations Human Rights Committee has taken the view that if the respondent state disputes the contention that domestic remedies have been exhausted, it is for the respondent state to give details of the remedies which are allegedly available and effective at the domestic level.[73] In the case of *Bazzano v Uruguay* the respondent government sought to discharge this burden by providing the texts of applicable domestic laws and procedures, but it was held that this was insufficient. The state was obliged to provide evidence of the extent to which these remedies were available and effective in practice in practice.[74]

The African Charter on Human and Peoples' Rights, the American Convention on Human Rights and the International Covenant on Civil and Political Rights all make explicit reference to the situation where achieving domestic remedies would be unduly delayed or prolonged.[75] There is no such express provision in the European Convention on Human Rights, but it is thought that where there was excessive or undue delay in achieving a remedy at the domestic level then this would not be regarded as an "effective" remedy.

(c) Anonymous or Abusive Petitions

The relevant international body may refuse to accept a complaint which is

---

[71] See, for example, the opinion of the European Commission on Human Rights in *Nielsen v Denmark*, 343/57, 2 YB 412.
[72] See, for examples of these points, *De Wilde, Ooms and Versyp v Belgium (No.1)*, European Court of Human Rights, Series A, No. 12 (1970), *Stogmüller v Austria*, European Court of Human Rights, Series A, No. 9 (1969), *Airey v Ireland*, European Court of Human Rights, Series A, No. 32 (1979), *Van Oosterwijck v Belgium*, European Court of Human Rights, Series A, No. 40 (1980).
[73] United Nations Document A/33/40.
[74] *Ibid.*, Annex A, para 4.
[75] International Covenant on Civil and Political Rights, Article 41(1)(c) (inter-state applications), Protocol, Article 5(2); American Convention on Human Rights, Article 46(2)(c); African Charter on Human and Peoples' Rights, Article 50 (inter-state communications), Article 56(5) (other communications).

anonymous or which is submitted in abusive terms, or which otherwise constitute an abuse of the right of petition.[76]

(d) Cases already under Consideration by Another International System

It is generally not possible to submit a case to one international system when it has already been submitted for consideration by another international body. So, for example, Article 5(2)(a) of the Protocol to the International Covenant on Civil and Political Rights provides that a communication shall not be considered by the Human Rights Committee unless it has ascertained that the same matter is not being examined under another procedure of international investigation or settlement. Article 27(2)(b) of the European Convention on Human Rights provides that the Commission shall not deal with any individual application which is "substantially the same as a matter which has already been examined by the Commission or had already been submitted to another procedure of international investigation or settlement and if it contains no relevant new information".

C. THE COMPETENT ORGANS

As we have already noted, each of the above systems has its own organs competent to receive complaints from individuals concerning violations of human rights. In the case of the International Covenant on Civil and Political Rights, this is the United Nations Human Rights Committee, which was created by the International Covenant. Article 1 of the first Optional Protocol to the Covenant provides that a state party to the Covenant that becomes a party to the present Protocol recognises the competence of the Committee to receive and consider communications from individuals subject to its jurisdiction who claim to be victims of a violation by that state party of any of the rights set forth in the Covenant. No communication may be received by the Committee if it concerns a state party to the Covenant which is not a party to the present Protocol. Article 2 of the protocol provides that, subject to the provisions of Article 1, individuals who claim that any of their rights enumerated in the Covenant have been violated and who have exhausted all available domestic remedies may submit a written communication to the Committee for consideration. The Committee is the only body which exercises functions under this Protocol. Its decisions are final, and not subject to review by any other international body.

In the case of the European Convention on Human Rights, Article 19 of the Convention provides that to ensure the observance of the engagements undertaken by the High Contracting Parties in the present Convention, there shall be set up a European Commission of Human Rights and a European Court of Human Rights. The procedure is initiated by an individual complaint being

---

[76] International Covenant on Civil and Political Rights, Article 41, Protocol, Article 3; European Convention on Human Rights, Article 27(1)(a), 27(2); American Convention on Human Rights, Article 46(1)(d), 47(a); African Charter on Human and Peoples' Rights, Article 56(1) and (3) (other communications under Article 55. The African Charter insists that the author of the communication be identified, even if he or she requests anonymity: Article 56(1).

presented to the Commission under Article 25 of the Convention. The Commission was intended to act as a filter, to ensure that the Court was not required to examine every alleged violation of the Convention. The eleventh protocol to the Convention contains provisions which will radically change the nature of the enforcement procedure under the Convention. When those procedures are implemented, the existing Commission and Court will be abolished to be replaced by a new court of human rights, to which individuals will have direct access, without the interposition of the Human Rights Commission.

The structure of the American Convention procedures is very similar to that of the European Convention. Under Article 44 of the Convention, any person or group of persons, or any non-governmental entity legally recognised in one or more member States of the Organisation, may lodge petitions with the Commission containing denunciations or complaints of violation of this Convention by a State Party. Article 61 of the Convention reveals the limited access to the Inter-American Court of Human Rights. Only the States Parties and the Commission have the right to submit a case to the Court.

So far as concerns the African Charter, Article 30 provides for the creation of an African Commission on Human Peoples' Rights to promote human and peoples' rights and ensure their protection in Africa. Article 47 of the Charter provide that one state may draw to the attention of the Commission alleged violations of the Charter by another state. It does not, however, explicitly refer to individual complaints. Rather it provides, in Article 55, for "other communications". These clearly include complaints by individuals, but the individual is given no right of direct access to the Commission. Instead, Article 55 provides that before each session, the Secretary of the Commission shall make a list of such "other communications" and transmit them to the members of the Commission. Whether or not such a communication is considered by the Commission is within the discretion of the Commission, although Article 55(2) provides that a communication shall be considered by the Commission if a simple majority of its members so decide.

D. REMEDIES FOR HUMAN RIGHTS VIOLATIONS

The remedies which can be granted for human rights violations vary according to the terms of the relevant treaty. In the vast majority of cases the only real remedy lies in the fact that an international body has upheld the applicant's claim that his or her rights have been violated. In certain circumstances, however, limited monetary compensation may be awarded by an international court. So for example, the European Court of Human Rights is empowered to award "just satisfaction" which may include financial compensation for the injury suffered by the applicant, and legal costs.

PART I

THE GENERAL FRAMEWORK FOR THE INTERNATIONAL PROTECTION OF HUMAN RIGHTS

SECTION ONE

THE UNITED NATIONS

1. THE HUMAN RIGHTS PROVISIONS OF THE CHARTER OF THE UNITED NATIONS

Signed at San Francisco: 26 June 1945

Entry into force: 24 October 1945

We the Peoples of the United Nations

Determined to save succeeding generations from the scourge of war, which twice in our lifetime has brought untold sorrow to mankind, and
to reaffirm faith in fundamental human rights, in the dignity and worth of the human person, in the equal rights of men and women and of nations large and small, and
to establish conditions under which justice and respect for the obligations arising from treaties and other sources of international law can be maintained, and
to promote social progress and better standards of life in larger freedom,
And for these ends to practice tolerance and live together in peace with one another as good neighbours, and
to unite our strength to maintain international peace and security, and
to ensure by the acceptance of principles and the institution of methods, that armed force shall not be used, save in the common interest, and
to employ international machinery for the promotion of the economic and social advancement of all peoples,
Have resolved to combine our efforts to accomplish these aims. Accordingly, our respective Governments, through representatives assembled in the city of San Francisco, who have exhibited their full powers found to be in good and due form, have agreed to the present Charter of the United Nations and do hereby establish an international organization to be known as the United Nations.

CHAPTER I
PURPOSES AND PRINCIPLES

Article 1

The Purposes of the United Nations are:

1. To maintain international peace and security, and to that end: to take effective collective measures for the prevention and removal of threats to the peace, and for the suppression of acts of aggression or other breaches of the peace, and to bring about by peaceful means, and in conformity with the principles of justice and international law, adjustment or settlement of international disputes or situations which might lead to a breach of the peace;
2. To develop friendly relations among nations based on respect for the principle of equal rights and self-determination of peoples, and to take other appropriate measures to strengthen universal peace;

3. To achieve international co-operation in solving international problems of an economic, social, cultural, or humanitarian character, and in promoting and encouraging respect for human rights and for fundamental freedoms for all without distinction as to race, sex, language, or religion; and
4. To be a centre for harmonising the actions of nations in the attainment of these common ends.

Article 2

The organization and its Members, in pursuit of the Purposes stated in Article 1, shall act in accordance with the following Principles.

1. The organization is based on the principle of the sovereign equality of all its Members.
2. All Members, in order to ensure to all of them the rights and benefits resulting from membership, shall fulfil in good faith the obligations assumed by them in accordance with the present Chapter.
3. All Members shall settle their international disputes by peaceful means in such a manner that international peace and security, and justice, are not endangered.
4. All Members shall refrain in their international relations from the threat or use of force against the territorial integrity or political independence of any state, or in any other manner inconsistent with the Purposes of the United Nations.
5. All Members shall give the United Nations every assistance in any action it takes in accordance with the present Charter, and shall refrain from giving assistance to any state against which the United Nations is taking preventive or enforcement action.
6. The Organization shall ensure that states which are not Members of the United Nations act in accordance with these Principles so far as may be necessary for the maintenance of international peace and security.
7. Nothing contained in the present Charter shall authorise the United Nations to intervene in matters which are essentially within the domestic jurisdiction of any state or shall require the Members to submit such matters to settlement under the present Charter; but this principle shall not prejudice the application of enforcement measures under Chapter VII.

CHAPTER II
MEMBERSHIP

Article 3

The original Members of the United Nations shall be the states which, having participated in the United Nations Conference on International Organization at San Francisco, or having previously signed the Declaration by United Nations of 1 January 1942, sign the present Chapter and ratify it in accordance with Article 110.

Article 4

1. Membership in the United Nations is open to all other peace-loving states which accept the obligations contained in the present Charter and, in the judgement of the Organization, are able and willing to carry out these obligations.
2. The admission of any such state to membership in the United Nations will be effected by a decision of the General Assembly upon the recommendation of the Security Council.

Article 5

A Member of the United Nations against which preventive or enforcement action has been taken by the Security Council may be suspended from the exercise of the right and privileges of membership by the General Assembly upon the recommendation of the Security Council. The exercise of these rights and privileges may be restored by the Security Council.

Article 6

A Member of the United Nations which has persistently violated the Principles contained in the present Charter may be expelled from the Organization by the General Assembly upon the recommendation of the Security Council.

CHAPTER III
ORGANS

Article 7

1. There are established as the principal organs of the United Nations: a General Assembly, a Security Council, an Economic and Social Council, a Trusteeship Council, an International Court of Justice, and a Secretariat.
2. Such subsidiary organs as may be found necessary may be established in accordance with the present Charter.

Article 8

The United Nations shall place no restrictions on the eligibility of men and women to participate in any capacity and under conditions of equality in its principal and subsidiary organs.

CHAPTER IV
THE GENERAL ASSEMBLY

Article 9

1. The General Assembly shall consist of all the Members of the United Nations.
2. Each Member shall have not more than five representatives in the General Assembly.

Article 10

The General Assembly may discuss any questions or any matters within the scope of the present Charter or relating to the powers and functions of any organs provided for in the present Charter, and, except as provided in Article 12, may make recommendations to the Members of the United Nations or to the Security Council or to both on any such questions or matters.

Article 11

1. The General Assembly may consider the general principles of co-operation in the maintenance of international peace and security, including the principles governing disarmament and the regulation of armaments, and may make recommendations with regard to such principles to the Members or to the Security Council or to both.
2. The General Assembly may discuss any questions relating to the maintenance of international peace and security brought before it by any Member of the United Nations, or by the Security Council, or by a state which is not a Member of the United Nations in Accordance with Article 35, paragraph 2, and, except as provided in Article 12, may make recommendations with regard to any such question to the state or states concerned or to the Security Council or to both. Any such question on which action is necessary shall be referred to the Security Council by the General Assembly either before or after discussion.
3. The General Assembly may call the attention of the Security Council to situations which are likely to endanger international peace and security.
4. The powers of the General Assembly set forth in this Article shall not limit the general scope of Article 10.

Article 12

1. While the Security Council is exercising in respect of any dispute or situation the functions assigned to it in the present Charter, the General Assembly shall not make any recommendation with regard to that dispute or situation unless the Security Council so requests.
2. The Secretary-General, with the consent of the Security Council, small notify the General Assembly at each session of any matters relative to the maintenance of international peace and security which are being dealt with by the Security Council and shall similarly notify the General Assembly, or the Members of the United Nations if the General Assembly is not in session, immediately the Security Council ceases to deal with such matters.

Article 13

1. The General Assembly shall initiate studies and make recommendations for the purpose of:

(a) promoting international co-operation in the political field and encouraging the progressive development of international law and its codification;

(b) promoting international co-operation in the economic, social, cultural, educational, and health fields, and assisting in the realisation of human rights and fundamental freedoms for all without distinction as a race, sex, language, or religion.

2. The further responsibilities, functions and powers of the General Assembly with respect to matters mentioned in paragraph 1(b) above are set forth in Chapters IX and X.

Article 14

Subject to the provisions of Article 12, the General Assembly may recommend measures for the peaceful adjustment of any situation, regardless of origin, which it deems likely to impair the general welfare or friendly relations among nations, including situations resulting from a violation of the provisions of the present Charter setting forth the Purposes and Principles of the United Nations.

CHAPTER IX
INTERNATIONAL ECONOMIC AND SOCIAL CO-OPERATION

Article 55

With a view to the creation of conditions of stability and well-being which are necessary for peaceful and friendly relations among nations based on respect for the principle of equal rights and self-determination of people, the United Nations shall promote:

(a) higher standards of living, full employment, and conditions of economic and social progress and development;

(b) solutions of international economic, social, health, and related problems; and international cultural and educational co-operation; and

(c) universal respect for, and observance of, human rights and fundamental freedoms for all without distinction as to race, sex, language, or religion.

Article 56

All Members pledge themselves to take joint and separate action in co-operation with the Organization for the achievement of the purposes set forth in Article 55.

CHAPTER X
THE ECONOMIC AND SOCIAL COUNCIL

Article 61

1. The Economic and Social Council shall consist of fifty-four Members of the United Nations elected by the General Assembly.

2. Subject to the provisions of paragraph 3, eighteen members of the Economic and Social Council shall be elected each year for a term of three years. A retiring member shall be eligible for immediate re-election...
4. Each member of the Economic and Social Council shall have one representative.

Article 62

1. The Economic and Social Council may make or initiate studies and reports with respect to international economic, social, cultural, educational, health, and related matters and may make recommendations with respect to any such matters to the General Assembly, to the Members of the United Nations, and to the specialised agencies concerned.
2. It may make recommendations for the purpose of promoting respect for, and observance of, human rights and fundamental freedoms for all.
3. It may prepare draft conventions for submission to the General Assembly, with respect to matters falling within its competence.
4. It may call, in accordance with the rules prescribed by the United Nations, international conferences on matters falling within its competence.

Article 65

The Economic and Social Council may furnish information to the Security Council and shall assist the Security Council upon its request.

Article 66

1. The Economic and Social Council shall perform such functions as fall within its competence in connexion with the carrying out of the recommendations of the General Assembly.
2. It may, with the approval of the General Assembly, perform services at the request of Members of the United Nations and at the request of specialised agencies.
3. It shall perform such other functions as are specified elsewhere in the present Charter or as may be assigned to it by the General Assembly.

Article 68

The Economic and Social Council shall set up Commissions in economic and social fields and for the promotion of human rights, and such other commissions as may be required for the performance of its functions.

2. UNIVERSAL DECLARATION OF HUMAN RIGHTS

Adopted and Proclaimed by the General Assembly: 10 December 1948

PREAMBLE

Whereas recognition of the inherent dignity and of the equal and inalienable rights of all members of the human family is the foundation of freedom, justice and peace in the world,

Whereas disregard and contempt for human rights have resulted in barbarous acts which have outraged the conscience of mankind, and the advent of a world in which human beings shall enjoy freedom of speech and believe and freedom from fear and want has been proclaimed as the highest aspiration of the common people,

Whereas it is essential, if man is not to be compelled to have recourse, as a last resort, to rebellion against tyranny and oppression, that human rights should be protected by the rule of law,

Whereas it is essential to promote the development of friendly relations between nations,

Whereas the peoples of the United Nations have in the Charter reaffirmed their faith in fundamental human rights, in the dignity and worth of the human person and in the equal rights of men and women and have determined to promote social progress and better standards of life in larger freedom,

Whereas Member States have pledged themselves to achieve, in co-operation with the United Nations, the promotion of universal respect for and observance of human rights and fundamental freedoms,

Whereas a common understanding of these rights and freedoms is of the greatest importance for the full realisation of this pledge,

Now, therefore,

The General Assembly

Proclaims this Universal Declaration of Human Rights as a common standard of achievement for all peoples and all nations, to the end that every individual and every organ of society, keeping this Declaration constantly in mind, shall strive by teaching and education to promote respect for these rights and freedoms and by progressive measures, national and international, to secure their universal and effective recognition and observance, both among the peoples of Member States themselves and among the peoples of territories under their jurisdiction.

Article 1

All human beings are born free and equal in dignity and rights. They are endowed with reason and conscience and should act towards one another in a spirit of brotherhood.

11

Article 2

Everyone is entitled to all the rights and freedoms set forth in this Declaration, without distinction of any kind, such as race, colour, sex, language, religion, political or other opinion, national or social origin, property, birth or other status. Furthermore, no distinction shall be made on the basis of the political, jurisdictional or international status of the country or territory to which a person belongs, whether it be independent, trust, non-self-governing or under any other limitation of sovereignty.

Article 3

Everyone has the right to life, liberty and security of person.

Article 4

No one shall be held in slavery or servitude, slavery and the slave trade shall be prohibited in all of their forms.

Article 5

No one shall be subject to torture or to cruel, inhuman or degrading treatment or punishment.

Article 6

Everyone has the right to recognition everywhere as a person before the law.

Article 7

All are equal before the law and are entitled without any discrimination to equal protection of the law. All are entitled to equal protection against any discrimination in violation of this Declaration and against any incitement to such discrimination.

Article 8

Everyone has the right to an effective remedy by the competent national tribunals for acts violating the fundamental rights granted him by the constitution or by law.

Article 9

No one shall be subjected to arbitrary arrest, detention or exile.

Article 10

Everyone is entitled to full equality to a fair and public hearing by an independent and impartial tribunal, in the determination of his rights and obligations and of any criminal charge against him.

Article 11

1. Everyone charged with a penal offence has the right to be presumed innocent until proved guilty according to law in a public trial at which he has had all the guarantees necessary for his defence.
2. No one shall be held guilty of any penal offence on account of any act or omission which did not constitute a penal offence, under national or international law, at the time when it was committed. Nor shall a heavier penalty be imposed than the one that was applicable at the time the penal offence was committed.

Article 12

No one shall be subjected to arbitrary interference with his privacy, family, home or correspondence, nor to attacks upon his honour and reputation. Everyone has the right to the protection of the law against such interference or attacks.

Article 13

1. Everyone has the right to freedom and movement and residence within the borders of each State.
2. Everyone has the right to leave any country, including his own, and to return to his country.

Article 14

1. Everyone has the right to seek and to enjoy in other countries asylum from persecution.
2. This right may not be invoked in the case of prosecutions genuinely arising from non-political crimes or from acts contrary to the purposes and principles of the United Nations.

Article 15

1. Everyone has the right to a nationality.
2. No one shall be arbitrarily deprived of his nationality nor denied the right to change his nationality.

Article 16

1. Men and women of full age, without any limitation due to race, nationality or religion, have the right to marry and to found a family. They are entitled to equal rights as to marriage, during marriage and at its dissolution.
2. Marriage shall be entered into only with the free and full consent of the intending spouses.
3. The family is the natural and fundamental group unit of society and is entitled to protection by society and the State.

Article 17

1. Everyone has the right to own property alone as well as in association with others.
2. No one shall be arbitrarily deprived of his property.

Article 18

Everyone has the right to freedom of thought, conscience and religion; this right includes freedom to change his religion or belief, and freedom, either alone or in community with others and in public or private, to manifest his religion or belief in teaching, practice, worship and observance.

Article 19

Everyone has the right to freedom of opinion and expression; this right includes freedom to hold opinions without interference and to seek, receive and impart information and ideas through any media and regardless of frontiers.

Article 20

1. Everyone has the right to freedom of peaceful assembly and association.
2. No one may be compelled to belong to an association.

Article 21

1. Everyone has the right to take part in the government of his country, directly or through freely chosen representatives.
2. Everyone has the right to equal access to public service in his country.
3. The will of the people shall be the basis of the authority of government; this will shall be expressed in periodic and genuine elections which shall be by universal and equal suffrage and shall be held by secret vote or by equivalent free voting procedures.

Article 22

Everyone, as a member of society, has the right to social security and is entitled to realisation, through national effort and international co-operation and in accordance with the organisation and resources of each State, of the economic, social and cultural rights indispensable for his dignity and the free development of his personality.

Article 23

1. Everyone has the right to work, to free choice of employment, to just and favourable conditions of work and to protection against unemployment.
2. Everyone, without any discrimination, has the right to equal pay for equal work.
3. Everyone who works has the right to just and favourable remuneration ensuring for himself and his family an existence worthy of human dignity, and supplemented, if necessary, by other means of social protection.
4. Everyone has the right to form and to join trade unions for the protection of his interests.

Article 24

Everyone has the right to rest and leisure, including reasonable limitation of working hours and periodic holidays with pay.

Article 25

1. Everyone has the right to a standard of living adequate for the health and well-being of himself and of his family, including food, clothing, housing and medical care and necessary social services, and the right to security in the event of unemployment, sickness, disability, widowhood, old age or other lack of livelihood in circumstances beyond his control.
2. Motherhood and childhood are entitled to special care and assistance. All children, whether born in or out of wedlock, shall enjoy the same social protection.

Article 26

1. Everyone has the right to education. Education shall be free, at least in the elementary and fundamental stages. Elementary education shall be compulsory. Technical and professional education shall be made generally available and higher education shall be equally accessible to all on the basis of merit.
2. Education shall be directed to the full development of the human personality and to the strengthening of respect for human rights and fundamental freedoms. It shall promote understanding, tolerance and friendship among all nations, racial or religious groups, and shall further the activities of the United Nations for the maintenance of peace.
3. Parents have a prior right to choose the kind of education that shall be given to their children.

Article 27

1. Everyone has the right freely to participate in the cultural life of the community, to enjoy the arts and to share in scientific advancement and its benefits.
2. Everyone has the right to the protection of the moral and material interests resulting from any scientific, literary or artistic production of which he is the author.

Article 28

Everyone is entitled to a social and international order in which the rights and freedoms set forth in this Declaration can be fully realised.

Article 29

1. Everyone has duties to the community in which alone the free and full development of his personality is possible.
2. In the exercise of his rights and freedoms, everyone shall be subject only to such limitations as are determined by law solely for the purpose of securing due recognition and respect for the rights and freedoms of other and of meeting the just requirements of morality, public order and the general welfare in a democratic society.
3. These rights and freedoms may in no case be exercised contrary to the purposes and principles of the United Nations.

Article 30

Nothing in this Declaration may be interpreted as implying for any State, group or person any right to engage in any activity or to perform any act aimed at the destruction of any of the rights and freedoms set forth herein.

3. INTERNATIONAL COVENANT ON CIVIL AND POLITICAL RIGHTS

Adopted and Opened for Signature, Ratification and Accession by General Assembly resolution 2200 A (XXI) of 16 December 1966

Entry into force: 23 March 1976, in accordance with Article 49

PREAMBLE

The States Parties to the present Covenant,

Considering that, in accordance with the principles proclaimed in the Charter of the United Nations, recognition of the inherent dignity and of the equal and inalienable rights of all members of the human family is the foundation of freedom, justice and peace in the world,

Recognizing that these rights derive from the inherent dignity of the human person,

Recognizing that, in accordance with the Universal Declaration of Human Rights, the ideal of free human beings enjoying civil and political freedom and freedom from fear and want can only be achieved if conditions are created whereby everyone may enjoy his civil and political rights, as well as his economic, social and cultural rights,

Considering the obligation of States under the Charter of the United Nations to promote universal respect for, and observance of, human rights and freedoms,

Realizing that the individual, having duties to other individuals and to the community to which he belongs, is under a responsibility to strive for the promotion and observance of the rights recognized in the present Covenant,

Agree upon the following articles:

PART I

Article 1

1. All peoples have the right of self-determination. By virtue of that right they freely determine their political status and freely pursue their economic, social and cultural development.
2. All peoples may, for their own ends, freely dispose of their natural wealth and resources without prejudice to any obligations arising out of international economic co-operation, based upon the principle of mutual benefit, and international law. In no case may a people be deprived of its own means of subsistence.
3. The States parties to the present Covenant, including those having

responsibility for the administration of Non-Self-Governing and Trust Territories, shall promote the realization of the right of self-determination, and shall respect that right, in conformity with the provisions of the Charter of the United Nations.

PART II

Article 2

1. Each State Party to the present Covenant undertakes to respect and to ensure to all individuals within its territory and subject to its jurisdiction the rights recognized in the present Covenant, without distinction of any kind, such as race, colour, sex, language, religion, political or other opinion, national or social origin, property, birth or other status.
2. Where not already provided for by existing legislative or other measures, each State Party to the present Covenant undertakes to take the necessary steps, in accordance with its constitutional processes and with the provisions of the present Covenant, to adopt such legislative or other measures as may be necessary to give effect to the rights recognized in the present Covenant.
3. Each State Party to the present Covenant undertakes:

    (a) To ensure that any person whose rights or freedoms are herein recognized are violated shall have an effective remedy, notwithstanding that the violation has been committed by persons acting in an official capacity;
    (b) To ensure that any person claiming such a remedy shall have his right thereto determined by competent judicial, administrative or legislative authorities, or by any other competent authority provided for by the legal system of the State, and to develop the possibilities of judicial remedy;
    (c) To ensure that the competent authorities shall enforce such remedies when granted.

Article 3

The States Parties to the present Covenant undertake to ensure the equal right of men and women to the enjoyment of all civil and political rights set forth in the present Covenant.

Article 4

1. In time of public emergency which threatens the life of the nation and the existence of which is officially proclaimed, the States parties to the present Covenant may take measures derogating from their obligations under the present Covenant to the extent strictly required by the exigencies of the situation, provided that such measures are not inconsistent with their other obligations under international law and do not involve discrimination solely on the ground of race, colour, sex, language, religion or social origin.

2. No derogation from articles 6, 7, 8 (paragraphs 1 and 2), 11, 15, 16 and 18 may be made under this provision.
3. Any State party to the present Covenant availing itself of the right of derogation shall immediately inform the other States Parties to the present Covenant, through the intermediary of the Secretary-General of the United Nations, of the provisions from which it has derogated and of the reasons by which it was actuated. A further communication shall be made, through the same intermediary, on the date on which it terminates such derogation.

Article 5

1. Nothing in the present Covenant may be interpreted as implying for any State, group or person any right to engage in any activity or perform any act aimed at the destruction of any of the rights and freedoms recognized herein or at their limitation to a greater extent than is provided for in the present Covenant.
2. There shall be no restriction upon or derogation from any of the fundamental human rights recognized or existing in any State Party to the present Covenant pursuant to law, conventions, regulations or custom on the pretext that the present Covenant does not recognize such rights or that it recognizes them to a lesser extent.

PART III

Article 6

1. Every human being has the inherent right to life. This right shall be protected by law. No one shall be arbitrarily deprived of his life.
2. In countries which have not abolished the death penalty, sentence of death may be imposed only for the most serious crimes in accordance with the law in force at the time of the commission of the crime and not contrary to the provisions of the present Covenant and to the Convention on the Prevention and Punishment of the Crime of Genocide. This penalty can only be carried out pursuant to a final judgement rendered by a competent court.
3. When deprivation of life constitutes the crime of genocide, it is understood that nothing in this article shall authorize any State Party to the present Covenant to derogate in any way from any obligation assumed under the provisions of the Convention on the Prevention and Punishment of the Crime of Genocide.
4. Anyone sentenced to death shall have the right to seek pardon or commutation of the sentence. Amnesty, pardon or commutation of the sentence of death may be granted in all cases.
5. Sentence of death shall not be imposed for crimes committed by persons below eighteen years of age and shall not be carried out on pregnant women.
6. Nothing in this article shall be invoked to delay or to prevent the abolition of capital punishment by any State Party to the present Covenant.

Article 7

No one shall be subjected to torture or to cruel, inhuman or degrading treatment or punishment. In particular, no one shall be subjected without his free consent to medical or scientific experimentation.

Article 8

1. No one shall be held in slavery; slavery and the slave-trade in all their forms shall be prohibited.
2. No one shall be held in servitude.
3. (a) No one shall be required to perform forced or compulsory labour;
   (b) Paragraph 3 (a) shall not be held to preclude, in countries where imprisonment with hard labour may be imposed as a punishment for a crime, the performance of hard labour in pursuance of a sentence to such punishment by a competent court;
   (c) For the purpose of this paragraph the term "forced or compulsory labour" shall not include:

   (i) Any work or service, not referred to in subparagraph (b), normally required of a person who is under detention in consequence of a lawful order of a court, or of a person during conditional release from such detention;
   (ii) Any service of a military character and, in countries where conscientious objection is recognized, any national service required by law of conscientious objectors;
   (iii) Any service exacted in cases of emergency or calamity threatening the life or well-being of the community;
   (iv) Any work or service which forms part of normal civil obligations.

Article 9

1. Everyone has the right to liberty and security of person. No one shall be subjected to arbitrary arrest or detention. No one shall be deprived of his liberty except on such grounds and in accordance with such procedure as are established by law.
2. Anyone who is arrested shall be informed, at the time of arrest, of the reasons for his arrest and shall be promptly informed of any charges against him.
3. Anyone arrested or detained on a criminal charge shall be brought promptly before a judge or other officer authorized by law to exercise judicial power and shall be entitled to trial within a reasonable time or to release. It shall not be the general rule that persons awaiting trial shall be detained in custody, but release may be subject to guarantees to appear for trial, at any other stage of the judicial proceedings, and, should occasion arise, for execution of the judgement.
4. Anyone who is deprived of his liberty by arrest or detention shall be entitled to take proceedings before a court, in order that that court may decide without

delay on the lawfulness of his detention and order his release if the detention is not lawful.

5. Anyone who has been the victim of unlawful arrest or detention shall have an enforceable right to compensation.

Article 10

1. All persons deprived of their liberty shall be treated with humanity and with respect for the inherent dignity of the human person.

2. (a) Accused persons shall, save in exceptional circumstances, be segregated from convicted persons and shall be subject to separate treatment appropriate to their status as unconvicted persons;
   (b) Accused juvenile persons shall be separated from adults and brought as speedily as possible for adjudication.

3. The penitentiary system shall comprise treatment of prisoners the essential aim of which shall be their reformation and social rehabilitation. Juvenile offenders shall be segregated from adults and be accorded treatment appropriate to their age and legal status.

Article 11

No one shall be imprisoned merely on the ground of inability to fulfil a contractual obligation.

Article 12

1. Everyone lawfully within the territory of a State shall, within that territory have the right to liberty of movement and freedom to choose his residence.
2. Everyone shall be free to leave any country, including his own.
3. The above-mentioned rights shall not be subject to any restrictions except those which are provided by law, are necessary to protect national security, public order (ordre public), public health or morals or the rights and freedoms of others, and are consistent with the other rights recognized in the present Covenant.
4. No one shall be arbitrarily deprived of the right to enter his own country.

Article 13

An alien lawfully in the territory of a State Party to the present Covenant may be expelled therefrom only in pursuance of a decision reached in accordance with law and shall, except where compelling reasons of national security otherwise require, be allowed to submit the reasons against his expulsion and to have his case reviewed by, and be represented for the purpose before, the competent authority or a person or persons especially designated by the competent authority.

Article 14

1. All persons shall be equal before the courts and tribunals. In the determination of any criminal charge against him, or of his rights and obligations in a suit of law, everyone shall be entitled to a fair and public hearing by a competent, independant and impartial tribunal established by law. The Press and the public may be excluded from all or part of a trial for reasons of morals, public order (ordre public) or national security in a democratic society, or when the interest of the private lives of the parties so requires, or to the extent strictly necessary in the opinion of the court in special circumstances where publicity would prejudice the interests of justice; but any judgment rendered in a criminal case or in a suit at law shall be made public except where the interest of juvenile persons otherwise requires or the proceedings concern matrimonial disputes of the guardianship of children.
2. Everyone charged with a criminal offence shall have the right to be presumed innocent until proved guilty according to law.
3. In the determination of any criminal charge against him, everyone shall be entitled to the following minimum guarantees, in full equality:

    (a) To be informed promptly and in detail in a language which he understands of the nature and cause of the charge against him;
    (b) To have adequate time and facilities for the preparation of his defence and to communicate with counsel of his own choosing;
    (c) To be tried without undue delay;
    (d) To be tried in his presence, and to defend himself in person or through legal assistance of his own choosing; to be informed, if he does not have legal assistance, of his right; and to have legal assistance assigned to him, in any case where the interests of justice so require, and without payment by him in any such case if he does not have sufficient means to pay for it;
    (e) To examine, or have examined, the witnesses against him and to obtain the attendance and examination of witnesses on his behalf under the same conditions as witnesses against him;
    (f) To have the free assistance of an interpreter if he cannot understand or speak the language used in court;
    (g) Not to be compelled to testify against himself or to confess guilt.

4. In the case of juvenile persons, the procedure shall be such as will take account of their age and the desirability of promoting their rehabilitation.
5. Everyone convicted of a crime shall have the right to his conviction and sentence being reviewed by a higher tribunal according to law.
6. When a person has by a final decision been convicted of a criminal offence and when subsequently his conviction has been reversed or he has been pardoned on the ground that a new or newly discovered fact shows conclusively that there has been a miscarriage of justice, the person who has suffered punishment as a result of such conviction shall be compensated according to law, unless it is proved that the non-disclosure of the unknown fact in time is wholly or partly attributable to him.
7. No one shall be liable to be tried or punished again for an offence for which he

has already been finally convicted or acquitted in accordance with the law and penal procedure of each country.

Article 15

1. No one shall be held guilty of any criminal offence on account of any act or omission which did not constitute a criminal offence, under national or international law, at the time when it was committed. Nor shall a heavier penalty be imposed than the one that was applicable at the time when the criminal offence was committed. If, subsequent to the commission of the offence, provision is made by law for the imposition of the lighter penalty, the offender shall benefit thereby.
2. Nothing in this article shall prejudice the trial and punishment of any person for any act or omission which, at the time when it was committed, was criminal according to the general principles of law recognized by the community of nations.

Article 16

Everyone shall have the right to recognition everywhere as a person before the law.

Article 17

1. No one shall be subjected to arbitrary or unlawful interference with his privacy, family, home or correspondence, nor to unlawful attacks on his honour and reputation.
2. Everyone has the right to the protection of the law against such interference or attacks.

Article 18

1. Everyone shall have the right to freedom of thought, conscience and religion. This right shall include freedom to have or to adopt a religion or belief of his choice, and freedom, either individually or in community with others and in public or private, to manifest his religion or belief in worship, observance, practice and teaching.
2. No one shall be subject to coercion which would impair his freedom to have or to adopt a religion or belief of his choice.
3. Freedom to manifest one's religion or beliefs may be subject only to such limitations as are prescribed by law and are necessary to protect public safety, order, health, or morals or the fundamental rights and freedoms of others.
4. The States Parties to the present Covenant undertake to have respect for the liberty of parents and, when applicable, legal guardians to ensure the religious and moral education of their children in conformity with their own convictions.

Article 19

1. Everyone shall have the right to hold opinions without interference.
2. Everyone shall have the right to freedom of expression; this right shall include freedom to seek, receive and impart information and ideas of all kinds, regardless of frontiers, either orally, in writing or in print, in the form of art, or through any other media of his choice.
3. The exercise of the rights provided for in paragraph 2 of this article carries with it special duties and responsibilities. It may therefore be subject to certain restrictions, but these shall only be such as are provided by law and are necessary:
   (a) For respect of the rights or reputations of others;
   (b) For the protection of national security or of public order (ordre public), or of public health or morals.

Article 20

1. Any propaganda for war shall be prohibited by law.
2. Any advocacy of national, racial or religious hatred that constitutes incitement to discrimination, hostility or violence shall be prohibited by law.

Article 21

The right of peaceful assembly shall be recognized. No restrictions may be placed on the exercise of this right other than those imposed in conformity with the law and which are necessary in a democratic society in the interests of national security or public safety, public order (ordre public), the protection of public health or morals or the protection of the rights and freedoms of others.

Article 22

1. Everyone shall have the right to freedom of association with others, including the right to form and join trade unions for the protection of his interests.
2. No restrictions may be placed on the exercise of this right other than those which are prescribed by law and which are necessary in a democratic society in the interests of national security or public safety, public order (ordre public), the protection of public health or morals or the protection of the rights and freedoms of others. This article shall not prevent the imposition of lawful restrictions on members of the armed forces and of the police in their exercise of this right.
3. Nothing in this article shall authorize States Parties to the International Labour Organisation Convention of 1948 concerning Freedom of Association and Protection of the Right to Organize to take legislative measures which would prejudice, or to apply the law in such a manner as to prejudice the guarantees provided for in that Convention.

Article 23

1. The family is the natural and fundamental group unit of society and is entitled to protection by society and the State.
2. The right of men and women of marriageable age to marry and to found a family shall be recognized.
3. No marriage shall be entered into without the free and full consent of the intending spouses.
4. States parties to the present Covenant shall take appropriate steps to ensure equality of rights and responsibilities of spouses as to marriage, during marriage and at its dissolution. In the case of dissolution, provision shall be made for the necessary protection of any children.

Article 24

1. Every child shall have, without any discrimination as to race, colour, sex, language, religion, national or social origin, property or birth, the right to such measures of protection as are required by his status as a minor, on the part of his family, society and the State.
2. Every child shall be registered immediately after birth and shall have a name.
3. Every child has the right to acquire a nationality.

Article 25

Every citizen shall have the right and the opportunity, without any of the distinctions mentioned in article 2 and without unreasonable restrictions:

   (a) To take part in the conduct of public affairs, directly or through freely chosen representatives;
   (b) To vote and to be elected at genuine periodic elections which shall be by universal and equal suffrage and shall be held by secret ballot, guaranteeing the free expression of the will of the electors;
   (c) To have access, on general terms of equality, to public service in his country.

Article 26

All persons are equal before the law and are entitled without any discrimination to the equal protection of the law. In this respect, the law shall prohibit any discrimination and guarantee to all persons equal and effective protection against discrimination on any ground such as race, colour, sex, language, religion, political or other opinion, national or social origin, property, birth or other status.

Article 27

In those States in which ethnic, religious or linguistic minorities exist, persons belonging to such minorities shall not be denied the right, in community with the other members of their group, to enjoy their own culture, to profess and practise their own religion, or to use their own language.

PART IV

Article 28

1. There shall be established a Human Rights Committee, (hereafter referred to in the present Covenant as the Committee). It shall consist of eighteen members and shall carry out the functions hereinafter provided.
2. The Committee shall be composed of nationals of the States Parties to the present Covenant who shall be persons of high moral character and recognized competence in the field of human rights, consideration being given to the usefulness of the participation of some persons having legal experience.
3. The members of the Committee shall be elected and shall serve in their personal capacity.

Article 29

1. The members of the Committee shall be elected by secret ballot from a list of persons possessing the qualifications prescribed in article 28 and nominated for the purpose by the States parties to the present Covenant.
2. Each State Party to the present Covenant may nominate not more than two persons. These persons shall be nationals of the nominating state.
3. A person shall be eligible for renomination.

Article 30

1. The initial election shall be held no later than six months after the date of the entry into force of the present Covenant.
2. At least four months before the date of each election to the Committee, other than an election to fill a vacancy declared in accordance with article 34, the Secretary-General of the United Nations shall address a written invitation to the States parties to the present Covenant to submit their nominations for membership of the Committee within three months.
3. The Secretary-General of the United Nations shall prepare a list in alphabetical order of all the persons thus nominated, with an indication of the States Parties which have nominated them, and shall submit it to the States Parties to the present Covenant no later than one month before the date of each election.
4. Elections of the members of the Committee shall be held at a meeting of the States Parties to the present Covenant convened by the Secretary-General of the United Nations at the Headquarters of the United Nations. At that meeting, for which two thirds of the States Parties to the present Covenant shall constitute a quorum, the persons elected to the Committee shall be those

nominees who obtain the largest number of votes and an absolute majority of the votes of the representatives of States Parties present and voting.

Article 31

1. The Committee may not include more than one national of the same State.
2. In the election of the Committee, consideration shall be given to equitable geographical distribution of membership and to the representation of the different forms of civilization and of the principal legal systems.

Article 32

1. The members of the Committee shall be elected for a term of four years. They shall be eligible for re-election if renominated. However, the terms of nine of the members elected at the first election shall expire at the end of two years; immediately after the first election, the names of these nine members shall be chosen by lot by the Chairman of the meeting referred to in article 30, paragraph 4.
2. Elections at the expiry of office shall be held in accordance with the preceding articles of this part of the present Covenant.

Article 33

1. If, in the unanimous opinion of the other members, a member of the Committee has ceased to carry out his functions for any cause other than absence of a temporary character, the Chairman of the Committee shall notify the Secretary-General of the United Nations, who shall then declare the seat of that member to be vacant.
2. In the event of the death or the resignation of a member of the Committee, the Chairman shall immediately notify the Secretary-General of the United Nations, who shall declare the seat vacant from the date of death or the date on which the resignation takes effect.

Article 34

1. When a vacancy is declared in accordance with article 33 and if the term of office of the member to be replaced does not expire within six months of the declaration of the vacancy, the Secretary-General of the United Nations shall notify each of the States Parties to the present Covenant, which may within two months submit nominations in accordance with article 29 for the purpose of filling the vacancy.
2. The Secretary-General of the United Nations shall prepare a list in alphabetical order of the persons thus nominated and shall submit it to the States Parties to the present Covenant. The election to fill the vacancy shall then take place in accordance with the relevant provisions of this part of the present Covenant.
3. A member of the Committee elected to fill a vacancy declared in accordance

with article 33 shall hold office for the remainder of the term of the member who vacated the seat on the Committee under the provisions of that article.

Article 35

The members of the Committee shall, with the approval of the General Assembly of the United Nations, receive emoluments from United Nations resources on such terms and conditions as the General Assembly may decide, having regard to the importance of the Committee's responsibilities.

Article 36

The Secretary-General of the United Nations shall provide the necessary staff and facilities for the effective performance of the functions of the Committee under the present Covenant.

Article 37

1. The Secretary-General of the United Nations shall convene the initial meeting of the Committee at the Headquarters of the United Nations.
2. After its initial meeting, the Committee shall meet at such times as shall be provided in its rules of procedure.
3. The Committee shall normally meet at the Headquarters of the United Nations or at the United Nations Office at Geneva.

Article 38

Every member of the Committee shall, before taking up his duties, make a solemn declaration in open committee that he will perform his functions impartially and conscientiously.

Article 39

1. The Committee shall elect its officers for a term of two years. They may be re-elected.
2. The Committee shall establish its own rules of procedure, but these rules shall provide, *inter alia*, that:

    (a) Twelve members shall constitute a quorum;
    (b) Decisions of the Committee shall be made by a majority vote of the members present.

Article 40

1. The States parties to the present Covenant undertake to submit reports on the measures they have adopted which give effect to the rights recognized herein and on the progress made in the enjoyment of those rights:

(a) Within one year of the entry into force of the present Covenant for the States Parties concerned;

(b) Thereafter whenever the Committee so requests.

2. All reports shall be submitted to the Secretary-General of the United Nations, who shall transmit them to the Committee for consideration. Reports shall indicate the factors and difficulties, if any, affecting the implementation of the present Covenant.

3. The Secretary-General of the United Nations may, after consultation with the Committee, transmit to the specialized agencies concerned copies of such parts of the reports as may fill within their field of competence.

4. The Committee shall study the reports submitted by the States Parties to the present Covenant. It shall transmit its reports, and such general comments as it may consider appropriate, to the States Parties. The Committee may also transmit to the Economic and Social Council these comments along with the copies of the reports it has received from States Parties to the present Covenant.

5. The States Parties to the present Covenant may submit to the Committee observations on any comments that may be made in accordance with paragraph 4 of this article.

Article 41

1. A State Party to the present Covenant may at any time declare under this article that it recognizes the competence of the Committee to receive and consider communications to the effect that a State Party claims that another State Party is not fulfilling its obligations under the present Covenant. Communications under this article may be received and considered only if submitted by a State Party which has made a declaration recognizing in regard to itself the competence of the Committee. No communication shall be received by the Committee if it concerns a State Party which has not made such a declaration. Communications received under this article shall be dealt with in accordance with the following procedure:

(a) If a State party to the present Covenant considers that another State Party is not giving effect to the provisions of the present Covenant, it may, by written communication, bring the matter to the attention of that State Party. Within three months after the receipt of the communication the receiving State shall afford the State which sent the communication an explanation, or any other statement in writing clarifying the matter which should include, to the extent possible and pertinent, reference to domestic procedures and remedies taken, pending, or available in the matter.

(b) If the matter is not adjusted to the satisfaction of both States Parties concerned within six months after the receipt by the receiving State of the initial communication, either State shall have the right to refer the matter to the Committee, by notice given to the Committee and to the other State.

(c) The Committee shall deal with a matter referred to it only after it has ascertained that all available domestic remedies have been invoked and exhausted in the matter, in conformity with the generally recognized principles of international law. This shall not be the rule where the application of the remedies is unreasonably prolonged.

(d) The Committee shall hold closed meetings when examining communications under this article.

(e) Subject to the provisions of sub-paragraph (c), the Committee shall make available its good offices to the States Parties concerned with a view to a friendly solution of the matter on the basis of respect for human rights and fundamental freedoms as recognized in the present Covenant.

(f) In any matter referred to it, the Committee may call upon the States Parties concerned, referred to in sub-paragraph (b), to supply any relevant information.

(g) The States parties concerned, referred to in sub-paragraph (b), shall have the right to be represented when the matter is being considered in the Committee and to make submissions orally and/or in writing.

(h) The Committee shall, within twelve months after the date of receipt of notice under sub-paragraph (b), submit a report:

(i) If a solution within the terms of sub-paragraph (e) is reached, the Committee shall confine its report to a brief statement of the facts and of the solution reached;

(ii) If a solution within the terms of sub-paragraph (e) is not reached, the Committee shall confine its report to a brief statement of the facts; the written submissions and record of the oral submissions made by the States Parties concerned shall be attached to the report.

In every matter, the report shall be communicated to the States Parties concerned.

2. The provisions of this article shall come into force when ten States parties to the present Covenant have made declarations under paragraph 1 of this Article Such declarations shall be deposited by the States Parties with the Secretary-General of the United Nations, who shall transmit copies thereof to the other States Parties. A declaration may be withdrawn at any time by notification to the Secretary-General. Such a withdrawal shall not prejudice the consideration of any matter which is the subject of a communication already transmitted under this article; no further communication by any State party shall be received after the notification of withdrawal of the declaration has been received by the Secretary-General, unless the State Party concerned has made a new declaration.

Article 42

1. (a) If a matter referred to the Committee in accordance with article 41 is not resolved to the satisfaction of the States Parties concerned, the Committee may, with the prior consent of the States Parties concerned, appoint an Ad hoc Conciliation Commission (hereinafter referred to as the Commission). The good offices of the Commission shall be made available

to the States Parties concerned with a view to an amicable solution of the matter on the basis of respect for the present Covenant;

(b) The Commission shall consist of five persons acceptable to the States Parties concerned. If the States Parties concerned fail to reach agreement within three months on all or part of the composition of the Commission, the members of the Commission concerning whom no agreement has been reached shall be elected by secret ballot by a two-thirds majority vote of the Committee from among its members.

2. The members of the Commission shall serve in their personal capacity. They shall not be nationals of the States Parties concerned, or of a State not party to the present Covenant, or of a State Party which has not made a declaration under article 41.

3. The Commission shall elect its own Chairman and adopt its own rules of procedure.

4. The meetings of the Commission shall normally be held at the Headquarters of the United Nations or at the United Nations Office at Geneva. However, they may be held at such other convenient places as the Commission may determine in consultation with the Secretary-General of the United Nations and the States Parties concerned.

5. The secretariat provided in accordance with article 36 shall also service the commissions appointed under this article.

6. The information received and collated by the Committee shall be made available to the Commission and the Commission may call upon the States Parties concerned to supply any other relevant information.

7. When the Commission has fully considered the matter, but in any event not later than twelve months after having been seized of the matter, it shall submit to the Chairman of the Committee a report for communication to the States Parties concerned:

(a) If the Commission is unable to complete its consideration of the matter within twelve months, it shall confine its report to a brief statement of the status of its consideration of the matter;

(b) If an amicable solution to the matter on the basis of respect for human rights as recognized in the present Covenant is reached, the Commission shall confine its report to a brief statement of the facts and of the solution reached;

(c) If a solution within the terms of sub-paragraph (b) is not reached, the Commission's report shall embody its findings on all questions of fact relevant to the issues between the States Parties concerned, and its views on the possibilities of an amicable solution of the matter. This report shall also contain the written submissions and a record of the oral submissions made by the States Parties concerned;

(d) If the Commission's report is submitted under sub-paragraph (c), the States Parties concerned shall, within three months of the receipt of the report, notify the Chairman of the Committee whether or not they accept the contents of the report of the Commission.

8. The provisions of this article are without prejudice to the responsibilities of the Committee under article 41.
9. The States Parties concerned shall share equally all the expenses of the members of the Commission in accordance with estimates to be provided by the Secretary-General of the United Nations.
10. The Secretary-General of the United Nations shall be empowered to pay the expenses of the members of the Commission, if necessary, before reimbursement by the States parties concerned, in accordance with paragraph 9 of this Article.

Article 43

The members of the Committee, and of the *ad hoc* conciliation commissions which may be appointed under article 42, shall be entitled to the facilities, privileges and immunities of experts on mission for the United Nations as laid down in the relevant sections of the Convention on the Privileges and Immunities of the United Nations.

Article 44

The provisions for the implementation of the present Convenant shall apply without prejudice to the procedures prescribed in the field of human rights by or under the constituent instruments and the conventions of the United Nations and of the specialized agencies and shall not prevent the States parties to the present Covenant from having recourse to other procedures for settling a dispute in accordance with general or special international agreements in force between them.

Article 45

The Committee shall submit to the General Assembly of the United Nations, through the Economic and Social Council, an annual report on its activities.

PART V

Article 46

Nothing in the present Covenant shall be interpreted as impairing the provisions of the Charter of the United Nations and of the constitutions of the specialized agencies which define the respective responsibilities of the various organs of the United Nations and of the specialized agencies in regard to the matters dealt with in the present Covenant.

Article 47

Nothing in the present Covenant shall be interpreted as impairing the inherent right of all peoples to enjoy and utilize fully and freely their natural wealth and resources.

PART VI

Article 48

1. The present Covenant is open for signature by any State Member of the United Nations or member of any of its specialized agencies, by any State Party to the Statute of the International Court of Justice, and by any other State which has been invited by the General Assembly of the United Nations to become a party to the present Covenant.
2. The present Covenant is subject to ratification. Instruments of ratification shall be deposited with the Secretary-General of the United Nations.
3. The present Covenant shall be open to accession by any State referred to in paragraph 1 of this article.
4. Accession shall be affected by the deposit of an instrument of accession with the Secretary-General of the United Nations.
5. The Secretary-General of the United Nations shall inform all States which have signed this Covenant or acceded to it, of the deposit of each instrument of ratification or accession.

Article 49

1. The present Covenant shall enter into force three months after the date of the deposit with the Secretary-General of the United Nations of the thirty-fifth instrument of ratification or instrument of accession.
2. For each State ratifying the present Covenant or acceding to it after the deposit of the thirty-fifth instrument of ratification or instrument of accession, the present Covenant shall enter into force three months after the date of the deposit of its own instrument of ratification or instrument of accession.

Article 50

The provisions of the present Covenant shall extend to all parts of federal States without any limitations or exceptions.

Article 51

1. Any State Party to the present Covenant may propose an amendment and file it with the Secretary-General of the United Nations. The Secretary-General of the United Nations shall thereupon communicate any proposed amendments to the States Parties to the present Covenant with a request that they notify him whether they favour a conference of States Parties for the purpose of considering and voting upon the proposals. In the event that at least one third of the States Parties favours such a conference, the Secretary-General shall convene the conference under the auspices of the United Nations. Any amendment adopted by a majority of the States Parties present and voting at the conference shall be submitted to the General Assembly of the United Nations for approval.

2. Amendments shall come into force when they have been approved by the General Assembly of the United Nations and accepted by a two-thirds majority of the States Parties to the present Covenant in accordance with their respective constitutional processes.
3. When amendments come into force, they shall be binding on those States Parties which have accepted them, other States Parties still being bound by the provisions of the present Covenant and any earlier amendment which they have accepted.

Article 52

Irrespective of the notifications made under article 48, paragraph 5, the Secretary-General of the United Nations shall inform all States referred to in paragraph 1 of the same article of the following particulars:

(a) Signatures, ratifications and accessions under article 48;
(b) The date of the entry into force of the present Covenant under article 49 and the date of the entry into force of any amendments under article 51.

Article 53

1. The present Covenant, of which the Chinese, English, French, Russian and Spanish texts are equally authentic, shall be deposited in the archives of the United Nations.
2. The Secretary-General of the United Nations shall transmit certified copies of the present Covenant to all States referred to in article 48.

4. OPTIONAL PROTOCOL TO THE INTERNATIONAL COVENANT ON CIVIL AND POLITICAL RIGHTS

Adopted and Opened for Signature, Ratification and Accession by General Assembly Resolution 2200 X (XXI) of 16 December 1966

Entry into force: 23 March 1976, in accordance with Article 9

The States parties to the present Protocol,

Considering that in order further to achieve the purposes of the Covenant on Civil and Political Rights (hereinafter referred to as the Covenant) and the implementation of its provisions it would be appropriate to enable the Human Rights Committee set up in part IV of the Covenant (hereinafter referred to as the Committee) to receive and consider, as provided in the present Protocol, communications from individuals claiming to be victims of violations of any of the rights set forth in the Covenant,

Have agreed as follows:

Article 1

A State Party to the Covenant that becomes a party to the present Protocol recognizes the competence of the Committee to receive and consider communications from individuals subject to its jurisdiction who claim to be victims of a violation by that State party of any of the rights set forth in the Covenant. No communication shall be received by the Committee if it concerns a State Party to the Covenant which is not a party to the present Protocol.

Article 2

Subject to the provisions of article 1, individuals who claim that any of their rights enumerated in the Covenant have been violated and who have exhausted all available domestic remedies may submit a written communication to the Committee for consideration.

Article 3

The Committee shall consider inadmissible any communication under the present Protocol which is anonymous, or which it considers to be an abuse of the right of submission of such communications or to be incompatible with the provisions of the Covenant.

Article 4

1. Subject to the provisions of article 3, the Committee shall bring any communications submitted to it under the present Protocol to the attention of the State Party to the present Protocol alleged to be violating any provision of the Covenant.
2. Within six months, the receiving State shall submit to the Committee written explanations or statements clarifying the matter and the remedy, if any, that may have been taken by the State.

Article 5

1. The Committee shall consider communications received under the present Protocol in the light of all written information made available to it by the individual and by the State Party concerned.
2. The Committee shall not consider any communication from an individual unless it has ascertained that:

   (a) The same matter is not being examined under another procedure of international investigation or settlement;
   (b) The individual has exhausted all available domestic remedies.

   This shall not be the rule where the application of the remedies is unreasonably prolonged.
3. The Committee shall hold closed meetings when examining communications under the present Protocol.
4. The Committee shall forward its views to the State Party concerned and to the individual.

Article 6

The Committee shall include in its annual report under article 45 of the Covenant a summary of its activities under the present Protocol.

Article 7

Pending the achievement of the objectives of resolution 1514 (XV) adopted by the General Assembly of the United Nations on 14 December 1960 concerning the Declaration on the Granting of Independence to Colonial Countries and Peoples, the provisions of the present Protocol shall in no way limit the right of petition granted to these peoples by the Charter of the United Nations and other international conventions and instruments under the United Nations and its specialized agencies.

Article 8

1. The present Protocol is open for signature by any State which has signed the Covenant.

2. The present Protocol is subject to ratification by any State which has ratified or acceded to the Covenant. Instruments of ratification shall be deposited with the Secretary-General of the United Nations.
3. The present Protocol shall be open to accession by any State which has ratified or acceded to the Covenant.
4. Accession shall be effected by the deposit of an instrument of accession with the Secretary-General of the United Nations.
5. The Secretary General of the United Nations shall inform all States which have signed the present Protocol or acceded to it of the deposit of each instrument of ratification or accession.

Article 9

1. Subject to the entry into force of the Covenant, the present Protocol shall enter into force three months after the date of the deposit with the Secretary-General of the United Nations of the tenth instrument of ratification or instrument of accession.
2. For each State ratifying the present Protocol or acceding to it after the deposit of the tenth instrument of ratification or instrument of accession, the present Protocol shall enter into force three months after the date of the deposit of its own instrument of ratification or instrument of accession.

Article 10

The provisions of the present Protocol shall extend to all parts of federal States without any limitations or exceptions.

Article 11

1. Any State Party to the present Protocol may propose an amendment and file it with the Secretary-General of the United Nations. The Secretary-General shall thereupon communicate any proposed amendments to the States Parties to the present Protocol with a request that they notify him whether they favour a conference of States Parties for the purpose of considering and voting upon the proposal. In the event that at least one third of the States Parties favours such a conference, the Secretary-General shall convene the conference under the auspices of the United Nations. Any amendment adopted by a majority of the States Parties present and voting at the conference shall be sumitted to the General Assembly of the United Nations for approval.
2. Amendments shall come into force when they have been approved by the General Assembly of the United Nations and accepted by a two-thirds majority of the States Parties to the present Protocol in accordance with their respective constitutional processes.
3. When amendments come into force, they shall be binding on those States Parties which have accepted them, other States Parties still being bound by the provisions of the present Protocol and any earlier amendment which they have accepted.

Article 12

1. Any State Party may denounce the present Protocol at any time by written notification addressed to the Secretary-General of the United Nations. Denunciation shall take effect three months after the date of receipt of the notification by the Secretary-General.
2. Denunciation shall be without prejudice to the continued application of the provisions of the present Protocol to any communication submitted under article 2 before the effective date of denunciation.

Article 13

Irrespective of the notifications made under article 8, paragraph 5, of the present Protocol, the Secretary-General of the United Nations shall inform all States referred to in article 48, paragraph 1, of the Covenant of the following particulars:

   (a) Signatures, ratifications and accessions under article 8;
   (b) The date of the entry into force of the present Protocol under article 9 and the date of the entry into force of any amendments under article 11;
   (c) Denunciations under article 12.

Article 14

1. The present Protocol, of which the Chinese, English, French, Russian and Spanish texts are equally authentic, shall be deposited in the archives of the United Nations.
2. The Secretary-General of the United Nations shall transmit certified copies of the present Protocol to all States referred to in article 48 of the Covenant.

5. INTERNATIONAL COVENANT ON ECONOMIC, SOCIAL AND CULTURAL RIGHTS

Adopted by General Assembly Resolution XXXXX on 16 December 1966

Entry into force: 3 January 1976, in accordance with Article 27

PREAMBLE

The States Parties to the present Covenant,

Considering that, in accordance with the principles proclaimed in the Charter of the United Nations, recognition of the inherent dignity and of the equal and inalienable rights of all members of the human family is the foundation of freedom, justice and peace in the world,

Recognizing that these rights derive from the inherent dignity of the human person,

Recognizing that, in accordance with the Universal Declaration of Human Rights, the ideal of free human beings enjoying freedom from fear and want can only be achieved if conditions are created whereby everyone may enjoy his economic, social and cultural rights, as well as his civil and political rights,

Considering the obligation of States under the Charter of the United Nations to promote universal respect for, and observance of, human rights and freedoms,

Realizing that the individual, having duties to other individuals and to the community to which he belongs, is under a responsibility to strive for the promotion and observance of the rights recognized in the present Covenant,

Agree upon the following articles:

PART I

Article 1

1. All peoples have the right of self-determination. By virtue of that right they freely determine their status and freely pursue their economic, social and cultural development.
2. All peoples may, for their own ends, freely dispose of their natural wealth and resources without prejudice to any obligations arising out of international economic co-operation, based upon the principle of mutual benefit, and international law. In no case may a people be deprived of its own means of subsistence.
3. The States Parties to the present Covenant, including those having responsibility for the administration of Non-Self-Governing and Trust Territories, shall promote the realization of the right of self-determination, and shall respect that right, in conformity with the provisions of the Charter of the United Nations.

PART II

Article 2

1. Each State Party to the present Covenant undertakes to take steps, individually and through international assistance and co-operation, especially economic and technical, to the maximum of its available resources, with a view to achieving progressively the full realization of the rights recognized in the present Covenant by all appropriate means, including particularly the adoption of legislative measures.
2. The States Parties to the present Covenant undertake to guarantee that the rights enunciated in the present Covenant will be exercised without discrimination of any kind as to race, colour, sex, language, religion, political or other opinion, national or social origin, property, birth or other status.
3. Developing countries, with due regard to human rights and their national economy, may determine to what extent they would guarantee the economic rights recognized in the present Covenant to non-nationals.

Article 3

The States Parties to the present Covenant undertake to ensure the equal right of men and women to the enjoyment of all economic, social and cultural rights set forth in the present Covenant.

Article 4

The States Parties to the present Covenant recognize that, in the enjoyment of those rights provided by the State in conformity with the present Covenant, the State may subject such rights only to such limitations as are determined by law only in so far as this may be compatible with the nature of these rights and solely for the purpose of promoting the general welfare in a democratic society.

Article 5

1. Nothing in the present Covenant may be interpreted as implying for any State, group or person any right to engage in any activity or to perform any act aimed at the destruction of any of the rights or freedoms recognized herein, or at their limitation to a greater extent than is provided for in the present Covenant.
2. No restriction upon or derogation from any of the fundamental human rights recognized or existing in any country in virtue of law, conventions, regulations or custom shall be admitted on the pretext that the present Covenant does not recognize such rights or that it recognizes them to a lesser extent.

PART III

Article 6

1. The States Parties to the present Covenant recognize the right to work, which includes the right of everyone to the opportunity to gain his living by work which he chooses or accepts, and will take appropriate steps to safeguard this right.
2. The steps to be taken by a State Party to the present Covenant to achieve the full realization of this right shall include technical and vocational guidance and training programmes, policies and techniques to achieve steady economic, social and cultural development and full and productive employment under conditions safe-guarding fundamental political and economic freedoms to the individual.

Article 7

The States Parties to the present Covenant recognize the right of everyone to the enjoyment of just and favourable conditions of work which ensure, in particular:

    (a) Remuneration which provides all workers, as a minimum, with:

        (i) Fair wages and equal remuneration for work of equal value without distinction of any kind, in particular women being guaranteed conditions of work not inferior to those enjoyed by men, with equal pay for equal work;

        (ii) A decent living for themselves and their families in accordance with the provisions of the present Covenant;

    (b) Safe and healthy working conditions;

    (c) Equal opportunity for everyone to be promoted in his employment to an appropriate higher level, subject to no considerations other than those of seniority and competence;

    (d) Rest leisure and reasonable limitation of working hours and periodic holidays with pay, as well as remuneration for public holidays.

Article 8

1. The States Parties to the present Covenant undertake to ensure:

    (a) The right of everyone to form trade unions and join the trade union of his choice, subject only to the rules of the organization concerned, for the promotion and protection of his economic and social interests. No restrictions may be placed on the exercise of this right other than those prescribed by law and which are necessary in a democratic society in the interests of national security or public order or for the protection of the rights and freedoms of others;

    (b) The right of trade unions to establish national federations or confederations and the right of the latter to form or join international trade-union organizations;

(c) The right of trade unions to function freely subject to no limitations other than those prescribed by law and which are necessary in a democratic society in the interests of national security or public order or for the protection of the rights and freedoms of others;

(d) The right to strike, provided that it is exercised in conformity with the laws of the particular country.

2. This article shall not prevent the imposition of lawful restrictions on the exercise of these rights by members of the armed forces or of the police or of the administration of the State.

3. Nothing in this article shall authorize States Parties to the International Labour Organisation Convention of 1948 concerning Freedom of Association and Protection of the Right to Organize to take legislative measures which would prejudice, or apply the law in such a manner as would prejudice, the guarantees provided for in that Convention.

Article 9

The States parties to the present Covenant recognize the right of everyone to social security, including social insurance.

Article 10

The States Parties to the present Covenant recognize that:

1. The widest possible protection and assistance should be accorded to the family, which is the natural and fundamental group unit of society, particularly for its establishment and while it is responsible for the care and education of dependent children. Marriage must be entered into with the free consent of the intending spouses.

2. Special protection should be accorded to mothers during a reasonable period before and after childbirth. During such period working mothers should be accorded paid leave or leave with adequate social security benefits.

3. Special measures of protection and assistance should be taken on behalf of all children and young persons without any discrimination for reasons of parentage or other conditions. Children and young persons should be protected from economic and social exploitation. Their employment in work harmful to their morals or health or dangerous to life or likely to hamper their normal development should be punishable by law. States should also set age limits below which the paid employment of child labour should be prohibited and punishable by law.

Article 11

1. The States Parties to the present Covenant recognize the right of everyone to an adequate standard of living for himself and his family, including adequate food, clothing and housing, and to the continuous improvement of living conditions. The States Parties will take appropriate steps to ensure the

realization of this right, recognizing to this effect the essential importance of international co-operation based on free consent.

2.   The States parties to the present Covenant, recognizing the fundamental right of everyone to be free from hunger, shall take, individually and through international co-operation, the measures, including specific programmes, which are needed.

(a)   To improve methods of production, conservation and distribution of food by making full use of technical and scientific knowledge, by disseminating knowledge of the principles of nutrition and by developing or reforming agrarian systems in such a way as to achieve the most efficient development and utilization of natural resources;

(b)   Taking into account the problems of both food-importing and food-exporting countries, to ensure an equitable distribution of world food supplies in relation to need.

Article 12

1.   The States Parties to the present Covenant recognize the right of everyone to the enjoyment of the highest attainable standard of physical and mental health.

2.   The steps to be taken by the States Parties to the present Covenant to achieve the full realization of this right shall include those necessary for:

(a)   The provision for the reduction of the stillbirth-rate and of infant mortality and for the healthy development of the child;

(b)   The improvement of all aspects of environmental and industrial hygiene;

(c)   The prevention, treatment and control of epidemic, endemic, occupational and other diseases;

(d)   The creation of conditions which would assure to all medical service and medical attention in the event of sickness.

Article 13

1.   The States Parties to the present Covenant recognize the right of everyone to education. They agree that education shall be directed to the full development of the human personality and the sense of its dignity, and shall strengthen the respect for human rights and fundamental freedoms. They further agree that education shall enable all persons to participate effectively in a free society, promote understanding, tolerance and friendship among all nations and all racial, ethnic or religious groups, and further the activities of the United Nations for the maintenance of peace.

2.   The States Parties to the present Covenant recognize that, with a view to achieving the full realization of this right:

(a)   Primary education shall be compulsory and available free to all;

(b)   Secondary education in its different forms, including technical and vocational secondary education, shall be made generally available and accessible to all by every appropriate means, and in particular by the progressive introduction of free education;

    (c) Higher education shall be made equally accessible to all, on the basis of capacity, by every appropriate means, and in particular by the progressive introduction of free education;

    (d) Fundamental education shall be encouraged or intensified as far as possible for those persons who have not received or completed the whole period of their primary education;

    (e) The development of a system of schools at all levels shall be actively pursued, an adequate fellowship system shall be established, and the material conditions of teaching staff shall be continuously improved.

3.   The States Parties to the present Covenant undertake to have respect for the liberty of parents and, when applicable, legal guardians to choose for their children schools, other than those established by the public authorities, which conform to such minimum educational standards as may be laid down or approved by the State and to ensure the religious and moral education of their children in conformity with their own convictions.

4.   No part of this article shall be construed so as to interfere with the liberty of individuals and bodies to establish and direct educational institutions, subject always to the observance of the principles set forth in paragraph 1 of this article and to the requirement that the education given in such institutions shall conform to such minimum standards as may be laid down by the State.

Article 14

Each State Party to the present Covenant which, at the time of becoming a Party, has not been able to secure in its metropolitan territory or other territories under its jurisdiction compulsory primary education, free of charge, undertakes, within two years to work out and adopt a detailed plan of action for the progressive implementation, within a reasonable number of years, to be fixed in the plan, of the principle of compulsory education free of charge for all.

Article 15

1.   The States Parties to the present Covenant recognize the right of everyone:

    (a) To take part in cultural life;

    (b) To enjoy the benefits of scientific progress and its applications;

    (c) To benefit from the protection of the moral and material interests resulting from any scientific, literary or artistic production of which he is the author.

2.   The steps to be taken by the States Parties to the present Covenant to achieve the full realization of this right shall include those necessary for the conservation, and development and the diffusion of science and culture.

3.   The States Parties to the present Covenant undertake to respect the freedom indispensable for scientific research and creative activity.

4. The States Parties to the present Covenant recognize the benefits to be derived from the encouragment and development of international contacts and co-operation in the scientific and cultural fields.

PART IV

Article 16

1. The States Parties to the present Covenant undertake to submit in conformity with this part of the Covenant reports on the measures which they have adopted and the progress made in achieving the observance of the rights recognized herein.
2. (a) All reports shall be submitted to the Secretary-General of the United Nations, who shall transmit copies to the Economic and Social Council for consideration in accordance with the provisions of the present Covenant;
   (b) The Secretary-General of the United Nations shall also transmit to the specialized agencies copies of the reports, or any relevant parts therefrom, from States Parties to the present Covenant which are also members of these specialized agencies in so far as these reports, or parts therefrom, relate to any matters which fall within the responsibilities of the said agencies in accordance with their constitutional instruments.

Article 17

1. The States Parties to the present Covenant shall furnish their reports in stages, in accordance with a programme to be established by the Economic and Social Council within one year of the entry into force of the present Covenant after consultation with the States parties and the specialized agencies concerned.
2. Reports may indicate factors and difficulties affecting the degree of fulfilment of obligations under the present Covenant.
3. Where relevant information has previously been furnished to the United Nations or to any specialized agency by any State party to the present Covenant, it will not be necessary to reproduce that information, but a precise reference to the information so furnished will suffice.

Article 18

Pursuant to its responsibilities under the Charter of the United Nations in the field of human rights and fundamental freedoms, the Economic and Social Council may make arrangements with the specialized agencies in respect of their reporting to it on the progress made in achieving the observance of the provisions of the present Covenant falling within the scope of their activities. These reports may include particulars of decisions and recommendations on such implementation adopted by their competent organs.

Article 19

The Economic and Social Council may transmit to the Commission of Human Rights for study and general recommendation or, as appropriate, for information the reports concerning human rights submitted by States in accordance with articles 16 and 17, and those concerning human rights submitted by the specialized agencies in accordance with article 18.

Article 20

The States Parties to the present Covenant and the specialized agencies concerned may submit comments to the Economic and Social Council on any general recommendation under article 19 or reference to such general recommendation in any report of the Commission on Human Rights or any documentation referred to therein.

Article 21

The Economic and Social Council may submit from time to time to the General Assembly reports with recommendations of a general nature and a summary of the information received from the States Parties to the present Covenant and the specialized agencies on the measures taken and the progress made in achieving general observance of the rights recognized in the present Covenant.

Article 22

The Economic and Social Council may bring to the attention of other organs of the United Nations, their subsidiary organs and specialized agencies concerned with furnishing technical assistance any matters arising out of the reports referred to in this part of the present Covenant which may assist such bodies in deciding, each within its field of competence, on the advisability of international measures likely to contribute to the effective progressive implementation of the present Covenant.

Article 23

The States parties to the present Covenant agree that international action for the achievement of the rights recognized in the present Covenant includes such methods as the conclusion of conventions, the adoption of recommendations, the furnishing of technical assistance and the holding of regional meetings and technical meetings for the purpose of consultation and study organized in conjunction with the Governments concerned.

Article 24

Nothing in the present Covenant shall be interpreted as impairing the provisions of the Charter of the United Nations and of the constitutions of the specialized agencies which define the respective responsibilities of the various organs of the

United Nations and of the specialized agencies in regard to the matters dealt with in the present Covenant.

Article 25

Nothing in the present Covenant shall be interpreted as impairing the inherent right of all peoples to enjoy and utilize fully and freely their natural wealth and resources.

PART V

Article 26

1. The present Covenant is open for signature by any State Member of the United Nations or member of any of its specialized agencies, by any State party to the Statute of the International Court of Justice, and by any other State which has been invited by the General Assembly of the United Nations to become a party to the present Covenant.
2. The present Covenant is subject to ratification. Instruments of ratification shall be deposited with the Secretary-General of the United Nations.
3. The present Covenant shall be open to accession by any State referred to in paragraph 1 of this article.
4. Accession shall be effected by the deposit of an instrument of accession with the Secretary-General of the United Nations.
5. The Secretary-General of the United Nations shall inform all States which have signed the present Covenant or acceded to it of the deposit of each instrument of ratification or accession.

Article 27

1. The present Covenant shall enter into force three months after the date of the deposit with the Secretary-General of the United Nations of the thirty-fifth instrument of ratification or instrument of accession.
2. For each State ratifying the present Covenant or acceding to it after the deposit of the thirty-fifth instrument of ratification or instrument of accession, the present Covenant shall enter into force three months after the date of the deposit of its own instrument of ratification or instrument of accession.

Article 28

The provisions of the present Covenant shall extend to all parts of federal States without any limitations or exceptions.

Article 29

1. Any State Party to the present Covenant may propose an amendment and file it with the Secretary-General of the United Nations. The Secretary-General shall thereupon communicate any proposed amendments to the States parties

to the present Covenant with a request that they notify him whether they favour a conference of States Parties for the purpose of considering and voting upon the proposals. In the event that at least one third of the States parties favours such a conference, the Secretary-General shall convene the conference under the auspices of the United Nations. Any amendment adopted by a majority of the States Parties present and voting at the conference shall be submitted to the General Assembly of the United Nations for approval.

2. Amendments shall come into force when they have been approved by the General Assembly of the United Nations and accepted by a two-thirds majority of the States parties to the present Covenant in accordance with their respective constitutional processes.

3. When amendments come into force they shall be binding on those States Parties which have accepted them, other States Parties still being bound by the provisions of the present Covenant and any earlier amendment which they have accepted.

Article 30

Irrespective of the notifications made under article 26, paragraph 5, the Secretary-General of the United Nations shall inform all States referred to in paragraph 1 of the same article of the following particulars:

(a) Signatures, ratifications and accessions under article 26;

(b) The date of the entry into force of the present Covenant under article 27 and the date of the entry into force of any amendments under article 29.

Article 31

1. The present Covenant, of which the Chinese, English, French, Russian and Spanish texts are equally authentic, shall be deposited in the archives of the United Nations.

2. The Secretary-General of the United Nations shall transmit certified copies of the present Covenant to all States referred to in article 26.

SECTION TWO

REGIONAL INSTRUMENTS

6. CONVENTION FOR THE PROTECTION OF HUMAN RIGHTS AND FUNDAMENTAL FREEDOMS

(European Convention on Human Rights)

Signed at Rome: 4 November 1950

Entry into force: 3 September 1953 in accordance with
Article 66(2)

Editors' Notes
The Text reproduced here is that of the Convention as amended by the Third, Fifth, Eighth, and Ninth Protocols to the Convention. All of these Protocols have entered into force. However, the Ninth Protocol, which amends Articles 31(2), 44, 45 and 48, has not been ratified by all parties to the Convention. Consequently, there are two operative versions of those provisions. The original provisions are set out here, followed by the provisions as amended by the Ninth Protocol in italics. Protocol No. 10 to the Convention, which removes the requirement of a two-thirds majority referred to in Article 32 (proceedings before the Council of Ministers) is not yet in force.

The Governments signatory hereto, being Members of the Council of Europe,

Considering the Universal Declaration of Human Rights proclaimed by the General Assembly of the United Nations on 10th December 1948;
Considering that this Declaration aims at securing the universal and effective recognition and observance of the Rights therein declared;
Considering that the aim of the Council of Europe is the achievement of greater unity between its Members and that one of the methods by which that aim is to be pursued is the maintenance and further realisation of Human Rights and Fundamental Freedoms;
Reaffirming their profound belief in those Fundamental Freedoms which are the foundation of justice and peace in the world and are best maintained on the one hand by an effective political democracy and on the other by a common understanding and observance of the Human Rights upon which they depend;
Being resolved, as the Governments of European countries which are like-minded and have a common heritage of political traditions, ideals, freedom and the rule of law to take the first steps for the collective enforcement of certain of the Rights stated in the Universal Declaration;
Have agreed as follows:

Article 1

The High Contracting Parties shall secure to everyone within their jurisdiction the rights and freedoms defined in Section I of this Convention.

SECTION I

Article 2

1. Everyone's right to life shall be protected by law. No one shall be deprived of his life intentionally save in the execution of a sentence of a court following his conviction of a crime for which this penalty is provided by law.
2. Deprivation of life shall not be regarded as inflicted in contravention of this Article when it results from the use of force which is no more than absolutely necessary:

   (a) in defence of any person from unlawful violence;
   (b) in order to effect a lawful arrest or to prevent the escape of a person lawfully detained;
   (c) in action lawfully taken for the purpose of quelling a riot or insurrection.

Article 3

No one shall be subjected to torture or to inhuman or degrading treatment or punishment.

Article 4

1. No one shall be held in slavery or servitude.
2. No one shall be required to perform forced or compulsory labour.
3. For the purpose of this Article the term "forced or compulsory labour" shall not include:

   (a) any work required to be done in the ordinary course of detention imposed according to the provisions of Article 5 of this Convention or during conditional release from such detention;
   (b) any service of a military character or, in case of conscientious objectors in countries where they are recognised, service exacted instead of compulsory military service;
   (c) any service exacted in case of an emergency or calamity threatening the life or well-being of the community;
   (d) any work or service which forms part of normal civic obligations.

Article 5

1. Everyone has the right to liberty and security of person. No one shall be deprived of his liberty save in the following cases and in accordance with a procedure prescribed by law:

    (a) the lawful detention of a person after conviction by a competent court;
    (b) the lawful arrest or detention of a person for non-compliance with the lawful order of a court or in order to secure the fulfilment of any obligation prescribed by law;
    (c) the lawful arrest or detention of a person effected for the purpose of bringing him before the competent legal authority on reasonable suspicion of having committed an offence or when it is reasonably considered necessary to prevent his committing an offence or fleeing after having done so;
    (d) the detention of a minor by lawful order for the purpose of educational supervision or his lawful detention for the purpose of bringing him before the competent legal authority;
    (e) the lawful detention of persons for the prevention of the spreading of infectious diseases, of persons of unsound mind, alcoholics or drug addicts or vagrants;
    (f) the lawful arrest or detention of a person to prevent his effecting an unauthorised entry into the country or of a person against whom action is being taken with a view to deportation or extradition.

2. Everyone who is arrested shall be informed promptly, in a language which he understands, of the reasons for his arrest and of any charge against him.

3. Everyone arrested or detained in accordance with the provisions of paragraph 1 (c) of this Article shall be brought promptly before a judge or other officer authorised by law to exercise judicial power and shall be entitled to trial within a reasonable time or to release pending trial. Release may be conditioned by guarantees to appear for trial.

4. Everyone who is deprived of his liberty by arrest or detention shall be entitled to take proceedings by which the lawfulness of his detention shall be decided speedily by a court and his release ordered if the detention is not lawful.

5. Everyone who has been the victim of arrest or detention in contravention of the provisions of this Article shall have an enforceable right to compensation.

Article 6

1. In the determination of his civil rights and obligations or of any criminal charge against him, everyone is entitled to a fair and public hearing within a reasonable time by an independent and impartial tribunal established by law. Judgment shall be pronounced publicly but the press and public may be excluded from all or part of the trial in the interest of morals, public order or national security in a democratic society, where the interests of juveniles or the protection of the private life of the parties so require, or to the extent

strictly necessary in the opinion of the court in special circumstances where publicity would prejudice the interests of justice.

2. Everyone charged with a criminal offence shall be presumed innocent until proved guilty according to law.

3. Everyone charged with a criminal offence has the following minimum rights:

    (a) to be informed promptly, in a language which he understands and in detail, of the nature and cause of the accusation against him;
    (b) to have adequate time and facilities for the preparation of his defence;
    (c) to defend himself in person or through legal assistance of his own choosing or, if he has not sufficient means to pay for legal assistance, to be given it free when the interests of justice so require;
    (d) to examine or have examined witnesses against him and to obtain the attendance and examination of witnesses on his behalf under the same conditions as witnesses against him;
    (e) to have the free assistance of an interpreter if he cannot understand or speak the language used in court.

Article 7

1. No one shall be held guilty of any criminal offence on account of any act or omission which did not constitute a criminal offence under national or international law at the time when it was committed. Nor shall a heavier penalty be imposed than the one that was applicable at the time the criminal offence was committed.

2. This article shall not prejudice the trial and punishment of any person for any act or omission which at the time when it was committed, was criminal according to the general principles of law recognized by civilised nations.

Article 8

1. Everyone has the right to respect for his private and family life, his home and his correspondence.

2. There shall be no interference by a public authority with the exercise of this right except such as is in accordance with the law and is necessary in a democratic society in the interests of national security, public safety or the economic well-being of the country, for the prevention of disorder or crime, for the protection of health or morals, or for the protection of the rights and freedoms of others.

Article 9

1. Everyone has the right to freedom of thought, conscience and religion, this right includes freedom to change his religion or belief and freedom, either alone or in community with others and in public or private, to manifest his religion or belief, in worship, teaching, practice and observance.

2. Freedom to manifest one's religion or beliefs shall be subject only to such

limitations as are prescribed by law and are necessary in a democratic society in the interests of public safety, for the protection of public order, health or morals, or for the protection of the rights and freedoms of others.

Article 10

1. Everyone has the right to freedom of expression. This right shall include freedom to hold opinions and to receive and impart information and ideas without interference by public authority and regardless of frontiers. This Article shall not prevent States from requiring the licensing of broadcasting, television or cinema enterprises.
2. The exercise of these freedoms, since it carries with it duties and responsibilities, may be subject to such formalities, conditions, restrictions or penalties as are prescribed by law and are necessary in a democratic society, in the interests of national security, territorial integrity or public safety, for the prevention of disorder or crime, for the protection of health or morals, for the protection of the reputation or rights of others, for preventing the disclosure of information received in confidence, or for maintaining the authority and impartiality of the judiciary.

Article 11

1. Everyone has the right to freedom of peaceful assembly and to freedom of association with others, including the right to form and to join trade unions for the protection of his interests.
2. No restrictions shall be placed on the exercise of these rights other than such as are prescribed by law and are necessary in a democratic society in the interests of national security or public safety, for the prevention of disorder or crime, for the protection of health or morals or for the protection of the rights and freedoms of others. This Article shall not prevent the imposition of lawful restrictions on the exercise of these rights by members of the armed forces, of the police or of the administration of the State.

Article 12

Men and women of marriageable age have the right to marry and to found a family, according to the national laws governing the exercise of this right.

Article 13

Everyone whose rights and freedoms as set forth in this Convention are violated shall have an effective remedy before a national authority notwithstanding that the violation has been committed by persons acting in an official capacity.

Article 14

The enjoyment of the rights and freedoms set forth in this Convention shall be secured without discrimination on any ground such as sex, race, colour, language, religion, political or other opinion, national or social origin, association with a national minority, property, birth or other status.

Article 15

1. In time of war or other public emergency threatening the life of the nation any High Contracting party may take measures derogating from its obligations under this Convention to the extent strictly required by the exigencies of the situation, provided that such measures are not inconsistent with its other obligations under international law.
2. No derogation from Article 2, except in respect of deaths resulting from lawful acts of war, or from Articles 3, 4 (paragraph 1) and 7 shall be made under this provision.
3. Any High Contracting Party availing itself of this right of derogation shall keep the Secretary General of the Council of Europe fully informed of the measures which it has taken and the reasons therefor. It shall also inform the Secretary General of the Council of Europe when such measures have ceased to operate and the provisions of the Convention are again being fully executed.

Article 16

Nothing in Articles 10, 11 and 14 shall be regarded as preventing the High Contracting parties from imposing restrictions on the political activity of aliens.

Article 17

Nothing in this Convention may be interpreted as implying for any State, group or person any right to engage in any activity or perform any act aimed at the destruction of any of the rights and freedoms set forth herein or at their limitation to a greater extent than is provided for in the Convention.

Article 18

The restrictions permitted under this Convention to the said rights and freedoms shall not be applied for any purpose other than those for which they have been prescribed.

SECTION II

Article 19

To ensure the observance of the engagements undertaken by the High Contracting Parties in the present Convention, there shall be set up:

(1) A European Commission of Human Rights hereinafter referred to as "the Commission";

(2) A European Court of Human Rights, hereinafter referred to as "the Court".

SECTION III

Article 20

1. The Commission shall consist of a number of members equal to that of the High Contracting Parties. No two members of the Commission may be nationals of the same State.

2. The Commission shall sit in plenary session. It may, however, set up Chambers, each composed of at least seven members. The Chambers may examine petitions submitted under Article 25 of this Convention which can be dealt with on the basis of established case law or which raise no serious question affecting the interpretation or application of the Convention. Subject to this restriction and to the provisions of paragraph 5 of this Article, the Chambers shall exercise all the powers conferred on the Commission by the Convention.

   The member of the Commission elected in respect of a High Contracting Party against which a petition has been lodged shall have the right to sit on a Chamber to which that petition has been referred.

3. The Commission may set up committees, each composed of at least three members, with the power, exercisable by a unanimous vote, to declare inadmissible or strike from its list of cases a petition submitted under Article 25, when such a decision can be taken without further examination.

4. A Chamber or committee may at any time relinquish jurisdiction in favour of the plenary Commission, which may also order the transfer to it of any petition referred to a Chamber or committee.

5. Only the plenary Commission can exercise the following powers:

   a. the examination of applications submitted under Article 24;
   b. the bringing of a case before the Court in accordance with Article 48;
   c. the drawing up of rules of procedure in accordance with Article 36.

Article 21

1. The members of the Commission shall be elected by the Committee of Ministers by an absolute majority of votes, from a list of names drawn up by the Bureau of the Consultative Assembly; each group of the Representatives

of the High Contracting Parties in the Consultative Assembly shall put forward three candidates, of whom two at least shall be its nationals.

2. As far as applicable, the same procedure shall be followed to complete the Commission in the event of other States subsequently becoming Parties to this Convention, and in filling casual vacancies.

3. The candidates shall be of high moral character and must either possess the qualifications required for appointment to high judicial office or be persons of recognised competence in national or international law.

Article 22

1. The members of the Commission shall be elected for a period of six years. They may be re-elected. However, of the members elected at the first election, the terms of seven members shall expire at the end of three years...

Article 23

The members of the Commission shall sit on the Commission in their individual capacity. During their term of office they shall not hold any position which is incompatible with their independence and impartiality as members of the Commission or the demands of this office.

Article 24

Any High Contracting Party may refer to the Commission, through the Secretary General of the Council of Europe, any alleged breach of the provisions of the Convention by another High Contracting Party.

Article 25

1. The Commission may receive petitions addressed to the Secretary General of the Council of Europe from any person, non-governmental organization or group of individuals claiming to be the victim of a violation by one of the High Contracting Parties of the rights set forth in this Convention, provided that the High Contracting Party against which the complaint has been lodged has declared that it recognises the competence of the Commission to receive such petitions. Those of the High Contracting Parties who have made such a declaration undertake not to hinder in any way the effective exercise of this right.

2. Such declarations may be made for a specific period.

3. The declarations shall be deposited with the Secretary General of the Council of Europe who shall transmit copies thereof to the High Contracting Parties and publish them.

4. The commission shall only exercise the powers provided for in this Article when at least six High Contracting Parties are bound by declarations made in accordance with the preceding paragraphs.

Article 26

The Commission may only deal with the matter after all domestic remedies have been exhausted, according to the generally recognised rules of international law, and within a period of six months from the date on which the final decision was taken.

Article 27

1. The Commission shall not deal with any petition submitted under Article 25 which

   (a) is anonymous, or
   (b) is substantially the same as a matter which has already been examined by the Commission or has already been submitted to another procedure of international investigation or settlement and if it contains no relevant new information.

2. The Commission shall consider inadmissible any petition submitted under Article 25 which it considers incompatible with the provisions of the present Convention, manifestly ill-founded, or an abuse of the right of petition.
3. The Commission shall reject any petition referred to it which it considers inadmissible under Article 26.

Article 28

1. In the event of the Commission accepting a petition referred to it:

   a. it shall, with a view to ascertaining the facts, undertake together with the representatives of the parties an examination of the petition and, if need be, an investigation, for the effective conduct of which the States concerned shall furnish all necessary facilities, after an exchange of views with the Commission;
   b. it shall at the same time place itself at the disposal of the parties concerned with a view to securing a friendly settlement of the matter on the basis of respect for Human Rights as defined in the Convention.

2. If the Commission succeeds in effecting a friendly settlement, it shall draw up a Report which shall be sent to the States concerned, to the Committee of Ministers and to the Secretary General of the Council of Europe for publication. This Report shall be confined to a brief statement of the facts and of the solution reached.

Article 29

After it has accepted a petition submitted under Article 25, the Commission may nevertheless decide by a majority of two-thirds of its members to reject the petition if, in the course of its examination, it finds that the existence of one of the grounds for non-acceptance provided for in Article 27 has been established.

In such a case, the decision shall be communicated to the parties.

Article 30

1. The Commission may at any stage of the proceedings decide to strike a petition out of its list of cases where the circumstances lead to the conclusion that:

   a. the applicant does not intend to pursue his petition, or
   b. the matter has been resolved, or
   c. for any other reason established by the Commission, it is no longer justified to continue the examination of the petition.

   However, the Commission shall continue the examination of a petition if respect for Human Rights as defined in the Convention so requires.

2. If the Commission decides to strike a petition out of its list after having accepted it, it shall draw up a Report which shall contain a statement of the facts and the decision striking out the petition together with the reasons therefor. The Report shall be transmitted to the parties, as well as to the Committee of Ministers for information. The Commission may publish it.

3. The Commission may decide to restore a petition to its list of cases if it considers that the circumstances justify such a course.

Article 31

1. If the examination of a petition has not been completed in accordance with Article 28 (paragraph 2), 29 or 30, the Commission shall draw up a Report on the facts and state its opinion as to whether the facts found disclose a breach by the State concerned of its obligations under the Convention. The individual opinions of members of the Commission on this point may be stated in the Report.

2. The Report shall be transmitted to the Committee of Ministers. It shall also be transmitted to the States concerned, who shall not be at liberty to publish it.

2. *[Inserted by 9th Protocol] The Report shall be transmitted to the Committee of Ministers. The Report shall also be transmitted to the States concerned, and, if it deals with a petition submitted under Article 25, the applicant. The States concerned and the applicant shall not be at liberty to publish it.*

3. In transmitting the Report to the Committee of Ministers the Commission may make such proposals as it thinks fit.

Article 32

1. If the question is not referred to the Court in accordance with Article 48 of this Convention within a period of three months from the date of the transmission of the Report to the Committee of Ministers, the Committee of Ministers shall decide by a majority of two-thirds of the members entitled to sit on the Committee whether there has been a violation of the convention.

2. In the affirmative case the Committee of Ministers shall prescribe a period during which the High Contracting Party concerned must take the measures required by the decision of the Committee of Ministers.

3. If the High Contracting Party concerned has not taken satisfactory measures within the prescribed period, the Committee of Ministers shall decide by the majority provided for in paragraph 1 above what effect shall be given to its original decision and shall publish the Report.
4. The High Contracting Parties undertake to regard as binding on them any decision which the Committee of Ministers may take in application of the preceding paragraphs.

Article 33

The Commission shall meet in camera.

Article 34

Subject to the provisions of Articles 20 (paragraph 3) and 29, the Commission shall take its decisions by a majority of the members present and voting.

Article 35

The Commission shall meet as the circumstances require. The meeting shall be convened by the Secretary General of the Council of Europe.

Article 36

The Commission shall draw up its own rules of procedure.

Article 37

The secretariat of the Commission shall be provided by the Secretary General of the Council of Europe.

SECTION IV

Article 38

The European Court of Human Rights shall consist of a number of judges equal to that of the Members of the Council of Europe. No two judges may be nationals of the same State.

Article 39

1. The members of the Court shall be elected by the Consultative Assembly by a majority of the votes cast from a list of persons nominated by the Members of the Council of Europe; each Member shall nominate three candidates, of whom two at least shall be its nationals.

2. As far as applicable, the same procedure shall be followed to complete the Court in the event of the admission of New Members of the Council of Europe, and in filling casual vacancies.
3. The candidates shall be of high moral character and must either possess the qualifications required for appointment to high judicial office or be jurisconsults of recognised competence.

Article 40

1. The members of the Court shall be elected for a period of nine years. They may be re-elected. However, of the members elected at the first election the terms of four members shall expire at the end of three years, and the terms of four more members shall expire at the end of six years.
2. The members whose terms are to expire at the end of the initial periods of three and six years shall be chosen by lot by the Secretary-General immediately after the first election has been completed.
3. In order to ensure that, as far as possible, one third of the membership of the Court shall be renewed every three years, the Consultative Assembly may decide, before proceeding to any subsequent election, that the term or terms of office of one or more members to be elected shall be for a period other than nine years but not more than twelve and not less than six years.
4. In cases where more than one term of office in involved and the Consultative Assembly applies the preceding paragraph, the allocation of terms of office shall be effected by the drawing of lots by the Secretary General immediately after the election.
5. The members of the Court shall hold office until replaced. After having been replaced, they shall continue to deal with such cases as they already have under consideration.
6. The members of the Court shall sit on the Court in their individual capacity. During their term of office they shall not hold any position which is incompatible with their independence and impartiality as members of the Court or the demands of this office.

Article 41

The Court shall elect its President and one or two Vice-Presidents for a period of three years. They may be re-elected.

Article 42

The members of the Court shall receive for each day of duty a compensation to be determined by the Committee of Ministers.

Article 43

For the consideration of each case brought before it the Court shall consist of a Chamber composed of nine judges. There shall sit as an *ex officio* member of the

Chamber the judge who is a national of any State party concerned, or, if there is none, a person of its choice who shall sit in the capacity of judge; the names of the other judges shall be chosen by lot by the President before the opening of the case.

Article 44

Only the High Contracting Parties and the Commission shall have the right to bring a case before the Court.

Article 44 *[Inserted by 9th Protocol]*

Only the High Contracting Parties, the Commission, and persons, non-governmental organisations or groups of individuals having submitted a petition under Article 25 shall have the right to bring a case before the Court.

Article 45

The jurisdiction of the Court shall extend to all cases concerning the interpretation and application of the present Convention which the High Contracting Parties or the Commission shall refer to it in accordance with Article 48.

Article 45 *[Inserted by 9th Protocol]*

The jurisdiction of the Court shall extend to all cases concerning the interpretation and application of the present Convention which are referred to it in accordance with Article 48.

Article 46

1. Any of the High Contracting Parties may at any time declare that it recognises as compulsory ipso facto and without special agreement the jurisdiction of the Court in all matters concerning the interpretation and application of the present Convention.
2. The declarations referred to above may be made unconditionally or on condition of reciprocity on the part of several or certain other High Contracting parties or for a specified period.
3. These declarations shall be deposited with the Secretary General of the Council of Europe who shall transmit copies thereof to the High Contracting Parties.

Article 47

The Court may only deal with a case after the Commission has acknowledged the failure of efforts for a friendly settlement and within the period of three months provided for in Article 32.

Article 48

The following may bring a case before the Court, provided that the High Contracting Party concerned, if there is only one, or the High Contracting Parties concerned, if there is more than one, are subject to the compulsory jurisdiction of the Court or, failing that, with the consent of the High Contracting Party concerned, if there is only one, or of the High Contracting Parties concerned if there is more than one:

(a) The Commission;
(b) a High Contracting Party whose national is alleged to be a victim;
(c) a High Contracting Party which referred the case to the Commission;
(d) a High Contracting Party against which the complaint has been lodged.

Article 48 [Inserted by 9th Protocol]

1. *The following may refer a case to the Court, provided that the High Contracting Party concerned, if there is only one, of the High Contracting Parties concerned, if there is more than one, are subject to the compulsory jurisdiction of the Court or failing that, with the consent of the High Contracting Party concerned, if there is only one, or of the High Contracting Parties concerned if there is more than one:*

   a. *The Commission;*
   b. *a High Contracting Party whose national is alleged to be a victim;*
   c. *a High Contracting Party which referred the case to the Commission;*
   d. *a High Contracting Party against whom the complaint has been lodged;*
   e. *the person, non-governmental organisation or group of individuals having lodged the complaint with the Commission.*

2. *If a case is referred to the Court only in accordance with paragraph 1.e, it shall first be submitted to a panel composed of three members of the Court. There shall sit as an ex-officio member of the panel the judge who is elected in respect of the High Contracting Party against which the complaint has been lodged, or, if there is none, a person of its choice who shall sit in the capacity of judge. If the complaint has been lodged against more than one High Contracting Party, the size of the panel shall be increased accordingly.*

   If the case does not raise a serious question affecting the interpretation or application of the Convention, and does not for any other reason warrant consideration by the Court, the panel may, by a unanimous vote, decide that it shall not be considered by the Court. In that event, the Committee of Ministers shall decide, in accordance with the provisions of Article 32, where there has been a violation of the Convention.

Article 49

In the event of dispute as to whether the Court has jurisdiction, the matter shall be settled by decision of the Court.

Article 50

If the Court finds that a decision or a measure taken by a legal authority or any other authority of a High Contracting Party, is completely or partially in conflict with the obligations arising from the present Convention, and if the internal law of the said Party allows only partial reparation to be made for the consequences of this decision or measure, the decision of the Court shall, if necessary, afford just satisfaction to the injured party.

Article 51

1. Reasons shall be given for the judgment of the Court.
2. If the judgment does not represent in whole or in part the unanimous opinion of the judges, any judge shall be entitled to deliver a separate opinion.

Article 52

The judgment of the Court shall be final.

Article 53

The High Contracting Parties undertake to abide by the decision of the Court in any case to which they are parties.

Article 54

The judgment of the Court shall be transmitted to the Committee of Ministers which shall supervise its execution.

Article 55

The Court shall draw up its own rules and shall determine its own procedure.

Article 56

1. The first election of the members of the Court shall take place after the declarations by the High Contracting Parties mentioned in Article 46 have reached a total of eight.
2. No case can be brought before the Court before this election.

SECTION V

Article 57

On receipt of a request from the Secretary General of the Council of Europe any High Contracting Party shall furnish an explanation of the manner in which its internal law ensures the effective implementation of any of the provisions of this Convention.

Article 58

The expenses of the Commission and the Court shall be borne by the Council of Europe.

Article 59

The members of the Commission and of the Court shall be entitled during the discharge of their functions, to the privileges and immunities provided for in Article 40 of the Statute of the Council of Europe and in the agreements made thereunder.

Article 60

Nothing in this Convention shall be construed as limiting or derogating from any of the human rights and fundamental freedoms which may be ensured under the laws of any High Contracting Party or under any other agreement to which it is a Party.

Article 61

Nothing in this Convention shall prejudice the powers conferred on the Committee of Ministers by the Statute of the Council of Europe.

Article 62

The High Contracting Parties agree that, except by special agreement, they will not avail themselves of treaties, conventions or declarations in force between them for the purpose of submitting, by way of petition, a dispute arising out of the interpretation or application of this Convention to a means of settlement other than those provided for in this Convention.

Article 63

1. Any State may at the time of its ratification or at any time thereafter declare by notification addressed to the Secretary General of the Council of Europe that the present Convention shall extend to all or any of the territories for whose international relations it is responsible.
2. The Convention shall extend to the territory or territories named in the notification as from the thirtieth day after the receipt of this notification by the Secretary General of the Council of Europe.
3. The provisions of this Convention shall be applied in such territories with due regard, however, to local requirements.
4. Any State which has made a declaration in accordance with paragraph 1 of this

Article may at any time thereafter declare on behalf of one or more of the territories to which the declaration relates that it accepts the competence of the Commission to receive petitions from individuals, non-governmental organisations or groups of individuals in accordance with Article 25 of the present Convention.

Article 64

1. Any State may, when signing this Convention or when depositing its instrument of ratification, make a reservation in respect to any particular provision of the Convention to the extent that any law then in force in its territory is not in conformity with the provision. Reservations of a general character shall not be permitted under this Article.
2. Any reservation made under this Article shall contain a brief statement of the law concerned.

Article 65

1. A High Contracting Party may denounce the present Convention only after the expiry of five years from the date on which it became a party to it and after six months' notice contained in a notification addressed to the Secretary General of the Council of Europe, who shall inform the other High Contracting Parties.
2. Such a denunciation shall not have the effect of releasing the High Contracting party concerned from its obligations under this Convention in respect of any act which, being capable of constituting a violation of such obligations, may have been performed by it before the date at which the denunciation became effective.
3. Any High Contracting Party which shall cease to be a Member of the Council of Europe shall cease to be a Party to this Convention under the same conditions.
4. The Convention may be denounced in accordance with the provisions of the preceding paragraphs in respect of any territory to which it has been declared to extend under the terms of Article 63.

Article 66

1. This Convention shall be open to the signature of the Members of the Council of Europe. It shall be ratified. Ratifications shall be deposited with the Secretary General of the Council of Europe.
2. The present Convention shall come into force after the deposit of ten instruments of ratification.
3. As regards any signatory ratifying subsequently, the Convention shall come into force at the date of the deposit of its instrument of ratification.
4. The Secretary General of the Council of Europe shall notify all the Members of the Council of Europe of the entry into force of the Convention, the names of the High Contracting Parties who have ratified it, and the deposit of all instruments of ratification which may be effected subsequently.

7. FIRST PROTOCOL TO THE CONVENTION FOR THE PROTECTION OF HUMAN RIGHTS AND FUNDAMENTAL FREEDOMS

Signed at Paris: 20 March 1955

Entry into force: 18 May 1954, in accordance with Article 6

The Governments signatory hereto, being Members of the Council of Europe,

Being resolved to take steps to ensure the collective enforcement of certain rights and freedoms other than those already included in Section 1 of the Convention for the Protection of Human Rights and Fundamental Freedoms signed at Rome on 4th November, 1950 (hereinafter referred to as "the Convention").

Have agreed as follows:

Article 1

Every natural or legal person is entitled to the peaceful enjoyment of his possessions. No one shall be deprived of his possessions except in the public interest and subject to the conditions provided for by law and by the general principles of international law.

The preceding provisions shall not, however, in any way impair the right of a State to enforce such laws as it deems necessary to control the use of property in accordance with the general interest or to secure the payment of taxes or other contributions or penalties.

Article 2

No person shall be denied the right to education. In the exercise of any functions which it assumes in relation to education and to teaching, the State shall respect that right of parents to ensure such education and teaching in conformity with their own religious and philosophical convictions.

Article 3

The High Contracting Parties undertake to hold free elections at reasonable intervals by secret ballot, under conditions which will ensure the free expression of the opinion of the people in the choice of the legislature.

Article 4

Any High contracting Party may at the time of signature or ratification or at any time thereafter communicate to the Secretary General of the Council of Europe a declaration stating the extent to which it undertakes that the provisions of the present Protocol shall apply to such of the territories for the international relations of which it is responsible as are named therein.

Any High Contracting Party which has communicated a declaration in virtue of the preceding paragraph may from time to time communicate a further declaration modifying the terms of any former declaration or terminating the application of the provisions of this Protocol in respect to any territory.

A declaration made in accordance with this Article shall be deemed to have been made in accordance with Paragraph (1) of Article 63 of the Convention.

Article 5

As between the High Contracting Parties the provisions of Articles 1, 2, 3 and 4 of this Protocol shall be regarded as additional Articles to the Convention and all the provisions of the Convention shall apply accordingly.

Article 6

[Signature, ratification etc. Ten ratifications required.]

8. SECOND PROTOCOL TO THE CONVENTION FOR THE PROTECTION OF HUMAN RIGHTS AND FUNDAMENTAL FREEDOMS

Conferring upon the European Court of Human Rights competence to give advisory opinions

Signed at Strasbourg: 6 May 1963

Entry into force: 21 September 1970, in accordance with Article 5(2)

The member States of the Council of Europe signatory hereto: ...

Considering that it is expedient to confer upon the Court competence to give advisory opinions subject to certain conditions,
Have agreed as follows:

Article 1

1. The Court may, at the request of the Committee of Ministers, give advisory opinions on legal questions concerning the interpretation of the Convention and the Protocols thereto.
2. Such opinions shall not deal with any question relating to the content or scope of the rights or freedoms defined in Section 1 of the Convention and in the Protocols thereto, or with any other question which the Commission, the Court or the Committee of Ministers might have to consider in consequence of any such proceedings as could be instituted in accordance with the Convention.
3. Decisions of the Committee of Ministers to request an advisory opinion of the Court shall require a two-thirds majority vote of the representatives entitled to sit on the Committee.

Article 2

The Court shall decide whether a request for an advisory opinion submitted by the Committee of Ministers is within its consultative competence as defined in Article 1 of this Protocol.

Article 3

1. For the consideration of requests for an advisory opinion, the Court shall sit in plenary session.
2. Reasons shall be given for advisory opinions of the Court.
3. If the advisory opinion does not represent in whole or in part the unanimous opinion of the judges, any judge shall be entitled to deliver a separate opinion.

4.   Advisory opinions of the Court shall be communicated to the Committee of Ministers.

Article 4

The powers of the Court under Article 55 of the Convention shall extend to the drawing up on such rules and the determination of such procedure as the Court may think necessary for the purposes of this Protocol.

Article 5

[Signature, ratification, etc. Article 5(2) provides that ratification by all Parties to the Convention is required for entry into effect.]

9. FOURTH PROTOCOL TO THE CONVENTION FOR THE PROTECTION OF HUMAN RIGHTS AND FUNDAMENTAL FREEDOMS

Securing certain rights and freedoms other than those already included in the Convention and in the first Protocol thereto

Signed at Strasbourg: 16 September 1963
Entry into force: 2 May 1968 in accordance with Article 7

The Governments signatory hereto, being Members of the Council of Europe,

Being resolved to take steps to ensure the collective enforcement of certain rights and freedoms other than those already included in Section I of the Convention for the Protection of Human Rights and Fundamental Freedoms signed at Rome on 4th November 1950 (hereinafter referred to as "the Convention") and in Articles 1 to 3 of the First protocol to the Convention, signed at Paris on 20th March 1952,
Have agreed as follows:

Article 1

No one shall be deprived of his liberty merely on the ground of inability to fulfil a contractual obligation.

Article 2

1. Everyone lawfully within the territory of a State shall, within that territory, have the right to liberty of movement and freedom to choose his residence.
2. Everyone shall be free to leave any country, including his own.
3. No restrictions shall be placed on the exercise of these rights other than such as are in accordance with law and are necessary in a democratic society in the interests of national security or public safety, for the maintenance of *ordre public*, for the prevention of crime, for the protection of health or morals, or for the protection of the rights and freedoms of others.
4. The rights set forth in paragraph 1 may also be subject, in particular areas, to restrictions imposed in accordance with law and justified by the public interest in a democratic society.

Article 3

1. No one shall be expelled, by means either of an individual or of a collective measure, from the territory of the State of which he is a national.
2. No one shall be deprived of the right to enter the territory of the State of which he is a national.

Article 4

Collective expulsion of aliens is prohibited.

Article 5

1. Any High Contracting Party may, at the time of signature or ratification of this Protocol, or at any time thereafter, communicate to the Secretary General of the Council of Europe a declaration stating the extent to which it undertakes that the provisions of this Protocol shall apply to such of the territories for the international relations of which it is responsible as are named therein.
2. Any High Contracting Party which has communicated a declaration in virtue of the preceding paragraph may, from time to time, communicate a further declaration modifying the terms of any former declaration or terminating the application of the provisions of this protocol in respect to any territory.
3. A declaration made in accordance with this Article shall be deemed to have been made in accordance with paragraph 1 of Article 63 of the Convention.
4. The territory of any State to which this Protocol applies by virtue of ratification or acceptance by that State, and each territory to which this Protocol is applied by virtue of a declaration by that State under this Article, shall be treated as separate territories for the purpose of the references in Article 2 and 3 to the territory of a State.

Article 6

1. As between the High Contracting Parties the provisions of Articles 1 to 5 of this Protocol shall be regarded as additional Articles to the Convention, and all the provisions of the Convention shall apply accordingly.
2. Nevertheless, the right of individual recourse recognised by a declaration made under Article 25 of the Convention, or the acceptance of the compulsory jurisdiction of the Court by a declaration made under Article 46 of the Convention, shall not be effective in relation to this Protocol unless the High Contracting Party concerned has made a statement recognising such right, or accepting such jurisdiction, in respect of all or any Articles 1 to 4 of the Protocol.

Article 7

1. [Signature, etc. Five ratifications required.]

10. SEVENTH PROTOCOL TO THE CONVENTION FOR THE PROTECTION OF HUMAN RIGHTS AND FUNDAMENTAL FREEDOMS

Signed at Strasbourg: 22 November 1984

Entry into force: 1 November 1988 in accordance with Article 9

The member States of the Council of Europe signatory hereto,

Being resolved to take further steps to ensure the collective enforcement of certain rights and freedoms by means of the Convention for the Protection of Human Rights and Fundamental Freedoms signed at Rome on 4 November 1950 (hereinafter referred to as "the Convention");

Have agreed as follows:

Article 1

1. An alien lawfully resident in the territory of a State shall not be expelled therefrom except in pursuance of a decision reached in accordance with law and shall be allowed:

    a. to submit reasons against his expulsion,
    b. to have his case reviewed, and
    c. to be represented for these purposes before the competent authority or a person or persons designated by that authority.

2. An alien may be expelled before the exercise of his rights under paragraph 1(a), (b) and (c) for this Article, when such expulsion is necessary in the interests of public order or is grounded on reasons of national security.

Article 2

1. Everyone convicted of a criminal offence by a tribunal shall have the right to have conviction or sentence reviewed by a higher tribunal. The exercise of this right, including the grounds on which it may be exercised, shall be governed by law.

2. This right may be subject to exceptions in regard to offences of a minor character, as prescribed by law, or in cases in which the person concerned was tried in the first instance by the highest tribunal or was convicted following an appeal against acquittal.

Article 3

When a person has by a final decision been convicted of a criminal offence and when subsequently his conviction has been reversed, or he has been pardoned, on the ground that a new or newly discovered fact shows conclusively that there has been a miscarriage of justice, the person who has suffered punishment as a result of such conviction shall be compensated according to the law or the practice of the State concerned, unless it is proved that the non-disclosure of the unknown fact in time is wholly or partly attributable to him.

Article 4

1. No one shall be liable to be tried or punished again in criminal proceedings under the jurisdiction of the same State for an offence for which he has already been finally acquitted or convicted in accordance with the law and penal procedure of that State.
2. The provisions of the preceding paragraph shall not prevent the re-opening of the case in accordance with the law and penal procedure of the State concerned, if there is evidence of new or newly discovered facts, or if there has been a fundamental defect in the previous proceedings, which could affect the outcome of the case.
3. No derogation from this Article shall be made under Article 15 of the Convention.

Article 5

1. Spouses shall enjoy equality of rights and responsibilities of a private law character between them, and in their relations with their children, as to marriage, during marriage and in the event of its dissolution. This Article shall not prevent States from taking such measures as are necessary in the interests of the children.

Article 6

[Territories to which State obligations may apply]

Article 7

1. As between the States Parties, the provisions of Article 1 to 6 of this Protocol shall be regarded as additional Articles to the Convention, and all the provisions of the Convention shall apply accordingly.
2. Nevertheless, the right of individual recourse recognised by a declaration made under Article 25 of the Convention, or the acceptance of the compulsory jurisdiction of the Court by a declaration made under Article 46 of the Convention, shall not be effective in relation to this Protocol unless the State concerned has made a statement recognising such right, or accepting such jurisdiction in respect to Articles 1 to 5 of this Protocol.

Article 8

[Signatures, ratifications etc]

Article 9

[Entry into force: seven ratifications required]

Article 10

[Notification of signatures, ratification etc]

11. PROTOCOL NO. 11
TO THE CONVENTION FOR THE PROTECTION OF HUMAN RIGHTS AND FUNDAMENTAL FREEDOMS, RESTRUCTURING THE CONTROL MACHINERY ESTABLISHED THEREBY

Not in force

The member States of the Council of Europe, signatories to this Protocol to the Convention for the Protection of Human Rights and Fundamental Freedoms, signed at Rome on 4 November 1950 (hereinafter referred to as "the Convention"),

Considering the urgent need to restructure the control machinery established by the Convention in order to maintain and improve the efficiency of its protection of human rights and fundamental freedoms, mainly in view of the increase in the number of applications and the growing membership of the Council of Europe;

Considering that it is therefore desirable to amend certain provisions of the Convention with a view, in particular, to replacing the existing European Commission and Court of Human Rights with a new permanent Court;

Having regard to Resolution No. 1 adopted at the European Ministerial Conference on Human Rights, held in Vienna on 19 and 20 March 1985;

Having regard to Recommendation 1194 (1992), adopted by the Parliamentary Assembly of the Council of Europe on 6 October 1992;

Having regard to the decision taken on reform of the Convention control machinery by the Heads of State and Government of the Council of Europe member States in the Vienna Declaration on 9 October 1993,

Have agreed as follows:

Article 1

The existing text of Sections II to IV of the Convention (Articles 19 to 56) and Protocol No. 2 conferring upon the European Court of Human Rights competence to give advisory opinions shall be replaced by the following Section II of the Convention (Articles 19 to 51):

"SECTION II – EUROPEAN COURT OF HUMAN RIGHTS

Article 19 – Establishment of the Court

To ensure the observance of the engagements undertaken by the High Contracting Parties in the Convention and the protocols thereto, there shall be set up a European Court of Human Rights, hereinafter referred to as 'the Court'. It shall function on a permanent basis.

77

Article 20 – Number of judges

The Court shall consist of a number of judges equal to that of the High Contracting Parties.

Article 21 – Criteria for office

1. The judges shall be of high moral character and must either possess the qualifications required for appointment to high judicial office or be jurisconsults of recognised competence.
2. The judges shall sit on the Court in their individual capacity.
3. During their term of office the judges shall not engage in any activity which is incompatible with their independence, impartiality or with the demands of a full-time office; all questions arising from the application of this paragraph shall be decided by the Court.

Article 22 – Election of judges

1. The judges shall be elected by the Parliamentary Assembly with respect to each High Contracting Party by a majority of votes cast from a list of three candidates nominated by the High Contracting Party.
2. The same procedure shall be followed to complete the Court in the event of the accession of new High Contracting Parties and in filling casual vacancies.

Article 23 – Terms of office

1. The judges shall be elected for a period of six years. They may be re-elected. However, the terms of office of one-half of the judges elected at the first election shall expire at the end of three years.
2. The judges whose terms of office are to expire at the end of the initial period of three years shall be chosen by lot by the Secretary General of the Council of Europe immediately after their election.
3. In order to ensure that, as far as possible, the terms of office of one-half of the judges are renewed every three years, the Parliamentary Assembly may decide, before proceeding to any subsequent election, that the term or terms of office of one or more judges to be elected shall be for a period other than six years but not more than nine and not less than three years.
4. In cases where more than one term of office is involved and where the Parliamentary Assembly applies the preceding paragraph, the allocation of the terms of office shall be effected by a drawing of lots by the Secretary General of the Council of Europe immediately after the election.
5. A judge elected to replace a judge whose term of office has not expired shall hold office for the remainder of his predecessor's term.
6. The terms of office of judges shall expire when they reach the age of 70.
7. The judges shall hold office until replaced. They shall, however, continue to deal with such cases as they already have under consideration.

Article 24 – Dismissal

No judge may be dismissed from his office unless the other judges decide by a majority of two-thirds that he has ceased to fulfill the required conditions.

Article 25 – Registry and legal secretaries

The Court shall have a registry, the functions and organisations of which shall be laid down in the rules of the Court. The Court shall be assisted by legal secretaries.

Article 26 – Plenary Court

The plenary Court shall

  (a) elect its President and one or two Vice-Presidents for a period of three years; they may be re-elected;
  (b) set up Chambers, constituted for a fixed period of time;
  (c) elect the Presidents of the Chambers of the Court; they may be re-elected;
  (d) adopt the rules of the Court; and
  (e) elect the Registrar and one or more Deputy Registrars.

Article 27 – Committees, Chambers and Grand Chamber

1. To consider cases brought before it, the Court shall sit in committees of three judges, in Chambers of seven judges and in a Grand Chamber of seventeen judges. The Court's Chambers shall set up committees for a fixed period of time.
2. There shall sit as an *ex officio* member of the Chamber and the Grand Chamber the judge elected in respect of the State Party concerned or, if there is none or if he is unable to sit, a person of its choice who shall sit in the capacity of judge.
3. The Grand Chamber shall also include the President of the Court, the Vice-Presidents, the Presidents of the Chambers and other judges chosen in accordance with the rules of the Court. When a case is referred to the Grand Chamber under Article 43, no judge from the Chamber which rendered the judgment shall sit in the Grand Chamber, with the exception of the President of the Chamber and the judge who sat in respect of the State Party concerned.

Article 28 – Declarations of Inadmissibility by committees

A committee may, by a unanimous vote, declare inadmissible or strike out of its list of cases an individual application submitted under Article 34 where such a decision can be taken without further examination. The decision shall be final.

Article 29 – Decisions by Chambers on admissibility and merits

1. If no decision is taken under Article 28, a Chamber shall decide on the admissibility and merits of individual applications submitted under Article 34.
2. A Chamber shall decide on the admissibility and merits of inter-State applications submitted under Article 33.
3. The decision on admissibility shall be taken separately unless the Court, in exceptional cases, decides otherwise.

Article 30 – Relinquishment of jurisdiction to the Grand Chamber

Where a case pending before a Chamber raises a serious question affecting the interpretation of the Convention or the protocols thereto, or where the resolution of a question before the Chamber might have a result inconsistent with a judgment previously delivered by the Court, the Chamber may, at any time before it has rendered its judgment, relinquish jurisdiction in favour of the Grand Chamber, unless one of the parties to the case objects.

Article 31 – Powers of the Grand Chamber

The Grand Chamber shall

(a) determine applications submitted either under Article 33 or Article 34 when a Chamber has relinquished jurisdiction under Article 30 or when the case has been referred to it under Article 43; and
(b) consider requests for advisory opinions submitted under Article 47.

Article 32 – Jurisdiction of the Court

1. The jurisdiction of the Court shall extend to all matters concerning the interpretation and application of the Convention and the protocols thereto which are referred to it as provided in Articles 33, 34 and 47.
2. In the event of dispute as to whether the Court has jurisdiction, the Court shall decide.

Article 33 – Inter-State cases

Any High Contracting Party may refer to the Court any alleged breach of the provisions of the Convention and the protocols thereto by another High Contracting Party.

Article 34 – Individual applications

The Court may receive applications from any person, non-governmental organisation or group of individuals claiming to be the victim of a violation by one of the High Contracting Parties of the rights set forth in the Convention or the protocols thereto. The High Contracting Parties undertake not to hinder in any way the effective exercise of this right.

Article 35 – Admissibility criteria

1. The Court may only deal with the matter after all domestic remedies have been exhausted, according to the generally recognised rules of international law, and within a period of six months from the date on which the final decision was taken.
2. The Court shall not deal with any individual application submitted under Article 34 that

    (a) is anonymous; or
    (b) is substantially the same as a matter that has already been examined by the Court or has already been submitted to another procedure of international investigation or settlement and contains no relevant new information.

3. The Court shall declare inadmissible any individual application submitted under Article 34 which it considers incompatible with the provisions of the Convention or the protocols thereto, manifestly ill-founded, or an abuse of the right of application.
4. The Court shall reject any application which it considers inadmissible under this Article. It may do so at any stage of the proceedings.

Article 36 – Third party intervention

1. In all cases before a Chamber or the Grand Chamber, a High Contracting Party one of whose nationals is an applicant shall have the right to submit written comments and to take part in hearings.
2. The President of the Court may, in the interest of the proper administration of justice, invite any High Contracting Party which is not a party to the proceedings or any person concerned who is not the applicant to submit written comments or take part in hearings.

Article 37 – Striking out applications

1. The Court may at any stage of the proceedings decide to strike an application out of its list of cases where the circumstances lead to the conclusion that

    (a) the applicant does not intend to pursue his application; or
    (b) the matter has been resolved; or
    (c) for any other reason established by the Court, it is no longer justified to continue the examination of the application.

    However, the Court shall continue the examination of the application if respect for human rights as defined in the Convention and the protocols thereto so requires.

2. The Court may decide to restore an application to its list of cases if it considers that the circumstances justify such a course.

Article 38 – Examination of the case and friendly settlement proceedings

1. If the Court declares the application admissible, it shall

    (a) pursue the examination of the case, together with the representatives of the parties, and if need be, undertake an investigation, for the effective conduct of which the States concerned shall furnish all necessary facilities;

    (b) place itself at the disposal of the parties concerned with a view to securing a friendly settlement of the matter on the basis of respect for human rights as defined in the Convention and the protocols thereto.

2. Proceedings conducted under paragraph 1.b shall be confidential.

Article 39 – Finding of a friendly settlement

If a friendly settlement is effected, the Court shall strike the case out of its list by means of a decision which shall be confined to a brief statement of the facts and of the solution reached.

Article 40 – Public hearings and access to documents

1. Hearings shall be public unless the Court in exceptional circumstances decides otherwise.
2. Documents deposited with the Registrar shall be accessible to the public unless the President of the Court decides otherwise.

Article 41 – Just satisfaction

If the Court finds that there has been a violation of the Convention or the protocols thereto, and if the internal law of the High Contracting Party concerned allows only partial reparation to be made, the Court shall, if necessary, afford just satisfaction to the injured party.

Article 42 – Judgments of Chambers

Judgments of Chambers shall become final in accordance with the provisions of Article 44, paragraph 2.

Article 43 – Referral to the Grand Chamber

1. Within a period of three months from the date of the judgment of the Chamber, any party to the case may, in exceptional cases, request that the case be referred to the Grand Chamber.
2. A panel of five judges of the Grand Chamber shall accept the request if the case raises a serious question affecting the interpretation or application of the

Convention or the protocols thereto, or a serious issue of general importance.

3. If the panel accepts the request, the Grand Chamber shall decide the case by means of a judgment.

Article 44 – Final judgments

1. The judgment of the Grand Chamber shall be final.
2. The judgment of a Chamber shall become final

    (a) when the parties declare that they will not request that the case be referred to the Grand Chamber; or
    (b) three months after the date of the judgment, if reference of the case to the Grand Chamber has not been requested; or
    (c) when the panel of the Grand Chamber rejects the request to refer under Article 43.

3. The final judgment shall be published.

Article 45 – Reasons for judgments and decisions

1. Reasons shall be given for judgments as well as for decisions declaring applications admissible or inadmissible.
2. If a judgment does not represent, in whole or in part, the unanimous opinion of the judges, any judge shall be entitled to deliver a separate opinion.

Article 46 – Binding force and execution of judgments

1. The High Contracting Parties undertake to abide by the final judgment of the Court in any case to which they are parties.
2. The final judgment of the Court shall be transmitted to the Committee of Ministers, which shall supervise its execution.

Article 47 – Advisory opinions

1. The Court may, at the request of the Committee of Ministers, give advisory opinions on legal questions concerning the interpretation of the Convention and the protocols thereto.
2. Such opinions shall not deal with any question relating to the content or scope of the rights or freedoms defined in Section I of the Convention and the protocols thereto, or with any other question which the Court or the Committee of Ministers might have to consider in consequence of any such proceedings as could be instituted in accordance with the Convention.
3. Decisions of the Committee of Ministers to request an advisory opinion of the Court shall require a majority vote of the representatives entitled to sit on the Committee.

Article 48 – Advisory jurisdiction of the Court

The Court shall decide whether a request for an advisory opinion submitted by the Committee of Ministers is within its competence as defined in Article 47.

Article 49 – Reasons for advisory opinions

1. Reasons shall be given for advisory opinions of the Court.
2. If the advisory opinion does not represent, in whole or in part, the unanimous opinion of the judges, any judge shall be entitled to deliver a separate opinion.
3. Advisory opinions of the Court shall be communicated to the Committee of Ministers.

Article 50 – Expenditure on the Court

The expenditure on the Court shall be borne by the Council of Europe.

Article 51 – Privileges and immunities of judges

The judges shall be entitled, during the exercise of their functions, to the privileges and immunities provided for in Article 40 of the Statute of the Council of Europe and in the agreements made thereunder."

Article 2

1. Section V of the Convention shall become Section III of the Convention; Article 57 of the Convention shall become Article 52 of the Convention; Articles 58 and 59 of the Convention shall be deleted, and Articles 60 to 66 of the Convention shall become Articles 53 to 59 of the Convention respectively.
2. Section I of the Convention shall be entitled "Rights and freedoms" and new Section III of the Convention shall be entitled "Miscellaneous provisions". Articles 1 to 18 and new Articles 52 to 59 of the Convention shall be provided with headings, as listed in the appendix to this Protocol.
3. In new Article 56, in paragraph 1, the words ", subject to paragraph 4 of this Article," shall be inserted after the word "shall"; in paragraph 4, the words "Commission to receive petitions" and "in accordance with Article 25 of the present Convention" shall be replaced by the words "Court to receive applications" and "as provided in Article 34 of the Convention" respectively. In new Article 58, paragraph 4, the words "Article 63" shall be replaced by the words "Article 56".
4. The Protocol to the Convention shall be amended as follows

    (a) the Articles shall be provided with the headings listed in the appendix to the present Protocol; and
    (b) in Article 4, last sentence, the words "of Article 63" shall be replaced by the words "of Article 56".

5. Protocol No. 4 shall be amended as follows

   (a) the Articles shall be provided with the headings listed in the appendix to the present Protocol;

   (b) in Article 5, paragraph 3, the words "of Article 63" shall be replaced by the words "of Article 56"; a new paragraph 5 shall be added, which shall read

   "Any State which has made a declaration in accordance with paragraph 1 or 2 of this Article may at any time thereafter declare on behalf of one or more of the territories to which the declaration relates that it accepts the competence of the Court to receive applications from individuals, non-governmental organisations or groups of individuals as provided in Article 34 of the Convention in respect of all or any of Articles 1 to 4 of this Protocol."; and

   (c) paragraph 2 of Article 6 shall be deleted.

6. Protocol No. 6 shall be amended as follows

   (a) the Articles shall be provided with the heading listed in the appendix to the present Protocol; and

   (b) in Article 4 the words "under Article 64" shall be replaced by the words "under Article 57".

7. Protocol No. 7 shall be amended as follows

   (a) the Articles shall be provided with the headings listed in the appendix to the present Protocol;

   (b) in Article 6, paragraph 4, the words "of Article 63" shall be replaced by the words "of Article 56"; a new paragraph 6 shall be added, which shall read

   "Any State which has made a declaration in accordance with paragraph 1 or 2 of this Article may at any time thereafter declare on behalf of one or more of the territories to which the declaration relates that it accepts the competence of the Court to receive applications from individuals, non-governmental Organisations or groups of individuals as provided in Article 34 of the Convention in respect of Articles 1 to 5 of this Protocol."; and

   (c) paragraph 2 of Article 7 shall be deleted.

8. Protocol No. 9 shall be repealed.

Article 3

[Signature, ratification etc.]

Article 4

This Protocol shall enter into force on the first day of the month following the expiration of a period of one year after the date on which all Parties to the Convention have expressed their consent to be bound by the Protocol in accordance with the provisions of Article 3. The election of new judges may take place, and any further necessary steps may be taken to establish the new Court, in accordance with the provisions of this Protocol from the date on which all Parties to the Convention have expressed their consent to be bound by the Protocol.

Article 5

1. Without prejudice to the provisions in paragraphs 3 and 4 below, the terms of office of the judges, members of the Commission, Registrar and Deputy Registrar shall expire at the date of entry into force of this Protocol.
2. Applications pending before the Commission which have not been declared admissible at the date of the entry into force of this Protocol shall be examined by the Court in accordance with the provisions of this Protocol.
3. Applications which have been declared admissible at the date of entry into force of this Protocol shall continue to be dealt with by members of the Commission within a period of one year thereafter. Any applications the examination of which has not been completed within the aforesaid period shall be transmitted to the Court which shall examine them as admissible cases in accordance with the provisions of this Protocol.
4. With respect to applications in which the Commission, after the entry into force of this Protocol, has adopted a report in accordance with former Article 31 of the Convention, the report shall be transmitted to the parties, who shall not be at liberty to publish it. In accordance with the provisions applicable prior to the entry into force of this Protocol, a case may be referred to the Court. The panel of the Grand Chamber shall determine whether one of the Chambers or the Grand Chamber shall decide the case. If the case is decided by a Chamber, the decision of the Chamber shall be final. Cases not referred to the Court shall be dealt with by the Committee of Ministers acting in accordance with the provisions of former Article 32 of the Convention.
5. Cases pending before the Court which have not been decided at the date of entry into force of this Protocol shall be transmitted to the Grand Chamber of the Court, which shall examine them in accordance with the provisions of this Protocol.
6. Cases pending before the Committee of Ministers which have not been decided under former Article 32 of the Convention at the date of entry into force of this Protocol shall be completed by the Committee of Ministers acting in accordance with that Article.

Article 6

Where a High Contracting Party had made a declaration recognising the competence of the Commission or the jurisdiction of the Court under former Article 25 or 46 of the Convention with respect to matters arising after or based on facts occurring subsequent to any such declaration, this limitation shall remain valid for the jurisdiction of the Court under this Protocol.

Article 7

[Notification of signatures, ratifications, entry into force, etc.]

12. EUROPEAN AGREEMENT RELATING TO PERSONS PARTICIPATING IN PROCEEDINGS OF THE EUROPEAN COMMISSION AND COURT OF HUMAN RIGHTS

Signed at London: 6 May 1969

Entry into force: 17 April 1971

Editors' Notes

A revised European Agreement relating to Persons Participating in Proceedings of the European Court of Human Rights was opened for signature on 5 March 1996. The revised *Agreement* is intended to take account of the changes to the control machinery of the Convention contained in Protocol 11 to the Convention. Article 8 of the Revised Agreement provides that it shall enter into force on the first day following the expiration of one month after the date on which ten member States of the Council of Europe have expressed their consent to be bound by the *Agreement* or on the date of entry into force of Protocol No. 11 to the Convention, whichever is the later.

PREAMBLE

The member States of the Council of Europe, signatory hereto,

Having regard to the Convention for the Protection of Human Rights and Fundamental Freedoms, signed at Rome on 4th November 1950 (hereinafter referred to as "the Convention");

Considering that it is expedient for the better fulfilment of the purposes of the Convention that persons taking part in proceedings before the European Commission of Human Rights (hereinafter referred to as "the Commission") or the European Court of Human Rights (hereinafter referred to as "the Court") shall be accorded certain immunities and facilities;

Desiring to conclude an Agreement for this purpose,

Have agreed as follows:

Article 1

1. The persons to whom this Agreement applies are:

    (a) agents of the Contracting Parties and advisers and advocates assisting them;

    (b) persons taking part in proceedings instituted before the Commission under Article 25 of the Convention, whether in their own name or as representatives of one of the applicants enumerated in the said Article 25;

    (c) barristers, solicitors or professors of law, taking part in proceedings in order to assist one of the persons enumerated in sub-paragraph (b) above;

(d) persons chosen by the delegates of the Commission to assist them in proceedings before the Court;

(e) witnesses, experts and other persons called upon by the Commission or the Court to take part in proceedings before the Commission of the Court.

2. For the purposes of this Agreement, the terms "Commission" and "Court" shall include a Sub-Commission or Chamber, or members of either body carrying out their duties under the terms of the Convention or of the rules of the Commission or of the Court, as the case may be; and the term "taking part in proceedings" shall include making communications with a view to a complaint against a State which has recognised the right of individual petition under Article 25 of the Convention.

3. If, in the course of the exercise by the Committee of Ministers of its functions under Article 32 of the Convention, any person mentioned in paragraph 1 of this Article is called upon to appear before, or to submit written statements to the Committee of Ministers, the provisions of this Agreement shall apply in relation to him.

Article 2

1. The persons referred to in paragraph 1 of Article 1 of this Agreement shall have immunity from legal process in respect of oral or written statements made, or documents or other evidence submitted by them before or to the Commission or the Court.

2. This immunity does not apply to the communication, outside the Commission or the Court, by or on behalf of any person entitled to immunity under the preceding paragraph, of any such statements, documents or evidence or any part hereof submitted by that person to the Commission or the Court.

Article 3

1. The Contracting Parties shall respect the right of the persons referred to in paragraph 1 of the Article 1 of this Agreement to correspond freely with the Commission and the Court.

2. As regards persons under detention, the exercise of this right shall in particular imply that:

(a) if their correspondence is examined by the competent authorities, its despatch and delivery shall nevertheless take place without undue delay and without alteration;

(b) such persons shall not be subject to disciplinary measures in any form on account of any communication sent through the proper channels to the Commission or the Court;

(c) such persons shall have the right to correspond, and consult out of hearing of other person, with a lawyer qualified to appear before the courts of the country where they are detained in regard to an application to the Commission, or any proceedings resulting therefrom.

3. In application of the preceding paragraphs, there shall be no interference by a public authority except such as is in accordance with the law and is necessary in a democratic society in the interests of national security, for the detection or prosecution of a criminal offence or for the protection of health.

Article 4

1. (a) The Contracting Parties undertake not to hinder the free movement and travel, for the purpose of attending and returning from proceedings before the Commission or the Court, of persons referred to in paragraph 1 of Article 1 of this Agreement whose presence has in advance been authorised by the Commission or the Court.
    (b) No restrictions shall be placed on their movement and travel other than such as are in accordance with the law and necessary in a democratic society in the interests of national security of public safety, for the maintenance of order public, for the prevention of crime, for the protection of health or morals, or for the protection of the rights and freedoms of others.

2. (a) Such persons shall not, in countries of transit and in the country where the proceedings take place, be prosecuted or detained or be subjected to any other restriction of their personal liberty in respect to acts or convictions prior to the commencement of the journey.
    (b) Any Contracting Party may at the time of signature or ratification of this Agreement declare that the provisions of this paragraph will not apply to its own nationals. Such a declaration may be withdrawn at any time by means of a notification addressed to the Secretary General of the Council of Europe.

3. The Contracting Parties undertake to re-admit on his return to their territory any such person who commenced his journey in the said territory.

4. The provisions of paragraphs 1 and 2 of this Article shall cease to apply when the person concerned has had for a period of 15 consecutive days from the date when his presence is no longer required by the Commission or the Court the opportunity of returning to the country from which his journey commenced.

5. Where there is any conflict between the obligations of a Contracting Party resulting from paragraph 2 of this Article and those resulting from a Council of Europe Convention or from an extradition treaty or other treaty concerning mutual assistance in criminal matters with other Contracting Parties, the provisions of paragraph 2 of this Article shall prevail.

Article 5

1. Immunities and facilities are accorded to the persons referred to in paragraph 1 of Article 1 of this Agreement solely in order to ensure for them the freedom of speech and the independence necessary for the discharge of their functions, tasks or duties, or the exercise of their rights in relation to the Commission of the Court.

2. (a) The Commission or the Court, as the case may be, shall alone be competent to waive, in whole or in part, the immunity provided for paragraph 1 of Article 2 of this Agreement; they have not only the right but the duty to waive immunity in any case where, in their opinion, such immunity would impede the course of justice and waiver in whole or in part would not prejudice the purpose defined in paragraph 1 of this Article.
    (b) The immunity may be waived by the Commission or by the Court, either *ex officio* or at the request, addressed to the Secretary General of the Council of Europe, of any Contracting Party or of any person concerned.
    (c) Decisions waiving immunity or refusing the waiver shall be accompanied by a statement of reasons.

3. If a Contracting Party certifies that waiver of the immunity provided for in paragraph 1 of Article 2 of this Agreement is necessary for the purpose of proceedings in respect of an offence against national security, the Commission or the Court shall waive immunity to the extent specified in the certificate.

4. In the event of the discovery of a fact which might, by its nature, have a decisive influence and which at the time of the decision refusing waiver of immunity was unknown to the author of the request, the latter may make a new request to the Commission or the Court.

Article 6

Nothing in this Agreement shall be construed as limiting or derogating from any of the obligations assumed by the Contracting Parties under the Convention.

Article 7

1. This Agreement shall be open to signature by the member States of the Council of Europe, who may become Parties to it either by:

    (a) signature without reservation in respect of ratification or acceptance, or
    (b) signature by ratification in respect of ratification or acceptance, followed by ratification or acceptance.

2. Instruments of ratification or acceptance shall be deposited with the Secretary General of the Council of Europe.

Article 8

1. This Agreement shall enter into force one month after the date on which five member States of the Council shall have become Parties to the Agreement, in accordance with the provisions of Article 7.

2. As regards any member States who shall subsequently sign the Agreement without reservation in respect of ratification or acceptance or who shall ratify or accept it, the Agreement shall enter into force one month after the date of such signature or after the date of the instrument of ratification or acceptance.

Article 9

1. Any Contracting Party may at the time of signature or when depositing its instrument of ratification or acceptance, specify the territory or territories to which this Agreement shall apply.
2. Any Contracting Party may, when depositing its instrument of ratification or acceptance or at any later date, by declaration addressed to the Secretary General of the Council of Europe, extend this Agreement to any other territory or territories specified in the declaration and for whose international relations it is responsible or on whose behalf it is authorized to give undertakings.
3. Any declaration made in pursuance of the preceding paragraph may, in respect of any territory mentioned in such declaration, be withdrawn according to the procedure laid down in Article 10 of this Agreement.

Article 10

1. This Agreement shall remain in force indefinitely.
2. Any Contracting Party may, insofar as it is concerned, denounce this Agreement by means of a notification addressed to the Secretary General of the Council of Europe.
3. Such denunciation shall take effect six months after the date of receipt by the Secretary General of such notification. Such a denunciation shall not have the effect of releasing the Contracting Parties concerned from any obligation which may have arisen under this Agreement in relation to any person referred to in paragraph 1 of Article 1.

Article 11

The Secretary General of the Council of Europe shall notify the Member States of the Council of:

(a) any signature without reservation in respect of ratification or acceptance;
(b) any signature with reservation in respect of ratification or acceptance;
(c) the deposit of any instrument of ratification or acceptance;
(d) any date of entry into force of this Agreement in accordance with Article 8 thereof;
(e) any declaration received in pursuance of the provisions of paragraph 2 of Article 4 and paragraphs 2 and 3 of Article 9;
(f) any notification of withdrawal of a declaration in pursuance of the provisions of paragraph 2 of Article 4 and any notification received in pursuance of the provisions of Article 10 and the date on which any denunciation takes effect.

13. RULES OF PROCEDURE OF THE EUROPEAN COMMISSION OF HUMAN RIGHTS

Entry into force: 28 June 1993

Revised version as adopted by the Commission: 12 February and 6 May 1993

The Commission,

Having regard to the Convention for the Protection of Human Rights and Fundamental freedoms and Protocols hereinafter called "the Convention",
Pursuant to Article 36 of the Convention,
Adopts the present Rules:

TITLE I – ORGANISATION OF THE COMMISSION

CHAPTER I – THE COMMISSION

Rule 1

1. The Commission sits in plenary session, in Chambers and in Committees set up under Article 20, paragraphs 2 and 3, of the Convention.
2. Unless otherwise stated, the terms "Commission" and "President" in these Rules shall mean "Chamber" and "President of the Chamber" in relation to cases referred to Chambers, and "Committee" and "President of the Committee" in relation to cases referred to Committees.

CHAPTER II – MEMBERS OF THE COMMISSION

Rule 2

1. The duration of the term of office of members of the Commission elected on 18 May 1954 shall be calculated as from this date. Similarly, the duration of the term of office of any member elected as a consequence of a State becoming a Party to the Convention after 18 May 1954 shall be calculated as from the election.
2. However, where members are re-elected on the expiry of their terms of office or are elected to replace a member whose term of office has expired or is about to expire, the duration of their term of office shall, in either case, be calculated as from the date of such expiry.

Rule 3

Before taking up their duties, members of the Commission shall, at the first meeting of the Commission at which they are present after their election, make the following solemn declaration:

"I solemnly declare that I will exercise all my powers and duties honourably and faithfully, impartially and conscientiously and that I will keep secret all Commission proceedings."

Rule 4

1. Members of the Commission shall take precedence after the President of the Commission and Presidents of Chambers according to the length of time they have been in office.
2. Members having the same length of time in office shall take precedence according to age.
3 Re-elected members shall take precedence having regard to the duration of their previous terms of office.

Rule 5

Resignation of a member shall be notified to the President of the Commission who shall transmit it to the Secretary General of the Council of Europe.

CHAPTER III – PRESIDENCY OF THE COMMISSION

Rule 6

1. The Commission shall elect its President in plenary session not later than the second session after the date of the entry into office of members elected at periodical elections of part of the Commission in accordance with Article 22, paragraph 1, of the Convention.
2. The term of office of the President of the Commission shall be three years.
3. If the President of the Commission, before the normal expiry of his term of office, ceases to be a member of the Commission or resigns from office, the Commission shall as soon as possible elect a successor to hold office for the remainder of the said term.
4. Each Chamber, voting separately, shall elect its President and Vice-President as soon as the Chambers have been constituted according to Rule 24, paragraph 3.
5. The term of office of the President of a Chamber shall be eighteen months. On the expiry of this term the presidency of the Chamber shall be assumed by the Vice-President for the remainder of the period for which the Chamber has been constituted. At the same time the Chamber concerned shall elect a new Vice-President.
6. A member of the Commission who has served as the President of a Chamber

shall not be eligible for re-election as President or Vice-President of a Chamber until eighteen months have elapsed since the end of his previous term of office.

7. The elections referred to in this Rule shall be by secret ballot, only the members present shall take part. Election shall be by an absolute majority of the members of the Commission or of the members of the Chamber concerned, as appropriate.

8. If no member receives such a majority, a second ballot shall take place. The member receiving the most votes shall then be elected. In the case of equal voting the member having precedence under Rule 4 shall be elected.

Rule 7

1. The President of the Commission shall direct the work of the Commission and preside at its plenary sessions.

2. The Presidents of Chambers shall preside at the meetings of the Chamber which has elected them.

3. Each Committee shall be presided over by the member taking precedence under Rule 4 of these Rules.

4. The term "President" shall in these Rules, where appropriate, include also any member acting as president.

Rule 8

1. The Presidents of Chambers, according to the order of precedence laid down in Rule 4, shall take the place of the President of the Commission if the latter is prevented from carrying out the duties of President or if the office of President is vacant.

2. The Vice-President of a Chamber shall take the place of the President of the Chamber which has elected him if the latter is prevented from carrying out his duties or if the office of President of Chamber is vacant.

3. The President of the Commission may delegate certain functions to the President of either Chamber.

Rule 9

1. If the President of the Commission and the Presidents of Chambers are at the same time prevented from carrying out their duties, or if their offices are at the same time vacant, the duties of President of the Commission shall be carried out by another member according to the order of precedence laid down in Rule 4.

2. If the President and Vice-President of the Chamber are prevented from carrying out their duties in respect of that Chamber, or if their offices are at the same time vacant, the duties of President shall be carried out by another member according to the order of precedence dawn in Rule 4.

Rule 10

Members of the Commission shall not preside in cases to which the High Contracting Party, of which they are nationals or in respect of which they were elected, is a party.

Rule 11

Where the President of the Commission or the Presidents of the Chambers for some special reason consider that they should not act as President in a particular case, they shall be replaced in accordance with the provisions of Rule 8, paragraph 1, and Rule 9.

CHAPTER IV – SECRETARIAT OF THE COMMISSION

Rule 12

1. The Secretariat of the Commission shall consist of the Secretary, the Deputy Secretary, and other staff members appointed under Article 37 of the Convention.
2. The Secretary and the Deputy Secretary to the Commission shall be appointed by the Secretary General of the Council of Europe on the proposal of the Commission.
3. The officials of the Secretariat of the Commission, other than the Secretary and the Deputy Secretary, shall be appointed by the Secretary-General, with the agreement of the President of the Commission or the Secretary acting on the President's instructions.

Rule 13

1. The Secretary to the Commission shall, under the general direction of the President, be responsible for the work of the Secretariat and, in particular:

    a. shall assist the Commission and its members in the fulfilment of their duties,
    b. shall be the channel for all communications concerning the Commission,
    c. shall have custody of the archives of the Commission.

2. The Secretary shall be responsible for the publication of:

    a. the decisions of the Commission,
    b. minutes of the Commission's sessions,
    c. any other document insofar as their publication in the official languages or in any other language is considered useful by the President.

Rule 14

A special register shall be kept at the Secretariat in which shall be entered the date of registration of each application and the date of the termination of the relevant proceedings before the Commission.

TITLE II – THE FUNCTIONING OF THE COMMISSION

CHAPTER I – GENERAL RULES

Rule 15

1. The seat of the Commission shall be in Strasbourg.
2. The Commission may decide, at any stage of the examination of an application, that it is necessary that an investigation or any other of its functions be carried out elsewhere by it or one or more of its members.

Rule 16

1. The Commission shall meet during at least sixteen weeks in each year.
2. The Commission shall, at the last session of each year at the latest, fix its sessions for the following year. It shall meet at other times by decision of the President as circumstances may require. It shall also meet if at least one third of the members so request.
3. Members who are prevented by illness or other serious reason from attending all or part of any session of the Commission or from fulfilling any other duty shall, as soon as possible, give notice thereof to the Secretary who shall inform the President.

Rule 17

1. All deliberations of the Commission shall be and shall remain confidential. Only the Secretary to the Commission, members of its Secretariat, interpreters, and persons providing technical or secretarial assistance to the Commission may be present at its meetings, unless the Commission decides otherwise.
2. The contents of all case-files, including all pleadings, shall be confidential. However, the decisions of the Commission on admissibility shall be available to the public, provided that the name or other means of identification of an applicant shall not be indicated, unless the Commission decides otherwise.
3. At any stage in the examination of an application, the Secretary may communicate information to the press to an extent compatible with the legitimate interests of the parties and subject to any special directions by the Commission.

Rule 18

1. After any deliberations and before a vote is taken on any matter in the Commission, the President may request members to state their opinions thereon, in the order of precedence laid down in Rule 4, starting with the junior member. The vote may also be taken in the same manner.
2. If the voting is equal, a roll call vote shall then be taken as provided in paragraph 1 of this Rule and the President shall have a casting vote.
3. In decisions on the admissibility of an application, or in expressing an opinion on a breach of the Convention, members shall not abstain.

Rule 19

1. The records of deliberations shall be limited to a record of the subject of the discussions, the votes taken, the names of those voting for and against a motion and any statements expressly made for insertion therein.
2. The records of hearings shall contain the names of the members present and of any persons appearing; they shall give a brief account of the course of the hearing and of any decision taken.
3. The draft minutes of the Commission's sessions shall be circulated to members and if no comments are received within a prescribed time-limit they shall be deemed to be adopted. Any such comments will be taken up at the next session.

Rule 20

1. Members shall not take part in the examination of an application before the Commission, where they

   a. have any personal interest in the case;
   b. have participated in any decision on the facts on which the application is based as adviser to any of the parties or as a member of any tribunal or body of enquiry.

2. If, in any case of doubt with regard to paragraph 1 of this Rule, or in any other circumstances which might appear to affect the impartiality of members in their examination of an application, they or the President consider that they should not take part, the Commission shall decide.

Rule 21

Where, for any special reason other than under Rule 20, members consider that they should not take part or continue to take part in the examination of a case, they shall inform the President.

Rule 22

Any member who, under the provisions of Rule 20 or Rule 21, does not take part in the examination of an application, shall not form part of the quorum during such examination.

CHAPTER II – THE PLENARY COMMISSION

Rule 23

1. A quorum of the Commission shall consist of a number of members equal to the majority of the members of the Commission.
2. However, seven members shall constitute a quorum when the Commission examines an application submitted under Article 25 of the Convention and:

   a. decides to act as provided in Rule 48, paragraph 2, or
   b. declares the application inadmissible or decides to strike it off its list of cases provided that notice of the application has not been given to the High Contracting Party concerned under Rule 48, paragraph 2 b.

3. Seven members shall also constitute a quorum when the Commission acts in pursuance of the Addendum to the present Rules (Legal aid).

CHAPTER III – THE CHAMBERS

Rule 24

1. There shall be two Chambers set up under Article 20, paragraph 2, of the Convention.
2. The composition of the Chambers shall be determined by the Commission.
3. The Chambers shall be constituted for three years as soon as possible following the election of the President of the Commission in accordance with Rule 6 of these Rules.
4. The Commission may make such special arrangements concerning the constitution of Chambers as it sees fit.

Rule 25

1. Where a member of the Commission elected in respect of the High Contracting Party against which a petition has been lodged is not a member of the Chamber to which that petition has been referred, but wishes to sit on that Chamber in accordance with Article 20, paragraph 2, last sentence, of the Convention, the President of the Chamber shall be so informed.
2. Where members of a Chamber cease to be members of the Commission before the expiration of the period for which the Chamber was constituted, their successors in the Commission shall succeed them as members of the Chamber.

Rule 26

1. A quorum of a Chamber shall be seven members.
2. As a rule, the Chambers meet during the sessions of the Commission.
3. Where circumstances require, the Chamber or, when it is not in session, its President, may decide that the Chamber may meet when the Commission is not in session.

CHAPTER IV – THE COMMITTEES

Rule 27

1. There shall be Committees set up under Article 20, paragraph 3, of the Convention.
2. The Committees shall be constituted once a year. The members shall be chosen by the drawing of lots.

Rule 28

1. The Committees shall each be composed of three members. The President of the Commission shall not be a member of a Committee.
2. The members of the Commission who shall sit on the Committees shall be distributed in three lists, following the order of precedence set out in Rule 4 of these Rules. Each Committee shall be composed of one member from each list, chosen in the above order of precedence.
3. The members of the Commission who have not been chosen to sit on Committees shall act as substitute Committee members.
4. If a member is prevented from attending, a substitute member shall sit in that member's place. If none of the substitute members is able to attend, a member appearing on the same list as the member prevented from attending shall sit on the Committee.

Rule 29

The Committees meet during the sessions of the Commission.

TITLE III – PROCEDURE

CHAPTER I – GENERAL RULES

Rule 30

1. The official languages of the Commission shall be English and French.
2. The President may authorise a member to speak in another language.
3. The President may permit the use by a party or a person representing that party of a language other than English or French, either in hearings or

documents. Any such document shall be submitted in an original and at least two copies.

4. The Secretary is authorised, in correspondence with an applicant, to employ a language other than English or French.

Rule 31

The High Contracting Parties shall be represented before the Commission by their agents who may have the assistance of advisers.

Rule 32

1. Persons, non-governmental organisations, or groups of individuals, may present and conduct applications under Article 25 of the Convention on their own behalf or through a representative appointed under paragraph 2 of this Rule.
2. Any such applicant may appoint, and be represented in proceedings before the Commission by, a lawyer or any other person, resident in a Convention country, unless the Commission at any stage decides otherwise.
3. Any such applicant or representative shall appear in person before the Commission:

   a. to present the application in a hearing fixed by the Commission; or
   b. for any other purpose, if invited by the Commission.

4. In the other provisions of these Rules the term "applicant" shall, where appropriate, include the applicant's representative.

Rule 33

The Commission shall deal with applications in the order in which they become ready for examination. It may, however, decide to give precedence to a particular application.

Rule 34

1. The Commission may, *proprio motu*, or at the request of a party, take any action which it considers expedient or necessary for the proper performance of its duties under the Convention.
2. The Commission may delegate one or more of its members to take any such action in its name, and in particular to hear witnesses or experts, to examine documents or to visit any locality. Such member or members shall duly report to the Commission.
3. In case of urgency when the Commission is not in session, the President of the Commission or, if he is prevented from carrying out his duties, the President of either Chamber, may take any necessary action on behalf of the Commission. As soon as the Commission is again in session, any action which has been taken under this paragraph shall be brought to its attention.

Rule 35

The Commission may, if it considers necessary, order the joinder of two or more applications.

Rule 36

The Commission, or when it is not in session, the President may indicate to the parties any interim measure the adoption of which seems desirable in the interest of the parties or the proper conduct of the proceedings before it.

CHAPTER II – HEARINGS

Rule 37

1. Hearings before the Commission shall be held in camera. Unless the Commission decides otherwise, no person shall be admitted, other than:

   a. the persons referred to in Rule 31 or 32;
   b. the individual applicant;
   c. any person being heard by the Commission as a witness;
   d. the persons referred to in Rule 17, paragraph 1.

2. If the applicant is a non-governmental organisation or group of individuals, the Commission shall ensure that those appearing are entitled to represent it.
3. When it considers it in the interest of the proper conduct of a hearing, the Commission may limit the number of the parties' representatives or advisers who may appear.
4. The parties shall inform the Commission at least ten days before the date of the opening of the hearing of the names and functions of the persons who will appear on their behalf at the hearing.
5. The provisions of the present Rule shall apply *mutatis mutandis* to hearings before delegates of the Commission.

Rule 38

1. Any individual applicant, expert or other person whom the Commission decides to hear as a witness, shall be summoned by the Secretary. The summons shall indicate:

   a. the parties to the application,
   b. the facts or issues regarding which the person concerned will be heard,
   c. the arrangements made, in accordance with Rule 42, paragraph 1 or 2, to reimburse the persons concerned for any expenses incurred by them.

2. Any such persons may, if they have not sufficient knowledge of English or French, be authorised by the President to speak in any other language.

Rule 39

1. After establishing the identity of the witnesses or experts the President or the principal delegate mentioned in Rule 34, paragraph 2, shall request them to take the following oath:

    a. for witnesses: "I swear that I will speak the truth, the whole truth and nothing but the truth."
    b. for experts: "I swear that my statement will be in accordance with my sincere belief."

2. Instead of taking the oath in the terms set out in paragraph 1 of this Rule, the witnesses or experts may make the following declaration:

    a. for witnesses: "I solemnly declare upon my honour and conscience that I will speak the truth, the whole truth and nothing but the truth."
    b. for experts: "I solemnly declare upon my honour and conscience that my statement will be in accordance with my sincere belief."

Rule 40

1. The President, or the principal delegate, shall conduct the hearing or examination of any persons heard. Any member may put questions to the parties or to the persons heard with the leave of the President or the principal delegate.
2. A party may, with the permission of the President or of the principal delegate, also put questions to any person heard.

Rule 41

1. The Secretary shall be responsible for the production of verbatim records of hearings before the Commission.
2. The parties or, where appropriate, their representatives shall receive a draft verbatim record of their submissions in order that they may propose corrections to the Secretary within a time-limit laid down by the President. After necessary corrections, if any, the text shall constitute certified matters of record.

Rule 42

1. The expenses incurred by any person who is heard by the Commission as a witness at the request of a party shall be borne either by that party or by the Council of Europe, as the Commission may decide. Where it is decided that the expenses shall be borne by the Council of Europe, the amount shall be fixed by the President of the Commission.
2. The expenses incurred by any such person whom the Commission hears *proprio motu* shall be fixed by the President and be borne by the Council of Europe.

3. Where the Commission decides to obtain written expert opinions, the costs, as agreed by the President, shall be borne by the Council of Europe.

4. Where the Commission decides to obtain written evidence, any costs incurred by the party who submits it shall be borne either by that party or by the Council of Europe, as the Commission may decide. Where it is decided that the costs shall be borne by the Council of Europe, the amount shall be agreed by the President of the Commission.

CHAPTER III – INSTITUTION OF PROCEEDINGS

Rule 43

1. Any application made under Articles 24 or 25 of the Convention shall be submitted in writing and shall be signed by the applicant or by the applicant's representative.

2. Where an application is submitted by a non-governmental organisation or by a group of individuals, it shall be signed by those persons competent to represent such organisation or group. The Commission shall determine any question as to whether the persons who have signed an application are competent to do so.

3. Where applicants are represented in accordance with Rule 32 of these Rules, a power of attorney or written authorisation shall be supplied by their representative or representatives.

Rule 44

1. Any application under Article 25 of the Convention shall be made on the application form provided by the Secretariat, unless the President decides otherwise. It shall set out:

   a. the name, age, occupation and address of the applicant;
   b. the name, occupation and address of the representative, if any;
   c. the name of the High Contracting Party against which the application is made;
   d. the object of the application and the provision of the Convention alleged to have been violated;
   e. a statement of the facts and arguments;
   f. any relevant documents and in particular the decisions, whether judicial or not, relating to the object of the application.

2. Applicants shall furthermore:

   a. provide information enabling it to be shown that the conditions laid down in Article 26 of the Convention have been satisfied;
   b. indicate whether they have submitted their complaints to any other procedure of international investigation or settlement;
   c. indicate in which of the official languages they wish to receive the Commission's decisions;

    d.   indicate whether they do or do not object to their identity being disclosed to the public;

    e.   declare that they will respect the confidentiality of the proceedings before the Commission.

3.   Failure to comply with the requirements set out under paragraphs 1 and 2 above may result in the application not being registered and examined by the Commission.

4.   The date of introduction of the application shall in general be considered to be the date of the first communication from the applicant setting out, even summarily, the object of the application. The Commission may nevertheless for good cause decide that a different date be considered to be the date of introduction.

5.   Applicants shall keep the Commission informed of any change of their address and of all circumstances relevant to the application.

CHAPTER IV – PROCEEDINGS ON ADMISSIBILITY

Rule 45

1.   Where, pursuant to Article 24 of the Convention, an application is brought before the Commission by a High Contracting Party, the President of the Commission shall give notice of such application to the High Contracting Party against which the claim is made and shall invite it to submit to the Commission its observations in writing on the admissibility of such application. The observations so obtained shall be communicated to the High Contracting Party which brought the application and it may submit written observations in reply.

2.   The Commission shall designate one or more of its members to submit a report on admissibility. Rule 47, paragraph 3, is, by analogy, applicable to this report.

3.   Before deciding upon the admissibility of the application the Commission may invite the parties to submit further observations, either in writing or at a hearing.

Rule 46

In any case of urgency, the Secretary to the Commission may, without prejudice to the taking of any other procedural steps, inform a High Contracting Party concerned in an application, by any available means, of the introduction of the application and of a summary of its objects.

Rule 47

1.   Any application submitted pursuant to Article 25 of the Convention shall be referred to a member of the Commission who, as rapporteur, shall examine the application and submit a report to the Commission on its admissibility and a proposal on the procedure to be adopted.

2. Rapporteurs, in their examination of the application:

    a. may request relevant information on matters connected with the application, from the applicant or the High Contracting Party concerned;
    b. shall communicate any information so obtained from the High Contracting party to the applicant for comments;
    c. shall decide whether to refer the application to a Committee.

3. The report of the rapporteur on the admissibility of the application shall contain:

    a. a statement of the relevant facts, including any information or comments obtained under paragraph 2 of this Rule;
    b. if necessary, an indication of the issues arising under the Convention in the application;
    c. a proposal on admissibility and on any other action to be taken, as the case may require.

Rule 48

1. The Commission shall consider the report of the rapporteur and may declare at once that the application is inadmissible or to be struck off its list.
2. Alternatively, the Commission may:

    a. request relevant information on matters connected with the application from the applicant or the High Contracting Party concerned. Any information so obtained from the High Contracting Party shall be communicated to the applicant for comments;
    b. give notice of the application to the High Contracting Party against which it is brought and invite that Party to present to the Commission written observations on the application. Any observations so obtained shall be communicated to the applicant for any written observations in reply.

Rule 49

1. An application shall be referred to a Chamber unless it has been referred to a Committee under Rule 47, paragraph 2 c, or its examination by a Chamber is excluded under Article 20, paragraph 2, of the Convention.
2. Applications shall normally be referred to the Chamber which includes the member of the Commission elected in respect of the High Contracting Party against which the application has been made.
3. If there is a reasoned request from a party that the application should be referred to the Plenary Commission, that request shall be considered by the Plenary Commission.
4. The members of the Commission shall be informed of the decisions of the Chambers.

Rule 50

Before deciding upon the admissibility of the application, the Commission may invite the parties:

   a.   to submit further observations in writing;
   b.   to submit further observations orally at a hearing on issues of admissibility and at the same time, if the Commission so decides, on the merits of the application.

Rule 51

Time limits shall be fixed by the rapporteur for any information or comments requested under Rule 47, paragraph 2, and by the Commission for any information, observations or comments requested under Rule 48, paragraph 2 and under Rule 50.

Rule 52

1.   The decision of the Commission shall be communicated by the Secretary of the Commission to the applicant and to the High Contracting Party or Parties concerned. However, in the case provided for in paragraph 1 of Rule 48 or where information has been obtained from the applicant only, the decision shall be communicated to the High Contracting Party or Parties concerned only at their request and provided that the Commission does not decide otherwise.
2.   The decision of the Commission shall state whether it was taken unanimously or by majority and shall be accompanied or followed by reasons.

CHAPTER V – PROCEDURE AFTER THE ADMISSION OF AN APPLICATION

Rule 53

1.   After deciding to admit an application, the Commission shall decide on the procedure to be followed:

   a.   for the examination of the application under Article 28, paragraph 1a, of the Convention;
   b.   with a view to securing a friendly settlement under Article 28, paragraph 1b, of the Convention.

2.   In order to accomplish its tasks under Article 28, paragraph 1a, of the Convention, the Commission may invite the parties to submit further evidence and observations.
3.   The Commission shall decide in each case whether observations should be submitted in writing or orally at a hearing.
4.   The President shall lay down the time-limits within which the parties shall submit evidence and written observations.

Rule 54

1. The Commission shall appoint one or more of its members as rapporteur.
2. The rapporteur may at any stage of the examination of an application under Article 25 of the Convention invite the parties to submit further written evidence and observations.
3. The rapporteur shall:

    a. draft such memoranda as may be required by the Commission for its consideration of the case before it;
    b. draft a Report for the Commission in accordance with Rule 57, Rule 60 or Rule 62, as the case may be.

Rule 55

The Commission may, when it sees fit, deliberate with a view to reaching a provisional opinion on the merits of the case.

Rule 56

Where the Commission decides to reject an application under Article 29 of the Convention, its decision shall be accompanied by reasons. The Secretary shall communicate the decision to the parties.

CHAPTER VI – THE REPORT OF THE COMMISSION

Rule 57

1. The Report provided for in Article 28, paragraph 2, of the Convention shall contain:

    a. a description of the parties, their representatives and advisers;
    b. a statement of the facts;
    c. the terms of the settlement reached.

2. The Report shall also contain the names of the President and members participating and shall be signed by the President and the Secretary.
3. The Report shall be sent to the High Contracting Party or Parties concerned, to the Committee of Ministers and to the Secretary General of the Council of Europe for publication. It shall also be sent to the applicant.

Rule 58

1. When the Commission has found that no friendly settlement in accordance with Article 28, paragraph 1b, of the Convention can be reached, it shall consider a draft Report drawn up by the Rapporteur on the basis of any provisional opinion reached by the Commission in its deliberations under Rule 55.

2. Where the Commission has been divided in its provisional opinion, the draft Report shall include alternative opinions, if the Commission so decides.

Rule 59

1. When the Commission considers the draft Report referred to in Rule 58, it shall adopt in the first place the parts of the Report in which it establishes the facts.
2. It shall then deliberate and vote on whether the facts found disclose any violation by the State concerned of its obligations under the Convention.
3. Only those members who have participated in the deliberations and votes provided for in this Rule shall be entitled to express their separate opinion in the Report.

Rule 60

1. The Report provided for in Article 31 of the Convention shall contain:
   a. a description of the parties, their representatives and advisers;
   b. a statement of the proceedings followed before the Commission;
   c. a statement of the facts established;
   d. the complaints declared admissible;
   e. the opinion of the Commission, with an indication of the number of members forming the majority, as to whether or not the facts found disclose any breach by the State concerned of its obligations under the Convention;
   f. the reasons upon which that opinion is based;
   g. any separate opinion of a member of the Commission.

2. The Report shall contain the names of the President and the members participating in the deliberations and vote provided for in Rule 59, paragraph 2. It shall be signed by the President and by the Secretary.
3. It shall be sent, together with any proposal under Article 31, paragraph 3, of the Convention, to the Committee of Ministers and to the High Contracting Party or Parties concerned.

Rule 61

1. After the adoption of the Report drawn up under Article 31 of the Convention the Commission shall decide in plenary session whether or not to bring the case before the European Court of Human Rights under Article 48a of the Convention.
2. Where the Commission decides to bring the case before the Court, it shall file its request with the Registry of the Court within three months after the transmission of the Report to the Committee of Ministers. It shall also inform the Committee of Ministers and the parties to the application.
3. Where the Commission decides not to bring the case before the Court, it shall so inform the Court, the Committee of Ministers and the parties to the application.

Rule 62

1. The Report provided for in Article 30, paragraph 2, of the Convention shall contain:

    a. a description of the parties, their representatives and advisers;
    b. a statement of the facts;
    c. a brief account of the proceedings;
    d. the terms of the decision striking out the application together with the reasons therefor.

2. The Report shall contain the names of the President and members who participated in the decision striking out the application. It shall be signed by the President and by the Secretary.
3. It shall be communicated to the Committee of Ministers of the Council of Europe for information and to the parties. The Commission may publish it.

TITLE IV – RELATIONS OF THE COMMISSION WITH THE COURT

Rule 63

1. The Commission shall assist the European Court of Human Rights in any case brought before the Court. When a case is referred to the Court the Commission shall appoint, at a plenary session, one or more delegates to take part in the consideration of the case before the Court. These delegates may be assisted by any person appointed by the Commission. In discharging their functions they shall act in accordance with such directives as they may receive from the Commission.
2. Until delegates have been appointed, the President may, if consulted by the Court, express views upon the procedure to be followed before the Court.

Rule 64

1. When, in pursuance of Article 48a of the Convention, the Commission decides to bring a case before the Court, it shall draw up a request indicating in particular:

    a. the parties to the proceedings before the Commission;
    b. the date on which the Commission adopted its Report;
    c. the date on which the Report was transmitted to the Committee of Ministers;
    d. the object of the request;
    e. the names and addresses of its delegates.

2. The Secretary of the commission shall transmit to the Registry of the Court forty copies of the request referred to in paragraph 1 of this Rule.

Rule 65

When, in pursuance of Article 48b, c or d of the Convention, a High Contracting Party brings a case before the Court, the Secretary of the Commission shall communicate to the Registry of the Court as soon as possible:

- a. the names and addresses of the Commission's delegates;
- b. any other information which the Commission may consider appropriate.

Rule 66

The Secretary to the Commission shall, as soon as the request referred to in Rule 64, paragraph 2, above, has been transmitted or the communication mentioned in Rule 33, paragraph 1c, of the Rules of Court, has been received, file with the Registry of the Court an adequate number of copies of the Commission's Report.

Rule 67

The Commission shall communicate to the Court, at its request, any memorial, evidence, document or information concerning the case, with the exception of documents relating to the attempt to secure a friendly settlement in accordance with Article 28, paragraph 1b, of the Convention. The communication of those documents shall be subject in each case to a decision of the Commission.

FINAL TITLE

Rule 68

1. Any Rule may be amended upon motion made after notice when such motion is carried at a plenary session of the Commission by a majority of all the members of the Commission. Notice of such a motion shall be delivered in writing to the Secretary of the Commission at least one month before the session where it is to be discussed On receipt of such notice of motion the Secretary shall be required to inform all members of the Commission at the earliest possible moment.
2. Any Rule may be suspended upon motion made without notice, provided that this decision is taken unanimously. The suspension of a Rule shall in this case be limited in its operation to the particular purpose for which such suspension has been sought.

ADDENDUM TO THE RULES OF PROCEDURE – LEGAL AID

Rule 1

The Commission may, either at the request of an applicant lodging an application under Article 25 of the Convention or *proprio motu*, grant free legal aid to that applicant in connection with the representation of the case:

a. where observations in writing on the admissibility of that application have been received from the High Contracting Party concerned in pursuance of Rule 48, paragraph 2 b, or where the time-limit for their submission has expired, or
b. where the application has been declared admissible.

Rule 2

Free legal aid shall only be granted where the Commission is satisfied:

a. that it is essential for the proper discharge of the Commission's duties;
b. that the applicant has not sufficient means to meet all or part of the costs involved.

Rule 3

1. In order to determine whether or not applicants have sufficient means to meet all or part of the costs involved, the Commission shall require them to complete a form of declaration stating their income, capital assets and any financial commitments in respect of dependants, or any other financial obligations. Such declaration shall be certified by the appropriate domestic authority or authorities.
2. Before making a grant of free legal aid, the Commission shall request the High Contracting Party concerned to submit its comments in writing.
3. The Commission shall, after receiving the information mentioned in paragraphs 1 and 2 above, decide whether or not to grant free legal aid and shall inform the parties accordingly.
4. The President shall fix the time-limits within which the parties shall be requested to supply the information referred to in this Rule.

Rule 4

1. Fees shall be payable only to a barrister-at-law, solicitor or professor of law or professionally qualified person of similar status. Fees may, where appropriate, be paid to more than one such lawyer as defined above.
2. Legal aid may be granted to cover not only lawyers' fees but also travelling and subsistence expenses and other necessary out-of-pocket expenses incurred by the applicant or appointed lawyer.

Rule 5

1. On the Commission deciding to grant legal aid, the Secretary shall, by agreement with the appointed lawyer, fix the rate of fees to be paid.
2. The Secretary shall as soon as possible notify the Secretary General of the Council of Europe of the rate of fees so agreed.

Rule 6

The Commission may, at any time, if it finds that the conditions set out in Rule 2 above are no longer satisfied, revoke its grant of free legal aid to an applicant, in whole or in part, and shall at once notify the parties thereof.

Rule 7

In case of urgency when the Commission is not in session, the President of the Commission or the President of either Chamber may exercise the powers conferred on the Commission by this Addendum. As soon as the Commission is again in session, any action which has been taken under this paragraph shall be brought to its attention.

NATIONAL AUTHORITIES COMPETENT TO CERTIFY THE INDIGENCE OF APPLICANTS FOR THE PURPOSES OF RULE 3 OF THE LEGAL AID ADDENDUM TO THE COMMISSION'S RULES OF PROCEDURE

Austria

The mayor of the locality where the applicant has his or her legal or actual residence.

Belgium

The direct taxation department of the district in which the applicant lives issues him with a certificate of income or, with his authorisation, express and in writing, issues such to another person or administrative department.

The request, accompanied by such authorisation, may be addressed either to the local direct taxation department or to the Administration centrale des contributions directes, 45 rue Belliard, B-1040 Brussels.

Denmark

The local tax authority.

Finland

The local social welfare authority.

France

The local tax authority for the applicant's place of residence.

Germany

None. The applicant submits a prescribed form, duly completed and with supporting documents, which the Commission submits to the Federal Ministry of Justice.

Greece

a. A certificate from the mayor or president of the district in which the applicant lives giving details of his family situation, his employment and his assets; and

b. A certificate from the tax authority showing the applicant has made a tax return for the previous three years with the results thereof.

Iceland

The Rikisskattstjóri (Director of Internal Revenue), Skúlagotu 57, IS-Reykjavik.

Ireland

The Chief Inspector, Department of Social Welfare, 101/104 Marlboro Street, IRL-Dublin 1.

Italy

a. Certification, by the responsible section of the tax authorities, of a declaration of means prepared by the applicant; or

b. certificate of indigence issued by the mayor of the municipality in which the applicant lives.

Luxembourg

On production of a certificate stating the amount of tax paid the previous year the College of Mayors and Aldermen of the municipality in which the applicant lives issues a certificate of indigence.

Malta

Dr. Joseph Mifsud, LL.D. The Law Courts, Valletta, Malta.

Netherlands

The local government *(gemeentebestuur)* in accordance with Article 11 of the Legal Aid Act *(Wet rechtsbiistand on- en minvermogenden)*.

Norway

The local tax authority *(ligningskontor)* of the district in which the applicant lives.

Portugal

The local government *(junta de frequesia)* for the district in which the applicant lives.

Spain

The district office of the Finance Minister *(Delegación de Hacienda)* for the district in which the applicant lives.

Sweden

The local tax authority *(lokala skattemyndigheten)* certifies the means of persons requesting free legal aid.

Switzerland

The local tax authority for the applicant's place of residence.

Turkey

    a.   The mayor of the municipality in which the applicant lives; or
    b.   The elders' council for the village or district in which the applicant lives (Article 468 of the Code of civil procedure).

United Kingdom

    a.   England and Wales: DHSS, Legal Aid Assessment Office, No. 3 The Pavilions, Ashton on Ribble, Preston PR2 2PA;
    b.   Scotland: The Scottish Legal Aid Board, 44 Drumsheugh Gardens, Edinburgh EH3 7SW.

14. EUROPEAN COURT OF HUMAN RIGHTS RULES OF COURT "A"

Adopted: 27 January 1994

Entry into force: 1 February 1994

The European Court of Human Rights,

Having regard to the Convention for the Protection of Human Rights and Fundamental Freedoms and the Protocols thereto,
Makes the present Rules:

Rule 1 (Definitions)

For the purposes of these Rules unless the context otherwise requires:

a. the term "Convention" means the Convention for the Protection of Human Rights and Fundamental Freedoms and the Protocols thereto;

b. the expression "Protocol No. 2" means Protocol No. 2 to the Convention conferring upon the European Court of Human Rights competence to give advisory opinions;

c. the expression "plenary Court" means the European Court of Human Rights sitting in plenary session;

d. the term "Chamber" means any Chamber constituted in pursuance of Article 43 of the Convention; the term "Grand Chamber" means the Chamber provided for under Rule 51;

e. the term "Court" means either the plenary Court, the Grand Chambers or the Chambers;

f. the expression *"ad hoc* judge" means any person, other than an elected judge, chosen by a Contracting Party in pursuance of Article 43 of the Convention to sit as a member of a Chamber;

g. the term "judge" or "judges" means the judges elected by the Consultative Assembly of the Council of Europe or *ad hoc* judges;

h. the term "Parties" means those Contracting Parties which are the applicant and respondent Parties;

i. the term "Commission" means the European Commission of Human Rights;

j. the expression "Delegates of the Commission" means the member or members of the Commission delegated by it to take part in the consideration of a case before the Court;

k. the term "applicant" means:

    — in Title I and in Rules 50, 53, 54 and 55 of the present Rules, the person, non-governmental organisation or group of individuals who

115

lodged a complaint with the Commission under Article 25 of the Convention;

— in Title II with the exception of Rules 50, 53, 54 and 55, such a person, organisation or group when he or it expressed the desire, in accordance with Rule 33, to take part in the proceedings pending before the Court;

l. the expression "report of the Commission" means the report provided for in Article 31 of the Convention;

m. the expression "Committee of Ministers" means the Committee of Ministers of the Council of Europe.

TITLE I – ORGANISATION AND WORKING OF THE COURT

CHAPTER I – JUDGES

Rule 2: Calculation of term of office

1. The duration of the term of office of an elected judge shall be calculated as from his election. However, when a judge is re-elected on the expiry of his term of office or is elected to replace a judge whose term of office has expired or is about to expire, the duration of his term of office shall, in either case, be calculated as from the date of such expiry.

2. In accordance with Article 40, paragraph 5, of the Convention, a judge elected to replace a judge whose term of office has not expired shall hold office for the remainder of his predecessor's term.

3. In accordance with Article 40, paragraph 6, of the Convention, an elected judge shall hold office until his successor has taken the oath or made the declaration provided for in Rule 3. Thereafter he shall continue to deal with any case in connection with which hearings or, failing that, deliberations have begun before him.

Rule 3: Oath or solemn declaration

1. Before taking up his duties, each elected judge shall, at the first sitting of the plenary Court at which he is present after his election or, in case of need, before the President, take the following oath or make the following solemn declaration:

    "I swear" – or "I solemnly declare" – "that I will exercise my functions as a judge honourably, independently and impartially and that I will keep secret all deliberations."

2. This act shall be recorded in minutes.

Rule 4: Obstacle to the exercise of the functions of judge

A judge may not exercise his functions while he is a member of a Government or while he holds a post or exercises a profession which is incompatible with his independence and impartiality. In case of need the plenary Court shall decide.

Rule 5: Precedence

1. Elected judges shall take precedence after the President and the Vice-President according to the date of their election; in the event of re-election, even if it is not an immediate re-election, the length of time during which the judge concerned previously exercised his functions as a judge shall be taken into account.
2. Judges elected on the same date shall take precedence according to age.
3. *Ad hoc* judges shall take precedence after the elected judges according to age.

Rule 6: Resignation

Resignation of a judge shall be notified to the President who shall transmit it to the Secretary General of the Council of Europe. Subject to the provisions of Rule 2, paragraph 3, resignation shall constitute vacation of office.

CHAPTER II – PRESIDENCY OF THE COURT

Rule 7: Election of the President and Vice-President

1. The Court shall elect its President and Vice-President for a period of three years, provided that such period shall not exceed the duration of their term of office as judges. They may be re-elected.
2. The President and Vice-President shall continue to exercise their functions until the election of their respective successors.
3. If the President or Vice-President ceases to be a member of the Court or resigns his office before its normal expiry, the plenary Court shall elect a successor for the remainder of the term of that office.
4. The elections referred to in this Rule shall be by secret ballot; only the elected judges who are present shall take part. If no judge receives an absolute majority of the elected judges present, a ballot shall take place between the two judges who have received most votes. In the case of equal voting, preference shall be given to the judge having precedence in accordance with Rule 5.

Rule 8: Functions of the President

The President shall direct the work and administration of the Court and shall preside at its sessions. He shall represent the Court and, in particular, be responsible for its relations with the authorities of the Council of Europe.

Rule 9: Functions of the Vice-President

The Vice-President shall take the place of the President if the latter is unable to carry out his functions or if the office of President is vacant.

Rule 10: Replacement of the President and Vice-President

If the President and Vice-President are at the same time unable to carry out their functions or if their offices are at the same time vacant, the office of President shall be assumed by another elected judge in accordance with the order of precedence provided for in Rule 5.

CHAPTER III – THE REGISTRY

Rule 11: Election of the Registrar

1. The plenary Court shall elect its Registrar after the President has in this respect consulted the Secretary General of the Council of Europe The candidates must possess the legal knowledge and the experience necessary to carry out the functions attaching to the post and must have an adequate working knowledge of the two official languages of the Court.
2. The Registrar shall be elected for a term of seven years. He may be re-elected.
3. The elections referred to in this Rule shall be by secret ballot; only the elected judges who are present shall take part. If no candidate receives an absolute majority of the elected judges present, a ballot shall take place between the two candidates who have received most votes. In the case of equal voting, preference shall be given to the older candidate.
4. Before taking up his functions, the Registrar shall take the following oath or make the following solemn declaration before the plenary Court or, if it is not in session, before the President:

   "I swear" – or "I solemnly declare" – "that I will exercise loyally, discreetly and conscientiously the functions conferred upon me as Registrar of the European Court of Human Rights."

   This act shall be recorded in minutes.

Rule 12: Election of the Deputy Registrar

1. The plenary Court shall also elect a Deputy Registrar according to the conditions and in the manner and for the term prescribed in Rule 11. It shall first consult the Registrar.
2. Before taking up his functions, the Deputy Registrar shall take an oath or make a solemn declaration before the plenary Court or, if it is not in session, before the President, in similar terms to those prescribed in respect of the Registrar. This act shall be recorded in minutes.

Rule 13: Other staff, equipment and facilities

The President, or the Registrar on his behalf, shall request the Secretary General of the Council of Europe to provide the Registrar with the staff, permanent or temporary, equipment and facilities necessary for the Court.

The officials of the registry, other than the Registrar and the Deputy Registrar, shall be appointed by the Secretary General, with the agreement of the President or of the Registrar acting on the President's instructions.

Rule 14: Functions of the Registrar

1. The Registrar shall assist the Court in the performance of its functions. He shall be responsible for the organisation and activities of the registry under the authority of the President.
2. The Registrar shall have the custody of the archives of the Court and shall be the channel for all communications and notifications made by, or addressed to, the Court in connection with the cases brought or to be brought before it.
3. The Registrar shall ensure that the dates of despatch and receipt of any communication or notification relating to the above mentioned cases may be easily verified. Communications or notifications addressed to the Agents of the Parties, to the Delegates of the Commission or to the representative, if any, of the applicant shall be considered as having been addressed to the Parties, to the Commission or to the applicant, as the case may be. The date of receipt shall be noted on each document received by the Registrar who shall transmit to the sender a receipt bearing this date and the number under which the document has been registered.
4. The Registrar shall, subject to the discretion attaching to his functions, reply to requests for information concerning the work of the Court, in particular from the press. He shall announce the date and time fixed for the hearings in open court and shall be responsible for making immediately available to the public all judgments delivered by the Court.
5. General instructions drawn up by the Registrar and sanctioned by the President shall provide for the working of the registry.

CHAPTER IV – THE WORKING OF THE COURT

Rule 15: Seat of the Court

The seat of the Court shall be at the seat of the Council of Europe at Strasbourg. The Court may, however, if it considers it expedient, exercise its functions elsewhere in the territories of the Member States of the Council of Europe.

Rule 16: Sessions of the plenary Court

The plenary sessions of the Court shall be convened by the President whenever the exercise of its functions under the Convention and under these Rules so requires. The President shall convene a plenary session if at least one-third of the members of the Court so request, and in any event once a year to consider administrative matters.

Rule 17: Quorum

1. The quorum of the plenary Court shall be two-thirds of the judges.
2. If there is no quorum, the President shall adjourn the sitting.

Rule 18: Public character of the hearings

The hearings shall be public unless the Court shall in exceptional circumstances decide otherwise.

Rule 19: Deliberations

1. The Court shall deliberate in private. Its deliberations shall remain secret.
2. Only the judges shall take part in the deliberations. The Registrar or his substitute, as well as such other officials of the registry and interpreters whose assistance is deemed necessary, shall be present. No other person may be admitted except by special decision of the Court.
3. Each judge present at such deliberations shall state his opinion and the reasons therefor.
4. Any question which is to be voted upon shall be formulated in precise terms in the two official languages and the text shall, if a judge so requests, be distributed before the vote is taken.
5. The minutes of the private sittings of the Court for deliberations shall remain secret; they shall be limited to a record of the subject of the discussions, the votes taken, the names of those voting for and against a motion and any statements expressly made for insertion in the minutes.

Rule 20: Votes

1. The decisions of the Court shall be taken by the majority of judges present.
2. The votes shall be cast in the inverse order to the order of precedence provided for in Rule 5.
3. If the voting is equal, the President shall have a second and casting vote.

CHAPTER V – THE CHAMBERS

Rule 21: Composition of the Court when constituted in a Chamber

1. When a case is brought before the Court either by the Commission or by a Contracting State having the right to do so under Article 48 of the Convention, the Court shall be constituted in a Chamber of nine judges.
2. On the reference of a case to the Court, the Registrar shall notify all the judges, including the newly-elected judges, that such a Chamber is to be constituted. If any judge, upon receiving such notification, believes that for

one of the reasons set out in Rule 24 he will be unable to sit, he shall so inform the Registrar. The President shall then draw up the list of judges available to constitute the Chamber.

3. There shall sit as *ex officio* members of the Chamber:

    a. in accordance with Article 43 of the Convention, every judge who has the nationality of a Party;
    b. the President of the Court, or, failing him, the Vice-President, provided that they do not sit by virtue of the preceding subparagraph.

4. The other judges named on the list provided for in paragraph 2 shall be called upon to complete the Chamber, as members or as substitutes, in the order determined by a drawing of lots effected by the President of the Court in the Presence of the Registrar.

5. The President of the Chamber shall be the judge sitting by virtue of paragraph 3.b or, failing one, a judge appointed under paragraph 4 as a member of the Chamber, in accordance with the order of precedence provided for in Rule 5.

    If the President of the Chamber is unable to sit or withdraws, he shall be replaced by the Vice-President or, if the same applies to him, by a judge appointed under paragraph 4 as a member of the Chamber, in accordance with the said order of precedence. However, where he is unable to sit or withdraws less than twenty-four hours before the opening of, or during or after, the hearing, his place shall be taken, in accordance with the said order of precedence, by one of the judges called upon to be present or present at the hearing.

6. If the President of the Court finds that two cases concern the same Party or Parties and raise similar issues, he may refer the second case to the Chamber already constituted, or in the course of constitution, for the consideration of the first case or, if there is none, proceed to the constitution of one Chamber to consider both cases.

Rule 22: Substitute judges

1. The substitute judges shall be called upon, in the order determined by the drawing of lots, to replace the judges appointed as members of the Chamber by virtue of Rule 21, paragraph 4.
2. Judges who have been so replaced shall cease to be members of the Chamber.
3. The substitute judges shall be supplied with the documents relating to the proceedings. The President may convoke one or more of them, according to the above order of precedence, to attend the hearings and deliberations.

Rule 23: *Ad hoc* judges

1. If the Court does not include a judge elected in respect of a Party or if the judge called upon to sit in that capacity is unable to sit or withdraws, the President of the Court shall invite that Party to inform him within thirty days whether it wishes to appoint to sit as judge either another elected judge or, as an *ad hoc* judge, any other person possessing the qualifications required under

Article 39, paragraph 3, of the Convention and, if so, to state at the same time the name of the person so appointed. The same rule shall apply if the person so appointed is unable to sit or withdraws.

2. The Party concerned shall be presumed to have waived such right of appointment if it does not reply within thirty days.

3. An *ad hoc* judge shall, at the opening of the first sitting fixed for the consideration of the case after he has been appointed, take the Oath or make the solemn declaration provided for in Rule 3. This act shall be recorded in minutes.

Rule 24: Inability to sit, withdrawal or exemption

1. Any judge who is prevented from taking part in sittings for which he has been convoked shall, as soon as possible, give notice thereof to the President of the Chamber or to the Registrar.

2. A judge may not take part in the consideration of any case in which he has a personal interest or has previously acted either as the agent, advocate or adviser of a Party or of a person having an interest in the case, or as member of a tribunal or commission of enquiry, or in any other capacity.

3. If a judge withdraws for one of the said reasons, or for some special reason, he shall inform the President who shall exempt him from sitting.

4. If the President considers that a reason exists for a judge to withdraw, he shall consult with the judge concerned; in the event of disagreement, the Court shall decide.

5. Any judge who has been called upon to sit on one or more recent cases may, at his own request, be exempted by the President from sitting on a new case.

Rule 25: Common interest

1. If several Parties have a common interest, the President of the Court may invite them to agree to appoint a single elected judge or *ad hoc* judge in accordance with Article 43 of the Convention. If the Parties are unable to agree, the President shall choose by lot, from among the persons proposed as judges by these Parties, the judge called upon to sit *ex officio*. The names of the other judges and substitute judges shall then be chosen by lot by the President from among the judges who have not been elected in respect of a Party.

2. In the event of dispute as to the existence of a common interest, the plenary Court shall decide.

CHAPTER VI – GENERAL RULES

Rule 26: Possibility of particular derogations

The provisions of this Title shall not prevent the Court from derogating from them for the consideration of a particular case after having consulted the Party or Parties, the Delegates of the Commission and the applicant.

Rule 27: Official languages

1. The official languages of the Court shall be English and French.
2. A Party may, not later than the consultation provided for in Rule 38, apply to the President for leave to use another language at the oral hearings. If such leave is granted by the President, the Party concerned shall be responsible for the interpretation into English or French of the oral arguments or statements made by its Agent, advocates or advisers and shall, to the extent which the President may determine in each case, bear the other extra expenses involved in the use of a non-official language.
3. The President may grant the applicant, as well as any person assisting the Delegates under Rule 29, paragraph 1, leave to use a non-official language. In that event, the Registrar shall make the necessary arrangements for the translation or interpretation into English and French of their comments or statements.
4. Any witness, expert or other person appearing before the Court may use his own language if he does not have sufficient knowledge of either of the two official languages. The Registrar shall, in that event, make the necessary arrangements for the interpretation into English and French of the statements of the witness, expert or other person concerned.
5. All judgments shall be given in English and in French; unless the Court decides otherwise, both texts shall be authentic.

Rule 28: Representation of the Parties

The Parties shall be represented by Agents who may have the assistance of advocates or advisers.

Rule 29: Relations between the Court and the Commission and release of the report of the Commission

1. The Commission shall delegate one or more of its members to take part in the consideration of a case before the Court. The Delegates may be assisted by other persons.
2. The Court shall, whether a case is referred to it by a Contracting Party or by the Commission, take into consideration the report of the latter.
3. Unless the President decides otherwise, the said report shall be made available to the public through the Registrar as soon as possible after the case has been brought before the Court.

Rule 30: Representation of the applicant

1. The applicant shall be represented by an advocate authorised to practise in any of the Contracting States and resident in the territory of one of them, or by any other person approved by the President. The President may, however, give leave to the applicant to present his own case, subject, if need be, to his being assisted by an advocate or other person as aforesaid.

2. Unless the President decides otherwise, the advocate or other himself if he seeks leave to present his own case, must have an adequate knowledge of one of the Court's official languages.

Rule 31: Communications, notifications and summonses addressed to persons other than the Agents of the Parties or the Delegates of the Commission

1. If, for any communication, notification or summons addressed to persons other than the Agents of the Parties or the Delegates of the Commission, the Court considers it necessary to have the assistance of the Government of the State on whose territory such communication, notification or summons is to have effect, the President shall apply directly to that Government in order to obtain the necessary facilities.

2. The same rule shall apply when the Court desires to make or arrange for the making of an investigation on the spot in order to establish the facts or to procure evidence or when it orders the appearance of a person resident in, or having to cross, that territory.

CHAPTER VII – INSTITUTION OF PROCEEDINGS

Rule 32: Filing of the application or request

1. Any Contracting Party which intends to bring a case before the Court under Article 48 of the Convention shall file with the registry an application, in forty copies, indicating:

    a. the parties to the proceedings before the Commission;
    b. the date on which the Commission adopted its report;
    c. the date on which the report was transmitted to the Committee of Ministers;
    d. the object of the application;
    e. the name and address of the person appointed as Agent.

2. If the Commission intends to bring a case before the Court under Article 48 of the Convention, it shall file with the registry a request, in forty copies, signed by its President and containing the particulars indicated in sub-paragraphs a, b, c and d of paragraph 1 of this Rule together with the names and addresses of the Delegates of the Commission.

Rule 33: Communication of the application or request

1. On receipt of an application or request, the Registrar shall transmit a copy thereof:

    a. to all the members of the Court, and also, as the case may be,
    b. to any Contracting Party mentioned in Article 48 of the Convention,
    c. to the Commission,

    d. to the person, non-governmental organisation or group of individuals who lodged the complaint with the Commission under Article 25 of the Convention.

He shall also inform the Committee of Ministers, through the Secretary General of the Council of Europe, of the filing of the application or request.

2. The communications provided for in sub-paragraphs a, b and d of paragraph 1 shall include a copy of the report of the Commission.

3. When making the communications provided for in sub-paragraphs b, c and d of paragraph 1, the Registrar shall invite:

    a. the Contracting Party against which the complaint has been lodged before the Commission to notify him within two weeks of the name and address of its Agent;

    b. any other Contracting Party which appears to have the right, under Article 48 of the Convention, to bring a case before the Court and which has not availed itself of that right, to inform him within four weeks whether it wishes to take part in the proceedings and, if so, to notify him at the same time of the name and address of its Agent;

    c. the Commission to notify him as soon as possible of the names and addresses of its Delegates;

    d. the person, non-governmental organisation or group of individuals who lodged the complaint with the Commission under Article 25 of the Convention to notify him within two weeks

        — whether he or it wishes to take part in the proceedings pending before the Court;

        — if so, of the name and address of the person appointed by him or it in accordance with Rule 30.

Rule 34: Question whether a Contracting Party has the right to bring a case before the Court

In the event of a dispute as to whether a Contracting Party has the right under Article 48 to bring a case before the Court, the President shall submit that question for decision to the Grand Chamber provided for in paragraph 2 of Rule 51 of these Rules, without prejudice to the possible application of paragraph 5 of Rule 51.

Rule 35: Notice of the composition of the Chamber

As soon as a Chamber has been constituted for the consideration of a case, the Registrar shall communicate its composition to the judges, to the Agents of the Parties, to the Commission and to the applicant.

Rule 36: Interim measures

1. Before the constitution of a Chamber, the President of the Court may, at the request of a Party, of the Commission, of the applicant or of any other person

concerned, or *proprio motu*, indicate to any Party and, where appropriate, the applicant, any interim measure which it is advisable for them to adopt. The Chamber when constituted or, if the Chamber is not in session, its President shall have the same power.

Notice of these measures shall be immediately given to the Committee of Ministers.

2. Where the Commission, pursuant to Rule 36 of its Rules of Procedure, has indicated an interim measure as desirable, its adoption or maintenance shall remain recommended to the Parties and, where appropriate, the applicant after the case has been brought before the Court, unless and until the President or the Chamber otherwise decides or until paragraph 1 of this Rule is applied.

CHAPTER VIII – EXAMINATION OF CASES

Rule 37: Written procedure

1. The proceedings before the Court shall, as a general rule, comprise as their first stage a written procedure in which memorials are filed by the Parties, the applicant and, if it so wishes, the Commission.

   As soon as possible after the reference of a case to the Court, the President shall consult the Agents of the Parties, the applicant and the Delegates of the Commission, or, if the latter have not yet been appointed, the President of the Commission, as to the organisation of the proceedings, unless, with their agreement, he directs that a written procedure is to be dispensed with, he shall lay down the time-limits for the filing of the memorials.

   No memorial or other document may be filed except within such time-limit (if any) or with the authorisation of the President or at his or the Chamber's request.

2. The President may, in the interests of the proper administration of justice, invite or grant leave to any Contracting State which is not a Party to the proceedings to submit written comments within a time limit and on issues which he shall specify. He may extend such an invitation or grant such leave to any person concerned other than the applicant.

3. Where two cases have been referred to the same Chamber under Rule 21, paragraph 6, the President of the Chamber may, in the interests of the proper administration of justice and after consulting the Agents of the Parties, the Delegates of the Commission and the applicants, order that the proceedings in both cases be conducted simultaneously, without prejudice to the decision of the Chamber on the joinder of the cases.

4. Memorials, comments and documents annexed thereto shall be filed with the registry; they shall be filed in forty copies when they are submitted by a Party, by another State or by the Commission. The Registrar shall transmit copies thereof to the judges, to the Agents of the Parties, to the Delegates of the Commission and to the applicant, as the case may be.

Rule 38: Fixing of the date of the hearing

The President of the Chamber shall, after consulting the Agents of the Parties, the Delegates of the Commission and the applicant, fix the date of the hearing. The Registrar shall notify them of the decision taken in this respect.

Rule 39: Conduct of hearings

The President of the Chamber shall direct hearings. He shall prescribe the order in which the Agents, advocates or advisers of the Parties, the Delegates of the Commission, any person assisting the Delegates in accordance with Rule 29, paragraph 1, and the applicant shall be called upon to speak.

Rule 40: Failure to appear at hearings

Where, without showing sufficient cause, a Party or the applicant fails to appear, the Chamber may, provided that it is satisfied that such a course is consistent with the proper administration of justice, proceed with the hearing.

Rule 41: Measures for taking evidence

1. The Chamber may, at the request of a Party, of the Delegates of the Commission, of the applicant or of a third party invited or granted leave to submit written comments under Rule 37, paragraph 2, or *proprio motu*, obtain any evidence which it considers capable of providing clarification on the facts of the case. The Chamber may, *inter alia*, decide to hear as a witness or expert or in any other capacity any person whose evidence or statements seem likely to assist it in the carrying out of its task.

   When the Chamber is not in session, the President of the Chamber may exercise, by way of preparatory measure, the powers set forth in the immediately foregoing sub-paragraph, without prejudice to the decision of the Chamber on the relevance of the evidence so taken or sought.

2. The Chamber may ask any person or institution of its choice to obtain information, express an opinion or make a report, upon any specific point.

3. Where a report drawn up in accordance with the preceding paragraphs has been prepared at the request of a Party, the costs relating thereto shall be borne by that Party unless the Chamber decides otherwise. In other cases, the Chamber shall decide whether such costs are to be borne by the Council of Europe, or awarded against an applicant, or a third party, at whose request the report was prepared. in all cases, the costs shall be taxed by the President.

4. The Chamber may, at any time during the proceedings, depute one or more of its members to conduct an enquiry, carry out an investigation on the spot or take evidence in some other manner.

Rule 42: Convocation of witnesses, experts and other persons; costs of their appearance

1. Witnesses, experts or other persons whom the Chamber or the President of the Chamber decides to hear shall be summoned by the Registrar If they appear at the request of a Party, the costs of their appearance shall be borne by that Party unless the Chamber decides otherwise. In other cases, the Chamber shall decide whether such costs are to be borne by the Council of Europe or awarded against an applicant, or a third party within the meaning of Rule 41, paragraph 1, at whose request the person summoned appeared. In all cases, the costs shall, if need be, be taxed by the President.

2. The summons shall indicate:

    –   the case in connection with which it has been issued;
    –   the object of the enquiry, expert opinion or other measures ordered by the Chamber or the President of the Chamber;
    –   any provisions for the payment of the sum due to the person summoned.

Rule 43: Oath or solemn declaration by witnesses and experts

1. After the establishment of his identity and before giving evidence, every witness shall take the following oath or make the following solemn declaration:

    "I swear" – or "I solemnly declare upon my honour and conscience" – "that I will speak the truth, the whole truth and nothing but the truth."

    This act shall be recorded in minutes.

2. After the establishment of his identity and before carrying out his task, every expert shall take the following oath or make the following solemn declaration:

    "I swear" – or "I solemnly declare" – "that I will discharge my duty as expert honourably and conscientiously."

    This act shall be recorded in minutes.

    This oath may be taken or this declaration made before the President of the Chamber, or before a judge or any public authority nominated by the President.

Rule 44: Objection to a witness or expert; hearing of a person for the purpose of information

The Chamber shall decide in the event of any dispute arising from an objection to a witness or expert. It may hear for the purpose of information a person who cannot be heard as a witness.

Rule 45: Questions put during hearings

1. The President or any judge may put questions to the Agents, advocates or advisers of the Parties, to the witnesses and experts, to the Delegates of the

Commission, to the applicant and to any other persons appearing before the Chamber.

2. The witnesses, experts and other persons referred to in Rule 41, paragraph 1, may, subject to the control of the President, be examined by the Agents, advocates or advisers of the Parties, by the Delegates of the Commission, by any person assisting the Delegates in accordance with Rule 29, paragraph 1, and by the applicant. In the event of an objection as to the relevance of a question put, the Chamber shall decide.

Rule 46: Failure to appear or false evidence

When, without good reason, a witness or any other person who has been duly summoned fails to appear or refuses to give evidence, the Registrar shall, on being so required by the President, inform that Contracting Party to whose jurisdiction such witness or other person is subject. The same provisions shall apply when a witness or expert has, in the opinion of the Chamber, violated the oath or solemn declaration provided for in Rule 43.

Rule 47: Verbatim record of hearings

1. The Registrar shall be responsible for the making of a verbatim record of each hearing. The verbatim record shall include:
   a. the composition of the Chamber at the hearing;
   b. a list of those appearing before the Court, that is to say, Agents, advocates and advisers of the Parties, Delegates of the Commission and persons assisting them, applicants, Contracting States and other persons referred to in Rule 37, paragraph 2;
   c. the surnames, forenames, description and address of each witness, expert or other person heard;
   d. the text of statements made, questions put and replies given;
   e. the text of any decision delivered by the Chamber during the hearing.

2. The Agents, advocates and advisers of the Parties, the Delegates of the Commission, the applicant and the witnesses, experts and other persons mentioned in Rules 29, paragraph 1, and 41, paragraph 1, shall receive the verbatim record of their arguments, statements or evidence, in order that they may, subject to the control of the Registrar or the President of the Chamber, make corrections, but in no case may such corrections affect the sense and bearing of what was said. The Registrar, in accordance with the instructions of the President, shall fix the time-limits granted for this purpose.

3. The verbatim record, once so corrected, shall be signed by the President and the Registrar and shall then constitute certified matters of record.

Rule 48: Preliminary objections

1. A Party wishing to raise a preliminary objection must file a statement setting out the objection and the grounds therefor not later than the time when that

Party informs the President of its intention not to submit a memorial or, alternatively, not later than the expiry of the time-limit laid down under Rule 37, paragraph 1, for the filing of its first memorial.

2. Unless the Chamber decides otherwise, the filing of a preliminary objection shall not have the effect of suspending the proceedings on the merits. In all cases, the Chamber shall, after following the procedure provided for under Chapter III herein, give its decision on the objection or join the objection to the merits.

Rule 49: Striking out of the list

1. When the Party which has brought the case before the Court notifies the Registrar of its intention not to proceed with the case and when the other Parties agree to such discontinuance, the Chamber shall, after consulting the Commission and the applicant, decide whether or not it is appropriate to approve the discontinuance and accordingly to strike the case out of its list.

2. When the Chamber is informed of a friendly settlement, arrangement or other fact of a kind to provide a solution of the matter, it may, after consulting, if necessary, the Parties, the Delegates of the Commission and the applicant, strike the case out of the list.

   The same shall apply where the circumstances warrant the conclusion that the applicant does not intend to pursue his complaints or if, for any other reason, further examination of the case is not justified.

3. The striking out of a case shall be effected by means of a judgment which the President shall forward to the Committee of Ministers in order to allow them to supervise, in accordance with Article 54 of the Convention, the execution of any undertakings which may have been attached to the discontinuance or solution of the matter.

4. The Chamber may, having regard to the responsibilities of the Court under Article 19 of the Convention, decide that, notwithstanding the notice of discontinuance, friendly settlement, arrangement or other fact referred to in paragraphs 1 and 2 of this Rule, it should proceed with the consideration of the case.

Rule 50: Question of the application of Article 50 of the Convention

1. Any claims which the applicant may wish to make under Article 50 of the Convention shall, unless the President otherwise directs, be set out in his memorial or, if he does not submit a memorial, in a special document filed at least one month before the date fixed pursuant to Rule 38 for the hearing.

2. The Chamber may, at any time during the proceedings, invite any Party, the Commission and the applicant to submit comments on this question.

Rule 51: Relinquishment of jurisdiction by the Chamber in favour of the Grand Chamber; and by the Grand Chamber in favour of the plenary Court

1. Where a case pending before a Chamber raises one or more serious questions affecting the interpretation of the Convention, the Chamber may, at any time

during the proceedings, relinquish jurisdiction in favour of a Grand Chamber. Relinquishment of jurisdiction shall be obligatory where the resolution of such a question or questions might have a result inconsistent with a judgment previously delivered by the Court. Reasons need not be given for the decision to relinquish jurisdiction.

2. The Grand Chamber shall comprise nineteen judges and be composed as follows:

    a. the President and the Vice-President(s) of the Court,
    b. the other members of the Chamber which has relinquished jurisdiction,
    c. additional judges appointed by means of a separate drawing of lots by the President of the Court in the presence of the Registrar immediately after the Chamber has relinquished jurisdiction.

3. The quorum of the Grand Chamber shall be seventeen judges.
4. The Grand Chamber, when the case has been referred to it, may either retain jurisdiction over the whole case or, after deciding the said question or questions, order that the case be referred back to the Chamber, which shall, in regard to the remaining part of the case, recover its original jurisdiction.
5. The Grand Chamber may exceptionally, when the issues raised are particularly serious or involve a significant change of existing case-law, relinquish jurisdiction in favour of the plenary Court, which for this purpose shall comprise all the judges.

    When a case is referred to the plenary Court, any *ad hoc* judge who is a member of the Grand Chamber shall sit as a judge on the plenary Court.

    The plenary Court, when the case has been referred to it, may either retain jurisdiction over the whole case or, after deciding the said question or questions, order that the case be referred back to the Grand Chamber, which shall, in regard to the remaining part of the case, recover its jurisdiction.

6. Any provisions governing the Chambers shall apply, *mutatis mutandis*, to proceedings before the Grand Chamber and the plenary Court.

CHAPTER IX – JUDGMENTS

Rule 52: Procedure by default

Where a Party fails to appear or to present its case, the Chamber shall, subject to the provisions of Rule 49, give a decision in the case.

Rule 53: Contents of the judgment

1. The judgment shall contain:

    a. the names of the President and the judges constituting the Chamber, and also the names of the Registrar and, where appropriate, the Deputy Registrar:
    b. the dates on which it was adopted and delivered;
    c. a description of the Party or Parties;

d. the names of the Agents, advocates or advisers of the Party or Parties;
e. the names of the Delegates of the Commission and of the persons assisting them;
f. the name of the applicant;
g. an account of the procedure followed;
h. the final submissions of the Party or Parties and, if any, of the Delegates of the Commission and of the applicant;
i. the facts of the case;
j. the reasons in point of law;
k. the operative provisions of the judgment;
l. the decision, if any, in respect of costs;
m. the number of judges constituting the majority;
n. where appropriate, a statement as to which of the two texts, English or French, is authentic.

2. Any judge who has taken part in the consideration of the case shall be entitled to annex to the judgment either a separate opinion, concurring with or dissenting from that judgment, or a bare statement of dissent.

Rule 54: Judgment on the application of Article 50 of the Convention

1. Where the Chamber finds that there is a breach of the Convention, it shall give in the same judgment a decision on the application of Article 50 of the Convention if that question, after being raised in accordance with Rule 50, is ready for decision, if the question is not ready for decision, the Chamber shall reserve it in whole or in part and shall fix the further procedure. If, on the other hand, this question has not been raised in accordance with Rule 50, the Chamber may lay down a time-limit for the applicant to submit any claims for just satisfaction that he may have.
2. For the purposes of ruling on the application of Article 50 of the Convention, the Chamber shall, as far as possible, be composed of those judges who sat to consider the merits of the case. Those judges who have ceased to be members of the Court shall be recalled in order to deal with the question in accordance with Article 40, paragraph 6, of the Convention; however, in the event of death, inability to sit, withdrawal or exemption from sitting, the judge concerned shall be replaced in the same manner as was applied for his appointment to the Chamber.
3. When the judgment finding a breach has been delivered under Rule 51 and does not contain a ruling on the application of Article 50 of the Convention, the plenary Court or the Grand Chamber may decide, without prejudice to the provisions of paragraph 1 above, to refer the question back to the Chamber.
4. If the Court is informed that an agreement has been reached between the injured party and the Party liable, it shall verify the equitable nature of such agreement and, where it finds the agreement to be equitable, strike the case out of the list by means of a judgment. Rule 49, paragraph 3, shall apply in such circumstances.

Rule 55: Signature, delivery and notification of the judgment

1. The judgment shall be signed by the President and by the Registrar.
2. The judgment shall be read out by the President, or by another judge delegated by him, at a public hearing in one of the two official languages. It shall not be necessary for the other judges to be present. The Agents of the Parties, the Delegates of the Commission and the applicant shall be informed in due time of the date and time of delivery of the judgment.

   However, in respect of a judgment striking a case out of the list or relating to the application of Article 50 of the Convention, the President may direct that the notification provided for under paragraph 4 of this Rule shall count as delivery.
3. The judgment shall be transmitted by the President to the Committee of Ministers.
4. The original copy, duly signed and sealed, shall be placed in the archives of the Court. The Registrar shall send certified copies to the Party or Parties, to the Commission, to the applicant, to the Secretary General of the Council of Europe, to the Contracting States and persons referred to in Rule 37, paragraph 2, and to any other person directly concerned.

Rule 56: Publication of judgments and other documents

1. The Registrar shall be responsible for the publication of:

   - judgments of the Court,
   - documents relating to the proceedings, including the report of the Commission but excluding any document which the President considers unnecessary or inadvisable to publish;
   - verbatim records of public hearings;
   - any document which the President considers useful to publish.

   Publication shall take place in the two official languages in the case of judgments, applications or requests instituting proceedings and the Commission's reports; the other documents shall be published in the official language in which they occur in the proceedings.
2. Documents deposited with the Registrar and not published shall be accessible to the public unless otherwise decided by the President either on his own initiative or at the request of a Party, of the Commission, of the applicant or of any other person concerned.

Rule 57: Request for interpretation of a judgment

1. A Party or the Commission may request the interpretation of a judgment within a period of three years following the delivery of that judgment.
2. The request shall state precisely the point or points in the operative provisions of the judgment on which interpretation is required. It shall be filed with the registry in forty copies.
3. The Registrar shall communicate the request, as appropriate, to any other Party, to the Commission and to the applicant, and shall invite them to submit

any written comments within a time-limit laid down by the President of the Chamber. The President of the Chamber shall also fix the date of the hearing should the Chamber decide to hold one.

Written comments shall be filed with the registry, they shall be filed in forty copies when they are submitted by a Party or by the Commission.

4. The request for interpretation shall be considered by the Chamber which gave the judgment and which shall, as far as possible, be composed of the same judges. Those judges who have ceased to be members of the Court shall be recalled in order to deal with the case in accordance with Article 40, paragraph 6, of the Convention; however, in the event of death, inability to sit, withdrawal or exemption from sitting, the judge concerned shall be replaced in the same manner as was applied for his appointment to the Chamber.

5. The Chamber shall decide by means of a judgment.

Rule 58: Request for revision of a judgment

1. A Party or the Commission may, in the event of the discovery of a fact which might by its nature have a decisive influence and which, when a judgment was delivered, was unknown both to the Court and to that Party or the Commission, request the Court, within a period of six months after that Party or the Commission, as the case may be, acquired knowledge of such fact, to revise that judgment.

2. The request shall mention the judgment of which the revision is requested and shall contain the information necessary to show that the conditions laid down in paragraph 1 have been complied with. It shall be accompanied by the original or a copy of all supporting documents. The request and supporting documents shall be filed with the registry in forty copies.

3. The Registrar shall communicate the request, as appropriate, to any other Party, to the Commission and to the applicant, and shall invite them to submit any written comments within a time-limit laid down by the President. The President shall also fix the date of the hearing should the Chamber decide to hold one.

Written comments shall be filed with the registry; they shall be filed in forty copies if they are submitted by a Party or by the Commission.

4. The request for revision shall be considered by a Chamber constituted in accordance with Article 43 of the Convention, which shall decide whether the request is admissible or not under paragraph 1 of this Rule. In the affirmative, the Chamber shall refer the request to the Chamber which gave the original judgment or, if in the circumstances that is not reasonably possible, it shall retain the request and examine the merits thereof.

5. The Chamber shall decide by means of a judgment.

CHAPTER X – ADVISORY OPINIONS

Rule 59

In proceedings in regard to advisory opinions the Court shall, in addition to the provisions of Protocol No. 2, apply the provisions which follow. It shall also apply the other provisions of these Rules to the extent to which it considers this to be appropriate.

Rule 60

The request for an advisory opinion shall be filed with the registry in forty copies. It shall state fully and precisely the question on which the opinion of the Court is sought, and also:

a.   the date on which the Committee of Ministers adopted the decision referred to in Article 1, paragraph 3, of Protocol No. 2;
b.   the names and addresses of the person or persons appointed by the Committee of Ministers to give the Court any explanations which it may require.

The request shall be accompanied by all documents likely to elucidate the question.

Rule 61

1.   On receipt of a request, the Registrar shall transmit a copy thereof to all the members of the Court and to the Commission.
2.   He shall inform the Contracting Parties that the Court is prepared to receive their written comments. The President may decide that, by reason of the nature of the question, a similar invitation is to be sent to the Commission.

Rule 62

1.   The President shall lay down the time-limits for the filing of written comments or other documents.
2.   Written comments or other documents shall be filed with the registry in sixty copies. The Registrar shall transmit copies thereof to all the members of the Court, to the Committee of Ministers, to each of the Contracting Parties and to the Commission.

Rule 63

After the closure of the written procedure, the President shall decide whether the Contracting Parties or the Commission which have submitted written comments are to be given an opportunity to develop them at an oral hearing held for the purpose.

Rule 64

If the Court considers that the request for an advisory opinion is not within its consultative competence as defined in Article 1 of Protocol No. 2, it shall so declare in a reasoned decision.

Rule 65

1. Advisory opinions shall be given by majority vote of the plenary Court. They shall mention the number of judges constituting the majority.
2. Any judge may, if he so desires, attach to the opinion of the Court either a separate opinion, concurring with or dissenting from the advisory opinion, or a bare statement of dissent.

Rule 66

The advisory opinion shall be read out by the President, or by another judge delegated by him, at a public hearing in one of the two official languages, prior notice having been given to the Committee of Ministers, to each of the Contracting Parties and to the Commission.

Rule 67

The opinion, as well as any decision given under Rule 64, shall be signed by the President and by the Registrar. The original copy, duly signed and sealed, shall be placed in the archives of the Court. The Registrar shall send certified copies to the Committee of Ministers, to the Contracting Parties, to the Commission and to the Secretary General of the Council of Europe.

Rule 68 Final clause

The present Rules shall enter into force on 1 January 1983. They shall, however, apply only to cases brought before the Court after that date.

ADDENDUM
RULES ON LEGAL AID TO APPLICANTS

The European Court of Human Rights,

Having regard to the Convention for the Protection of Human Rights and Fundamental Freedoms and the Protocols thereto;
Having regard to the Rules of Court,
Adopts the present addendum to the Rules of Court:

Rule 1: Definitions

1. For the purposes of the present addendum:

   a. the term "applicant" is to be understood as meaning the person, non-governmental organisation or group of individuals who, after lodging a complaint with the Commission under Article 25 of the Convention, has expressed the desire, in accordance with Rule 33 of the Rules of Court, to take part in the proceedings before the Court;

b.   the term "President" is to be understood as meaning the President of the Court until the constitution of the Chamber or in the event of relinquishment of jurisdiction under Rule 51 of the Rules of Court, and the President of the Chamber in all other instances.

2.   Subject to the foregoing, the terms used herein shall, unless the context otherwise requires, have the same meaning as they have in the Rules of Court.

Rule 2: Requests for information regarding legal aid before the Commission

1.   Unless the information is already available to him, the Registrar shall enquire whether or not the applicant applied for, and, if so, whether or not he was granted, legal aid in connection with the representation of his case before the Commission pursuant to the addendum to the Rules of Procedure of the Commission.

2.   At the same time the Registrar may, on the instructions of the President, ask the Commission to produce to the Court the file relating to the grant or refusal, if any, of legal aid to the applicant.

Rule 3: Continuation in force of a grant made by the Commission

1.   Subject to the provisions of Rule 5 herein, where the applicant has been granted legal aid in connection with the representation of his case before the Commission, that grant shall continue in force for the purposes of his representation before the Court.

2.   The President may, however, instruct the Registrar to obtain from the applicant information evidencing that the conditions laid down in Rule 4, paragraph 2, herein are fulfilled. The Registrar shall bring any information so obtained to the attention of the Agents of the Parties and the Delegates of the Commission, in order to give them the opportunity to verify its correctness.

Rule 4: Grant of legal aid by the President

1.   Where the applicant did not receive a grant of legal aid in connection with the representation of his case before the Commission or had such grant revoked, the President may at any time, at the request of the applicant, grant free legal aid to the applicant for the purposes of his representation before the Court.

2.   Legal aid may be so granted only where the President is satisfied that:

   a.   the applicant lacks sufficient means to meet all or part of the costs involved; and

   b.   such a course is necessary for the proper conduct of the case before the Court

3.   In order to determine whether or not the applicant lacks the sufficient means, the Registrar shall ask him to complete a form of declaration stating his income, capital assets and any financial commitments in respect of dependants, or any other financial obligations. Such declaration shall be certified by the

appropriate domestic authority or authorities. This certified declaration may be replaced by a certificate of indigence delivered by the appropriate domestic authority or authorities as listed in the appendix to this addendum.

4. Before the President makes a grant of legal aid, the Registrar shall request the Agents of the Parties and the Delegates of the Commission to submit their comments in writing.

5. After receiving the information mentioned in paragraphs 3 and 4 and, if appropriate, Rule 2, paragraph 2, above, the President shall decide whether or not legal aid is to be granted and to what extent. The Registrar shall notify the applicant, the Agents of the Parties and the Delegates of the Commission accordingly.

6. The Registrar, on the instructions of the President, shall fix the time-limits within which the information referred to in this Rule is to be supplied.

Rule 5: Revocation or variation of a grant

The President may, if he is satisfied that the conditions stated in Rule 4, paragraph 2, are no longer fulfilled, at any time revoke or vary, in whole or in part a grant of legal aid made or continued in force under the present addendum. The Registrar shall at once notify the applicant, the Agents of the Parties and the Delegates of the Commission accordingly.

Rule 6: Fees and expenses payable

1. Fees shall be payable only to the advocates or other persons appointed in accordance with Rule 30 of the Rules of Court.

2. Legal aid may be granted to cover not only fees for representation but also travelling and subsistence expenses and other necessary out-of-pocket expenses incurred by the applicants or by their representatives.

3. After consulting the representatives, the Registrar shall, on the instructions of the President, fix the amount of fees to be paid. The Registrar shall also in each case decide what particular expenses referred to above at paragraph 2 are to be covered by the grant of legal aid.

Rule 7: Derogation from procedural requirements

In case of urgency, the President may sanction a derogation from the procedural requirements of this addendum provided that the derogation in question is essential for the proper conduct of the case before the Court.

Rule 8: Entry into force and transitional arrangements

This addendum shall come into force at a date to be fixed by the President of the Court. Pending such entry into force, the grant of legal aid to an applicant in connection with the representation of his case before the Court shall continue to be governed by the addendum to the Rules of Procedure of the Commission.

APPENDIX
NATIONAL AUTHORITIES COMPETENT TO DELIVER A
CERTIFICATE OF INDIGENCE

The declaration of means referred to in Rule 4, paragraph 3, of the addendum to the Rules of Court A (Rules on legal aid to applicants) may be replaced by a certificate of indigence delivered by the appropriate domestic authority or authorities. The competent domestic authorities are as follows:

Austria

The mayor of the locality where the applicant has his or her legal or actual residence.

Belgium

The direct taxation department of the district in which the applicant lives issues him with a certificate of income or, with his authorisation, express and in writing, issues such to another person or administrative department.

The request, accompanied by such authorisation, may be addressed either to the local direct taxation department or to the Administration centrale des contributions directes, 45, rue Belliard, B-1040 Bruxelles.

Cyprus

The Social Welfare Services, Ministry of Labour and Social Insurance.

Czech Republic

The social welfare authority in the municipality of the applicant's place of domicile.

Denmark

The local tax authority.

Finland

The social welfare authority in the municipality of the applicant's place of domicile.

France

The mayor of the municipality in which the applicant lives.

Germany

None. The applicant submits a prescribed form, duly completed and with supporting documents, which is forwarded to the Federal Ministry of Justice.

Greece

a. A certificate from the mayor or president of the district in which the applicant lives giving details of his family situation, his employment and his assets; and
b. A certificate from the tax authority showing that the applicant has made a tax return for the previous three years with the results thereof.

Hungary

None. In court proceedings, the applicant, the tax authorities, and the applicant's employer complete a prescribed form and attach supporting documents, if any. The applicant then submits this group of documents to the proceeding court.

Iceland

The *Rikisskattstóri* (Director of Internal Revenue), Skúlagotu 57, IS-Reykjavik.

Ireland

The Chief Inspector, Department of Social Welfare, 101/104 Marlboro Street, IRL-Dublin 1.

Italy

a. Certification, by a responsible section of the tax authorities, of a declaration of means prepared by the applicant; or
b. Certificate of indigence issued by the mayor of the municipality in which the applicant lives.

Liechtenstein

The Court of Justice (Fürstliches Landgericht).

Luxembourg

On production of a certificate stating the amount of tax paid the previous year, the College of Mayor and Aldermen of the municipality in which the applicant lives issues a certificate of indigence.

Netherlands

The local government *(gemeentebestuur)* in accordance with Article 11 of the Legal Aid Act *(Wet Rechtsbijstand on- en minvermogenden)*.

Norway

The local tax authority *(ligningskontor)* of the district in which the applicant lives.

Portugal

The local government *(junta de frequesia)* for the district in which the applicant lives.

San Marino

The certificate of indigence is issued by the office of the Secretary of State for Internal Affairs following a declaration made by the San Marinese tax office.

Spain

The district office of the Finance Minister *(Delegación de Hacienda)* for the district in which the applicant lives.

Sweden

The local tax authority *(lokala skattemyndigheten)* certifies the means of persons requesting free legal aid.

Switzerland

The local tax authority for the applicant's place of residence.

Turkey

a. The mayor of the municipality in which the applicant lives; or
b. The elders' council for the village or district in which the applicant lives (Article 468 of the Code of Civil Procedure).

United Kingdom

a. England and Wales
   DHSS, Legal Aid Assessment Office, No.3 The Pavilions, Ashton on Ribble, Preston PR2 2PA;
b. Scotland
   The Scottish Legal Aid Board, 44 Drumsheugh Gardens, Edinburgh EH3 7SW.

The relevant information concerning four States − Bulgaria, Malta, Poland and Slovakia − has not yet been communicated to the registry of the Court.

RULES OF COURT "B"

Adopted: 9 January 1994 and applicable to cases concerning States bound by Protocol No 9 to the Convention

Entry into force: 2 October 1994, in accordance with Rule 70

Editors' Notes

As indicated above, Protocol Nine to the Convention has not been ratified by all parties to the Convention. The amendments to the Convention do, however, necessitate different Rules of Court for those States which have ratified that Protocol. Those Rules are set out below, to the extent that they differ from the Rules applicable to cases concerning States which are not bound by Protocol Nine.

The European Court of Human Rights,

Having regard to the Convention for the Protection of Human Rights and Fundamental Freedoms and the Protocols thereto,

Having regard to the Rules of Court that entered into force on 1 January 1983 ("Rules of Court A"), which apply to cases concerning States not bound by Protocol No. 9 to the said Convention,

Makes the present Rules ("Rules of Court B"), which apply to cases concerning States bound by Protocol No. 9:

Rule 1: Definitions

For the purposes of these Rules unless the context otherwise requires:

a. the term "Convention" means the Convention for the Protection of Human Rights and Fundamental Freedoms and the Protocols thereto;

b. the expression "Protocol No. 2" means Protocol No. 2 to the Convention conferring upon the European Court of Human Rights competence to give advisory opinions;

c. the expression "plenary Court" means the European Court of Human Rights sitting in plenary session;

d. the term "Chamber" means any Chamber constituted in pursuance of Article 43 of the Convention; the term "Grand Chamber" means the Chamber provided for under Rule 53;

e. the term "Court" means either the plenary Court, the Grand Chamber or the Chambers;

f. the expression "Screening Panel" means the Panel provided for in Article 48, paragraph 2, of the Convention;

g. the expression 'ad hoc judge' means any person, other than an elected judge, chosen by a Contracting Party in pursuance of Article 43 or Article

48, paragraph 2, of the Convention to sit as a member of a Chamber or of a Screening Panel;

h. the term "judge" or "judges" means the judges elected by the Consultative Assembly of the Council of Europe or *ad hoc* judges;

i. the term "parties" means:

   - the applicant or respondent Contracting Parties;
   - the private party (the person, non-governmental organisation or group of individuals) who lodged a complaint with the European Commission of Human Rights under Article 25 and whose case has been referred to the Court;

j. the term "Commission" means the European Commission of Human Rights;

k. the expression "Delegates of the Commission" means the member or members of the Commission delegated by it to take part n the consideration of a case before the Court;

l. the expression "report of the Commission" means the report provided for in Article 31 of the Convention;

m. the expression "Committee of Ministers" means the Committee of Ministers of the Council of Europe.

TITLE I – ORGANISATION AND WORKING OF THE COURT

CHAPTER I – JUDGES

Rule 2: Calculation of term of office

[As Rules of Court "A", Rule 2]

Rule 3: Oath or solemn declaration

[As Rules of Court "A", Rule 3]

Rule 4: Obstacle to the exercise of the functions of judge

[As Rules of Court "A", Rule 4]

Rule 5: Precedence

[As Rules of Court "A", Rule 5]

Rule 6: Resignation

[As Rules of Court "A", Rule 6]

CHAPTER II – PRESIDENCY OF THE COURT

Rule 7: Election of the President and Vice-President

[As Rules of Court "A", Rule 7]

Rule 8: Functions of the President

[As Rules of Court "A", Rule 8]

Rule 9: Functions of the Vice-President

[As Rules of Court "A", Rule 9]

Rule 10: Replacement of the President and Vice-President

[As Rules of Court "A", Rule 10]

CHAPTER III – THE REGISTRY

Rule 11: Election of the Registrar

[As Rules of Court "A", Rule 11]

Rule 12: Election of the Deputy Registrar

[As Rules of Court "A", Rule 12]

Rule 13: Other staff, equipment and facilities

[As Rules of Court "A", Rule 13]

Rule 14: Functions of the Registrar

[As Rules of Court "A", Rule 14, except that paragraph 3 of Rules of Court "B", Rule 14 reads as follows:

"3. Communications or notifications addressed to the Agents or advocates of the parties and to the Delegates of the Commission shall be considered as having been addressed to the parties or to the Commission as the case may be."]

CHAPTER IV – THE WORKING OF THE COURT

Rule 15: Seat of the Court

[As Rules of Court "A", Rule 15]

Rule 16: Sessions of the plenary Court

[As Rules of Court "A", Rule 16]

Rule 17: Quorum

[As Rules of Court "A", Rule 17]

Rule 18: Public character of the hearings

[As Rules of Court "A", Rule 17]

Rule 19: Deliberations

[As Rules of Court "A", Rule 19, except that paragraph 1 of Rules of Court "B", Rule 19 reads as follows:

"1. The Court and the Screening Panels shall deliberate in private. Their deliberations shall remain secret."

Rule 20: Votes

[As Rules of Court "A", Rule 20]

CHAPTER V – THE CHAMBERS

Rule 21: Composition of the Court when constituted in a Chamber

1. For the consideration of any case referred to it under one or more of the sub-paragraphs of Article 48, paragraph 1, of the Convention, the Court shall be constituted in a Chamber of nine judges.
2. On the reference of a case to the Court, the Registrar shall notify all the judges, including the newly-elected judges, that such a Chamber is to be constituted. If any judge, upon receiving such notification, believes that for one of the reasons set out in Rule 24 he will be unable to sit, he shall so inform the Registrar. The President shall then draw up the list of judges available to constitute the Chamber.
3. There shall sit as *ex officio* members of the Chamber:

   a. every judge elected in respect of an applicant or respondent Contracting Party or, failing him, a person appointed pursuant to Rule 23, paragraph 1;
   b. the President of the Court, or, failing him, the Vice-President provided that they do not sit by virtue of the preceding subparagraph.

4. The other judges named on the list provided for in paragraph 2 shall be called upon to complete the Chamber, as members or as substitutes, in the order determined by a drawing of lots effected by the President of the Court in the presence of the Registrar.

5. The President of the Chamber shall be the judge sitting by virtue of paragraph 3.b or, failing one, a judge appointed under paragraph 4 as a member of the Chamber, in accordance with the order of precedence provided for in Rule 5.

    If the President of the Chamber is unable to sit or withdraws, he shall be replaced by the Vice-president or, if the same applies to him, by a judge appointed under paragraph 4 as a member of the Chamber, in accordance with the said order of precedence. However, where he is unable to sit or withdraws less than twenty-four hours before the opening of, or during or after, the hearing, his place shall be taken, in accordance with the said order of precedence, by one of the judges called upon to be present or present at the hearing.

6. If the President of the Court finds that two cases concern the same Contracting Party or Parties and raise similar issues, he may refer the second case to the Chamber already constituted, or in the course of constitution, for the consideration of the first case or, if there is none, proceed to the constitution of one Chamber to consider both cases.

Rule 22: Substitute judges

[As Rules of Court "A", Rule 22]

Rule 23: *Ad hoc* judges

1. If the Court does not include a judge elected in respect of a Contracting Party or if the judge called upon to sit in that capacity is unable to sit or withdraws, the President of the Court shall invite that Party to inform him within thirty days whether it wishes to appoint to sit as judge either another elected judge or, as an *ad hoc* judge, any other person possessing the qualifications required under Article 39, paragraph 3, of the Convention and, if so, to state at the same time the name of the person so appointed. The same rule shall apply if the person so appointed is unable to sit or withdraws.

2. The Contracting Party concerned shall be presumed to have waived such right of appointment if it does not reply within thirty days.

3. An *ad hoc* judge shall, at the opening of the first sitting fixed for the consideration of the case after he has been appointed, take the oath or make the solemn declaration provided for in Rule 3. This act shall be recorded in minutes.

Rule 24: Inability to sit, withdrawal or exemption

[As Rules of Court "A", Rule 24]

Rule 25: Common interest

1. If several applicant or respondent Contracting Parties have a common interest, the President of the Court may invite them to agree to appoint a single elected judge or *ad hoc* judge in accordance with Article 43 of the Convention. If the

Parties are unable to agree, the President shall choose by lot, from among the persons proposed as judges by these Parties, the judge called upon to sit *ex officio*. The names of the other judges and substitute judges shall then be chosen by lot by the President from among the judges who have not been elected in respect of an applicant or respondent Contracting Party.

2. In the event of dispute as to the existence of a common interest, the plenary Court shall decide.

CHAPTER VI – THE SCREENING PANELS

Rule 26: Composition of the Screening Panels

1. Any case referred to the Court by virtue solely of Article 48, paragraph 1.e of the Convention shall first be submitted to a Screening Panel.
2. There shall sit as an *ex officio* member of the Panel:

   a. any Judge elected in respect of a respondent Contracting Party,
   b. failing him, that is to say in one of the instances specified in Rule 23, paragraph l, d person appointed under that same provision.

3. The other two members shall be the first two judges designated by the drawing of lots provided for in Rule 21, paragraph 4. If one of these judges is unable to sit or withdraws, he shall be replaced by one of the remaining members of the Chamber in accordance with the order determined by the aforementioned drawing of lots.
4. The Chairman of the Panel shall be one of the judges appointed under paragraph 3 above, in accordance with the order of precedence provided for in Rule 5.
5. In the event of Rule 21, paragraph 6, being applied, the Panel already constituted, or in the course of constitution, for the consideration of the first case shall also consider the second case.

TITLE II – PROCEDURE

CHAPTER I – GENERAL RULES

Rule 27: Possibility of particular derogations

The provisions of this title shall not prevent the Court from derogating from them for the consideration of a particular case after having consulted the parties and the Delegates of the Commission.

Rule 28: Official languages

1. The official languages of the Court shall be English and French.

2.   An applicant or respondent Contracting Party may, not later than the consultation provided for in Rule 40, apply to the President of the Chamber for leave to use another language at the hearing. If such leave is granted by the President, the Party concerned shall be responsible for the interpretation into English or French of the oral arguments or statements made by its Agent, advocates or advisers and shall, to the extent which the President may determine in each case, bear the other extra expenses involved in the use of a non-official language.

3.   The President may grant the private party, as well as any person assisting the Delegates under Rule 30, paragraph 1, leave to use a non-official language. In that event, the Registrar shall make the necessary arrangements for the translation or interpretation into English and French of their comments or statements.

4.   Any witness, expert or other person appearing before the Court may use his own language if he does not have sufficient knowledge of either of the two official languages. The Registrar shall, in that event, make the necessary arrangements for the interpretation into English and French of the statements of the witness, expert or other person concerned.

5.   All judgments shall be given in English and in French; unless the Court decides otherwise, both texts shall be authentic.

Rule 29: Representation of the applicant or respondent Contracting Parties

The applicant or respondent Contracting Parties shall be represented by Agents who may have the assistance of advocates or advisers.

Rule 30: Relations between the Court and the Commission and release of the report of the Commission

1.   The Commission shall delegate one or more of its members to take part in the consideration of a case before the Court. The Delegates may be assisted by other persons.

2.   In every case referred to it, the Court shall take into consideration the report of the Commission.

3.   Unless the President decides otherwise, the said report shall be made available to the public through the Registrar:

   a.   in cases referred to the Court by virtue solely of Article 48, paragraph 1.e, of the Convention, as soon as possible after the Screening Panel has decided not to decline consideration of the case pursuant to paragraph 2 of the same Article;

   b.   in other cases as soon as possible after the reference of the case to the Court.

Rule 31: Representation of private parties

1.   Any private party shall be represented by an advocate authorised to practise

in any of the Contracting States and resident on the territory of one of them, or by any other person approved by the President. A private party may however present his own case before the Screening Panel and, if the President gives leave to do so, in the ensuing proceedings, subject, if need be, to his being assisted by an advocate or other person as aforesaid.

2. Unless the President decides otherwise, the advocate or other person representing or assisting the private party, or the latter himself if he presents his own case or seeks leave to do so, must have an adequate knowledge of one of the Court's official languages.

Rule 32: Communications, notifications and summonses addressed to persons other than the Agents or advocates of the parties or the Delegates of the Commission

1. If, for any communication, notification or summons addressed to persons other than the Agents or advocates of the parties or the Delegates of the Commission, the Court considers it necessary to have the assistance of the Government of the State on whose territory such communication, notification or summons is to have effect, the President shall apply directly to that Government in order to obtain the necessary facilities.

2. The same rule shall apply when the Court desires to make or arrange for the making of an investigation on the spot in order to establish the facts or to procure evidence or when it orders the appearance of a person resident in, or having to cross, that territory.

CHAPTER II – INSTITUTION OF PROCEEDINGS

Rule 33: Cases referred to the Court by a Contracting Party or by the Commission

1. Any Contracting Party which intends to refer a case to the Court under Article 48, paragraph 1.b, c or d of the Convention shall file with the registry an application, in forty copies, indicating:

   a. the parties to the proceedings before the Commission;
   b. the date on which the Commission adopted its report;
   c. the date on which the report was transmitted to the Committee of Ministers;
   d. the object of the application;
   e. the name and address of the person appointed as Agent.

2. If the Commission intends to refer a case to the Court under Article 48, paragraph 1.a, of the Convention, it shall file with the registry a request, in forty copies, signed by its President and containing the particulars indicated in sub-paragraphs a, b, c and d of paragraph 1 of this Rule together with the names and addresses of the delegates of the Commission.

Rule 34: Cases referred to the Court by a private party

1. If a private party intends to refer a case to the Court under Article 48, paragraph 1.e, of the Convention, he shall file with the registry an application containing the particulars indicated in sub-paragraphs a, b and c of Rule 33, paragraph 1, and specifying:

   a. the object of the application, and in particular the serious question affecting the interpretation or application of the Convention which, in his opinion, the case raises or the other reasons for which, in his opinion, the case warrants consideration by the Court;
   b. the name and address of any person appointed by him pursuant to Rule 31.

2. On receipt of such application the Registrar shall notify accordingly

   a. all members of the Court;
   b. any Contracting Party mentioned in Article 48 of the Convention;
   c. the Commission;
   d. the Committee of Ministers.

3. As soon as it becomes established that the case has been referred to the Court by virtue solely of Article 48, paragraph 1e, of the Convention, the Screening Panel shall proceed to examine the application; it shall do so solely on the basis of the existing case-file.

4. If the case does not raise a serious question affecting the interpretation or application of the Convention and does not for any other reason warrant consideration by the Court, the Panel may, by a unanimous vote, decide to decline consideration of the case.

   In that event, the Panel shall deliver a briefly reasoned decision signed by the President and the Registrar. The original copy thereof shall be placed in the archives of the Court. The Registrar shall send certified copies to the private party, to the respondent Contracting Party, to the Commission and to the Committee of Ministers. This notification shall count as delivery.

Rule 35: Communication of the application or request

1. If a case has been referred to the Court by a Contracting Party or the Commission, the Registrar shall transmit a copy of the application or request:

   a. to all members of the Court and, as appropriate,
   b. to any Contracting Party mentioned in Article 48 of the Convention,
   c. to the Commission,
   d. to the private party.

   The communications provided for in sub-paragraphs a, b and d above shall be accompanied by a copy of the report of the Commission. The Registrar shall in addition inform the Committee of Ministers of the filing of the application or request.

2. If a case has been referred to the Court by virtue solely of Article 48,

paragraph 1.e, of the Convention and thereafter the Screening Panel has decided not to decline consideration of the case, the Registrar shall immediately transmit a copy of the application:

a.   to the respondent Contracting Party, together with a copy of the report of the Commission,

b.   to the Commission.

The Registrar shall in addition inform the parties, the Commission and the Committee of Ministers of the decision of the Screening Panel.

3.   When making the communications provided for in sub-paragraphs b to d of paragraph 1 and in paragraph 2, the Registrar shall invite, as appropriate:

a.   the respondent Contracting Party in the proceedings before the Commission to notify him within two weeks of the name and address of its Agent;

b.   any other Contracting Party which appears to have the right, under Article 48 of the Convention, to bring a case before the Court and which has not availed itself of that right, to inform him, within four weeks, whether it wishes to take part in the proceedings and, if so, to notify him at the same time of the name and address of its Agent;

c.   the Commission to notify him as soon as possible of the names and addresses of its Delegates;

d.   the private party to notify him within two weeks of the name and address of any person whom he may wish to appoint pursuant to Rule 31.

Rule 36: Question whether a Contracting Party has the right to bring a case before the Court

In the event of a dispute as to whether a Contracting Party has the right under Article 48 to bring a case before the Court, the President shall submit that question for decision to the Grand Chamber provided for in paragraph 2 of Rule 53 of these Rules, without prejudice to the possible application of paragraph 5 of Rule 53.

Rule 37: Notice of the composition of the Chamber

As soon as a Chamber has been constituted for the consideration of a case, the registrar shall communicate its composition to the judges, to the Agents and advocates of the parties and to the Commission.

Rule 38: Interim measures

1.   Before the constitution of a Chamber, the President of the Court may, at the request of a party, of the Commission or of any other person concerned, or *proprio motu*, indicate to any Contracting Party and, where appropriate, the private party, any interim measure which it is advisable for them to adopt. The Chamber when constituted or, if the Chamber is not in session, its President shall have the same power.

Notice of these measures shall be immediately given to the Committee of Ministers.
2. Where the Commission, pursuant to Rule 36 of its Rules of Procedure, has indicated an interim measure as desirable, its adoption or maintenance shall remain recommended to the Contracting Parties and, where appropriate, the private party after the case has been brought before the Court, unless and until the President or the Chamber otherwise decides or until paragraph 1 of this Rule is applied.

CHAPTER III – EXAMINATION OF CASES

Rule 39: Written procedure

1. The proceedings before the Court shall, as a general rule, comprise as their first stage a written procedure in which memorials are filed by the parties and, if it so wishes, the Commission.
    As soon as possible after the reference of a case to the Court, the President shall consult the Agents and advocates of the parties and the Delegates of the Commission, or, if the latter have not yet been appointed, the President of the Commission, as to the organisation of the proceedings, unless, with their agreement, he directs that a written procedure is to be dispensed with, he shall lay down the time-limits for the filing of the memorials.
    No memorial or other document may be filed except within such time-limit (if any) or with the authorisation of the President or at his or the Chamber's request.
2. The President may, in the interests of the proper administration of justice, invite or grant leave to any Contracting State which is not a Party to the proceedings to submit written comments within a time-limit and on issues which he shall specify. He may extend such an invitation or grant such leave to any person concerned other than the private party.
3. Where two cases have been referred to the same Chamber under Rule 21, paragraph 6, the President of the Chamber may, in the interests of the proper administration of justice and after consulting the Agents and advocates of the parties and the Delegates of the Commission, order that the proceedings in both cases be conducted simultaneously, without prejudice to the decision of the Chamber on the joinder of the cases.
4. Memorials, comments and documents annexed thereto shall be filed with the registry; they shall be filed in forty copies when they are submitted by an applicant or respondent Contracting Party, by another State or by the Commission. The Registrar shall transmit copies thereof to the judges, to the Agents and advocates of the parties and to the Delegates of the Commission, as the case may be.

Rule 40: fixing of the date of the hearing

The President of the Chamber shall, after consulting the Agents and advocates of the parties and the Delegates of the Commission, fix the date of the hearing. The Registrar shall notify them of the decision taken in this respect.

Rule 41: Conduct of hearings

The President of the Chamber shall direct hearings. He shall prescribe the order in which the Agents, advocates or advisers of the parties, the Delegates of the Commission and any person assisting the Delegates in accordance with Rule 30, paragraph 1, shall be called upon to speak.

Rule 42: Failure to appear at hearings

Where, without showing sufficient cause, a party fails to appear, the Chamber may, provided that it is satisfied that such a course is consistent with the proper administration of justice, proceed with the hearing.

Rule 43: Measures for taking evidence

1. The Chamber may, at the request of a party, of the Delegates of the Commission or of a third party invited or granted leave to submit written comments under Rule 39, paragraph 2, or *proprio motu*, obtain any evidence which it considers capable of providing clarification on the facts of the case. The Chamber may, *inter alia*, decide to hear as a witness or expert or in any other capacity any person whose evidence or statements seem likely to assist it in the carrying out of its task.

   When the Chamber is not in session, the President of the Chamber may exercise, by way of preparatory measure, the powers set forth in the immediately foregoing sub-paragraph, without prejudice to the decision of the Chamber on the relevance of the evidence so taken or sought.
2. The Chamber may ask any person or institution of its choice to obtain information or express an opinion or make a report, upon any specific point.
3. Where a report drawn up in accordance with the preceding paragraphs has been prepared at the request of an applicant or respondent Contracting Party, the costs relating thereto shall be borne by that Party unless the Chamber decides otherwise. In other cases, the Chamber shall decide whether such costs are to be borne by the Council of Europe, or awarded against a private party, or a third party, at whose request the report was prepared. In all cases, the costs shall be taxed by the President.
4. The Chamber may, at any time during the proceedings, depute one or more of its members to conduct an enquiry, carry out an investigation on the spot or take evidence in some other manner.

Rule 44: Convocation of witnesses, experts and other persons, costs of their appearance

1. Witnesses, experts or other persons whom the Chamber or the President of the Chamber decides to hear shall be summoned by the Registrar. If they appear at the request of an applicant or respondent Contracting Party, the costs of their appearance shall be borne by that Party unless the Chamber decides otherwise. In other cases, the Chamber shall decide whether such costs

are to be borne by the Council of Europe or awarded against a private party, or a third party within the meaning of Rule 43, paragraph 1, at whose request the person summoned appeared. In all cases, the costs shall, if need be, be taxed by the President.

2. The summons shall indicate:

    —   the case in connection with which it has been issued;
    —   the object of the enquiry, expert opinion or other measure ordered by the Chamber or the President of the Chamber;
    —   any provisions for the payment of the sum due to the person summoned.

Rule 45: Oath or solemn declaration by witnesses and experts

[As Rules of Court "A", Rule 43]

Rule 46: Objection to a witness or expert; hearing of a person for the purpose of information

[As Rules of Court "A", Rule 44]

Rule 47: Questions put during hearings

1. The President or any judge may put questions to the Agents, advocates or advisers of the parties, to the witnesses and experts, to the Delegates of the Commission and to any other persons appearing before the Chamber.
2. The witnesses, experts and other persons referred to in Rule 43, paragraph 1, may, subject to the control of the President, be examined by the Agents, advocates or advisers of the parties, by the Delegates of the Commission and by any person assisting the Delegates in accordance with Rule 30, paragraph 1. In the event of an objection as to the relevance of a question put, the Chamber shall decide.

Rule 48: Failure to appear or false evidence

[As Rules of Court "A", Rule 46]

Rule 49: Verbatim record of hearings

1. The Registrar shall be responsible for the making of a verbatim record of each hearing. The verbatim record shall include:

    a. the composition of the Chamber at the hearing;
    b. a list of those appearing before the Court, that is to say, Agents, advocates and advisers of the parties, Delegates of the Commission and persons assisting them, Contracting States and other persons referred to in Rule 39, paragraph 2;

   c.   the surnames, forenames, description and address of each witness, expert or other person heard;

   d.   the text of statements made, questions put and replies given;

   e.   the text of any decision delivered by the Chamber during the hearing.

2.   The Agents, advocates and advisers of the parties, the Delegates of the Commission and the witnesses, experts and other persons mentioned in Rules 30, paragraph 1, and 43, paragraph 1, shall receive the verbatim record of their arguments, statements or evidence, in order that they may, subject to the control of the Registrar or the President of the Chamber, make corrections, but in no case may such corrections affect the sense and bearing of what was said. The Registrar, in accordance with the instructions of the President, shall fix the time-limits granted for this purpose.

3.   The verbatim record, once so corrected, shall be signed by the President and the Registrar and shall then constitute certified matters of record.

Rule 50: Preliminary objections

1.   A party wishing to raise a preliminary objection must file a statement setting out the objection and the grounds therefor not later than the time when that party informs the President of its intention not to submit a memorial or, alternatively, not later than the expiry of the time-limit laid down under Rule 39, paragraph 1, for the filing of its first memorial.

2.   Unless the Chamber decides otherwise, the filing of a preliminary objection shall not have the effect of suspending the proceedings on the merits. In all cases, the Chamber shall, after following the procedure provided for under Chapter III herein, give its decision on the objection or join the objection to the merits.

Rule 51: Striking out of the list

1.   When a party which has brought the case before the Court notifies the Registrar of its intention not to proceed with the case and when the other party or parties agree to such discontinuance, the Chamber shall, after consulting the Commission, decide whether or not it is appropriate to approve the discontinuance and accordingly to strike the case out of its list.

2.   When the Chamber is informed of a friendly settlement, arrangement or other fact of a kind to provide a solution of the matter, it may, after consulting, if necessary, the parties and the Delegates of the Commission, strike the case out of the list.

     The same shall apply where the circumstances warrant the conclusion that a party who filed an application by virtue of Article 48, paragraph 1.e, of the Convention does not intend to pursue the application or if, for any other reason, further examination of the case is not justified.

3.   The striking out of a case shall be effected by means of a judgment which the President shall forward to the Committee of Ministers in order to allow them to supervise, in accordance with Article 54 of the Convention, the execution

of any undertakings which may have been attached to the discontinuance or solution of the matter.

4.   The Chamber may, having regard to the responsibilities of the Court under Article 19 of the Convention, decide that, notwithstanding the notice of discontinuance, friendly settlement, arrangement or other fact referred to in paragraphs 1 and 2 of this Rule, it should proceed with the consideration of the case.

Rule 52: Question of the application of Article 50 of the Convention

1.   Any claims which the private party may wish to make under Article 50 of the Convention shall, unless the President otherwise directs, be set out in his memorial or, if he does not submit a memorial, in a special document filed at least one month before the date fixed pursuant to Rule 40 for the hearing.
2.   The Chamber may, at any time during the proceedings, invite any party and the Commission to submit comments on this question.

Rule 53: Relinquishment of jurisdiction by the Chamber in favour of the Grand Chamber; and by the Grand Chamber in favour of the plenary Court

[As Rules of Court "A", Rule 51]

CHAPTER IV – JUDGMENTS

Rule 54: Procedure by default

Where a party fails to appear or to present its case, the Chamber shall, subject to the provisions of Rule 51, give a decision in the case.

Rule 55: Contents of the judgment

1.   The judgment shall contain:

   a.   the names of the President and the judges constituting the Chamber, and also the names of the Registrar and, where appropriate, the Deputy Registrar;
   b.   the dates on which it was adopted and delivered;
   c.   a description of the party or parties,
   d.   the names of the Agents, advocates or advisers of the party or parties;
   e.   the names of the Delegates of the Commission and of the persons assisting them;
   f.   an account of the procedure followed;
   g.   the final submissions of the party or parties and, if any, of the Delegates of the Commission;
   h.   the facts of the case;
   i.   the reasons in point of law;
   j.   the operative provisions of the judgment;
   k.   the decision, if any, in respect of costs;

l.   the number of judges constituting the majority;
m.   where appropriate, a statement as to which of the two texts, English or French, is authentic.

2.   Any judge who has taken part in the consideration of the case shall be entitled to annex to the judgment either a separate opinion, concurring with or dissenting from that judgment, or a bare statement of dissent.

Rule 56: Judgment on the application of Article 50 of the Convention

1.   Where the Chamber finds that there is a breach of the Convention, it shall give in the same judgment a decision on the application of Article 50 of the Convention if that question after being raised in accordance with Rule 52, is ready for decision; if the question is not ready for decision, the Chamber shall reserve it in whole or in part and shall fix the further procedure. If, on the other hand, this question has not been raised in accordance with Rule 52, the Chamber may lay down a time-limit for the private party to submit any claims for just satisfaction that he may have.
2.   For the purposes of ruling on the application of Article 50 of the Convention, the Chamber shall, as far as possible, be composed of those judges who sat to consider the merits of the case. Those judges who have ceased to be members of the Court shall be recalled in order to deal with the question in accordance with Article 40, paragraph 6, of the Convention; however, in the event of death, inability to sit, withdrawal or exemption from sitting, the judge concerned shall be replaced in the same manner as *was* applied for his appointment to the Chamber.
3.   When the judgment finding a breach has been delivered under Rule 53 and does not contain a ruling on the application of Article 50 of the Convention, the plenary Court or the Grand Chamber may decide, without prejudice to the provisions of paragraph 1 above, to refer the question back to the Chamber.
4.   If the Court is informed that an agreement has been reached between the injured party and Contracting Party liable, it shall verify the equitable nature of such agreement and, where it finds the agreement to be equitable, strike the case out of the list by means of a judgment. Rule 51, paragraph 3, shall apply in such circumstances.

Rule 57: Signature, delivery and notification of the judgment

1.   The judgment shall be signed by the President and by the Registrar.
2.   The judgment shall be read out by the President, or by another judge delegated by him, at a public hearing in one of the two official languages. It shall not be necessary for the other judges to be resent. The Agents and advocates of the parties and the Delegates of the Commission shall be informed in due time of the date and time of delivery of the judgment.

   However, in respect of a judgment striking a case out of the list or relating to the application of Article 50 of the Convention, the President may direct that the notification provided for under paragraph 4 of this Rule shall count as delivery.

3. The judgment shall be transmitted by the President to the Committee of Ministers.
4. The original copy, duly signed and sealed, shall be placed in the archives of the Court. The Registrar shall send certified copies to the parties, to the Commission, to the Secretary General of the Council of Europe, to the Contracting States and persons referred to in Rule 39, paragraph 2, and to any other person directly concerned.

Rule 58: Publication of judgments and other documents

[As Rules of Court "A", Rule 56]

Rule 59: Request for interpretation of a judgment

1. A party or the Commission may request the interpretation of a judgment within a period of three years following the delivery of that judgment.
2. The request shall state precisely the point or points in the operative provisions of the judgment on which interpretation is required.
   It shall be filed with the registry in forty copies when it has been submitted by a Contracting Party.
3. When the request has been submitted by a private party, a Screening Panel may decide, by a unanimous vote, to reject it on the ground that there is no reason to warrant its consideration by the Court. The Panel shall in principle be composed of the judges who delivered the decision provided for in Rule 35, paragraph 2; if and in so far as that is not reasonably possible in the circumstances, Rule 26 shall apply *mutatis mutandis*.
4. When the request has been submitted by a Contracting Party or by the Commission, the Registrar shall communicate it, as appropriate, to any other party and to the Commission and shall invite them to submit any written comments within a time-limit laid down by the President of the Chamber. The President of the Chamber shall also fix the date of the hearing should the Chamber decide to hold one.
   Written comments shall be filed with the registry; they shall be filed in forty copies when they are submitted by a Contracting Party or by the Commission.
5. If the Screening Panel does not reject the request or if it has been submitted by a Contracting Party or by the Commission, it shall be considered by the Chamber which gave the judgment and which shall, as far as possible, be composed of the same judges. Those judges who have ceased to be members of the Court shall be recalled in order to deal with the case in accordance with Article 40, paragraph 6, of the Convention; however, in the event of death, inability to sit, withdrawal or exemption from sitting, the judge concerned shall be replaced in the same manner as was applied for his appointment to the chamber.
6. The Chamber shall decide by means of a judgment.

Rule 60: Request for revision of a judgment

1. A party or the Commission may, in the event of the discovery of a fact which might by its nature have a decisive influence and which, when a judgment was delivered, was unknown both to the Court and to that party or the Commission, request the Court, within a period of six months after that party or the Commission, as the case may be, acquired knowledge of such fact, to revise that judgment.

2. The request shall mention the judgment of which the revision is requested and shall contain the information necessary to show that the conditions laid down in paragraph 1 have been complied with. It shall be accompanied by the original or a copy of all supporting documents The request and supporting documents shall be filed with the registry; they shall be filed in forty copies when they have been submitted by a Contracting Party.

3. When the request has been submitted by a private party, it shall be considered by a Screening Panel composed as provided in Rule 59, paragraph 4. The Panel shall, in the event of declaring the request admissible under paragraph 1 of this Rule, refer the request to the Chamber which gave the original judgment or, if in the circumstances that is not reasonably possible, to a Chamber constituted in accordance with Article 43 of the Convention.

4. When the request has been submitted by a Contracting Party or by the Commission, the Registrar shall communicate it, as appropriate, to any other party and to the Commission, and shall invite them to submit any written comments within a time-limit laid down by the President. The President shall also fix the date of the hearing should the Chamber decide to hold one.

    Written comments shall be filed with the registry; they shall be filed in forty copies if they are submitted by a Contracting Party or by the Commission.

5. In the cases provided for in the preceding paragraph, the request shall be considered by a Chamber constituted in accordance with Article 43 of the Convention. This Chamber shall, in the event of its declaring the request admissible under paragraph 1 of this Rule, refer the request to the Chamber which gave the original judgment or, if in the circumstances that is not reasonably possible, it shall retain the request and consider the merits thereof.

6. The Chamber shall decide by means of a judgment.

CHAPTER V – ADVISORY OPINIONS

Rule 61

[As Rules of Court "A", Rule 59]

Rule 62

[As Rules of Court "A", Rule 60]

Rule 63

[As Rules of Court "A", Rule 61]

Rule 64

[As Rules of Court "A", Rule 62]

Rule 65

[As Rules of Court "A", Rule 63]

Rule 66

[As Rules of Court "A", Rule 64]

Rule 67

[As Rules of Court "A", Rule 65]

Rule 68

[As Rules of Court "A", Rule 66]

Rule 69

The opinion, as well as any decision given under Rule 66, shall be signed by the President and by the Registrar. The original copy, duly signed and sealed, shall be placed in the archives of the Court. The Registrar shall send certified copies to the Committee of Ministers, to the Contracting Parties, to the Commission and to the Secretary General of the Council of Europe.

Rule 70 Final clause

The present Rules shall enter into force the day after the entry into force of Protocol No. 9 to the Convention. They shall, however, apply only to cases brought before the Court after that date.

15. RULES ADOPTED BY THE COMMITTEE OF MINISTERS FOR THE APPLICATION OF ARTICLES 32 AND 54 OF THE EUROPEAN CONVENTION ON HUMAN RIGHTS

RULES FOR THE APPLICATION OF ARTICLE 32

Text approved by the Committee of Ministers at the 181st meeting of the Ministers' Deputies in June 1969 and amended at the 215th (November 1972), 245th (May 1975), 307th (September 1979), 409th (June 1987), 449th (December 1990) and 451st (January 1991) meetings and at the special meeting of the Ministers' Deputies on 19 December 1991.

A. RULES OF SUBSTANCE

Rule 1

When exercising its functions under Article 32 of the Convention, the Committee of Ministers is entitled to discuss the substance of any case on which the Commission has submitted a report, for example by considering written or oral statements of the parties and hearing of witnesses (see Rule 4).

Rule 2

The representative of any member state on the Committee of Ministers shall be fully qualified to take part in exercising the functions and powers set forth in Article 32 of the Convention, even if that state has not yet ratified the Convention.

Rule 3

Each representative on the Committee of Ministers has an intrinsic right to make submissions and deposit documents. Consequently, the representative on the Committee of Ministers of a government which was not a party to the proceedings before the Commission, may play a full part in the proceedings before the Committee of Ministers.

Rule 4

While the Committee of Ministers must have all the necessary powers to reach a decision on a report of the Commission, nevertheless, it may not itself wish to undertake the task of taking evidence, etc., should the need arise. The procedure to be followed in such a case will be decided *ad hoc*.

RULE 53

Rule 6

The Committee of Ministers considers that the Commission is not entitled to make proposals under Article 31, paragraph 3, of the Convention in cases where it considers that there has not been a violation of the Convention.

Rule 6 *bis*

Prior to taking a decision under Article 32, paragraph 1, of the Convention, the Committee of Ministers may be informed of a friendly settlement, arrangement or other fact of a kind to provide a solution of the matter. In that event, it may decide to discontinue its examination of the case, after satisfying itself that the solution envisaged is based on respect for human rights as defined in the Convention.

B. PROCEDURAL RULES

Rule 7

If the chairmanship of the Committee of Ministers is held by the representative of a state which is party to a dispute referred to the Committee of Ministers, that representative shall step down from the chair during the discussion of the Commission's report.

Rule 8

The Chairman of the Committee shall obtain the opinion of the representatives of the State Party or States Parties to the dispute in regard to the procedure to be followed, and the Committee shall specify, if necessary, in what order and within what time-limits any written submissions or other documents are to be deposited.

Rule 9

1. During the examination of the case and before taking the decision mentioned in Article 32, paragraph 1, of the Convention, the Committee of Ministers may, if it deems advisable, request the Commission for information on particular points in the report which it has transmitted to the Committee.
2. After taking a decision under Article 32, paragraph 1, to the effect that there has been a violation of the Convention, the Committee of Ministers may request the Commission to make proposals concerning in particular the appropriateness, nature and extent of just satisfaction for the injured party.
3. This Rule applies not only to inter-state disputes but also when the Committee of Ministers is considering the report of the Commission on an individual application.

Rule 9 *bis*

When a vote is taken in accordance with Article 32, paragraph 1, and the majority required to decide whether there has been a violation of the Convention has not been attained, a second and final vote shall be taken at one of the three following meetings of the Committee of Ministers.

Rule 9 *ter*

1. The Commission's report shall be published when the Committee of Ministers has completed consideration of the case under Article 32, paragraph 1.
2. The Committee of Ministers may, by way of exception and without prejudice to Article 32, paragraph 3, decide not to publish a report of the Commission or a part thereof upon a reasoned request of a Contracting Party or of the Commission.

Rule 10

In the matter of voting, the rules laid down in Article 20 of the Statute should, in general, apply. In particular

   a.   the parties to the dispute shall have the right to vote;
   b.   decisions taken in pursuance of Rule 6 *bis* require a two-thirds majority of the representatives casting a vote and a majority of the representatives entitled to sit on the Committee;
   c.   certain questions of procedure, such as in what order and within what time-limits any written submissions or other documents are to be deposited, shall be determined by a simple majority of the representatives entitled to sit on the Committee.

Rule 11

The decision taken under Article 32, paragraph 1, will be published in the form of a resolution adopted by a two-thirds majority of the representatives casting a vote and a majority of the representatives entitled to sit on the Committee.

APPENDIX – OTHER POINTS DISCUSSED BY THE COMMITTEE OF MINISTERS

1. With reference to Rule 3 above, the Committee of Ministers reserved its position on the possibility that the representative of a government which had not been a party to the proceedings before the Commission might make a request to the Committee of Ministers which had not been made before the Commission (for example, a request for damages).
2. In connection with Rule 4, the Committee of Ministers considered that while it must have all the necessary powers to reach a decision on a case submitted to it, nevertheless it is not well-equipped to take evidence, etc. and ought not

normally to undertake such tasks. If therefore it should become necessary for the Committee of Ministers to take evidence, etc. when it is considering a case under Article 32, there are the following possibilities:

a. to conclude a Protocol to the Convention conferring on the Commission the power to undertake such tasks on behalf of the Committee of Ministers;

b. to invite the Commission to undertake these tasks on its behalf, since the Commission is in its nature better equipped to do so, if the Commission agrees to this procedure;

c. the Committee of Ministers could take evidence, etc. in plenary sessions (possibly with alternate members) or appoint a subcommittee for the purpose;

d. under Article 17 of the Statute, the Committee of Ministers may set up advisory and technical committees for specific purposes.

The Committee of Ministers decided not to adopt the first of these possibilities but to leave the choice open for a decision *ad hoc* should the need arise.

2 *bis.* The Committee of Ministers decided that in every case in which it finds there has been a violation of the Convention, it would consider, taking into account any proposals from the Commission, whether just satisfaction should be afforded to the injured party and, if necessary, indicate measures on this subject to the state concerned.

3. a. The Committee of Ministers decided not to establish a procedure permitting the communication to an applicant of the report of the Commission on his application, or the communication to the Committee of Ministers of the applicant's observations on the report.

   b. The communication to an individual applicant of the complete text or extracts from the report of the Commission should take place only as an exceptional measure (for example, where the Committee of Ministers wishes to obtain the observations of the applicant), only on a strictly confidential basis, and only with the consent of the state against which the application was lodged.

   c. Since the individual applicant is not a party to the proceedings before the Committee of Ministers under Article 32 of the Convention, he has no right to be heard by the Committee of Ministers or to have any written communication considered by the Committee.

   This should be explained by the Secretary General to the applicant when he writes to inform him that the report of the Commission on his case has been transmitted to the Committee of Ministers in accordance with the provisions of Article 31 of the Convention.

   d. If communications from the individual applicant intended for the Committee of Ministers are nevertheless received, the Secretary General should acknowledge their receipt and explain to the applicant why they will not form part of the proceedings before the Committee of Ministers and cannot be considered as a document in the case. In appropriate cases, the Secretary General might add that it is possible for the applicant to submit a new application to the Commission if he wishes to invoke important new information.

4. The Committee of Ministers decided not to make provisions in its Rules for participation by delegates of the Commission in its proceedings, since the Commission considered that such participation would be outside its powers as defined in the Convention.

The Committee of Ministers at the 307th meeting of the Ministers' Deputies (September 1979) adopted the following additional Rules:

a. An individual applicant ought normally to be informed of the outcome of the examination of his case before the Committee of Ministers. It would be for the Committee of Ministers to decide in each particular case on the information to be communicated and on the procedure to be followed;

b. a decision to inform an individual applicant about the outcome of his case should be taken, in accordance with Article 21 b of the Statute, by unanimous vote;

c. the Committee of Ministers could indicate in its communication to the applicant if any of the information conveyed to him is to be treated as confidential.

RULES FOR THE APPLICATION OF ARTICLE 54

Text approved by the Committee of Ministers at the 254th Meeting of the Ministers' Deputies in February 1976.

Rule 1

When a judgment of the Court is transmitted to the Committee of Ministers in accordance with Article 54 of the Convention, the case shall be inscribed on the agenda of the Committee without delay.

Rule 2

a. When, in the judgment transmitted to the Committee of Ministers in accordance with Article 54 of the Convention, the Court decides that there has been a violation of the Convention and/or affords just satisfaction to the injured party under Article 50 of the Convention, the Committee shall invite the state concerned to inform it of the measures which it has taken in consequence of the judgment, having regard to its obligation under Article 53 of the Convention to abide by the judgment.

b. If the state concerned informs the Committee of Ministers that it is not yet in a position to inform it of the measures taken, the case shall be automatically inscribed on the agenda of a meeting of the Committee taking place not more than six months later, unless the Committee of

Ministers decides otherwise; the same Rule will be applied on expiration of this and any subsequent period.

Rule 3

The Committee of Ministers shall not regard its functions under Article 54 of the Convention as having been exercised until it has taken note of the information supplied in accordance with Rule 2 and, when just satisfaction has been afforded, until it has satisfied itself that the state concerned has awarded this just satisfaction to the injured party.

Rule 4

The decision in which the Committee of Ministers declares that its functions under Article 54 of the Convention have been exercised shall take the form of a resolution.

16. EUROPEAN SOCIAL CHARTER

Signed at Turin: 18 October 1961

Entry into force: 26 February 1965 in accordance with Article 35(1)

Editors' Notes

Substantial amendments to the Charter were proposed in the Protocol Amending the Social Charter, of 21 October 1991. That Protocol is not yet in force, but the amendments have been inserted at the appropriate points. A complete revision of the Charter has been proposed by a Revised Charter, opened for signature on 3 May 1996. Where that document makes minor amendments to the original charter, these are indicated in the text. The more substantial changes are set out as an addendum to the main text.

PREAMBLE

The Governments signatory hereto, being Members of the Council of Europe,

Considering that the aim of the Council of Europe is the achievement of greater unity between its Members for the purpose of safeguarding and realising the ideals and principles which are their common heritage and of facilitating their economic and social progress, in particular by the maintenance and further realisation of human rights and fundamental freedoms;

Considering that in the European Convention for the protection of Human Rights and Fundamental Freedoms signed at Rome on 4th November 1950, and the *Protocol thereto signed at Paris on 20th March 1952,*[1] the member States of the Council of Europe agreed to secure to their populations the civil and political rights and freedoms therein specified;

Considering that in the European Social Charter opened for signature in Turin on 18 October 1961 and the Protocols thereto, the member States of the Council of Europe agreed to secure to their populations the social rights specified therein in order to improve their standard of living and their social well-being;[2]

Recalling that the Ministerial Conference on Human Rights held in Rome on 5 November 1990 stressed the need, on the one hand, to preserve the indivisible nature of all human rights, be they civil, political, economic, social or cultural and, on the other hand, to give the European Social Charter fresh impetus;[3]

Resolved, as was decided during the Ministerial Conference held in Turin on 21 and 22 October 1991, to update and adapt the substantive contents of the Charter in order to take

---

[1] In the Revised Charter the italicised words are replaced by the words "Protocols thereto".
[2] Inserted by the 1996 Revisions.
[3] Inserted by the 1996 Revisions.

account in particular of the fundamental social changes which have occurred since the text was adopted;[4]

Recognising the advantage of embodying in a Revised Charter, designed progressively to take the place of the European Social Charter, the rights guaranteed by the Charter as amended, the rights guaranteed by the Additional Protocol of 1988 and to add new rights,[5]

Considering that the enjoyment of social rights should be secured without discrimination on grounds of race, colour, sex, religion, political opinion, national extraction or social origin;[6]

Being resolved to make every effort in common to improve the standard of living and to promote the social well-being of both their urban and rural populations by means of appropriate institutions and action;[7]

Have agreed as follows:

PART I

The Contracting Parties accept as the aim of their policy, to be pursued by all appropriate means, both national and international in character, the attainment of conditions in which the following rights and principles may be effectively realised:

1. Everyone shall have the opportunity to earn his living in an occupation freely entered upon.
2. All workers have the right to just conditions of work.
3. All workers have the right to safe and healthy working conditions.
4. All workers have the right to a fair remuneration sufficient for a decent standard of living for themselves and their families.
5. All workers and employers have the right to freedom of association in national or international organisations for the protection of their economic and social interests.
6. All workers and employers have the right to bargain collectively.
7. Children and young persons have the right to a special protection against physical and moral hazards to which they are exposed.
8. Employed women in case of maternity, and other employed women as appropriate, have the right to a special protection in their work.
[8. *Employed women, in case of maternity, have the right to a special protection.*][8]
9. Everyone has the right to appropriate facilities for vocational guidance with a view to helping him choose an occupation suited to his personal aptitude and interests.
10. Everyone has the right to appropriate facilities for vocational training.
11. Everyone has the right to benefit from any measures enabling him to enjoy the highest possible standard of health attainable.

[4] Inserted by the 1996 Revisions.
[5] Inserted by the 1996 Revisions.
[6] Deleted in the 1996 Revisions.
[7] Deleted in the 1996 Revisions.
[8] Replaces existing Article 8.

12. All workers and their dependants have the right to social security.
13. Anyone without adequate resources has the right to social and medical assistance.
14. Everyone has the right to benefit from social welfare services.
15. Disabled persons have the right to vocational training, rehabilitation and resettlement, whatever the origin and nature of their disability.

[*15 Disabled persons have the right to independence, social integration and participation in the life of the community.*][9]

16. The family as a fundamental unit of society has the right to appropriate social, legal and economic protection to ensure its full development.
17. Mothers and children, irrespective of marital status and family relations, have the right to appropriate social and economic protection.

[*17. Children and young persons have the right to appropriate social, legal and economic protection.*][10]

18. The nationals of anyone of the Contracting[11] Parties have the right to engage in any gainful occupation in the territory of any one of the others on a footing of equality with the nationals of the latter, subject to restrictions based on cogent economic or social reasons.
19. Migrant workers who are nationals of a Contracting Party and their families have the right to protection and assistance in the territory of any other Contracting Party.

[*20. All Workers have the right to equal opportunities and equal treatment in matters of employment and occupation without discrimination on the grounds of sex.*]

[*21. Workers have the right to be informed and to be consulted within the undertaking.*]

[*22. Workers have the right to take part in the determination and improvement of the working conditions and working environment in the undertaking.*]

[*23. Every elderly person has the right to social protection.*]

[*24. All workers have the right to protection in cases of termination of employment.*]

[*25. All workers have the right to protection of their claims in the event of the insolvency of their employer.*]

[*26. All workers have the right to dignity at work.*]

[*27. All persons with family responsibilities and who are engaged or wish to engage in employment have a right to do so without being subject to discrimination and as far as possible without conflict between their employment and family responsibilities.*]

[*28. Workers' representatives in undertakings have the right to protection against act prejudicial to them and should be afforded appropriate facilities to carry out their functions.*]

[*29. All workers have the right to be informed and consulted in collective redundancy procedures.*]

[*30. Everyone has the right to protection against poverty and social exclusion.*]

[*31. Everyone has the right to housing.*][12]

---

[9] Replaces existing Article 15.

[10] Replaces existing Article 17.

[11] Throughout the Revised Charter the word "Contracting" has been omitted from the terms "Contracting Party" and "Contracting Parties".

[12] Paragraphs 20 to 31 contain new provisions, inserted by the 1996 Revisions.

PART II

The Contracting Parties undertake, as provided for in Part III, to consider themselves bound by the obligations laid down in the following articles and paragraphs.

Article 1: The right to work

With a view to ensuring the effective exercise of the right to work, the Contracting Parties undertake:

1. to accept as one of their primary aims and responsibilities the achievement and maintenance of as high and stable a level of employment as possible, with a view to the attainment of full employment;
2. to protect effectively the right of the worker to earn his living in an occupation freely entered upon;
3. to establish or maintain free employment services for all workers;
4. to provide or promote appropriate vocational guidance, training and rehabilitation.

Article 2: The right to just conditions of work

With a view of ensuring the effective exercise of the right to just conditions of work, the Contracting Parties undertake:

1. to provide for reasonable daily and weekly working hours, the working week to be progressively reduced to the extent that the increase of productivity and other relevant factors permit;
2. to provide for public holidays with pay;
3. to provide for a minimum of two [four][13] weeks annual holiday with pay;
4. to provide for additional paid holidays or reduced working hours for workers engaged in dangerous or unhealthy occupations as prescribed;
    [4. *to eliminate risks in inherently dangerous or unhealthy occupations, and where it had not yet been possible to eliminate or reduce sufficiently these risks, to provide for either a reduction of working hours or additional paid holidays for workers engaged in such occupations;*][14]
5. to ensure a weekly rest period which shall, as far as possible, coincide with the day recognised by tradition or custom in the country or region concerned as a day of rest.
    [6. *to ensure that workers are informed in written form, as soon as possible, and in any event not later than two months after the date of commencing their employment, of the essential aspects of the contract or employment relationship;*]
    [7. *to ensure that workers performing night work benefit from measures which take account of the special nature of the work.*][15]

---

[13] As inserted by the 1996 Revisions.
[14] Replaces existing Article 2(4).
[15] Paragraphs 6 and 7 of Article 2 inserted by the 1996 Revisions.

Article 3: The right to safe and healthy working conditions

With a view to ensuring the effective exercise of the right to safe and healthy working conditions, the Contracting Parties undertake [*in consultation with employers' and workers' organisations*][16]:

[1. *to formulate, implement and periodically review a coherent national policy on occupational safety, occupational health and the working environment. The primary aim of this policy shall be to improve occupational safety and health and to prevent accidents and injury to health arising out of, linked with or occurring in the course of work, particularly by minimising the causes of hazards inherent in the working environment;*][17]

1. to issue safety and health regulations;
2. to provide for the enforcement of such regulations by measures of supervision;
3. to consult, as appropriate, employers' and workers' organisations on measures intended to improve industrial safety and health.[18]

[4. *to promote the progressive development of occupational health services for all workers with essentially preventive and advisory functions.*][19]

Article 4: The right to a fair remuneration

With a view to ensuring the effective exercise of the right to a fair remuneration, the Contracting Parties undertake:

1. to recognise the right of workers to a remuneration such as will give them and their families a decent standard of living;
2. to recognise the right of workers to an increased rate of remuneration for overtime work, subject to exceptions in particular cases;
3. to recognise the right of men and women workers to equal pay for work of equal value;
4. to recognise the right of all workers to a reasonable period of notice for termination of employment;
5. to permit deductions from wages only under conditions and to the extent prescribed by national laws or regulations or fixed by collective agreements or arbitration awards.

    The exercise of these rights shall be achieved by freely concluded, collective agreements, by statutory wage-fixing machinery, or by other means appropriate to national conditions.

---

[16] Words inserted by the 1996 Revisions.
[17] New paragraph inserted by the 1996 Revisions.
[18] Paragraph deleted by the 1996 Revisions.
[19] New paragraph inserted by the 1996 Revisions.

Article 5: The right to organise

With a view to ensuring or promoting the freedom of workers and employers to form local, national or international organizations for the protection of their economic and social interests and to join those organisations, the Contracting Parties undertake that national law shall not be such as to impair nor shall it be so applied as to impair this freedom. The extent to which the guarantees provided for in this article shall apply to the police shall be determined by national laws or regulations. [*The principle governing the application to the members of the armed forces of these guarantees and the extent to which they shall apply to persons in this category shall equally be determined by national laws or regulations.*][20]

Article 6: The right to bargain collectively

With a view to ensuring the effective exercise of the right to bargain collectively, the Contracting Parties undertake:

1. to promote joint consultation between workers and employers;
2. to promote, where necessary and appropriate, machinery for voluntary negotiations between employers or employers' organisations and workers' organisations, with a view to the regulations of terms and conditions of employment by means of collective agreements;
3. to promote the establishment and use of appropriate machinery for conciliation and voluntary arbitration for the settlement of labour disputes; and recognise:
4. the right of workers and employers to collective action in cases of conflicts of interest, including the right to strike, subject to obligations that might arise out of collective agreements previously entered into.

Article 7: The right of children and young persons to protection

With a view to ensuring the effective exercise of the right of children and young persons to protection, the Contracting Parties undertake:

1. to provide that the minimum age of admission to employment shall be 15 years, subject to exceptions for children employed in prescribed light work without harm to their health, morals or education;
[2. *to provide that the minimum age of admission to employment shall be 18 years with respect to prescribed occupations regarded as dangerous or unhealthy;*][21]
2. to provide that a higher minimum age of admission to employment shall be fixed with respect to prescribed occupations regarded as dangerous or unhealthy;[22]
3. to provide that persons who are still subject to compulsory education shall not be employed in such work as would deprive them of the full benefit of their education;

---

[20] Words inserted by the 1996 Revisions.
[21] New paragraph inserted by the 1996 Revisions.
[22] Paragraph deleted in the 1996 Revisions.

4. to provide that the working hours of persons under 16 [18][23] years of age shall be limited in accordance with the needs of their development, and particularly with their need for vocational training;
5. to recognise the right of young workers and apprentices to a fair wage or other appropriate allowances;
6. to provide that the time spent by young persons in vocational training during the normal working hours, with the consent of the employer, shall be treated as forming part of the working day;
7. to provide that employed persons of under 18 years of age shall be entitled to not less than three weeks' [to a minimum of four weeks'][24] annual holiday with pay;
8. to provide that persons under 18 years of age shall not be employed in night work with the exception of certain occupations provided for by national laws or regulations;
9. to provide that persons under 18 years of age employed in occupations prescribed by national laws or regulations shall be subject to regular medical control;
10. to ensure special protection against physical and moral dangers to which children and young persons are exposed, and particularly against those resulting directly or indirectly from their work.

Article 8: The right of employed women to protection

With a view to ensuring the effective exercise of the right of employed women to protection, the Contracting Parties undertake:

1. to provide either by paid leave, by adequate social security benefits or by benefits from public funds for women to take leave before and after childbirth up to a total of at least 12 weeks;
2. to consider it as unlawful for an employer to give a woman notice of dismissal during her absence on maternity leave or to give her notice of dismissal at such a time that the notice would expire during such absence;
3. to provide that mothers who are nursing their infants shall be entitled to sufficient time off for this purpose;
4. (a) to regulate the employment of women workers on night work in industrial employment;
    (b) to prohibit the employment of women workers in underground mining, and, as appropriate, on all other work which is unsuitable for them by reason of its dangerous, unhealthy, or arduous nature.

Article 9: The right to vocational guidance

With a view to ensuring the effective exercise of the right to vocational guidance, the Contracting Parties undertake to provide or promote, as necessary, a service

---

[23] Substituted by the 1996 Revisions.
[24] As amended by the 1996 Revisions.

which will assist all persons, including the handicapped, to solve problems related to occupational choice and progress with due regard to the individual's characteristics and their relation to occupational opportunity: this assistance should be available free of charge, both to young persons, including school children, and to adults.

Article 10: The right to vocational training

With a view to ensuring the effective exercise of the right to vocational training, the Contracting Parties undertake:

1. to provide or promote, as necessary, the technical and vocational training of all persons, including the handicapped, in consultation with employers' and workers' organisations, and to grant facilities for access to higher technical and university education, based solely on individual aptitude;
2. to provide or promote a system of apprenticeship and other systematic arrangements for training young boys and girls in their various employments;
3. to provide or promote, as necessary:

   (a) adequate and readily available training facilities for adult workers;
   (b) special facilities for the re-training of adult workers needed as a result of technological development or new trends in employment;

[4. *to provide or promote, as necessary, special measures for the retraining and reintegration of the long-term unemployed.*][25]
4. to encourage the full utilisation of the facilities provided by appropriate measures such as:

   (a) reducing or abolishing any fees or charges;
   (b) granting financial assistance in appropriate cases;
   (c) including in the normal working hours time spent on supplementary training taken by the worker, at the request of his employer, during employment;
   (d) ensuring, through adequate supervision, in consultation with the employers' and workers' organisations, the efficiency of apprenticeship and other training arrangements for young workers, and the adequate protection of young workers generally.

Article 11: The right to protection of health

With a view to ensuring the effective exercise of the right to protection of health, the Contracting Parties undertake, either directly or in co-operation with public or private organisations, to take appropriate measures designed *inter alia*:

1. to remove as far as possible the causes of ill-health;
2. to provide advisory and educational facilities for the promotion of health and the encouragement of individual responsibility of matters of health;

---

[25] New paragraph 4 inserted by the 1996 Revisions.

3. to prevent as far as possible epidemic, endemic and other diseases [*as well as accidents*].[26]

Article 12: The right to social security

With a view to ensuring the effective exercise of the right to social security, the Contracting Parties undertake:

1. to establish or maintain a system of social security;
2. to maintain the social security system at a satisfactory level at least equal to that required for ratification of International Labour Convention (No. 102) Concerning Minimum Standards of Social Security;
[2. *to maintain the social security system at a satisfactory level at least equal to that necessary for the ratification of the European Code of Social Security;*][27]
3. to endeavour to raise progressively the system of social security to a higher level;
4. to take steps, by the conclusion of appropriate bilateral and multilateral agreements, or by other means, and subject to the conditions laid down in such agreements, in order to ensure:

    (a) equal treatment with their own nationals of the nationals of other Contracting Parties in respect of social security rights, including the retention of benefits arising out of social security legislation, whatever movements the persons protected may undertake between the territories of the Contracting Parties;
    (b) the granting, maintenance and resumption of social security rights by such means as the accumulation of insurance or employment periods completed under the legislation of each of the Contracting Parties.

Article 13: The right to social and medical assistance

With a view to ensuring the effective service of the right to social and medical assistance, the Contracting Parties undertake:

1. to ensure that any person who is without adequate resources and who is unable to secure such resources either by his own efforts or from other sources, in particular by benefits under a social security scheme, be granted adequate assistance, and, in case of sickness, the care necessitated by his condition;
2. to ensure that persons receiving such assistance shall not, for that reason, suffer from a diminution of their political or social rights;
3. to provide that everyone may receive by appropriate public or private services such advice and personal help as may be required to prevent to remove, or to alleviate personal or family want;
4. to apply the provisions referred to in paragraphs 1, 2 and 3 of this Article on

---

[26] Words inserted by the 1996 Revisions.
[27] Amended paragraph 2 inserted by the 1996 Revisions.

an equal footing with their nationals to nationals of other Contracting Parties lawfully within their territories, in accordance with their obligations under the European Convention on Social and Medical Assistance, signed at Paris on 11th December 1953.

Article 14: The right to benefit from social welfare services

With a view to ensuring the effective exercise of the right to benefit from social welfare services, the Contracting Parties undertake:

1. to promote or provide services which, by using methods of social work, would contribute to the welfare and development of both individuals and groups in the community, and to their adjustment to the social environment;
2. to encourage the participation of individuals and voluntary or other organisations in the establishment and maintenance of such services.

Article 15: The right of physically or mentally disabled persons to vocational training, rehabilitation and social resettlement

With a view to ensuring the effective exercise of the right of the physically or mentally disabled to vocational training, rehabilitation and resettlement, the Contracting Parties undertake:

1. to take adequate measures for the provision of training facilities, including where necessary, specialised institutions, public or private;
2. to take adequate measures for the placing of disabled persons in employment, such as specialised placing services, facilities for sheltered employment and measures to encourage employers to admit disabled persons to employment.

Article 16: The right of the family to social, legal and economic protection

With a view to ensuring the necessary conditions for the full development of the family which is a fundamental unit of society, the Contracting Parties undertake to promote the economic, legal and social protection of family life by such means as social and family benefits, fiscal arrangements, provision of family housing, benefits for the newly married, and other appropriate means.

Article 17: The right of mothers and children to social and economic protection

With a view to ensuring the effective exercise of the right of mothers and children to social and economic protection, the Contracting Parties will take all appropriate and necessary measures to that end, including the establishment or maintenance of appropriate institutions or services.

Article 18: The right to engage in a gainful occupation in the territory of other Contracting Parties

With a view to ensuring the effective exercise of the right to engage in a gainful occupation in the territory of any other Contracting Party, the Contracting Parties undertake:

1. to apply existing regulations in a spirit of liberality;
2. to simplify existing formalities and to reduce or abolish chancery dues and other charges payable by foreign workers or their employers;
3. to liberalise, individually or collectively, regulations governing the employment of foreign workers;
   and recognise:
4. the right of their nationals to leave the country to engage in a gainful occupation in the territories of the other Contracting Parties.

Article 19: The right of migrant workers and their families to protection and assistance

With a view to ensuring the effective exercise of the right of migrant workers and their families to protection and assistance in the territory of any other Contracting Party, the Contracting Parties undertake:

1. to maintain or to satisfy themselves that there are maintained adequate and free services to assist such workers, particularly in obtaining accurate information, and to take all appropriate steps, so far as national laws and regulations permit, against misleading propaganda relating to emigration and immigration;
2. to adopt appropriate measures within their own jurisdiction to facilitate the departure, journey and reception of such workers and their families, and to provide, within their own jurisdiction, appropriate services for health, medical attention and good hygienic conditions during the journey;
3. to promote co-operation, as appropriate, between social services, public and private, in emigration and immigration countries;
4. to secure for such workers lawfully within their territories, insofar as such matters are regulated by law or regulations or are subject to the control of administrative authorities, treatment not less favourable than that of their own nationals in respect to the following matters:

   (a) remuneration and other employment and working conditions;
   (b) membership of trade unions and enjoyment of the benefits of collective bargaining;
   (c) accommodation;

5. to secure for such workers lawfully within their territories treatment not less favourable than that of their own nationals with regard to employment taxes, dues or contributions payable in respect of employed persons;
6. to facilitate as far as possible the reunion of the family of a foreign worker permitted to establish himself in the territory;

7. to secure for such workers lawfully within their territories treatment not less favourable than that of their own nationals with regard to legal proceedings relating to matters referred to in this article;
8. to secure that such workers lawfully residing within their territories are not expelled unless they endanger national security or offend against public interest or morality;
9. to permit, within legal limits, the transfer of such parts of the earnings and savings of such workers as they may desire;
10. to extend the protection and assistance provided for in this Article to self-employed migrants insofar as such measures apply.
[11. *to promote and facilitate the teaching of the national language of the receiving state or, if there are several, one of these languages, to migrant workers and members of their families;*]
[12. *to promote and facilitate, as far as practicable, the teaching of the migrant worker's mother tongue to the children of the migrant worker.*][28]

PART III[29]

UNDERTAKINGS

Article 20

1. Each of the Contracting Parties undertakes:

    (a) to consider Part I of this Charter as a declaration of the aims which it will pursue by all appropriate means, as stated in the introductory paragraph of that Part;

    (b) to consider itself bound by at least five of the following Articles of Part II of this Charter: Articles 1, 5, 6, 12, 13, 16 and 19;

    (c) in addition to the Articles selected by it in accordance with the preceding sub-paragraph, to consider itself bound by such number of Articles or numbered paragraphs of Part II of the Charter as it may select, provided that the total number of Articles or numbered paragraphs by which it is bound is not less than 10 Articles or 45 numbered paragraphs.

2. The Articles or paragraphs selected in accordance with sub-paragraphs (b) and (c) of paragraph 1 of this Article shall be notified to the Secretary-General of the Council of Europe at the time when the instrument of ratification or approval of the Contracting Party concerned is deposited.

3. Any Contracting Party may, at a later date, declare by notification to the Secretary-General that it considers itself bound by any Articles or any numbered paragraphs of Part II of the Charter which it has not already accepted under the terms of paragraph 1 of this Article. Such undertaking

---

[28] Paragraphs 11 and 12 of this article inserted by the 1996 Revisions.
[29] Part III of the revised Charter does not begin until after revised Article 31.

subsequently given shall be deemed to be an integral part of the ratification or approval, and shall have the same effect as from the thirtieth day after the date of the notification.

4. The Secretary-General shall communicate to all the signatory Governments and to the Director-General of the International Labour Office any notification which he shall have received pursuant to this Part of the Charter.

5. Each Contracting Party shall maintain a system of labour inspection appropriate to national conditions.

PART IV

REPORTS CONCERNING ACCEPTED PROVISIONS

Article 21

The Contracting Parties shall send to the Secretary-General of the Council of Europe a report at two-yearly intervals, in a form to be determined by the Committee of Ministers, concerning the application of such provisions of Part II of the Charter as they have accepted.

REPORTS CONCERNING PROVISIONS WHICH ARE NOT ACCEPTED

Article 22

The Contracting Parties shall send to the Secretary-General, at appropriate intervals as requested by the Committee of Ministers, reports relating to the provisions of Part II of the Charter which they did not accept at the time of their ratification or approval or in a subsequent notification. The Committee of Ministers shall determine from time to time in respect of which provisions such reports shall be requested and the form of the reports to be provided.

COMMUNICATION OF COPIES

Article 23

1. Each Contracting Party shall communicate copies of its reports referred to in Articles 21 and 22 to such of its national organisations as are members of the international organisations of employers and trade unions to be invited under Article 27, paragraph 2, to be represented at meetings of the Sub-committee of the Governmental Social Committee.

2. The Contracting Parties shall forward to the Secretary-General any comments on the said reports received from these national organisations, if so requested by them.

[Article 23 – Communication of copies of reports and comments

1   *When sending to the Secretary General a report pursuant to Articles 21 and 22, each Contracting Party shall forward a copy of that report to such of its national organisations as are members of the international organisations of employers and trade unions invited, under Article 27, paragraph 2, to be represented at meetings of the Governmental Committee. Those organisations shall send to the Secretary General any comments on the reports of the Contracting Parties. The Secretary General shall send a copy of those comments to the Contracting Parties concerned, who might wish to respond.*

2.   *The Secretary General shall forward a copy of the reports of the Contracting Parties to the international non-governmental organisations which have consultative status with the Council of Europe and have particular competence in the matters governed by the present Charter.*

3.   *The reports and comments referred to in Articles 21 and 22 and in the present article shall be made available to the public on request.]*[30]

EXAMINATION OF THE REPORTS

Article 24

1.   The reports sent to the Secretary-General in accordance with Articles 21 and 22 shall be examined by a Committee of Experts, who shall have also before them any comments forwarded to the Secretary-General in accordance with paragraph 2 of Article 23.

[Article 24 – Examination of the reports

1.   *The reports sent to the Secretary General in accordance with Articles 21 and 22 shall be examined by a Committee of Independent Experts constituted pursuant to Article 25. The committee shall also have before it any comments forwarded to the Secretary General in accordance with paragraph 1 of Article 23. On completion of its examination, the Committee of Independent Experts shall draw up a report containing its conclusions.*

2.   *With regard to the reports referred to in Article 21, the Committee of Independent Experts shall assess from a legal standpoint the compliance of national law and practice with the obligations arising from the Charter for the Contracting Parties concerned.*

3.   *The Committee of Independent Experts may address requests for additional information and clarification directly to Contracting Parties. In this connection the Committee of Independent Experts may also hold, if necessary, a meeting with the representatives of a Contracting Party, either on its own initiative or at the request of the Contracting Party concerned. The organisations referred to in paragraph 1 of Article 23 shall be kept informed.*

[30] Amended Article 23 as proposed by article 1 of the Protocol Amending the Charter, 21 October 1991 (not yet in force).

4. *The conclusions of the Committee of Independent Experts shall be made public and communicated by the Secretary General to the Governmental Committee, to the Parliamentary Assembly and to the organisations which are mentioned in paragraph 1 of Article 23 and paragraph 2 of Article 27.]*[31]

Article 25: Committee of Experts

1. The Committee of Experts shall consist of not more than seven members appointed by the Committee of Ministers from a list of independent experts of the highest integrity and of recognised competence in international social questions, nominated by the Contracting Parties.
2. The members of the Committee shall be appointed for a period of six years. They may be reappointed. However, the members first appointed, the terms of office of two members shall expire at the end of four years.
3. The members whose terms of office are to expire at the end of the initial period of four years shall be chosen by lot by the Committee of Ministers immediately after the first appointment has been made.
4. A member of the Committee of Experts appointed to replace a member whose term of office has not expired shall hold office for the remainder of his predecessor's term.

[Article 25 – Committee of Independent Experts

1. *The Committee of Independent Experts shall consist of at least nine members elected by the Parliamentary Assembly by a majority of votes cast from a list of experts of the highest integrity and of recognised competence in national and international social questions, nominated by the Contracting Parties. The exact number of members shall be determined by the Committee of Ministers.*
2. *The members of the committee shall be elected for a period of six years. They may stand for re-election once.*
3. *A member of the Committee of Independent Experts elected to replace a member whose term of office has not expired shall hold office for the remainder of his predecessor's term.*
4. *The members of the committee shall sit in their individual capacity. Throughout their term of office, they may not perform any function incompatible with the requirements of independence, impartiality and availability inherent in their office.]*[32]

Article 26: Participation of the International Labour Organisation

The International Labour Organisation shall be invited to nominate a representative to participate in a consultative capacity in the deliberations of the Committee of Experts.

---

[31] Amended article 24 as proposed by article 2 of the Protocol Amending the Charter, 21 October 1991 (not yet in force).
[32] Amended article 25 as proposed by article 3 of the Protocol Amending the Charter, 21 October 1991 (not yet in force).

Article 27: Sub-committee of the Governmental Social Committee

1. The reports of the Contracting Parties and the conclusions of the Committee of Experts shall be submitted for examination to a Sub-committee of the Governmental Social Committee of the Council of Europe.
2. The Sub-committee shall be composed of one representative of each of the Contracting Parties. It shall invite no more than two international organisations of employers and no more than two international trade union organisations as it may designate to be represented as observers in a consultative capacity at its meetings. Moreover, it may consult no more than two representatives of international non-governmental organisations having consultative status with the Council of Europe, in respect of questions with which the organisations are particularly qualified to deal, such as social welfare, and the economic and social protection of the family.
3. The Sub-committee shall present to the Committee of Ministers a report containing its conclusions and append the report of the Committee of Experts.

[Article 27 – Governmental Committee

1. *The reports of the Contracting Parties, the comments and information communicated in accordance with paragraphs 1 of Article 23 and 3 of Article 24, and the reports of the Committee of Independent Experts shall be submitted to a Governmental Committee.*
2. *The committee shall be composed of one representative of each of the Contracting Parties. It shall invite no more than two international organisations of employers and no more than two international trade union organisations to send observers in a consultative capacity to its meetings.*

    Moreover, it may consult representatives of international non-governmental organisations which have consultative status with the Council of Europe and have particular competence in the matters governed by the present Charter.
3. *The Governmental Committee shall prepare the decisions of the Committee of Ministers. In particular, in the light of the reports of the Committee of Independent Experts and of the Contracting Parties, it shall select, giving reasons for its choice, on the basis of social, economic and other policy considerations the situations which should, in its view, be the subject of recommendations to each Contracting Party concerned, in accordance with Article 28 of the Charter. It shall present to the Committee of Ministers a report which shall be made public.*

    On the basis of its findings on the implementation of the Social Charter in general, the Governmental Committee may submit proposals to the Committee of Ministers aiming at studies to be carried out on social issues and on articles of the Charter which possibly might be updated.][33]

---

[33] Amended article 27 as proposed by article 4 of the Protocol Amending the Charter, 21 October 1991 (not yet in force).

Article 28: Consultative Assembly

The Secretary-General of the Council of Europe shall transmit to the Consultative Assembly, the Conclusions of the Committee of Experts. The Consultative Assembly shall communicate its views on these Conclusions to the Committee of Ministers.

[Article 28: Committee of Ministers

1. *The Committee of Ministers shall adopt, by a majority of two-thirds of those voting, with entitlement to voting limited to the Contracting Parties, on the basis of the report of the Governmental Committee, a resolution covering the entire supervision cycle and containing individual recommendations to the Contracting Parties concerned.*
2. *Having regard to the proposals made by the Governmental Committee pursuant to paragraph 4 of Article 27, the Committee of Ministers shall take such decisions as it deems appropriate.]*[34]

Article 29: Committee of Ministers

By a majority of two-thirds of the members entitled to sit on the Committee, the Committee of Ministers may, on the basis of the report of the Sub-committee, and after consultation with the Consultative Assembly, make to each Contracting Party any necessary recommendations.

[Article 29: Parliamentary Assembly

The Secretary General of the Council of Europe shall transmit to the Parliamentary Assembly, with a view to the holding of periodical plenary debates, the reports of the Committee of Independent Experts and of the Governmental Committee, as well as the resolutions of the Committee of Ministers.][35]

PART V

DEROGATIONS IN TIME OF WAR OR PUBLIC EMERGENCY

Article 30

1. In time of war or other public emergency threatening the life of the nation any Contracting Party may take measures derogating from its obligations under this Charter to the extent strictly required by the exigencies of the situation,

---

[34] Amended article 28 as proposed by article 5 of the Protocol Amending the Charter, 21 October 1991 (not yet in force).
[35] Amended article 29 as proposed by article 6 of the Protocol Amending the Charter, 21 October 1991 (not yet in force).

provided that such measures are not inconsistent with its other obligations under international law.

2. Any Contracting Party which has availed itself of this right of derogation shall, within a reasonable lapse of time, keep the Secretary-General of the Council of Europe fully informed of the measures taken and of the reasons therefore. It shall likewise inform the Secretary-General when such measures have ceased to operate and the provisions of the Charter which it has accepted are again being fully executed.

3. The Secretary-General shall in turn inform other Contracting Parties and the Director-General of the International Labour Office of all communications received in accordance with paragraph 2 of this Article.

RESTRICTIONS

Article 31

1. The rights and principles set forth in Part I when effectively realised, and their effective exercise as provided for in Part II, shall not be subject to any restrictions or limitations not specified in those Parts except such as are prescribed by law and are necessary in a democratic society for the protection of the rights and freedoms of others or for the protection of public interest, national security, public health, or morals.

2. The restrictions permitted under this Charter to the rights and obligations set forth herein shall not be applied for any purpose other than that for which they have been prescribed.

RELATIONS BETWEEN THE CHARTER AND DOMESTIC LAW OR
INTERNATIONAL AGREEMENTS

Article 32

The provisions of this Charter shall not prejudice the provisions of domestic law or of any bilateral or multilateral treaties, conventions or agreements which are already in force, or may come into force, under which more favourable treatment would be accorded to the persons protected.

IMPLEMENTATION BY COLLECTIVE AGREEMENTS

Article 33

1. In member States where the provisions of paragraphs 1, 2, 3, 4, and 5 of Article 2, paragraphs 4, 6 and 7 of Article 7 and paragraphs 1, 2, 3, and 4 of Article 10 of Part II of this Charter are matters normally left to agreements between employers and employers' organisations and workers' organisations, or are normally carried out otherwise than by law, the undertakings of those paragraphs may be given and compliance with them shall be treated as

effective if their provisions are applied through such agreements or other means to the great majority of the workers concerned.

2. In member States where these provisions are normally the subject of legislation, the undertakings concerned may likewise be given and compliance with them shall be regarded as effective if the provisions are applied by law to the great majority of the workers concerned.

TERRITORIAL APPLICATION

Article 34

1. This Charter shall apply to the metropolitan territory of each Contracting Party. Each signatory Government may, at the time of signature or of the deposit of its instrument of ratification or approval specify, by declaration addressed to the Secretary-General of the Council of Europe, the territory which shall be considered to be its metropolitan territory for this purpose.
2. Any Contracting Party may, at the time of ratification or approval of this Charter or at any time thereafter, declare by notification addressed to the Secretary-General of the Council of Europe, that the Charter shall extend in whole or in part to a non-metropolitan territory or territories specified in the said declaration for whose international relations it is responsible or for which it assumes international responsibility. It shall specify in the declaration the Articles or paragraphs of Part II of the Charter which it accepts as binding in respect of the territories named in the declaration.
3. The Charter shall extend to the territory or territories named in the aforesaid declaration as from the thirtieth day after the date on which the Secretary-General shall have received notification of such declaration.
4. Any Contracting Party may declare at a later date by notification addressed to the Secretary-General of the Council of Europe, that in respect of one or more of the territories to which the Charter has been extended in accordance with paragraph 2 of this Article, it accepts as binding any Articles or any numbered paragraphs which it has not already accepted in respect of that territory or territories. Such undertakings subsequently given shall be deemed to be an integral part of the original declaration in respect of the territory concerned, and shall have the same effect as from the thirtieth day after the date of the notification.
5. The Secretary-General shall communicate to the other signatory Governments and to the Director-General of the International Labour Office any notification transmitted to him in accordance with this Article.

SIGNATURE, RATIFICATION AND ENTRY INTO FORCE

Article 35

1. This Charter shall be open for signature by the Members of the Council of Europe. It shall be ratified or approved. Instruments of ratification or approval shall be deposited with the Secretary-General of the Council of Europe.

2. This charter shall come into force as from the thirtieth day after the date of deposit of the fifth instrument of ratification or approval.

3. In respect of any signatory Government ratifying subsequently, the Charter shall come into force as from the thirtieth day after the date of deposit of its instrument of ratification or approval.

4. The Secretary-General shall notify all the Members of the Council of Europe and the Director-General of the International Labour Office, of the entry into force of the Charter, the names of the Contracting Parties which have ratified or approved it and the subsequent deposit of any instruments of ratification or approval.

AMENDMENTS

Article 36

Any Member of the Council of Europe may propose amendments to this Charter in a communication addressed to the Secretary-General of the Council of Europe. The Secretary-General shall transmit to the other Members of the Council of Europe any amendments so proposed, which shall then be considered by the Committee of Ministers and submitted to the Consultative Assembly for opinion. Any amendments approved by the Committee of Ministers shall enter into force as from the thirtieth day after all the Contracting Parties have informed the Secretary-General of their acceptance. The Secretary-General shall notify all the Members of the Council of Europe and the Director-General of the International Labour Office of the entry into force of such amendments.

DENUNCIATION

Article 37

1. Any Contracting Party may denounce this Charter only at the end of a period of five years from the date on which the Charter entered into force for it or at the end of any successive period of two years, and, in each case, after giving six months' notice to the Secretary-General of the Council of Europe, who shall inform the other Parties and the Director-General of the International Labour Office accordingly. Such denunciation shall not affect the validity of the Charter in respect of the other Contracting Parties provided that at all times there are not less than five such Contracting Parties.

2. Any Contracting Party may, in accordance with the provisions set out in the preceding paragraph, denounce any Article or paragraph of Part II of the Charter accepted by it provided that the number of Articles or paragraphs by which this Contracting Party is bound shall never be less than 10 in the former case and 45 in the latter and that this number of Articles or paragraphs shall continue to include the Articles selected by the Contracting Party among those to which special reference is made in Article 20, paragraph 1, subparagraph (b).

3. Any Contracting Party may denounce the present Charter or any of the

Articles or paragraphs of Part II of the Charter, under the conditions specified in paragraph 1 of this Article in respect of any territory to which the said Charter is applicable by virtue of a declaration made in accordance with paragraph 2 of Article 34.

APPENDIX

Article 38

The Appendix to this Charter shall form an integral part of it. In witness whereof, the undersigned, being duly authorised thereto, have signed this Charter. Done at Turin, this 18th day of October 1961, in English and French both texts being equally authoritative in a single copy which shall be deposited within the archives of the Council of Europe. The Secretary-General shall transmit certified copies to each of the Signatories.

ADDENDUM: PROVISIONS INSERTED BY THE 1996 REVISED EUROPEAN SOCIAL CHARTER

In addition to the amendments noted in the text above, and to those contained in the Additional Protocol to the European Social Charter, 1988 (below), the following new or substantially revised articles are inserted into the Charter by the 1996 revisions:

Article 8: The right of employed women to protection of maternity[36]

With a view to ensuring the effective exercise of the right of employed women to the protection of maternity, the Contracting Parties undertake:

1. *to provide either by paid leave, by adequate social security benefits or by benefits from public funds for women to take leave before and after childbirth up to a total of at least fourteen weeks;*
2. *to consider it as unlawful for an employer to give a woman notice of dismissal during the period from the time she notifies her employer that she is pregnant until the end of her maternity leave, or to give her notice of dismissal at such time that the notice would expire during such a period;*
3. *to provide that mothers who are nursing their infants shall be entitled to sufficient time off for this purpose;*
4. *to regulate the employment in night work of pregnant women, women who have recently given birth and women nursing their infants;*
5. *to prohibit the employment of pregnant women, women who have recently given birth or who are nursing their infants in underground mining and all other work which is unsuitable by reason of its dangerous, unhealthy or arduous nature and to take appropriate measures to protect the employment rights of these women.*

---

[36] Revised article 8 inserted by the 1996 Revision.

187

Article 15: The right of persons with disabilities to independence, social integration and participation in the life of the community[37]

With a view to ensuring to persons with disabilities, irrespective of age and the nature and origin of their disabilities, the effective exercise of the right to independence, social integration and participation in the life of the community, in particular:

1. to take the necessary measures to provide persons with disabilities with guidance, education and vocational training in the framework of general schemes wherever possible or, where this is not possible, through specialised bodies, public or private;
2. to promote their access to employment though all measures tending to encourage employers to hire and keep in employment persons with disabilities in the ordinary working environment and to adjust the working conditions to the needs of the disabled or, where this is not possible by reason of the disability, by arranging for or creating sheltered employment according to the level of disability. In certain cases, such measures may require recourse to specialised placement and support services.
3. to promote their full social integration and participation in the life of the community in particular through measures, including technical aids, aiming to overcome barriers to communication and mobility and enabling access to transport, housing, cultural activities and leisure.

Article 17: The right of children and young persons to social, legal and economic protection

With a view to ensuring the effective exercise of the right of children and young persons to grow up in an environment which encourages the full development of their personality and of their physical and mental capacities, the Parties undertake, either directly or in co-operation with public and private organisations, to take all appropriate and necessary measures designed:

1. (a) to ensure that children and young persons, taking account of the rights and duties of their parents, have the care, the assistance, the education and the training they need, in particular by providing for the establishment or maintenance of institutions and services sufficient and adequate for this purpose;
   (b) to protect children and young persons against negligence, violence or exploitation;
   (c) to provide protection and special aid from the state for children and young persons temporarily or definitively deprived of their family's support;

2. to provide to children and young persons a free primary and secondary education as well as to encourage regular attendance at schools.[38]

Article 24: The right to protection in cases of termination of employment[39]

With a view to ensuring the effective exercise of the right of workers to protection in cases of termination of employment, the Parties undertake to recognise:

---

[37] Revised article 15 inserted by the 1996 Revisions.
[38] New article 17.
[39] New article 24.

(a) the right of all workers not to have their employment terminated without valid reasons for such termination connected with their capacity or conduct based on the operational requirements of the undertaking, establishment or service;

(b) the right of workers whose employment is terminated without a valid reason to adequate compensation or other appropriate relief.

To this end, the Parties undertake to ensure that a worker who considers that his employment has been terminated without a valid reason shall have the right to appeal to an impartial body.

Article 25: The right of workers to the protection of their claim in the event of the insolvency of their employer[40]

With a view to ensuring the effective exercise of the right of workers to the protection of their claims in the event of the insolvency of their employer, the Parties undertake to provide that workers' claims arising from contracts of employment or employment relationships be guaranteed by a guarantee institution or by any other effective form of protection.

Article 26: The right to dignity at work[41]

With a view to ensuring the effective exercise of the right of all workers to protection of their dignity at work, the Parties undertake, in consultation with employers' and workers' organisations:

(1) to promote awareness, information and prevention of sexual harassment in the workplace or in relation to work and to take all appropriate measures to protect such workers from such conduct;

(2) to promote awareness, information and prevention of recurrent reprehensible or distinctly negative and offensive actions directed against individual workers in the workplace or in relation to work and to take all appropriate measures to protect workers from such conduct.

Article 27: The right of workers with family responsibilities to equal opportunities and equal treatment[42]

With a view to ensuring the effective exercise of the right to equality of opportunity and treatment for men and women workers with family responsibilities and between such workers and other workers, the Parties undertake:

(1) to take appropriate measures:

(a) to enable workers with family responsibilities to enter and remain in employment, as well as to re-enter employment after an absence due to those responsibilities, including measures in the field of vocational guidance and training;

---

[40] New article 25.
[41] New article 26.
[42] New article 27.

   (b)   to take account of their needs in terms of conditions of employment and social security;

   (c)   to develop or promote services, public or private, in particular child day-care services and other childcare arrangements;

(2)   to provide a possibility for either parent to obtain, during a period after maternity leave, parental leave to take care of a child, the duration and conditions of which should be determined by national legislation, collective agreements or practice;

(3)   to ensure that family responsibilities shall not, as such, constitute a valid reason for termination of employment.

Article 28: The right of workers' representatives to protection in the undertaking and facilities to be accorded to them

With a view to ensuring the effective exercise of the right of workers' representatives to carry out their functions, the Parties undertake to ensure that in the undertaking:

   (a)   they enjoy effective protection against acts prejudicial to them, including dismissal, based on their status or activities as workers' representatives within the undertaking;

   (b)   they are afforded such facilities as may be appropriate in order to enable them to carry out their functions promptly and efficiently, account being taken of the industrial relations system of the country and the needs, size and capabilities of the undertaking concerned.

Article 29: The right to information and consultation in collective redundancy procedures

With a view to ensuring the effective exercise of the right of workers to be informed and consulted in situations of collective redundancies, the Parties undertake to ensure that employers shall inform and consult workers' representatives, in good time prior to such collective redundancies, on ways and means of avoiding collective redundancies or limiting their occurrence and mitigating their consequences, for example by recourse to accompanying social measures aimed, in particular, at aid for the redeployment or retraining of the workers concerned.

Article 30: The right to protection against poverty and social exclusion

With a view to ensuring the effective exercise of the right to protection against poverty and social exclusion, the Parties undertake:

   (a)   to take measures within the framework of an overall and co-ordinated approach to promote the effective access of persons who live or risk living in a situation of social exclusion or poverty, as well as their families, to, in particular, employment, housing, training, education, culture and social and medical assistance;

   (b)   to review these measures with a view to their adaptation if necessary.

Article 31: The right to housing

With a view to ensuring the effective exercise of the right to housing, the Parties undertake to take measures designed:

1. *to promote access to housing of an adequate standard.*
2. *to prevent and reduce homelessness with a view to its gradual elimination;*
3. *to make the price of housing accessible to those without adequate resources.*

PART III

Article A: Undertakings

1   *Subject to the provisions of Article B below, each of the Parties undertakes:*

   (a)   *to consider Part I of this Charter as a declaration of the aims which it will pursue by all appropriate means, as stated in the introductory paragraph of that part;*

   (b)   *to consider itself bound by at least six of the following nine articles of Part 11 of this Charter: Articles 1, 5, 6, 7, 12, 13, 16, 19 and 20;*

   (c)   *to consider itself bound by an additional number of articles or numbered paragraphs of Part 11 of the Charter which it may select, provided that the total number of articles or numbered paragraphs by which it is bound is not less than sixteen articles or sixty-three numbered paragraphs.*

2.   *The articles or paragraphs selected in accordance with sub-paragraphs b and c of paragraph 1 of this article shall be notified to the Secretary General of the Council of Europe at the time when the instrument of ratification, acceptance or approval is deposited.*

3.   *Any Party may, at a later date, declare by notification addressed to the Secretary General that it considers itself bound by any articles or any numbered paragraphs of Part 11 of the Charter which it has not already accepted under the terms of paragraph 1 of this article. Such undertakings subsequently given shall be deemed to be an integral part of the ratification, acceptance or approval and shall have the same effect as from the first day of the month following the expiration of a period of one month after the date of the notification.*

4.   *Each Party shall maintain a system of labour inspection appropriate to national conditions.*

Article B: Links with the European Social Charter and the 1988 Additional Protocol

1   *No Contracting Party to the European Social Charter or Party to the Additional Protocol of 5 May 1988 may ratify, accept or approve this Charter without considering itself bound by at least the Provisions corresponding to the provisions of the European Social Charter and, where appropriate, of the Additional Protocol, to which it was bound.*

2.   *Acceptance of the obligations of any provision of this Charter shall, from the date of entry into force of those obligations for the Party concerned, result in the*

corresponding provision of the European Social Charter and, where appropriate, of its Additional Protocol of 1988 ceasing to apply to the Party concerned in the event of that Party being bound by the first of those instruments or by both instruments.

PART IV

Article C: Supervision of the implementation of the undertakings contained in this Charter

The implementation of the legal obligations contained in this Charter shall be submitted to the same supervision as the European Social Charter.

Article D: Collective complaints

1. The provisions of the Additional Protocol to the European Social Charter providing for a system of collective complaints shall apply to the undertakings given in this Charter for the States which have ratified the said Protocol.
2. Any State which is not bound by the Additional Protocol to the European Social Charter providing for a system of collective complaints may when depositing its instrument of ratification, acceptance or approval of this Charter or at any time thereafter, declare by notification addressed to the Secretary General of the Council of Europe, that it accepts the supervision of its obligations under this Charter following the procedure provided for in the said Protocol.

PART V

Article E: Non-discrimination

The enjoyment of the rights set forth in this Charter shall be secured without discrimination on any ground such as race, colour, sex, language, religion, political or other opinion, national extraction or social origin, health, association with a national minority, birth or other status.

Article F: Derogations in time of war or public emergency

1. In time of war or other public emergency threatening the life of the nation any Party may take measures derogating from its obligations under this Charter to the extent strictly required by the exigencies of the situation, provided that such measures are not inconsistent with its other obligations under international law.
2. Any Party which has availed itself of this right of derogation shall, within a reasonable lapse of time, keep the Secretary General of the Council of Europe fully informed of the measures taken and of the reasons therefor. It shall likewise inform the Secretary General when such measures have ceased to operate and the provisions of the Charter which it has accepted are again being fully executed.

Article G: Restrictions

1. *The rights and principles set forth in Part I when effectively realised, and their effective exercise as provided for in Part II, shall not be subject to any restrictions or limitations not specified in those parts, except such as are prescribed by law and are necessary in a democratic society for the protection of the rights and freedoms of others or for the protection of public interest, national security, public health, or morals.*

    The restrictions permitted under this Charter to the rights and obligations set forth herein shall not be applied for any purpose other than that for which they have been prescribed.

Article H: Relations between the Charter and domestic law or international agreements

The provisions of this Charter shall not prejudice the provisions of domestic law or of any bilateral or multilateral treaties, conventions or agreements which are already in force, or may come into force, under which more favourable treatment would be accorded to the persons protected.

Article I: Implementation of the undertakings given

1. *Without prejudice to the methods of implementation foreseen in these articles the relevant provisions of Articles 1 to 31 of Part II of this Charter shall be implemented by:*

    (a) *laws or regulations;*
    (b) *agreements between employers or employers' organisations and workers' organisations;*
    (c) *a combination of those two methods;*
    (d) *other appropriate means.*

    Compliance with the undertakings deriving from the provisions of paragraphs 1, 2, 3, 4, 5 and 7 of Article 2, paragraphs 4, 6 and 7 of Article 7, paragraphs 1, 2, 3 and 5 of Article 10 and Articles 21 and 22 of Part II of this Charter shall be regarded as effective if the provisions are applied, in accordance with paragraph 1 of this article, to the great majority of the workers concerned.

Article J: Amendments

1. *Any amendment to Parts I and II of this Charter with the purpose of extending the rights guaranteed in this Charter as well as any amendment to Parts III to VI, proposed by a Party or by the Governmental Committee, shall be communicated to the Secretary General of the Council of Europe and forwarded by the Secretary General to the Parties to this Charter.*
2. *Any amendment proposed in accordance with the provisions of the preceding paragraph shall be examined by the Governmental Committee which shall submit the text adopted to the Committee of Ministers for approval after consultation with*

the Parliamentary Assembly. After its approval by the Committee of Ministers this text shall be forwarded to the Parties for acceptance.

3. Any amendment to Part I and to Part II of this Charter shall enter into force, in respect of those Parties which have accepted it, on the first day of the month following the expiration of a period of one month after, the date on which three Parties have informed the Secretary General that they have accepted it.

   In respect of any Party which subsequently accepts it, the amendment shall enter into force on the first day of the month following the expiration of a period of one month after the date on which that Party has informed the Secretary General of its acceptance.

4. Any amendment to Parts III to VI of this Charter shall enter into force on the first day of the have informed the Secretary General that they have accepted it.

PART VI

Article K: Signature, ratification and entry into force

1. This Charter shall be open for Signature by the member States of the Council of Europe. It shall be subject to ratification, acceptance or approval. Instruments of ratification, acceptance or approval shall be deposited with the Secretary General of the Council of Europe.

2. This Charter shall enter into force on the first day of the month following the expiration of a period of one month after the date on which three member States of the Council of Europe have expressed their consent to be bound by this Charter in accordance with the preceding paragraph.

3. In respect of any member State which subsequently expresses its consent to be bound by this Charter, it shall enter into force on the first day of the month following the expiration of a period of one month after the date of the deposit of the instrument of ratification, acceptance or approval.

Article L: Territorial application

1. This Charter shall apply to the metropolitan territory of each Party. Each signatory may, at the time of signature or of the deposit of its instrument of ratification, acceptance or approval, specify, by declaration addressed to the Secretary General of the Council of Europe, the territory which shall be considered to be its metropolitan territory for this purpose.

2. Any signatory may, at the time of signature or of the deposit of its instrument of ratification, acceptance or approval, or at any time thereafter, declare by notification addressed to the Secretary General of the Council of Europe, that the Charter shall extend in whole or in part to a non-metropolitan territory or territories specified in the said declaration for whose international relations it is responsible or for which it assumes international responsibility, It shall specify in the declaration the articles or paragraphs of Part II of the Charter which it accepts as binding in respect of the territories named in the declaration.

3.   *The Charter shall extend its application to the territory or territories named in the aforesaid declaration as from the first day of the month following the expiration of a period of one month after the date of receipt of the notification of such declaration.*

4.   *Any Party may declare at a later date by notification addressed to the Secretary General of the Council of Europe that, in respect of one or more of the territories to which the Charter has been applied in accordance with paragraph 2 of this article, it accepts as binding any articles or any numbered paragraphs which it has not already accepted in respect of that territory or territories. Such undertakings subsequently given shall be deemed to be an integral part of the original declaration in respect of the territory concerned, and shall have the same effect as from the first day of the month following the expiration of a period of one month after the date of receipt of such notification by the Secretary General.*

Article M: Denunciation

1.   *Any Party may denounce this Charter only at the end of a period of five years from the date on which the charter entered into force for it, or at the end of any subsequent period of two years, and in either case after giving six months' notice to the Secretary General of the Council of Europe who shall inform the other Parties accordingly.*

2.   *Any Party may, in accordance with the Provisions set out in the preceding paragraph, denounce any article or paragraph of Part II of the Charter accepted by it provided that the number of articles or paragraphs by which this Party is bound shall never be less than sixteen in the former case and sixty three in the latter and that this number of articles or paragraphs shall continue to include the articles selected by the Party among those to which special reference is made in Article A, paragraph 1, sub-paragraph b.*

3.   *Any Party may denounce the present Charter or any of the articles or paragraphs of Part II of the Charter under the conditions specified in paragraph 1 of this article in respect of any territory to which the said Charter is applicable, by virtue of a declaration made in accordance with paragraph 2 of Article L.*

Article N: Appendix

The appendix to this Charter shall form an integral part of it.

Article O: Notifications

The Secretary General of the Council of Europe shall notify the member States of the Council and the Director General of the International Labour Office of:

  — *any signature;*
  — *the deposit of any instrument of ratification, acceptance or approval;*
  — *any date of entry into force of this Charter in accordance with Article K;*
  — *any declaration made in application of Articles A, paragraphs 2 and 3, D, paragraphs 1 and 2, F, paragraph 2, L, paragraphs 1, 2, 3 and 4;*
  — *any amendment in accordance with Article J;*
  — *any denunciation in accordance with Article M;*
  — *any other act, notification or communication relating to this Charter.*

APPENDIX TO THE REVISED EUROPEAN SOCIAL CHARTER
SCOPE OF THE REVISED EUROPEAN SOCIAL CHARTER IN
TERMS OF PERSONS PROTECTED

1. *Without prejudice to Article 12, paragraph 4, and Article 13, paragraph 4, the persons covered by Articles 1 to 17 and 20 to 31 include foreigners only in so far as they are nationals of other Parties lawfully resident or working regularly within the territory of the Party concerned, subject to the understanding that these articles are to be interpreted in the light of the provisions of Articles 18 and 19.*

    This interpretation would not prejudice the extension of similar facilities to other persons by any of the Parties.

2. *Each Party will grant to refugees as defined in the Convention relating to the Status of Refugees, signed in Geneva on 28 July 1951 and in the Protocol of 31 January 1967, and lawfully staying in its territory, treatment as favourable as possible, and in any case not less favourable than under the obligations accepted by the Party under the said convention and under any other existing international instruments applicable to those refugees.*

3. *Each Party will grant to stateless persons as defined in the Convention on the Status of Stateless Persons done in New York on 28 September 1954 and lawfully staying in its territory, treatment as favourable as possible and in any case not less favourable than under the obligations accepted by the Party under the said instrument and under any other existing international instruments applicable to those stateless persons.*

PART I, PARAGRAPH 18, AND PART II, ARTICLE 18, PARAGRAPH 1

It is understood that these provisions are not concerned with the question of entry into the territories of the Parties and do not prejudice the provisions of the European Convention on Establishment, signed in Paris on 13 December 1955.

PART II

Article 1, paragraph 2

This provision shall not be interpreted as prohibiting or authorising any union security clause or practice.

Article 2, paragraph 6

Parties may provide that this provision shall not apply:

(a) *to workers having a contract or employment relationship with a total duration not exceeding one month and/or with a working week not exceeding eight hours;*

(b) *where the contract or employment relationship is of a casual and/or specific*

196

nature, provided, in these cases, that its non-application is justified by objective considerations.

Article 3, paragraph 4

It is understood that for the purposes of this provision the functions, organisation and conditions of operation of these services shall be determined by national laws or regulations, collective agreements or other means appropriate to national conditions.

Article 4, paragraph 4

This provision shall be so understood as not to prohibit immediate dismissal for any serious offence.

Article 4, paragraph 5

It is understood that a Party may give the undertaking required in this paragraph if the great majority of workers are not permitted to suffer deductions from wages either by law or through collective agreements or arbitration awards, the exceptions being those persons not so covered.

Article 6, paragraph 4

It is understood that each Party may, insofar as it is concerned, regulate the exercise of the right to strike by law, provided that any further restriction that this might place on the right can be justified under the terms of Article G.

Article 7, paragraph 2

This provision does not prevent Parties from providing in their legislation that young persons not having reached the minimum age laid down may perform work in so far as it is absolutely necessary for their vocational training where such work is carried out in accordance with conditions prescribed by the competent authority and measures are taken to protect the health and safety of these young persons.

Article 7, paragraph 8

It is understood that a Party may give the undertaking required in this paragraph if it fulfils the spirit of the undertaking by providing by law that the great majority of persons under eighteen years of age shall not be employed in night work.

Article 8, paragraph 2

This provision shall not be interpreted as laying down an absolute prohibition. Exceptions could be made, for instance, in the following cases:

(a) if an employed woman has been guilty of misconduct which justifies breaking off the employment relationship;

(b) if the undertaking concerned ceases to operate;

(c) if the period prescribed in the employment contract has expired.

Article 12, paragraph 4

The words "and subject to the conditions laid down in such agreements" in the introduction to this paragraph are taken to imply inter alia that with regard to benefits which are available independent of any insurance contribution, a Party may require the completion of a prescribed period of residence before granting such benefits to nationals of other Parties.

Article 13, paragraph 4

Governments not Parties to the European Convention on Social and Medical Assistance may ratify the Charter in respect of this paragraph provided that they grant to nationals of other Parties a treatment which is in conformity with the provisions of the said convention.

Article 16

It is understood that the protection afforded in this provision covers single-parent families.

Article 17

It is understood that this provision covers all persons below the age of 18 years, unless under the law applicable to the child majority is attained earlier, without prejudice to the other specific provisions provided by the Charter, particularly Article 7.

This does not imply an obligation to provide compulsory education up to the above-mentioned age.

Article 19, paragraph 6

For the purpose of applying this provision, the term "family of a foreign worker" is understood to mean at least the worker's spouse and unmarried children as long as the latter are considered to be minors of the receiving State and are dependent on the migrant worker.

Article 20

1. It is understood that social security matters, as well as other provisions relating to unemployment benefit, old age benefit and survivor's benefit, may be excluded from the scope of this article.
2. Provisions concerning the protection of women, particularly as regards pregnancy, confinement and the post-natal period, shall not be deemed to be discrimination as referred to in this article.
3. This article shall not prevent the adoption of specific measures aimed at removing de facto inequalities.

4.   *Occupational activities which, by reason of their nature or the context in which they are carried out, can be entrusted only to persons of a particular sex may be excluded from the scope of this article or some of its provisions. This provision is not to be interpreted as requiring the Parties to embody in laws or regulations a list of occupations which, by reason of their nature or the context in which they are carried out, may be reserved to persons of a particular sex.*

Articles 21 and 22

1.   *For the purpose of the application of these articles, the term "workers' representatives" means persons who are recognised as such under national legislation or practice.*
2.   *The terms "national legislation and practice" embrace as the case may be, in addition to laws and regulations, collective agreements, other agreements between employers and workers' representatives, customs as well as relevant case law.*
3.   *For the purpose of the application of these articles, the term "undertaking" is understood as referring to a set of tangible and intangible components, with or without legal personality, formed to produce goods or provide services for financial gain and with power to determine its own market policy.*
4.   *It is understood that religious communities and their institutions may be excluded from the application of these articles, even if these institutions are "undertakings" with the meaning of paragraph 3. Establishments pursuing activities which are inspired by certain ideals or guided by certain moral concepts, ideals and concepts which are protected by national legislation, may be excluded from the application of these articles to such an extent as is necessary to protect the orientation of the undertaking.*
5.   *It is understood that where in a state the rights set out in these articles are exercised in the various establishments of the undertaking, the Party concerned is to be considered as fulfilling the obligations deriving from these provisions.*
6.   *The Parties may exclude from the field of application of these articles, those undertakings employing less than a certain number of workers, to be determined by national legislation or practice.*

Article 22

1.   *This provision affects neither the powers and obligations of states as regards the adoption of health and safety regulations for workplaces, nor the powers and responsibilities of the bodies in charge of monitoring their application.*
2.   *The terms "social and socio-cultural services and facilities" are understood as referring to the social and/or cultural facilities for workers provided by some undertakings such as welfare assistance, sports fields, rooms for nursing mothers, libraries, children's holiday camps, etc.*

Article 23, paragraph 1

For the purpose of the application of this paragraph, the term "for as long as possible" refers to the elderly person's physical, psychological and intellectual capacities.

Article 24

1. It is understood that for the purposes of this article the terms "termination of employment" and "terminated" mean termination of employment at the initiative of the employer.
2. It is understood that this article covers all workers but that a Party may exclude from some or all of its protection the following categories of employed persons:

    (a) workers engaged under a contract of employment for a specified period of time or a specified task;
    (b) workers undergoing a period of probation or a qualifying period of employment, provided that this is determined in advance and is of a reasonable duration;
    (c) workers engaged on a casual basis for a short period.

3. For the purpose of this article the following, in particular, shall not constitute valid reasons for termination of employment:

    (a) trade union membership or participation in union activities outside working hours, or, with the consent of the employer, within working hours;
    (b) seeking office as, acting or having acted in the capacity of a workers' representative;
    (c) the filing of a complaint or the participation in proceedings against an employer involving alleged violation of laws or regulations or recourse to competent administrative authorities;
    (d) race, colour, sex, marital status, family responsibilities, pregnancy, religion, political opinion, national extraction or social gain;
    (e) maternity or parental leave;
    (f) temporary absence from work due to illness or injury.

4. It is understood that compensation or other appropriate relief in case of termination of employment without valid reasons shall be determined by national laws or regulations, collective agreements or other means appropriate to national conditions.

Article 25

1. It is understood that the competent national authority may, by way of exemption and after consulting organisations of employers and workers, exclude certain categories of workers from the protection provided in this provision by reason of the special nature of their employment relationship.
2. It is understood that the definition of the term "insolvency" must be determined by national law and practice.
3. The workers' claims covered by this provision shall include at least:

    (a) the workers' claims for wages relating to a prescribed period, which shall not be less than three months under a privilege system and eight weeks under a guarantee system, prior to the insolvency or to the termination of employment;
    (b) the workers' claims for holiday pay due as a result of work performed during the year in which the insolvency or the termination of employment occurred;

(c)   the workers' claims for amounts due in respect of other types of paid absence relating to a prescribed period, which shall not be less than three months under a privilege system and eight weeks under a guarantee system, prior to the insolvency or the termination of the employment.

4.   National laws or regulations may limit the protection of workers' claims to a prescribed amount, which shall be of a socially acceptable level.

Article 26

It is understood that this article does not require that legislation be enacted by the Parties. It is understood that paragraph 2 does not cover sexual harassment.

Article 27

It is understood that this article applies to men and women workers with family responsibilities in relation to their dependent children as well as in relation to other members of their immediate family who clearly need their care or support where such responsibilities restrict their possibilities of preparing for, entering, participating in or advancing in economic activity. The terms "dependent children" and "other members of their immediate family who clearly need their care and support" mean persons defined as such by the national legislation of the Party concerned.

Articles 28 and 29

For the purpose of the application of this article, the term "workers' representatives" means persons who are recognised as such under national legislation or practice.

PART III

It is understood that the Charter contains legal obligations of an international character, the application of which is submitted solely to the supervision provided for in Part IV thereof.

Article A, paragraph 1

It is understood that the numbered paragraphs may include articles consisting of only one paragraph.

Article B, paragraph 2

For the purpose of paragraph 2 of Article B, the provisions of the revised Charter correspond to the provisions of the Charter with the same article or paragraph number with the exception of:

(a)   Article 3, paragraph 2, of the revised Charter which corresponds to Article 3, paragraphs 1 and 3, of the Charter;

(b) Article 3, paragraph 3, of the revised Charter which corresponds to Article 3, paragraphs 2 and 3, of the Charter;

(c) Article 10, paragraph 5, of the revised Charter which corresponds to Article 10, paragraph 4, of the Charter.

(d) Article 17, paragraph 1, of the revised Charter which corresponds to Article 17 of the Charter.

PART V

Article E

A differential treatment based on an objective and reasonable justification shall not be deemed discriminatory.

Article F

The terms "in time of war or other public emergency" shall be so understood as to cover also the threat of war.

Article I

It is understood that workers excluded in accordance with the appendix to Articles 21 and 22 are not taken into account in establishing the number of workers concerned.

Article J

The term "amendment" shall be extended so as to cover also the addition of new articles to the Charter.

17. ADDITIONAL PROTOCOL TO THE EUROPEAN SOCIAL CHARTER

Done at Strasbourg on 5 May 1988

Entry into force: 4 September 1992, in accordance with Article 10(2)

PREAMBLE

The member States of the Council of Europe signatory hereto.

Resolved to take new measures to extend the protection of the social and economic rights guaranteed by the European Social Charter, opened for signature in Turin on 18 October 1961 (hereinafter referred to as "the Charter"),
Have agreed as follows:

PART I

The Parties accept as the aim of their policy to be pursued by all appropriate means, both national and international in character, the attainment of conditions in which the following rights and principles may be effectively realised:

1. All workers have the right to equal opportunities and equal treatment in matters of employment and occupation without discrimination on the grounds of sex.
2. Workers have the right to be informed and to be consulted within the undertaking.
3. Workers have the right to take part in the determination and improvement of the working conditions and working environment in the undertaking.
4. Every elderly person has the right to social protection.

PART II

The Parties undertake, as provided for in Part III, to consider themselves bound by the obligations laid down in the following articles:

Article 1: Right to equal opportunities and equal treatment in matters of employment and occupation without discrimination on the grounds of sex[1]

With a view to ensuring the effective exercise of the right to equal opportunities and equal treatment in matters of employment and occupation without discrimination on the grounds of sex, the Parties undertake to recognise that

---

[1] Paragraph 1 of this article forms the whole of Article 20 in the 1996 revised Social Charter.

right and to take appropriate measures to ensure or promote its application in the following fields:

- access to employment, protection against dismissal and occupational resettlement;
- vocational guidance. training, retraining and rehabilitation;
- terms of employment and working conditions including remuneration;
- career development including promotion.

2. Provisions concerning the protection of women, particularly as regards pregnancy, confinement and the post-natal period, shall not be deemed to be discrimination as referred to in paragraph 1 of this Article.
3. Paragraph 1 of this Article shall not prevent the adoption of specific measures aimed at removing *de facto* inequalities.
4. Occupational activities which, by reason of their nature or the context in which they are carried out, can be entrusted only to persons of a particular sex may be excluded from the scope of this Article or some of its provisions.

Article 2: Right to information and consultation[2]

1. With a view to ensuring the effective exercise of the right of workers to be informed and consulted within the undertaking, the Parties undertake to adopt or encourage measures enabling workers or their representatives, in accordance with national legislation and practice:

   a. to be informed regularly or at the appropriate time and in a comprehensible way about the economic and financial situation of the undertaking employing them, on the understanding that the disclosure of certain information which could be prejudicial to the undertaking may be refused or subject to confidentiality; and
   b. to be consulted in good time on proposed decisions which could substantially affect the interests of workers, particularly on those decisions which could have an important impact on the employment situation in the undertaking.

2. The Parties may exclude from the field of application of paragraph 1 of this Article, those undertakings employing less than a certain number of workers to be determined by national legislation or practice.

Article 3: Right to take part in the determination and improvement of the working conditions and working environment[3]

1. With a view to ensuring the effective exercise of the right of workers to take part in the determination and improvement of the working conditions and working environment in the undertaking, the Parties undertake to adopt or

---

[2] Article 21 in the 1996 revised Social Charter.
[3] Article 22 in the 1996 revised Social Charter.

encourage measures enabling workers or their representatives, in accordance with national legislation and practice, to contribute:

a. to the determination and the improvement of the working conditions, work organisation and working environment;
b. to the protection of health and safety within the undertaking;
c. to the organisation of social and socio-cultural services and facilities within the undertaking;
d. to the supervision of the observance of regulations on these matters.

2. The Parties may exclude from the field of application of paragraph 1 of this Article, those undertakings employing less than a certain number of workers to be determined by national legislation or practice.

Article 4: Right of elderly persons to social protection[4]

With a view to ensuring the effective exercise of the right of elderly persons to social protection, the Parties undertake to adopt or encourage either directly or in co-operation with public or private organisations, appropriate measures designed in particular:

1. to enable elderly persons to remain full members of society for as long as possible, by means of:

a. adequate resources enabling them to lead a decent life and play an active part in public, social and cultural life;
b. provision of information about services and facilities available for elderly persons and their opportunities to make use of them;

2. to enable elderly persons to choose their life-style freely and to lead independent lives in their familiar surroundings for as long as they wish and are able, by means of:

a. provision of housing suited to their needs and their state of health or of adequate support for adapting their housing;
b. the health care and the services necessitated by their state;

3. to guarantee elderly persons living in institutions appropriate support, while respecting their privacy, and participation in decisions concerning living conditions in the institution.

---

[4] Article 23 in the 1996 revised Social Charter.

PART III

Article 5: Undertakings

1. Each of the Parties undertakes:

    a. to consider Part I of this Protocol as a declaration of the aims which it will pursue by all appropriate means, as stated in the introductory paragraph of that Part;

    b. to consider itself bound by one or more articles of Part II of this Protocol.

2. The article or articles selected in accordance with sub-paragraph b of paragraph I of this Article, shall be notified to the Secretary General of the Council of Europe at the time when the instrument of ratification, acceptance or approval of the Contracting State concerned is deposited.

3. Any Party may, at a later date, declare by notification to the Secretary General that it considers itself bound by any articles of Part II of this Protocol which it has not already accepted under the terms of paragraph I of this Article. Such undertakings subsequently given shall be deemed to be an integral part of the ratification, acceptance or approval, and shall have the same effect as from the thirtieth day after the date of the notification.

PART IV

Article 6: Supervision of compliance with the undertakings given

The Parties shall submit reports on the application of those provisions of Part II of this Protocol which thev have accepted in the reports submitted be virtue of Article 21 of the Charter.

PART V

Article 7: Implementation of the undertakings given

1. The relevant Provisions of Articles I to 4 of Part II of this Protocol may be implemented by:

    a. laws or regulations;

    b. agreements between employers or employers' organisations and workers' organisations;

    c. a combination of those two methods; or

    d. other appropriate means.

2. Compliance with the undertakings deriving from Articles 2 and 3 of Part II of this Protocol shall be regarded as effective if the provisions are applied, in accordance with paragraph 1 of this Article, to the great majority of the workers concerned.

Article 8: Relations between the Charter and this Protocol

1. The provisions of this Protocol shall not prejudice the provisions of the Charter.
2. Articles 22 to 32 and Article 36 of the Charter shall apply *mutatis mutandis* to this Protocol.

Article 9: Territorial application

1. This Protocol shall apply to the metropolitan territory of each Party. Any State may, at the time of signature or when depositing its instrument of ratification, acceptance or approval, specify by declaration addressed to the Secretary General of the Council of Europe, the territory which shall be considered to be its metropolitan territory for this purpose.
2. Any Contracting State may, at the time of ratification, acceptance or approval of this Protocol or at any time thereafter, declare by notification addressed to the Secretary General of the Council of Europe that the Protocol shall extend in whole or in part to a non-metropolitan territory or territories specified in the said declaration for whose international relations it is responsible or for which it assumes international responsibility. It shall specify in the declaration the article or articles of Part II of this Protocol which it accepts as binding in respect of the territories named in the declaration.
3. This Protocol shall enter into force in respect of the territory or territories named in the aforesaid declaration as from the thirtieth day after the date on which the Secretary General shall have notification of such declaration.
4. Any Party may declare at a later date by notification addressed to the Secretary General of the Council of Europe, that, in respect of one or more of the territories to which this Protocol has been extended in accordance with paragraph 2 of this Article, it accepts as binding any articles which it has not already accepted in respect of that territory or territories. Such undertakings subsequently given shall be deemed to be an integral part of the original declaration in respect of the territory concerned, and shall have the same effect as from the thirtieth day after the date on which the Secretary General shall have notification of such declaration.

Article 10: Signature, ratification, acceptance, approval and entry into force

1. This Protocol shall be open for signature by member States of the Council of Europe who are signatories to the Charter. It is subject to ratification, acceptance or approval. No member State of the Council of Europe shall ratify, accept or approve this Protocol except at the same time as or after ratification of the Charter. Instruments of ratification, acceptance or approval shall be deposited with the Secretary General of the Council of Europe.
2. This Protocol shall enter into force on the thirtieth day after the date of deposit of the third instrument of ratification, acceptance or approval.
3. In respect of any signatory State ratifying subsequently, this Protocol shall

come into force as from the thirtieth day after the date of deposit of its instrument of ratification, acceptance or approval.

Article 11: Denunciation

1. Any Party may denounce this Protocol only at the end of a period of five years from the date on which the Protocol entered into force for it, or at the end of any successive period of two years, and, in each case, after giving six months' notice to the Secretary General of the Council of Europe. Such denunciation shall not affect the validity of the Protocol in respect of the other Parties provided that at all times there are not less than three state Parties.
2. Any Party may, in accordance with the provisions set out in the preceding paragraph, denounce any article of Part II of this Protocol accepted by it, provided that the number of articles by which this Party is bound shall never be less than one.
3. Any Party may denounce this Protocol or any of the articles of Part II of the Protocol, under the conditions specified in paragraph I of this Article, in respect of any territory to which the Protocol is applicable by virtue of a declaration made in accordance with paragraphs 2 and 4 of Article 9.
4. Any Party bound by the Charter and this Protocol, which denounces the Charter in accordance with the provisions of paragraph I of Article 37 thereof, will be considered to have denounced the Protocol likewise.

Article 12: Notifications

The Secretary General of the Council of Europe shall notify the member States of the Council and the Director General of the International Labour Office of:

a. any signature;
b. the deposit of any instrument of ratification, acceptance or approval;
c. any date of entry into force of this Protocol in accordance with Articles 9 and 10;
d. any other act, notification or communication relating to this Protocol.

Article 13: Appendix

The Appendix to this Protocol shall form an integral part of it.

18. COUNCIL OF EUROPE: PROTOCOL AMENDING THE EUROPEAN SOCIAL CHARTER PROVIDING FOR A SYSTEM OF COLLECTIVE COMPLAINTS

Done at Strasbourg: 9 November 1995

PREAMBLE

The member States of the Council of Europe, signatories to this Protocol to the European Social Charter opened for signature in Turin on 18 October 1961 (hereinafter referred to as "the Charter");

Resolved to take new measures to improve the effective enforcement of the social rights guaranteed by the Charter;

Considering that this aim could be achieved in particular by the establishment of a collective complaints procedure, which, inter alia, would strengthen the participation of management and labour and of non-governmental organisations.

Have agreed as follows:

Article 1

The Contracting Parties to this Protocol recognise the right of the following organisations to submit complaints alleging unsatisfactory application of the Charter:

a. international organisations of employers and trade unions referred to in paragraph 2 of Article 27 of the Charter;

b. other international non-governmental organisations which have consultative status with the Council of Europe and have been put on a list established for this purpose by the Governmental Committee;

c. representative national organisations of employers and trade unions within the jurisdiction of the Contracting Party against which they have lodged a complaint.

Article 2

1. Any Contracting State may also, when it expresses its consent to be bound by this Protocol in accordance with the provisions of Article 13, or at any moment thereafter, declare that it recognises the right of any other representative national non-governmental organisation within its jurisdiction, which has particular competence in the matters governed by the Charter, to lodge complaints against it.

2. Such declarations may be made for a specific period.

3. The declarations shall be deposited with the Secretary General of the Council of Europe who shall transmit copies thereof to the Contracting Parties and publish them.

Article 3

The international non-governmental organisations and the national non-governmental organisations referred to in Article 1b and Article 2 respectively may submit complaints in accordance with the procedure prescribed by the aforesaid provisions only in respect of those matters regarding which they have been recognised as having particular competence.

Article 4

The complaint shall be lodged in writing, relate to a provision of the Charter accepted by the Contracting Party concerned and indicate in what respect the latter has not ensured the satisfactory application of this provision.

Article 5

Any complaint shall be addressed to the Secretary General who shall acknowledge receipt of it, notify it to the Contracting Party concerned and immediately transmit it to the Committee of Independent Experts.

Article 6

The Committee of Independent Experts may request the Contracting Party concerned and the organisation which lodged the complaint to submit written information and observations on the admissibility of the complaint within such time-limit as it shall prescribe.

Article 7

1. If it decides that a complaint is admissible, the Committee of Independent Experts shall notify the Contracting Parties to the Charter through the Secretary General. It shall request the Contracting Party concerned and the organisation which lodged the complaint to submit, within such time-limit as it shall prescribe, all relevant written explanations or information, and the other Contracting Parties to this Protocol, the comments they wish to submit, within the same time-limit.
2. If the complaint has been lodged by a national organisation of employers or a national trade union or by another national or international non-governmental organisation, the Committee of Independent Experts shall notify the international organisations of employers or trade unions referred to in paragraph 2 of Article 27 of the Charter, through the Secretary General, and invite them to submit observations within such time-limit as it shall prescribe.
3. On the basis of the explanations, information or observations submitted under paragraphs 1 and 2 above, the Contracting Party concerned and the organisation which lodged the complaint may submit any additional written information or observations within such time limit as the Committee of Independent Experts shall prescribe.

4. In the course of the examination of the complaint, the Committee of Indepen-
    dent Experts may organise a hearing with the representatives of the parties.

Article 8

1. The Committee of Independent Experts shall draw up a report in which it shall
    describe the steps taken by it to examine the complaint and present its
    conclusions as to whether or not the Contracting Party concerned has ensured
    the satisfactory application of the provision of the Charter referred to in the
    complaint.
2. The report shall be transmitted to the Committee of Ministers. It shall also be
    transmitted to the organisation that lodged the complaint and to the
    Contracting Parties to the Charter, which shall not be at liberty to publish it.
    It shall be transmitted to the Parliamentary Assembly and be made public at
    the same time as the resolution referred to in Article 9 or no later than four
    months after it has been transmitted to the Committee of Ministers.

Article 9

1. On the basis of the report of the Committee of Independent Experts, the
    Committee of Ministers shall adopt a resolution by a majority of those voting.
    If the Committee of Independent Experts finds that the Charter has not been
    applied in a satisfactory manner, the Committee of Ministers shall adopt, by a
    majority of two-thirds of those voting, a recommendation addressed to the
    Contracting Party concerned. In both cases, entitlement to voting shall be
    limited to the Contracting Parties to the Charter.
2. At the request of the Contracting Party concerned, the Committee of
    Ministers may decide, where the report of the Committee of Independent
    Experts raises new issues, by a two-thirds majority of the Contracting Parties
    to the Charter, to consult the Governmental Committee.

Article 10

The Contracting Party concerned shall provide information on the measures it has
taken to give effect to the Committee of Ministers' recommendation, in the next
report which it submits to the Secretary General under Article 21 of the Charter.

Article 11

Articles 1 to 10 of this Protocol shall apply also to the articles of Part II of the First
Additional Protocol to the Charter in respect of the States Parties to that Protocol,
to the extent that these articles have been accepted.

Article 12

The States Parties to this Protocol consider that the appendix to the Charter
relating to Part III reads as follows:

"It is understood that the Charter contains legal obligations of an inter-national character, the application of which is submitted solely to the super-vision provided for in Part IV thereof and in the provisions of this Protocol."

Article 13

1. This Protocol shall be open for signature by member States of the Council of Europe signatories to the Charter, which may express their consent to be bound by:

    a. signature without reservation as to ratification, acceptance or approval; or
    b. signature subject to ratification, acceptance or approval, followed by ratification, acceptance or approval.

2. A member State of the Council of Europe may not express its consent to be bound by this Protocol without simultaneously or previously ratifying the Charter.
3. Instruments of ratification, acceptance or approval shall be deposited with the Secretary General of the Council of Europe.

Article 14

1. This Protocol shall enter into force on the first day of the month following the expiration of a period of one month after the date on which five member States of the Council of Europe have expressed their consent to be bound by the Protocol in accordance with the provisions of Article 12.
2. In respect of any member State which subsequently expresses its consent to be bound by it, the Protocol shall enter into force on the first day of the month following the expiration of a period of one month after the date of the deposit of the instrument of ratification, acceptance or approval.

Article 15

1. Any Party may at any time denounce this Protocol by means of a notification addressed to the Secretary General of the Council of Europe.
2. Such denunciation shall become effective on the first day of the month following the expiration of a period of twelve months after the date of receipt of such notification by the Secretary General.

Article 16

The Secretary General of the Council of Europe shall notify all the member States of the Council of:

a. any signature;
b. the deposit of any instrument of ratification, acceptance or approval;
c. the date of entry into force of this Protocol in accordance with Article 14;
d. any other act, notification or declaration relating to this Protocol.

19. AMERICAN DECLARATION OF THE RIGHTS AND DUTIES OF MAN

OAS resolution XXX
Adopted by the Ninth International Conference of American States (1948)

Whereas:

The American peoples have acknowledged the dignity of the individual, and their national constitutions recognise that juridical and political institutions, which regulate life in human society, have as their principal aim the protection of the essential rights of man and the creation of circumstances that will permit him to achieve spiritual and material progress and attain happiness;

The American States have on repeated occasions recognised that the essential rights of man are not derived from the fact that he is a national of a certain state, but are based upon attributes of his human personality;

The international protection of the rights of man should be the principal guide of an evolving American law;

The affirmation of essential human rights by the American States together with the guarantees given by the internal regimes of the states establish the initial system of protection considered by the American States as being suited to the present social and juridical conditions, not without a recognition on their part that they should increasingly strengthen that system in the international field as conditions become more favourable.

The Ninth International Conference of American States

Agrees

To adopt the following

American Declaration of the Rights and Duties of Man

PREAMBLE

All men are born free and equal, in dignity and in rights, and, being endowed by nature with reason and conscience, they should conduct themselves as brothers one to another.

The fulfilment of duty by each individual is a prerequisite to the rights of all. Rights and duties are interrelated in every social and political activity of man. While rights exalt individual liberty, duties express the dignity of that liberty.

Duties of a juridical nature presuppose others of a moral nature which support them in principle and constitute their basis.

Inasmuch as spiritual development is the supreme end of human existence and the highest expression thereof, it is the duty of man to serve that end with all his strength and resources.

Since culture is the highest social and historical expression of that spiritual development, it is the duty of man to preserve, practice and foster culture by every means within his power.

And, since moral conduct constitutes the noblest flowering of culture, it is the duty of every man always to hold it in high respect.

CHAPTER ONE. RIGHTS

Article I: Right to life, liberty and personal security

Every human being has the right to life, liberty and the security of his person.

Article II: Right to equality before the law

All persons are equal before the law and have the rights and duties established in this Declaration, without distinction as to race, sex, language, creed or any other factor.

Article III: Right to religious freedom and worship

Every person has the right freely to profess a religious faith, and to manifest and practice it both in public and in private.

Article IV: Right to freedom of investigation, opinion, expression and dissemination

Every person has the right to freedom of investigation, of opinion, and of the expression and dissemination of ideas, by any medium whatsoever.

Article V: Right to protection of honour, personal reputation and private and family life

Every person has the right to the protection of the law and against abusive attacks upon his honour, his reputation, and his private and family life.

Article VI: Rights to the family and to protection thereof

Every person has the right to establish a family, the basic element of society, and to receive protection therefor.

Article VII: Right to protection for mothers and children

All women, during pregnancy and the nursing period, and all children have the right to special protection, care and aid.

Article VIII: Right to residence and movement

Every person has the right to fix his residence within the territory of the state of which he is a national, to move about freely within such territory, and not to leave it except by his own will.

Article IX: Right to inviolability of home

Every person has the right to the inviolability of his home.

Article X: Right to the inviolability and transmission of correspondence

Every person has the right to the inviolability and transmission of his correspondence.

Article XI: Right to the preservation of health and to well-being

Every person has the right to the preservation of his health through sanitary and social measures relating to food, clothing, housing and medical care, to the extent permitted by public and community resources.

Article XII: Right to education

Every person has the right to an education, which should be based on the principles of liberty, morality and human solidarity. Likewise every person has the right to an education that will prepare him to attain a decent life, to raise his standard of living, and to be a useful member of society.

The right to an education includes the right to equality of opportunity in every case, in accordance with natural talents, merit and the desire to utilise the resources that the state or the community is in a position to provide.

Every person has the right to receive, free, at least a primary education.

Article XIII: Right to the benefits of culture

Every person has the right to take part in the cultural life of the community, to enjoy the arts, and to participate in the benefits that result from intellectual progress, especially scientific discoveries.

He likewise has the right to the protection of his moral and material interests as regards his inventions or any literary, scientific or artistic works of which he is the author.

Article XIV: Right to work and to fair remuneration

Every person has the right to work, under proper conditions, and to follow his vocation freely, in so far as existing conditions of employment permit.

Every person who works has the right to receive such remuneration as will, in proportion to his capacity and skill, assure him a standard of living suitable for himself and for his family.

Article XV: Right to leisure time and to the use thereof

Every person has the right to leisure time, to wholesome recreation, and to the opportunity for advantageous use of his free time to his spiritual, cultural and physical benefit.

Article XVI: Right to social security

Every person has the right to social security which will protect him from the consequences of unemployment, old age, and disabilities arising from causes beyond his control that make it physically or mentally impossible for him to earn a living.

Article XVII: Right to recognition of juridical personality and of civil rights

Every person has the right to be recognised everywhere as a person having rights and obligations, and to enjoy the basic civil rights.

Article XVIII: Right to fair trial

Every person may resort to the courts to ensure respect for his legal rights. There should likewise be available to him a simple, brief procedure whereby the courts will protect him from acts of authority that, to his prejudice, violate any fundamental constitutional rights.

Article XIX: Right to nationality

Every person has the right to the nationality to which he is entitled by law and to change it, if he so wishes, for the nationality of any other country that is willing to grant it to him.

Article XX: Right to vote and to participate in government

Every person having legal capacity is entitled to participate in the government of his country, directly or through his representatives, and to take part in popular elections, which shall be by secret ballot, and shall be honest, periodic and free.

Article XXI: Right to assembly

Every person has the right to assemble peaceably with others in a formal public meeting or an informal gathering, in connection with matters of common interest of any nature.

Article XXII: Right to association

Every person has the right to associate with others to promote, exercise and protect his legitimate interests of a political, economic, religious, social, cultural, professional, labor union or other nature.

Article XXIII: Right to property

Every person has a right to own such private property as meets the essential needs of decent living and helps to maintain the dignity of the individual and of the home.

Article XXIV: Right of petition

Every person has the right to submit respectful petitions to any competent authority, for reasons of either general or private interest, and the right to obtain a prompt decision thereon.

Article XXV: Right of protection from arbitrary arrest

No person may be deprived of his liberty except in the cases and according to the procedures established by pre-existing law.

No person may be deprived of liberty for non-fulfilment of obligations of a purely civil character.

Every individual who has been deprived of his liberty has the right to have the legality of his detention ascertained without delay by a court, and the right to be tried without undue delay or, otherwise, to be released. He also has the right to humane treatment during the time he is in custody.

Article XXVI: Right to due process of law

Every accused person is presumed to be innocent until proven guilty.

Every person accused of an offence has the right to be given an impartial and public hearing, and to be tried by courts previously established in accordance with pre-existing laws, and not to receive cruel, infamous or unusual punishment.

Article XXVII: Right to asylum

Every person has the right, in case of pursuit not resulting from ordinary crimes, to seek and receive asylum in foreign territory, in accordance with the laws of each country and with international agreements.

Article XXVIII: Scope of the rights of man

The rights of man are limited by the rights of others, by the security of all, and by the just demands of the general welfare and the advancement of democracy.

CHAPTER TWO. DUTIES

Article XXIX: Duties to society

It is the duty of the individual so to conduct himself in relation to others that each and every one may fully form and develop his personality.

Article XXX: Duties toward children and parents

It is the duty of every person to aid, support, educate and protect his minor children, and it is the duty of children to honour their parents always and to aid, support and protect them when they need it.

Article XXXI: Duties to receive instruction

It is the duty of every person to acquire at least an elementary education.

Article XXXII: Duty to vote

It is the duty of every person to vote in the popular elections of the country of which he is a national, when he is legally capable of doing so.

Article XXXIII: Duty to obey the law

It is the duty of every person to obey the law and other legitimate commands of the authorities of his country and those of the country in which he may be.

Article XXXIV: Duty to serve the community and the nation

It is the duty of every able-bodied person to render whatever civil and military service his country may require for its defence and preservation, and in case of public disaster, to render such services as may be in his power.

It is likewise his duty to hold any public office to which he may be elected by popular vote in the state of which he is a national.

Article XXXV: Duties with respect to social security and welfare

It is the duty of every person to cooperate with the state and the community with respect to social security and welfare, in accordance with his ability and with existing circumstances.

Article XXXVI: Duty to pay taxes

It is the duty of every person to pay the taxes established by law for the support of public services.

Article XXXVII: Duty to work

It is the duty of every person to work, as far as his capacity and possibilities permit, in order to obtain the means of livelihood or to benefit his community.

Article XXXVIII: Duty to refrain from political activities in a foreign country

It is the duty of every person to refrain from taking part in political activities, that according to law, are reserved exclusively to the citizens of the state in which he is an alien.

20. AMERICAN CONVENTION ON HUMAN RIGHTS ("PACT OF SAN JOSÉ")

Signed at San José: 22 November 1969

OAS TS 36

Entry into force: 18 July 1978

PREAMBLE

The American States signatory to the present Convention,

Reaffirming their intention to consolidate in this hemisphere, within the framework of democratic institutions, a system of personal liberty and social justice based on respect for the essential rights of man;

Recognising that the essential rights of man are not derived from one's being a national of a certain state but are based upon attributes of the human personality, and that they therefore justify international protection in the form of a Convention reinforcing or complementing the protection provided by the domestic law of the American States;

Considering that these principles have been set forth in the Charter of the Organisation of American States, in the American Declaration of the Rights and Duties of Man, and in the Universal Declaration of Human Rights, and that they have been reaffirmed and refined in other international instruments, world-wide as well as regional in scope;

Reiterating that, in accordance with the Universal Declaration of Human Rights, the ideal of free men enjoying freedom from fear and want can be achieved only if conditions are created whereby everyone may enjoy his economic, social and cultural rights, as well as his civil and political rights; and

Considering that the Third Special Inter-American Conference (Buenos Aires, 1967) approved the incorporation into the Charter of the Organisation itself of broader standards with respect to economic, social and educational rights and resolved that an inter-American Convention on human rights should determine the structure, competence and procedure of the organs responsible for these matters; *Have agreed* upon the following:

PART I
STATE OBLIGATIONS AND RIGHTS PROTECTED

CHAPTER I
GENERAL OBLIGATIONS

Article 1: Obligation to respect rights

1. The States Parties to this Convention undertake to respect the rights and freedoms recognised herein and to ensure to all persons subject to their jurisdiction the free and full exercise of those rights and freedoms, without any discrimination for reasons of race, colour, sex, language, religion, political or other opinion, national or social origin, economic status, birth, or any other social condition.
2. For the purposes of this Convention, "person" means every human being.

Article 2: Domestic legal effects

Where the exercise of any of the rights or freedoms referred to in Article 1 is not already ensured by legislative or other provisions, the States Parties undertake to adopt, in accordance with their constitutional processes and the provisions of this Convention, such legislative or other measures as may be necessary to give effect to those rights or freedoms.

CHAPTER II
CIVIL AND POLITICAL RIGHTS

Article 3: Right to juridical personality

Every person has the right to recognition as a person before the law.

Article 4: Right to life

1. Every person has the right to have his life respected. This right shall be protected by law, and, in general, from the moment of conception. No one shall be arbitrarily deprived of his life.
2. In countries that have not abolished the death penalty, this may be imposed only for the most serious crimes and pursuant to a final judgment rendered by a competent court and in accordance with a law establishing such punishment, enacted prior to the commission of the crime. Its application shall not be extended to crimes to which it does not presently apply.
3. The death penalty shall not be re-established in states that have abolished it.
4. In no case shall capital punishment be inflicted for political offences or related common crimes.
5. Capital punishment shall not be imposed upon persons who, at the time the crime was committed, were under 18 years of age or over 70 years of age; nor shall it be applied to pregnant women.

6.   Every person condemned to death shall have the right to apply for amnesty, pardon, or commutation of sentence, which may be granted in all cases. Capital punishment shall not be imposed while such a petition is pending a decision by the competent authority.

Article 5: Freedom from torture

1.   Every person has the right to have his physical, mental and moral integrity respected.
2.   No one shall be subjected to torture or to cruel, inhuman or degrading punishment or treatment. All persons deprived of their liberty shall be treated with respect for the inherent dignity of the human person.
3.   Punishment shall not be extended to any person other than the criminal.
4.   Accused persons shall, save in exceptional circumstances, be segregated from convicted persons and shall be subject to separate treatment appropriate to their status as unconvicted persons.
5.   Minors while subject to criminal proceedings shall be separated from adults and brought before specialised tribunals, as speedily as possible, so that they may be treated in accordance with their status as minors.
6.   Punishments consisting of deprivation of liberty shall have as an essential aim the reform and social readaptation of the prisoners.

Article 6: Freedom from slavery

1.   No one shall be subject to slavery or to involuntary servitude, which are prohibited in all their forms, as are the slave trade and traffic in women.
2.   No one shall be required to perform forced or compulsory labour. This provision shall not be interpreted to mean that, in those countries in which the penalty established for certain crimes is deprivation of liberty at forced labour, the carrying out of such a sentence imposed by a competent court is prohibited. Forced labour shall not adversely affect the dignity or the physical or intellectual capacity of the prisoner.
3.   For the purposes of this article the following do not constitute forced or compulsory labour:

     a.   any work or service normally required of a person imprisoned in execution of a sentence or formal decision passed by the competent judicial authority. Such work or service shall be carried out under the supervision and control of public authorities, and any persons performing such work or service shall not be placed at the disposal of any private party, company, or juridical person;
     b.   any military service and, in countries in which conscientious objectors are recognised, any national service that the law may provide for in lieu of that service;
     c.   any service exacted in time of danger or calamity that threatens the existence or the well-being of the community; or
     d.   any work or service that forms part of normal civic obligations.

Article 7: Right to personal liberty

1. Every person has the right to personal liberty and security.
2. No one shall be deprived of his physical liberty except for the reasons and under the conditions established beforehand by the constitution of the State Party concerned or a law established pursuant thereto.
3. No one shall be subject to arbitrary arrest or imprisonment.
4. Anyone who is detained shall be informed of the reasons for his detention and shall be promptly notified of the charge or charges against him.
5. Any person detained shall be brought promptly before the judge or other officer authorised by law to exercise judicial power and shall be entitled to trial within a reasonable time or to be released without prejudice to continuation of the proceedings. His release may be subject to guarantees to assure his appearance for trial.
6. Anyone who is deprived of his liberty shall be entitled to recourse to a competent court, in order that the court may decide without delay on the lawfulness of his arrest or detention and order his release if the arrest or detention is unlawful. In States parties whose laws provide that anyone who believes himself to be threatened with deprivation of his liberty is entitled to recourse to a competent court in order that it may decide on the lawfulness of such threat, his remedy may not be restricted or abolished. The interested party or another person in his behalf is entitled to seek these remedies.
7. No one shall be detained for debt. This principle shall not limit the orders of a competent judicial authority issued for non-fulfilment of duties of support.

Article 8: Right to a fair trial

1. Every person shall have the right to a hearing with due guarantees and within a reasonable time, by a competent, independent and impartial tribunal, previously established by law, in the substantiation of any accusation of a criminal nature made against him or for the determination of his rights or obligations of a civil, labour, fiscal or any other nature.
2. Every person accused of a serious crime has the right to be presumed innocent so long as his guilt has not been proven according to law. During the proceedings, every person is entitled, with full equality, to the following minimum guarantees:

    a. the right of the accused to be assisted without charge by a translator or interpreter, if he does not understand or does not speak the language of the tribunal or court;
    b. prior notification in detail to the accused of the charges against him;
    c. adequate time and means for the preparation of his defence;
    d. the right of the accused to defend himself personally or to be assisted by legal counsel of his own choosing, and to communicate freely and privately with his counsel;
    e. the inalienable right to be assisted by counsel provided by the State, paid or not as the domestic law provides, if the accused does not defend

       himself personally or engage his own counsel within the time period established by law;

  f.   the right of the defence to examine witnesses present in the court and to obtain the appearance, as witnesses, of experts or other persons who may throw light on the facts;

  g.   the right not to be compelled to be a witness against himself or to plead guilty; and

  h.   the right to appeal the judgment to a higher court.

3.   A confession of guilt by the accused shall be valid only if it is made without coercion of any kind.

4.   An accused person, acquitted by a non-appealable judgment, shall not be subjected to a new trial for the same cause.

5.   Criminal procedure shall be public, except in so far as may be necessary to protect the interests of justice.

Article 9: Freedom from *ex post facto* laws

No one shall be convicted of any act or omission that did not constitute a criminal offence, under the applicable law, at the time it was committed. A heavier penalty shall not be imposed than the one that was applicable at the time the criminal offence was committed. If subsequent to the commission of the offence the law provides for the imposition of a lighter punishment, the guilty person shall benefit therefrom.

Article 10: Right to compensation

1.   Every person shall have the right to be compensated in accordance with the law in the event he has been sentenced by a final judgment through a miscarriage of justice.

Article 11: Right to privacy

1.   Everyone has the right to have his honour respected and his dignity recognised.

2.   No one may be the object of arbitrary or abusive interference with his private life, his family, his home, or his correspondence, or of unlawful attacks on his honour or reputation.

3.   Everyone has a right to the protection of the law against such interference or attacks.

Article 12: Freedom of conscience and religion

1.   Everyone has the right to freedom of conscience and of religion. This right includes freedom to maintain or to change one's religion or beliefs, and freedom to profess or disseminate one's religion or beliefs either individually or together with others, in public or in private.

2. No one shall be subject to restrictions that might impair his freedom to maintain or to change his religion or beliefs.
3. Freedom to manifest one's religion and beliefs may be subject only to the limitations prescribed by law that are necessary to protect public safety, order, health, or morals, or the rights or freedoms of others.
4. Parents or guardians, as the case may be, have the right to provide for religious and moral education of their children, or wards, that is in accord with their own convictions.

Article 13: Freedom of thought and expression

1. Everyone has the right to freedom of thought and expression. This right includes freedom to seek, receive, and impart information and ideas of all kinds, regardless of frontiers, either orally, in writing, in print, in the form of art, or through any other medium of one's choice.
2. The exercise of the right provided for in the foregoing paragraph shall not be subject to prior censorship but shall be subject to subsequent imposition of liability, which shall be expressly established by law and be necessary in order to ensure:

   a. respect for the rights or reputations of others, or
   b. the protection of national security, public order, or public health or morals.

3. The right of expression may not be restricted by indirect methods or means, such as the abuse of government or private controls over newsprint, radio broadcasting frequencies, or implements or equipment used in the dissemination of information, or by any other means tending to impede the communication and circulation of ideas and opinions.
4. Notwithstanding the provisions of paragraph 2 above, public entertainments may be subject by law to prior censorship, for the sole purpose of regulating access to them for the moral protection of childhood and adolescence.
5. Any propaganda for war and any advocacy of national, racial, or religious hatred that constitute incitements to lawless violence or any other similar illegal action against any person or group of persons on any grounds including those of race, colour, religion, language, or national origin shall be considered as offences punishable by law.

Article 14: Right of reply

1. Anyone injured by inaccurate or offensive statements or ideas disseminated to the public in general by a legally regulated medium of communication has the right to reply or make a correction using the same communication outlet, under such conditions as the law may establish.
2. The correction or reply shall not in any case remit other legal liabilities that may have been incurred.
3. For the effective protection of honour and reputation, every publication and every newspaper, motion picture, radio and television company shall have a person responsible, who is not protected by immunities or special privileges.

Article 15: Right of assembly

The right of peaceful assembly, without arms, in recognised. No restrictions may be placed on the exercise of this right other than those imposed in conformity with the law and necessary in a democratic society in the interests of national security or public safety or public order, or to protect public health or morals or the rights or freedoms of others.

Article 16: Freedom of association

1. Everyone has the right to associate freely for ideological, religious, political, economic, labour, social, cultural, sports or other purposes.
2. Exercise of this right shall be subject only to such restrictions established by law as may be necessary in a democratic society, in the interests of national security, public safety, or public order, or to protect public health or morals or the rights and freedoms of others.
3. The provisions of this article do not bar the imposition of legal restrictions, including even deprivation of the exercise of the right of association, on members of the armed forces and the police.

Article 17: Rights of the family

1. The family is the natural and fundamental group unit of society and is entitled to protection by society and the state.
2. The right of men and women of marriageable age to marry and to raise a family shall be recognised, if they meet the conditions required by domestic laws, in so far as such conditions do not affect the principle of non-discrimination established in this Convention.
3. No marriage shall be entered into without the free and full consent of the intending spouses.
4. The States Parties shall take appropriate steps to ensure the equality of rights and the adequate balancing of responsibilities of the spouses as to marriage, and in the event of its dissolution. In case of dissolution, provision shall be made for the necessary protection of any children solely on the basis of their best interests.
5. The law shall recognise equal rights for children born out of wedlock and those born in wedlock.

Article 18: Right to a name

Every person has the right to a given name and to the surnames of his parents or that of one of them. The law shall regulate the manner in which this right shall be ensured for all, by the use of assumed names if necessary.

Article 19: Rights of the child

Every minor child has the right to the measures of protection required by his condition as a minor, on the part of his family, society and the State.

Article 20: Right to nationality

1. Every person has the right to a nationality.
2. Every person has the right to the nationality of the State in which territory he was born if he does not have the right to any other nationality.
3. No one shall be arbitrarily deprived of his nationality or of the right to change it.

Article 21: Right to property

1. Everyone has the right to the use of and enjoyment of his property. The law may subordinate such use and enjoyment to the interest of society.
2. No one shall be deprived of his property except upon payment of just compensation, for reasons of public utility or social interest and in the cases and according to the forms established by law.
3. Usury and any other form of exploitation of man by man shall be prohibited by law.

Article 22: Freedom of movement and residence

1. Every person lawfully in the territory of a State party shall have the right to move about in it and to reside in it subject to the provisions of the law.
2. Every person has the right to leave the country freely, including his own.
3. The exercise of the foregoing rights may be restricted only pursuant to a law, to the extent indispensable in a democratic society in order to prevent crime or to protect national security, public safety, public order, public morals, public health, or the rights or freedoms of others.
4. The exercise of the rights recognised in paragraph 1 may also be restricted by law in designated zones for reasons of public interest.
5. No one can be expelled from the territory of the State of which he is a national or be deprived of the right to enter it.
6. An alien lawfully in the territory of a State Party to this Convention may be expelled from it only pursuant to a decision reached in accordance with law.
7. Every person has the right to seek and be granted asylum in a foreign territory, in accordance with the legislation of the State and international conventions, in the event he is being pursued for political or related common crimes.
8. In no case may an alien be deported or returned to a country, regardless of whether or not it is his country of origin, if in that country his right to life or personal freedom is in danger of being violated because of his race, nationality, religion, social status, or political opinions.
9. The collective expulsion of aliens is prohibited.

Article 23: Right to participate in Government

1. Every citizen shall enjoy the following rights and opportunities:

    a. to take part in the conduct of public affairs, directly or through freely chosen representatives;
    b. to vote and to be elected at genuine periodic elections, which shall be by universal and equal suffrage and by secret ballot that guarantees the free expression of the will of the voters; and
    c. to have access, under general conditions of equality, to the public service of his country.

2. The law may regulate the exercise of the rights and opportunities referred to in the preceding paragraph, exclusively on the basis of age, nationality, residence, language, education, civil and mental capacity and conviction by a competent judge in criminal proceedings.

Article 24: Right to equal protection

All persons are equal before the law. Consequently, they are entitled, without discrimination, to equal protection of the law.

Article 25: Right to judicial protection

1. Everyone has the right to simple and prompt recourse, or any other effective recourse, to a competent court of tribunal for protection against acts that violate his fundamental rights recognised by the Constitution or laws of a State or by this Convention, even though such violation may have been committed by persons acting in the course of their official duties.
2. The States Parties undertake:

    a. to ensure that any person claiming such remedy shall have his right thereto determined by the competent authority provided for by the legal system of the State;
    b. to develop the possibilities of judicial remedy, and
    c. to ensure that the competent authorities shall enforce such remedies when granted.

CHAPTER III
ECONOMIC, SOCIAL AND CULTURAL RIGHTS

Article 26: Progressive development

The States Parties undertake to adopt measures, both internally and through international co-operation, especially those of an economic and technical nature, with a view to achieving progressively by legislation or other appropriate means, the full realisation of the rights implicit in the economic, social, educational, scientific and cultural standards set forth in the Charter of the Organisation of American States as amended by the Protocol of Buenos Aires.

CHAPTER IV
SUSPENSION OF GUARANTEES, INTERPRETATION AND APPLICATION

Article 27: Suspension of guarantees

1. In time of war, public danger, or other emergency that threatens the independence or security of a State Party, it may take measures derogating from its obligations under the present Convention to the extent and for the period of time strictly required by the exigencies of the situation, provided that such measures are not inconsistent with its other obligations under international law and do not involve discrimination on the ground of race, colour, sex, language, religion or social origin.
2. The foregoing provision does not authorise any suspension of the following Articles: Article 3 (Right to juridical personality); Article 4 (Right to life); Article 5 (Right to humane treatment); Article 6 (Freedom from slavery); Article 9 (Freedom from ex post facto laws); Article 12 (Freedom of conscience and religion); Article 17 (Rights of the family); Article 18 (Right to a name); Article 19 (Rights of the Child); Article 20 (Right to nationality); and Article 23 (Right to participate in Government), or of the judicial guarantees essential for the protection of such rights.
3. Any State Party availing itself of the right of suspension shall immediately inform the other States Parties, through the Secretary General of the Organisation of American States, of the provision the application of which it has suspended, the reasons that gave rise to the suspension and the date set for the determination of such suspension.

Article 28: Federal Clause

Where a State Party is constituted as a federal State, the national government of such State Party shall implement all the provisions of the Convention over whose subject matter it exercises legislative and judicial jurisdiction.

With respect to the provisions over whose subject matter the constituent units of the federal State have jurisdiction, the national government shall immediately take suitable measures, in accordance with its constitution and its laws, to the end that the competent authorities of the constituent units may adopt appropriate provisions for the fulfilment of this Convention.

Whenever two or more States Parties agree to form a federation or other type of association they shall take care that the resulting federal or other compact contains the provisions necessary for continuing and rendering effective the standards of this Convention in the new State that is organised.

Article 29: Restrictions regarding interpretation

No provision of this Convention shall be interpreted as:

a. permitting any State Party, group or person to suppress the enjoyment or exercise of the rights and freedoms recognised in this Convention or to restrict them to a greater extent than is provided for herein;

b.   restricting the enjoyment or exercise of any right or freedom recognised by virtue of the laws of any State Party or by virtue of another Convention to which one of the said States is a party;

c.   precluding other rights or guarantees that are inherent in the human personality or derived from representative democracy as a form of government; or

d.   excluding or limiting the effect that the American Declaration of the Rights and Duties of Man and other international acts of the same nature may have.

Article 30: Scope of restrictions

The restrictions that, pursuant to this Convention, may be placed on the enjoyment or exercise of the rights or freedoms recognised herein may not be applied except in accordance with laws enacted for reasons of general interest and for the purpose of which the restrictions have been established.

Article 31: Recognition of other rights

Other rights and freedoms recognised by virtue of the procedures established in Articles 76 and 77 may be included in the system of protection of this Convention.

CHAPTER V
PERSONAL RESPONSIBILITIES

Article 32: Relations between duties and rights

1.   Every person has responsibilities to his family, his community, and mankind.
2.   The rights of each person are limited by the rights of others, by the security of all, and by the just demands of the general welfare, in a democratic society.

PART II
MEANS OF PROTECTION

CHAPTER VI
COMPETENT ORGANS

Article 33

The following organs shall be competent to hear matters relating to the fulfilment of the commitments made by the States Parties to this Convention.

a.   the Inter-American Commission on Human Rights, referred to as "The Commission"; and

b.   the Inter-American Court of Human Rights, referred to as "The Court".

CHAPTER VII
INTER-AMERICAN COMMISSION ON HUMAN RIGHTS

Section 1. Organisation

Article 34

The Inter-American Commission on Human Rights shall be composed of seven members, who shall be persons of high moral character and recognised competence in the field of human rights.

Article 35

The Commission shall represent all the member countries of the Organisation of American States.

Article 36

1. The members of the Commission shall be elected in a personal capacity by the General Assembly of the Organisation from a list of candidates proposed by the governments of the member States.
2. Each of those governments may propose up to three candidates, who may be nationals of the States proposing them or of any other member States of the Organisation of American States. When a slate of three is proposed, at least one of the candidates shall be a national of a State other than the one proposing the slate.

Article 37

1. The members of the Commission shall be elected for a term of four years and may be re-elected only once, but the terms of three of the members chosen in the first election shall expire at the end of two years. Immediately following that election the General Assembly shall determine the names of those three members by lot.
2. No two nationals of the same State may be members of the Commission.

Article 38

Vacancies that may occur on the Commission for reasons other than the normal expiration of a term shall be filled by the Permanent Council of the Organisation in accordance with the provisions of the Statute of the Commission.

Article 39

The Commission shall prepare its Statute, which shall be submitted to the General Assembly for approval, and it shall also establish its own Regulations.

231

Article 40

Secretariat services for the Commission shall be furnished by the appropriate specialised unit of the General Secretariat of the organisation. This unit shall be provided with the resources required to accomplish the tasks assigned to it by the Commission.

Section 2. Functions

Article 41

The main functions of the Commission shall be to promote respect for and defence of human rights. In the exercise of its mandate, it shall have the following functions and powers:

  a. to develop an awareness of human rights among the people of America;
  b. to make recommendations to the governments of the member States, when it considers such action advisable, for the adoption of progressive measures in favour of human rights within the framework of their domestic law and constitutional provisions as well as appropriate measures to further the observance of those rights;
  c. to prepare such studies or reports as it considers advisable in the performance of its duties;
  d. to request the governments of the member States to supply it with information on the measures adopted by them in matters of human rights;
  e. to respond, through the General Secretariat of the Organisation of American States, to inquiries made by the member States on matters related to human rights and, within the limits of its possibilities, to provide those States with the advisory services they request;
  f. to take action on petitions and other communications pursuant to its authority, in accordance with the provisions of Article 44 through 51 of this Convention, and
  g. to submit an annual report to the General Assembly of the Organisation of American States.

Article 42

The States Parties shall transmit to the Commission a copy of each of the reports and studies that they submit annually to the Executive Committees of the Inter-American Economic and Social Council and the Inter-American Council for Education, Science and Culture, in their respective fields, so that the Commission may watch over the promotion of the rights implicit in the economic, social, educational, scientific and cultural standards set forth in the Charter of the Organisation of American States as amended by the Protocol of Buenos Aires.

Article 43

The States Parties undertake to provide the Commission with such information as it may request of them as to the manner in which their domestic law ensures the effective application of any provisions of this Convention.

Section 3. Competence

Article 44

Any person or group of persons, or any non-governmental entity legally recognised in one or more member States of the Organisation, may lodge petitions with the Commission containing denunciations or complaints of violation of this Convention by a State Party.

Article 45

1. Any State Party may, when it deposits its instrument of ratification or of adherence to this Convention, or at any later time, declare that it recognises the competence of the Commission to receive, and examine communications in which a State Party alleges that another State Party has committed a violation of a human right set forth in this Convention.
2. Communications presented by virtue of this article may be admitted and examined only if they are presented by a State Party that has made a declaration recognising the aforementioned competence of the Commission. The Commission shall not admit any communication against a State Party that has not made such a declaration.
3. A declaration concerning recognition of competence may be made to be valid for an indefinite time, for a specific period or for a specific case.
4. The declarations shall be deposited in the General Secretariat of the Organisation of American States, which shall transmit copies thereof to member States of that Organisation.

Article 46

1. Admission by the Commission of a petition or communication lodged in accordance with Articles 44 and 45 shall be subject to the following requirements:

    a. that the remedies of domestic law have been pursued and exhausted, in accordance with generally recognised principles of international law;
    b. that the petition is lodged within a period of six months from the date on which the party alleging violation of his rights was notified of the final decision;
    c. that the subject of the petition or communications is not pending before another international procedure for settlement; and
    d. that, in the case of Article 44, the petition contains the name, nationality,

profession, domicile and signature of the person or persons or of the legal representative of the entity lodging the petition.

2. The provisions of paragraphs 1.a and 1.b of this article shall not be applicable when:

   a. the domestic legislation of the state concerned does not afford due process of law for the protection of the right or rights that have allegedly been violated;
   b. the party alleging violation of his right has been denied access to the remedies of domestic jurisdiction or has been prevented from exhausting them; or
   c. there has been unwarranted delay in rendering a final judgment under the aforementioned remedies.

Article 47

The Commission shall consider inadmissible any petition or communication submitted under Articles 44 or 45 if:

   a. any of the requirements indicated in Article 46 has not been met;
   b. the petition or communication does not state facts that tend to establish a violation of the rights guaranteed by this Convention;
   c. the statements of the petitioner or the State indicate that the petition or communication is manifestly groundless or obviously out of order; or
   d. the petition or communication is substantially the same as one previously studied by the Commission or another international Organisation.

Section 4. Procedure

Article 48

1. When the Commission receives a petition or communication alleging violation of any of the rights protected by this Convention, is shall proceed as follows:

   a. If it considers the petition or communication admissible, it shall request information from the government of the State which has been indicated as being the authority responsible for the alleged violations and shall furnish that government a transcript of the pertinent portions of the petition or communication. This information shall be submitted within a reasonable period to be determined by the Commission in accordance with the circumstances of each case.
   b. After the information has been received, or after the period established has elapsed and the information has not been received, the Commission shall ascertain whether the grounds for the petition or communication still exist. If they do not, the Commission shall order the record to be closed.
   c. The Commission may also declare the petition or communication inadmissible or out of order on the basis of information or evidence subsequently received.

d. If the record has not been closed, the Commission shall, with the knowledge of the parties, examine the matter set forth in the petition or communication in order to verify the fact. If necessary and advisable, the Commission shall conduct an investigation, for the effective conduct of which it shall request, and the interested States shall furnish to it, all necessary facilities.

e. The Commission may request the State concerned to furnish any pertinent information and, if so requested, shall hear oral statements or receive written statements from the parties concerned.

f. The Commission shall place itself at the disposal of the parties concerned with a view to reaching a friendly settlement of the matter on the basis of respect for the human rights recognised in this Convention.

2. However, in serious and urgent cases, only the presentation of a petition or communication that fulfils all the formal requirements of admissibility shall be necessary in order for the Commission to conduct an investigation with the prior consent of the State in whose territory a violation has allegedly been committed.

Article 49

If a friendly settlement has been reached in accordance with paragraph 1.f of Article 48, the Commission shall draw up a report, which shall be transmitted to the petitioner and to the States Parties to this Convention and then communicated to the Secretary General of the Organisation of American States for publication. This report shall contain a brief statement of the facts and of the solution reached. If any party in the case so requests, the fullest possible information shall be provided to it.

Article 50

1. If a settlement is not reached, the Commission shall, within the time limit established by its Statute, draw up a report setting forth the facts and stating its conclusions. If the report, in whole or in part, does not represent the unanimous agreement of the members of the Commission, any member may attach to it a separate opinion. The written and oral statements made by the parties in accordance with paragraph 1.e of Article 48 shall also be attached to the report.

2. The report shall be transmitted to the States concerned, which shall not be at liberty to publish it.

3. In transmitting the report, the Commission may make such proposals and recommendations as it sees fit.

Article 51

1. If, within a period of three months from the date of the transmittal of the report of the Commission to the States concerned, the matter has not either

been settled or submitted by the Commission or by the State concerned to the Court and its jurisdiction accepted, the Commission may, by the vote of an absolute majority of its members, set forth its opinion and conclusions concerning the question submitted for its consideration.

2. Where appropriate, the Commission shall make pertinent recommendations and shall prescribe a period within which the state is to take the measures that are incumbent upon it to remedy the situation examined.

3. When the prescribed period has expired, the Commission shall decide by the vote of an absolute majority of its members whether the State has taken adequate measures and whether to publish its report.

CHAPTER VIII
INTER-AMERICAN COURT OF HUMAN RIGHTS

Section 1. Organisation

Article 52

1. The Court shall consist of seven judges, nationals of the member States of the Organisation, elected in an individual capacity from among jurists of the highest moral authority and of recognised competence in the field of human rights, who possess the qualifications required for the exercise of the highest judicial functions in conformity with the law of the State of which they are nationals or of the State that proposes them as candidates.

2. No two judges may be nationals of the same State.

Article 53

1. The judges of the Court shall be elected by secret ballot by an absolute majority vote of the States Parties to the Convention in General Assembly of the Organisation, from a panel of candidates proposed by those States.

2. Each of the States Parties may propose up to three candidates, nationals of the State that proposes them or of any other member State of the Organisation of American States. When a slate of three is proposed, at least one of the candidates shall be a national of a State other than the one proposing the slate.

Article 54

1. The judges of the Court shall be elected for a term of six years and may be re-elected only once. The term of three of the judges chosen in the first election shall expire at the end of three years. Immediately after the election, the names of the three judges shall be determined by lot in the General Assembly.

2. A judge elected to replace a judge whose term has not expired shall complete the term of the latter.

3. The judges shall continue in office until the expiration of their term. However, they shall continue to serve with regard to cases that they have begun to hear

and that are still pending, for which purposes they shall not be replaced by the newly-elected judges.

Article 55

1. If a judge is a national of any of the States Parties to a case submitted to the Court, he shall retain his right to hear that case.
2. If one of the judges called upon to hear a case should be a national of one of the States Parties in the case, any other State party in the case may appoint a person of its choice to serve on the Court as an *ad hoc* judge.
3. If among the judges called upon to hear a case none is a national of any of the States Parties to the case, each of the latter may appoint an *ad hoc* judge.
4. An *ad hoc* judge shall possess the qualifications indicated in Article 52.
5. If several States parties to the Convention should have the same interest in a case, they shall be considered as a single party for purposes of the above provisions. In case of doubt, the Court shall decide.

Article 56

Five judges shall constitute a quorum for the transaction of business by the Court.

Article 57

The Commission shall appear at all cases before the Court.

Article 58

1. The Court shall have its seat at the place determined by the States Parties to the Convention in the General Assembly of the Organisation; however, it may convene in the territory of any member State of the Organisation of American States when a majority of the Court considers it desirable, and with the prior consent of the States concerned. The seat of the Court may be changed by the States Parties to the Convention in the General Assembly, by a two-thirds vote.
2. The Court shall appoint its own Secretary.
3. The Secretary shall have his office at the place where the Court has its seat and shall attend the meetings that the Court may hold away from its seat.

Article 59

The Court shall establish its own secretariat, which shall function under the direction of the Secretary of the Court, in accordance with the administrative standards of the General Secretariat of the Organisation in all matters not incompatible with the independence of the Court. The staff of the Court's Secretariat shall be appointed by the Secretary General of the Organisation, in consultation with the Secretary of the Court.

Article 60

The Court shall draw up its statute and it shall submit it to the General Assembly for approval. It shall adopt its own Rules of Procedure.

Section 2. Jurisdiction and functions

Article 61

1. Only the States Parties and the Commission shall have the right to submit a case to the Court.
2. In order for the Court to hear a case, it is necessary that the procedures set forth in Articles 48 to 50 shall have been exhausted.

Article 62

1. A State Party may, upon depositing its instrument of ratification or accession to this Convention, or at any subsequent time, declare that it recognises as binding, ipso facto, and not requiring special agreement, the jurisdiction of the Court on all matters relating to the interpretation or application of this Convention.
2. Such declaration may be made unconditionally, or on the condition of reciprocity, for a specified period, or for specific cases. It shall be presented to the Secretary General of the Organisation who shall transmit copies thereof to the other member States of the Organisation and to the Secretary of the Court.
3. The jurisdiction of the Court shall comprise all cases concerning the interpretation and application of the provisions of this Convention that are submitted to it, provided that the States Parties to the case recognise or have recognised such jurisdiction, whether by special declaration pursuant to the preceding paragraphs, or by a special agreement.

Article 63

1. If the Court finds that there has been a violation of a right or freedom protected by this Convention, the Court shall rule that the injured party be ensured the enjoyment of his right or freedom that was violated. It shall also rule, if appropriate, that the consequences of the measure or situation that constituted the breach of such right or freedom be remedied and that fair compensation be paid to the injured party.
2. In cases of extreme gravity and urgency, and when necessary to avoid irreparable damage to persons, the Court shall adopt such provisional measures as it deems pertinent in the matters it has under consideration. With respect to a case not yet submitted to the Court, it may act at the request of the Commission.

Article 64

The member States of the Organisation may consult the Court regarding the interpretation of this Convention or of other treaties concerning the protection of human rights in the American States. Within their spheres of competence, the organs listed in Chapter X of the Charter of the Organisation of American States, as amended by the Protocol of Buenos Aires, may in like manner consult the Court.

The Court, at the request of a member State of the Organisation, may provide that State with opinions regarding the compatibility of any of its domestic laws and the aforesaid international instruments.

Article 65

To each regular session of the General Assembly of the Organisation of American States the Court shall submit, for the Assembly's consideration, a report on its work during the previous year. It shall specify, in particular, the cases in which a State has not complied with its judgments and make any pertinent recommendations.

Article 66

1. Reasons shall be given for the judgment of the Court.
2. If the judgment does not represent in whole or in part the unanimous opinion of the judges, any judge shall be entitled to have his dissenting or separate opinion attached to the judgment.

Article 67

The judgment of the Court shall be final and not subject to appeal. In case of disagreement as to the meaning or scope of the judgment, the Court shall interpret it at the request of any of the parties, provided the request is made within ninety days from the date of notification of the judgment.

Article 68

1. The States Parties to the Convention undertake to comply with the judgment of the Court in any case to which they are parties.
2. That part of a judgment that stipulates compensatory damages may be executed in the country concerned in accordance with the domestic procedure governing the execution of judgments against the State.

Article 69

The parties to the case shall be notified of the judgment of the Court and it shall be transmitted to the States Parties to the Convention.

CHAPTER IX
COMMON PROVISIONS

Article 70

The judges of the Court and the members of the Commission shall enjoy, from the moment of their election and throughout their term of office, the immunities extended to diplomatic agents in accordance with international law. During the exercise of their official function they shall, in addition, enjoy the diplomatic privileges necessary for the performance of their duties.

At no time shall the judges of the Court or the members of the Commission be held liable for any decisions or opinions issued in the exercise of their functions.

Article 71

The position of judge of the Court or member of the Commission is incompatible with any other activity that might affect the independence or impartiality of a judge or member, as determined in the respective statutes.

Article 72

The judges of the Court and the members of the Commission shall receive emoluments and travel allowances in the form and under the conditions set forth in their statutes, with due regard for the importance and independence of their office. Such emoluments and travel allowances shall be determined in the budget of the Organisation of American States, which shall also include the expenses of the Court and its secretariat. To this end, the Court shall draw up its own budget and submit it to the General Assembly through the General Secretariat. The latter may not introduce any changes in it.

Article 73

The General Assembly may, only at the request of the Commission or the Court, as the case may be, determine sanctions to be applied against members of the Commission or judges of the Court when there are justifiable grounds for such action as set forth in the respective statutes. A vote of a two-thirds majority of the member States of the Organisation shall be required for a decision in the case of members of the Commission and, in the case of judges of the Court, a two-thirds majority vote of the States Parties to the Convention shall also be required.

PART III
GENERAL AND TRANSITORY PROVISIONS

CHAPTER X
SIGNATURE, RATIFICATION, RESERVATIONS, AMENDMENTS, PROTOCOLS AND
DENUNCIATION

Article 74

1. This Convention shall be open for signature and ratification by or adherence of any member State of the Organisation of American States.
2. Ratification of or adherence to this Convention shall be made by the deposit of an instrument of ratification or adherence with the General Secretariat of the Organisation of American States. As soon as eleven States have deposited their instruments of ratification or adherence, the Convention shall enter into force. With respect to any State that ratifies or adheres thereafter, the Convention shall enter into force on the date of the deposit of its instrument of ratification or adherence.
3. The Secretary General shall inform all member States of the Organisation of the entry into force of the Convention.

Article 75

This Convention shall be subject to reservations only in conformity with the provisions of the Vienna Convention on the Law of Treaties signed on May 23, 1969.

Article 76

1. Proposals to amend this Convention may be submitted by the General Assembly for the action it deems appropriate by any State party directly, and by the Commission or the Court through the Secretary General.
2. Amendments shall enter into force for the States ratifying them on the date when two-thirds of the States parties to this Convention have deposited their respective instruments of ratification. With respect to the other States Parties, the amendments shall enter into force on the dates on which they deposit their respective instruments of ratification.

Article 77

1. In accordance with Article 31, any State Party and the Commission may submit proposed Protocols to this Convention for consideration by the States Parties at the General Assembly with a view to gradually including other rights and freedoms within its system of protection.
2. Each Protocol shall determine the manner of its entry into force and shall be applied only among the States Parties to it.

Article 78

1. The States Parties may denounce this Convention at the expiration of a five-year period starting from the date of its entry into force and by means of notice given one year in advance. Notice of the denunciation shall be addressed to the Secretary General of the Organisation of American States, who shall inform the other States Parties.
2. Such a denunciation shall not have the effect of releasing the State Party concerned from the obligations contained in this Convention with respect to any act that may constitute a violation of those obligations and that has been taken by that State prior to the effective date of denunciation.

CHAPTER XI
TRANSITORY PROVISIONS

Section 1. Inter-American Commission on Human Rights

Article 79

Upon the entry into force of this Convention, the Secretary General shall, in writing, request each member State of the Organisation to present, within ninety days, its candidates for membership on the Inter-American Commission on Human Rights. The Secretary General shall prepare a list in alphabetical order of the candidates presented, and transmit it to the member States of the Organisation at least thirty days prior to the next session of the General Assembly.

Article 80

The members of the Commission shall be elected by secret ballot of the General Assembly from the list of candidates referred to in Article 79. The candidates who obtain the largest number of votes and an absolute majority of the votes of the representatives of the member States shall be declared elected. Should it become necessary to have several ballots in order to elect all the members of the Commission, the candidates who receive the smallest number of votes shall be eliminated successively, in the manner determined by the General Assembly.

Section 2. Inter-American Court of Human Rights

Article 81

Upon the entry into force of this Convention, the Secretary General shall, in writing, request each State Party to present, within ninety days, its candidates for membership on the Inter-American Court of Human Rights. The Secretary General shall prepare a list in alphabetical order of the candidates presented and transmit it to the States Parties at least thirty days prior to the next session of the General Assembly.

Article 82

The judges of the Court shall be elected from the list of candidates referred to in Article 81, by secret ballot of the States Parties to the Convention in the General Assembly. The candidates who obtain the largest number of votes and an absolute majority of the votes of the representatives of the States Parties shall be declared elected. Should it become necessary to have several ballots in order to elect all the judges of the Court the candidates who receive the smallest number of votes shall be eliminated successively, in the manner determined by the States Parties.

21. ADDITIONAL PROTOCOL TO THE AMERICAN CONVENTION ON HUMAN RIGHTS IN THE AREA OF ECONOMIC, SOCIAL AND CULTURAL RIGHTS ("PROTOCOL OF SAN SALVADOR")

Signed at San Salvador: 17 November 1988

OAS TS 69

Not in force

PREAMBLE

The States Parties to the American Convention on Human Rights "Pact of San José, Costa Rica",

Reaffirming their intention to consolidate in this hemisphere, within the framework of democratic institutions, a system of personal liberty and social justice based on respect for the essential rights of man;

Recognizing that the essential rights of man are not derived from one's being a national of a certain State, but are based upon attributes of the human person, for which reason they merit international protection in the form of a convention reinforcing or complementing the protection provided by the domestic law of the American States;

Considering the close relationship that exists between economic, social and cultural rights, and civil and political rights, in that the different categories of rights constitute an indivisible whole based on the recognition of the dignity of the human person, for which reason both require permanent protection and promotion if they are to be fully realized, and the violation of some rights in favor of the realization of others can never be justified;

Recognizing the benefits that stem from the promotion and development of cooperation among states and international relations;

Recalling that, in accordance with the Universal Declaration of Human Rights and the American Convention on Human Rights, the ideal of free human beings enjoying freedom from fear and want can only be achieved if conditions are created whereby everyone may enjoy his economic, social and cultural rights as well as his civil and political rights;

Bearing in mind that, although fundamental economic, social and cultural rights have been recognized in earlier international instruments of both world and regional scope, it is essential that those right be reaffirmed, developed, perfected and protected in order to consolidate in America, on the basis of full respect for the rights of the individual, and democratic representative form of government as well as the right of its peoples to develop, self-determination, and the free disposal of their wealth and natural resources; and

Considering that the American Convention on Human Rights provides that draft additional protocols to that Convention may be submitted for consideration to the Stated Parties, meeting together on the occasion of the General Assembly of the Organization of American States, for the purpose of gradually incorporating other rights and freedoms into the protective system thereof;

Have agreed upon the following Additional Protocol to the American Convention on Human Rights "Protocol of San Salvador":

Article 1: Obligation to adopt measures

The States Parties to this Additional Protocol to the American Convention on Human Rights undertake to adopt the necessary measures, both domestically and through cooperation among the States, especially economic and technical, to the extent allowed by their available resources, and taking into account their degree of development, for the purpose of achieving progressively and pursuant to their internal legislations, the full observance of the rights recognized in this Protocol.

Article 2: Obligation to enact domestic legislation

If the exercise of the rights set forth in this Protocol is not already guaranteed by legislative or other provisions, the States Parties undertake to adopt, in accordance with their constitutional processes and the provisions of this Protocol, such legislative or other measures as may be necessary for making those rights a reality.

Article 3: Obligation of nondiscrimination

The States Parties to this Protocol undertake to guarantee the exercise of the rights set forth herein without discrimination of any kind for reasons related to race, color, sex, language, religion, political or other opinions, national or social origin, economic status, birth or any other social condition.

Article 4: Inadmissibility of restrictions

A right which is recognized or in effect in a State by virtue of its internal legislation or international conventions may not be restricted or curtailed on the pretext that this Protocol does not recognize the right or recognizes it to a lesser degree.

Article 5: Scope of restrictions and limitations

The States Parties may establish restrictions and limitations on the enjoyment and exercise of the rights established herein by means of laws promulgated for the purpose of preserving the general welfare in a democratic society only to the extent that they are not incompatible with the purpose and reason underlying those rights.

Article 6: Right to work

1. Everyone has the right to work, which includes the opportunity to secure the means for living a dignified and decent existence by performing a freely elected or accepted lawful activity.
2. The States Parties undertake to adopt measures that will make the right to work fully effective, especially with regard to the achievement of full employment, vocational guidance, and the development of technical and vocational training projects, in particular those directed to the disabled. The States Parties also undertake to implement and strengthen programs that help to ensure suitable family care, so that women may enjoy a real opportunity to exercise the right to work.

Article 7: Just, equitable and satisfactory conditions of work

The States Parties to this Protocol recognize that the right to work to which the foregoing article refers presupposes that everyone shall enjoy that right under just, equitable and satisfactory conditions, which the States Parties undertake to guarantee in their internal legislation, particularly with respect to:

    a.   Remuneration which guarantees, as a minimum, to all workers dignified and decent living conditions for them and their families and fair and equal wages for equal work, without distinction;

    b.   The right of every worker to follow his vocation and to devote himself to the activity that best fulfills his expectations and to change employment in accordance with the pertinent national regulations;

    c.   The right of every worker to promotion or upward mobility in his employment, for which purpose account shall be taken of his qualifications, competence, integrity and seniority;

    d.   Stability of employment, subject to the nature of each industry and occupation and the causes for just separation. In cases of unjustified dismissal, the worker shall have the right to indemnity or to reinstatement on the job or any other benefits provided by domestic legislation;

    e.   Safety and hygiene at work;

    f.   The prohibition of night work or unhealthy or dangerous working conditions and, in general, of all work which jeopardizes health, safety or morals, for persons under 18 years of age. As regards minors under the age of 16, the work day shall be subordinated to the provisions regarding compulsory education and in no case shall work constitute an impediment to school attendance or a limitation on benefiting from education received;

    g.   A reasonable limitation of working hours, both daily and weekly. The days shall be shorter in the case of dangerous or unhealthy work or of night work;

    h.   Rest, leisure and paid vacations as well as remuneration for national holidays.

Article 8: Trade union rights

1. The States Parties shall ensure:

    a. The right of workers to organize trade unions and to join the union of their choice for the purpose of protecting and promoting their interests. As an extension of that right, the States Parties shall permit trade unions to establish national federations or confederations, or to affiliate with those that already exist, as well as to form international trade union organizations and to affiliate with that of their choice. The States Parties shall also permit trade unions, federations and confederations to function freely;
    b. The right to strike.

2. The exercise of the rights set forth above may be subject only to restrictions established by law, provided that such restrictions are characteristic of a democratic society and necessary for safeguarding public order or for protecting public health or morals or the rights and freedoms of others. Members of the armed forces and the police and of other essential public services shall be subject to limitations and restrictions established by law.
3. No one may be compelled to belong to a trade union.

Article 9: Right to social security

1. Everyone shall have the right to social security protecting him from the consequences of old age and of disability which prevents him, physically or mentally, from securing the means for a dignified and decent existence. In the event of the death of a beneficiary, social security benefits shall be applied to his dependents.
2. In the case of persons who are employed, the right to social security shall cover at least medical care and an allowance or retirement benefit in the case of work accidents or occupational disease and, in the case of women, paid maternity leave before and after childbirth.

Article 10: Right to health

1. Everyone shall have the right to health, understood to mean the enjoyment of the highest level of physical, mental and social well-being.
2. In order to ensure the exercise of the right to health, the States Parties agree to recognize health as a public good, and particularly, to adopt the following measures to ensure that right:

    a. Primary health care, that is, essential health care made available to all individuals and families of the community;
    b. Extension of the benefits of health services to all individuals subject to the State's jurisdiction;
    c. Universal immunization against the principal infectious diseases;
    d. Prevention and treatment of endemic, occupational and other diseases;
    e. Education of the population on the prevention and treatment of health problems; and

f.   Satisfaction of the health needs of the highest risk groups and of those whose poverty makes them the most vulnerable.

Article 11: Right to a healthy environment

1.   Everyone shall have the right to live in a healthy environment and to have access to basic public services.
2.   The States Parties shall promote the protection, preservation and improvement of the environment.

Article 12: Right to food

1.   Everyone has the right to adequate nutrition which guarantees the possibility of enjoying the highest level of physical, emotional and intellectual development.
2.   In order to promote the exercise of this right and eradicate malnutrition, the States Parties undertake to improve methods of production, supply and distribution of food, and to this end, agree to promote greater international cooperation in support of the relevant national policies.

Article 13: Right to education

1.   Everyone has the right to education.
2.   The States Parties to this Protocol agree that education should be directed towards the full development of the human personality and human dignity and should strengthen respect for human rights, ideological pluralism, fundamental freedoms, justice and peace. They further agree that education ought to enable everyone to participate effectively in a democratic and pluralistic society and achieve a decent existence and should foster understanding, tolerance and friendship among all nations and all racial, ethnic or religious groups and promote activities for the maintenance of peace.
3.   The States Parties to this Protocol recognize that in order to achieve the full exercise of the right of education:

   a.   Primary education should be compulsory and accessible to all without cost;
   b.   Secondary education in its different forms, including technical and vocational secondary education, should be made generally available and accessible to all by every appropriate means, and in particular, by the progressive introduction of free education;
   c.   Higher education should be made equally accessible to all on the basis of individual capacity, by every appropriate means, and in particular, by the progressive introduction of free education;
   d.   Basic education should be encouraged or intensified as far as possible for those persons who have not received or completed the whole cycle of primary instruction;
   e.   Programs of special education should be established for the handicapped,

so as to provide special instruction and training to persons with physical disabilities or mental deficiencies.

4. In conformity with the domestic legislation of the States Parties, parents should have the right to select the type of education to be given to their children, provided that it conforms to the principles set forth above.
5. Nothing is this Protocol shall be interpreted as a restriction of the freedom of individuals and entities to establish and direct educational institutions in accordance with the domestic legislation of the States Parties.

Article 14: Right to the benefits of culture

1. The States Parties to this Protocol recognize the right of everyone:

    a. To take part in the cultural and artistic life of the community;
    b. To enjoy the benefits of scientific and technological progress;
    c. To benefit from the protection of moral and material interests deriving from any scientific, literary or artistic production of which he is the author.

2. The steps to be taken by the States Parties to this Protocol to ensure the full exercise of this right shall include those necessary for the conservation, development and dissemination of science, culture and art.
3. The States Parties to this Protocol undertake to respect the freedom indispensable for scientific research and creative activity.
4. The States Parties to this Protocol recognize the benefits to be derived from the encouragement and development of international cooperation and relations in the fields of science, arts and culture, and accordingly agree to foster greater international cooperation in these fields.

Article 15: Right to the formation and the protection of families

1. The family is the natural and fundamental element of society and ought to be protected by the State, which should see to the improvement of its spiritual and material conditions.
2. Everyone has the right to form a family, which shall be exercised in accordance with the provisions of the pertinent domestic legislation.
3. The States Parties hereby undertake to accord adequate protection to the family unit and in particular:

    a. To provide special care and assistance to mothers during a reasonabale period before and after childbirth;
    b. To guarantee adequate nutrition for children at the nursing stage and during school attendance years;
    c. To adopt special measures for the protection of adolescents in order to ensure the full development of their physical, intellectual and moral capacities;
    d. To undertake special programs of family training so as to help create a stable and positive environment in which children will receive and

develop the values of understanding, solidarity, respect and responsibility.

Article 16: Rights of children

Every child, whatever his parentage, has the right to the protection that his status as a minor requires from his family, society and the State. Every child has the right to grow under the protection and responsibility of his parents; save in exceptional, judicially-recognized circumstances, a child of young age ought not to be separated from his mother. Every child has the right to free and compulsory education, at least in the elementary phase, and to continue his training at higher levels of the educational system.

Article 17: Protection of the elderly

Everyone has the right to special protection in old age. With this in view, the States Parties agree to take progressively the necessary steps to make his right a reality and, particularly, to:

   a.   Provide suitable facilities, as well as food and specialized medical care, for elderly individuals who lack them and are unable to provide them for themselves;
   b.   Undertake work programs specifically designed to give the elderly the opportunity to engage in a productive activity suited to their abilities and consistent with their vocations or desires;
   c.   Foster the establishment of social organizations aimed at improving the quality of life for the elderly.

Article 18: Protection of the handicapped

Everyone affected by a diminution of his physical or mental capacities is entitled to receive special attention designed to help him achieve the greatest possible development of his personality. The States parties agree to adopt such measures as may be necessary for this purpose and, especially, to:

   a.   Undertake programs specifically aimed at providing the handicapped with the resources and environment needed for attaining this goal, including work programs consistent with their possibilities and freely accepted by them or their legal representatives, as the case may be;
   b.   Provide special training to the families of the handicapped in order to help them solve the problems of coexistence and convert them into active agents in the physical, mental and emotional development of the later;
   c.   Include the consideration of solutions to specific requirements arising from needs of this group as a priority component of their urban development plans;
   d.   Encourage the establishment of social groups in which the handicapped can be helped to enjoy a fuller life.

Article 19: Means of protection

1. Pursuant to the provisions of this article and the corresponding rules to be formulated for this purpose by the General Assembly of the Organization of American States, the States Parties to this Protocol undertake to submit periodic reports on the progressive measures they have taken to ensure due respect for the rights set forth in this Protocol.

2. All reports shall be submitted to the Secretary General of the OAS, who shall transmit them to the Inter-American Economic and Social Council and the Inter-American Council for Education, Science and Culture so that they may examine them in accordance with the provisions of this article. The Secretary General shall send a copy of such reports to the Inter-American Commission on Human Rights.

3. The Secretary General of the Organization of American States shall also transmit to the specialized organizations of the inter-American system of which the States Parties to the present Protocol are members, copies or pertinent portions of the reports submitted, insofar as they relate to matters within the purview of those organizations, as established by their constituent instruments.

4. The specialized organizations of the inter-American system may submit reports to the Inter-American Economic and Social Council and the Inter-American Council for Education, Science and Culture relative to compliance with the provisions of the present Protocol in their fields of activity.

5. The annual reports submitted to the General Assembly by the Inter-American Economic and Social Council and the Inter-American Council for Education, Science and Culture shall contain a summary of the information received from the States parties to the present Protocol and the specialized organizations concerning the progressive measures adopted in order to ensure respect for the rights acknowledged in the Protocol itself and the general recommendations they consider to be appropriate in this respect.

6. Any instance in which the rights established in paragraph a) of Article 8 and in Article 13 are violated by action directly attributable to a State Party to this Protocol may give rise, through participation of the Inter-American Commission on Human Rights and, when applicable, of the Inter-American Court of Human Rights, to application of the system of individual petitions governed by Article 44 through 51 and 61 through 69 of the American Convention on Human Rights.

7. Without prejudice to the provisions of the preceding paragraph, the Inter-American Commission on Human Rights may formulate such observations and recommendations as it deems pertinent concerning the status of the economic, social and cultural rights established in the present Protocol in all or some of the States Parties, which it may include in its Annual Report to the General Assembly or in a social report, whichever it considers more appropriate.

8. The Councils and the Inter-American Commission on Human Rights, in discharging the functions conferred upon them in this article, shall take into account the progressive nature of the observance of the rights subject to protection by this Protocol.

Article 20: Reservations

The States Parties may, at the time of approval, signature, ratification or accession, make reservations to one or more specific provisions of this Protocol, provided that such reservations are not incompatible with the object and purpose of the Protocol.

Article 21: Signature, ratification or accession. Entry into effect

1. This Protocol shall remain open to signature and ratification or accession by any State Party to the American Convention on Human Rights.
2. Ratification of or accession to this Protocol shall be effected by depositing an instrument of ratification or accession with the General Secretariat of the Organization of American States.
3. The protocol shall enter into effect when eleven States have deposited their respective instruments of ratification or accession.
4. The Secretary General shall notify all the member States of the Organization of American States of the entry of the Protocol into effect.

Article 22: Inclusion of other rights and expansion of those recognized

1. Any State Party and the Inter-American Commission on Human Rights may submit for the consideration of the States Parties meeting on the occasion of the General Assembly proposed amendments to include the recognition of other rights or freedoms or to extend or expand rights or freedoms recognized in this Protocol.
2. Such Amendments shall enter into effect for the States that ratify them on the date of deposit of the instrument of ratification corresponding to the number representing two third of the States Parties to this Protocol. For all other States Parties they shall enter into effect on the date on which they deposit their respective instrument of ratification.

22. INTER-AMERICAN COMMISSION AND COURT ON HUMAN RIGHTS

22–I STATUTE OF THE INTER-AMERICAN COMMISSION ON HUMAN RIGHTS

O.A.S. Res. 447 (IX-0/79), O.A.S. Off. Rec. OEA/Ser.P/IX.0.2/80, Vol. 1 at 88, Annual Report of the Inter-American Commission on Human Rights, OEA/Ser.L/ V/11.50 doc.13 rev. 1 at 10 (1980), reprinted in Basic Documents Pertaining to Human Rights in the Inter-American System, OEA/Ser.L.V/II.82 doc.6 rev.1 at 93 (1992).

I. NATURE AND PURPOSES

Article 1

1. The Inter-American Commission on Human Rights is an organ of the Organization of the American States, created to promote the observance and defense of human rights and to serve as consultative organ of the Organization in this matter.
2. For the purposes of the present Statute, human rights are understood to be:

    a. The rights set forth in the American Convention on Human Rights, in relation to the States Parties thereto;
    b. The rights set forth in the American Declaration of the Rights and Duties of Man, in relation to the other member states.

II. MEMBERSHIP AND STRUCTURE

Article 2

1. The Inter-American Commission on Human Rights shall be composed of seven members, who shall be persons of high moral character and recognized competence in the field of human rights.
2. The Commission shall represent all the member states of the Organization.

Article 3

1. The members of the Commission shall be elected in a personal capacity by the General Assembly of the Organization from a list of candidates proposed by the governments of the member states.
2. Each government may propose up to three candidates, who may be nationals of the state proposing them or of any other member state of the Organization.

When a slate of three is proposed, at least one of the candidates shall be a national of a state other then the proposing state.

Article 4

1. At least six months prior to completion of the terms of office for which the members of the Commission were elected, the Secretary General shall request, in writing, each member state of the Organization to present its candidates within 90 days.
2. The Secretary General shall prepare a list in alphabetical order of the candidates nominated, and shall transmit it to the member states of the Organization at least thirty days prior to the next General Assembly.

Article 5

The members of the Commission shall be elected by secret ballot of the General Assembly from the list of candidates referred to in Article 3(2). The candidates who obtain the largest number of votes and an absolute majority of the votes of the member states shall be declared elected. Should it become necessary to hold several ballots to elect all the members of the Commission, the candidates who receive the smallest number of votes shall be eliminated successively, in the manner determined by the General Assembly.

Article 6

The members of the Commission shall be elected for a term of four years and may be reelected only once. Their terms of office shall begin on January 1 of the year following the year in which they are elected.

Article 7

No two nationals of the same state may be members of the Commission.

Article 8

1. Membership on the Inter-American Commission on Human Rights is incompatible with engaging in other functions that might affect the independence or impartiality of the member or the dignity or prestige of his post on the Commission.
2. The Commission shall consider any case that may arise regarding incompatibility in accordance with the provisions of the first paragraph of this Article, and in accordance with the procedures provided by its Regulations. If the Commission decides, by an affirmative vote of a least five of its members, that a case of incompatibility exists, it will submit the case, with its background, to the General Assembly for decision.
3. A declaration of incompatibility by the General Assembly shall be adopted by a majority of two thirds of the member states of the Organization and shall

occasion the immediate removal of the member of the Commission from his post, but it shall not invalidate any action in which he may have participated.

Article 9

The duties of the members of the Commission are:

1. Except when justifiably prevented, to attend the regular and special meetings the Commission holds at its permanent headquarters or in any other place to which it may have decided to move temporarily.
2. To serve, except when justifiably prevented, on the special committees which the Commission may form to conduct on-site observations, or to perform any other duties within their ambit.
3. To maintain absolute secrecy about all matters which the Commission deems confidential.
4. To conduct themselves in their public and private life as befits the high moral authority of the office and the importance of the mission entrusted to the Commission.

Article 10

1. If a member commits a serious violation of any of the duties referred to in Article 9, the Commission, on the affirmative vote of five of its members, shall submit the case to the General Assembly of the Organization, which shall decide whether he should be removed from office.
2. The Commission shall hear the member in question before taking its decision.

Article 11

1. When a vacancy occurs for reasons other than the normal completion of a member's term of office, the Chairman of the Commission shall immediately notify the Secretary General of the Organization, who shall in turn inform the member states of the Organization.
2. In order to fill vacancies, each government may propose a candidate within a period of 30 days from the date of receipt of the Secretary-General's communication that a vacancy has occurred.
3. The Secretary General shall prepare an alphabetical list of the candidates and shall transmit it to the Permanent Council of the Organization, which shall fill the vacancy.
4. When the term of office is due to expire within six months following the date on which a vacancy occurs, the vacancy shall not be filled.

Article 12

1. In those member states of the Organization that are Parties to the American Convention on Human Rights, the members of the Commission shall enjoy, from the time of their election and throughout their term of office, such immunities as

are granted to diplomatic agents under international law. While in office, they shall also enjoy the diplomatic privileges required for the performance of their duties.

2. In those member states of the Organization that are not Parties to the American Convention on Human Rights, the members of the Commission shall enjoy the privileges and immunities pertaining to their posts that are required for them to perform their duties with independence.

3. The system of privileges and immunities of the members of the Commission may be regulated or supplemented by multilateral or bilateral agreements between the Organization and the member states.

Article 13

The members of the Commission shall receive travel allowances and *per diem* and fees, as appropriate, for their participation in the meetings of the Commission or in other functions which the Commission, in accordance with its Regulations, entrusts to them, individually or collectively. Such travel and *per diem* allowances and fees shall be included in the budget of the Organization, and their amounts and conditions shall be determined by the General Assembly.

Article 14

1. The Commission shall have a Chairman, a First Vice-Chairman and a Second Vice-Chairman, who shall be elected by an absolute majority of its members for a period of one year; they may be re-elected only once in each four-year period.

2. The Chairman and the two Vice-Chairmen shall be the officers of the Commission, and their functions shall be set forth in the Regulations.

Article 15

The Chairman of the Commission may go to the Commission's headquarters and remain there for such time as may be necessary for the performance of his duties.

III. HEADQUARTERS AND MEETINGS

Article 16

1. The headquarters of the Commission shall be in Washington, D.C.

2. The Commission may move to and meet in the territory of any American State when it so decides by an absolute majority of votes, and with the consent, or at the invitation of the government concerned.

3. The Commission shall meet in regular and special sessions, in conformity with the provisions of the Regulations.

Article 17

1. An absolute majority of the members of the Commission shall constitute a quorum.
2. In regard to those States that are Parties to the Convention, decisions shall be taken by an absolute majority vote of the members of the Commission in those cases established by the American Convention on Human Rights and the present Statute. In other cases, an absolute majority of the members present shall be required.
3. In regard to those States that are not Parties to the Convention, decisions shall be taken by an absolute majority vote of the members of the Commission, except in matters of procedure, in which case, the decisions shall be taken by simple majority.

IV. FUNCTIONS AND POWERS

Article 18

The Commission shall have the following powers with respect to the member states of the Organization of American States:

a. to develop an awareness of human rights among the peoples of the Americas;
b. to make recommendations to the governments of the states on the adoption of progressive measures in favor of human rights in the framework of their legislation, constitutional provisions and international commitments, as well as appropriate measures to further observance of those rights;
c. to prepare such studies or reports as it considers advisable for the performance of its duties;
d to request that the governments of the states provide it with reports on measures they adopt in matters of human rights;
e. to respond to inquiries made by any member state through the General Secretariat of the Organization on matters related to human rights in the state and, within its possibilities, to provide those states with the advisory services they request;
f. to submit an annual report to the General Assembly of the Organization, in which due account shall be taken of the legal regime applicable to those States Parties to the American Convention on Human Rights and of that system applicable to those that are not Parties;
g. to conduct on-site observations in a state, with the consent or at the invitation of the government in question; and
h. to submit the program-budget of the Commission to the Secretary General, so that he may present it to the General Assembly.

Article 19

With respect to the States Parties to the American Convention on Human Rights, the Commission shall discharge its duties in conformity with the powers granted under the Convention and in the present Statute, and shall have the following powers in addition to those designated in Article 18:

    a.   to act on petitions and other communications, pursuant to the provisions of Articles 44 to 51 of the Convention;

    b.   to appear before the Inter-American Court of Human Rights in cases provided for in the Convention;

    c.   to request the Inter-American Court of Human Rights to take such provisional measures as it considers appropriate in serious and urgent cases which have not yet been submitted to it for consideration, whenever this becomes necessary to prevent irreparable injury to persons;

    d.   to consult the Court on the interpretation of the American Convention on Human Rights or of other treaties concerning the protection of human rights in the American states; to submit additional draft protocols to the American Convention on Human Rights to the General Assembly, in order to progressively include other rights and freedoms under the system of protection of the Convention; and

    e.   to submit to the General Assembly, through the Secretary General, proposed amendments to the American Convention on Human Rights, for such action as the General Assembly deems appropriate.

Article 20

In relation to those member states of the Organization that are not parties to the American Convention on Human Rights, the Commission shall have the following powers, in addition to those designated in Article 18:

    a.   particular attention to the observance of the human rights referred to in Articles I, II, III, IV, XVIII, XXV, and XXVI of the American Declaration of the Rights and Duties of Man;

    b   to examine communications submitted to it and any other available information, to address the government of any member state not a Party to the Convention for information deemed pertinent by this Commission, and to make recommendations to it, when it finds this appropriate, in order to bring about more effective observance of fundamental human rights; and

    c.   to verify, as a prior condition to the exercise of the powers granted under subparagraph b. above, whether the domestic legal procedures and remedies of each member state not a Party to the Convention have been duly applied and exhausted.

V. SECRETARIAT

Article 21

1. The Secretariat services of the Commission shall be provided by a specialized administrative unit under the direction of an Executive Secretary. This unit shall be provided with the resources and staff required to accomplish the tasks the Commission may assign to it.
2. The Executive Secretary, who shall be a person of high moral character and recognized competence in the field of human rights, shall be responsible for the work of the Secretariat and shall assist the Commission in the performance of its duties in accordance with the Regulations.
3. The Executive Secretary shall be appointed by the Secretary General of the Organization, in consultation with the Commission. Furthermore, for the Secretary General to be able to remove the Executive Secretary, he shall consult with the Commission and inform its members of the reasons for his decision.

VI. STATUTE AND REGULATIONS

Article 22

1. The present Statute may be amended by the General Assembly.
2. The Commission shall prepare and adopt its own Regulations, in accordance with the present Statute.

Article 23

1. In accordance with the provisions of Articles 44 to 51 of the American Convention on Human Rights, the Regulations of the Commission shall determine the procedure to be followed in cases of petitions or communications alleging violation of any of the rights guaranteed by the Convention, and imputing such violation to any State Party to the Convention.
2. If the friendly settlement referred to in Articles 44–51 of the Convention is not reached, the Commission shall draft, within 180 days, the report required by Article 50 of the Convention.

Article 24

1. The Regulations shall establish the procedure to be followed in cases of communications containing accusations or complaints of violations of human rights imputable to States that are not Parties to the American Convention on Human Rights.
2. The Regulations shall contain, for this purpose, the pertinent rules established in the Statute of the Commission approved by the Council of the Organization in resolutions adopted on May 25 and June 8, 1960, with the

modifications and amendments introduced by Resolution XXII of the Second Special Inter-American Conference, and by the Council of the Organization at its meeting held on April 24, 1968, taking into account resolutions P/RES. 253 (343/78), "Transition from the present Inter-American Commission on Human Rights to the Commission provided for in the American Convention on Human Rights," adopted by the Permanent Council of the Organization on September 20, 1979.

VII. TRANSITORY PROVISIONS

Article 25

Until the Commission adopts its new Regulations, the current Regulations (OEA/ Ser.L/VII. 17, doc. 26) shall apply to all the member states of the Organization.

Article 26

1. The present Statute shall enter into effect 30 days after its approval by the General Assembly.
2. The Secretary General shall order immediate publication of the Statute, and shall give it the widest possible distribution.

22–II STATUTE OF THE INTER-AMERICAN COURT ON HUMAN RIGHTS

O.A.S. Res. 448 (IX-0/79), O.A.S. Off. Rec. OEA/Ser.P/IX.0.2/80, Vol. 1 at 98, Annual Report of the Inter-American Court on Human Rights, OEA/Ser.L/V.III.3 doc. 13 corr. 1 at 16 (1980), reprinted in Basic Documents Pertaining to Human Rights in the Inter-American System, OEA/Ser.L.V/II.82 doc.6 rev.1 at 133 (1992).

CHAPTER I
GENERAL PROVISIONS

Article 1: Nature and Legal Organization

The Inter-American Court of Human Rights is an autonomous judicial institution whose purpose is the application and interpretation of the American Convention on Human Rights. The Court exercises its functions in accordance with the provisions of the aforementioned Convention and the present Statute.

Article 2: Jurisdiction

The Court shall exercise adjudicatory and advisory jurisdiction:

1. Its adjudicatory jurisdiction shall be governed by the provisions of Articles 61, 62 and 63 of the Convention, and
2. Its advisory jurisdiction shall be governed by the provisions of Article 64 of the Convention.

Article 3: Seat

1. The seat of the Court shall be San José, Costa Rica; however, the Court may convene in any member state of the Organization of American States (OAS) when a majority of the Court considers it desirable, and with the prior consent of the State concerned.
2. The seat of the Court may be changed by a vote of two-thirds of the States Parties to the Convention, in the OAS General Assembly.

CHAPTER II
COMPOSITION OF THE COURT

Article 4: Composition

1. The Court shall consist of seven judges, nationals of the member states of the OAS, elected in an individual capacity from among jurists of the highest moral authority and of recognized competence in the field of human rights, who possess the qualifications required for the exercise of the highest judicial functions under the law of the State of which they are nationals or of the State that proposes them as candidates.
2. No two judges may be nationals of the same State.

Article 5: Judicial Terms

The judges of the Court shall be elected for a term of six years and may be reelected only once.

1. A judge elected to replace a judge whose term has not expired shall complete that term.
2. The terms of office of the judges shall run from January 1 of the year following that of their election to December 31 of the year in which their terms expire.
3. The judges shall serve until the end of their terms. Nevertheless, they shall continue to hear the cases they have begun to hear and that are still pending, and shall not be replaced by the newly elected judges in the handling of those cases.

Article 6: Election of the Judges – Date

1. Election of judges shall take place, insofar as possible, during the session of the OAS General Assembly immediately prior to the expiration of the term of the outgoing judges.
2. Vacancies on the Court caused by death, permanent disability, resignation or

dismissal of judges shall, insofar as possible, be filled at the next session of the OAS General Assembly. However, an election shall not be necessary when a vacancy occurs within six months of the expiration of a term.

3. If necessary in order to preserve a quorum of the Court, the States Parties to the Convention, at a meeting of the OAS Permanent Council, and at the request of the President of the Court, shall appoint one or more interim judges who shall serve until such time as they are replaced by elected judges.

Article 7: Candidates

1. Judges shall be elected by the States Parties to the Convention, at the OAS General Assembly, from a list of candidates nominated by those States.
2. Each State Party may nominate up to three candidates, nationals of the state that proposes them or of any other member state of the OAS.
3. When a slate of three is proposed, at least one of the candidates must be a national of a state other than the nominating state.

Article 8: Election – Preliminary Procedures

1. Six months prior to expiration of the terms to which the judges of the Court were elected, the Secretary General of the OAS shall address a written request to each State Party to the Convention that it nominate its candidates within the next ninety days.
2. The Secretary General of the OAS shall draw up an alphabetical list of the candidates nominated, and shall forward it to the States Parties, if possible, at least thirty days before the next session of the OAS General Assembly.
3. In the case of vacancies on the Court, as well as in cases of the death or permanent disability of a candidate, the aforementioned time periods shall be shortened to a period that the Secretary General of the OAS deems reasonable.

Article 9: Voting

1. The judges shall be elected by secret ballot and by an absolute majority of the States Parties to the Convention, from among the candidates referred to in Article 7 of the present Statute.
2. The candidates who obtain the largest number of votes and an absolute majority shall be declared elected. Should several ballots be necessary, those candidates who receive the smallest number of votes shall be eliminated successively, in the manner determined by the States Parties.

Article 10: Ad Hoc Judges

1. If a judge is a national of any of the States Parties to a case submitted to the Court, he shall retain his right to hear that case.
2. If one of the judges called upon to hear a case is a national of one of the States Parties to the case, any other State Party to the case may appoint a person to serve on the Court as an *ad hoc* judge.

3. If among the judges called upon to hear a case, none is a national of the States Parties to the case, each of the latter may appoint an *ad hoc* judge. Should several States have the same interest in the case, they shall be regarded as a single party for purposes of the above provisions. In case of doubt, the Court shall decide.
4. The right of any State to appoint an *ad hoc* judge shall be considered relinquished if the State should fail to do so within thirty days following the written request from the President of the Court.
5. The provisions of Articles 4, 11, 15, 16, 18, 19 and 20 of the present Statute shall apply to *ad hoc* judges.

Article 11: Oath

1. Upon assuming office, each judge shall take the following oath or make the following solemn declaration: "I swear" – or "I solemnly declare" – "that I shall exercise my functions as a judge honorably, independently and impartially and that I shall keep secret all deliberations."
2. The oath shall be administered by the President of the Court and, if possible, in the presence of the other judges.

CHAPTER III
STRUCTURE OF THE COURT

Article 12: Presidency

1. The Court shall elect from among its members a President and Vice-President who shall serve for a period of two years; they may be reelected.
2. The President shall direct the work of the Court, represent it, regulate the disposition of matters brought before the Court, and preside over its sessions.
3. The Vice-President shall take the place of the President in the latter's temporary absence, or if the office of the President becomes vacant. In the latter case, the Court shall elect a new Vice-President to serve out the term of the previous Vice-President.
4. In the absence of the President and the Vice-President, their duties shall be assumed by other judges, following the order of precedence established in Article 13 of the present Statute.

Article 13: Precedence

1. Elected judges shall take precedence after the President and Vice-President according to their seniority in office.
2. Judges having the same seniority in office shall take precedence according to age.
3. *Ad hoc* and interim judges shall take precedence after the elected judges, according to age. However, if an *ad hoc* or interim judge has previously served as an elected judge, he shall have precedence over any other *ad hoc* or interim judge.

Article 14: Secretariat

1. The Secretariat of the Court shall function under the immediate authority of the Secretary, in accordance with the administrative standards of the OAS General Secretariat, in all matters that are not incompatible with the independence of the Court.
2. The Secretary shall be appointed by the Court. He shall be a full-time employee serving in a position of trust to the Court, shall have his office at the seat of the Court and shall attend any meetings that the Court holds away from its seat.
3. There shall be an Assistant Secretary who shall assist the Secretary in his duties and shall replace him in his temporary absence.
4. The Staff of the Secretariat shall be appointed by the Secretary General of the OAS, in consultation with the Secretary of the Court.

CHAPTER IV
RIGHTS, DUTIES AND RESPONSIBILITIES

Article 15: Privileges and Immunities

1. The judges of the Court shall enjoy, from the moment of their election and throughout their term of office, the immunities extended to diplomatic agents under international law. During the exercise of their functions, they shall, in addition, enjoy the diplomatic privileges necessary for the performance of their duties.
2. At no time shall the judges of the Court be held liable for any decisions or opinions issued in the exercise of their functions.
3. The Court itself and its staff shall enjoy the privileges and immunities provided for in the Agreement on Privileges and Immunities of the Organization of American States, of May 15, 1949, mutatis mutandis, taking into account the importance and independence of the Court.
4. The provision of paragraphs 1, 2 and 3 of this article shall apply to the States Parties to the Convention. They shall also apply to such other member states of the OAS as expressly accept them, either in general or for specific cases.
5. The system of privileges and immunities of the judges of the Court and of its staff may be regulated or supplemented by multilateral or bilateral agreements between the Court, the OAS and its member states.

Article 16: Service

1. The judges shall remain at the disposal of the Court, and shall travel to the seat of the Court or to the place where the Court is holding its sessions as often and for as long a time as may be necessary, as established in the Regulations.
2. The President shall render his service on a permanent basis.

Article 17: Emoluments

1. The emoluments of the President and the judges of the Court shall be set in accordance with the obligations and incompatibilities imposed on them by Articles 16 and 18, and bearing in mind the importance and independence of their functions.
2. The *ad hoc* judges shall receive the emoluments established by Regulations, within the limits of the Court's budget.
3. The judges shall also receive per diem and travel allowances, when appropriate.

Article 18: Incompatibilities

1. The position of judge of the Inter-American Court of Human Rights is incompatible with the following positions and activities:

    a. Members or high-ranking officials of the executive branch of government, except for those who hold positions that do not place them under the direct control of the executive branch and those of diplomatic agents who are not Chiefs of Missions to the OAS or to any of its member states;
    b. Officials of international organizations;
    c. Any others that might prevent the judges from discharging their duties, or that might affect their independence or impartiality, or the dignity and prestige of the office.

2. In case of doubt as to incompatibility, the Court shall decide. If the incompatibility is not resolved, the provisions of Article 73 of the Convention and Article 20(2) of the present Statute shall apply.
3. Incompatibilities may lead only to dismissal of the judge and the imposition of applicable liabilities, but shall not invalidate the acts and decisions in which the judge in question participated.

Article 19: Disqualification

1. Judges may not take part in matters in which, in the opinion of the Court, they or members of their family have a direct interest or in which they have previously taken part as agents, counsel or advocates, or as members of a national or international court or an investigatory committee, or in any other capacity.
2. If a judge is disqualified from hearing a case or for some other appropriate reason considers that he should not take part in a specific matter, he shall advise the President of his disqualification. Should the latter disagree, the Court shall decide.
3. If the President considers that a judge has cause for disqualification or for some other pertinent reason should not take part in a given matter, he shall advise him to that effect. Should the judge in question disagree, the Court shall decide.
4. When one or more judges are disqualified pursuant to this article, the President may request the States Parties to the Convention, in a meeting of the OAS Permanent Council, to appoint interim judges to replace them.

Article 20: Disciplinary Regime

1. In the performance of their duties and at all other times, the judges and staff of the Court shall conduct themselves in a manner that is in keeping with the office of those who perform an international judicial function. They shall be answerable to the Court for their conduct, as well as for any violation, act of negligence or omission committed in the exercise of their functions.
2. The OAS General Assembly shall have disciplinary authority over the judges, but may exercise that authority only at the request of the Court itself, composed for this purpose of the remaining judges. The Court shall inform the General Assembly of the reasons for its request.
3. Disciplinary authority over the Secretary shall lie with the Court, and over the rest of the staff, with the Secretary, who shall exercise that authority with the approval of the President.
4. The Court shall issue disciplinary rules, subject to the administrative regulations of the OAS General Secretariat insofar as they may be applicable in accordance with Article 59 of the Convention.

Article 21: Resignation – Incapacity

1. Any resignation from the Court shall be submitted in writing to the President of the Court. The resignation shall not become effective until the Court has accepted it.
2. The Court shall decide whether a judge is incapable of performing his functions.
3. The President of the Court shall notify the Secretary General of the OAS of the acceptance of a resignation or a determination of incapacity, for appropriate action.

CHAPTER V
THE WORKINGS OF THE COURT

Article 22: Sessions

1. The Court shall hold regular and special sessions.
2. Regular sessions shall be held as determined by the Regulations of the Court.
3. Special sessions shall be convoked by the President or at the request of a majority of the judges.

Article 23: Quorum

1. The quorum for deliberations by the Court shall be five judges.
2. Decisions of the Court shall be taken by a majority vote of the judges present.
3. In the event of a tie, the President shall cast the deciding vote.

Article 24: Hearings, Deliberations, Decisions

1. The hearings shall be public, unless the Court, in exceptional circumstances, decides otherwise.
2. The Court shall deliberate in private. Its deliberations shall remain secret, unless the Court decides otherwise.
3. The decisions, judgments and opinions of the Court shall be delivered in public session, and the parties shall be given written notification thereof. In addition, the decisions, judgments and opinions shall be published, along with judges' individual votes and opinions and with such other data or background information that the Court may deem appropriate.

Article 25: Rules and Regulations

1. The Court shall draw up its Rules of Procedure.
2. The Rules of Procedure may delegate to the President or to Committees of the Court authority to carry out certain parts of the legal proceedings, with the exception of issuing final rulings or advisory opinions. Rulings or decisions issued by the President or the Committees of the Court that are not purely procedural in nature may be appealed before the full Court.
3. The Court shall also draw up its own Regulations.

Article 26: Budget, Financial System

1. The Court shall draw up its own budget and shall submit it for approval to the General Assembly of the OAS, through the General Secretariat. The latter may not introduce any changes in it.
2. The Court shall administer its own budget.

CHAPTER VI
RELATIONS WITH GOVERNMENTS AND ORGANIZATIONS

Article 27: Relations with the Host Country, Governments and Organizations

1. The relations of the Court with the host country shall be governed through a headquarters agreement. The seat of the Court shall be international in nature.
2. The relations of the Court with governments, with the OAS and its organs, agencies and entities and with other international governmental organizations involved in promoting and defending human rights shall be governed through special agreements.

Article 28: Relations with the Inter-American Commission on Human Rights

The Inter-American Commission on Human Rights shall appear as a party before the Court in all cases within the adjudicatory jurisdiction of the Court, pursuant to Article 2(1) of the present Statute.

Article 29: Agreements of Cooperation

1. The Court may enter into agreements of cooperation with such nonprofit institutions as law schools, bar associations, courts, academies and educational or research institutions dealing with related disciplines in order to obtain their cooperation and to strengthen and promote the juridical and institutional principles of the Convention in general and of the Court in particular.
2. The Court shall include an account of such agreements and their results in its Annual Report to the OAS General Assembly.

Article 30: Report to the OAS General Assembly

The Court shall submit a report on its work of the previous year to each regular session of the OAS General Assembly. It shall indicate those cases in which a State has failed to comply with the Court's ruling. It may also submit to the OAS General Assembly proposals or recommendations on ways to improve the inter-American system of human rights, insofar as they concern the work of the Court.

CHAPTER VII
FINAL PROVISIONS

Article 31: Amendments to the Statute

The present Statute may be amended by the OAS General Assembly, at the initiative of any member state or of the Court itself.

Article 32: Entry into Force

The present Statute shall enter into force on January 1, 1980.

22–III REGULATIONS OF THE INTER-AMERICAN COMMISSION ON HUMAN RIGHTS

Reprinted in Basic Documents Pertaining to Human Rights in the Inter-American System, OEA/Ser.L.V/II.82 doc.6 rev.1 at 103 (1992).

TITLE I
ORGANIZATION OF THE COMMISSION

CHAPTER I
NATURE AND COMPOSITION

Article 1: Nature and Composition

1. The Inter-American Commission on Human Rights is an autonomous entity of

the Organization of American States whose principal function is to promote the observance and defense of human rights and to serve as an advisory body to the Organization in this area.

2. The Commission represents all the member states of the Organization.
3. The Commission is composed of seven members elected in their individual capacity by the General Assembly of the Organization who shall be persons of high moral standing and recognized competence in the field of human rights.

CHAPTER II
MEMBERSHIP

Article 2: Duration of the term of office

1. The members of the Commission shall be elected for four years and may be re-elected only once.
2. In the event that new members of the Commission are not elected to replace those completing their term of office, the latter shall continue to serve until the new members are elected.

Article 3: Precedence

The members of the Commission shall follow the Chairman and Vice-Chairmen in order of precedence according to their length of service. When there are two or more members with equal seniority, precedence shall be determined according to age.

Article 4: Incompatibility

1. The position of member of the Inter-American Commission on Human Rights is incompatible with the exercise of activities which could affect the independence, impartiality, dignity or prestige of membership on the Commission.
2. The Commission, with the affirmative vote of at least five of its members, shall decide if a situation of incompatibility exists.
3. The Commission, prior to taking a decision, shall hear the member who is considered to be in a situation of incompatibility.
4. The decision with respect to the incompatibility, together with all the background information, shall be sent to the General Assembly by means of the Secretary General of the Organization for the purposes set forth in Article 8, (3), of the Commission's Statute.

Article 5: Resignation

In the event that a member resigns, his resignation shall be presented to the Chairman of the Commission who shall notify the Secretary General of the Organization for the appropriate purposes.

CHAPTER III
OFFICERS

Article 6: Composition and functions

The Commission shall have as its officers a Chairman, a first Vice-Chairman, and a second Vice-Chairman, who shall perform the functions set forth in these regulations.

Article 7: Elections

1. In the election for each of the posts referred to in the preceding article, only members present shall participate.
2. Elections shall be by secret ballot. However, with the unanimous consent of the members present, the Commission may decide on another procedure.
3. The vote of an absolute majority of the members of the Commission shall be required for election to any of the posts referred to in Article 6.
4. Should it be necessary to hold more than one ballot for election to any of these posts, the names receiving the lowest number of votes shall be eliminated successively.
5. Elections shall be held on the first day of the Commission's first session of the new calendar year.

Article 8: Duration of Mandate

1. The board of officers shall hold office for a year and may be reelected only once in every four year period.
2. The mandate of the board of officers extends from the date of their election until the elections held the following year for the new board, pursuant to Article 7, paragraph 5.
3. In case the mandate of the Chairman or any of the Vice Chairmen expires, the provisions of Article 9, paragraphs 3 and 4 will apply.

Article 9: Resignation, Vacancy and Replacements

1. If the Chairman resigns from his post or ceases to be a member of the Commission, the Commission shall elect a successor to fill the post for the remainder of the term of office at the first meeting held after the date on which it is notified of the resignation or vacancy.
2. The same procedure shall be applied in the event of the resignation of either of the Vice-Chairmen, or if a vacancy occurs.
3. The First Vice-Chairman shall serve as Chairman until the Commission elects a new Chairman under the provisions of paragraph 1 of this article.
4. The First Vice-Chairman shall also replace the Chairman if the latter is temporarily unable to perform his duties. The Second Vice-Chairman shall replace the Chairman in the event of the absence or disability of the First Vice-Chairman, or if that post is vacant.

Article 10: Functions of the Chairman

The Duties of the Chairman shall be:

a.   to represent the Commission before all the other organs of the Organization and other institutions;

b.   to convoke regular and special meetings of the Commission in accordance with the Statute and these Regulations;

c.   to preside over the sessions of the Commission and submit to it, for consideration, all matters appearing on the agenda of the work schedule approved for the corresponding session;

d.   to give the floor to the members in the order in which they have requested it;

e.   to rule on points of order that may arise during the discussions of the Commission. If any member so requests, the Chairman's ruling shall be submitted to the Commission for its decision;

f.   to submit to a vote matters within his competence, in accordance with the pertinent provisions of these Regulations;

g.   to promote the work of the Commission and see to compliance with its program-budget;

h.   to present a written report to the Commission at the beginning of its regular or special sessions on what he has done during its recesses to carry out the functions assigned to him by the Statute and by these Regulations;

i.   to see to compliance with the decisions of the Commission;

j.   to attend the meetings of the General Assembly of the Organization and, as an observer, those of the United Nations Commission on Human Rights; further, he may participate in the activities of other entities concerned with protecting and promoting respect for human rights;

k.   to go to the headquarters of the Commission and remain there for as long as he considers necessary to carry out his functions;

l.   to designate special committees, *ad hoc* committees, and subcommittees composed of several members, to carry out any mandate within his area of competence;

m.   to perform any other functions that may be conferred upon him in these Regulations.

Article 11: Delegation of Functions

The Chairman may delegate to one of the Vice-Chairmen or to another member of the Commission the functions specified in Article 8(a), (j), and (m).

CHAPTER IV
SECRETARIAT

Article 12: Composition

The Secretariat of the Commission shall be composed of an Executive Secretary, an Assistant Executive Secretary, and the professional, technical, and administrative staff needed to carry out its activities.

Article 13: Functions of the Executive Secretary

1. The functions of the Executive Secretary shall be:

   a. to direct, plan, and coordinate the work of the Secretariat;
   b. to prepare the draft work schedule for each session in consultation with the Chairman;
   c. to provide advisory services to the Chairman and members of the Commission in the performance of their duties;
   d. to present a written report to the Commission at the beginning of each session, on the activities of the Secretariat since the preceding session, and on any general matters that may be of interest to the Commission;
   e. to implement the decisions entrusted to him by the Commission or by the Chairman.

2. The Assistant Executive Secretary shall replace the Executive Secretary in the event of his absence or disability.
3. The Executive Secretary, the Assistant Executive Secretary and the staff of the Secretariat must observe strict discretion in all matters that the Commission considers confidential.

Article 14: Functions of the Secretariat

1. The Secretariat shall prepare the draft reports, resolutions, studies and any other papers entrusted to it by the Commission or by the Chairman, and shall see that the summary minutes of the sessions of the Commission and any documents considered by it are distributed among its members.
2. The Secretariat shall receive petitions addressed to the Commission and, when appropriate, shall request the necessary information from the governments concerned and, in general, it shall make the necessary arrangements to initiate any proceedings to which such petitions may give rise.

CHAPTER V
FUNCTIONING OF THE COMMISSION

Article 15: Sessions

1. The Commission shall meet for a period not to exceed a total of eight weeks a year, divided into however many regular meetings the Commission may

272

decide, without prejudice to the fact that it may convoke special sessions at the decision of its Chairman, or at the request of an absolute majority of its members.

2. The sessions of the Commission shall be held at its headquarters. However, by an absolute majority vote of its members, the Commission may decide to meet elsewhere, with the consent of or at the invitation of the government concerned.

3. Any member who because of illness or for any other serious reason is unable to attend all or part of any session or meeting of the Commission, or to fulfill any other functions, must notify the Executive Secretary to this effect as soon as possible, and he shall so inform the Chairman.

Article 16: Meetings

1. During the sessions, the Commission shall hold as many meetings as necessary to carry out its activities.

2. The length of the meetings shall be determined by the Commission subject to any changes that, for justifiable reasons, are decided on by the Chairman after consulting with the members of the Commission.

3. The meetings shall be closed unless the Commission decides otherwise.

4. The date and time for the next meeting shall be set at each meeting.

Article 17: Working Groups

1. When the Commission considers it advisable, prior to the beginning of every regular session a working group shall convene to prepare the draft resolutions and other decisions on petitions and communications which are dealt with under Title II, Chapters I, II and III of the present Regulations and which are to be considered by the full Commission during the session. Said Working Group will be composed of three members, designated by the Chairman of the Commission, following a rotation policy, when possible.

2. The Commission, with a vote of the absolute majority of its members, shall determine the formation of other working groups the purpose of which shall be the consideration of specific subjects which will then be considered by the full Commission. Each working group will be made up of no more than three members, who will be designated by the Chairman. As far as possible, these working groups will meet immediately before or after each session for the period of time the Commission determines.

Article 18: Quorum for Meetings

The presence of an absolute majority of the members of the Commission shall be necessary to constitute a quorum.

Article 19: Discussion and Voting

1. The meetings shall conform primarily to the Regulations and secondarily, to the pertinent provisions of the Regulations of the Permanent Council of the Organization of American States.

2. Members of the Commission may not participate in the discussion, investigation, deliberation or decision of a matter submitted to the Commission in the following cases:

   a. if they were nationals or permanent residents of the State which is subject of the Commission's general or specific consideration, or if they were accredited to, or carrying out, a special mission, as diplomatic agents, on behalf of said State;

   b. if previously they have participated in any capacity in a decision concerning the same facts on which the matter is based or have acted as an adviser to, or representative of, any of the parties involved in the decision.

3. When any member thinks that he should abstain from participating in the study or decision of a matter, he shall so inform the Commission, which shall decide if the withdrawal is warranted.

4. Any member may raise the issue of the withdrawal of another member provided that it is based upon reasons formulated in paragraph 2 of this article.

5. Any member who has withdrawn from the case shall not participate in the discussion, investigation, deliberation or decision of the matter even though the reason for the withdrawal has been superseded.

6. During the discussion of a given subject, any member may raise a point of order, which shall be ruled upon immediately by the Chairman or, when appropriate, by the majority of the members present. The discussion may be ended at any time, as long as the members have had the opportunity to express their opinion.

7. Once the discussion has been terminated, and if there is no consensus on the subject submitted to the Commission for deliberation, the Chairman shall put the matter to a vote in the reverse order of precedence among the members.

8. The Chairman shall announce the results of the vote and shall declare (as approved) the proposal that has the majority of votes. In the case of a tie, the Chairman shall decide.

9. Any doubt which may arise as regards the application or interpretation of the present article shall be resolved by the Commission.

Article 20: Special Quorum to take Decisions

1. Decisions shall be taken by an absolute majority vote of the members of the Commission in the following cases:

   a. to elect the executive officers of the Commission;

   b. for matters where such a majority is required under the provisions of the Convention, the Statute or these Regulations;

c. to adopt a report on the situation of human rights in a specific state;
d. for any amendment or interpretation on the application of these Regulations.

2. To take decisions regarding other matters, a majority vote of members present shall be sufficient.

Article 21: Explanation of Vote

1. Whether or not members agree with the decisions of the majority, they shall be entitled to present a written explanation of their vote, which shall be included following that decision.
2. If the decision concerns the approval of a report or draft, the explanation of the vote shall be included after that report or draft.
3. When the decision does not appear in a separate document, the explanation of the vote shall be included in the minutes of the meeting, following the decision in question.

Article 22: Minutes of the Meetings

1. Summary minutes shall be taken of each meeting. They shall state the day and time at which it was held, the names of the members present, the matters dealt with, the decisions taken, the names of those voting for and against each decision, and any statement made by a member especially for inclusion in the minutes.
2. The Secretariat shall distribute copies of the summary minutes of each meeting to the members of the Commission, who may present their observations to the Secretariat prior to the meeting at which they are to be approved.

Article 23: Compensation for Special Services

The Commission may assign any of its members, with the approval of an absolute majority, the preparation of a special study or other specific papers to be carried out individually outside the sessions. Such work shall be compensated in accordance with funds available in the budget. The amount of the fees shall be set on the basis of the number of days required for preparation and drafting of the paper.

Article 24: Program-budget

1. The proposed program-budget of the Commission shall be prepared by its Secretariat in consultation with the Chairman and shall be governed by the Organization's current budgetary standards.
2. The Executive Secretary will advise the Commission of said program-budget.

TITLE II PROCEDURES

CHAPTER I
GENERAL PROVISIONS

Article 25: Official Languages

1. The official languages of the Commission shall be Spanish, French, English and Portuguese. The working languages shall be those decided on by the Commission every two years, in accordance with the languages spoken by its members.
2. A member of the Commission may allow omission of the interpretation of debates and the preparation of documents in his language.

Article 26: Presentation of Petitions

1. Any person or group of persons or nongovernmental entity legally recognized in one or more of the member states of the Organization may submit petitions to the Commission, in accordance with these Regulations, on one's own behalf or on behalf of third persons, with regard to alleged violations of a human right recognized, as the case may be, in the American Convention on Human Rights or in the American Declaration of the Rights and Duties of Man.
2. The Commission may also, motu proprio, take into consideration any available information that it considers pertinent and which might include the necessary factors to begin processing a case which in its opinion fulfills the requirements for the purpose.

Article 27: Form

1. The petition shall be lodged in writing.
2. The petitioner may appoint, in the petition itself, or in another written petition, an attorney or other person to represent him before the Commission.

Article 28: Special Missions

The Commission may designate one or more of its members or staff members of the Secretariat to take specific measures, investigate facts or make the necessary arrangements for the Commission to perform its functions.

Article 29: Precautionary Measures

1. The Commission may, at its own initiative, or at the request of a party, take any action it considers necessary for the discharge of its functions.
2. In urgent cases, when it becomes necessary to avoid irreparable damage to persons, the Commission may request that provisional measures be taken to avoid irreparable damage in cases where the denounced facts are true.

3. If the Commission is not in session, the Chairman, or in his absence, one of the Vice-Chairmen, shall consult with the other members, through the Secretariat, on implementation of the provisions of paragraphs 1 and 2 above. If it is not possible to consult within a reasonable time, the Chairman shall take the decision on behalf of the Commission and shall so inform its members immediately.
4. The request for such measures and their adoption shall not prejudice the final decision.

Article 30: Initial Processing

1. The Secretariat of the Commission shall be responsible for the study and initial processing of petitions lodged before the Commission and that fulfill all the requirements set forth in the Statute and in these Regulations.
2. If a petition or communication does not meet the requirements called for in these Regulations, the Secretariat of the Commission may request the petitioner or his representative to complete it.
3. If the Secretariat has any doubt as to the admissibility of a petition, it shall submit it for consideration to the Commission or to the Chairman during recesses of the Commission.

CHAPTER II
PETITIONS AND COMMUNICATIONS REGARDING STATES PARTIES TO
THE AMERICAN CONVENTION ON HUMAN RIGHTS

Article 31: Condition for Considering the Petition

The Commission shall take into account petitions regarding alleged violations by a state party of human rights defined in the American Convention on Human Rights, only when they fulfill the requirements set forth in that Convention, in the Statute and in these Regulations.

Article 32: Requirements for the Petitions

Petitions addressed to the Commission shall include:

a. the name, nationality, profession or occupation, postal address, or domicile and signature of the person or persons making the denunciation; or in cases where the petitioner is a nongovernmental entity, its legal domicile or postal address, and the name and signature of its legal representative or representatives;
b. an account of the act or situation that is denounced, specifying the place and date of the alleged violations and, if possible, the name of the victims of such violations as well as that of any official that might have been appraised of the act or situation that was denounced;
c. an indication of the state in question which the petitioner considers

responsible, by commission or omission, for the violation of a human right recognized in the American Convention on Human Rights in the case of States Parties thereto, even if no specific reference is made to the article alleged to have been violated;

d.   information on whether the remedies under domestic law have been exhausted or whether it has been impossible to do so.

Article 33: Omission of Requirements

Without prejudice to the provisions of Article 26, if the Commission considers that the petition is inadmissible or incomplete, it shall notify the petitioner, whom it shall ask to complete the requirements omitted in the petition.

Article 34: Initial Processing

1.   The Commission, acting initially through its Secretariat, shall receive and process petitions lodged with it in accordance with the standards set forth below:

   a.   it shall enter the petition in a register especially prepared for that purpose, and the date on which it was received shall be marked on the petition or communication itself;

   b.   it shall acknowledge receipt of the petition to the petitioner, indicating that it will be considered in accordance with the Regulations;

   c.   if it accepts, in principle, the admissibility of the petition, it shall request information from the government of the State in question and include the pertinent parts of the petitions.

2.   In serious or urgent cases or when it is believed that the life, personal integrity or health of a person is in imminent danger, the Commission shall request the promptest reply from the government, using for this purpose the means it considers most expeditious.

3.   The request for information shall not constitute a prejudgment with regard to the decision the Commission may finally adopt on the admissibility of the petition.

4.   In transmitting the pertinent parts of a communication to the government of the State in question, the identity of the petitioner shall be withheld, as shall any other information that could identify him, except when the petitioner expressly authorizes in writing the disclosure of his identity.

5.   The Commission shall request the affected government to provide the information requested within 90 days after the date on which the request is sent.

6.   The government of the State in question may, with justifiable cause, request a 30 day extension, but in no case shall extensions be granted for more than 180 days after the date on which the first communication is sent to to government of the State concerned.

7.   The pertinent parts of the reply and the documents provided by the government shall be made known to the petitioner or to his representative, who shall be asked to submit his observations and any available evidence to the contrary within 30 days.

8. On receipt of the information or documents requested, the pertinent parts shall be transmitted to the government, which shall be allowed to submit its final observations within 30 days.

Article 35: Preliminary Questions

The Commission shall proceed to examine the case and decide on the following matters:

    a. whether the remedies under domestic law have been exhausted, and it may determine any measures it considers necessary to clarify any remaining doubts;

    b. other questions related to the admissibility of the petition or its manifest inadmissibility based upon the record or submission of the parties;

    c. whether grounds for the petition exist or subsist, and if not, to order the file closed.

Article 36: Examination by the Commission

The record shall be submitted by the Secretariat to the Commission for consideration at the first session held after the period referred to in Article 31, paragraph 5, if the government has not provided the information on that occasion, or after the periods indicated in paragraphs 7 and 8 have elapsed if the petitioner has not replied or if the government has not submitted its final observations.

Article 37: Exhaustion of Domestic Remedies

1. For a petition to be admitted by the Commission, the remedies under domestic jurisdiction must have been invoked and exhausted in accordance with the general principles of international law.

2. The provisions of the preceding paragraph shall not be applicable when:

    a. the domestic legislation of the State concerned does not afford due process of law for protection of the right or rights that have allegedly been violated;

    b. the party alleging violation of his rights has been denied access to the remedies under domestic law or has been prevented from exhausting them;

    c. there has been unwarranted delay in rendering a final judgment under the aforementioned remedies.

3. When the petitioner contends that he is unable to prove exhaustion as indicated in this Article, it shall be up to the government against which this petition has been lodged to demonstrate to the Commission that the remedies under domestic law have not previously been exhausted, unless it is clearly evident from the background information contained in the petition.

Article 38: Deadline for the Presentation of Petitions

1. The Commission shall refrain from taking up those petitions that are lodged after the six-month period following the date on which the party whose rights have allegedly been violated has been notified of the final ruling in cases where the remedies under domestic law have been exhausted.

2. In the circumstances set forth in Article 34, (2) of these Regulations, the deadline for presentation of a petition to the Commission shall be within a reasonable period of time, in the Commission's judgment, as from the date on which the alleged violation of rights has occurred, considering the circumstances of each specific case.

Article 39: Duplication of Procedures

1. The Commission shall not consider a petition in cases where the subject of the petition:

   a. is pending settlement in another procedure under an international governmental organization of which the State concerned is a member;

   b. essentially duplicates a petition pending or already examined and settled by the Commission or by another international governmental organization of which the state concerned is a member.

2. The Commission shall not refrain from taking up and examining a petition in cases provided for in paragraph 1 when:

   a. the procedure followed before the other organization or agency is one limited to an examination of the general situation on human rights in the state in question and there has been no decision on the specific facts that are the subject of the petition submitted to the Commission, or is one that will not lead to an effective settlement of the violation denounced;

   b. the petitioner before the Commission or a family member is the alleged victim of the violation denounced and the petitioner before the organizations in reference is a third party or a nongovernmental entity having no mandate from the former.

Article 40: Separation and Combination of Cases

1. Any petition that states different facts that concern more than one person, and that could constitute various violations that are unrelated in time and place shall be separated and processed as separate cases, provided the requirements set forth in Article 32 are met.

2. When two petitions deal with the same facts and persons, they shall be combined and processed in a single file.

Article 41: Declaration of Inadmissibility

The Commission shall declare inadmissible any petition when:

a.   any of the requirements set forth in Article 32 of these Regulations has not been met;
b.   when the petition does not state facts that constitute a violation of rights referred to in Article 31 of these Regulations in the case of States Parties to the American Convention on Human Rights;
c.   the petition is manifestly groundless or inadmissible on the basis of the statement by the petitioner himself or the government.

Article 42: Presumption

The facts reported in the petition whose pertinent parts have been transmitted to the government of the State in reference shall be presumed to be true if, during the maximum period set by the Commission under the provisions of Article 34 paragraph 5, the government has not provided the pertinent information, as long as other evidence does not lead to a different conclusion.

Article 43: Hearing

1.   If the file has not been closed and in order to verify the facts, the Commission may conduct a hearing following a summons to the parties and proceed to examine the matter set forth in the petition.
2.   At that hearing, the Commission may request any pertinent information from the representative of the State in question and shall receive, if so requested, oral or written statements presented by the parties concerned.

Article 44: On-site Investigation

1.   If necessary and advisable, the Commission shall carry out an on-site investigation, for the effective conduct of which it shall request, and the States concerned shall furnish to it, all necessary facilities.
2.   However, in serious and urgent cases, only the presentation of a petition or communication that fulfills all the formal requirements of admissibility shall be necessary in order for the Commission to conduct an on-site investigation with the prior consent of the State in whose territory a violation has allegedly been committed.
3.   Once the investigatory stage has been completed, the case shall be brought for consideration before the Commission, which shall prepare its decision in a period of 180 days.

Article 45: Friendly Settlement

1.   At the request of any of the parties, or on its own initiative, the Commission shall place itself at the disposal of the parties concerned, at any stage of the examination of a petition, with a view to reaching a friendly settlement of the matter on the basis of respect for the human rights recognized in the American Convention on Human Rights.

2. In order for the Commission to offer itself as an organ of conciliation for a friendly settlement of the matter it shall be necessary for the positions and allegations of the parties to be sufficiently precise; and in the judgment of the Commission, the nature of the matter must be susceptible to the use of the friendly settlement procedure.

3. The Commission shall accept the proposal to act as an organ of conciliation for a friendly settlement presented by one of the parties if the circumstances described in the above paragraph exist and if the other party to the dispute expressly accepts the procedure.

4. The Commission, upon accepting the role of an organ of conciliation for a friendly settlement shall designate a Special Commission or an individual from among its members. The Special Commission or the member so designated shall inform the Commission within the time period set by the Commission.

5. The Commission shall fix a time for the reception and gathering of evidence, it shall set dates for the holding of hearings, if appropriate, it shall plan an on-site observation, which will be carried out following the receipt of consent of the State to be visited and it shall fix a time for the conclusion of the procedure, which the Commission may extend.

6. If a friendly settlement is reached, the Commission shall prepare a report which shall be transmitted to the parties concerned and referred to the Secretary General of the Organization of American States for publication. This report shall contain a brief statement of the facts and of the solution reached. If any party in the case so requests, it shall be provided with the fullest possible information.

7. In a case where the Commission finds, during the course of processing the matter, that the case, by its very nature, is not susceptible to a friendly settlement; or finds that one of the parties does not consent to the application of this procedure; or does not evidence good will in reaching a friendly settlement based on the respect for human rights, the Commission, at any stage of the procedure shall declare its role as organ of conciliation for a friendly settlement to have terminated.

Article 46: Preparation of the Report

1. If a friendly settlement is not reached, the Commission shall examine the evidence provided by the government in question and the petitioner, evidence taken from witnesses to the facts or that obtained from documents, records, official publications, or through an on-site investigation.

2. After the evidence has been examined, the Commission shall prepare a report stating the facts and conclusions regarding the case submitted to it for its study.

Article 47: Proposals and Recommendations

1. In transmitting the report, the Commission may make such proposals and recommendations as it sees fit.

2. If, within a period of three months from the date of the transmittal of the report of the Commission to the States concerned, the matter has not been

settled or submitted by the Commission, or by the State concerned, to the Court and its jurisdiction accepted, the Commission may, by the vote of an absolute majority of its members, set forth its opinion and conclusions concerning the question submitted for its consideration.

3. The Commission may make the pertinent recommendations and prescribe a period within which the government in question must take the measures that are incumbent upon it to remedy the situation examined.

4. If the report does not represent, in its entirety, or, in part, the unanimous opinion of the members of the Commission, any member may add his opinion separately to that report.

5. Any verbal or written statement made by the parties shall also be included in the report.

6. The report shall be transmitted to the parties concerned, who shall not be authorized to publish it.

Article 48: Publication of the Report

1. When the prescribed period has expired, the Commission shall decide by the vote of an absolute majority of its members whether the State has taken suitable measures and whether to publish its report.

2. That report may be published by including it in the Annual Report to be presented by the Commission to the General Assembly of the Organization or in any other way the Commission may consider suitable.

Article 49: Communications from a Government

1. Communications presented by the government of a State Party to the American Convention on Human Rights, which has accepted the competence of the Commission to receive and examine such communications against other States Parties, shall be transmitted to the State Party in question, whether or not it has accepted the competence of the Commission. Even if it has not accepted such competence, the communication shall be transmitted so that the State can exercise its option under the provisions of Article 45, (3) of the Convention to recognize the Commission's competence in the specific case that is the subject of the communication.

2. Once the State in question has accepted the competence of the Commission to take up the communication of the other State Party, the corresponding procedure shall be governed by the provisions of Chapter II insofar as they may be applicable.

Article 50: Referral of the Case to the Court

1. If a State Party to the Convention has accepted the Court's jurisdiction in accordance with Article 62 of the Convention, the Commission may refer the case to the Court, subsequent to transmittal of the report referred to in Article 46 of these Regulations to the government of the State in question.

2. When it is ruled that the case is to be referred to the Court, the Executive

Secretary of the Commission shall immediately notify the Court, the petitioner and the government of the State in question.

3. If the State Party has not accepted the Court's jurisdiction, the Commission may call upon that State to make use of the option referred to in Article 62, paragraph 2 of the Convention to recognize the Court's jurisdiction in the specific case that is the subject of the report.

CHAPTER III

PETITIONS CONCERNING STATES THAT ARE NOT PARTIES TO THE AMERICAN CONVENTION ON HUMAN RIGHTS

Article 51: Receipt of the Petitions

The Commission shall receive and examine any petition that contains a denunciation of alleged violations of the human rights set forth in the American Declaration of the Rights and Duties of Man, concerning the member states of the Organization that are not parties to the American Convention on Human Rights.

Article 52: Applicable Procedure

The procedure applicable to petitions concerning member states of the Organization that are not parties to the American Convention on Human Rights shall be that provided for in the General Provisions included in Chapter I of Title II, in Articles 32 to 43 of these Regulations, and in the articles indicated below.

Article 53: Final Decision

1. In addition to the facts and conclusions, the Commission's final decision shall include any recommendations the Commission deems advisable and a deadline for their implementation.
2. That decision shall be transmitted to the State in question or to the petitioner.
3. If the State does not adopt the measures recommended by the Commission within the deadline referred to in paragraphs 1 or 3, the Commission may publish its decision.
4. The decision referred to in the preceding paragraph may be published in the Annual Report to be presented by the Commission to the General Assembly of the Organization or in any other manner the Commission may see fit.

Article 54: Request for Reconsideration

1. When the State in question or the petitioner, prior to the expiration of the 90 day deadline, invokes new facts or legal arguments which have not been previously considered, it may request a reconsideration of the conclusions or recommendations of the Commission's Report. The Commission shall decide to maintain or modify its decision, fixing a new deadline for compliance, where appropriate.
2. The Commission, if it considers it necessary, may request the State in question

or the petitioner, as the case may be, to present any observations for reconsideration.

3. The reconsideration procedure may be utilized only once.
4. The Commission shall consider the request for reconsideration during the first regular session following its presentation.
5. If the State does not adopt the measures recommended by the Commission within the deadline referred to in paragraph 1, the Commission may publish its decision in conformity with Articles 48(2) and 53(4) of the present Regulations.

CHAPTER IV
ON-SITE OBSERVATIONS

Article 55: Designation of the Special Commission

On-site observations shall be carried out in each case by a Special Commission named for that purpose. The number of members of the Special Commission and the designation of its Chairman shall be determined by the Commission. In cases of great urgency, such decisions may be made by the Chairman subject to the approval of the Commission.

Article 56: Disqualification

A member of the Commission who is a national of or who resides in the territory of the State in which the on-site observation is to be carried out shall be disqualified from participating therein.

Article 57: Schedule of Activities

The Special Commission shall organize its own activities. To that end, it may appoint its own members and, after hearing the Executive Secretary, any staff members of the Secretariat or personnel necessary to carry out any activities related to its mission.

Article 58: Necessary Facilities

In extending an invitation for an on-site observation or in giving its consent, the government shall furnish to the Special Commission all necessary facilities for carrying out its mission. In particular, it shall bind itself not to take any reprisals of any kind against any persons or entities cooperating with the Special Commission or providing information or testimony.

Article 59: Other Applicable Standards

Without prejudice to the provisions in the preceding article, any on-site observation agreed upon by the Commission shall be carried out in accordance with the following standards:

a.   the Special Commission or any of its members shall be able to interview freely and in private, any persons, groups, entities or institutions, and the government shall grant the pertinent guarantees to all those who provide the Commission with information, testimony or evidence of any kind;

b.   the members of the Special Commission shall be able to travel freely throughout the territory of the country, for which purpose the government shall extend all the corresponding facilities, including the necessary documentation;

c.   the government shall ensure the availability of local means of transportation;

d.   the members of the Special Commission shall have access to the jails and all other detention and interrogation centers and shall be able to interview in private those persons imprisoned or detained;

e.   the government shall provide the Special Commission with any document related to the observance of human rights that it may consider necessary for the presentation of its reports;

f.   the Special Commission shall be able to use any method appropriate for collecting, recording or reproducing the information it considers useful;

g.   the government shall adopt the security measures necessary to protect the Special Commission;

h.   the government shall ensure the availability of appropriate lodging for the members of the Special Commission;

i.   the same guarantees and facilities that are set forth here for the members of the Special Commission shall also be extended to the Secretariat staff;

j.   any expenses incurred by the Special Committee, any of its members and the Secretariat staff shall be borne by the Organization, subject to the pertinent provisions.

CHAPTER V
GENERAL AND SPECIAL REPORTS

Article 60: Preparation of Draft Reports

The Commission shall prepare the general or special draft reports that it considers necessary.

Article 61: Processing and Publication

1.   The reports prepared by the Commission shall be transmitted as soon as possible through the General Secretariat of the Organization to the government or pertinent organs of the Organization.

2.   Upon adoption of a report by the Commission, the Secretariat shall publish it in the manner determined by the Commission in each instance, except as provided for in Article 47, paragraph 6, of these Regulations.

Article 62: Report on Human Rights in a State

The preparation of reports on the status of human rights in a specific state shall meet the following standards:

    a. after the draft report has been approved by the Commission, it shall be transmitted to the government of the member state in question so that it may make any observations it deems pertinent;

    b. the Commission shall indicate to that government the deadline for presentation of its observations;

    c. when the Commission receives the observations from the government, it shall study them and, in light thereof, may uphold its report or change it and decide how it is to be published;

    d. if no observation has been submitted on expiration of the deadline by the government, the Commission shall publish the report in the manner it deems suitable.

Article 63: Annual Report

The Annual Report presented by the Commission to the General Assembly of the Organization shall include the following:

    a. a brief account of the origin, legal basis, structure and purposes of the Commission as well as the status of the American Convention;

    b. a summary of the mandates and recommendations conferred upon the Commission by the General Assembly and the other competent organs, and of the status of implementation of such mandates and recommendations;

    c. a list of the meetings held during the period covered by the report and of other activities carried out by the Commission to achieve its purposes, objectives, and mandates;

    d. a summary of the activities of the Commission carried out in cooperation with other organs of the Organization and with regional or world organizations of the same type, and the results achieved through these activities;

    e. a statement on the progress made in attaining the objectives set forth in the American Declaration of the Rights and Duties of Man and the American Convention on Human Rights;

    f. a report on the areas in which measures should be taken to improve observance of human rights in accordance with the aforementioned Declaration and Convention;

    g. any observations that the Commission considers pertinent with respect to petitions it has received, including those processed in accordance with the Statute and the present Regulations which the Commission decides to publish as reports, resolutions, or recommendations;

    h. any general or special report that the Commission considers necessary with regard to the situation of human rights in the member states, noting in such reports the progess achieved and difficulties that have arisen in the effective observance of human rights;

i.   any other information, observation, or recommendation that the Commission considers advisable to submit to the General Assembly and any new program that implies additional expense.

Article 64: Economic, Social and Cultural Rights

1.   The States Parties shall forward to the Commission copies of the reports and studies referred to in Article 42 of the American Convention on Human Rights on the same date on which they submit them to the pertinent organs.
2.   The Commission may request annual reports from the other member states regarding the economic, social, and cultural rights recognized in the American Declaration of the Rights and Duties of Man.
3.   Any person, group of persons, or organization may present reports, studies or other information to the Commission on the situation of such rights in all or any of the member states.
4.   If the Commission does not receive the information referred to in the preceding paragraphs or considers it inadequate, it may send questionnaires to all or any of the member states, setting a deadline for the reply or it may turn to other available sources of information.
5.   Periodically, the Commission may entrust to experts or specialized entities studies on the situation of one or more of the aforementioned rights in a specific country or group of countries.
6.   The Commission shall make the pertinent observations and recommendations on the situation of such rights in all or any of the member states and shall include them in the Annual Report to the General Assembly or in a Special Report, as it considers most appropriate.
7.   The recommendations may include the need for economic aid or some other form of cooperation to be provided among the member states, as called for in the Charter of the Organization and in other agreements of the inter-American system.

CHAPTER VI
HEARING BEFORE THE COMMISSION

Article 65: Decision to Hold Hearing

On its own initiative, or at the request of the person concerned, the Commission may decide to hold hearings on matters defined by the Statute as within its jurisdiction.

Article 66: Purpose of the Hearings

Hearings may be held in connection with a petition or communication alleging a violation of a right set forth in the American Convention on Human Rights or in the American Declaration on the Rights and Duties of Man or in order to receive information of a general or particular nature related to the situation of human rights in one State or in a group of American states.

Article 67: Hearings on Petitions or Communications

1. Hearings on cases concerning violations of human rights and which the Commission is examining pursuant to the procedures established in Chapters II and III of Title II of these Regulations, will have as their purpose the receipt of testimony oral or written of the parties, relative to the additional information regarding the admissibility of the case, the possibility of applying the friendly settlement procedure, the verification of the facts or the merits of the matter submitted to the Commission for consideration, or as regards any other matter pertinent to the processing of the case.
2. To implement the provisions of the previous article, the Commission may invite the parties to attend a hearing, or one of the parties may request that a hearing be held.
3. If one of the two parties requests a hearing for the purposes indicated above, the Secretariat shall immediately inform the other party of that petition, and when the hearing date is set, shall invite the other party to attend, unless the Commission considers that there are reasons warranting a confidential hearing.
4. The Government shall furnish the appropriate guarantees to all persons attending a hearing or providing the Commission with information, testimony or evidence of any kind during a hearing.

Article 68: Hearings of a General Nature

1. Persons who are interested in presenting testimony or information of a general nature to the Commission shall indicate, prior to the meeting, to the Executive Secretary that they wish to appear before the next session of the Commission.
2. In their petition, interested persons shall give their reasons for desiring to appear, a summary of the information they will furnish, and the approximate time required for their testimony.
3. The Executive Secretary shall, in consultation with the Chairman of the Commission, accede to the request for a hearing, unless the information presented by the interested person reveals that the hearing bears no relation to matters within the Commission's competence or if the purpose of the hearing and its circumstances are substantially the same as an earlier one.
4. The Executive Secretary shall, in consultation with the Chairperson of the Commission, draw up a schedule and propose the time and date for the general hearings to be held during the session, and shall submit them to the Commission for approval on the first day of the session.

Article 69: Conduct of Hearings

The Commission shall, in each case, decide which of its members will take part in the hearing.

Article 70: Attendance at Hearings

1. Hearings shall be private, unless the Commission decides that other persons should attend.
2. Hearings called specifically to review a petition shall be held in private, in the presence of the parties or their representatives, unless they agree that the hearing should be public.

TITLE III
RELATIONS WITH THE INTER-AMERICAN COURT OF HUMAN RIGHTS

CHAPTER I
DELEGATES, ADVISERS, WITNESSES, AND EXPERTS

Article 71: Delegates and Assistants

1. The Commission shall delegate one or more of its members to represent it and participate as delegates in the consideration of any matter before the Inter-American Court of Human Rights.
2. In appointing such delegates, the Commission shall issue any instructions it considers necessary to guide them in the Court's proceedings.
3. When it designates more than one delegate, the Commission shall assign to one of them the responsibility of settling situations that are not foreseen in the instructions, or of clarifying any doubts raised by a delegate.
4. The delegates may be assisted by any person designated by the Commission. In the discharge of their functions, the advisers shall act in accordance with the instructions of the delegates.

Article 72: Witnesses and Experts

1. The Commission may also request the Court to summon other persons as witnesses or experts.
2. The summoning of such witnesses or experts shall be in accordance with the Regulations of the Court.

CHAPTER II
PROCEDURE BEFORE THE COURT

Article 73: Presentation of the Case

1. When, in accordance with Article 61 of the American Convention on Human Rights, the Commission decides to bring a case before the Court, it shall submit a request in accordance with the provisions of the Statute and the Regulations of the Court, and specifying:

a.   the parties who will be intervening in the proceedings before the Court;
b.   the date on which the Commission approved its report;
c.   the names and addresses of its delegates;
d.   a summary of the case;
e.   the grounds for requesting a ruling by the Court.

2.   The Commissions's request shall be accompanied by certified copies of the items in the file that the Commission or its delegate considers pertinent.

Article 74: Transmittal of other Elements

The Commission shall transmit to the Court, at its request, any other petition, evidence, document, or information concerning the case, with the exception of documents concerning futile attempts to reach a friendly settlement. The transmittal of documents shall in each case be subject to the decision of the Commission, which shall withhold the name and identity of the petitioner.

Article 75: Notification of the Petitioner

When the Commission decides to refer a case to the Court, the Executive Secretary shall immediately notify the petitioner and alleged victim of the Commission's decision and offer him the opportunity of making observations in writing on the request submitted to the Court. The Commission shall decide on the action to be taken with respect to these observations.

Article 76: Provisional Measures

1.   In cases of extreme gravity and urgency, and when it becomes necessary to avoid irreparable damage to persons in a matter that has not yet been submitted to the Court for consideration, the Commission may request it to adopt any provisional measures it deems pertinent.
2.   When the Commission is not in session, that request may be made by the Chairman, or in his absence by one of the Vice-Chairmen, in order of precedence.

TITLE IV
FINAL PROVISIONS

Article 77: Calendar Computation

All time periods set forth in the present Regulations – in numbers of days – will be understood to be counted as calendar days.

Article 78: Interpretation

Any doubt that might arise with respect to the interpretation of these Regulations shall be resolved by an absolute majority of the members of the Commission.

Article 79: Amendment of the Regulations

The Regulations may be amended by an absolute majority of the members of the Commission.

23. RULES OF PROCEDURE OF THE INTER-AMERICAN COURT ON HUMAN RIGHTS

Annual Report of the Inter-American Court of Human Rights, 1991, O.A.S. Doc. OEA/Ser.L/V/III.25 doc.7 at 18 (1992), reprinted in Basic Documents Pertaining to Human Rights in the Inter-American System, OEA/Ser.L.V/II.82 doc.6 rev.1 at 145 (1992).

Article 1: Purpose

1. These Rules regulate the organization and establish the procedures of the Inter-American Court of Human Rights.
2. The Court may adopt such other Rules as are necessary to carry out its functions.
3. In the absence of a provision in these Rules or in case of doubt as to their interpretation, the Court shall decide.

Article 2: Definitions

For the purposes of these Rules:

    a. the term "Court" means the Inter-American Court of Human Rights;

    b. the term "Convention" means the American Convention on Human Rights (Pact of San José, Costa Rica);

    c. the term "Statute" means the Statute of the Court approved by the General Assembly of the Organization of American States on October 31, 1979 (AG/RES. 448 [IX-O/79]), as amended;

    d. the expression "Permanent Commission" means the Permanent Commission of the Court;

    e. the expression "titular judge" means any judge elected in pursuance of Articles 53 and 54 of the Convention;

    f. the expression "*ad hoc* judge" means any judge appointed in pursuance of Article 55 of the Convention;

    g. the expression "interim judge" means any judge appointed in pursuance of Articles 6(3) and 19(4) of the Statute;

    h. the expression "Contracting states" means the States which have ratified or adhered to the Convention;

    i. the expression "member states" means the States which are Members of the Organization of American States;

    j. the expression "parties to the case" means the parties in a case before the Court;

    k. the term "Commission" means the Inter-American Commission on Human Rights;

    l. the expression "Delegates of the Commission" means the persons designated by the Commission to represent it before the Court;

    m. the term "Agent" means the person designated by a State to represent it before the Court;

n. the expression "original claimant" means the person, group of persons, or non-govermental entity that instituted the original petition with the Commission pursuant to Article 44 of the Convention;

o. the term "victim" means the person whose rights under the Convention are alleged to have been violated;

p. the expression "Report of the Commission" means the report provided for in Article 50 of the Convention;

q. the acronym "OAS" means the Organization of American States;

r. the expression "General Assembly" means the General Assembly of the OAS;

s. the expression "Permanent Council" means the Permanent Council of the OAS;

t. the expression "Secretary General" means the Secretary General of the OAS;

u. the term "Secretary" means the Secretary of the Court;

v. the expression "Deputy Secretary" means the Deputy Secretary of the Court;

w. the term "Secretariat" means the Secretariat of the Court.

TITLE I
ORGANIZATION AND FUNCTIONING OF THE COURT

CHAPTER I
THE PRESIDENCY

Article 3: Election of the President and Vice-President

1. The President and Vice-President are elected by the Court for a period of two years. Their terms begin on July 1 of the corresponding year. The election shall be held during the regular session nearest to that date.

2. The election referred to in this Article shall be by secret ballot of the titular judges present. The judge who wins four or more votes shall be deemed elected. If no candidate receives the required number of votes, a ballot shall take place between the two judges who have received the most votes. In the case of a tie vote, the judge having precedence in accordance with Article 13 of the Statute shall be deemed elected.

Article 4: Functions of the President

1. The functions of the President are

    a. to represent the Court;

    b. to preside over the meetings of the Court and to submit for its consideration the topics of the agenda;

    c. to direct and promote the work of the Court;

    d. to rule on points of order that may arise during the meetings of the Court.

If any judge so requests, the point of order shall be decided by a majority vote;

e.   to present, at the beginning of each regular or special session, a report to the Court on the activities he has carried out as President during the recess between sessions;

f.   to exercise such other functions as are conferred upon him by the Statute or these Rules, or entrusted to him by the Court.

2.   In specific cases, the President may delegate the representation to which paragraph 1(a) of this Article refers to the Vice-President or any of the judges or, if necessary, to the Secretary or Deputy Secretary.

3.   If the President is a national of one of the parties to a case before the Court or in special situations in which he considers it appropriate, he shall relinquish the Presidency for that particular case. The same rule shall apply to the Vice-President or to any judge called upon to exercise the Presidency.

Article 5: Functions of the Vice-President

1.   The Vice-President shall replace the President in the latter's temporary absence and shall assume the Presidency when the absence is permanent. In the latter case, the Court shall elect a Vice-President to serve out that term. The same procedure shall be followed if the absence of the Vice-President is permanent.

2.   In the absence of the President and the Vice-President, their functions shall be assumed by the other judges in the order of precedence established in Article 13 of the Statute.

Article 6: Commissions

1.   The Permanent Commission is composed of the President, the Vice-President and a third judge appointed by the President. The President may appoint a fourth judge for specific cases or on a permanent basis. The Permanent Commission assists the President in the exercise of his functions.

2.   The Court may appoint other commissions for specific matters. In urgent cases, they may be appointed by the President if the Court is not in session.

3.   In performing their functions, the commissions shall be governed, wherever relevant, by the provisions of these Rules.

CHAPTER II
THE SECRETARIAT

Article 7: Election of the Secretary

1.   The Court shall elect its Secretary. The Secretary must possess the legal qualifications required for the position, a good command of the working languages of the Court and the experience necessary to carry out his functions.

2. The Secretary shall be elected for a period of five years and may be reelected. He may be freely removed at any time if the Court so decides by the vote of no less than four judges. The vote shall be by secret ballot.
3. The Secretary shall be elected in the manner provided for in Article 3(2) of these Rules.

Article 8: Deputy Secretary

1. The Deputy Secretary shall be appointed, at the proposal of the Secretary of the Court, in the manner provided for in the Statute. He shall assist the Secretary in the performance of his functions and substitute for him in his temporary absences.
2. If the Secretary and Deputy Secretary are both unable to perform their functions, the President may appoint an Acting Secretary.

Article 9: Oath

1. The Secretary and Deputy Secretary shall take an oath before the President.
2. The staff of the Secretariat, including any persons carrying out interim or temporary functions, shall, upon assuming their functions, take an oath before the President undertaking to respect the confidential nature of any facts that may come to their attention in performing such functions. If the President is not present at the seat of the Court, the Secretary shall administer the oath.
3. All oaths shall be recorded in a document that shall be signed by the person being sworn and the person administering the oath.

Article 10: Functions of the Secretary

The functions of the Secretary are:

    a.   to notify the judgments, advisory opinions, decisions and other rulings of the Court;
    b.   to announce the hearings of the Court;
    c.   to record the minutes of the meetings of the Court;
    d.   to attend all meetings of the Court held at the seat or away from it;
    e.   to deal with the correspondence of the Court;
    f.   to direct the administration of the Court, pursuant to the instructions of the President;
    g.   to prepare the draft programs, regulations and budgets of the Court;
    h.   to plan, direct and co-ordinate the work of the staff of the Court;
    i.   to carry out the tasks assigned to him by the Court or the President;
    j.   to perform any other duties provided for by the Statute or these Rules.

CHAPTER III
FUNCTIONING OF THE COURT

Article 11: Regular Sessions

The Court shall meet in two regular sessions each year, one in each semester, on the dates decided upon by the Court at the immediately preceding session. The President may change these dates in exceptional circumstances.

Article 12: Special Sessions

Special sessions may be convoked by the President on his own initiative or at the request of a majority of the judges.

Article 13: Quorum

The quorum for the deliberations of the Court is five judges.

Article 14: Hearings, Deliberations and Decisions

1. The hearings shall be public and shall be held at the seat of the Court. When exceptional circumstances warrant it, the Court may decide to hold a hearing in private or at some other location. The Court shall decide who is permitted to attend such hearings. Even in these exceptional cases, however, minutes shall be kept in the manner prescribed in Article 42 of these Rules.
2. The Court shall deliberate in private and its deliberations shall remain secret. Only the judges shall take part in the deliberations, although the Secretary and Deputy Secretary or their substitutes may be present, as well as such other Secretariat staff as may be required. No other persons may be admitted except by special decision of the Court and after having taken an oath.
3. Any question which is to be voted upon shall be formulated in precise terms in one of the working languages. At the request of any of the judges, the text thereof shall be translated by the Secretariat into the other working languages and distributed prior to the vote.
4. The minutes of the deliberations of the Court shall be limited to a statement of the subject of the discussion and the decisions that were taken. Dissenting votes and declarations made for the record shall also be noted.

Article 15: Decisions and Voting

1. The President shall present, point by point, the matters to be voted upon. Each judge shall vote either in the affirmative or the negative; abstentions shall not be permitted.
2. The votes shall be cast in inverse order to the order of precedence established in Article 13 of the Statute.
3. The decisions of the Court shall be made by a majority of the judges present.
4. In the event of a tie, the President shall have a second and casting vote.

Article 16: Continuation in Office by the Judges

Judges whose terms have expired shall continue to exercise their functions in cases that they have begun to hear and that are still pending. However, in the event of death, resignation, inability to sit, withdrawal, or exemption from sitting, the judge in question shall be substituted by the judge who was selected to replace him, if applicable, or by the judge who has precedence among the new judges elected upon expiration of the term of the judge to be replaced.

Article 17: Interim Judges

Interim judges, appointed in pursuance of Articles 6(3) and 19(4) of the Statute, shall have the same rights and functions as titular judges, except for the limitations expressly established.

Article 18: Ad Hoc Judges

1. In a case arising under Articles 55(2) or 55(3) of the Convention and 10(2) or 10(3) of the Statute, the President, acting through the Secretariat, shall invite the States referred to in those provisions to appoint an *ad hoc* judge within thirty days following the Agent's receipt of the written invitation. The invitation may also be delivered to the Embassy of the State in question in Costa Rica or, if the State is not represented there, to its Delegation to the OAS in Washington, D. C., United States of America. The President shall also bring the relevant provisions to the attention of the States concerned.
2. When it appears that two or more States have a common interest, the President shall invite them to appoint a single *ad hoc* judge in accordance with Article 10 of the Statute. If no agreement has been communicated to the Court within the thirty-day period following receipt of the written invitation by the last of these States to receive it at the location stipulated in the preceding paragraph, each State shall have fifteen days in which to submit a candidate. Thereafter, and if several candidates have been presented, the President shall choose by lot one *ad hoc* judge, and shall communicate the result to the interested parties.
3. If the interested States fail to exercise their rights within the periods provided for in the preceding paragraphs, they shall be deemed to have waived such rights.
4. The Secretary shall communicate the appointment of the *ad hoc* judges to the parties to the case.
5. Ad hoc judges shall take an oath at the first meeting devoted to the consideration of the case for which they have been appointed.
6. Ad hoc judges shall receive honoraria for days worked, consistent with the budgetary policies of the Court.

Article 19: Disqualification, Withdrawal or Exemption

1. Disqualifications, withdrawals or exemptions of the judges shall be governed by the provisions of Article 19 of the Statute.

2. Motions for disqualifications and withdrawal must be filed prior to the first hearing of the case. However, if the grounds therefor were not known at that time, such motions may be submitted to the Court at the first possible opportunity to enable it to rule on the matter immediately.
3. When, for whatever reason, a judge is not present at one of the hearing or at other stages of the proceedings, the Court may decide to exempt him from continuing to hear the case, taking into account all the circumstances it deems relevant.

TITLE II PROCEDURE

CHAPTER I
GENERAL RULES

Article 20: Official Languages

1. The official languages of the Court are those of the OAS.
2. The working languages shall be those agreed upon by the Court every three years, taking into account the languages spoken by the judges. In a specific case, however, the language of one of the parties may also be adopted as a working language, provided it is one of the official languages.
3. The working languages shall be determined at the beginning of the proceedings in each case, unless they are the same as those already being employed by the Court.
4. The Court may authorize any person appearing before it to use his own language if he does not have sufficient knowledge of the working languages. In these circumstances, however, the Court shall make the necessary arrangements to ensure that an interpreter is present to translate that testimony into the working languages.
5. The Court shall, in all cases, determine the authentic text.

Article 21: Representation of the States

1. The States Parties to a case shall be represented by an Agent, who may be assisted by any person of his choice.
2. If a State replaces its Agent, it shall notify the Court of that fact.
    The substitution shall only take effect once the notification has been received at the seat of the Court.
3. A Deputy Agent may be designated. His actions shall have the same validity as those of the Agent.
4. When appointing its Agent, the State in question shall notify the address to which all relevant communications shall be deemed to have been officially transmitted.

Article 22: Representation of the Commission

1. The Commission shall be represented by the Delegates whom it shall have designated for that purpose. The Delegates may be assisted by any person of their choice.
2. If the attorneys retained by the original claimant, by the alleged victim or by the next of kin of the victim are among the persons selected by the Delegates to assist them, pursuant to the preceding paragraph, this fact shall be brought to the attention of the Court.

Article 23: Co-operation by the States

1. The States Parties to a case have the obligation to cooperate in order to ensure that all notices, communications or summonses addressed to persons subject to their jurisdiction are duly executed. They shall also expedite compliance with summonses by persons who either reside in or need to pass through their territory.
2. The same rule shall apply to any proceedings that the Court decides to carry out or order in the territory of a State Party to the case.
3. When the performance of any of the measures referred to in the preceding paragraphs requires the co-operation of any other State, the President shall request the government in question to provide the requisite assistance.

Article 24: Interim Measures

1. At any stage of the proceeding involving cases of extreme gravity and urgency and when necessary to avoid irreparable damage to persons, the Court may, at the request of a party or on its own motion, order whatever provisional measures it deems appropriate, pursuant to Article 63(2) of the Convention.
2. With respect to matters not yet submitted to it, the Court may act at the request of the Commission.
3. Such request may be presented to the President, to any judge of the Court or to the Secretariat, by any means of communication. The recipient of the request shall immediately bring it to the attention of the President.
4. If the Court is not sitting, the President shall convoke it immediately. Pending the meeting of the Court, the President, in consultation with the Permanent Commission and, if possible, with the other judges, shall call upon the government concerned to adopt the necessary urgent measures and to act so as to permit any provisional measures subsequently ordered by the Court to have the requisite effect.
5. In its Annual Report to the General Assembly, the Court shall include a statement regarding the provisional measures ordered during the period covered by the report. If such measures have not been duly executed, the Court shall make whatever recommendations it deems appropriate.

Article 25: Procedure by Default

1. When a party fails to appear in or to continue with a case, the Court shall, on its own motion, take whatever measures are necessary to complete consideration of the case.
2. When a party enters a case at a later stage of the proceedings, it shall take the proceedings at that stage.

CHAPTER II
INSTITUTION OF THE PROCEEDINGS

Article 26: Filing of the Application

For a case to be referred to the Court under Article 61(1) of the Convention, an application shall be filed with the Secretariat, in ten copies, indicating:

1. the appointment of the Agent or Delegates, pursuant to Articles 21 and 22 of these Rules;
2. when the case is referred by a State, it shall, if pertinent, present its objections to the opinion of the Commission;
3. when the case is referred by the Commission, it shall include, in addition, the report referred to in Article 50 of the Convention;
4. when the case is before the Commission, the following information shall also be provided:

    a. the parties to the case;
    b. the date of the report of the Commission to which Article 50 of the Convention refers;

5. the purpose of the application, a statement of the facts, the supporting evidence, the legal arguments and relevant conclusions.

Article 27: Preliminary Review of the Application

When during a preliminary review of the application the President finds that the basic requirements have not been met, he shall request the applicant to correct any deficiencies within twenty days.

Article 28: Communications of the Application

1. On receipt of the application, the Secretary shall give notice thereof and transmit copies to the following:

    a. the President and the judges of the Court;
    b. the respondent State;
    c. the Commission, when it is not also the applicant;
    d. the original claimant, if known;
    e. the victim or his next of kin, if applicable.

2. The Secretary shall inform the other Contracting States and the Secretary General of the filing of the application.
3. When giving the notice, the Secretary shall request that, within a period of two weeks, the respondent States designate their Agent and, if appropriate, the Commission appoint its Delegates, in accordance with Articles 21 and 22 of these Rules. Until the Delegates are duly appointed, the Commission shall be deemed to be properly represented by its President for all purposes in the case.

CHAPTER III
EXAMINATION OF THE CASES

Article 29: Written Proceedings

1. The respondent State shall always have the right to file a written answer to the application within three months following notification thereof.
2. The President shall consult the Agents and the Delegates on whether they consider other steps in the written proceedings to be necessary. If the response is in the affirmative, he shall fix the deadlines for the filing of the documents.
3. The documents to which this article refers shall be filed with the Secretariat in ten copies. The Secretary shall transmit them to the persons indicated in Article 28(1) of these Rules.

Article 30: Joinder of Cases

1. The Court may, at any stage of the proceedings, direct the joinder of cases that are interrelated.
2. It may also order the joinder of the written or oral proceedings of several cases, including the examination of witnesses.
3. After consulting the Agents and the Delegates, the President may direct that the proceedings in two or more cases be conducted simultaneously, without prejudice to the decision of the Court regarding the joinder of the cases.

Article 31: Preliminary Objections

1. Preliminary objections may be filed only within thirty days following notification of the application.
2. The document setting out the preliminary objections shall be filed with the Secretariat in ten copies and shall set out the facts on which the objection is based, the legal arguments, and the conclusions and supporting documents, as well as any evidence which the party filing the objection may wish to produce.
3. The Secretary shall immediately transmit the preliminary objections to the persons indicated in Article 28(1) of these Rules.
4. The presentation of preliminary objections shall not cause the suspension of the proceedings on the merits, unless the Court expressly decides otherwise.
5. Any parties to the case wishing to submit briefs regarding the preliminary objections may do so within thirty days after receipt of the communication.

302

6.   The Court may, if it deems it appropriate, convene a special hearing relating to the preliminary objections, after which it shall rule on the objections or order that they be joined to the merits.

Article 32: Oral Proceedings

The President shall, after consulting the Agents and the Delegates, fix the date for the opening of the oral proceedings.

Article 33: Conduct of the Hearings

The President shall direct the hearings. He shall prescribe the order in which the persons listed in Articles 21 and 22 of these Rules shall be heard.

Article 34: Measures for Taking Evidence

1.   The Court may, at the request of a party or on its own motion, obtain any evidence which it considers likely to clarify the facts of the case. In particular, it may decide to hear as a witness or expert witness, or in any other capacity, any person whose evidence, statements or opinion it deems useful.
2.   The Court may, at any time during the proceedings, request the parties to provide any type of evidence available to them or any explanation or statement that, in its judgment, would be likely to clarify the facts of the case.
3.   The Court may, at any time during the proceedings, designate any person, office, commission or authority of its choice to obtain information, express an opinion or make a report on any given point. These reports may not be published without the authorization of the Court.
4.   The Court may, at any time during the proceedings, designate one or more of its members to conduct an inquiry, carry out an investigation on the spot or take evidence in some other manner.

Article 35: Cost of Requested Evidence

The party requesting the production of evidence shall defray the cost thereof.

Article 36: Convocation of Witnesses, Expert Witnesses and Other Persons

1.   Witnesses, expert witnesses, or other persons whom the Court decides to hear, shall be summoned by the Secretary.
2.   The summons shall indicate:

     a.   the name, status and other particulars of the person summoned;
     b.   the name of the parties;
     c.   the object of the inquiry, expert opinion, or any other measure ordered by the Court or by the President;
     d.   the provisions made for the reimbursement of the expenses incurred by the person summoned.

Article 37: Oath or Solemn Declaration by Witnesses and Expert Witnesses

1. After his identity has been established and before giving evidence, every witness shall take an oath or make a solemn declaration as follows:

    "I swear" – or "I solemnly declare" – "upon my honor and conscience that I will speak the truth, the whole truth and nothing but the truth."

2. After his identity has been established and before carrying out his task, every expert witness shall take an oath or make a solemn declaration along the following lines:

    "I swear" – or "I solemnly declare" – "that I will discharge my duty as an expert witness honorably and conscientiously."

3. This oath shall be taken or this declaration made before the Court or before the President or any of the judges who have been so delegated by the Court.

Article 38: Disqualification of a Witness

1. The disqualification of a witness shall take place before he testifies, unless the grounds for the disqualification become known only thereafter.
2. If the Court considers it necessary, it may nevertheless hear, for purposes of information, a person who is not qualified to be heard as a witness.
3. The Court shall assess the value of the testimony and of the disqualification.

Article 39: Objection to an Expert Witness

1. The grounds for disqualification applicable to judges under Article 19(1) of the Statute shall also apply to expert witnesses.
2. Objections shall be presented within fifteen days following notification of the appointment of the expert witness in question.
3. If the expert witness who has been challenged contests the grounds invoked against him, the Court shall decide, except that when the Court is not in session the President, in consultation with the Permanent Commission, may order the evidence to be presented. The Court shall be informed thereof and shall have the final decision on the value of the evidence.
4. When it becomes necessary to appoint a new expert witness, the Court shall decide. Nevertheless, if there is urgency in obtaining the evidence, the President, in consultation with the Permanent Commission, shall make the appointment and inform the Court accordingly. The Court shall have the final decision in assessing the value of the evidence.

Article 40: Failure to Appear or False Evidence

1. When, without good reason, a witness or any other person who has been duly summoned fails to appear or refuses to give evidence, the State having jurisdiction over such witness or other person shall be informed accordingly. The same provision shall apply when a witness or expert witness has, in the

opinion of the Court, violated the oath or solemn declaration mentioned in Article 37 of these Rules.

2. States shall not institute proceedings nor take reprisals against any persons on account of their testimony before the Court. However, the Court may request the States to take the measures provided for in their domestic legislation against those who, in the opinion of the Court, have violated their oath.

Article 41: Questions Put During the Hearings

1. The judges may ask any person appearing before the Court whatever questions they deem appropriate.
2. The witnesses, expert witnesses and any other persons referred to in Article 36 of these Rules may, subject to the control of the President, be examined by the Agents and the Delegates or, at their request, by the persons referred to in articles 21 and 22 of these Rules.
3. The President is empowered to rule on the relevance of the questions posed and to excuse the person to whom the questions are addressed from replying, unless the Court shall decide otherwise.

Article 42: Minutes of the Hearings

1. Minutes shall be made of each hearing and shall contain the following:

    a. the names of the judges present;
    b. the names of those persons referred to in Articles 21 and 22 of these Rules who are present at the hearing;
    c. the names and other relevant information concerning the witnesses, expert witnesses and other persons appearing at the hearing;
    d. the declarations expressly made for insertion in the minutes by the states parties or the Commission;
    e. the declarations of the witnesses, expert witnesses and other persons appearing at the hearing, as well as the questions put to them and their replies;
    f. the text of the questions put by the judges and the responses thereto;
    g. the text of any decisions rendered by the Court during the hearing.

2. The Agents and Delegates, as well as the witnesses, expert witnesses and other persons appearing at the hearing, shall receive a copy of their arguments, statements or testimony, to enable them, subject to the control of the Secretary, to correct any material errors appearing in the transcript of the hearing. The Secretary, in accordance with the instructions of the President, shall fix the time limits granted for this purpose.
3. The minutes shall be signed by the President and the Secretary, who shall attest to their accuracy.
4. Copies of the minutes shall be transmitted to the Agents and to the Delegates.

Article 43: Discontinuance

1. When the party which has filed the case notifies the Court of its intention not to proceed with it, the Court, after having obtained the opinions of the other parties thereto and the persons referred to in Article 22(2) of these Rules, shall decide whether it is appropriate to approve the discontinuance and, accordingly, to strike the case off its list.
2. When the parties to a case inform the Court that there exists a friendly settlement, arrangement or other fact capable of providing a solution of the matter, the Court may strike the case off its list after having obtained the opinion of the persons referred to in Article 22(2) of these Rules.
3. Notwithstanding the existence of the conditions indicated in the two preceding paragraphs, the Court, mindful of its responsibility to protect human rights, may decide that it should proceed with the consideration of the case.

Article 44: Application of Article 63(1) of the Convention

1. Article 63(1) of the Convention may be invoked at any stage of the proceedings, even when reference thereto was not made in the application.
2. The Court may invite the persons referred to in Article 22(2) of the Rules to submit briefs regarding the application of Article 63(1) of the Convention.

Article 45: Decisions

1. The judgments and interlocutory decisions for discontinuance of a case shall be rendered by the Court.
2. All other decisions shall be rendered by the Court, if it is sitting, or by the President, if it is not, unless otherwise provided. The decisions of the President may be appealed to the Court.

CHAPTER IV
JUDGMENTS

Article 46: Contents of the Judgment

1. A judgment shall contain:

    a. the names of the President, the judges who rendered it, and the Secretary and Deputy Secretary;
    b. the date on which it was delivered at a hearing;
    c. the identification of the parties;
    d. the names of the persons referred to in Articles 21 and 22 of these Rules;
    e. a description of the proceedings;
    f. the submissions of the States Parties to the case and of the Commission;
    g. the facts of the case;
    h. the legal arguments;

    i.   the operative provisions of the judgment;
    j.   the allocation of compensation, if any, without prejudice to what is provided for in the Article that follows;
    k.   the decision, if any, in regard to costs;
    l.   the names of the judges constituting the majority;
    m. a statement indicating which text is authentic.

2.   Any judge who has taken part in the consideration of the case is entitled to append to the judgment a dissenting or concurring opinion.

      These opinions shall be submitted within a time-limit to be fixed by the President, to enable the other judges to take cognizance thereof before the judgment is handed down.

Article 47: Judgment Relating to Article 63(1) of the Convention

1.   When the Court finds that there is a breach of the Convention, it shall in the same judgment decide on the application of Article 63(1) of the Convention if that question is ready for decision. If the question is not ready for decision, the Court shall reserve its decision thereon in whole or in part and shall determine the further proceedings.
2.   For the purposes of ruling on the application of Article 63(1) of the Convention, the Court shall, as far as possible, be composed of the same judges who rendered the judgment on the merits of the case. However, in the event of death, resignation, disability, withdrawal or exemption, the judge concerned shall be replaced in the manner provided for in Article 16 of these Rules.
3.   If the Court is informed that the injured party and the party adjudged to be responsible have reached an agreement that conforms to its judgment on the merits, it shall verify the fairness of the agreement and, pursuant to Article 43 of these Rules, decide accordingly.

Article 48: Delivery and Communication of the Judgment

1.   When the case is ready for a decision, the Court shall meet in private. A preliminary vote shall be taken and a date fixed for the deliberation and final vote.
2.   After the final deliberation, the Court shall take a final vote, approve the wording of the judgment, and fix the date of the public hearing at which it shall be communicated to the parties.
3.   Until the aforementioned communication, the texts, the legal arguments and the votes shall all remain secret.
4.   The judgments shall be signed by all of the judges who participated in the voting and by the Secretary. A judgment signed by only a majority of the judges shall, however, be valid.
5.   The dissenting or concurring opinions referred to in Article 46(2) of these Rules shall be signed by the judges who support them and by the Secretary.
6.   The judgment shall conclude with an order, signed by the President and the

Secretary and sealed by the latter, providing for the communication and execution of the judgment.

7. The originals of the judgments shall be deposited in the archives of the Court. The Secretary shall send certified copies to the States Parties to the case, to the Commission, to the President of the Permanent Council, to the Secretary General, to the persons referred to in Article 22(2) of these Rules, and to any interested persons who request them.

8. The Secretary shall transmit the judgment to all the Contracting States.

Article 49: Publication of Judgments and Other Decisions

1. The Secretary shall be responsible for the publication of:

   a. the judgments and other decisions of the Court;
   b. documents relating to the proceedings, including the report of the Commission, but excluding any particulars bearing on attempts to reach a friendly settlement and any documents which the President considers irrelevant or inappropriate to publish;
   c. the record of the hearings;
   d. any other document whose publication the President considers useful.

2. The judgments shall be published in the working languages used in each case; all other documents shall be published in their original language.

3. Documents deposited with the Secretariat regarding cases already adjudicated shall be accessible to the public, unless otherwise decided by the Court.

Article 50: Application for an Interpretation of a Judgment

1. Applications for an interpretation pursuant to Article 67 of the Convention shall be filed with the Secretariat in ten copies and shall state with precision the issues relating to the meaning or scope of the judgment on which the interpretation is requested.

2. The Secretary shall transmit the application for interpretation to the States Parties to the case and to the Commission, as appropriate, and shall invite them to submit, in ten copies, any written comments they deem relevant within a time-limit laid down by the President.

3. When considering an application for interpretation, the Court shall be composed, whenever possible, of the same judges who adjudicated the case whose interpretation is being sought. However, in the event of death, resignation, disability, withdrawal or exemption, the judge affected shall be replaced in accordance with Article 16 of these Rules.

4. An application for interpretation shall not suspend the effect of the judgment.

5. The Court shall determine the procedure to be followed and shall render its decision by means of a judgment.

TITLE III ADVISORY OPINIONS

Article 51: Interpretation of the Convention

1. Requests for an advisory opinion under Article 64(1) of the Convention shall state with precision the specific questions on which the opinion of the Court is sought.
2. Requests for an advisory opinion submitted by a member state or by the Commission shall, in addition, identify the provisions to be interpreted, the considerations giving rise to the request, and the names and addresses of the Agent or of the Delegates appointed under Articles 21 and 22 of these Rules.
3. If the advisory opinion is sought by an OAS organ other than the Commission, the request shall also specify, in addition to the information listed in the preceding paragraph, how it relates to its sphere of competence.

Article 52: Interpretation of Other Treaties

1. If the interpretation requested refers to other treaties concerning the protection of human rights in the American states, as provided for in Article 64(1) of the Convention, the application shall indicate the name of, and parties to, the treaty, the specific questions on which the opinion of the Court is sought, and the considerations giving rise to the request.
2. When the request is submitted by one of the organs of the OAS, the application shall also indicate how the request relates to its sphere of competence.

Article 53: Interpretation of Domestic Laws

1. Request for advisory opinions presented pursuant to Article 64(2) of the Convention shall indicate the following:

    a. The provisions of domestic law and of the Convention or of other treaties concerning the protection of human rights to which the request relates;
    b. the specific questions on which the opinion of the Court is sought;
    c. the name and address of the applicant's Agent;
    d. appointed pursuant to Article 21 of these Rules.

2. Copies of the domestic laws referred to in the request shall accompany the application.

Article 54: Procedure

1. On receipt of a request for an advisory opinion, the Secretary shall transmit copies thereof to all the member states, to the Commission, to the Secretary General and to the OAS organs whose spheres of competence relate to the subject of the request, if appropriate.
2. The President shall fix the time-limits for the filing of written comments by interested parties.

309

3. The President may invite or authorize any interested party to submit a written opinion on the issues covered by the request. If the request is governed by Article 64(2) of the Convention, he may do so after consulting with the Agent.

4. At the conclusion of the written proceedings, the Court shall decide whether there should be oral proceedings and shall fix the date for such a hearing, unless it Delegates the latter task to the President. In cases governed by Article 64(2) of the Convention, a prior consultation with the Agent is required.

Article 55: Application by Analogy

The Court shall apply the provisions of Title II of these Rules to advisory proceedings, to the extent that it deems them to be compatible.

Article 56: Adoption and Content of Advisory Opinions

1. The adoption of advisory opinions shall be governed by Article 48 of these Rules.

2. Advisory opinions shall contain the following:

   a. the names of the President, the judges who rendered the opinion, and the Secretary and Deputy Secretary;
   b. the date on which it was delivered at a public hearing, if applicable;
   c. the issues presented to the Court;
   d. a summary of the considerations giving rise to the request;
   e. a description of the proceedings;
   f. the legal arguments;
   g. the names of the judges constituting the majority;
   h. the opinion of the Court;
   i. a statement indicating which text is authentic.

3. Any judge who has taken part in the deliberations on the advisory opinion request is entitled to append to the opinion of the Court a concurring or dissenting opinion. These opinions shall be submitted within a time-limit to be fixed by the President, to enable the other judges to take cognizance thereof before the advisory opinion is rendered.

4. Advisory opinions may be delivered in public.

TITLE IV
FINAL AND TRANSITORY PROVISIONS

Article 57: Abrogation and Modification of the Rules of Procedure

These Rules may be amended by the vote of an absolute majority of the titular judges of the Court. Upon entry into force, they shall abrogate the previous Rules of Procedure.

Article 58: Entry into Force

These Rules, whose Spanish and English versions are equally authentic, shall enter into force on August 1, 1991. They shall only apply for cases brought before the Court after that date.

24. AFRICAN CHARTER ON HUMAN AND PEOPLES' RIGHTS

Adopted by the 18th Assembly of the Heads of State and Government of the
Organisation of African Unity: 27 June 1981 at Nairobi

Entry into force: 21 October 1986, in accordance with Article 63(3)

PREAMBLE

The African States members of the Organization of African Unity, parties to the
present convention entitled "African Charter on Human and Peoples' Rights",

Recalling Decision 115 (XVI) of the Assembly of Heads of State and
Government at its Sixteenth Ordinary Session held in Monrovia, Liberia, from
17 to 20 July 1979 on the preparation of "a preliminary draft on an African Charter
on Human and Peoples' Rights providing inter alia for the establishment of bodies
to promote and protect human and peoples' rights";

Considering the Charter of the Organization of African Unity, which stipulates
that "freedom, equality, justice and dignity are essential objectives for the
achievement of the legitimate aspiration of the African peoples";

Reaffirming the pledge they solemnly made in Article 2 of the said Charter to
eradicate all forms of colonialism from Africa, to co-ordinate and intensify their co-
operation and efforts to achieve a better life for the peoples of Africa and to
promote international co-operation having due regard to the Charter of the United
Nations and the Universal Declaration of Human Rights;

Taking into consideration the virtues of their historical tradition and the values of
African civilisation which should inspire and characterise their reflection on the
concept of human and peoples' rights;

Recognising on the one hand, that fundamental human rights stem from the
attributes of human beings, which justifies their national and international
protection and on the other hand that the reality and respect of peoples' rights
should necessarily guarantee human rights;

Considering that the enjoyment of rights and freedoms also implies the
performance of duties on the part of everyone;

Convinced that it is henceforth essential to pay particular attention to the right
to develop and that civil and political rights cannot be dissociated from economic,
social and cultural rights in their conception as well as universality and that the
satisfaction of economic, social and cultural rights is a guarantee for the enjoyment
of civil and political rights;

Conscious of their duty to achieve the total liberation of Africa, the peoples of
which are still struggling for their dignity and genuine independence, and
undertaking to eliminate colonialism, neo-colonialism, apartheid, zionism and to

dismantle aggressive foreign military bases and all forms of discrimination, particularly those based on race, ethnic group, colour, sex, language, religion or particular opinion;

Reaffirming their adherence to the principles of human and peoples' rights and freedoms contained in the declarations, conventions and other instruments adopted by the Organization of African Unity, the Movement of Non-Aligned Countries and the United Nations;

Firmly convinced of the duty to promote and protect human and peoples' rights and freedoms taking into account the importance traditionally attached to these rights and freedoms of Africa;

Have agreed as follows:

PART I
RIGHTS AND DUTIES

CHAPTER I
HUMAN AND PEOPLES' RIGHTS

Article 1

The Member States of the Organisations of African Unity parties to the present Charter shall recognise the right, duties and freedoms enshrined in this Charter and shall undertake to adopt legislative or other measures to give effect to them.

Article 2

Every individual shall be entitled to the enjoyment of the rights and freedoms recognized and guaranteed in the present Charter without distinction of any kind such as race, ethnic group, colour, sex, language, religion, political or any other opinion, national and social origin, fortune, birth or other status.

Article 3

1. Every individual shall be equal before the law.
2. Every individual shall be entitled to equal protection of the law.

Article 4

Human beings are inviolable. Every human being shall be entitled to respect for his life and the integrity of his person. No one may be arbitrarily deprived of this right.

Article 5

Every individual shall have the right to the respect of the dignity inherent in a human being and to the recognition of his legal status. All forms of exploitation and degradation of man particularly slavery, slave trade, torture, cruel, inhuman or degrading punishment and treatment shall be prohibited.

Article 6

Every individual shall have the right to liberty and to the security of his person. No one may be deprived of his freedom except for reasons and conditions previously laid down by law. In particular, no one may be arbitrarily arrested or detained.

Article 7

1. Every individual shall have the right to have his cause heard. This comprises:

   (a) The right to an appeal to competent national organs against acts violating his fundamental rights as recognized and guaranteed by conventions, laws, regulations and customs in force;
   (b) The right to be presumed innocent until proved guilty by a competent court or tribunal;
   (c) The right to defence, including the right to be defended by counsel of his choice;
   (d) the right to be tried within a reasonable time by an impartial court or tribunal.

2. No one may be condemned for an act or omission which did not constitute a legally punishable offence at the time it was committed. No penalty may be inflicted for an offence for which no provision was made at the time it was committed. Punishment is personal and can be imposed only on the offender.

Article 8

Freedom of conscience, the profession and free practice of religion shall be guaranteed. No one may, subject to law and order, be submitted to measures restricting the exercise of these freedoms.

Article 9

1. Every individual shall have the right to receive information.
2. Every individual shall have the right to express and disseminate his opinions within the law.

Article 10

1. Every individual shall have the right to free association provided that he abides by the law.

2. Subject to the obligation of solidarity provided for in Article 29 no one may be compelled to join an association.

Article 11

Every individual shall have the right to assemble freely with others. The exercise of this right shall be subject only to necessary restrictions provided for by law in particular those enacted in the interest of national security, the safety, health, ethics and rights and freedoms of others.

Article 12

1. Every individual shall have the right to freedom of movement and residence within the borders of a State provided he abides by the law.
2. Every individual shall have the right to leave any country including his own, and to return to his country. This right may only be subject to restrictions, provided for by law for the protection of national security, law and order, public health or morality.
3. Every individual shall have the right, when persecuted, to seek and obtain asylum in other countries in accordance with the laws of those countries and international conventions.
4. A non-national legally admitted in a territory of a State Party to the present Charter, may only be expelled from it by virtue of a decision taken in accordance with the law.
5. The mass expulsion of non-nationals shall be prohibited. Mass expulsion shall be that which is aimed at national, racial, ethnic or religious groups.

Article 13

1. Every citizen shall have the right to freely participate in the government of his country, either directly or through freely chosen representatives in accordance with the provisions of the law.
2. Every citizen shall have the right of access to public service of his country.
3. Every individual shall have the right of access to public property and services in strict equality of all persons before the law.

Article 14

The right to property shall be guaranteed. It may only be encroached upon in the interest of public need or in the general interest of the community and in accordance with the provisions of appropriate laws.

Article 15

Every individual shall have the right to work under equitable and satisfactory conditions and shall receive equal pay for equal work.

Article 16

1. Every individual shall have the right to enjoy the best attainable state of physical and mental health.

Article 17

1. Every individual shall have the right to education.
2. Every individual may freely take part in the cultural life of his community;
3. The promotion and protection of morals and traditional values recognized by the community shall be the duty of the State.

Article 18

1. The family shall be the natural unit and basis of society. It shall be protected by the State.
2. The State shall have the duty to assist the family which is the custodian of morals and traditional values recognized by the community.
3. The State shall ensure the elimination of every discrimination against women and also ensure the protection of the rights of the woman and the child as stipulated in international declarations and conventions.
4. The aged and the disabled shall also have the right to special measures of protection in keeping with their physical or moral needs.

Article 19

All peoples shall be equal; they shall enjoy the same respect and shall have the same rights. Nothing shall justify the domination of a people by another.

Article 20

1. All people shall have the right to existence. They shall have the unquestionable and inalienable right to self-determination. They shall freely determine their political status and shall pursue their economic and social development according to the policy they have freely chosen.
2. Colonized or oppressed peoples shall have the right to free themselves from the bonds of domination by resorting to any means recognized by the international community.
3. All peoples shall have the right to the assistance of the States Parties to the present Charter in their liberation struggle against foreign domination, be it political, economic or cultural.

Article 21

1. All peoples shall freely dispose of their wealth and natural resources. This right shall be exercised in the exclusive interest of the people. In no case shall a people be deprived of it.

2. In case of spoliation the dispossessed people shall have the right to the lawful recovery of its property as well as to an adequate compensation.
3. The free disposal of wealth and natural resources shall be exercised without prejudice to the obligation of promoting international economic co-operation based on mutual respect, equitable exchange and the principles of international law.
4. States Parties to the present Charter shall individually and collectively exercise the right to free disposal of their wealth and natural resources with a view to strengthening African unity and solidarity.
5. State Parties to the present Charter shall undertake to eliminate all forms of foreign economic exploitation particularly that practised by international monopolies so as to enable their peoples to fully benefit from the advantages derived from their national resources.

Article 22

1. All people shall have the right to their economic, social and cultural development with due regard to their freedom and identity and in the equal enjoyment of the common heritage of mankind.
2. States shall have the duty, individually or collectively, to ensure the exercise of the right to development.

Article 23

1. All people shall have the right to national and international peace and security. The principles of solidarity and friendly relations implicitly affirmed by the Charter of the United Nations and reaffirmed by that of the Organization of African Unity shall govern relations between States.
2. For the purpose of strengthening peace, solidarity and friendly relations, States Parties to the present Charter shall ensure that:

   (a) any individual enjoying the right of asylum under Article 12 of the present Charter shall not engage in subversive activities against his country of origin or any other State party to the present Charter;
   (b) their territories shall not be used as bases for subversive or terrorist activities against the people of any other State party to the present Charter.

Article 24

All peoples shall have the right to a general satisfactory environment favourable to their development.

Article 25

States parties to the present Charter shall have the duty to promote and ensure through teaching, education and publication, the respect of the rights and freedoms contained in the present Charter and to see to it that these freedoms and rights as well as corresponding obligations and duties are understood.

Article 26

States parties to the present Charter shall have the duty to guarantee the independence of the Courts and shall allow the establishment and improvement of appropriate national institutions entrusted with the promotion and protection of the rights and freedoms guaranteed by the present Charter.

CHAPTER II
DUTIES

Article 27

1. Every individual shall have duties towards his family and society, the State and other legally recognized communities and the international community.
2. The rights and freedoms of each individual shall be exercised with due regard to the rights of others, collective security, morality and common interest.

Article 28

Every individual shall have the duty to respect and consider his fellow beings without discrimination, and to maintain relations aimed at promoting, safe-guarding and reinforcing mutual respect and tolerance.

Article 29

The individual shall also have the duty:

1. To preserve the harmonious development of the family and to work for the cohesion and respect of the family, to respect his parents at all times, to maintain them in case of need;
2. To serve his national community by placing his physical and intellectual abilities at its service;
3. Not to compromise the security of the State whose national or resident he is;
4. To preserve and strengthen social and national solidarity, particularly when the latter is threatened;
5. To preserve and strengthen the national independence and the territorial integrity of his country and to contribute to its defence in accordance with the law;
6. To work to the best of his abilities and competence, and to pay taxes imposed by law in the interest of the society;
7. To preserve and strengthen positive African cultural values in his relations with other members of the society, in the spirit of tolerance, dialogue and consultation and, in general, to contribute to the promotion of the moral well being of society;

8. To contribute to the best of his abilities, at all times and at all levels, to the promotion and achievement of African unity.

PART II
MEASURES OF SAFEGUARD

CHAPTER I
ESTABLISHMENT AND ORGANIZATION OF THE AFRICAN COMMISSION ON HUMAN AND PEOPLES' RIGHTS

Article 30

An African Commission on Human Peoples' Rights, hereinafter called "the Commission", shall be established within the Organization of African Unity to promote human and peoples' rights and ensure their protection in Africa.

Article 31

1. The Commission shall consist of eleven members chosen from amongst African personalities of the highest reputation, known for their high morality, integrity, impartiality and competence in matters of human and peoples' rights; particular consideration being given to persons having legal experience.
2. The members of the Commission shall serve in their personal capacity.

Article 32

The Commission shall not include more than one national of the same State.

Article 33

The members of the Commission shall be elected by secret ballot by the Assembly of Heads of State and Government, from a list of persons nominated by the States parties to the present Charter.

Article 34

Each State party to the present Charter may not nominate more than two candidates. The candidates must have the nationality of one of the States parties to the present Charter. When two candidates are nominated by a State, one of them may not be a national of that State.

Article 35

1. The Secretary General of the Organization of African Unity shall invite States parties to the present Charter at least four months before the elections to nominate candidates;
2. The Secretary General of the Organization of African Unity shall make an alphabetical list of the persons thus nominated and communicate it to the Heads of State and Government at least one month before the elections.

Article 36

The members of the Commission shall be elected for a six year period and shall be eligible for re-election. However, the term of office of four of the members elected at the first election shall terminate after two years and the term of office of three others, at the end of four years.

Article 37

Immediately after the first election, the Chairman of the Assembly of Heads of State and Government of the Organization of African Unity shall draw lots to decide the names of those members referred to in Article 36.

Article 38

After their election, the members of the Commission shall make a solemn declaration to discharge their duties impartially and faithfully.

Article 39

1. In case of death or resignation of a member of the Commission, the Chairman of the Commission shall immediately inform the Secretary General of the Organization of African Unity, who shall declare the seat vacant from the date of death or from the date on which the resignation takes effect.
2. If, in the unanimous opinion of other members of the Commission, a member has stopped discharging his duties for any reason other than a temporary absence, the Chairman of the Commission shall inform the Secretary General of the Organization of African Unity, who shall then declare the seat vacant.
3. In each of the cases anticipated above, the Assembly of Heads of State and Government shall replace the member whose seat became vacant for the remaining period of his term unless the period is less than six months.

Article 40

Every member of the Commission shall be in office until the date his successor assumes office.

Article 41

The Secretary General of the Organization of African Unity shall appoint the Secretary of the Commission. He shall also provide the staff and services necessary for the effective discharge of the duties of the Commission. The Organization of African Unity shall bear the cost of the staff and services.

Article 42

1. The Commission shall elect its Chairman and Vice Chairman for a two-year period. They shall be eligible for re-election.
2. The Commission shall lay down its rules of procedure.
3. Seven members shall form the quorum.
4. In case of an equality of votes, the Chairman shall have a casting vote.
5. The Secretary General may attend the meetings of the Commission. He shall neither participate in deliberations nor shall he be entitled to vote. The Chairman of the Commission may, however, invite him to speak.

Article 43

In discharging their duties, members of the Commission shall enjoy diplomatic privileges and immunities provided for in the General Convention on the Privileges and Immunities of the Organization of African Unity.

Article 44

Provision shall be made for the emoluments and allowances of the members of the Commission in the Regular Budget of the Organization of African Unity.

Article 45

The functions of the Commission shall be:

1. To promote Human and Peoples' Rights and in particular:

    (a) To collect documents, undertake studies and researches on African problems in the field of human and peoples' rights, organise seminars, symposia and conferences, disseminate information, encourage national and local institutions concerned with human and peoples' rights, and should the case arise, give its views or make recommendations to Governments.
    (b) To formulate and lay down, principles and rules aimed at solving legal problems relating to human and peoples' rights and fundamental freedoms upon which African Governments may base their legislations.
    (c) Co-operate with other African and international institutions concerned with the promotion and protection of human and peoples' rights.

2. Ensure the protection of human and peoples' rights under conditions laid down by the present Charter.
3. Interpret all the provisions of the present Charter at the request of a State Party, an institution of the OAU or an African organization recognized by the OAU.
4. Perform any other tasks which may be entrusted to it by the Assembly of Heads of State and Government.

CHAPTER III
PROCEDURE OF THE COMMISSION

Article 46

The Commission may resort to any appropriate method of investigation; it may hear from the Secretary General of the Organization of African Unity or any other person capable of enlightening it.

COMMUNICATION FROM STATES

Article 47

If a State party to the present Charter has good reasons to believe that another State party to this Charter has violated the provisions of the Charter, it may draw, by written communication, the attention of that State to the matter. This communication shall also be addressed to the Secretary General of the OAU and to the Chairman of the Commission. Within three months of the receipt of the communication, the State to which the communication is addressed shall give the enquiring State, written explanation or statements elucidating the matter. This should include as much as possible relevant information relating to the laws and rules of procedure applied and applicable and the redress already given or course of action available.

Article 48

If within three months from the date on which the original communication is received by the State to which it is addressed, the issue is not settled to the satisfaction of the two states involved through bilateral negotiation or by any other peaceful procedure, either State shall have the right to submit the matter to the Commission through the Chairman and shall notify the other State involved.

Article 49

Notwithstanding the provisions of Article 47, if a State party to the present Charter considers that another State party has violated the provisions of the Charter, it may refer the matter directly to the Commission by addressing a communication to the Chairman, to the Secretary General or the Organization of African Unity and the State concerned.

Article 50

The Commission can only deal with a matter submitted to it after making sure that all local remedies, if they exist, have been exhausted, unless it is obvious to the Commission that the procedure of achieving these remedies would be unduly prolonged.

Article 51

1. The Commission may ask the States concerned to provide it with all relevant information.
2. When the Commission is considering the matter, States concerned may be represented before it and submit written or oral representations.

Article 52

After having obtained from the States concerned and from other sources all the information it deems necessary and after having tried all appropriate means to reach an amicable solution based on the respect of Human and Peoples' Rights, the Commission shall prepare, within a reasonable period of time from the notification referred to in Article 48, a report stating the facts and its findings. This report shall be sent to the State concerned and communicated to the Assembly of Heads of State and Government.

Article 53

While transmitting its report, the Commission may make to the Assembly of Heads of State and Government such recommendations as it deems useful.

Article 54

The Commission shall submit to each Ordinary Session of the Assembly of Heads of State and Government a report on its activities.

OTHER COMMUNICATIONS

Article 55

1. Before each Session, the Secretary of the Commission shall make a list of the communications other than those of State parties to the present Charter and transmit them to the Members of the Commission, who shall indicate which communications should be considered by the Commission.
2. A communication shall be considered by the Commission if a simple majority of its members so decide.

Article 56

Communications relating to human and peoples' rights referred to in Article 55 received by the Commission, shall be considered if they:

1. indicate their authors even if the latter request anonymity,
2. are compatible with the Charter of the organization of African Unity or with the present Charter,
3. are not written in disparaging or insulting language directed against the State concerned and its institutions or to the Organization of African Unity,
4. are not based exclusively on news disseminated through the mass media,
5. are sent after exhausting local remedies, if any, unless it is obvious that this procedure is unduly prolonged,
6. are submitted within a reasonable period from the time local remedies are exhausted or from the date the Commission is seized of the matter, and
7. do not deal with cases which have been settled by these States involved in accordance with the principles of the Charter of the United Nations, or the Charter of the organization of African Unity or the provisions of the present Charter.

Article 57

Prior to any substantive consideration, all communications shall be brought to the knowledge of the State concerned by the Chairman of the Commission.

Article 58

1. When it appears after deliberations of the Commission that one or more communications apparently reveal the existence of a series of serious or massive violations of human and peoples' rights, the Commission shall draw the attention of the Assembly of Heads of State and Government to them.
2. The Assembly of Heads of State and Government may then request the Commission to undertake an in-depth study of these situations and make a factual report, accompanied by its finding and recommendations.
3. A case of emergency duly noticed by the Commission shall be submitted by the latter to the Chairman of the Assembly of Heads of State and Government who may request an in-depth study.

Article 59

1. All measures taken within the provisions of the present Charter shall remain confidential until such a time as the Assembly of Heads of State and Government shall otherwise decide.
2. However, the report shall be published by the Chairman of the Commission upon the decision of the Assembly of Heads of State and Government.
3. The report on the activities of the Commission shall be published by its Chairman after it has been considered by the Assembly of Heads of State and Government.

CHAPTER IV
APPLICABLE PRINCIPLES

Article 60

The Commission shall draw inspiration from international law on human and peoples' rights, particularly from the provisions of various African instruments on human and peoples' rights, the Charter of the United Nations, the Charter of the organization of African Unity, the Universal Declaration of Human Rights, other instruments adopted by the United Nations and by African countries in the field of human and peoples' rights as well as from the provisions of various instruments adopted within the Specialised Agencies of the United Nations of which the parties to the present Charter are members.

Article 61

The Commission shall also take into consideration, as subsidiary measures to determine the principles of law, other general or special international conventions, laying down rules expressly recognized by member States of the Organization of African Unity, African practices consistent with international norms on human and peoples' rights, customs generally accepted as law, general principles of law recognized by African states as well as legal precedents and doctrine.

Article 62

Each State party shall undertake to submit every two years, from the date and present Charter comes into force, a report on the legislative or other measures taken with a view to giving effect to the rights and freedoms recognized and guaranteed by the present Charter.

Article 63

1. The present Charter shall be open to signature, ratification or adherence of the member states of the Organization of African Unity.
2. The instruments of ratification or adherence to the present Charter shall be deposited with the Secretary General of the organization of African Unity.
3. The present Charter shall come into force three months after the reception by the Secretary General of the instruments of ratification or adherence by a simple majority of the member states of the Organization of African Unity.

PART III
GENERAL PROVISIONS

Article 64

1. After the coming into force of the present Charter, members of the Commission shall be elected in accordance with the relevant Articles of the present Charter.
2. The Secretary General of the organization of African Unity shall convene the first meeting of the Commission at the Headquarters of the Organization within three months of the constitution of the Commission. Thereafter, the Commission shall be convened by its Chairman whenever necessary but at least once a year.

Article 65

For each of the States that will ratify or adhere to the present Charter after its coming into force, the Charter shall take effect three months after the date of the deposit by that State of its instrument of Ratification or adherence.

Article 66

Special protocols or agreements may, if necessary, supplement the provisions of the present Charter.

Article 67

The Secretary General of the Organization of African Unity shall inform member states of the Organization of the deposit of each instrument of ratification or adherence.

Article 68

The present Charter may be amended or revised if a State party makes a written request to that effect to the Secretary General of the organization of African Unity. The Assembly of Heads of State and Government may only consider the draft amendment after all the States parties have been duly informed of it and the Commission has given its opinion on it at the request of the sponsoring State. The amendment shall be approved by a simple majority of the States parties, it shall come into force for each State which has accepted it in accordance with its constitutional procedure three months after the Secretary General has received notice of the acceptance.

25. RULES OF PROCEDURE OF THE AFRICAN COMMISSION ON HUMAN AND PEOPLES' RIGHTS

Adopted: 13 February 1988

The African Commission on Human and Peoples' Rights,

Considering the African Charter on Human and Peoples' Rights,
Acting on the strength of Article 42 (2) of the Charter,
Hereby adopts the present Rules:

PART ONE
GENERAL PROVISIONS: ORGANIZATION OF THE COMMISSION

CHAPTER I – SESSIONS

Rule 1: Number of Sessions

The African Commission on Human and Peoples' Rights hereinafter referred to as "the Commission" shall hold the Sessions which may be necessary to enable it to carry out satisfactorily its functions in conformity with the African Charter on Human and Peoples' Rights (hereinafter referred to as "the Charter").

Rule 2: Opening Date

The Commission shall normally hold two ordinary sessions a year each lasting two weeks.

The ordinary sessions of the Commission shall be convened on a date fixed by the Commission on the proposal of its Chairman and in consultation with the Secretary-General of the Organization of African Unity (hereinafter referred to as "the Secretary-General").

The Secretary-General may change, under exceptional circumstances, the opening date of a session, in consultation with the Chairman of the Commission.

Rule 3: Extraordinary sessions

1. Extraordinary sessions shall be convened on decisions of the Commission. When the Commission is not in Session, the Chairman may convene extraordinary sessions in consultation with the members of the Commission. The Chairman of the Commission shall also convene extraordinary sessions:

   (a) At the request of the majority of the members of the Commission;
   (b) At the request of the current Chairman of the Organization African Unity.

2. Extraordinary Sessions shall be convened as soon as possible on a date fixed by the Chairman, in consultation with the Secretary-General and the other members of the Commission.

Rule 4: Place of Meetings

The Sessions shall normally be held at the Headquarters of the Commission. The Commission may, in consultation with the Secretary-General, decide to hold a Session in another place.

Rule 5: Notification of the Opening Date of the Sessions

The Secretary-General shall inform members of the Commission of the date of the first sitting of each Session and its venue. This notification should be sent, in the case of an Ordinary Session, at least eight (8) weeks and, the case of an Extraordinary Session, at least three (3) weeks, if possible, before the Session.

CHAPTER II – AGENDA

Rule 6: Drawing up the Provisional Agenda

1. The Provisional Agenda for each Ordinary Session shall be drawn up by the Secretary-General, in consultation with the Chairman of the Commission in accordance with the provisions of the Charter and these Rules.
2. The provisional Agenda shall include, if necessary, items "Communications from States", and "Other Communications" in conformity with the provisions of Article 55 of the Charter. It should not contain any information relating to such communications.
3. Except what has been specified above on the communications, the Provisional Agenda shall include all the items listed by the present Rules of Procedure as well as the items proposed:
    (a) By the Commission at a previous Session;
    (b) By the Chairman of the Commission or another member of the Commission;
    (c) By a State Party to the Charter;
    (d) By the Assembly of Heads of State and Government (or the Council of Ministers of the Organization of African Unity);
    (e) By the Secretary-General of the Organization of African Unity for every issue relating to the functions assigned to him by the Charter;
    (f) By a national liberation movement recognized by the Organization of African Unity or by a non-governmental organization;
    (g) By a specialized institution of which the States Parties to the Charter are members.
4. The items to be included in the provisional agenda under sub-paragraphs b, c, f and g of paragraph 3 must be communicated to the Secretary-General, accompanied by essential documents, not later than eight (8) weeks before the first sitting of each Session.

5.   (a)   All national liberation movements or non-governmental organizations wishing to propose the inclusion of an item in the Provisional Agenda must inform the Secretary-General at least ten (10) weeks before the opening of the meeting. Before formally proposing the inclusion of an item in the Provisional Agenda, the observations likely to be made by the Secretary-General must duly be taken into account.

(b)   The proposal, accompanied by essential documents, must formally be submitted not later than eight (8) weeks before the opening of the Session.

(c)   All proposals made under the provisions of the present paragraph shall be included in the Provisional Agenda of the Commission, if at least two-thirds (2/3) of the members present and voting so decide.

6.   The Provisional Agenda of the Extraordinary Session of the Commission shall include only the item proposed to be considered at that Extraordinary Session.

Rule 7: Transmission and Distribution of the Provisional Agenda

1.   The Provisional Agenda and the essential documents relating to each item shall be distributed to the members of the Commission by the Secretary-General who shall endeavour to transmit them to members at least six (6) weeks before the opening of the Session.

2.   The Secretary-General shall communicate the Provisional Agenda of that session and have the essential documents relating to each Agenda item distributed at least six weeks before the opening of the Session of the Commission to the members of the Commission, member States Party to the Charter, to the current Chairman of the Organization of African Unity.

3.   The provisional agenda shall also be sent to the specialised agencies non-governmental organizations and to the national liberation movement concerned with the agenda.

4.   In exceptional cases, the Secretary-General, may, while giving reasons in writing, have the essential documents relating to some items the Provisional Agenda distributed at least four (4) weeks prior to the opening of the Session.

Rule 8: Adoption of the Agenda

At the beginning of each session, the Commission shall, if necessary after the election of officers in conformity with Rule 18, adopt the agenda of the Session on the basis of the Provisional Agenda referred to in Rule 6.

Rule 9: Revision of the Agenda

The Commission may, during the Session, revise the Agenda if need be, adjourn, cancel or amend items. During the Session, only urgent important issues may be added to the Agenda.

Rule 10: Draft Provisional Agenda for the Next Session

The Secretary-General shall, at each session of the Commission, submit a Draft Provisional Agenda for the next session of the Commission, indicating with respect to each item, the documents to be submitted on that item and the decisions of the deliberative organ which authorized the preparation, so as to enable the Commission to consider these documents as regards the contribution they make to its proceedings, as well as their agency and relevance to the prevailing situation.

CHAPTER III – MEMBERS OF THE COMMISSION

Rule 11: Composition of the Commission

The Commission shall be composed of eleven (11) members elected by the Assembly of Heads of State and Government hereinafter referred to as "the Assembly", in conformity with the relevant provisions of the Charter.

Rule 12: Status of the Members

1. The members of the Commission shall be the eleven (11) persons appointed in conformity with the provisions of Article 31 of the Charter.
2. Each member of the Commission shall sit on the Commission in a personal capacity. No member may be represented by another person.

Rule 13: Term of Office of the Members

1. The term of office of the members of the Commission elected on 29 July 1987 shall begin from that date. The term of office of the members of the Commission elected at subsequent elections shall take effect the day following the expiry date of the term of office of the members of the Commission they shall replace.
2. However if a member is re-elected at the expiry of his or her term of office, or elected to replace a member whose term of office expired or will expire, the term of office shall begin from that expiry date.
3. In conformity with Article 39 (3) of the Charter, the member elected to replace a member whose term of office has not expired, shall complete the term of office of his or her predecessor, unless the remaining term of office is less than six (6) months. In the latter case, there shall be no replacement.

Rule 14: Cessation of Functions

1. If in the unanimous opinion of the other members of the Commission, a member has stopped discharging his duties for any reason other than a temporary absence, the Chairman of the Commission shall inform the Secretary-General of the Organization of African Unity, who shall then declare the seat vacant.
2. In case of the demise or resignation of a member of the Commission, the

Chairman shall immediately inform the Secretary-General who shall declare the seat vacant from the date of the demise or from that on which the resignation took effect. The member of the Commission who resigns shall address a written notification of his or her resignation directly to the Chairman or to the Secretary-General and steps to declare his or her seat vacant shall only be taken after receiving the said notification. The resignation shall make the seat vacant.

Rule 15: Vacant Seat

Every seat declared vacant in conformity with Rule 15 of the present Rules of Procedure shall be filled on the basis of Article 39 of the Charter.

Rule 16: Oath

Before coming into office, every member of the Commission shall make the following solemn commitment at a public sitting:

"I swear to carry out my duties well and faithfully in all impartiality".

CHAPTER IV – OFFICERS

Rule 17: Election of Officers

1. The Commission shall elect among its members a Chairman and Vice-Chairman.
2. The elections referred to in the present Rule shall be held by secret ballot. Only the members present shall vote. The member who shall obtain a two-thirds majority of the votes of the members present and voting shall be elected.
3. If no member obtains this two-thirds majority, a second and third and fourth ballot shall be held. The member having the largest number of votes at the fifth ballot shall be elected.
4. The officers of the Commission shall be elected for a period of two (2) years. They shall be eligible for re-election. None of them, may, however, exercise his or her functions if he or she ceases to be a member of the Commission.

Rule 18: Powers of the Chairman

The Chairman shall carry out the functions assigned to him by the Charter, the Rules of Procedure and the decisions of the Commission. In the exercise of his functions the Chairman shall be under the authority of the Commission.

Rule 19: Absence of the Chairman

The Vice-Chairman shall replace the Chairman during a session if the latter is unable to attend the whole or part of a sitting of a session.

Rule 20: Functions of the Vice-Chairman

The Vice-Chairman, acting in the capacity of the Chairman, shall have the same rights and the same duties as the Chairman.

Rule 21: Cessation of the Functions of an Officer

If any of the officers ceases to carry out his or her functions or declares that he or she is no longer able to exercise the functions of a member of the Commission or is no longer in a position, for one reason or another, to serve as an officer, a new officer shall be elected for the remaining term of office his or her predecessor.

CHAPTER V – SECRETARIAT

Rule 22: Functions of the Secretary-General

1. The Secretary-General or his representative may attend the meetings of the Commission. He shall participate neither in the deliberations, nor in the voting. He may, however, be called upon by the Chairman of the Commission to address the meeting. He may make written or oral statements at the sittings of the Commission.
2. He shall appoint, in consultation with the Chairman of the Commission, a Secretary of the Commission.
3. He shall, in consultation with the Chairman, provide the Commission with the necessary staff, material means and services for it to carry out effectively the functions and missions assigned to it under the Charter.
4. The Secretary-General shall take all the necessary steps for the meetings of the Commission.
5. The Secretary-General shall bring immediately to the knowledge of the members of the Commission all the issues that would be submitted to them for consideration.

Rule 23: Estimates

Before the Commission shall approve a proposal entailing expenses, the Secretary-General shall prepare and distribute, as soon as possible, to the members of the Commission, the financial implications of the proposal. It shall be incumbent on the Chairman to draw the attention of the members to those implications so that they discuss them when the proposal is considered by the Commission.

Rule 24: Financial Rules

The Financial Rules adopted pursuant to the provisions of Article 41 and 44 of the Charter, shall be appended to the present Rules of Procedure.

Rule 25: Powers of the Secretary of the Commission

The Secretary of the Commission hereinafter referred to as "the Secretary" shall be responsible for the activities of the Secretariat under the general supervision of the Chairman, and, in particular:

(a) He/she shall assist the Commission and its members in the exercise of their functions;
(b) He/she shall serve as an intermediary for all the communications concerning the Commission;
(c) He/she shall be the custodian of the archives of the Commission.

Rule 26: Records of Cases

A special record, with a reference number and initial, in which is entered the date of the registration and communication of each petition and that of the closure of the procedure relating to them before the Commission, shall be kept at the Secretariat.

Rule 27: Financial Responsibility

The Organization of African Unity shall bear the expenses of the staff and the means and services placed at the disposal of the Commission to carry out its functions.

CHAPTER VI – SUBSIDIARY BODIES

Rule 28: Establishment of Committees and Working Groups

1. The Commission may during a session, taking into account the provisions of the Charter and in consultation with the Secretary-General establish, if it deems it necessary for the exercise of its functions, committees or working groups, composed of the members of the Commission send them any agenda item for consideration and report.
2. These committees or working groups may, with the prior consent of the Secretary-General, be authorized to sit when the Commission is in session.
3. The members of the committees or working groups shall be appointed by the Chairman subject to the approval of the absolute majority the other members of the Commission.

Rule 29: Establishment of Sub-Commissions

1. The Commission may establish sub-Commissions of experts, with the prior approval of the Assembly.
2. Unless the Assembly decides otherwise, the Commission shall determine the functions and composition of each sub-Commission.

Rule 30: Officers of the Subsidiary bodies

Unless the Commission decides otherwise, the subsidiary bodies of the Commission shall elect their own officers.

Rule 31: Rules of Procedure

The Rules of Procedure of the Commission shall apply, as far as possible, to the proceedings of its subsidiary bodies.

CHAPTER VII – PUBLIC SESSIONS AND PRIVATE SESSIONS

Rule 32: General principle

The sittings of the Commission and of its subsidiary bodies shall be private and shall be held *"in camera"*.

Rule 33: Publication of Proceedings

At the end of each private sitting, the Commission or its subsidiary bodies may issue a communiqué through the Secretary-General.

CHAPTER VIII – LANGUAGES

Rule 34: Working Languages

The working languages of the Commission and of all its institutions shall be those of the Organization of African Unity.

Rule 35: Interpretation

1. An address delivered in one of the working languages shall be interpreted in the other working languages.
2. Any person addressing the Commission in a language other than one of the working languages, shall, in principle, ensure the interpretation into one of the working languages. The interpreters of the Secretariat may take the interpretation of the original language as source language for their interpretation in the other working languages.

Rule 36: Languages to be used for Minutes of Proceedings

The summary minutes of the sittings of the Commission shall be drafted in the working languages.

Rule 37: Languages to be used for resolutions and other official decisions

All the official decisions of the Commission shall be communicated in the working languages, which requirement shall also apply to the other official documents of the Commission.

CHAPTER IX – MINUTES AND REPORTS

Rule 38: Tape Recording of the Sessions

The Secretariat shall record and conserve the tapes of the sessions of the Commission. It may also record and conserve the tapes of the sessions of the committees, working groups and sub-commissions if the Commission so decides.

Rule 39: Summary Minutes of the Sessions

1. The Secretariat shall draft the summary minutes of the private and public sessions of the Commission and of its subsidiary bodies. It shall distribute them as soon as possible in draft form to the members of the Commission and to all other participants in the session. All those participants may, in the seven (7) working days following the receipt of draft minutes of the session, submit corrections to the Secretariat. The Chairman may, in special circumstances, in consultation with Secretary-General, extend the time for the submission of corrections.
2. Where the corrections are contested, the minutes of the Chairman of the Commission or the Chairman of the subsidiary body, whose minutes they shall resolve the disagreement after having listened to, if necessary, the recording of the discussions. If the disagreement persists, the Commission or the subsidiary body shall decide. The corrections shall be published in a separate distinct volume after the closure of the session.

Rule 40: Distribution of the Minutes of Private Sessions and Public Sessions

1. The final summary minutes of the public and private sessions shall be documents intended for general distribution unless, in exceptional circumstances, the Commission decides otherwise.
2. The minutes of the private sessions of the Commission shall be distributed forthwith to all members of the Commission and to any other participants in the sessions.

Rule 41: Reports to be submitted after each session

The Commission shall submit to the current Chairman of the Organization of African Unity, a report on the deliberations of each session. This report shall contain a brief summary of the recommendation and statements on the issues to which the Commission would like to draw the attention of the current Chairman and member States of the Organization of African Unity.

Rule 42: Submission of official decisions and reports

The text of the decisions and reports officially adopted by the Commission shall be distributed to all the members of the Commission as soon possible.

CHAPTER X – CONDUCT OF THE DEBATES

Rule 43: Quorum

The quorum shall be constituted by seven (7) members of the Commission, as specified in Article 42 (3) of the Charter.

Rule 44: General powers of the Chairman

In addition to the powers entrusted to him under other provisions of the present Rules of Procedure, the Chairman shall have the responsibility of declaring each session of the Commission open and closed; he shall direct the debates, ensure the application of the present Rules of Procedure, grant the use of the floor, submit to a vote matters under discussion and announce the result of the vote taken. Subject to the provisions of the present Rules of Procedure, the Chairman shall direct the discussions of the Commission and ensure order during meetings. The Chairman may during the discussion of an agenda item, propose to the Commission to limit the time accorded to speakers, as well as the number of interventions of each speaker on the same issue and close the list of speakers. He shall rule on points of order. He shall also have the power to propose the adjournment and the closure of debates as well as the adjournment and suspension of a sitting. The debates shall deal solely with the issue submitted to the Commission and the Chairman may call to order a speaker whose remarks are irrelevant to the matter under discussion.

Rule 45: Points of Order

1. During the discussion of any matter a member may, at any time, raise a point of order and the point of order shall be immediately decided by the Chairman, in accordance with the Rules of Procedure. If a member appeals against the decision, the appeal shall immediately be put to the vote and if the Chairman's ruling is not set aside by the simple majority of the members present, it shall be maintained.
2. A member raising a point of order cannot, in his or her comments, deal with the substance of the matter under discussion.

Rule 46: Adjournment of Debates

During the discussion of any matter, a member may move the adjournment of the debate on the matter under discussion. In addition to the proposer of the motion one member may speak in favour of and one against the motion after which the motion shall be immediately put to the vote.

Rule 47: Limit of the Time accorded to Speakers

The Commission may limit the time accorded to each speaker on any matter. When the time allotted for debates is limited and a speaker spends more than the time accorded, the Chairman shall immediately call him to order.

Rule 48: Closing of the list of speakers

The Chairman may, during a debate, read out the list of speakers and with the approval of the Commission, declare the list closed. Where there are no more speakers, the Chairman shall, with the approval of the Commission, declare the debate closed. This closure shall have the same effect as one decided by the Commission.

Rule 49: Closure of Debate

A member may, at any time, move the closure of the debate on the matter under discussion, even if the other members or representatives have expressed the desire to take the floor. The authorization to take the floor on the closure of the debate shall be given only to two speakers against closure, after which the motion shall immediately be put to the vote.

Rule 50: Suspension or Adjournment of the Meeting

During the discussion of any matter, a member may move the suspension or adjournment of the meeting. No discussion on any such motion shall be permitted and it shall immediately be put to the vote.

Rule 51: Order of the Motions

Subject to the provisions of Rule 45 of the present Rules of Procedure the following motions shall have precedence in the following order over the other proposals or motions before the meeting:

    (a) To suspend the meeting;
    (b) To adjourn the meeting;
    (c) To adjourn the debate on the item under discussion;
    (d) For the closure of the debate on the item under discussion.

Rule 52: Submission of Proposals and Amendments of Substance

Unless the Commission decides otherwise, the proposals, amendments or motions of substance made by members shall be submitted in writing to the Secretariat; if a member so requests they shall be considered at the first sitting following their submission.

Rule 53: Decisions on Competence

Subject to the provisions of Rule 45 of the present Rules of Procedure, any motion tabled by a member for a decision on the competence of the Commission to adopt a proposal submitted to it shall immediately be put to the vote before the said proposal is put to the vote.

Rule 54: Withdrawal of a Proposal or a Motion

The sponsor of a motion or a proposal may still withdraw it before it is put to the vote, on condition that it has not been amended. A motion or a proposal thus withdrawn may be submitted again by another member.

Rule 55: New Consideration of Proposals

When a proposal is adopted or rejected, it shall not be considered again at the same session, unless the Commission decides otherwise. When a member moves the new consideration of a proposal, only one member may speak in favour of and one against the motion, after which it shall immediately be put to the vote.

Rule 56: Interventions

1. No member may take the floor at a meeting of the Commission without prior authorization of the Chairman. Subject to Rules 50, 49, 45 and 48 the Chairman shall grant the use of the floor to the speakers in the order in which it has been requested.
2. The debates shall deal solely with the matter submitted to the Commission and the Chairman may call to order a speaker whose remarks are irrelevant to the matter under discussion.
3. The Chairman may limit the time accorded to speakers and the number of interventions which each member may make on the same issue, in accordance with Rule 44 of the present Rules.
4. Only two members in favour of the motion and two against the motion for fixing such time limits shall be granted the use of the floor after which the motion shall immediately be put to the vote. For questions of procedure the time accorded to each speaker shall not exceed five minutes, unless the Chairman decides otherwise. When the time allotted for discussions is limited and a speaker exceeds the time accorded the Chairman shall immediately call him to order.

Rule 57: Right of Reply

The right of reply shall be granted by the Chairman to any member requesting it. The member must try, while exercising this right, to be as brief as possible and to take the floor preferably at the end of the sitting at which this right has been requested.

Rule 58: Congratulations

Congratulations addressed to newly elected members of the Commission shall only be presented by the Chairman or a member designated by the latter. Those addressed by newly elected officers shall only be presented by the outgoing Chairman or a member designated him.

Rule 59: Condolences

Condolences shall be exclusively presented by the Chairman on behalf of all the members. The Chairman may, with the consent of the Commission, send a message of condolence on behalf of all the members of the Commission.

CHAPTER XI – VOTING AND ELECTIONS

Rule 60: Right to Vote

Each member of the Commission shall have one vote. In the event of an equal number of votes the Chairman shall have the casting vote.

Rule 61: Requests for a Vote

A proposal or a motion submitted to the decision of the Commission shall be put to the vote if a member so requests. If no member asks for a vote, the Commission may adopt a proposal or a motion without a vote.

Rule 62: Required Majority

1. Except where the Charter or other Rule of the present Rules of Procedure provide otherwise, decisions of the Commission shall be by the simple majority of the members present and voting.
2. For the purpose of the present Rules of Procedure, the expression "members present and voting" shall mean members voting for or against. Members who abstain from voting shall be considered as non-voting members.
3. Nevertheless decisions may be taken by consensus before resorting to voting, subject to compliance with the provisions of the Charter and Rules of Procedure and that the process for reaching that consensus does not unduly delay the proceedings of the Commission.

Rule 63: Method of Voting

1. Subject to the provisions of Rule 68, the Commission, unless it decides otherwise shall normally vote by show of hands, but any member may request a roll-call vote, which shall be taken in the alphabetical order of the names of the members of the Commission beginning with the member whose name is drawn by lot by the Chairman. In all the votes by roll-call each member shall

reply "yes", "no" or "abstention". The Commission may decide to hold a secret ballot.

2. In case of a vote by roll-call, the vote of each member participating in the ballot shall be recorded in the minutes.

Rule 64: Explanation of Vote

Members may make brief statements for the sole purpose of explaining their vote, before the beginning of the vote or once the vote has been taken. The member who is the sponsor of a proposal or a motion cannot explain his vote on that proposal or motion unless it has been amended.

Rule 65: Rules to be Observed while Voting

When the ballot begins, it may not be interrupted except if a member raises a point of order relating to the manner in which the ballot is conducted. The Chairman may allow members to intervene briefly, whether before the ballot begins or when it is closed, but solely to explain their vote.

Rule 66: Separation of Proposals and Amendments

The separation of proposals and amendments shall be done if so requested. The parts of the proposals or of the amendments which have been adopted shall later be put to the vote as a whole; if all the operative parts of a proposal have been rejected, the proposal shall be considered to have been rejected as a whole.

Rule 67: Amendment

An amendment shall simply comprise an addition to or a deletion of another proposal or a change in a part of the said proposal.

Rule 68: Order of Vote on Amendments

When an amendment to a proposal is moved, the amendment shall be voted on first. When two or more amendments are moved to a proposal, the Commission shall first vote on the amendment furthest removed in substance from the original proposal and then on the amendment next furthest removed therefrom and so on until all the amendments have been put to the vote. Nevertheless, when the adoption of an amendment shall necessarily imply the rejection of another amendment, the latter shall not be put to the vote. If one or several amendments are adopted, the amended proposal shall then be put to the vote.

Rule 69: Order of Vote on the Proposals

1. If two or more proposals are made on the same matter, the Commission, unless it decides otherwise, shall vote on these proposals in the order in which they have been submitted.

2. After each vote the Commission may decide whether it shall put the next proposal to the vote.
3. However, motions which do not require the opinion of Commission on the substance of the proposals shall be considered previous issues and put to the vote before the said proposals.

Rule 70: Elections

Elections shall be held by secret ballot, unless the Commission otherwise decides when the election concerns one post for which only one candidate has been proposed and that candidate or the list of candidates has been agreed upon.

Rule 71: Majority required to be Elected

1. When one post must be filled by election the candidate who in the first ballot obtains the majority of the votes cast and the largest number of votes shall be elected.
2. If the number of the candidates having a majority are fewer than the number of vacant posts, another round of voting shall be conducted for the posts which remain vacant.

CHAPTER XII – PARTICIPATION OF NON-MEMBERS OF THE COMMISSION

Rule 72: Participation of States in the Deliberations

1. The Commission may invite any State to participate in the discussion of any issue that is of particular interest to that State.
2. A subsidiary body of the Commission may invite any State to participate in the discussion of any issue that is of particular interest to that State.
3. A State thus invited shall have no voting right, but may submit proposals which may be put to the vote at the request of any member of Commission or of the subsidiary body concerned.

Rule 73: Participation of National Liberation Movements

The Commission may invite any national liberation movement recognized by the Organization of African Unity or by virtue of resolutions adopted by the Assembly to participate, without voting rights, in the discussion of any issue which is of particular interest to this movement.

Rule 74: Participation of Specialized Institutions and Consultations with the latter

1. Pursuant to the agreements concluded between the Organization of African Unity and the Specialized Institutions, the latter shall have the right to:

(a) Be represented in the public sessions of the Commission and of its subsidiary bodies;

(b) Participate, without voting rights, through their representatives in deliberations on issues which are of interest to them and to submit, on these issues, proposals which may be put to the vote at the request of any member of the Commission or the interested subsidiary body.

2. Before placing an issue submitted by a Specialized Institution on the provisional agenda, the Secretary General should initiate such preliminary consultations as may be necessary, with this institution.

3. When an issue proposed for inclusion in the provisional agenda of a session or which has been added to the agenda of a session pursuant to Rule 5 of the present Rules of Procedure, contains a proposal requesting the Organization of African Unity to undertake additional activities relating to issues concerning directly one or several Specialized Institutions, the Secretary-General should enter into consultation with the Institutions concerned and inform the Commission of the ways and means of ensuring co-ordinated utilization of the resources of the various Institutions.

4. When at a meeting of the Commission, a proposal calling upon the Organization of African Unity to undertake additional activities relating to issues directly concerning one or several Specialized Institutions, the Secretary General, after consulting as far as possible, the representatives of the interested institutions, should draw the attention of the Commission to the effects of that proposal.

5. Before taking a decision on the proposals mentioned above, the Commission shall make sure that the Institutions concerned have been duly consulted.

Rule 75: Participation of other Inter-governmental Organizations

Representatives of Inter-governmental Organizations to which the Organization of African Unity has granted permanent observer status and other Inter-governmental Organizations permanently designated by the Organization of African Unity or invited by the Commission, may participate, without voting rights, in the deliberations of the Commission on issues falling within the framework of the activities of these organizations.

CHAPTER XIII – CONSULTATIONS WITH NON-GOVERNMENTAL
ORGANIZATIONS AND REPRESENTATION OF THESE ORGANIZATIONS

Rule 76: Representation

Non-governmental organizations may appoint authorized observers to participate in the public sessions of the Commission and of its sub-bodies. The non-Governmental Organizations on the list as established the Commission may send observers to these sessions where issues falling within their area of activity are being considered.

Rule 77: Consultation

1. The Commission may consult the non-governmental organization either directly or through one or several committees set up for this purpose. In any case, these consultations may be held at the invitation of the commission or at the request of the organization.
2. Upon recommendation of the Secretary General and at the request of the Commission, organizations on the above-mentioned list may also be heard by the Commission.

CHAPTER XIV – PUBLICATION AND DISTRIBUTION OF THE REPORTS AND OTHER OFFICIAL DOCUMENTS OF THE COMMISSION

Rule 78: Report of the Commission

Within the framework of the procedure for communications by States parties to the Charter, referred to in Articles 47 and 49 of the Charter, the Commission shall submit to the Assembly a report containing, where possible, such recommendations it shall deem necessary. The report shall be confidential. However, it shall be published by the Chairman of the Commission if the Assembly so decides.

Rule 79: Periodical reports of Member States

Periodical reports and other information submitted by States party to the Charter as requested under Article 62 of the Charter, shall be documents for general distribution. The same thing shall apply to other information supplied by a State party to the Charter, unless this State shall declare otherwise.

Rule 80: Reports on the activities of the Commission

1. As stipulated in Article 54 of the Charter, the Commission shall each year submit to the Assembly a report on its deliberations in which it shall include a summary of its activities.
2. The report shall be published by the Chairman after the Assembly has considered it.

PART TWO
PROVISIONS RELATING TO THE FUNCTIONS OF THE COMMISSION

CHAPTER XV – PROMOTIONAL ACTIVITIES REPORTS SUBMITTED BY STATES PARTIES TO THE CHARTER UNDER ARTICLE 62 OF THE CHARTER

Rule 81: Contents of Reports

1. States parties to the Charter shall submit reports on measures they have taken to give effect to the rights recognized by the Charter and on the progress made with regard to the enjoyment of these rights. The reports should indicate, where possible, the factors and difficulties impeding the implementation of the provisions of the Charter.
2. Whenever the Commission shall request States parties to the Charter to submit reports as provided for by Article 62 of the Charter, it shall fix the date for the presentation of these reports.
3. The Commission may, through the Secretary-General, inform States parties to the Charter of its wishes regarding the form and the contents of the reports to be submitted under Article 62 of the Charter.

Rule 82: Transmission of the Reports

1. The Secretary-General may, after consultation with the Commission, communicate to the Specialized Institutions concerned, copies of all parts of the reports which may relate to their areas of competence, produced by member States of these institutions.
2. The Commission may invite the Specialized Institutions to which the Secretary-General has communicated parts of the reports, to submit observations relating to these parts within a time limit that it may specify.

Rule 83: Submission of Reports

The Commission shall inform, as early as possible, member States parties to the Charter, through the Secretary-General, of the opening date, duration and venue of the Session at which their respective reports shall be considered. Representatives of the States parties to the Charter may participate in the sessions of the Commission at which their reports shall be considered. The Commission may also inform a State party to the Charter from which it wanted complementary information, that it may authorize its representative to participate in a specific session. This representative shall be able to reply to questions put to him by the Commission and in statements on reports already submitted by this State. He may also furnish additional information from his State.

Rule 84: Non-submission of Reports

1. The Secretary-General, shall, at each session, inform the Commission of all cases of non-submission of reports or of additional information requested pursuant to Rules 81 and 85 of the Rules of Procedure. In such cases, the Commission may, through the Secretary-General, send to the State party to the Charter concerned, a report relating to the submission of the report or additional information.
2. If, after the reminder referred to in paragraph 1 of this Rule, the State party to the Charter does not submit the report or the additional information requested pursuant to Rules 81 and 85 of the Rules of Procedure, the Commission shall point it out in its annual report to the Assembly.

Rule 85: Examination of information contained in reports

1. When considering a report submitted by a State party to the Charter under Article 62 of the Charter, the Commission should first make sure that the report provides all the necessary information pursuant to the provisions of Rule 81 of the Rules of Procedure.
2. If, in the opinion of the Commission, a report submitted by a State party to the Charter does not contain adequate information, the Commission may request this State to furnish the additional information required, indicating the date by which the information needed should be submitted.
3. If, following consideration of the reports, and the information submitted by a State party to the Charter, the Commission decides that a State has not discharged some of its obligations under the Charter, it may address any general observations to the State concerned as it may think necessary.

Rule 86: Adjournment and Transmission of the Reports

1. The Commission shall, through the Secretary General, communicate to States parties to the Charter for comments, its general observations made following the consideration of the reports and the information submitted by States parties to the Charter. The Commission may when necessary, fix a time limit for the submission of the comments by States parties to the Charter.
2. The Commission may also transmit to the Assembly, the observations mentioned in paragraph 1 of this Rule, accompanied by copies of the reports it has received from the States parties to the Charter as well as the comments supplied by the latter, if possible.

CHAPTER XVI – PROTECTION ACTIVITIES
COMMUNICATIONS FROM THE STATES PARTIES TO THE CHARTER

Section I. Procedure for the Consideration of Communications Received in Conformity with Article 47 of the Charter: Procedure for Communication

Rule 87: Purpose of the Procedure

1. Any communication submitted under Article 47 of the Charter should be submitted to the Secretary General and the Chairman of the Commission.
2. The communication referred to above should be in writing and contain a detailed and comprehensive statement of the actions denounced as well as the provisions of the Charter alleged to have been violated.
3. The notification of the communication to the State party to the Charter, the Secretary-General and the Chairman of the Commission shall be done through a registered letter accompanied by an acknowledgement receipt form or through any recognized technical means.

Rule 88: Register of Communications

The Secretary General shall keep a permanent register for all communications received under Article 47 of the Charter.

Rule 89: Reply and time limit

1. The reply of the State party to the Charter seized of a written communication should reach the requesting State party to the Charter within 3 months following the receipt of the notification of the communication.
2. It shall be accompanied in particular by:

   (a) Written explanations, declarations or statements relating to the issues raised;
   (b) Possible indications and measures taken to end the situation denounced;
   (c) Indications on the law and rules of procedure applicable or applied;
   (d) Indications on the local procedures for appeal already used, in process or still open.

Rule 90: Non-settlement of the issue

1. If within three (3) months from the date on which the notification of the original communication is received by the addressee State, the issue has not been settled to the satisfaction of the two interested parties, through selected channel of negotiation or through any other peaceful means selected by common consent of the parties, the issue shall be referred to the Commission, in accordance with the provisions of Article 47 of the Charter.
2. The issue shall also be referred to the Commission if the State party to the Charter fails to react to the request made under of the Charter, within the same 3 months' period of time.

Rule 91: Seisin of the Commission

On the expiry of the 3 months' time limit referred to in Article 47 of the Charter, and in the absence of a satisfactory reply, or if the addressee State party to the Charter fails to react to the request, a party may submit the communication to the Commission through notification addressed to its Chairman, and to the other interested Parties and to the Secretary-General.

Section II. Procedure for the Consideration of the Communications Received in Conformity with Articles 48 and 49 of the Charter: Procedure for Communication-Complaint

Rule 92: Seisin of the Commission

1. Any communication submitted under Articles 48 and 49 of the Charter may be submitted to the Commission by any one of the States parties through notification addressed to the Chairman Commission, the Secretary-General and the State party concerned.
2. The notification referred to in paragraph 1 of the present Rule shall contain information on the following elements:

   (a) Measures taken to try to resolve the issue pursuant to Article 48 of the Charter including the text of the initial communication and a written explanation from the interested States parties to the Charter to the issue;
   (b) Measures taken to exhaust local procedures for appeal;
   (c) Any other procedure for international investigation or international settlement to which the interested States parties have resorted.

Rule 93: Permanent Register of Communications

The Secretary-General shall keep a permanent register for all communications received by the Commission under Articles 48 and 49 of the Charter.

Rule 94: Seisin of the Members of the Commission

The Secretary-General shall immediately inform members of the Commission of any notification received pursuant to Rule 91 of the Rules of Procedure and shall send to them, as early as possible, a copy of the notification as well as the relevant information.

Rule 95: Closed Sessions and Press Releases

1. The Commission shall consider the communications referred to in Articles 48 and 49 of the Charter in closed session.
2. After consulting the interested States parties to the Charter, the Commission may issue through the Secretary-General, releases on its activities at a closed session for the attention of the media and the public.

Rule 96: Consideration of the Communication

The Commission shall consider a communication only when:

(a) The procedure offered to the States parties by Article 47 of the Charter has been exhausted;

(b) The time limit set in Article 48 of the Charter has expired;

(c) The Commission is certain that all local remedies, if they exist, have been utilized and exhausted, pursuant to the generally recognized principles of international law, or that the process of achieving these remedies would extend beyond reasonable time limits or has been unduly prolonged.

Rule 97: Friendly Settlement

Subject to Rule 96 of the present Rules of Procedure, the Commission shall place its good offices at the disposal of the interested States parties to the Charter with a view to reaching a friendly settlement of the issue based on respect for human rights and fundamental liberties, as recognized by the Charter.

Rule 98: Additional Information

The Commission, through the Secretary-General, may request the States parties concerned, or one of them, to communicate additional information or observations orally or in writing. The Commission shall fix a time limit for the submission of the written information or observations.

Rule 99: Representation of States parties to the Charter

1. The States parties to the Charter concerned shall have the right to be represented during the consideration of the issue by the Commission and to submit observations orally and in writing or in either form.

2. The Commission shall notify, as soon as possible, the States Parties concerned, through the Secretary-General, of the opening date, the duration and the venue of the session at which the issue will be examined.

3. The procedure to be followed for the presentation of oral or written observations shall be determined by the Commission.

Rule 100: Report of the Commission

1. The Commission shall adopt a report pursuant to Article 52 of the Charter within a reasonable time limit which should not exceed 12 months following the notification referred to in Article 48 of the Charter and Rule 90 of the present Rules of Procedure.

2. The provisions of paragraph 1 of Rule 99 of these Rules of Procedure shall not apply to the deliberations of the Commission, relating the adoption of the report.

3. The report referred to above shall concern the decisions and conclusions that the Commission will reach.

4. The report of the Commission shall be communicated to the States parties concerned through the Secretary-General.
5. The report of the Commission shall be sent to the Assembly through the Secretary-General, together with such recommendations as it shall deem useful.

CHAPTER XVII – OTHER COMMUNICATIONS
PROCEDURE FOR THE CONSIDERATION OF THE COMMUNICATIONS RECEIVED IN CONFORMITY WITH ARTICLE 55 OF THE CHARTER

Section I. Transmission of Communications to the Commission

Rule 101: Seisin of the Commission

1. Pursuant to these Rules of Procedure, the Secretary General shall transmit to the Commission the communications submitted to him for consideration by the Commission in accordance with the Charter.
2. No communication concerning a State which is not a party to the Charter shall be received by the Commission or placed on a list under Rule 102 of the present Rules.

Rule 102: List of Communications

1. The Secretary of the Commission shall prepare lists of communications submitted to the Commission pursuant to Rule 101 above, to which he shall attach a brief summary of their contents and regularly cause lists to be distributed to members of the Commission. In addition, the Secretary shall keep a permanent register of all these communications.
2. The full text of each communication referred to the Commission shall be communicated to each member of the Commission on request.

Rule 103: Request for Clarifications

1. The Commission, through the Secretary-General, may request the author of a communication to furnish clarifications on the applicability of the Charter to his communication, and to specify in particular:

    (a) His name, address, age and profession verifying his true identity, should he request the Commission to remain anonymous;
    (b) The name of the State party referred to in the communication;
    (c) The purpose of the communication;
    (d) The provision(s) of the Charter allegedly violated;
    (e) "De facto" means of law;
    (f) The measures taken by the author to exhaust local remedies;
    (g) The extent to which the same issue is already being considered by another international investigating or settlement body.

2. When asking for clarification or information, the Secretary-General shall fix an appropriate time limit for the author to submit the communication so as to avoid undue delay in the procedure provided for by the Charter.
3. The Commission may adopt a questionnaire for use by the author of the communication in providing the above-mentioned information.
4. The request for clarification referred to in paragraph 1 of this Rule shall not prevent the inclusion of the communication on the lists mentioned in paragraph 1 of Rule 102 above.

Rule 104: Distribution of Communications

For each communication recorded, the Secretary-General shall prepare as soon as possible, a summary of the relevant information received, which shall be distributed to the members of the Commission.

Section II. General Provisions governing the Consideration of the Communications by the Commission or its Subsidiary Bodies

Rule 105: Private Sessions

The sessions of the Commission or of its subsidiary bodies during which the communications are examined as provided for in the Charter shall be considered private. The sessions during which the Commission may consider general issues, such as the application procedure of the Charter, may be public, if the Commission so desires.

Rule 106: Press Releases

The Commission may issue, through the Secretary General and for the attention of the media and the public, releases on the activities of the Commission in its private session.

Rule 107: Incompatibilities

1. No member shall take part in the consideration of a communication by the Commission:
   (a) If he has any personal interest in the case; or
   (b) If he has participated, in any capacity, in the adoption of any decision relating to the case which is the subject of the communication.

2. Any issue relating to the application of paragraph 1 above shall be resolved by the Commission.

Rule 108: Withdrawal of a Member

If, for any reason, a member considers that he should not take part or continue to take part in the consideration of a communication, he shall inform the Chairman of his decision to withdraw.

350

Rule 109: Provisional Measures

Before making its final views known to the Assembly on the communication, the Commission may inform the State party concerned of its views on the appropriateness of taking provisional measures to avoid irreparable prejudice being caused to the victim of the alleged violation. In so doing, the Commission shall inform the State party that the expression of its views on the adoption of those provisional measures does not imply a decision on the substance of the communication.

Rule 110: Information to the State party to the Charter

Prior to any substantive consideration, every communication should be made known to the State concerned through the Chairman of the Commission, pursuant to Article 57 of the Charter.

Section III. Procedures to Determine Admissibility

Rule 111: Time limits for consideration of the admissibility

The Commission shall decide, as early as possible and pursuant to the following provisions, whether or not the communication shall be admissible under the Charter.

Rule 112: Order of Consideration of the Communications

1. Unless otherwise decided, the Commission shall consider communications in the order they are received by the Secretariat.
2. The Commission may decide, if it deems it proper, to consider jointly two or more communications.

Rule 113: Working Groups

The Commission may set up one or several working groups, composed of three of its members at most, to submit recommendations on the conditions of admissibility stipulated in Article 56 of the Charter.

Rule 114: Admissibility of Communications

1. Communications may be submitted to the Commission by:
    (a) An alleged victim of a violation by a State party to the Charter of one of the rights enunciated in the Charter or, in his name, when it appears that he is unable to submit the communication himself;
    (b) An individual or an organization alleging, with supporting evidence, cases of serious or gross violations of human and peoples' rights.

2. The Commission may accept such communications from any individual or organization irrespective of where they are.
3. In order to decide on the admissibility of a communication, pursuant to the provisions of the Charter, the Commission shall ensure:

    (a) That the communication indicates the identity of the author even if he requests the Commission to be anonymous, in which case the Commission shall not disclose his name;

    (b) That the author alleges himself to be a victim of a violation, by a State party of any one of the rights enunciated in the Charter and, if necessary, that the communication is submitted in the name of an individual who is a victim (or individuals who are victims) who is unable to submit a communication or to authorize it to be done;

    (c) That the communication does not constitute an abuse of the right to submit a communication under the Charter;

    (d) That the communication is not incompatible with the provisions of the Charter;

    (e) That the communication is not limited solely to information published or disseminated through the mass communication media;

    (f) That the same issue is not already being considered by another international investigating or settlement body;

    (g) That the alleged victim has exhausted all the available local remedies or that the processes of such remedies are taking an unduly long time;

    (h) That the communication has been submitted within a reasonable time limit from the time the local remedies have been exhausted or from a period decided by the Commission.

Rule 115: Additional Information

1. The Commission or a working group set up under Rule 113, may, through the Secretary-General, request the State party concerned or the author of the communication to submit in writing additional information or observations relating to the issue of admissibility of the communication. The Commission or the working group shall fix a time limit for the submission of the information or observations to avoid the issue dragging on too long.
2. A communication may be declared admissible only on condition that the State party concerned has received the text of the communication and that it has been given the opportunity to submit the information and observations pursuant to paragraph 1 of this Rule.
3. A request made under paragraph 1 of this Rule should indicate clearly that the request does not mean that any decision whatsoever has been taken on the issue of admissibility.

Rule 116: Decision of the Commission on Admissibility

1. If the Commission decides that a communication is inadmissible under the Charter, it shall make its decision known as early as possible, through the

Secretary-General, to the author of the communication and, if the communication has been transmitted to a State party concerned, to that State.

2. If the Commission has declared a communication inadmissible under the Charter, it may reconsider this decision at a later date if it is seized by the interested individual or on his behalf, of a written request containing the information to the effect that the grounds for the inadmissibility have ceased to exist.

Section IV. Procedures for the Consideration of Communications

Rule 117: Proceedings

1. If the Commission decides that a communication is admissible under the Charter, its decision and the text of the relevant documents shall as soon as possible be submitted to the State party concerned, through the Secretary-General. The author of the communication shall also be informed of the Commission's decision through the Secretary-General.

2. The State party to the Charter concerned shall, within the 4 ensuing months, submit in writing to the Commission, explanations or statements elucidating the issue under consideration and indicating, if possible, measures it was able to take to remedy the situation.

3. All explanations or statements submitted by a State party pursuant to the present Rule shall be communicated, through the Secretary-General, to the author of the communication who may submit in writing additional information and observations within a time limit fixed by the Commission.

4. The Commission may review the decision by which it has declared a communication admissible, in the light of the explanations and statements submitted by the State party under the present Rule.

Rule 118: Final Decision of the Commission

1. If the communication is admissible, the Commission shall consider it in the light of all the information that the individual and the State party concerned has submitted in writing; it shall make known its observations on this issue. To this end, the Commission may refer the communication to a working group, composed of 3 of its members at most, which shall submit recommendations to it.

2. The observations of the Commission shall be communicated to the Assembly through the Secretary General.

3. The Assembly or its Chairman may request the Commission to conduct an in-depth study on these cases and to submit a factual report accompanied by its findings and recommendations, in accordance with the provisions of Article 58 subparagraph 2 of the Charter.

FINAL CHAPTER
AMENDMENT AND SUSPENSION OF THE RULES OF PROCEDURE

Rule 119: Method of Amendment

Only the Commission may modify the present Rules of Procedure.

Rule 120: Method of Suspension

The Commission may suspend temporarily the application of any of the present Rules of Procedure, on condition that such a suspension shall not be incompatible with any applicable decision of the Commission or the Assembly or with any relevant provision of the Charter and that the proposal shall have been submitted 24 hours in advance. This condition may be set aside if no member opposes it. Such a suspension may take place only with a specific and precise object in view and should be limited to the duration necessary to achieve that aim.

DELIBERATED AND ADOPTED by the Commission at its second session held in Dakar. Senegal, on 13 February 1988.

PART II

HUMAN RIGHTS AND THE
ADMINISTRATION OF JUSTICE

SECTION ONE

CRIME AND PUNISHMENT

Chapter 1: Personnel

26. UNITED NATIONS: CODE OF CONDUCT FOR LAW ENFORCEMENT OFFICIALS

Adopted by General Assembly resolution 34/169 (1979)

Editors' Notes

The Code of Conduct was adopted by the United Nations General Assembly in 1979 without a vote. The articles are couched in broad terms supplemented with commentaries so as to promote domestic implementation.[1] The definition of "Law Enforcement Officials" contained in Article 1 includes members of the armed forces in the recognition that the military are sometimes involved in operations concerning public order. Article 8 of the Code enjoins officials to "respect the law and the present Code" and that where a violation of the Code has, or is about to occur, the official should report the matter to their superior officer. The Code reiterates the prohibition of torture (Article 5) and reflects values contained within the Standard Minimum Rules for the Treatment of Prisoners.[2] Similar, but not identical, provisions are included in the Council of Europe's Declaration on the Police 1979.

The General Assembly,

Considering that the purposes proclaimed in the Charter of the United Nations include the achievement of international co-operation in promoting and encouraging respect for human rights and for fundamental freedoms for all without distinction as to race, sex, language or religion,

Recalling, in particular, the Universal Declaration of Human Rights and the International Covenants on Human Rights,

Recalling also the Declaration on the Protection of All Persons from Being Subjected to Torture and Other Cruel, Inhuman or Degrading Treatment or Punishment, adopted by the General Assembly in its resolution 3452(XXX) of 9 December 1975,

Mindful that the nature of the functions of law enforcement in the defence of public order and the manner in which those functions are exercised have a direct impact on the quality of life of individuals as well as of society as a whole,

Conscious of the important task which law enforcement officials are performing diligently and with dignity, in compliance with the principles of human rights,

Aware, nevertheless, of the potential for abuse which the exercise of such duties entails,

---

[1] ECOSOC have adopted guidelines for the implementation of the Code, ECOSOC Res. 1989/61, UN Doc. E/1989/89.

[2] See further: Rodley, N. (1987). The Treatment of Prisoners under International Law. Oxford, Oxford University Press. pp.279-288.

Recognising that the establishment of a code of conduct for law enforcement officials is only one of several important measures for providing the citizenry served by law enforcement officials with protection of all their rights and interests,

Aware that there are additional important principles and prerequisites for the humane performance of law enforcement functions, namely:

(a) That, like all agencies of the criminal justice system, every law enforcement agency should be representative of and responsible and accountable to the community as a whole,

(b) That the effective maintenance of ethical standards among law enforcement officials depends on the existence of a well-conceived, popularly accepted and humane system of laws,

(c) That every law enforcement official is part of the criminal justice system, the aim of which is to prevent and control crime, and that the conduct of every functionary within the system has an impact on the entire system,

(d) That every law enforcement agency, in fulfilment of the first premise of every profession, should be held to the duty of disciplining itself in complete conformity with the principles and standards herein provided and that the actions of law enforcement officials should be responsive to public scrutiny, whether exercised by a review board, a ministry, a procuracy, the judiciary, an ombudsman, a citizens' committee or any combination thereof, or any other reviewing agency,

(e) That standards as such lack practical value unless their content and meaning, through education and training and through monitoring, become part of the creed of every law enforcement official,

Adopts the Code of Conduct for Law Enforcement Officials set forth in the annex to the present resolution and decides to transmit it to Governments with the recommendation that favourable consideration should be given to its use within the framework of national legislation or practice as a body of principles for observance by law enforcement officials.

ANNEX
CODE OF CONDUCT FOR LAW ENFORCEMENT OFFICIALS

Article 1

Law enforcement officials shall at all times fulfil the duty imposed upon them by law, by serving the community and by protecting all persons against illegal acts, consistent with the high degree of responsibility required by their profession.

Commentary:

(a) The term "law enforcement officials" includes all officers of the law, whether appointed or elected, who exercise police powers, especially the powers of arrest or detention.

(b) In countries where police powers are exercised by military authorities, whether uniformed or not, or by State security forces, the definition of law enforcement officials shall be regarded as including officers of such services.

(c) Service to the community is intended to include particularly the rendition of services of assistance to those members of the community who by reason of personal, economic, social or other emergencies are in need of immediate aid.

(d) This provision is intended to cover not only all violent, predatory and harmful acts, but extends to the full range of prohibitions under penal statutes. It extends to conduct by persons not capable of incurring criminal liability.

Article 2

In the performance of their duty, law enforcement officials shall respect and protect human dignity and maintain and uphold the human rights of all persons.

Commentary:

(a) The human rights in question are identified and protected by national and international law. Among the relevant international instruments are the Universal Declaration of Human Rights, the International Covenant on Civil and Political Rights, the Declaration on the Protection of All Persons from Being Subjected to Torture and Other Cruel, Inhuman or Degrading Treatment or Punishment, the United Nations Declaration on the Elimination of All Forms of Racial Discrimination, the International Convention on the Elimination of All Forms of Racial Discrimination, the International Convention on the Suppression and Punishment of the Crime of Apartheid, Convention on the Prevention and Punishment of the Crime of Genocide, the Standard Minimum Rules for the Treatment of prisoners and the Vienna Convention on Consular Relations.

(b) National commentaries to this provision should indicate regional or national provisions identifying and protecting these rights.

Article 3

Law enforcement officials may use force only when strictly necessary and to the extent required for the performance of their duty.

Commentary:

(a) This provision emphasises that the use of force by law enforcement officials should be exceptional; while it implies that law enforcement officials may be authorised to use force as is reasonably necessary under the circumstances for the prevention of crime or in effecting or assisting in the lawful arrest of offenders or suspected offenders, no force going beyond that may be used.

(b) National law ordinarily restricts the use of force by law enforcement officials in accordance with a principle of proportionality. It is to be understood that such national principles of proportionality are to be respected in the interpretation of this provision. In no case should this provision be interpreted to authorize the use of force which is disproportionate to the legitimate objective to be achieved.

(c) The use of firearms is considered an extreme measure. Every effort should be made to exclude the use of firearms, especially against children. In general, firearms should not be used except when a suspected offender offers armed resistance or otherwise jeopardises the lives of others and less extreme measures are not sufficient to restrain or apprehend the suspected offender. In every instance in which a firearm is discharged, a report should be made promptly to the competent authorities.

Article 4

Matters of a confidential nature in the possession of law enforcement officials shall be kept confidential, unless the performance of duty or the needs of justice strictly require otherwise.

Commentary:

By the nature of their duties, law enforcement officials obtain information which may relate to private lives or be potentially harmful to the interests, and especially the reputation, of others. Great care should be exercised in safeguarding and using such information, which should be disclosed only in the performance of duty or to serve the needs of justice. Any disclosure of such information for other purposes is wholly improper.

Article 5

No law enforcement official may inflict, instigate or tolerate any act of torture or other cruel, inhuman or degrading treatment or punishment, nor may any law enforcement official invoke superior orders or exceptional circumstances such as a state of war or a threat of war, a threat to national security, internal political instability or any other public emergency as a justification of torture or other cruel, inhuman or degrading treatment or punishment.

Commentary:

(a) This prohibition derives from the Declaration on the Protection of All Persons from Being Subjected to Torture and Other Cruel, Inhuman or Degrading Treatment or Punishment, adopted by the General Assembly, according to which:

"[Such an act is] an offence to human dignity and shall be condemned as a denial of the purposes of the Charter of the United Nations and as a violation of the human rights and fundamental freedom proclaimed in the Universal Declaration of Human Rights [and other international human rights instruments.]"

(b)   The Declaration defines torture as follows:

"... torture means any act by which severe pain or suffering, whether physical or mental, is intentionally inflicted by or at the instigation of a public official on a person for such purposes as obtaining from him or a third person information or confession, punishing him for an act he has committed or is suspected of having committed, or intimidating him or other persons. It does not include pain or suffering arising only from, inherent in or incidental to, lawful sanctions to the extent consistent with the Standard Minimum Rules for the Treatment of Prisoners."

(c)   The term "cruel, inhuman or degrading treatment or punishment" has not been defined by the General Assembly but should be interpreted so as to intend the widest possible protection against abuses, whether physical or mental.

Article 6

Law enforcement officials shall ensure the full protection of the health of persons in their custody and, in particular, shall take immediate action to secure medical attention whenever required.

Commentary:

(a)   "medical attention", which refers to services rendered by any medical personnel, including certified medical practitioners and paramedics, shall be secured when needed or requested.
(b)   While the medical personnel are likely to be attached to the law enforcement operation, law enforcement officials must take into account the judgement of such personnel when they recommend providing the person in custody with appropriate treatment through, or in consultation with, medical personnel from outside the law enforcement operation.
(c)   It is understood that law enforcement officials shall also secure medical attention for victims of violations of law or of accidents occurring in the course of violations of law.

Article 7

Law enforcement officials shall not commit any act of corruption. They shall also rigorously oppose and combat all such acts.

Commentary:

(a)   Any act of corruption, in the same way as any other abuse of authority, is incompatible with the profession of law enforcement officials. The law must be enforced fully with respect to any law enforcement official who commits an act of corruption, as Governments cannot expect to enforce the law among their citizens if they cannot, or will not, enforce the law against their own agents and within their agencies.

(b) While the definition of corruption must be subject to national law, it should be understood to encompass the commission or omission of an act in the performance of or in connection with one's duties, in response to gifts, promises or incentives demanded or accepted, or the wrongful receipt of these once the act has been committed or omitted.

(c) The expression "act of corruption" referred to above should be understood to encompass attempted corruption.

Article 8

Law enforcement officials shall respect the law and the present Code. They shall also, to the best of their capability, prevent and rigorously oppose any violations of them.

Law enforcement officials who have reason to believe that a violation of the present Code has occurred or is about to occur shall report the matter to their superior authorities and, where necessary, to other appropriate authorities or organs vested with reviewing or remedial power.

Commentary:

(a) This Code shall be observed whenever it has been incorporated into national legislation or practice. If legislation or practice contains stricter provisions then those stricter provisions shall be observed.

(b) The article seeks to preserve the balance between the need for internal discipline of the agency on which public safety is largely dependent, on the one hand, and the need for dealing with violations of basic human rights, on the other. Law enforcement officials shall report violations within the chain of command and take other lawful action outside the chain of command only when no other remedies are available or effective. It is understood that law enforcement officials shall not suffer administrative or other penalties because they have reported that a violation of this Code has occurred or is about to occur.

(c) The term "appropriate authorities or organs vested with reviewing or remedial power" refers to any authority or organ existing under national law, whether internal to the law enforcement agency or independent thereof, with statutory, customary or other power to review grievances and complaints arising out of violations within the purview of this Code.

(d) In some countries, the mass media may be regarded as performing complaint review functions similar to those described in subparagraph (c) above. Law enforcement officials may, therefore, be justified if, as a last resort and in accordance with the laws and customs of their countries and with the provisions of article 4 of the present Code, they bring violations to the attention of public opinion through the mass media.

(e) Law enforcement officials who comply with the provisions of this Code deserve the respect, the full support and the co-operation of the community and of the law enforcement agency in which they serve, as well as the law enforcement profession.

27. UNITED NATIONS: BASIC PRINCIPLES ON THE USE OF FORCE AND FIREARMS BY LAW ENFORCEMENT OFFICIALS

Eighth United Nations Congress on the Prevention of Crime and the Treatment of Offenders, Havana, 27 August to 7 September 1990, U.N. Doc. A/CONF.144/28/Rev.1 at 112 (1990)

Editors' Notes
The Principles on the Use of Force and Firearms by Law Enforcement Officials were among a range of items submitted by the Eighth Congress on the Prevention of Crime and the Treatment of Offenders to the United Nations General Assembly, who adopted them 1990.

The Principles supplement and add detail to the circumstances in which force may be used as provided for in Article 3 of the Code of Conduct for Law Enforcement Officials.[1] Among the Principles, which are formulated for the guidance of member states in promoting the role of law enforcement officials, are that a policy of differentiated response should be adopted to differing circumstances (Principle 2), that the minimum force required should be used to control the particular circumstances (Principles 4, 13 and 15), and that officials should not use firearms except in self defence or in the defence of others, to prevent a particularly serious crime involving grave threat to life or to prevent escape (Principle 9). Even under these circumstances, lethal use of force should only be used where unavoidable. As well as promoting restraint in the use of force among law enforcement officers, the Principles also include provisions calling for effective training and support for those officers (Principles 18-21).

Whereas the work of law enforcement officials* is a social service of great importance and there is, therefore, a need to maintain and, whenever necessary, to improve the working conditions and status of these officials,

Whereas a threat to the life and safety of law enforcement officials must be seen as a threat to the stability of society as a whole,

Whereas law enforcement officials have a vital role in the protection of the right to life, liberty and security of the person, as guaranteed in the Universal Declaration of Human Rights and reaffirmed in the International Covenant on Civil and Political Rights,

Whereas the Standard Minimum Rules for the Treatment of Prisoners provide for the circumstances in which prison officials may use force in the course of their duties,

---

[1] Supra.

* In accordance with the commentary to article 1 of the Code of Conduct for Law Enforcement Officials, the term "law enforcement officials" includes all officers of the law, whether appointed or elected, who exercise police powers, especially the powers of arrest or detention.

Whereas article 3 of the Code of Conduct for Law Enforcement Officials provides that law enforcement officials may use force only when strictly necessary and to the extent required for the performance of their duty,

Whereas the preparatory meeting for the Seventh United Nations Congress on the Prevention of Crime and the Treatment of Offenders, held at Varenna, Italy, agreed on elements to be considered in the course of further work on restraints on the use of force and firearms by law enforcement officials,

Whereas the Seventh Congress, in its resolution 14, inter alia, emphasises that the use of force and firearms by law enforcement officials should be commensurate with due respect for human rights,

Whereas the Economic and Social Council, in its resolution 1986/10, section IX, of 21 May 1986, invited Member States to pay particular attention in the implementation of the Code to the use of force and firearms by law enforcement officials, and the General Assembly, in its resolution 41/149 of 4 December 1986, inter alia, welcomed this recommendation made by the Council,

Whereas it is appropriate that, with due regard to their personal safety, consideration be given to the role of law enforcement officials in relation to the administration of justice, to the protection of the right to life, liberty and security of the person, to their responsibility to maintain public safety and social peace and to the importance of their qualifications, training and conduct,

The basic principles set forth below, which have been formulated to assist Member States in their task of ensuring and promoting the proper role of law enforcement officials, should be taken into account and respected by Governments within the framework of their national legislation and practice, and be brought to the attention of law enforcement officials as well as other persons, such as judges, prosecutors, lawyers, members of the executive branch and the legislature, and the public.

General provisions

1. Governments and law enforcement agencies shall adopt and implement rules and regulations on the use of force and firearms against persons by law enforcement officials. In developing such rules and regulations Governments and law enforcement agencies shall keep the ethical issues associated with the use of force and firearms constantly under review.
2. Governments and law enforcement agencies should develop a range of means as broad as possible and equip law enforcement officials with various types of weapons and ammunition that would allow for a differentiated use of force and firearms. These should include the development of non-lethal incapacitating weapons for use in appropriate situations, with a view to increasingly restraining the application of means capable of causing death or injury to persons. For the same purpose, it should also be possible for law enforcement officials to be equipped with self-defensive equipment such as shields, helmets, bullet-proof vests and bullet-proof means of transportation, in order to decrease the need to use weapons of any kind.
3. The development and deployment of non-lethal incapacitating weapons should be carefully evaluated in order to minimise the risk of endangering

uninvolved persons, and the use of such weapons should be carefully controlled.

4. Law enforcement officials, in carrying out their duty, shall, as far as possible, apply non-violent means before resorting to the use of force and firearms. They may use force and firearms only if other means remain ineffective or without any promise of achieving the intended result.

5. Whenever the lawful use of force and firearms is unavoidable, law enforcement officials shall:

   (a) Exercise restraint in such use and act in proportion to the seriousness of the offence and the legitimate objective to be achieved;
   (b) Minimise damage and injury, and respect and preserve human life;
   (c) Ensure that assistance and medical aid are rendered to any injured or affected persons at the earliest possible moment;
   (d) Ensure that relatives or close friends of the injured or affected person are notified at the earliest possible moment.

6. Where injury or death is caused by the use of force and firearms by law enforcement officials, they shall report the incident promptly to their superiors, in accordance with principle 22.

7. Governments shall ensure that arbitrary or abusive use of force and firearms by law enforcement officials is punished as a criminal offence under their law.

8. Exceptional circumstances such as internal political instability or any other public emergency may not be invoked to justify any departure from these basic principles.

Special provisions

9. Law enforcement officials shall not use firearms against persons except in self-defence or defence of others against the imminent threat of death or serious injury, to prevent the perpetration of a particularly serious crime involving grave threat to life, to arrest a person presenting such a danger and resisting their authority, or to prevent his or her escape, and only when less extreme means are insufficient to achieve these objectives. In any event, intentional lethal use of firearms may only be made when strictly unavoidable in order to protect life.

10. In the circumstances provided for under principle 9, law enforcement officials shall identify themselves as such and give a clear warning of their intent to use firearms, with sufficient time for the warning to be observed, unless to do so would unduly place the law enforcement officials at risk or would create a risk of death or serious harm to other persons, or would be clearly inappropriate or pointless in the circumstances of the incident.

11. Rules and regulations on the use of firearms by law enforcement officials should include guidelines that:

   (a) Specify the circumstances under which law enforcement officials are authorised to carry firearms and prescribe the types of firearms and ammunition permitted;

(b) Ensure that firearms are used only in appropriate circumstances and in a manner likely to decrease the risk of unnecessary harm;

(c) Prohibit the use of those firearms and ammunition that cause unwarranted injury or present an unwarranted risk;

(d) Regulate the control, storage and issuing of firearms, including procedures for ensuring that law enforcement officials are accountable for the firearms and ammunition issued to them;

(e) Provide for warnings to be given, if appropriate, when firearms are to be discharged;

(f) Provide for a system of reporting whenever law enforcement officials use firearms in the performance of their duty.

Policing unlawful assemblies

12. As everyone is allowed to participate in lawful and peaceful assemblies, in accordance with the principles embodied in the Universal Declaration of Human Rights and the International Covenant on Civil and Political Rights, Governments and law enforcement agencies and officials shall recognise that force and firearms may be used only in accordance with principles 13 and 14.

13. In the dispersal of assemblies that are unlawful but non-violent, law enforcement officials shall avoid the use of force or, where that is not practicable, shall restrict such force to the minimum extent necessary.

14. In the dispersal of violent assemblies, law enforcement officials may use firearms only when less dangerous means are not practicable and only to the minimum extent necessary. Law enforcement officials shall not use firearms in such cases, except under the conditions stipulated in principle 9.

Policing persons in custody or detention

15. Law enforcement officials, in their relations with persons in custody or detention, shall not use force, except when strictly necessary for the maintenance of security and order within the institution, or when personal safety is threatened.

16. Law enforcement officials, in their relations with persons in custody or detention, shall not use firearms, except in self-defence or in the defence of others against the immediate threat of death or serious injury, or when strictly necessary to prevent the escape of a person in custody or detention presenting the danger referred to in principle 9.

17. The preceding principles are without prejudice to the rights, duties and responsibilities of prison officials, as set out in the Standard Minimum Rules for the Treatment of Prisoners, particularly rules 33, 34 and 54.

Qualifications, training and counselling

18. Governments and law enforcement agencies shall ensure that all law enforcement officials are selected by proper screening procedures, have appropriate moral, psychological and physical qualities for the effective

exercise of their functions and receive continuous and thorough professional training. Their continued fitness to perform these functions should be subject to periodic review.

19. Governments and law enforcement agencies shall ensure that all law enforcement officials are provided with training and are tested in accordance with appropriate proficiency standards in the use of force.

    Those law enforcement officials who are required to carry firearms should be authorised to do so only upon completion of special training in their use.

20. In the training of law enforcement officials, Governments and law enforcement agencies shall give special attention to issues of police ethics and human rights, especially in the investigative process, to alternatives to the use of force and firearms, including the peaceful settlement of conflicts, the understanding of crowd behaviour, and the methods of persuasion, negotiation and mediation, as well as to technical means, with a view to limiting the use of force and firearms. Law enforcement agencies should review their training programmes and operational procedures in the light of particular incidents.

21. Governments and law enforcement agencies shall make stress counselling available to law enforcement officials who are involved in situations where force and firearms are used.

Reporting and review procedures

22. Governments and law enforcement agencies shall establish effective reporting and review procedures for all incidents referred to in principles 6 and 11 (f). For incidents reported pursuant to these principles, Governments and law enforcement agencies shall ensure that an effective review process is available and that independent administrative or prosecutorial authorities are in a position to exercise jurisdiction in appropriate circumstances. In cases of death and serious injury or other grave consequences, a detailed report shall be sent promptly to the competent authorities responsible for administrative review and judicial control.

23. Persons affected by the use of force and firearms or their legal representatives shall have access to an independent process, including a judicial process. In the event of the death of such persons, this provision shall apply to their dependants accordingly.

24. Governments and law enforcement agencies shall ensure that superior officers are held responsible if they know, or should have known, that law enforcement officials under their command are resorting, or have resorted, to the unlawful use of force and firearms, and they did not take all measures in their power to prevent, suppress or report such use.

25. Governments and law enforcement agencies shall ensure that no criminal or disciplinary sanction is imposed on law enforcement officials who, in compliance with the Code of Conduct for Law Enforcement Officials and these basic principles, refuse to carry out an order to use force and firearms, or who report such use by other officials.

26. Obedience to superior orders shall be no defence if law enforcement officials

knew that an order to use force and firearms resulting in the death or serious injury of a person was manifestly unlawful and had a reasonable opportunity to refuse to follow it. In any case, responsibility also rests on the superiors who gave the unlawful orders.

In countries where police powers are exercised by military authorities, whether uniformed or not, or by State security forces, the definition of law enforcement officials shall be regarded as including officers of such services.

28. UNITED NATIONS: GUIDELINES ON THE ROLE OF PROSECUTORS

Eighth United Nations Congress on the Prevention of Crime and the
Treatment of Offenders, Havana, 27 August to 7 September 1990,
U.N. Doc. A/CONF.144/28/Rev.1 at 189 (1990)

Editors' Notes
Adopted by the United Nations in 1990, the Guidelines on the Role of Prosecutors
follow on from the Basic Principles on the Role of Lawyers in both format and
content,[1] and sets out standards for prosecutors to promote "the effectiveness,
impartiality and fairness of prosecutors in criminal proceedings".[2]

Whereas in the Charter of the United Nations the peoples of the world affirm,
inter alia, their determination to establish conditions under which justice can be
maintained, and proclaim as one of their purposes the achievement of international
co-operation in promoting and encouraging respect for human rights and
fundamental freedoms without distinction as to race, sex, language or religion,

Whereas the Universal Declaration of Human Rights enshrines the principles of
equality before the law, the presumption of innocence and the right to a fair and
public hearing by an independent and impartial tribunal,

Whereas frequently there still exists a gap between the vision underlying those
principles and the actual situation,

Whereas the organization and administration of justice in every country should
be inspired by those principles, and efforts undertaken to translate them fully into
reality,

Whereas prosecutors play a crucial role in the administration of justice, and rules
concerning the performance of their important responsibilities should promote
their respect for and compliance with the above-mentioned principles, thus
contributing to fair and equitable criminal justice and the effective protection of
citizens against crime,

Whereas it is essential to ensure that prosecutors possess the professional
qualifications required for the accomplishment of their functions, through
improved methods of recruitment and legal and professional training, and through
the provision of all necessary means for the proper performance of their role in
combating criminality, particularly in its new forms and dimensions,

Whereas the General Assembly, by its resolution 34/169 of 17 December 1979,
adopted the Code of Conduct for Law Enforcement Officials, on the
recommendation of the Fifth United Nations Congress on the Prevention of
Crime and the Treatment of Offenders,

Whereas in resolution 16 of the Sixth United Nations Congress on the

---

[1] *Infra.*
[2] See preamble.

Prevention of Crime and the Treatment of Offenders, the Committee on Crime Prevention and Control was called upon to include among its priorities the elaboration of guidelines relating to the independence of judges and the selection, professional training and status of judges and prosecutors.

Whereas the Seventh United Nations Congress on the Prevention of Crime and the Treatment of Offenders adopted the Basic Principles on the Independence of the Judiciary, subsequently endorsed by the General Assembly in its resolutions 40/32 of 29 November 1985 and 40/146 of 13 December 1985.

Whereas the Declaration of Basic Principles of Justice for Victims of Crime and Abuse of Power, recommends measures to be taken at the international and national levels to improve access to justice and fair treatment, restitution, compensation and assistance for victims of crime.

Whereas, in resolution 7 of the Seventh Congress the Committee was called upon to consider the need for guidelines relating, inter alia, to the selection, professional training and status of prosecutors, their expected tasks and conduct, means to enhance their contribution to the smooth functioning of the criminal justice system and their co-operation with the police, the scope of their discretionary powers, and their role in criminal proceedings, and to report thereon to future United Nations congresses.

The Guidelines set forth below, which have been formulated to assist Member States in their tasks of securing and promoting the effectiveness, impartiality and fairness of prosecutors in criminal proceedings, should be respected and taken into account by Governments within the framework of their national legislation and practice, and should be brought to the attention of prosecutors, as well as other persons, such as judges, lawyers, members of the executive and the legislature and the public in general. The present Guidelines have been formulated principally with public prosecutors in mind, but they apply equally, as appropriate, to prosecutors appointed on an *ad hoc* basis.

Qualifications, selection and training

1. Persons selected as prosecutors shall be individuals of integrity and ability, with appropriate training and qualifications.
2. States shall ensure that:

   (a) Selection criteria for prosecutors embody safeguards against appointments based on partiality or prejudice, excluding any discrimination against a person on the grounds of race, colour, sex. Language, religion, political or other opinion, national, social or ethnic origin, property, birth, economic or other status, except that it shall not be considered discriminatory to require a candidate for prosecutorial office to be a national of the country concerned;

   (b) Prosecutors have appropriate education and training and should be made aware of the ideals and ethical duties of their office, of the constitutional and statutory protections for the rights of the suspect and the victim, and of human rights and fundamental freedoms recognized by national and international law.

Status and conditions of service

3. Prosecutors, as essential agents of the administration of justice, shall at all times maintain the honour and dignity of their profession.
4. States shall ensure that prosecutors are able to perform their professional functions without intimidation, hindrance, harassment, improper interference or unjustified exposure to civil, penal or other liability.
5. Prosecutors and their families shall be physically protected by the authorities when their personal safety is threatened as a result of the discharge of prosecutorial functions.
6. Reasonable conditions of service of prosecutors, adequate remuneration and, where applicable, tenure, pension and age of retirement shall be set out by law or published rules or regulations.
7. Promotion of prosecutors, wherever such a system exists, shall be based on objective factors, in particular professional qualifications, ability, integrity and experience, and decided upon in accordance with fair and impartial procedures.

Freedom of expression and association

8. Prosecutors like other citizens are entitled to freedom of expression, belief, association and assembly. In particular, they shall have the right to take part in public discussion of matters concerning the law, the administration of justice and the promotion and protection of human rights and to join or form local, national or international organisations and attend their meetings, without suffering professional disadvantage by reason of their lawful action or their membership in a lawful organization.

    In exercising these rights, prosecutors shall always conduct themselves in accordance with the law and the recognized standards and ethics of their profession.
9. Prosecutors shall be free to form and join professional associations or other organisations to represent their interests, to promote their professional training and to protect their status.

Role in criminal proceedings

10. The office of prosecutors shall be strictly separated from judicial functions.
11. Prosecutors shall perform an active role in criminal proceedings, including institution of prosecution and, where authorised by law or consistent with local practice, in the investigation of crime, supervision over the legality of these investigations, supervision of the execution of court decisions and the exercise of other functions as representatives of the public interest.
12. Prosecutors shall, in accordance with the law, perform their duties fairly, consistently and expeditiously, and respect and protect human dignity and uphold human rights, thus contributing to ensuring due process and the smooth functioning of the criminal justice system.
13. In the performance of their duties, prosecutors shall:

(a) Carry out their functions impartially and avoid all political, social, religious, racial, cultural, sexual or any other kind of discrimination;

(b) Protect the public interest, act with objectivity, take proper account of the position of the suspect and the victim, and pay attention to all relevant circumstances, irrespective of whether they are to the advantage or disadvantage of the suspect;

(c) Keep matters in their possession confidential, unless the performance of duty or the needs of justice require otherwise;

(d) Consider the views and concerns of victims when their personal interests are affected and ensure that victims are informed of their rights in accordance with the Declaration of Basic Principles of Justice for Victims of Crime and Abuse of Power.

14. Prosecutors shall not initiate or continue prosecution, or shall make every effort to stay proceedings, when an impartial investigation shows the charge to be unfounded.

15. Prosecutors shall give due attention to the prosecution of crimes committed by public officials, particularly corruption, abuse of power, grave violations of human rights and other crimes recognized by international law and, where authorised by law or consistent with local practice, the investigation of such offences.

16. When prosecutors come into possession of evidence against suspects that they know or believe on reasonable grounds was obtained through recourse to unlawful methods, which constitute a grave violation of the suspect's human rights, especially involving torture or cruel, inhuman or degrading treatment or punishment, or other abuses of human rights, they shall refuse to use such evidence against anyone other than those who used such methods, or inform the Court accordingly, and shall take all necessary steps to ensure that those responsible for using such methods are brought to justice.

Discretionary functions

17. In countries where prosecutors are vested with discretionary functions, the law or published rules or regulations shall provide guidelines to enhance fairness and consistency of approach in taking decisions in the prosecution process, including institution or waiver of prosecution.

Alternatives to prosecution

18. In accordance with national law, prosecutors shall give due consideration to waiving prosecution, discontinuing proceedings conditionally or unconditionally, or diverting criminal cases from the formal justice system, with full respect for the rights of suspect(s) and the victim(s). For this purpose, States should fully explore the possibility of adopting diversion schemes not only to alleviate excessive court loads, but also to avoid the stigmatisation of pre-trial detention, indictment and conviction, as well as the possible adverse effects of imprisonment.

19. In countries where prosecutors are vested with discretionary functions as to the decision whether or not to prosecute a juvenile, special considerations shall be given to the nature and gravity of the offence, protection of society and the personality and background of the juvenile.

    In making that decision, prosecutors shall particularly consider available alternatives to prosecution under the relevant juvenile justice laws and procedures. Prosecutors shall use their best efforts to take prosecutory action against juveniles only to the extent strictly necessary.

Relations with other government agencies or institutions

20. In order to ensure the fairness and effectiveness of prosecution, prosecutors shall strive to cooperate with the police, the courts, the legal profession, public defenders and other government agencies or institutions.

Disciplinary proceedings

21. Disciplinary offences of prosecutors shall be based on law or lawful regulations. Complaints against prosecutors which allege that they acted in a manner clearly out of the range of professional standards shall be processed expeditiously and fairly under appropriate procedures.

    Prosecutors shall have the right to a fair hearing. The decision shall be subject to independent review.
22. Disciplinary proceedings against prosecutors shall guarantee an objective evaluation and decision. They shall be determined in accordance with the law, the code of professional conduct and other established standards and ethics and in the light of the present Guidelines.

Observance of the Guidelines

23. Prosecutors shall respect the present Guidelines. They shall also, to the best of their capability, prevent and actively oppose any violations thereof.
24. Prosecutors who have reason to believe that a violation of the present Guidelines has occurred or is about to occur shall report the matter to their superior authorities and, where necessary, to other appropriate authorities or organs vested with reviewing or remedial power.

29. UNITED NATIONS: BASIC PRINCIPLES ON THE ROLE OF LAWYERS

Eighth United Nations Congress on the Prevention of Crime and the Treatment of Offenders, Havana, 27 August to 7 September 1990, U.N. Doc. A/CONF.144/28/Rev.1 at 118 (1990)

Editors' Notes
The Basic Principles on the Role of Lawyers were adopted by the United Nations in 1990. The preamble to the Basic Principles makes it clear that the role of lawyers should be seen in the context of rights of due process and access to legal representation included within the international "bill of rights"[1] and other sets of standards adopted by the United Nations. The Basic Principles include standards for the provision of legal representation, the qualification and training of lawyers, professional immunity, freedom of expression and association, the need for an association of lawyers and guidelines for the imposition of disciplinary measures.

Whereas in the Charter of the United Nations the peoples of the world affirm, inter alia, their determination to establish conditions under which justice can be maintained, and proclaim as one of their purposes the achievement of international co-operation in promoting and encouraging respect for human rights and fundamental freedoms without distinction as to race, sex, language or religion,

Whereas the Universal Declaration of Human Rights enshrines the principles of equality before the law, the presumption of innocence, the right to a fair and public hearing by an independent and impartial tribunal, and all the guarantees necessary for the defence of everyone charged with a penal offence,

Whereas the International Covenant on Civil and Political Rights proclaims, in addition, the right to be tried without undue delay and the right to a fair and public hearing by a competent, independent and impartial tribunal established by law,

Whereas the International Covenant on Economic, Social and Cultural Rights recalls the obligation of States under the Charter to promote universal respect for, and observance of, human rights and freedoms.

Whereas the Body of Principles for the Protection of All Persons under Any Form of Detention or Imprisonment provides that a detained person shall be entitled to have the assistance of, and to communicate and consult with, legal counsel,

Whereas the Standard Minimum Rules for the Treatment of Prisoners recommend, in particular, that legal assistance and confidential communication with counsel should be ensured to untried prisoners.

Whereas the Safeguards Guaranteeing Protection of Those Facing the Death Penalty reaffirm the right of everyone suspected or charged with a crime for which

---

[1] *Supra.*

capital punishment may be imposed to adequate legal assistance at all stages of the proceedings, in accordance with article 14 of the International Covenant on Civil and Political Rights,

Whereas the Declaration of Basic Principles of Justice for Victims of Crime and Abuse of Power recommends measures to be taken at the international and national levels to improve access to justice and fair treatment, restitution, compensation and assistance for victims of crime.

Whereas adequate protection of the human rights and fundamental freedoms to which all persons are entitled, be they economic, social and cultural, or civil and political, requires that all persons have effective access to legal services provided by an independent legal profession,

Whereas professional associations of lawyers have a vital role to play in upholding professional standards and ethics, protecting their members from persecution and improper restrictions and infringements, providing legal services to all in need of them, and co-operating with governmental and other institutions in furthering the ends of justice and public interest.

The Basic Principles on the Role of Lawyers, set forth below, which have been formulated to assist Member States in their task of promoting and ensuring the proper role of lawyers, should be respected and taken into account by Governments within the framework of their national legislation and practice and should be brought to the attention of lawyers as well as other persons, such as judges, prosecutors, members of the executive and the legislature, and the public in general. These principles shall also apply, as appropriate, to persons who exercise the functions of lawyers without having the formal status of lawyers.

Access to lawyers and legal services

1. All persons are entitled to call upon the assistance of a lawyer of their choice to protect and establish their rights and to defend them in all stages of criminal proceedings.
2. Governments shall ensure that efficient procedures and responsive mechanisms for effective and equal access to lawyers are provided for all persons within their territory and subject to their jurisdiction, without distinction of any kind, such as discrimination based on race, colour, ethnic origin, sex, language, religion, political or other opinion, national or social origin, property, birth, economic or other status.
3. Governments shall ensure the provision of sufficient funding and other resources for legal services to the poor and, as necessary, to other disadvantaged persons. Professional associations of lawyers shall cooperate in the organization and provision of services, facilities and other resources.
4   Governments and professional associations of lawyers shall promote programmes to inform the public about their rights and duties under the law and the important role of lawyers in protecting their fundamental freedoms.

    Special attention should be given to assisting the poor and other disadvantaged persons so as to enable them to assert their rights and where necessary call upon the assistance of lawyers.

Special safeguards in criminal justice matters

5. Governments shall ensure that all persons are immediately informed by the competent authority of their right to be assisted by a lawyer of their own choice upon arrest or detention or when charged with a criminal offence.
6. Any such persons who do not have a lawyer shall, in all cases in which the interests of justice so require, be entitled to have a lawyer of experience and competence commensurate with the nature of the offence assigned to them in order to provide effective legal assistance, without payment by them if they lack sufficient means to pay for such services.
7. Governments shall further ensure that all persons arrested or detained, with or without criminal charge, shall have prompt access to a lawyer, and in any case not later than forty-eight hours from the time of arrest or detention.
8. All arrested, detained or imprisoned persons shall be provided with adequate opportunities, time and facilities to be visited by and to communicate and consult with a lawyer, without delay, interception or censorship and in full confidentiality. Such consultations may be within sight, but not within the hearing, of law enforcement officials.

Qualifications and training

9. Governments, professional associations of lawyers and educational institutions shall ensure that lawyers have appropriate education and training and be made aware of the ideals and ethical duties of the lawyer and of human rights and fundamental freedoms recognized by national and international law.
10. Governments, professional associations of lawyers and educational institutions shall ensure that there is no discrimination against a person with respect to entry into or continued practice within the legal profession on the grounds of race, colour, sex, ethnic origin, religion, political or other opinion, national or social origin, property, birth, economic or other status, except that a requirement, that a lawyer must be a national of the country concerned, shall not be considered discriminatory.
11. In countries where there exist groups, communities or regions whose needs for legal services are not met, particularly where such groups have distinct cultures, traditions or languages or have been the victims of past discrimination, Governments, professional associations of lawyers and educational institutions should take special measures to provide opportunities for candidates from these groups to enter the legal profession and should ensure that they receive training appropriate to the needs of their groups.

Duties and responsibilities

12. Lawyers shall at all times maintain the honour and dignity of their profession as essential agents of the administration of justice.
13. The duties of lawyers towards their clients shall include:

    (a) Advising clients as to their legal rights and obligations, and as to the working of the legal system in so far as it is relevant to the legal rights and obligations of the clients;

(b) Assisting clients in every appropriate way, and taking legal action to protect their interests;

(c) Assisting clients before courts, tribunals or administrative authorities, where appropriate.

14. Lawyers, in protecting the rights of their clients and in promoting the cause of justice, shall seek to uphold human rights and fundamental freedoms recognized by national and international law and shall at all times act freely and diligently in accordance with the law and recognized standards and ethics of the legal profession.

15. Lawyers shall always loyally respect the interests of their clients.

Guarantees for the functioning of lawyers

16. Governments shall ensure that lawyers

   (a) are able to perform all of their professional functions without intimidation, hindrance, harassment or improper interference;

   (b) are able to travel and to consult with their clients freely both within their own country and abroad; and

   (c) shall not suffer, or be threatened with, prosecution or administrative, economic or other sanctions for any action taken in accordance with recognized professional duties, standards and ethics.

17. Where the security of lawyers is threatened as a result of discharging their functions, they shall be adequately safeguarded by the authorities.

18. Lawyers shall not be identified with their clients or their clients' causes as a result of discharging their functions.

19. No court or administrative authority before whom the right to counsel is recognized shall refuse to recognise the right of a lawyer to appear before it for his or her client unless that lawyer has been disqualified in accordance with national law and practice and in conformity with these principles.

20. Lawyers shall enjoy civil and penal immunity for relevant statements made in good faith in written or oral pleadings or in their professional appearances before a court, tribunal or other legal or administrative authority.

21. It is the duty of the competent authorities to ensure lawyers access to appropriate information, files and documents in their possession or control in sufficient time to enable lawyers to provide effective legal assistance to their clients. Such access should be provided at the earliest appropriate time.

22. Governments shall recognise and respect that all communications and consultations between lawyers and their clients within their professional relationship are confidential.

Freedom of expression and association

23. Lawyers like other citizens are entitled to freedom of expression, belief,

association and assembly. In particular, they shall have the right to take part in public discussion of matters concerning the law, the administration of justice and the promotion and protection of human rights and to join or form local, national or international organisations and attend their meetings, without suffering professional restrictions by reason of their lawful action or their membership in a lawful organization.

In exercising these rights, lawyers shall always conduct themselves in accordance with the law and the recognized standards and ethics of the legal profession.

Professional associations of lawyers

24. Lawyers shall be entitled to form and join self-governing professional associations to represent their interests, promote their continuing education and training and protect their professional integrity. The executive body of the professional associations shall be elected by its members and shall exercise its functions without external interference.
25. Professional associations of lawyers shall cooperate with Governments to ensure that everyone has effective and equal access to legal services and that lawyers are able, without improper interference, to counsel and assist their clients in accordance with the law and recognized professional standards and ethics.

Disciplinary proceedings

26. Codes of professional conduct for lawyers shall be established by the legal profession through its appropriate organs, or by legislation, in accordance with national law and custom and recognized international standards and norms.
27. Charges or complaints made against lawyers in their professional capacity shall be processed expeditiously and fairly under appropriate procedures. Lawyers shall have the right to a fair hearing, including the right to be assisted by a lawyer of their choice.
28. Disciplinary proceedings against lawyers shall be brought before an impartial disciplinary committee established by the legal profession, before an independent statutory authority, or before a court, and shall be subject to an independent judicial review.
29. All disciplinary proceedings shall be determined in accordance with the code of professional conduct and other recognized standards and ethics of the legal profession and in the light of these principles.

30. UNITED NATIONS: BASIC PRINCIPLES ON THE INDEPENDENCE OF THE JUDICIARY

Adopted by General Assembly resolutions 40/32 (1985) and 40/146 (1985)

Editors' Notes

The Basic Principles on the Independence of the Judiciary were adopted by the United Nations General Assembly in 1985 and emphasise that the independence of the judiciary should be guaranteed by the state and enshrined in the Constitution or the law of the country (Principle 1). The Basic Principles suggest that "everyone be entitled to a fair and public hearing by a competent, independent and impartial tribunal, in accordance with the principles proclaimed in the Universal Declaration of Human Rights, the International Covenant on Civil and Political Rights and other United Nations Documents".[1]

The Basic Principles outline in broad terms criteria concerning the status of judges and their qualifications, selection, training, conditions of service and tenure, and professional secrecy and immunity. The Basic Principles also underline that judges should enjoy freedom of expression and association (Principles 8 and 9) and that they shall be free from undue disciplinary procedures (Principles 17–20). In reviewing the use of the Basic Principles, the Commission on Crime Prevention and Criminal Justice found that they were widely applied with only a few countries "struggling to improve the fundamental guarantees to ensure the independence of the judiciary in all its aspects".[2]

The Basic Principles are just one example of the standards and norms established by the United Nations, many of which are the recent product of work by the Congresses on the prevention of crime and the treatment of offenders and the Commission on Crime Prevention and Criminal Justice.

Whereas in the Charter of the United Nations the peoples of the world affirm, inter alia, their determination to establish conditions under which justice can be maintained to achieve international co-operation in promoting and encouraging respect for human rights and fundamental freedoms without any discrimination,

Whereas the Universal Declaration of Human Rights enshrines in particular the principles of equality before the law, of the presumption of innocence and of the right to a fair and public hearing by a competent, independent and impartial tribunal established by law,

Whereas the International Covenants on Economic, Social and Cultural Rights and on Civil and Political Rights both guarantee the exercise of those rights, and in addition, the Covenant on Civil and Political Rights further guarantees the right to be tried without undue delay,

---

[1] UN Commission on Crime Prevention and Criminal Justice, Fifth Session, Vienna, 21–31 May 1996. Item 7 of the Provisional Agenda, para. 13. UN Doc. E/CN.15/1996/1.

[2] *Ibid.* para. 14.

Whereas frequently there still exists a gap between the vision underlying those principles and the actual situation,

Whereas the organization and administration of justice in every country should be inspired by those principles, and efforts should be undertaken to translate them fully into reality,

Whereas rules concerning the exercise of judicial office should aim at enabling judges to act in accordance with those principles,

Whereas judges are charged with the ultimate decision of life, freedoms, rights, duties and property of citizens,

Whereas the Sixth United Nations Congress on the Prevention of Crime and the Treatment of Offenders, by its resolution 16, called upon the Committee on Crime Prevention and Control to include among its priorities the elaboration of guidelines relating to the independence of judges and the selection, professional training and status of judges and prosecutors,

Whereas it is, therefore, appropriate that consideration be first given to the role of judges in relation to the system of justice and to the importance of their selection, training and conduct,

The following basic principles, formulated to assist Member States in their task of securing and promoting the independence of the judiciary should be taken into account and respected by Governments within the framework of their national legislation and practice and be brought to the attention of judges, lawyers, members of the executive and the legislature and the public in general. The principles have been formulated principally with professional judges in mind, but they apply equally, as appropriate, to lay judges, where they exist.

Independence of the judiciary

1. The independence of the judiciary shall be guaranteed by the State and enshrined in the Constitution or the law of the country. It is the duty of all governmental and other institutions to respect and observe the independence of the judiciary.
2. The judiciary shall decide matters before them impartially, on the basis of facts and in accordance with the law, without any restrictions, improper influences, inducements, pressures, threats or interferences, direct or indirect, from any quarter or for any reason.
3. The judiciary shall have jurisdiction over all issues of a judicial nature and shall have exclusive authority to decide whether an issue submitted for its decision is within its competence as defined by law.
4. There shall not be any inappropriate or unwarranted interference with the judicial process, nor shall judicial decisions by the courts be subject to revision. This principle is without prejudice to judicial review or to mitigation or commutation by competent authorities of sentences imposed by the judiciary, in accordance with the law.
5. Everyone shall have the right to be tried by ordinary courts or tribunals using established legal procedures. Tribunals that do not use the duly established procedures of the legal process shall not be created to displace the jurisdiction belonging to the ordinary courts or judicial tribunals.

6. The principle of the independence of the judiciary entitles and requires the judiciary to ensure that judicial proceedings are conducted fairly and that the rights of the parties are respected.

7. It is the duty of each Member State to provide adequate resources to enable the judiciary to properly perform its functions.

Freedom of expression and association

8. In accordance with the Universal Declaration of Human Rights, members of the judiciary are like other citizens entitled to freedom of expression, belief, association and assembly; provided, however, that in exercising such rights, judges shall always conduct themselves in such a manner as to preserve the dignity of their office and the impartiality and independence of the judiciary.

9. Judges shall be free to form and join associations of judges or other organizations to represent their interests, to promote their professional training and to protect their judicial independence.

Qualifications, selection and training

10. Persons selected for judicial office shall be individuals of integrity and ability with appropriate training or qualifications in law. Any method of judicial selection shall safeguard against judicial appointments for improper motives. In the selection of judges, there shall be no discrimination against a person on the grounds of race, colour, sex, religion, political or other opinion, national or social origin, property, birth or status, except that a requirement, that a candidate for judicial office must be a national of the country concerned, shall not be considered discriminatory.

Conditions of service and tenure

11. The term of office of judges, their independence, security, adequate remuneration, conditions of service, pensions and the age of retirement shall be adequately secured by law.

12. Judges, whether appointed or elected, shall have guaranteed tenure until a mandatory retirement age or the expiry of their term of office, where such exists.

13. Promotion of judges, wherever such a system exists, should be based on objective factors, in particular ability, integrity and experience.

14. The assignment of cases to judges within the court to which they belong is an internal matter of judicial administration.

Professional secrecy and immunity

15. The judiciary shall be bound by professional secrecy with regard to their deliberations and to confidential information acquired in the course of their duties other than in public proceedings, and shall not be compelled to testify on such matters.

16. Without prejudice to any disciplinary procedure or to any right of appeal or to compensation from the State, in accordance with national law, judges should enjoy personal immunity from civil suits for monetary damages for improper acts or omissions in the exercise of their judicial functions.

Discipline, suspension and removal

17. A charge or complaint made against a judge in his/her judicial and professional capacity shall be processed expeditiously and fairly under an appropriate procedure. The judge shall have the right to a fair hearing. The examination of the matter at its initial stage shall be kept confidential, unless otherwise requested by the judge.
18. Judges shall be subject to suspension or removal only for reasons of incapacity or behaviour that renders them unfit to discharge their duties.
19. All disciplinary, suspension or removal proceedings shall be determined in accordance with established standards of judicial conduct.
20. Decisions in disciplinary, suspension or removal proceedings shuld be subject to an independent review. This principle may not apply to the decisions of the highest court and those of the legislature in impeachment or similar proceedings.

31. UNITED NATIONS: STANDARD MINIMUM RULES FOR THE TREATMENT OF PRISONERS

Adopted by the First United Nations Congress on the Prevention of Crime and
the Treatment of Offenders, 30 August 1955
Approved by ECOSOC resolution 663(XXIV) 1957;
and amended by ECOSOC resolution 2076(LXII) 1977

Editors' Notes

International standards for the treatment of prisoners have steadily evolved since the United Nations was established.[1] Despite these developments, no treaty actually imposes binding obligations upon states in their treatment of those in custody outside of war. The third Geneva Convention of 1949 deals expressly with the treatment of prisoners of war[2] and establishes a series of standards, the basis of which is that prisoners of war "must at all times be treated humanely".[3] On a wider scale, treaty provisions also expressly proscribe the use of torture and various mechanisms have been established to prevent those in detention being subjected to practices amounting to torture and other cruel, inhuman and degrading treatment.[4]

The lack of a convention dealing specifically with the treatment of prisoners and prisoner's rights as a whole has meant that various sets of guidelines and model standards formulated by the United Nations are of particular significance in indicating standards agreed by a consensus of the international community.

The Standard Minimum Rules for the Treatment of Prisoners were the first of these guidelines, adopted by the First UN Congress on the Prevention of Crime and Treatment of Offenders and endorsed by the Economic and Social Council (ECOSOC) in 1957. The Rules provide for a basic principle of impartiality and non-discrimination (Rule 6) and go on to outline specific aspects of prison conditions from food to recreational facilities. The Rules describe the appropriate treatment for specific categories of prisoners, including prisoners serving sentences, insane and mentally abnormal prisoners, those under arrest or on remand pending trial and civil prisoners. In 1977, an ECOSOC resolution added an additional provision (Rule 95), ensuring that people arrested or imprisoned without charge should be subject to the Standard Minimum Rules. Whilst not binding in international law, the

---

[1] Rodley, N. (1987). *The Treatment of Prisoners under International Law*. Oxford, Oxford University Press.

[2] See: Convention Relative to the Treatment of Prisoners of War 1949, *infra*

[3] *Ibid.* Article 13.

[4] See: UN Convention against Torture and other Cruel, Inhuman and Degrading Treatment or Punishment; Inter-American Convention to Prevent and Punish Torture; European Convention for the Prevention of Torture and Inhuman or Degrading Treatment or Punishment, *infra*, and notes attached thereto. See also: Kaiser, G. (1995). "Detention in Europe and the European Committee for the Prevention of Torture". 1 Eur.J.Crime. Cr.L.Cr.J. 2.

Standard Minimum Rules are considered of use in guidance as to the requirements of Article 10 of the International Covenant on Civil and Political Rights, requiring humane treatment and a prison system with the essential aim of "reformation and rehabilitation".[5]

Since the Rules were adopted, the UN has regularly surveyed the implementation of the Rules, and from 1984 member states have been required to formally report on their progress on implementation.[6] The principles underlying the Rules were reaffirmed by a United Nations General Assembly Resolution on Basic Principles for the Treatment of Prisoners.[7]

Preliminary observations

1. The following rules are not intended to describe in detail a model system of penal institutions. They seek only, on the basis of the general consensus of contemporary thought and the essential elements of the most adequate systems of today, to set out what is generally accepted as being good principle and practice in the treatment of prisoners and the management of institutions.

2. In view of the great variety of legal, social, economic and geographical conditions of the world, it is evident that not all of the rules are capable of application in all places and at all times. They should, however, serve to stimulate a constant endeavour to overcome practical difficulties in the way of their application, in the knowledge that they represent, as a whole, the minimum conditions which are accepted as suitable by the United Nations.

3. On the other hand, the rules cover a field in which thought is constantly developing. They are not intended to preclude experiment and practices, provided these are in harmony with the principles and seek to further the purposes which derive from the text of the rules as a whole. It will always be justifiable for the central prison administration to authorize departures from the rules in this spirit.

4. (1) Part I of the rules covers the general management of institutions, and is applicable to all categories of prisoners, criminal or civil, untried or convicted, including prisoners subject to "security measures" or corrective measures ordered by the judge.

    (2) Part II contains rules applicable only to the special categories dealt with in each section. Nevertheless, the rules under section A, applicable to prisoners under sentence, shall be equally applicable to categories of prisoners dealt with in section B, C and D, provided they do not conflict with the rules governing those categories and are for their benefit.

---

[5] See also: Council of Europe Standard Minimum Rules for the Treatment of Prisoners 1973.
[6] Committee on Crime Prevention and Control, Procedures for the Effective Implementation of the Standard Minimum Rules for the Treatment of Prisoners. UN Doc. E/1984/84.
[7] Basic Principles for the Treatment of Prisoners, UN Doc, A/Res/45/49 (1990).

5. (1) The rules do not seek to regulate the management of institutions set aside for young persons such as Borstal institutions or correctional schools, but in general part I would be equally applicable in such institutions.

   (2) The category of young prisoners should include at least all young persons who come within the jurisdiction of juvenile courts. As a rule, such young persons should not be sentenced to imprisonment.

PART I
RULES OF GENERAL APPLICATION

Basic principle

6. (1) The following rules shall be applied impartially. There shall be no discrimination on grounds of race, colour, sex, language, religion, political or other opinion, national or social origin, property, birth or other status.

   (2) On the other hand, it is necessary to respect the religious beliefs and moral precepts of the group to which a prisoner belongs.

Register

7. (1) In every place where persons are imprisoned there shall be kept a bound registration book with numbered pages in which shall be entered in respect of each prisoner received:

   (a) Information concerning his identity;
   (b) The reasons for his commitment and the authority therefor;
   (c) The day and hour of his admission and release.

   (2) No person shall be received in an institution without a valid commitment order of which the details shall have been previously entered in the register.

8. The different categories of prisoners shall be kept in separate institutions or parts of institutions taking account of their sex, age, criminal record, the legal reason for their detention and the necessities of their treatment. Thus,

   (a) Men and women shall so far as possible be detained in separate institutions; in an institution which received both men and women the whole of the premises allocated to women shall be entirely separate;
   (b) Untried prisoners shall be kept separate from convicted prisoners;
   (c) Persons imprisoned for debt and other civil prisoners shall be kept separate from persons imprisoned by reason of a criminal offence;
   (d) Young prisoners shall be kept separate from adults.

Accommodation

9. (1) Where sleeping accommodation is in individual cells or rooms, each prisoner shall occupy by night a cell or room by himself. If for special

387

reasons, such as temporary overcrowding, it becomes necessary for the central prison administration to make an exception to this rule, it is not desirable to have two prisoners in a cell or room.

(2) Where dormitories are used, they shall be occupied by prisoners carefully selected as being suitable to associate with one another in those conditions. There shall be regular supervision by night, in keeping with the nature of the institutions.

10. All accommodation provided for the use of prisoners and in particular all sleeping accommodation shall meet all requirements of health, due regard being paid to climatic conditions and particularly to cubic content of air, minimum floor space, lighting, heating and ventilation.

11. In all places where prisoners are required to live or work,

   (a) The windows shall be large enough to enable the prisoners to read or work by natural light, and shall be so constructed that they can allow the entrance of fresh air whether or not there is artificial ventilation;

   (b) Artificial light shall be provided sufficient for the prisoners to read or work without injury to eyesight.

12. The sanitary installations shall be adequate to enable every prisoner to comply with the needs of nature when necessary and in a clean and decent manner.

13. Adequate bathing and shower installations shall be provided so that every prisoner may be enabled and required to have a bath or shower, at a temperature suitable to the climate, as frequently as necessary for general hygiene according to season and geographical region, but at least once a week in a temperate climate.

14. All parts of an institution regularly used by prisoners shall be properly maintained and kept scrupulously clean at all times.

Personal hygiene

15. Prisoners shall be required to keep their persons clean, and to this end they shall be provided with water and with such toilet articles as are necessary for health and cleanliness.

16. In order that prisoners may maintain a good appearance compatible with this self-respect, facilities shall be provided for the proper care of the hair and beard, and men shall be enabled to shave regularly.

Clothing and bedding

17. (1) Every prisoner who is not allowed to wear his own clothing shall be provided with an outfit of clothing suitable for the climate and adequate to keep him in good health. Such clothing shall in no manner be degrading or humiliating.

   (2) All clothing shall be clean and kept in proper condition. Underclothing shall be changed and washed as often as necessary for the maintenance of hygiene.

(3) In exceptional circumstances, whenever a prisoner is removed outside the institution for an authorised purpose, he shall be allowed to wear his own clothing or other inconspicuous clothing.

18. If prisoners are allowed to wear their own clothing, arrangements shall be made on their admission to the institution to ensure that it shall be clean and fit for use.

19. Every prisoner shall, in accordance with local or national standards, be provided with a separate bed, and with separate and sufficient bedding which shall be clean when issued, kept in good order and changed often enough to ensure its cleanliness.

Food

20. (1) Every prisoner shall be provided by the administration at the usual hours with food of nutritional value adequate for health and strength, of wholesome quality and well prepared and served.

(2) Drinking water shall be available to every prisoner whenever he needs it.

21. (1) Every prisoner who is not employed in outdoor work shall have at least one hour of suitable exercise in the open air daily if the weather permits.

(2) Young prisoners, and others of suitable age and physique, shall receive physical and recreational training during the period of exercise. To this end space, installations and equipment should be provided.

Medical services

22. (1) At every institution there shall be available the services of at least one qualified medical officer who should have some knowledge of psychiatry. The medical services should be organised in close relationship to the general health administration of the community or nation. They shall include a psychiatric service for the diagnosis and, in proper cases, the treatment of states of mental abnormality.

(2) Sick prisoners who require specialist treatment shall be transferred to specialized institutions or to civil hospitals. Where hospital facilities are provided in an institution, their equipment, furnishings and pharmaceutical supplies shall be proper for the medical care and treatment of sick prisoners, and there shall be a staff of suitable trained officers.

(3) The services of a qualified dental officer shall be available to every prisoner.

23. (1) In women's institutions there shall be special accommodation for all necessary pre-natal and post-natal care and treatment. Arrangements shall be made wherever practicable for children to be born in a hospital outside the institution. If a child is born in prison, this fact shall not be mentioned in the birth certificate.

(2) Where nursing infants are allowed to remain in the institution with their mothers, provision shall be made for a nursery staffed by qualified

persons, where the infants shall be placed when they are not in the care of their mothers.

24. The medical officer shall see and examine every prisoner as soon as possible after his admission and thereafter as necessary, with a view particularly to the discovery of physical or mental illness and the taking of all necessary measures; the segregation of prisoners suspected of infectious or contagious conditions; the noting of physical or mental defects which might hamper rehabilitation, and the determination of the physical capacity of every prisoner for work.

25. (1) The medical officer shall have the care of the physical and mental health of the prisoners and should daily see all sick prisoners, all who complain of illness, and any prisoner to whom his attention is specially directed.

    (2) The medical officer shall report to the director whenever he considers that a prisoner's physical or mental health has been or will be injuriously affected by continued imprisonment or by any condition of imprisonment.

26. (1) The medical officer shall regularly inspect and advise the director upon:

    (a) The quantity, quality, preparation and service of food;
    (b) The hygiene and cleanliness of the institution and the prisoners;
    (c) The sanitation, heating, lighting and ventilation of the institution;
    (d) The suitability and cleanliness of the prisoners' clothing and bedding;
    (e) The observance of the rules concerning physical education and sports, in cases where there is no technical personnel in charge of these activities.

    (2) The director shall take into consideration the reports and advice that the medical officer submits according to rules 25(2) and 26 and, in case he concurs with the recommendations made, shall take immediate steps to give effect to those recommendations; if they are not within his competence or if he does not concur with them, he shall immediately submit his own report and the advice of the medical officer to higher authority.

Discipline and punishment

27. Discipline and order shall be maintained with firmness, but with no more restriction than is necessary for safe custody and well-ordered community life.

28. (1) No prisoner shall be employed, in the service of the institution, in any disciplinary capacity.

    (2) This rule shall not, however, impede the proper functioning of systems based on self-government, under which specified social, educational or sports activities or responsibilities are entrusted, under supervision, to prisoners who are formed into groups for the purposes of treatment.

29. The following shall always be determined by the law or by the regulation of the competent administrative authority:

(a) Conduct constituting a disciplinary offence;

(b) The types and duration of punishment which may be inflicted;

(c) The authority competent to impose such punishment.

30. (1) No prisoner shall be punished except in accordance with the terms of such law or regulation, and never twice for the same offence.

(2) No prisoner shall be punished unless he has been informed of the offence alleged against him and given a proper opportunity of presenting his defence. The competent authority shall conduct a thorough examination of the case.

(3) Where necessary and practicable the prisoner shall be allowed to make his defence through an interpreter.

31. Corporal punishment, punishment by placing in a dark cell, and all cruel, inhuman or degrading punishments shall be completely prohibited as punishments for disciplinary offences.

32. (1) Punishment by close confinement or reduction of diet shall never be inflicted unless the medical officer has examined the prisoner and certified in writing that he is fit to sustain it.

(2) The same shall apply to any other punishment that may be prejudicial to the physical or mental health of a prisoner. In no case may such punishment be contrary to or depart from the principle stated in rule 31.

(3) The medical officer shall visit daily prisoners undergoing such punishments and shall advise the director if he considers the termination or alteration of the punishment necessary on grounds of physical or mental health.

Instruments of restraint

33. Instruments of restraint such as handcuffs, chains, irons and strait-jackets, shall never be applied as a punishment. Furthermore, chains or irons shall not be used as restraints. Other instruments of restraint shall not be used except in the following circumstances;

(a) As a precaution against escape during a transfer, provided that they shall be removed when the prisoner appears before a judicial or administrative authority;

(b) On medical grounds by direction of the medical officer;

(c) By order of the director, if other methods of control fail, in order to prevent a prisoner from injuring himself or others or from damaging property; in such instances the director shall at once consult the medical officer and report to the higher administrative authority.

34. The patterns and manner of use of instruments of restraint shall be decided by the central prison administration. Such instruments must not be applied for any longer time than is strictly necessary.

Information to and complaints by prisoners

35. (1) Every prisoner on admission shall be provided with written information about the regulations governing the treatment of prisoners of his category, the disciplinary requirements of the institution, the authorised methods of seeking information and making complaints, and all such other matters as are necessary to enable him to understand both his rights and his obligations and to adapt himself to the life of the institution.
    (2) If a prisoner is illiterate, the aforesaid information shall be conveyed to him orally.

36. (1) Every prisoner shall have the opportunity each week day of making requests or complaints to the director of the institution or the officer authorised to represent him.
    (2) It shall be possible to make requests or complaints to the inspector of prisons during his inspection. The prisoner shall have the opportunity to talk to the inspector or to any other inspecting officer without the director or other members of the staff being present.
    (3) Every prisoner shall be allowed to make a request or complaint, without censorship as to substance but in proper form, to the central prison administration, the judicial authority or other proper authorities through approved channels.
    (4) Unless it is evidently frivolous or groundless, every request or complaint shall be promptly dealt with and replied to without undue delay.

Contact with the outside world

37. Prisoners shall be allowed under necessary supervision to communicate with their family and reputable friends at regular intervals, both by correspondence and by receiving visits.

38. (1) Prisoners who are foreign nationals shall be allowed reasonable facilities to communicate with the diplomatic and consular representatives of the State to which they belong.
    (2) Prisoners who are nationals of States without diplomatic or consular representation in the country and refugees or stateless persons shall be allowed similar facilities to communicate with the diplomatic representative of the State which takes charge of their interests or any national or international authority whose task it is to protect such persons.

39. Prisoners shall be kept informed regularly of the more important items of news by the reading of newspapers, periodicals or special institutional publications, by hearing wireless transmissions, by lectures or by any similar means as authorised or controlled by the administration.

Books

40. Every institution shall have a library for the use of all categories of prisoners, adequately stocked with both recreational and instructional books, and prisoners shall be encouraged to make full use of it.

Religion

41. (1) If the institution contains a sufficient number of prisoners of the same religion, a qualified representative of that religion shall be appointed or approved. If the number of prisoners justifies it and conditions permit, the arrangement should be on a full-time basis.

    (2) A qualified representative appointed or approved under paragraph (1) shall be allowed to hold regular services and to pay pastoral visits in private to prisoners of his religion at proper times.

    (3) Access to a qualified representative of any religion shall not be refused to any prisoner. On the other hand, if any prisoner should object to a visit of any religious representative, his attitude shall be fully respected.

42. So far as practicable, every prisoner shall be allowed to satisfy the needs of his religious life by attending the services provided in the institution and having in his possession the books of religious observance and instruction of his denomination.

Retention of prisoners' property

43. (1) All money, valuables, clothing and other effects belonging to a prisoner which under the regulations of the institution he is not allowed to retain shall on his admission to the institution be placed in safe custody. An inventory thereof shall be signed by the prisoner. Steps shall be taken to keep them in good condition.

    (2) On the release of the prisoner all such articles and money shall be returned to him except in so far as he has been authorised to spend money or send any such property out of the institution, or it has been found necessary on hygienic grounds to destroy any article of clothing. The prisoner shall sign a receipt for the articles and money returned to him.

    (3) Any money or effects received for a prisoner from outside shall be treated in the same way.

    (4) If a prisoner brings in any drugs or medicine, the medical officer shall decide what use shall be made of them.

Notification of death, illness, transfer, etc.

44. (1) Upon the death or serious illness of, or serious injury to a prisoner, or his removal to an institution for the treatment of mental affections, the director shall at once inform the spouse, if the prisoner is married, or the nearest relative and shall in any event inform any other person previously designated by the prisoner.

(2) A prisoner shall be informed at once of the death or serious illness of any near relative. In case of the critical illness of a near relative, the prisoner should be authorised, whenever circumstances allow, to go to his bedside either under escort of alone.

(3) Every prisoner shall have the right to inform at once his family of his imprisonment or his transfer to another institution.

Removal of prisoners

45. (1) When the prisoners are being removed to or from an institution, they shall be exposed to public view as little as possible, and proper safeguards shall be adopted to protect them from insult, curiosity and publicity in any form.

(2) The transport of prisoners in conveyances with inadequate ventilation or light, or in any way which would subject them to unnecessary physical hardship, shall be prohibited.

(3) The transport of prisoners shall be carried out at the expense of the administration and equal conditions shall obtain for all of them.

Institutional personnel

46. (1) The prison administration, shall provide for the careful selection of every grade of the personnel, since it is on their integrity, humanity, professional capacity and personal suitability for the work that the proper administration of the institutions depends.

(2) The prison administration shall constantly seek to awaken and maintain in the minds both of the personnel and of the public the conviction that this work is a social service of great importance, and to this end all appropriate means of informing the public should be used.

(3) To secure the foregoing ends, personnel shall be appointed on a full-time basis as professional prison officers and have civil service status with security of tenure subject only to good conduct, efficiency and physical fitness. Salaries shall be adequate to attract and retain suitable men and women; employment benefits and conditions of service shall be favourable in view of the exacting nature of the work.

47. (1) The personnel shall possess an adequate standard of education and intelligence.

(2) Before entering on duty, the personnel shall be given a course of training in their general and specific duties and be required to pass theoretical and practical tests.

(3) After entering on duty and during their career, the personnel shall maintain and improve their knowledge and professional capacity by attending courses of in-service training to be organised at suitable intervals.

48. All members of the personnel shall at all times so conduct themselves and perform their duties as to influence the prisoners for good by their example and to command their respect.

49. (1) So far as possible, the personnel shall include a sufficient number of specialists such as psychiatrists, psychologists, social workers, teachers and trade instructors.

    (2) The services of social workers, teachers and trade instructors shall be secured on a permanent basis, without thereby excluding part-time or voluntary workers.

50. (1) The director of an institution should be adequately qualified for his task by character, administrative ability, suitable training and experience.

    (2) He shall devote his entire time to his official duties and shall not be appointed on a part-time basis.

    (3) He shall reside on the premises of the institution or in its immediate vicinity.

    (4) When two or more institutions are under the authority of one director, he shall visit each of them at frequent intervals. A responsible resident official shall be in charge of each of these institutions.

51. (1) The director, his deputy, and the majority of the other personnel of the institution shall be able to speak the language of the greatest number of prisoners, or a language understood by the greatest number of them.

    (2) Whenever necessary, the services of an interpreter shall be used.

52. (1) In institutions which are large enough to require the services of one or more full-time medical officers, at least one of them shall reside on the premises of the institution or in its immediate vicinity.

    (2) In other institutions the medical officer shall visit daily and shall reside near enough to be able to attend without delay in cases of urgency.

53. (1) In an institution for both men and women, the part of the institution set aside for women shall be under the authority of a responsible woman officer who shall have the custody of the keys of all that part of the institution.

    (2) No male member of the staff shall enter the part of the institution set aside for women unless accompanied by a woman officer.

    (3) Women prisoners shall be attended and supervised only by women officers. This does not, however, preclude male members of the staff, particularly doctors and teachers, from carrying out their professional duties in institutions or parts of institutions set aside for women.

54. (1) Officers of the institutions shall not, in their relations with the prisoners, use force except in self-defence or in cases of attempted escape, or active or passive physical resistance to an order based on law or regulations. Officers who have recourse to force must use no more than is strictly necessary and must report the incident immediately to the director of the institution.

    (2) Prison officers shall be given special physical training to enable them to restrain aggressive prisoners.

    (3) Except in special circumstances, staff performing duties which bring them into direct contact with prisoners should not be armed. Furthermore, staff

should in no circumstances be provided with arms unless they have been trained in their use.

Inspection

55. There shall be a regular inspection of penal institutions and services by qualified and experienced inspectors appointed by a competent authority. Their task shall be in particular to ensure that these institutions are administered in accordance with existing laws and regulations and with a view to bringing about the objectives of penal and correctional services.

PART II
RULES APPLICABLE TO SPECIAL CATEGORIES

A. PRISONERS UNDER SENTENCE

Guiding principles

56. The guiding principles hereafter are intended to show the spirit in which penal institutions should be administered and the purposes at which they should aim, in accordance with the declaration made under Preliminary Observation 1 of the present text.
57. Imprisonment and other measures which result in cutting off an offender from the outside world are afflictive by the very fact of taking from the person the right of self-determination by depriving him of his liberty. Therefore the prison system shall not, except as incidental to justifiable segregation or the maintenance of discipline, aggravate the suffering inherent in such a situation.
58. The purpose and justification of a sentence of imprisonment or a similar measure deprivative of liberty is ultimately to protect society against crime. This end can only be achieved if the period of imprisonment is used to ensure, so far as possible, that upon his return to society the offender is not only willing but able to lead a law-abiding and self-supporting life.
59. To this end, the institution should utilise all the remedial, educational, moral, spiritual and other forces and forms of assistance which are appropriate and available, and should seek to apply them according to the individual treatment needs of the prisoners.

60. (1) The regime of the institution should seek to minimise any differences between prison life and life at liberty which tend to lessen the responsibility of the prisoners or the respect due to their dignity as human beings.
    (2) Before the completion of the sentence, it is desirable that the necessary steps be taken to ensure for the prisoner a gradual return to life in society. This aim may be achieved, depending on the case, by a pre-release regime organised in the same institution or in another appropriate institution, or

396

by release on trial under some kind of supervision which must not be entrusted to the police but should be combined with effective social aid.

61. The treatment of prisoners should emphasise not their exclusion from the community, but their continuing part in it. Community agencies should, therefore, be enlisted wherever possible to assist the staff of the institution in the task of social rehabilitation of the prisoners. There should be in connection with every institution social workers charged with the duty of maintaining and improving all desirable relations of a prisoner with his family and with valuable social agencies. Steps should be taken to safeguard, to the maximum extent compatible with the law and the sentence, the rights relating to civil interests, social security rights and other social benefits of prisoners.

62. The medical service of the institution shall seek to detect and shall treat any physical or mental illnesses or defects which may hamper a prisoner's rehabilitation. All necessary medical, surgical and psychiatric services shall be provided to that end.

63. (1) The fulfilment of these principles requires individualisation of treatment and for this purpose a flexible system of classifying prisoners in groups; it is therefore desirable that such groups should be distributed in separate institutions suitable for the treatment of each group.

    (2) These institutions need not provide the same degree of security for every group. It is desirable to provide varying degrees of security according to the needs of different groups. Open institutions, by the very fact that they provide no physical security against escape but rely on the self-discipline of the inmates, provide the conditions most favourable to rehabilitation for carefully selected prisoners.

    (3) It is desirable that the number of prisoners in closed institutions should not be so large that the individualisation of treatment is hindered. In some countries it is considered that the population of such institutions should not exceed five hundred. In open institutions the population should be as small as possible.

    (4) On the other hand, it is undesirable to maintain prisons which are so small that proper facilities cannot be provided.

64. The duty of society does not end with a prisoner's release. There should, therefore, be governmental or private agencies capable of lending the released prisoner efficient after-care directed towards the lessening of prejudice against him and towards his social rehabilitation.

Treatment

65. The treatment of persons sentenced to imprisonment or a similar measure shall have as its purpose, so far as the length of the sentence permits, to establish in them the will to lead law-abiding and self-supporting lives after their release and to fit them to do so. The treatment shall be such as will encourage their self-respect and develop their sense of responsibility.

66. (1) To these ends, all appropriate means shall be used, including religious care in the countries where this is possible, education, vocational guidance and training, social casework, employment counselling, physical development and strengthening of moral character, in accordance with the individual needs of each prisoner, taking account of his social and criminal history, his physical and mental capacities and aptitudes, his personal temperament, the length of his sentence and his prospects after release.

(2) For every prisoner with a sentence of suitable length, the director shall receive, as soon as possible after his admission, full reports on all the matters referred to in the foregoing paragraph. Such reports shall always include a report by a medical officer, wherever possible qualified in psychiatry, on the physical and mental condition of the prisoner.

(3) The reports and other relevant documents shall be placed in an individual file. This file shall be kept up to date and classified in such a way that it can be consulted by the responsible personnel whenever the need arises.

Classification and individualisation

67. The purposes of classification shall be:

(a) To separate from others those prisoners who, by reason of their criminal records or bad characters, are likely to exercise a bad influence;

(b) To divide the prisoners into classes in order to facilitate their treatment with a view to their social rehabilitation.

68. So far as possible separate institutions or separate sections of an institution shall be used for the treatment of the different classes of prisoners.

69. As soon as possible after admission and after a study of the personality of each prisoner with a sentence of suitable length, a programme of treatment shall be prepared for him in the light of the knowledge obtained about his individual needs, his capacities and dispositions.

Privileges

70. Systems of privileges appropriate for the different classes of prisoners and the different methods of treatment shall be established at every institution, in order to encourage good conduct, develop a sense of responsibility and secure the interest and co-operation of the prisoners in their treatment.

Work

71. (1) Prison labour must not be of an affective nature.

(2) All prisoners under sentence shall be required to work, subject to their physical and mental fitness as determined by the medical officer.

(3) Sufficient work of a useful nature shall be provided to keep prisoners actively employed for a normal working day.

(4) So far as possible the work provided shall be such as will maintain or increase the prisoner's ability to earn an honest living after release.

(5) Vocational training in useful trades shall be provided for prisoners able to profit thereby and especially for young prisoners.

(6) Within the limits compatible with proper vocational selection and with the requirements of institutional administration and discipline, the prisoners shall be able to choose the type of work they wish to perform.

72. (1) The organization and methods of work in the institutions shall resemble as closely as possible those of similar work outside institutions, so as to prepare prisoners for the conditions of normal occupational life.

(2) The interests of the prisoners and of their vocational training, however, must not be subordinated to the purpose of making a financial profit from an industry in the institution.

73. (1) Preferably institutional industries and farms shall be operated directly by the administration and not by private contractors.

(2) Where prisoners are employed in work not controlled by the administration, they shall always be under the supervision of the institution's personnel. Unless the work is for other departments of the government the full normal wages for such work shall be paid to the administration by the persons to whom the labour is supplied, account being taken of the output of the prisoners.

74. (1) The precautions laid down to protect the safety and health of free workmen shall be equally observed in situations.

(2) Provision shall be made to indemnify prisoners against industrial injury, including occupational disease, on terms not less favourable than those extended by law to free workmen.

75. (1) The maximum daily and weekly working hours of the prisoners shall be fixed by law or by administrative regulation, taking into account local rules or custom in regard to the employment of free workmen.

(2) The hours so fixed shall leave one rest day a week and sufficient time for education and other activities required as part of the treatment and rehabilitation of the prisoners.

76. (1) There shall be a system of equitable remuneration of the work of prisoners.

(2) Under the system prisoners shall be allowed to spend at least a part of their earnings on approved articles for their own use and to send a part of their earnings to their family.

(3) The system should also provide that a part of the earnings should be set aside by the administration so as to constitute a savings fund to be handed over to the prisoner on his release

Education and recreation

77. (1) Provision shall be made for the future education of all prisoners capable of profiting thereby, including religious instruction in the countries where this is possible. The education of illiterates and young prisoners shall be compulsory and special attention shall be paid to it by the administration.

(2) So far as practicable, the education of prisoners shall be integrated with the educational system of the country so that after their release they may continue their education without difficulty.

78. Recreational and cultural activities shall be provided in all institutions for the benefit of the mental and physical health of prisoners.

Social relations and after-care

79. Special attention shall be paid to the maintenance and improvement of such relations between a prisoner and his family as are desirable in the best interests of both.

80. From the beginning of a prisoner's sentence consideration shall be given to his future after release and he shall be encouraged and assisted to maintain or establish such relations with persons or agencies outside the institution as may promote the best interests of his family and his own social rehabilitation.

81. (1) Services and agencies, governmental or otherwise, which assist released prisoners to re-establish themselves in society shall ensure, so far as it possible and necessary, that released prisoners be provided with appropriate documents and identification papers, have suitable homes and work to go to, are suitable and adequately clothed having regard to the climate and season, and have sufficient means to reach their destination and maintain themselves in the period immediately following their release.

(2) The approved representatives of such agencies shall have all necessary access to the institution and to prisoners and shall be taken into consultation as to the future of a prisoner from the beginning of his sentence.

(3) It is desirable that the activities of such agencies shall be centralised or co-ordinated as far as possible in order to secure the best use of their efforts.

B. INSANE AND MENTALLY ABNORMAL PRISONERS

82. (1) Persons who are found to be insane shall not be detained in prisons and arrangements shall be made to remove them to mental institutions as soon as possible.

(2) Prisoners who suffer from other mental diseases or abnormalities shall be observed and treated in specialized institutions under medical management.

(3) During their stay in a prison, such prisoners shall be placed under the special supervision of a medical officer.

(4) The medical or psychiatric service of the penal institutions shall provide for the psychiatric treatment of all other prisoners who are in need of such treatment.

83. It is desirable that steps should be taken, by arrangement with the appropriate agencies, to ensure if necessary the continuation of psychiatric treatment after release and the provision of social-psychiatric after-care.

C. PRISONERS UNDER ARREST OR AWAITING TRIAL

84. (1) Persons arrested or imprisoned by reason of a criminal charge against them, who are detained either in police custody or in prison custody (jail) but have not yet been tried and sentenced, will be referred to as "untried prisoners" hereinafter in these rules.

    (2) Unconvicted prisoners are presumed to be innocent and shall be treated as such.

    (3) Without prejudice to legal rules for the protection of individual liberty or prescribing the procedure to be observed in respect of untried prisoners, these prisoners shall benefit by a special regime which is described in the following rules in its essential requirements only.

85. (1) Untried prisoners shall be kept separate from convicted prisoners.

    (2) Young untried prisoners shall be kept separate from adults and shall in principle be detained in separate institutions.

86. Untried prisoners shall sleep singly in separate rooms, with the reservation of different local custom in respect of the climate.

87. Within the limits compatible with the good order of the institution, untried prisoners may, if they so desire, have their food procured at their own expense from the outside, either through the administration or through their family or friends. Otherwise, the administration shall provide their food.

88. (1) An untried prisoner shall be allowed to wear his own clothing if it is clean and suitable.

    (2) If he wears prison dress, it shall be different from that supplied to convicted prisoners.

89. An untried prisoner shall always be offered opportunity to work, but shall not be required to work. If he chooses to work, he shall be paid for it.

90. An untried prisoner shall be allowed to procure at his own expense or at the expense of a third party such books, newspapers, writing materials and other means of occupation as are compatible with the interests of the administration of justice and the security and good order of the institution.

91. An untried prisoner shall be allowed to be visited and treated by his own doctor or dentist if there is reasonable ground for his application and he is able to pay any expenses incurred.

92. An untried prisoner shall be allowed to inform immediately his family of his detention and shall be given all reasonable facilities for communicating with his family and friends, and for receiving visits from them, subject only to restrictions and supervision as are necessary in the interests of the administration of justice and of the security and good order of the institution.

93. For the purposes of his defence, an untried prisoner shall be allowed to apply for free legal aid where such aid is available and to receive visits from his legal adviser with a view to his defence and to prepare and hand to him confidential instructions. For these purposes, he shall if he so desires be supplied with writing material. Interviews between the prisoner and his legal adviser may be within sight but not within the hearing of a police or institution official.

D. Civil Prisoners

94. In countries where the law permits imprisonment for debt, or by order of a court under any other non-criminal process, persons so imprisoned shall not be subject to any greater restriction or severity than is necessary to ensure safe custody and good order. Their treatment shall be not less favourable than that of untried prisoners, with the reservation, however, that they may possibly be required to work.

E. Persons Arrested or Detained Without Charge

95. Without prejudice to the provisions of article 9 of the International Covenant on Civil and Political Rights, persons arrested or imprisoned without charge shall be accorded the same protection as that accorded under part I and part II, section C. Relevant provisions of part II, section A, shall likewise be applicable where their application may be conducive to the benefit of this special group of persons in custody, provided that no measures shall be taken implying that re-education or rehabilitation is in any way appropriate to persons not convicted of any criminal offence.

32. UNITED NATIONS: BODY OF PRINCIPLES FOR THE PROTECTION OF ALL PERSONS UNDER ANY FORM OF DETENTION OR IMPRISONMENT

Adopted by General Assembly resolution 43/173 (1988)

Editors' Notes

The Body of Principles was adopted by the United Nations General Assembly in 1988 to supplement the general protections provided by the Standard Minimum Rules for the Treatment of Prisoners.[1] The Body of Principles is primarily aimed at protecting the physical safety of prisoners. The Principles reaffirm the values expressed elsewhere that those in detention should be treated humanely and with respect for their dignity (Principle 1),[2] and the prohibition on the use of torture, cruel, inhuman and degrading treatment (Principle 6).[3] Unlike the Standard Minimum Rules, the Body of Principles is not supported by any procedures for implementation or reporting.

Scope of the body of principles

These principles apply for the protection of all persons under any form of detention or imprisonment.

Use of terms

For the purposes of the Body of Principles:

   (a) "Arrest" means the act of apprehending a person for the alleged commission of an offence or by the action of an authority;

   (b) "Detained person" means any person deprived of personal liberty except as a result of conviction for an offence;

   (c) "Imprisoned person" means any person deprived of personal liberty as a result of conviction for an offence;

   (d) "Detention" means the condition of detained persons as defined above;

   (e) "Imprisonment" means the condition of imprisoned persons as defined above;

   (f) The words "a judicial or other authority" means a judicial or other authority under the law whose status and tenure should afford the strongest possible guarantees of competence, impartiality and independence.

---

[1] *Supra.*

[2] See: International Covenant on Civil and Political Rights, Article 10; Standard Minimum Rules for the Treatment of Prisoners, Rule 60; Code of Conduct for Law Enforcement Officials, Article 2, *supra.*

[3] See also: The Principles of Medical Ethics Relevant to the Role of Health Personnel, Particularly Physicians, in the Protection of Prisoners and Detainees against Torture and other Cruel, Inhuman or Degrading Treatment of Punishment, UN Doc. A/37/51 (1982)

Principle 1

All persons under any form of detention or imprisonment shall be treated in a humane manner and with respect for the inherent dignity of the human person.

Principle 2

Arrest, detention or imprisonment shall only be carried out strictly in accordance with the provisions of the law and by competent officials or persons authorised for that purpose.

Principle 3

There shall be no restriction upon or derogation from any of the human rights of persons under any form of detention or imprisonment recognized or existing in any State pursuant to law, conventions, regulations or custom on the pretext that this Body of Principles does not recognise such rights or that it recognises them to a lesser extent.

Principle 4

Any form of detention or imprisonment and all measures affecting the human rights of a person under any form of detention or imprisonment shall be ordered by, or be subject to the effective control of, a judicial or other authority.

Principle 5

1. These principles shall be applied to all persons within the territory of any given State, without distinction of any kind, such as race, colour, sex, language, religion or religious belief, political or other opinion, national, ethnic or social origin, property, birth or other status.
2. Measures applied under the law and designed solely to protect the rights and special status of women, especially pregnant women and nursing mothers, children and juveniles, aged, sick or handicapped persons shall not be deemed to be discriminatory. The need for, and the application of, such measures shall always be subject to review by a judicial or other authority.

Principle 6

No person under any form of detention or imprisonment shall be subjected to torture or to cruel, inhuman or degrading treatment or punishment.* No

---

* The term "cruel, inhuman or degrading treatment or punishment" should be interpreted so as to extend the widest possible protection against abuses, whether physical or mental, including the holding of a detained or imprisoned person in conditions which deprive him, temporarily or permanently, of the use of any of his natural senses, such as sight or hearing, or of his awareness of place and the passing of time.

circumstance whatever may be invoked as a justification for torture or other cruel, inhuman or degrading treatment or punishment.

Principle 7

1. States should prohibit by law any act contrary to the rights and duties contained in these principles, make any such act subject to appropriate sanctions and conduct impartial investigations upon complaints.
2. Officials who have reason to believe that a violation of this Body of Principles has occurred or is about to occur shall report the matter to their superior authorities and, where necessary, to other appropriate authorities or organs vested with reviewing or remedial powers.
3. Any other person who has ground to believe that a violation of this Body of Principles has occurred or is about to occur shall have the right to report the matter to the superiors of the officials involved as well as to other appropriate authorities or organs vested with reviewing or remedial powers.

Principle 8

Persons in detention shall be subject to treatment appropriate to their unconvicted status. Accordingly, they shall, whenever possible, be kept separate from imprisoned persons.

Principle 9

The authorities which arrest a person, keep him under detention or investigate the case shall exercise only the powers granted to them under the law and the exercise of these powers shall be subject to recourse to a judicial or other authority.

Principle 10

Anyone who is arrested shall be informed at the time of his arrest of the reason for his arrest and shall be promptly informed of any charges against him.

Principle 11

1. A person shall not be kept in detention without being given an effective opportunity to be heard promptly by a judicial or other authority. A detained person shall have the right to defend himself or to be assisted by counsel as prescribed by law.
2. A detained person and his counsel, if any, shall receive prompt and full communication of any order of detention, together with the reasons therefor.
3. A judicial or other authority shall be empowered to review as appropriate the continuance of detention.

Principle 12

1. There shall be duly recorded:

    (a) The reasons for the arrest;
    (b) The time of the arrest and the taking of the arrested person to a place of custody as well as that of his first appearance before a judicial or other authority;
    (c) The identity of the law enforcement officials concerned;
    (d) Precise information concerning the place of custody.

2. Such records shall be communicated to the detained person, or his counsel, if any, in the form prescribed by law.

Principle 13

Any person shall, at the moment of arrest and at the commencement of detention or imprisonment, or promptly thereafter, be provided by the authority responsible for his arrest, detention or imprisonment, respectively with information on and an explanation of his rights and how to avail himself of such rights.

Principle 14

A person who does not adequately understand or speak the language used by the authorities responsible for his arrest, detention or imprisonment is entitled to receive promptly in a language which he understands the information referred to in principle 10, principle 11, paragraph 2, principle 12, paragraph 1, and principle 13 and to have the assistance, free of charge, if necessary, of an interpreter in connection with legal proceedings subsequent to his arrest.

Principle 15

Notwithstanding the exceptions contained in principle 16, paragraph 4, and principle 18, paragraph 3, communication of the detained or imprisoned person with the outside world, and in particular his family or counsel, shall not be denied for more than a matter of days.

Principle 16

1. Promptly after arrest and after each transfer from one place of detention or imprisonment to another, a detained or imprisoned person shall be entitled to notify or to require the competent authority to notify members of his family or other appropriate persons of his choice of his arrest, detention or imprisonment or of the transfer and of the place where he is kept in custody.
2. If a detained or imprisoned person is a foreigner, he shall also be promptly informed of his right to communicate by appropriate means with a consular post or the diplomatic mission of the State of which he is a national or which is otherwise entitled to receive such communication in accordance with

international law or with the representative of the competent international organization, if he is a refugee or is otherwise under the protection of an intergovernmental organization.

3. If a detained or imprisoned person is a juvenile or is incapable of understanding his entitlement, the competent authority shall on its own initiative undertake the notification referred to in the present principle. Special attention shall be given to notifying parents or guardians.

4. Any notification referred to in the present principle shall be made or permitted to be made without delay. The competent authority may however delay a notification for a reasonable period where exceptional needs of the investigation so require.

Principle 17

1. A detained person shall be entitled to have the assistance of a legal counsel. He shall be informed of his right by the competent authority promptly after arrest and shall be provided with reasonable facilities for exercising it.

2. If a detained person does not have a legal counsel of his own choice, he shall be entitled to have a legal counsel assigned to him by a judicial or other authority in all cases where the interests of justice so require and without payment by him if he does not have sufficient means to pay.

Principle 18

1. A detained or imprisoned person shall be entitled to communicate and consult with his legal counsel.

2. A detained or imprisoned person shall be allowed adequate time and facilities for consultation with his legal counsel.

3. The right of a detained or imprisoned person to be visited by and to consult and communicate, without delay or censorship and in full confidentiality, with his legal counsel may not be suspended or restricted save in exceptional circumstances, to be specified by law or lawful regulations, when it is considered indispensable by a judicial or other authority in order to maintain security and good order.

4. Interviews between a detained or imprisoned person and his legal counsel may be within sight, but not within the hearing, of a law enforcement official.

5. Communications between a detained or imprisoned person and his legal counsel mentioned in the present principle shall be inadmissible as evidence against the detained or imprisoned person unless they are connected with a continuing or contemplated crime.

Principle 19

A detained or imprisoned person shall have the right to be visited by and to correspond with, in particular, members of his family and shall be given adequate opportunity to communicate with the outside world, subject to reasonable conditions and restrictions as specified by law or lawful regulations.

Principle 20

If a detained or imprisoned person so requests, he shall if possible be kept in a place of detention or imprisonment reasonably near his usual place of residence.

Principle 21

1. It shall be prohibited to take undue advantage of the situation of a detained or imprisoned person for the purpose of compelling him to confess, to incriminate himself otherwise or to testify against any other person.
2. No detained person while being interrogated shall be subject to violence, threats or methods of interrogation which impair his capacity of decision or his judgement.

Principle 22

No detained or imprisoned person shall, even with his consent, be subjected to any medical or scientific experimentation which may be detrimental to his health.

Principle 23

1. The duration of any interrogation of a detained or imprisoned person and of the intervals between interrogations as well as the identity of the officials who conducted the interrogations and other persons present shall be recorded and certified in such form as may be prescribed by law.
2. A detained or imprisoned person, or his counsel when provided by law, shall have access to the information described in paragraph 1 of the present principle.

Principle 24

A proper medical examination shall be offered to a detained or imprisoned person as promptly as possible after his admission to the place of detention or imprisonment, and thereafter medical care and treatment shall be provided whenever necessary. This care and treatment shall be provided free of charge.

Principle 25

A detained or imprisoned person or his counsel shall, subject only to reasonable conditions to ensure security and good order in the place of detention or imprisonment, have the right to request or petition a judicial or other authority for a second medical examination or opinion.

Principle 26

The fact that a detained or imprisoned person underwent a medical examination, the name of the physician and the results of such an examination shall be duly recorded. Access to such records shall be ensured. Modalities therefore shall be in accordance with relevant rules of domestic law.

Principle 27

Non-compliance with these principles in obtaining evidence shall be taken into account in determining the admissibility of such evidence against a detained or imprisoned person.

Principle 28

A detained or imprisoned person shall have the right to obtain within the limits of available resources, if from public sources, reasonable quantities of educational, cultural and informational material, subject to reasonable conditions to ensure security and good order in the place of detention or imprisonment.

Principle 29

1. In order to supervise the strict observance of relevant laws and regulations, places of detention shall be visited regularly by qualified and experienced persons appointed by, and responsible to, a competent authority distinct from the authority directly in charge of the administration of the place of detention or imprisonment.
2. A detained or imprisoned person shall have the right to communicate freely and in full confidentiality with the persons who visit the places of detention or imprisonment in accordance with paragraph 1 of the present principle, subject to reasonable conditions to ensure security and good order in such places.

Principle 30

1. The types of conduct of the detained or imprisoned person that constitute disciplinary offences during detention or imprisonment, the description and duration of disciplinary punishment that may be inflicted and the authorities competent to impose such punishment shall be specified by law or lawful regulations and duly published.
2. A detained or imprisoned person shall have the right to be heard before disciplinary action is taken. He shall have the right to bring such action to higher authorities for review.

Principle 31

The appropriate authorities shall endeavour to ensure, according to domestic law, assistance when needed to dependent and, in particular, minor members of the families of detained or imprisoned persons and shall devote a particular measure of care to the appropriate custody of children left without supervision.

Principle 32

1. A detained person or his counsel shall be entitled at any time to take proceedings according to domestic law before a judicial or other authority to challenge the lawfulness of his detention in order to obtain his release without delay, if it is unlawful.
2. The proceedings referred to in paragraph 1 of the present principle shall be simple and expeditious and at no cost for detained persons without adequate means. The detaining authority shall produce without unreasonable delay the detained person before the reviewing authority.

Principle 33

1. A detained or imprisoned person or his counsel shall have the right to make a request or complaint regarding his treatment, in particular in case of torture or other cruel, inhuman or degrading treatment, to the authorities responsible for the administration of the place of detention and to higher authorities and, when necessary, to appropriate authorities vested with reviewing or remedial powers.
2. In those cases where neither the detained or imprisoned person nor his counsel has the possibility to exercise his rights under paragraph 1 of the present principle, a member of the family of the detained or imprisoned person or any other person who has knowledge of the case may exercise such rights.
3. Confidentiality concerning the request or complaint shall be maintained if so requested by the complainant.
4. Every request or complaint shall be promptly dealt with and replied to without undue delay. If the request or complaint is rejected or, in case of inordinate delay, the complainant shall be entitled to bring it before a judicial or other authority. Neither the detained or imprisoned person nor any complainant under paragraph 1 of the present principle shall suffer prejudice for making a request or complaint.

Principle 34

Whenever the death or disappearance of a detained or imprisoned person occurs during his detention or imprisonment, an inquiry into the cause of death or disappearance shall be held by a judicial or other authority, either on its own motion or at the instance of a member of the family of such a person or any person who has knowledge of the case. When circumstances so warrant, such an inquiry shall be held on the same procedural basis whenever the death or disappearance occurs shortly after the termination of the detention or imprisonment. The findings of such inquiry or a report thereon shall be made available upon request, unless doing so would jeopardize an ongoing criminal investigation.

Principle 35

1. Damage incurred because of acts or omissions by a public official contrary to the rights contained in these principles shall be compensated according to the applicable rules or liability provided by domestic law.
2. Information required to be recorded under these principles shall be available in accordance with procedures provided by domestic law for use in claiming compensation under the present principle.

Principle 36

1. A detained person suspected of or charged with a criminal offence shall be presumed innocent and shall be treated as such until proved guilty according to law in a public trial at which he has had all the guarantees necessary for his defence.
2. The arrest or detention of such a person pending investigation and trial shall be carried out only for the purposes of the administration of justice on grounds and under conditions and procedures specified by law. The imposition of restrictions upon such a person which are not strictly required for the purpose of the detention or to prevent hindrance to the process of investigation or the administration of justice, or for the maintenance of security and good order in the place of detention shall be forbidden.

Principle 37

A person detained on a criminal charge shall be brought before a judicial or other authority provided by law promptly after his arrest. Such authority shall decide without delay upon the lawfulness and necessity of detention. No person may be kept under detention pending investigation or trial except upon the written order of such an authority. A detained person shall, when brought before such an authority, have the right to make a statement on the treatment received by him while in custody.

Principle 38

A person detained on a criminal charge shall be entitled to trial within a reasonable time or to release pending trial.

Principle 39

Except in special cases provided for by law, a person detained on a criminal charge shall be entitled, unless a judicial or other authority decides otherwise in the interest of the administration of justice, to release pending trial subject to the conditions that may be imposed in accordance with the law. Such authority shall keep the necessity of detention under review.

411

General clause

Nothing in this Body of Principles shall be construed as restricting or derogating from any right defined in the International Covenant on Civil and Political Rights.

33. COUNCIL OF EUROPE: EUROPEAN PRISON RULES

Recommendation (87) 3 of the Committee of Ministers on European Prison
Rules

Adopted: 12 February 1987

Editors' Notes

The European Prison Rules revise and extend the Council of Europe's Standard
Minimum Rules for the Treatment of Prisoners, which in turn were derived from the
UN Standard Minimum Rules of 1957.[1] The new European Rules, which are non-
binding, are far more comprehensive than the Standard Minimum Rules and were
formulated so as to take account of the developments in the practice and
philosophy of prison management.[2] Part I of the Rules restate the basic principles
for the treatment of prisoners including the concept that due respect for human
dignity is a fundamental concern (Rule 1). Part II of the Rules amount to a code of
practice for the management of prisons so as to give effect to those principles in
Part I. Part III of the Rules deal with the main ideas of recruitment, selection,
training, status and role of the personnel of the prison service. Part IV of the Rules
sets out the valid aims and objectives of imprisonment, stressing the goals of
providing prisoners with the social and practical skills to return to the community
and minimising the negative aspects of detention. To this end, Rule 70 states that
the preparation of prisoners for release should begin as soon as possible. It is
unfortunate that this section is broadly labelled as "treatment", which perhaps
implies the notion of criminality as a medical or psychiatric affliction.

The Committee of Ministers, under the terms of Article 15(b) of the Statute of the
Council of Europe,

Considering the importance of establishing common principles regarding penal
policy among the member states of the Council of Europe;

Noting that, although considerable progress has been made in developing non-
custodial alternatives for dealing with offenders, the deprivation of liberty remains
a necessary sanction in criminal justice systems;

Considering the important role of international rules in the practice and
philosophy of prison treatment and management;

Noting, however, that significant social trends and changes in regard to prison
treatment and management have made it desirable to reformulate the Standard
Minimum Rules for the Treatment of Prisoners of the Council of Europe
(Resolution (73)5) so as to support and encourage the best of these developments
and offer scope for future progress,

---

[1] UN Standard Minimum Rules for the Treatment of Prisoners, *supra.*
[2] Explanatory Memorandum Relating to the European Prison Rules, Council of Europe, Addendum I
rev. to CDPC (86)6, at 22 (1987).

Recommends that the governments of member states be guided in their internal legislation and practice by the principles set out in the text of the European Prison Rules, appended to the present Recommendations, with a view to their progressive implementation with special emphasis on the purposes set out in the preamble and the rules of basic principle in Part I, and to give the widest possible circulation to this text.

APPENDIX TO RECOMMENDATION NO. R(87)3
THE EUROPEAN PRISON RULES

REVISED EUROPEAN VERSION OF THE STANDARD MINIMUM RULES FOR THE TREATMENT OF PRISONERS

PREAMBLE

The purpose of these rules are:

a. to establish a range of minimum standards for all those aspects of prison administration that are essential to human conditions and positive treatment in modern and progressive systems;

b. to serve as a stimulus to prison administrations to develop policies and management style and practice based on good contemporary principles of purpose and equity;

c. to encourage in prison staffs professional attitudes that reflect the important social and moral qualities of their work and to create conditions in which they can optimise their own performance to the benefit of society in general, the prisoners in their care and their own vocational satisfaction;

d. to provide realistic basic criteria against which prison administrations and those responsible for inspecting the conditions and management of prisons can make valid judgments of performance and measure progress towards higher standards.

It is emphasised that the rules do not constitute a model system and that, in practice, many European prison services are already operating well above many of the standards set out in the rules and that others are striving, and will continue to strive, to do so. Wherever there are difficulties or practical problems to be overcome in the application of the rules, the Council of Europe has the machinery and the expertise available to assist with advice and the fruits of the experience of the various prison administrations within its sphere.

In these rules, renewed emphasis has been placed on the precepts of human dignity, the commitment of prison administrations to humane and positive treatment, the importance of staff roles and effective modern management approaches. They are set out to provide ready reference, encouragement and guidance to those who are working at all levels of prison administration. The explanatory memorandum that accompanies the rules is intended to ensure the understanding, acceptance and flexibility that are necessary to achieve the highest realistic level of implementation beyond the basic standards.

PART I
THE BASIC PRINCIPLES

1. The deprivation of liberty shall be effected in material and moral conditions which ensure respect for human dignity and are in conformity with these rules.
2. The rules shall be applied impartially. There shall be no discrimination on grounds of race, colour, sex, language, religion, political or other opinion, national or social origin, birth, economic or other status. The religious beliefs and moral precepts of the group to which a prisoner belongs shall be respected.
3. The purpose of the treatment of persons in custody shall be such as to sustain their health and self-respect and, so far as the length of sentence permits, to develop their sense of responsibility and encourage those attitudes and skills that will assist them to return to society with the best chance of leading law-abiding and self-supporting lives after their release.
4. There shall be regular inspections of penal institutions and services by qualified and experienced inspectors appointed by a competent authority. Their task shall be, in particular, to monitor whether and to what extent these institutions are administered in accordance with existing laws and regulations, the objectives of the prison services and the requirements of these rules.
5. The protection of the individual rights of prisoners with special regard to the legality of the execution of detention measures shall be secured by means of a control carried out, according to national rules, by a judicial authority or other duly constituted body authorised to visit the prisoners and not belonging to the prison administration.
6. 1. These rules shall be made readily available to staff in the national languages;
    2. They shall also be available to prisoners in the same languages and in other languages so far as is reasonable and practicable.

PART II
THE MANAGEMENT OF PRISON SYSTEMS

Reception and registration

7. 1. No person shall be received in an institution without a valid commitment order.
    2. The essential details of the commitment and reception shall immediately be recorded.

8. In every place where persons are imprisoned a complete and secure record of the following information shall be kept concerning each prisoner received:

    a. information concerning the identity of the prisoner;
    b. the reasons for commitment and the authority therefore;
    c. the day and hour of admission and release.

9. Reception arrangements shall conform with the basic principles of the rules and shall assist prisoners to resolve their urgent personal problems.

10. 1. As soon as possible after reception, full reports and relevant information about the personal situation and training programme of each prisoner with a sentence of suitable length in preparation for ultimate release shall be drawn up and submitted to the director for information or approval as appropriate.

    2. Such reports shall always include reports by a medical officer and the personnel in direct charge of the prisoner concerned.

    3. The reports and information concerning prisoners shall be maintained with due regard to confidentiality on an individual basis, regularly kept up to date and only accessible to authorised persons.

The allocation and classification of prisoners

11. 1. In allocating prisoners to different institutions or regimes, due account shall be taken of their judicial and legal situation (untried or convicted prisoner, first offender or habitual offender, short sentence or long sentence), of the special requirements of their treatment, of their medical needs, their sex and age.

    2. Males and females shall in principle be detained separately, although they may participate together in organised activities as part of an established treatment programme.

    3. In principle, untried prisoners shall be detained separately from convicted prisoners unless they consent to being accommodated or involved together in organised activities beneficial to them.

    4. Young prisoners shall be detained under conditions which as far as possible protect them from harmful influences and which take account of the needs peculiar to their age.

12. The purposes of classification or re-classification of prisoners shall be:

    a. to separate from others those prisoners who, by reasons of their criminal records or their personality, are likely to benefit from that or who may exercise a bad influence; and

    b. to assist in allocating prisoners to facilities their treatment and social resettlement taking into account the management and security requirements.

13. So far as possible separate institutions or separate sections of an institution shall be used to facilitate the management of different treatment regimes or the allocation of specific categories of prisoners.

Accommodation

14. 1. Prisoners shall normally be lodged during the night in individual cells except in cases where it is considered that there are advantages in sharing accommodation with other prisoners.

2. Where accommodation is shared it shall be occupied by prisoners suitable to associate with others in those conditions. There shall be supervision by night, in keeping with the nature of the institution.

15. The accommodation provided for prisoners, and in particular all sleeping accommodation, shall meet the requirements of health and hygiene, due regard being paid to climatic conditions and especially the cubic content of air, a reasonable amount of space, lighting, heating and ventilation.

16. In all places where prisoners are required to live or work:

    a. the windows shall be large enough to enable the prisoners inter alia, to read or work by natural light in normal conditions. They shall be so constructed that they can allow the entrance of fresh air except where there is an adequate air conditioning system. Moreover, the windows shall, with due regard to security requirements, present in their size, location and construction as normal an appearance as possible;
    b. artificial light shall satisfy recognized technical standards.

17. The sanitary installations and arrangements for access shall be adequate to enable every prisoner to comply with the needs of nature when necessary and in clean and decent conditions.

18. Adequate bathing and showering installations shall be provided so that every prisoner may be enabled and required to have a bath or shower, at a temperature suitable to the climate, as frequently as necessary for general hygiene according to season and geographical region, but at least once a week. Wherever possible there shall be free access at all reasonable times.

19. All parts of an institution shall be properly maintained and kept clean at all times.

Personal hygiene

20. Prisoners shall be required to keep their persons clean, and to this end they shall be provided with water and with such toilet articles as are necessary for health and cleanliness.

21. For reasons of health and in order that prisoners may maintain a good appearance and preserve their self-respect, facilities shall be provided for the proper care of the hair and beard, and men shall be enabled to shave regularly.

Clothing and bedding

22. 1. Prisoners who are not allowed to wear their own clothing shall be provided with an outfit of clothing suitable for the climate and adequate to keep them in good health. Such clothing shall in no manner be degrading or humiliating.
    2. All clothing shall be clean and kept in proper condition. Underclothing shall be changed and washed as often as necessary for the maintenance of hygiene.
    3. Whenever prisoners obtain permission to go outside the institution, they

shall be allowed to wear their own clothing or other inconspicuous clothing.

23. On the admission of prisoners to an institution, adequate arrangements shall be made to ensure that their personal clothing is kept in good condition and fit for use.

24. Every prisoner shall be provided with a separate bed and separate and appropriate bedding which shall be kept in good order and changed often enough to ensure its cleanliness.

Food

25. 1. In accordance with the standards laid down by the health authorities, the administration shall provide the prisoners at the normal times with food which is suitably prepared and presented, and which satisfies in quality and quantity the standards of dietetics and modern hygiene and takes into account their age, health, the nature of their work, and so far as possible, religious or cultural requirements.
   2. Drinking water shall be available to every prisoner.

Medical services

26. 1. At every institution there shall be available the services of at least one qualified general practitioner. The medical services should be organised in close relation with the general health administration of the community or nation. They shall include a psychiatric service for the diagnosis and, in proper cases, the treatment of states of mental abnormality.
   2. Sick prisoners who require specialist treatment shall be transferred to specialised institutions or to civil hospitals. Where hospital facilities are provided in an institution, their equipment, furnishings and pharmaceutical supplies shall be suitable for the medical care and treatment of sick prisoners, and there shall be a staff of suitably trained officers.
   3. The services of a qualified dental officer shall be available to every prisoner.

27. Prisoners may not be submitted to any experiments which may result in physical or moral injury.

28. 1. Arrangements shall be made wherever practicable for children to be born in a hospital outside the institution. However, unless special arrangements are made, there shall in penal institutions be the necessary staff and accommodation for the confinement and post-natal care of pregnant women. If a child is born in prison, this fact shall not be mentioned in the birth certificate.
   2. Where infants are allowed to remain in the institution with their mothers, special provision shall be made for a nursery staffed by qualified persons, where the infants shall be placed when they are not in the care of their mothers.

29. The medical officer shall see and examine every prisoner as soon as possible after admission and thereafter as necessary, with a view particularly to the discovery of physical or mental illness and the taking of all measures necessary for medical treatment, the segregation of prisoners suspected of infectious or contagious conditions; the noting of physical or mental defects which might impede resettlement after release; and the determination of the fitness of every prisoner to work.

30. 1. The medical officer shall have the care of the physical and mental health of the prisoners and shall see, under the conditions and with a frequency consistent with hospital standards, all sick prisoners, all who report illness or injury and any prisoner to whom attention is specially directed.

    2. The medical officer shall report to the director whenever it is considered that a prisoner's physical or mental health has been or will be adversely affected by continued imprisonment or by any condition of imprisonment.

31. 1. The medical officer or a competent authority shall regularly inspect and advise the director upon:

    a. the quantity, quality, preparation and serving of food and water;
    b. the hygiene and cleanliness of the institution and prisoners;
    c. the sanitation, heating, lighting and ventilation of the institution;
    d. the suitability and cleanliness of the prisoners' clothing and bedding.

    2. The director shall consider the reports and advice that the medical officer submits according to Rules 30, paragraph 2, and 31, paragraph 1, and, when in concurrence with the recommendations made, shall take immediate steps to give effect to those recommendations; if they are not within the director's competence or if the director does not concur with them, the director shall immediately submit a personal report and the advice of the medical officer to higher authority.

32. The medical services of the institution shall seek to detect and shall treat any physical or mental illness or defects which may impede a prisoner's resettlement after release. All necessary medical, surgical and psychiatric services including those available in the community shall be provided to the prisoner to that end.

Discipline and punishment

33. Discipline and order shall be maintained in the interests of safe custody, ordered community life and the treatment objectives of the institution.

34. 1. No prisoner shall be employed, in the service of the institution, in any disciplinary capacity.

    2. This rule shall not, however, impede the proper functioning of arrangements under which specified social, educational or sports activities or responsibilities are entrusted under supervision to prisoners who are formed into groups for the purposes of their participation in regime programmes.

35. The following shall be provided for and determined by the law or by the regulation of the competent authority:

    a.   conduct constituting a disciplinary offence;
    b.   the types and duration of punishment which may be imposed;
    c.   the authority competent to impose such punishment;
    d.   access to, and the authority of, the appellate process.

36. 1.   No prisoner shall be punished except in accordance with the terms of such law or regulation, and never twice for the same act.
    2.   Reports of misconduct shall be presented promptly to the competent authority who shall decide on them without undue delay.
    3.   No prisoner shall be punished unless informed of the alleged offence and given a proper opportunity of presenting a defence.
    4.   Where necessary and practicable prisoners shall be allowed to make their defence through an interpreter.

37. Collective punishments, corporal punishment, punishment by placing in a dark cell, and all cruel, inhuman or degrading punishment shall be completely prohibited as punishments for disciplinary offences.

38. 1.   Punishment by disciplinary confinement and any other punishment which might have an adverse effect on the physical or mental health of the prisoner shall only be imposed if the medical officer, after examination, certifies in writing that the prisoner is fit to sustain it.
    2.   In no case may such punishment be contrary to, or depart from, the principles stated in Rule 37.
    3.   The medical officer shall visit daily prisoners under-going such punishment and shall advise the director if the termination or alteration of the punishment is considered necessary on grounds of physical or mental health.

Instruments of restraint

39. The use of chains and irons shall be prohibited. Handcuffs, restraint-jackets and other body restraints shall never be applied as a punishment. They shall not be used except in the following circumstances:

    a.   if necessary, as a precaution against escape during a transfer, provided that they shall be removed when the prisoner appears before a judicial or administrative authority unless that authority decides otherwise;
    b.   on medical grounds by direction and under the supervision of the medical officer;
    c.   by order of the director, if other methods of control fail, in order to protect a prisoner from self-injury, injury to others or to prevent serious damage to property; in such instances the director shall at once consult the medical officer and report to the higher administrative authority.

40. The patterns and manner of use of the instruments of restraint authorised in

the preceding paragraph shall be decided by law or regulation. Such instruments must not be applied for any longer time than is strictly necessary.

Information to, and complaints by, prisoners

41. 1.   Every prisoner shall on admission be provided with written information about the regulations governing the treatment of prisoners of the relevant category, the disciplinary requirements of the institution, the authorised methods of seeking information and making complaints, and all such other matters as are necessary to understand the rights and obligations of prisoners and to adapt to the life of the institution.
    2.   If a prisoner cannot understand the written information provided, this information shall be explained orally.

42. 1.   Every prisoner shall have the opportunity every day to make requests or complaints to the director of the institution or the officer authorised to act in that capacity.
    2.   A prisoner shall have the opportunity to talk to, or to make requests or complaints to, an inspector of prisons or to any other duly constituted authority entitled to visit the prison without the director or other members of the staff being present. However, appeals against formal decisions may be restricted to the authorised procedures.
    3.   Every prisoner shall be allowed to make a request or complaint, under confidential cover, to the central prison administration, the judicial authority or other proper authorities.
    4.   Every request or complaint addressed or referred to a prison authority shall be promptly dealt with and replied to by his authority without undue delay.

Contact with the outside world

43. 1.   Prisoners shall be allowed to communicate with their families and, subject to the needs of treatment, security and good order, persons or representatives of outside organisations and to receive visits from these persons as often as possible.
    2.   To encourage contact with the outside world there shall be a system of prison leave consistent with the treatment objectives of Part IV of these rules.

44. 1.   Prisoners who are foreign nationals should be informed, without delay, of their right to request contact and be allowed reasonable facilities to communicate with the diplomatic or consular representative of the state to which they belong. The prison administration should co-operate fully with such representatives in the interests of foreign nationals in prison who may have special needs.
    2.   Prisoners who are nationals of states without diplomatic or consular representation in the country and refugees or stateless persons shall be allowed similar facilities to communicate with the diplomatic representa-

tive of the state which takes charge of their interests or national or international authority whose task it is to serve the interests of such persons.

45. Prisoners shall be allowed to keep themselves informed regularly of the news by reading newspapers, periodicals and other publications, by radio or television transmissions, by lectures or by any similar means as authorised or controlled by the administration. Special arrangements should be made to meet the needs of foreign nationals and linguistic difficulties.

Religious and moral assistance

46. So far as practicable, every prisoner shall be allowed to satisfy the needs of his religious, spiritual and moral life by attending the services or meetings provided in the institution and having in his possession any necessary books or literature.

47. 1. If the institution contains a sufficient number of prisoners of the same religion, a qualified representative of that religion shall be appointed and approved. If the number of prisoners justifies it and conditions permit, the arrangement should be on a full-time basis.
    2. A qualified representative appointed or approved under paragraph 1 shall be allowed to hold regular services and activities and to pay pastoral visits in private to prisoners of his religion at proper times.
    3. Access to a qualified representative of any religion shall not be refused to any prisoner. If any prisoner should object to a visit to any religious representative, the prisoner shall be allowed to refuse it.

Retention of prisoners' property

48. 1. All money, valuables, and other effects belonging to prisoners which under the regulations of the institution they are not allowed to retain shall on admission to the institution be placed in safe custody. An inventory thereof shall be signed by the prisoner. Steps shall be taken to keep them in good condition. If it has been found necessary to destroy any article, this shall be recorded and the prisoner informed.
    2. On the release of the prisoner, all such articles and money shall be returned except insofar as there have been authorised withdrawals of money or the authorised sending of any such property out of the institution, or it has been found necessary on hygienic grounds to destroy any article. The prisoner shall sign a receipt for the articles and money returned.
    3. As far as practicable, any money or effects received for a prisoner from outside shall be treated in the same way unless they are intended for and permitted for use during imprisonment.
    4. If a prisoner brings in any medicines, the medical officer shall decide what use shall be made of them.

Notification of death, illness, transfer, etc.

49. 1. Upon the death or serious illness of or serious injury to a prisoner, or removal to an institution for the treatment of mental illness or abnormalities, the director shall at once inform the spouse, if the prisoner is married, or the nearest relative and shall in any event inform any other person previously designated by the prisoner.
    2. A prisoner shall be informed at once of the death or serious illness of any near relative. In these cases and whenever circumstances allow, the prisoner should be authorised to visit this sick relative or see the deceased either under escort of alone.
    3. All prisoners shall have the right to inform at once their families of imprisonment or transfer to another institution.

Removal of prisoners

50. 1. When prisoners are being removed to or from an institution, they shall be exposed to public view as little as possible, and proper safeguards shall be adopted to protect them from insult, curiosity and publicity in any form.
    2. The transport of prisoners in conveyances with inadequate ventilation or light, or in any way which would subject them to unnecessary physical hardship or dignity shall be prohibited.
    3. The transport of prisoners shall be carried out at the expense of the administration and in accordance with duly authorised regulations.

PART III

Personnel

51. In view of the fundamental importance of the prison staffs to the proper management of the institutions and the pursuit of their organisational and treatment objectives, prison administrations shall give high priority to the fulfilment of the rules concerning personnel.
52. Prison staff shall be continually encouraged through training, consultative procedures and a positive management style to aspire to humane standards, higher efficiency and a committed approach to their duties.
53. The prison administration shall regard it as an important task continually to inform public opinion on the roles of the prison system and the work of the staff, so as to encourage public understanding of the importance of their contribution to society.
54. 1. The prison administration shall provide for the careful selection on recruitment or in subsequent appointments of all personnel. Special emphasis shall be given to their integrity, humanity, professional capacity and personal suitability for the work.
    2. Personnel shall normally be appointed on a permanent basis as professional prison staff and have civil service status with security of

tenure subject only to good conduct, efficiency, good physical and mental health and an adequate standard of education. Salaries shall be adequate to attract and retain suitable men and women; employment benefits and conditions of service shall be favourable in view of the exacting nature of the work.

3. Whenever it is necessary to employ part-time staff, these criteria should apply to them as far as that is appropriate.

55. 1. On recruitment or after an appropriate period of practical experience, the personnel shall be given a course of training in their general and specific duties and be required to pass theoretical and practical tests unless their professional qualifications made that unnecessary.

2. During their career, all personnel shall maintain and improve their knowledge and professional capacity by attending courses of in-service training to be organised by the administration at suitable intervals.

3. Arrangements should be made for wider experience and training for personnel whose professional capacity would be improved by this.

4. The training of all personnel should include instruction in the requirements and application of the European Prison Rules and the European Convention on Human Rights.

56. All members of the personnel shall be expected at all times so to conduct themselves and perform their duties as to influence the prisoners for good by their example and to command their respect.

57. 1. So far as possible the personnel shall include a sufficient number of specialists such as psychiatrists, psychologists, social workers, teachers, trade, physical education and sports instructors.

2. These and other specialist staff shall normally be employed on a permanent basis. This shall not preclude part-time or voluntary workers when that is appropriate and beneficial to the level of support and training they can provide.

58. 1. The prison administration shall ensure that every institution is at all times in the full charge of the director, the deputy director or other authorised official.

2. The director of an institution should be adequately qualified for that post by character, administrative ability, suitable professional training and experience.

3. The director shall be appointed on a full-time basis and be available or accessible as required by the prison administration in its management instructions.

4. When two or more institutions are under the authority of each director, each shall be visited at frequent intervals. A responsible official shall be in charge of each of these institutions.

59. The administration shall introduce forms of organisation and management systems to facilitate communication between the different categories of staff in an institution with a view to ensuring co-operation between the various

services, in particular, with respect to the treatment and re-socialisation of prisoners.

60. 1. The director, deputy, and the majority of the other personnel of the institution shall be able to speak the language of the greatest number of prisoners, or a language understood by the greatest number of them.
    2. Whenever necessary and practicable the services of an interpreter shall be used.

61. 1. Arrangements shall be made to ensure at all times that a qualified and approved medical practitioner is able to attend without delay in cases of urgency.
    2. In institutions not staffed by one or more full-time medical officers, a part-time medical officer or authorised staff of a health service shall visit regularly.

62. The appointment of staff in institutions or parts of institutions housing prisoners of the opposite sex is to be encouraged.

63. 1. Staff of the institutions shall not use force against prisoners except in self-defence or in cases of attempted escape or active or passive physical resistance to an order based on law or regulations. Staff who have recourse to force must use no more than is strictly necessary and must report the incident immediately to the director of the institution.
    2. Staff shall as appropriate be given special technical training to enable them to restrain aggressive prisoners.
    3. Except in special circumstances, staff performing duties which bring them into direct contact with prisoners should not be armed. Furthermore, staff should in no circumstances be provided with arms unless they have been fully trained in their use.

PART IV

Treatment objectives and regimes

64. Imprisonment is by the deprivation of liberty a punishment in itself. The conditions of imprisonment and the prison regimes shall not, therefore, except in incidental to justifiable segration or the maintenance of discipline, aggravate the suffering inherent in this.

65. Every effort shall be made to ensure that the regimes of the institutions are signed and managed so as:

    a. to ensure that the conditions of life are compatible with human dignity and acceptable standards in the community;
    b. to minimise the detrimental effect of imprisonment and the differences between prison life and life at liberty which tend to diminish the self-respect or sense of personal responsibility of prisoners;
    c. to sustain and strengthen those links with relatives and the outside

community that will promote the best interests of prisoners and their families;

    d.   to provide opportunities for prisoners to develop skills and aptitudes that will improve their prospects of successful resettlement after release.

66. To these ends all the remedial, educational, moral, spiritual and other resources that are appropriate should be made available and utilised in accordance with the individual treatment needs of prisoners. Thus the regimes should include:

    a.   spiritual support and guidance and opportunities for relevant work, vocational guidance and training, education, physical education, the development of social skills, counselling, group and recreational activities;

    b.   arrangements to ensure that these activities are organised, so far as possible, to increase contacts with and opportunities within the outside community so as to enhance the prospects for social resettlement after release;

    c.   procedures for establishing and reviewing individual treatment and training programmes for prisoners after full consultations among the relevant staff and with individual prisoners who should be involved in these as far as is practicable;

    d.   communications systems and a management style that will encourage appropriate and positive relationships between staff and prisoners that will improve the prospects for effective and supportive regimes and treatment programmes.

67. 1.   Since the fulfilment of these objectives requires individualisation of treatment and, for this purpose, a flexible system of allocation, prisoners should be placed in separate institutions or units where each can receive the appropriate treatment and training.

    2.   The type, size, organisation and capacity of these institutions or units should be determined essentially by the nature of the treatment to be provided.

    3.   It is necessary to ensure that prisoners are located with due regard to security and control but such measures should be the minimum compatible with safety and comprehend the special needs of the prisoner. Every effort should be made to place prisoners in institutions that are open in character or provide ample opportunities for contacts with the outside community. In the case of foreign nationals, links with people of their own nationality in the outside community are to be regarded as especially important.

68. As soon as possible after administration and after a study of the personality of each prisoner with a sentence of a suitable length, a programme of treatment in a suitable institution shall be prepared in the light of the knowledge obtained about individual needs, capacities and dispositions, especially proximity to relatives.

69. 1.   Within the regime, prisoners shall be given the opportunity to participate

in activities of the institution likely to develop their sense of responsibility, self-reliance and to stimulate interest in their own treatment.

2. Efforts should be made to develop methods of encouraging co-operation with and the participation of the prisoners in their treatment. To this end prisoners shall be encouraged to assume, within the limits specified in Rule 34, responsibilities in certain sectors of the institution's activity.

70. 1. The preparation of prisoners for release should begin as soon as possible after reception in a penal institution. Thus, the treatment of prisoners should emphasise not their exclusion from the community but their continuing part in it. Community agencies and social workers should, therefore, be enlisted wherever possible to assist the staff of the institution in the task of social rehabilitation of the prisoners particularly maintaining and improving the relationships with their families, with other persons and with the social agencies. Steps should be taken to safeguard, to the maximum extent compatible with the law and the sentence, the rights relating to civil interests, social security rights and other social benefits of prisoners.

2. Treatment programmes should include provision for prison leave which should also be granted to the greatest extent possible on medical, educational, occupational, family and other social grounds.

3. Foreign nationals should not be excluded from arrangements for prison leave solely on account of their nationality. Furthermore, every effort should be made to enable them to participate in regime activities together so as to alleviate their feelings of isolation.

Work

71. 1. Prison work should be seen as a positive element in treatment, training and institutional management.

2. Prisoners under sentence may be required to work, subject to their physical and mental fitness as determined by the medical officer.

3. Sufficient work of a useful nature, or if appropriate other purposeful activities shall be provided to keep prisoners actively employed for a normal working day.

4. So far as possible the work provided shall be such as will maintain or increase the prisoner's ability to earn a normal living after release.

5. Vocational training in useful trades shall be provided for prisoners able to profit thereby and especially for young prisoners.

6. Within the limits compatible with proper vocational selection and with the requirements of institutional administration and discipline, the prisoners shall be able to choose the type of employment in which they wish to participate.

72 1. The organisation and methods of work in the institutions shall resemble as closely as possible those of similar work in the community so as to prepare prisoners for the conditions of normal occupational life. It should

thus be relevant to contemporary working standards and techniques and organised to function within modern management systems and production processes.

2. Although the pursuit of financial profit from industries in the institutions can be valuable in raising standards and improving the quality and relevance of training, the interests of the prisoners and of their treatment must not be subordinated to that purpose.

73. Work for prisoners shall be assured by the prison administration:

   a. either on its own premises, workshops and farms, or
   b. in co-operation with private contractors inside or outside the institution in which case the full normal wages for such shall be paid by the persons to whom the labour is supplied, account being taken of the output of the prisoners.

74. 1. Safety and health precautions for prisoners shall be similar to those that apply to workers outside.
   2. Provision shall be made to indemnify prisoners against industrial injury, including occupational disease, on terms not less favourable than those extended by law to workers outside.

75. 1. The maximum daily and weekly working hours of the prisoners shall be fixed in conformity with local rules or custom in regard to the employment of free workmen.
   2. Prisoners should have at least one rest-day a week and sufficient time for education and other activities required as part of their treatment and training for social resettlement.

76. 1. There shall be a system of equitable remuneration of the work of prisoners.
   2. Under the system prisoners shall be allowed to spend at least a part of their earnings on approved articles for their own use and to allocate a part of their earnings to their family or for other approved purposes.
   3. The system may also provide that a part of the earnings be set aside by the administration so as to constitute a savings fund to be handed over to the prisoner on release.

Education

77. A comprehensive education programme shall be arranged in every institution to provide opportunities for all prisoners to pursue at least some of their individual needs and aspirations. Such programmes should have as their objectives the improvement of the prospects for successful social resettlement, the morale and attitudes of prisoners and their self-respect.

78. Education should be regarded as a regime activity that attracts the same status and basic remuneration within the regime as work, provided that it takes place in normal working hours and is part of an authorised individual treatment programme.

79. Special attention should be given by prison administrations to the education

428

of young prisoners, those of foreign origin or with particular cultural or ethnic needs.

80. Specific programmes of remedial education should be arranged for prisoners with special problems such as illiteracy or innumeracy.

81. So far as practicable, the education of prisoners shall:

   a.   be integrated with the educational system of the country so that after their release they may continue their education without difficulty;
   b.   take place in outside educational institutions.

82. Every institution shall have a library for the use of all categories of prisoners, adequately stocked with a wide range of both recreational and instructional books, the prisoners shall be encouraged to make full use of it. Wherever possible the prison library should be organised in co-operation with community library services.

Physical education, exercise, sport and recreation

83. The prison regimes shall recognise the importance to physical and mental health of properly organised activities to ensure physical fitness, adequate exercise and recreational opportunities.

84. Thus a properly organised programme of physical education, sport and other recreational activity should be arranged within the framework and objectives of the treatment and training regime. To this end space, installations and equipment should be provided.

85. Prison administrations should ensure that prisoners who participate in these programmes are physically fit to do so. Special arrangements should be made, under medical direction, for remedial physical education and therapy for those prisoners who need it.

86. Every prisoner who is not employed in outdoor work, or located in an open institution, shall be allowed, if the weather permits, at least one hour of walking or suitable exercise in the open air daily, as far as possible, sheltered from inclement weather.

Pre-release preparation

87. All prisoners should have the benefit of arrangements designed to assist them in returning to society, family life and employment after release. Procedure and special courses should be devised to this end.

88. In the case of those prisoners with longer sentences, steps should be taken to ensure a gradual return to life in society. This aim may be achieved, in particular, by a pre-release regime organised in the same institution or in another appropriate institution, or by conditional release under some kind of supervision combined with effective social support.

89. 1.   Prison administrations should work closely with the social services and agencies that assist released prisoners to re-establish themselves in society, in particular with regard to family life and employment.

2. Steps must be taken to ensure that on release prisoners are provided, as necessary, with appropriate documents and identification papers, and assisted in finding suitable homes and work to go to. They should also be provided with immediate means of subsistence, be suitably and adequately clothed having regard to the climate and season, and have sufficient means to reach their destination.

3. The approved representatives of the social agencies or services should be afforded all necessary access to the institution and to prisoners with a view to making a full contribution to the preparation for release and after-care programme of the prisoner.

PART V

Additional rules for special categories

90. Prison administrations should be guided by the provisions of the rules as a whole so far as they can appropriately and in practice be applied for the benefit of those special categories of prisoners for which additional rules are provided hereafter.

Untried prisoners

91. Without prejudice to legal rules for the protection of individual liberty or prescribing the procedure to be observed in respect of untried prisoners, these prisoners, who are presumed to be innocent until they are found guilty, shall be afforded the benefits that may derive from Rule 90 and treated without restrictions other than those necessary for the penal procedure and the security of the institution.

92. 1. Untried prisoners shall be allowed to inform their families of their detention immediately and give all reasonable facilities for communication with family and friends and persons with whom it is in their legitimate interest to enter into contact.

    2. They shall also be allowed to receive visits from them under humane conditions subject only to such restrictions and supervision as are necessary in the interests of the administration of justice and of the security and good order of the institution.

    3. If an untried prisoner does not wish to inform any of these persons, the prison administration should not do so on its own initiative unless there are good overriding reasons as, for instance, the age, state of mind or any other incapacity of the prisoner.

93. Untried prisoners shall be entitled, as soon as imprisoned, to choose a legal representative, or shall be allowed to apply for free legal aid where such aid is available and to receive visits from that legal adviser with a view to their defence and to prepare and hand to the legal adviser, and to receive, confidential instructions. On request, they shall be given all necessary facilities for this purpose. In particular, they shall be given the free assistance of an

interpreter for all essential contacts with the administration and for their defence. Interviews between prisoners and their legal advisers may be within sight but not within hearing, either direct or indirect, of the police or institution staff. The allocation of untried prisoners shall be in conformity with the provisions of Rule 11, paragraph 3.

94. Except where there are circumstances that make it undesirable, untried prisoners shall be given the opportunity of having separate rooms.

95. 1. Untried prisoners shall be given the opportunity of wearing their own clothing if it is clean and suitable.
    2. Prisoners who do not avail themselves of this opportunity, shall be supplied with suitable dress.
    3. If an untried prisoner does not with to inform any of these persons, the prison administration should not do so on its own initiative unless there are good overriding reasons as, for instance, the age, state of mind or any other incapacity of the prisoner.

96. Untried prisoners shall, whenever possible, be offered the opportunity to work but shall not be required to work. Those who choose to work shall be paid as other prisoners. If educational or trade training is available, untried prisoners shall be encouraged to avail themselves of these opportunities.

97. Untried prisoners shall be allowed to procure at their own expense or at the expense of a third party such books, newspapers, writing materials and other means of occupation as are compatible with the interests of the administration of justice and the security and good order of the institution.

98. Untried prisoners shall be given the opportunity of being visited and treated by their own doctor or dentist if there is reasonable ground for the application. Reasons should be given if the application is refused. Such costs as are incurred shall not be the responsibility of the prison administration.

Civil prisoners

99. In countries where the law permits imprisonment by order of a court under any non-criminal process, persons so imprisoned shall not be subjected to any greater restriction or severity than is necessary to ensure safe custody and good order. Their treatment shall not be less favourable that that of untried prisoners, with the reservation, however, that they may be required to work.

Insane and mentally abnormal prisoners

100. 1. Persons who are found to be insane should not be detained in prisons and arrangements shall be made to remove them to appropriate establishments for the mentally ill as soon as possible.
    2. Specialised institutions or sections under medical management should be available for the observation and treatment of prisoners suffering gravely from other mental disease or abnormality.
    3. The medical or psychiatric service of the penal institutions shall provide for the psychiatric treatment of all prisoners who are in need of such treatment.

4. Action should be taken, by arrangement with the appropriate community agencies, to ensure where necessary the continuation of psychiatric treatment after release and the provision of social psychiatric after-care.

34. UNITED NATIONS: GENERAL ASSEMBLY RESOLUTION ON UN STANDARD MINIMUM RULES FOR NON-CUSTODIAL MEASURES

Adopted by General Assembly resolution 45/110 (1990)

Editors' Notes

The Standard Minimum Rules for Non-Custodial Measures (Tokyo Rules) were adopted by the United Nations General Assembly in 1990, following their recommendation by the Eighth Congress on the Prevention of Crime and the Treatment of Offenders. The Tokyo Rules complement the United Nations Rules on the Treatment of Prisoners[1] by promoting the use of non-custodial measures as an alternative to prison (Rule 1). The Rules encourage states to increase the range of non-custodial measures available (Rule 2) and to avoid the use of pre-trial detention where possible (Rule 5). Rule 8 lists a range of non-custodial measures that states might wish to adopt as alternatives to detention and similar recommendations are listed in respect of post-sentence measures (Rule 9). Rules are also set out in relation to the supervision and conditions of any non-custodial sentence (Part V), the status of staff (Part VI) and the research and planning behind policies of non-custodial sentencing (Part VIII). The preamble to the Rules requests that member states report on the implementation of the rules every five years.

PREAMBLE

The General Assembly,

Bearing in mind the Universal Declaration of Human Rights and the International Covenant on Civil and Political Rights, as well as other international human rights instruments pertaining to the rights of persons in conflict with the law,

Bearing in mind also the Standard Minimum Rules for the Treatment of Prisoners, adopted by the First United Nations Congress on the Prevention of Crime and the Treatment of Offenders, and the important contribution of those Rules to national policies and practices,

Recalling resolution 8 of the Sixth United Nations Congress on the Prevention of Crime and the Treatment of Offenders on alternatives to imprisonment,

Recalling also resolution 16 of the Seventh United Nations Congress on the Prevention of Crime and the Treatment of Offenders on the reduction of the prison population, alternatives to imprisonment, and social integration of offenders,

Recalling further section XI of Economic and Social Council resolution 1986/10 of 21 May 1986, on alternatives to imprisonment, in which the Secretary-General was requested to prepare a report on alternatives to imprisonment for the Eighth

---

[1] *Supra.*

United Nations Congress on the Prevention of Crime and the Treatment of Offenders and to study that question with a view to the formulation of basic principles in that area, with the assistance of the United Nations institutes for the prevention of crime and the treatment of offenders,

Recognizing the need to develop local, national, regional and international approaches and strategies in the field of non-institutional treatment of offenders and the need to formulate standard minimum rules, as emphasized in the section of the report of the Committee on Crime Prevention and Control on its fourth session, concerning the methods and measures likely to be most effective in preventing crime and improving the treatment of offenders,

Convinced that alternatives to imprisonment can be an effective means of treating offenders within the community to the best advantage of both the offenders and society,

Aware that the restriction of liberty is justifiable only from the viewpoints of public safety, crime prevention, just retribution and deterrence and that the ultimate goal of the criminal justice system is the reintegration of the offender into society,

Emphasizing that the increasing prison population and prison overcrowding in many countries constitute factors that create difficulties for the proper implementation of the Standard Minimum Rules for the Treatment of Prisoners,

Noting with appreciation the work accomplished by the Committee on Crime Prevention and Control, as well as by the Interregional Preparatory Meeting for the Eighth United Nations Congress on the Prevention of Crime and the Treatment of Offenders on topic II, "Criminal justice policies in relation to problems of imprisonment, other penal sanctions and alternative measures", and by the regional preparatory meetings for the Eighth Congress,

Expressing its gratitude to the United Nations Asia and Far East Institute for the Prevention of Crime and the Treatment of Offenders for the work accomplished in the development of standard minimum rules for non-custodial measures, as well as to the various intergovernmental and non-governmental organizations involved, in particular, the International Penal and Penitentiary Foundation for its contribution to the preparatory work,

1. Adopts the United Nations Standard Minimum Rules for Non-custodial Measures, contained in the annex to the present resolution, and approves the recommendation of the Committee on Crime Prevention and Control that the Rules should be known as "the Tokyo Rules";
2. Recommends the Tokyo Rules for implementation at the national, regional and interregional levels, taking into account the political, economic, social and cultural circumstances and traditions of countries;
3. Calls upon Member States to apply the Tokyo Rules in their policies and practice;
4. Invites Member States to bring the Tokyo Rules to the attention of, in particular, law enforcement officials, prosecutors, judges, probation officers, lawyers, victims, offenders, social services and non-governmental organizations involved in the application of non-custodial measures, as well as members of the executive, the legislature and the general public;

5. Requests Member States to report on the implementation of the Tokyo Rules every five years, beginning in 1994;
6. Urges the regional commissions, the United Nations institutes for the prevention of crime and the treatment of offenders, specialized agencies and other entities within the United Nations system, other intergovernmental organizations concerned and non-governmental organizations in consultative status with the Economic and Social Council to be actively involved in the implementation of the Tokyo Rules;
7. Calls upon the Committee on Crime Prevention and Control to consider, as a matter of priority, the implementation of the present resolution;
8. Requests the Secretary-General to take the necessary steps to prepare a commentary to the Tokyo Rules, which is to be submitted to the Committee on Crime Prevention and Control at its twelfth session for approval and further dissemination, paying special attention to the legal safeguards, the implementation of the Rules and the development of similar guidelines at the regional level;
9. Invites the United Nations institutes for the prevention of crime and the treatment of offenders to assist the Secretary-General in that task;
10. Urges intergovernmental and non-governmental organizations and other entities concerned to remain actively involved in this initiative;
11. Requests the Secretary-General to take steps, as appropriate, to ensure the widest possible dissemination of the Tokyo Rules, including their transmission to Governments, interested intergovernmental and non-governmental organizations and other parties concerned;
12. Also requests the Secretary-General to prepare every five years, beginning in 1994, a report on the implementation of the Tokyo Rules for submission to the Committee on Crime Prevention and Control;
13. Further requests the Secretary-General to assist Member States, at their request, in the implementation of the Tokyo Rules and to report regularly thereon to the Committee on Crime Prevention and Control;
14. Requests that the present resolution and the text of the annex be brought to the attention of all United Nations bodies concerned and be included in the next edition of the United Nations publication entitled *Human Rights: A Compilation of International Instruments.*

UNITED NATIONS STANDARD MINIMUM RULES FOR NON-CUSTODIAL MEASURES (THE TOKYO RULES)

I GENERAL PRINCIPLES

1. Fundamental aims

1.1 The present Standard Minimum Rules provide a set of basic principles to promote the use of non-custodial measures, as well as minimum safeguards for persons subject to alternatives to imprisonment.

1.2 The Rules are intended to promote greater community involvement in the management of criminal justice, specifically in the treatment of offenders, as well as to promote among offenders a sense of responsibility towards society.

1.3 The Rules shall be implemented taking into account the political, economic, social and cultural conditions of each country and the aims and objectives of its criminal justice system.

1.4 When implementing the Rules, Member States shall endeavour to ensure a proper balance between the rights of individual offenders, the rights of victims, and the concern of society for public safety and crime prevention.

1.5 Member States shall develop non-custodial measures within their legal systems to provide other options, thus reducing the use of imprisonment, and to rationalize criminal justice policies, taking into account the observance of human rights, the requirements of social justice and the rehabilitation needs of the offender.

2. The scope of non-custodial measures

2.1 The relevant provisions of the present Rules shall be applied to all persons subject to prosecution, trial or the execution of a sentence, at all stages of the administration of criminal justice. For the purposes of the Rules, these persons are referred to as "offenders", irrespective of whether they are suspected, accused or sentenced.

2.2 The Rules shall be applied without any discrimination on the grounds of race, colour, sex, age, language, religion, political or other opinion, national or social origin, property, birth or other status.

2.3 In order to provide greater flexibility consistent with the nature and gravity of the offence, with the personality and background of the offender and with the protection of society and to avoid unnecessary use of imprisonment, the criminal justice system should provide a wide range of non-custodial measures, from pre-trial to post-sentencing dispositions. The number and types of non-custodial measures available should be determined in such a way that consistent sentencing remains possible.

2.4 The development of new non-custodial measures should be encouraged and closely monitored and their use systematically evaluated.

2.5 Consideration shall be given to dealing with offenders in the community, avoiding as far as possible resort to formal proceedings or trial by a court, in accordance with legal safeguards and the rule of law.

2.6 Non-custodial measures should be used in accordance with the principle of minimum intervention.

2.7 The use of non-custodial measures should be part of the movement towards depenalization and decriminalization instead of interfering with or delaying efforts in that direction.

3. Legal safeguards

3.1 The introduction, definition and application of non-custodial measures shall be prescribed by law.

3.2   The selection of a non-custodial measure shall be based on an assessment of established criteria in respect of both the nature and gravity of the offence and the personality, the background of the offender, the purposes of sentencing and the rights of victims.

3.3   Discretion by the judicial or other competent independent authority shall be exercised at all stages of the proceedings by ensuring full accountability and only in accordance with the rule of law.

3.4   Non-custodial measures imposing an obligation on the offender, applied before or instead of formal proceedings or trial, shall require the offender's consent.

3.5   Decisions on the imposition of non-custodial measures shall be subject to review by a judicial or other competent independent authority, upon application by the offender.

3.6   The offender shall be entitled to make a request or complaint to a judicial or other competent independent authority on matters affecting his or her individual rights in the implementation of non-custodial measures.

3.7   Appropriate machinery shall be provided for the recourse and, if possible, redress of any grievance related to non-compliance with internationally recognized human rights.

3.8   Non-custodial measures shall not involve medical or psychological experimentation on, or undue risk of physical or mental injury to, the offender.

3.9   The dignity of the offender subject to non-custodial measures shall be protected at all times.

3.10   In the implementation of non-custodial measures, the offender's rights shall not be restricted further than was authorized by the competent authority that rendered the original decision.

3.11   In the application of non-custodial measures, the offender's right to privacy shall be respected, as shall be the right to privacy of the offender's family.

3.12   The offender's personal records shall be kept strictly confidential and closed to third parties. Access to such records shall be limited to persons directly concerned with the disposition of the offender's case or to other duly authorized persons.

Saving clause

4.1 Nothing in the present Rules shall be interpreted as precluding the application of the Standard Minimum Rules for the Treatment of Prisoners, the United Nations Standard Minimum Rules for the Administration of Juvenile Justice (The Beijing Rules), the Body of Principles for the Protection of All Persons under Any Form of Detention or Imprisonment or any other human rights instruments and standards recognized by the international community and relating to the treatment of offenders and the protection of their basic human rights.

II. PRE-TRIAL STAGE

5. Pre-trial dispositions

5.1 Where appropriate and compatible with the legal system, the police, the prosecution service or other agencies dealing with criminal cases should be empowered to discharge the offender if they consider that it is not necessary to proceed with the case for the protection of society, crime prevention or the promotion of respect for the law and the rights of victims. For the purpose of deciding upon the appropriateness of discharge or determination of proceedings, a set of established criteria shall be developed within each legal system. For minor cases the prosecutor may impose suitable non-custodial measures, as appropriate.

6. Avoidance of pre-trial detention

6.1 Pre-trial detention shall be used as a means of last resort in criminal proceedings, with due regard for the investigation of the alleged offence and for the protection of society and the victim.

6.2 Alternatives to pre-trial detention shall be employed at as early a stage as possible. Pre-trial detention shall last no longer than necessary to achieve the objectives stated under rule 5.1 and shall be administered humanely and with respect for the inherent dignity of human beings.

6.3 The offender shall have the right to appeal to a judicial or other competent independent authority in cases where pre-trial detention is employed.

III. TRIAL AND SENTENCING STAGE

7. Social inquiry reports

7.1 If the possibility of social inquiry reports exists, the judicial authority may avail itself of a report prepared by a competent, authorized official or agency. The report should contain social information on the offender that is relevant to the person's pattern of offending and current offences. It should also contain information and recommendations that are relevant to the sentencing procedure. The report shall be factual, objective and unbiased, with any expression of opinion clearly identified.

8. Sentencing dispositions

8.1 The judicial authority, having at its disposal a range of non-custodial measures, should take into consideration in making its decision the rehabilitative needs of the offender, the protection of society and the interests of the victim, who should be consulted whenever appropriate.

8.2 Sentencing authorities may dispose of cases in the following ways:

(a) Verbal sanctions, such as admonition, reprimand and warning;
(b) Conditional discharge;
(c) Status penalties;
(d) Economic sanctions and monetary penalties, such as fines and day-fines;
(e) Confiscation or an expropriation order;
(f) Restitution to the victim or a compensation order;
(g) Suspended or deferred sentence;
(h) Probation and judicial supervision;
(i) A community service order;
(j) Referral to an attendance centre;
(k) House arrest;
(l) Any other mode of non-institutional treatment;
(m) Some combination of the measures listed above.

IV. POST-SENTENCING STAGE

9. Post-sentencing dispositions

9.1 The competent authority shall have at its disposal a wide range of post-sentencing alternatives in order to avoid institutionalization and to assist offenders in their early reintegration into society.

9.2 Post-sentencing dispositions may include:

(a) Furlough and half-way houses;
(b) Work or education release;
(c) Various forms of parole;
(d) Remission;
(e) Pardon.

9.3 The decision on post-sentencing dispositions, except in the case of pardon, shall be subject to review by a judicial or other competent independent authority, upon application of the offender.

9.4 Any form of release from an institution to a non-custodial programme shall be considered at the earliest possible stage.

V. IMPLEMENTATION OF NON-CUSTODIAL MEASURES

10. Supervision

10.1 The purpose of supervision is to reduce reoffending and to assist the offender's integration into society in a way which minimizes the likelihood of a return to crime.

10.2 If a non-custodial measure entails supervision, the latter shall be carried out by a competent authority under the specific conditions prescribed by law.

10.3 Within the framework of a given non-custodial measure, the most suitable type of supervision and treatment should be determined for each individual case aimed at assisting the offender to work on his or her offending. Supervision and treatment should be periodically reviewed and adjusted as necessary.

10.4 Offenders should, when needed, be provided with psychological, social and material assistance and with opportunities to strengthen links with the community and facilitate their reintegration into society.

11. Duration

11.1 The duration of a non-custodial measure shall not exceed the period established by the competent authority in accordance with the law.

11.2 Provision may be made for early termination of the measure if the offender has responded favourably to it.

12. Conditions

12.1 If the competent authority shall determine the conditions to be observed by the offender, it should take into account both the needs of society and the needs and rights of the offender and the victim.

12.2 The conditions to be observed shall be practical, precise and as few as possible, and shall be aimed at reducing the likelihood of an offender relapsing into criminal behaviour and at increasing the offender's chances of social integration, taking into account the needs of the victim.

12.3 At the beginning of the application of a non-custodial measure, the offender shall receive an explanation, orally and in writing, of the conditions governing the application of the measure, including the offender's obligations and rights.

12.4 The conditions may be modified by the competent authority under the established statutory provisions, in accordance with the progress made by the offender.

13. Treatment process

13.1 Within the framework of a given non-custodial measure, in appropriate cases, various schemes, such as case-work, group therapy, residential programmes and the specialized treatment of various categories of offenders, should be developed to meet the needs of offenders more effectively.

13.2 Treatment should be conducted by professionals who have suitable training and practical experience.

13.3 When it is decided that treatment is necessary, efforts should be made to understand the offender's background, personality, aptitude, intelligence, values and, especially, the circumstances leading to the commission of the offence.

13.4 The competent authority may involve the community and social support systems in the application of non-custodial measures.

13.5 Case-load assignments shall be maintained as far as practicable at a manageable level to ensure the effective implementation of treatment programmes.

13.6 For each offender, a case record shall be established and maintained by the competent authority.

14. Discipline and breach of conditions

14.1 A breach of the conditions to be observed by the offender may result in a modification or revocation of the non-custodial measure.

14.2 The modification or revocation of the non-custodial measure shall be made by the competent authority; this shall be done only after a careful examination of the facts adduced by both the supervising officer and the offender.

14.3 The failure of a non-custodial measure should not automatically lead to the imposition of a custodial measure.

14.4 In the event of a modification or revocation of the non-custodial measure, the competent authority shall attempt to establish a suitable alternative non-custodial measure. A sentence of imprisonment may be imposed only in the absence of other suitable alternatives.

14.5 The power to arrest and detain the offender under supervision in cases where there is a breach of the conditions shall be prescribed by law.

14.6 Upon modification or revocation of the non-custodial measure, the offender shall have the right to appeal to a judicial or other competent independent authority.

VI. STAFF

15. Recruitment

15.1 There shall be no discrimination in the recruitment of staff on the grounds of race, colour, sex, age, language, religion, political or other opinion, national or social origin, property, birth or other status. The policy regarding staff recruitment should take into consideration national policies of affirmative action and reflect the diversity of the offenders to be supervised.

15.2 Persons appointed to apply non-custodial measures should be personally suitable and, whenever possible, have appropriate professional training and practical experience. Such qualifications shall be clearly specified.

15.3 To secure and retain qualified professional staff, appropriate service status, adequate salary and benefits commensurate with the nature of the work should be ensured and ample opportunities should be provided for professional growth and career development.

16. Staff training

16.1 The objective of training shall be to make clear to staff their responsibilities with regard to rehabilitating the offender, ensuring the offender's rights and protecting society. Training should also give staff an understanding of the need to co-operate in and co-ordinate activities with the agencies concerned.

16.2 Before entering duty, staff shall be given training that includes instruction on the nature of non-custodial measures, the purposes of supervision and the various modalities of the application of non-custodial measures.

16.3 After entering on duty, staff shall maintain and improve their knowledge and professional capacity by attending in-service training and refresher courses. Adequate facilities shall be made available for that purpose.

VII. VOLUNTEERS AND OTHER COMMUNITY RESOURCES

17. Public participation

17.1 Public participation should be encouraged as it is a major resource and one of the most important factors in improving ties between offenders undergoing non-custodial measures and the family and community. It should complement the efforts of the criminal justice administration.

17.2 Public participation should be regarded as an opportunity for members of the community to contribute to the protection of their society.

18. Public understanding and co-operation

18.1 Government agencies, the private sector and the general public should be encouraged to support voluntary organizations that promote non-custodial measures.

18.2 Conferences, seminars, symposia and other activities should be regularly organized to stimulate awareness of the need for public participation in the application of non-custodial measures.

18.3 All forms of the mass media should be utilized to help to create a constructive public attitude, leading to activities conducive to a broader application of non-custodial treatment and the social integration of offenders.

18.4 Every effort should be made to inform the public of the importance of its role in the implementation of non-custodial measures.

19. Volunteers

19.1 Volunteers shall be carefully screened and recruited on the basis of their aptitude for and interest in the work involved. They shall be properly trained for the specific responsibilities to be discharged by them and shall have access to support and counselling from, and the opportunity to consult with, the competent authority.

19.2 Volunteers should encourage offenders and their families to develop meaningful ties with the community and a broader sphere of contact by providing counselling and other appropriate forms of assistance according to their capacity and the offenders' needs.

19.3 Volunteers shall be insured against accident, injury and public liability when carrying out their duties. They shall be reimbursed for authorized expenditures incurred in the course of their work. Public recognition should be extended to them for the services they render for the well-being of the community.

VIII. RESEARCH, PLANNING, POLICY FORMULATION AND EVALUATION

20. Research and planning

20.1 As an essential aspect of the planning process, efforts should be made to involve both public and private bodies in the organization and promotion of research on the non-custodial treatment of offenders.

20.2 Research on the problems that confront clients, practitioners, the community and policy makers should be carried out on a regular basis.

20.3 Research and information mechanisms should be built into the criminal justice system for the collection and analysis of data and statistics on the implementation of non-custodial treatment for offenders.

21. Policy formulation and programme development

21.1 Programmes for non-custodial measures should be systematically planned and implemented as an integral part of the criminal justice system within the national development process.

21.2 Regular evaluations should be carried out with a view to implementing non-custodial measures more effectively.

21.3 Periodic reviews should be conducted to assess the objectives, functioning and effectiveness of non-custodial measures.

22. Linkages with relevant agencies and activitie

22.1 Suitable mechanisms should be evolved at various levels to facilitate the establishment of linkages between services responsible for non-custodial measures, other branches of the criminal justice system, social development and welfare agencies, both governmental and non-governmental, in such fields as health, housing, education and labour, and the mass media.

23. International co-operation

23.1 Efforts shall be made to promote scientific co-operation between countries in the field of non-institutional treatment. Research, training, technical assistance and the exchange of information among Member States on non-custodial measures should be strengthened, through the United Nations institutes for the prevention of crime and the treatment of offenders, in close collaboration with the Crime Prevention and Criminal Justice Branch of the Centre for Social Development and Humanitarian Affairs of the United Nations Secretariat.

23.2 Comparative studies and the harmonization of legislative provisions should be furthered to expand the range of non-institutional options and facilitate their application across national frontiers, in accordance with the Model Treaty on the Transfer of Supervision of Offenders Conditionally Sentenced or Conditionally Released.

Chapter 3: The Death Penalty

Editors' Notes: Instruments Outlawing the Use of the Death Penalty and Treatment of those facing the Death Penalty.

Despite about half of the countries in the world retaining the use of the death penalty,[1] there has been a progressive universal and regional trend to restrict the use of the death penalty, as reflected by the instruments included in the present volume. The right to life as set out in the text of the International Covenant on Civil and Political Rights[2] has not been construed as prohibiting the use of the death penalty *per se*, however it is followed by a series of clauses which restrict its use and encourage abolition.

Since the Covenant, steady discussion within the United Nations has consistently sought to restrict the use of the death penalty. In 1984, the Economic and Social Council adopted the Safeguards Guaranteeing the Rights of those facing the Death Penalty which set out recommendations concerning basic procedural rights of the accused during the trial process and that when capital punishment is imposed, it should inflict the minimum possible suffering. However, studies have concluded that the broad, non-binding provisions of the Safeguards are not being effectively translated into enforceable rights.[3]

In 1989, the United Nations General Assembly adopted the Second Optional Protocol to the International Covenant on Civil and Political rights aiming at the abolition of the death penalty by a narrow majority. Parties to the Protocol undertake that no one within the state's jurisdiction will be executed (Article 1). The only exception is provided for the implementation of the death penalty during war time for a conviction for war crimes (Article 2). Under Article 3 of the Protocol, parties must submit reports on implementation to the UN Human Rights Committee. Provision is also made for complaints by state parties (Article 4) and individuals on a limited basis (Article 5).

Prior to the United Nations Protocol, the Council of Europe also sought to abolish the death penalty in its Sixth Protocol to the European Convention on Human Rights in 1985. The European Court of Human Rights has indicated that Article 2 of the European Convention did not preclude the death penalty.[4] The Protocol to the American Convention on Human Rights to Abolish the Death Penalty supplements the Inter-American Convention with a similar prohibition. Article 2 of both the European and American Protocols allow states to declare an exception with regard to serious military crimes.

While it may be premature to declare that the use of the death penalty is contrary to customary international law, it is clear that the way in which it is imposed can amount to inhuman and degrading treatment.[5] It has further been

---

[1] Amnesty International (1995). *Facts and Figures on the Death Penalty*. London, Amnesty International.
[2] *Supra*, Article 6.
[3] See: Hood, R. (1989). *The Death Penalty A Worldwide Perspective*. Oxford, Clarendon Press. p.83.
[4] *Soering v United Kingdom*, Ser. A, No. 161 (1989), para. 103.
[5] *Ibid*, para. 104.

suggested that emerging international law prohibits capital punishment for juveniles,[6] and the Inter-American Commission on Human Rights has concluded that the use of the death penalty for children is proscribed by a norm of *jus cogens.*[7]

35. UNITED NATIONS: SAFEGUARDS GUARANTEEING THE PROTECTION OF THE RIGHTS OF THOSE FACING THE DEATH PENALTY

Approved by Economic and Social Council resolution 1984/50 (1984)

1. In countries which have not abolished the death penalty, capital punishment may be imposed only for the most serious crimes, it being understood that their scope should not go beyond international crimes with lethal or other extremely grave consequence.
2. Capital punishment may be imposed only for crime for which the death penalty is prescribed by law at the time of its commission, it being understood that if, subsequent to the commission of the crime, provision is made by law for the imposition of a lighter penalty, the offender shall benefit thereby.
3. Persons below 18 years of age at the time of the commission of the crime shall not be sentenced to death, nor shall the death sentence be carried out on pregnant women, or on new mothers, or on persons who have become insane.
4. Capital punishment may be imposed only when the guilt of the person charged is based upon clear and convincing evidence leaving no room for an alternative explanation of the facts.
5. Capital punishment may only be carried out pursuant to a final judgement rendered by a competent court after legal process which gives all possible safeguards to ensure a fair trial, at least equal to those contained in article 14 of the International Covenant on Civil and Political Rights, including the right of anyone suspected of or charged with a crime for which capital punishment may be imposed to adequate legal assistance at all stages of the proceedings.
6. Anyone sentenced to death shall have the right to appeal to a court of higher jurisdiction, and steps should be taken to ensure that such appeals shall become mandatory.
7. Anyone sentenced to death shall have the right to seek pardon, or commutation of sentence; pardon or commutation of sentence may be granted in all cases of capital punishment.
8. Capital punishment shall not be carried out pending any appeal or other recourse procedure or other proceeding relating to pardon or commutation of the sentence.
9. Where capital punishment occurs, it shall be carried out so as to inflict the minimum possible suffering.

[6] Naldi, G. (1991). 'United Nations seeks to Abolish the Death Penalty'. 40 ICLQ 948, p.951.
[7] *Application of the death penalty on juveniles in the US (Roach and Pinkerton v US).* Res.3/87, Case no. 9647.

36. COUNCIL OF EUROPE: SIXTH PROTOCOL TO THE CONVENTION FOR THE PROTECTION OF HUMAN RIGHTS AND FUNDAMENTAL FREEDOMS CONCERNING THE ABOLITION OF THE DEATH PENALTY

Opened for signature at Strasbourg: 28 April 1983

ETS 114

Entry into force: 1 March 1985

The member States of the Council of Europe, signatory to this Protocol to the Convention for the Protection of Human Rights and Fundamental Freedoms, signed at Rome on 4 November 1950 (hereinafter referred to as "the Convention"),

Considering that the evolution that has occurred in several member States of the Council of Europe expresses a general tendency in favour of abolition of the death penalty,

Have agreed as follows:

Article 1

The death penalty shall be abolished. No one shall be condemned to such penalty or executed.

Article 2

A State may make provision in its law for the death penalty in respect to acts committed in time of war or of imminent threat of war; such penalty shall be applied only in the instances laid down in the law and in accordance with its provisions. The State shall communicate to the Secretary of the Council of Europe the relevant provisions of that law.

Article 3

No derogation from the provisions of this Protocol shall be made under Article 15 of the Convention.

Article 4

No reservation may be made under Article 64 of the Convention in respect to the provisions of this Protocol.

Article 5

[Extension of obligations to other territories]

Article 6

As between the States parties the provisions of Article 1 to 5 of this Protocol shall be regarded as additional articles to the Convention and all the provisions of the Convention shall apply accordingly.

Article 7

[Signature, ratification etc]

Article 8

1. [Entry into force]

Article 9

[Notification of signatures, ratifications, denunciations, etc.]

37. UNITED NATIONS: SECOND OPTIONAL PROTOCOL TO THE INTERNATIONAL COVENANT ON CIVIL AND POLITICAL RIGHTS, AIMING AT THE ABOLITION OF THE DEATH PENALTY

Opened for signature: 15 December 1989

General Assembly resolution 44/128

Entry into force: 11 July 1991

The States Parties to the present Protocol,

Believing that abolition of the death penalty contributes to enhancement of human dignity and progressive development of human rights,

Recalling article 3 of the Universal Declaration of Human Rights adopted on 10 December 1948 and article 6 of the International Covenant on Civil and Political Rights adopted on 16 December 1966,

Noting that article 6 of the International Covenant on Civil and Political Rights refers to abolition of the death penalty in terms that strongly suggest that abolition is desirable,

Convinced that all measures of abolition of the death penalty should be considered as progress in the enjoyment of the right to life,

Desirous to undertake hereby an international commitment to abolish the death penalty,

Have agreed as follows:

Article 1

1. No one within the jurisdiction of a State Party to the present Protocol shall be executed.
2. Each State Party shall take all necessary measures to abolish the death penalty within its jurisdiction.

Article 2

1. No reservation is admissible to the present Protocol, except for a reservation made at the time of ratification or accession that provides for the application of the death penalty in time of war pursuant to a conviction for a most serious crime of a military nature committed during wartime.
2. The State Party making such a reservation shall at the time of ratification or accession communicate to the Secretary-General of the United Nations the relevant provisions of its national legislation applicable during wartime.
3. The State Party having made such a reservation shall notify the Secretary-

General of the United Nations of any beginning or ending of a state of war applicable to its territory.

Article 3

The States Parties to the present Protocol shall include in the reports they submit to the Human Rights Committee, in accordance with article 40 of the Covenant, information on the measures that they have adopted to give effect to the present Protocol.

Article 4

With respect to the States Parties to the Covenant that have made a declaration under article 41, the competence of the Human Rights Committee to receive and consider communications when a State Party claims that another State Party is not fulfilling its obligations shall extend to the provisions of the present Protocol, unless the State Party concerned has made a statement to the contrary at the moment of ratification or accession.

Article 5

With respect to the States Parties to the first Optional Protocol to the International Covenant on Civil and Political Rights adopted on 16 December 1966, the competence of the Human Rights Committee to receive and consider communications from individuals subject to its jurisdiction shall extend to the provisions of the present Protocol, unless the State Party concerned has made a statement to the contrary at the moment of ratification or accession.

Article 6

1. The provisions of the present Protocol shall apply as additional provisions to the Covenant.
2. Without prejudice to the possibility of a reservation under article 2 of the present Protocol, the right guaranteed in article 1, paragraph 1, of the present Protocol shall not be subject to any derogation under article 4 of the Covenant.

Article 7

1. The present Protocol is open for signature by any State that has signed the Covenant.
2. The present Protocol is subject to ratification by any State that has ratified the Covenant or acceded to it. Instruments of ratification shall be deposited with the Secretary-General of the United Nations.
3. The present Protocol shall be open to accession by any State that has ratified the Covenant or acceded to it.
4. Accession shall be effected by the deposit of an instrument of accession with the Secretary-General of the United Nations.

5.   The Secretary-General of the United Nations shall inform all States that have signed the present Protocol or acceded to it of the deposit of each instrument of ratification or accession.

Article 8

1.   The present Protocol shall enter into force three months after the date of the deposit with the Secretary-General of the United Nations of the tenth instrument of ratification or accession.
2.   For each State ratifying the present Protocol or acceding to it after the deposit of the tenth instrument of ratification or accession, the present Protocol shall enter into force three months after the date of the deposit of its own instrument of ratification or accession.

Article 9

The provisions of the present Protocol shall extend to all parts of federal States without any limitations or exceptions.

Article 10

The Secretary-General of the United Nations shall inform all States referred to in article 48, paragraph 1, of the Covenant of the following particulars:

   (a)   Reservations, communications and notifications under article 2 of the present Protocol;
   (b)   Statements made under articles 4 or 5 of the present Protocol;
   (c)   Signatures, ratifications and accessions under article 7 of the present Protocol;
   (d)   The date of the entry into force of the present Protocol under article 8 thereof.

Article 11

1.   The present Protocol, of which the Arabic, Chinese, English, French, Russian and Spanish texts are equally authentic, shall be deposited in the archives of the United Nations.
2.   The Secretary-General of the United Nations shall transmit certified copies of the present Protocol to all States referred to in article 48 of the Covenant.

38. ORGANIZATION OF AMERICAN STATES: PROTOCOL TO THE AMERICAN CONVENTION ON HUMAN RIGHTS TO ABOLISH THE DEATH PENALTY

Opened for signature: 8 June 1990

OAS TS 73 (1990)

Entry into force: 28 August 1991

PREAMBLE

The States Parties to this protocol,

Considering:

That Article 4 of the American Convention on Human Rights recognizes the right to life and restricts the application of the death penalty;

That everyone has the inalienable right to respect for his life, a right that cannot be suspended for any reason;

That the tendency among the American States is to be in favor of abolition of the death penalty;

That application of the death penalty has irrevocable consequences, forecloses the correction of judicial error, and precludes any possibility of changing or rehabilitating those convicted;

That the abolition of the death penalty helps to ensure more effective protection of the right to life;

That an international agreement must be arrived at that will entail a progressive development of the American Convention on Human Rights, and That States Parties to the American Convention on Human Rights have expressed their intention to adopt an international agreement with a view to consolidating the practice of not applying the death penalty in the Americas,

Have agreed to sign the following Protocol to the American Convention on Human Rights to abolish the death penalty.

Article 1

The States Parties to this Protocol shall not apply the death penalty in their territory to any person subject to their jurisdiction.

Article 2

1. No reservations may be made to this Protocol. However, at the time of

452

ratification or accession, the States Parties to this instrument may declare that they reserve the right to apply the death penalty in wartime in accordance with international law, for extremely serious crimes of a military nature.

2. The State Party making this reservation shall, upon ratification or accession, inform the Secretary General of the Organization of American States of the pertinent provisions of its national legislation applicable in wartime, as referred to in the preceding paragraph.

3. Said State Party shall notify the Secretary General of the Organization of American States of the beginning or end of any state of war in effect in its territory.

Article 3

[Signature and ratification]

Article 4

[Entry into force]

39. UNITED NATIONS: CONVENTION ON THE RIGHTS OF THE CHILD (EXCERPTS)

Opened for signature at New York: 20 November 1989 by
General Assembly resolution 44/25 (1989)

Entry into force: 2 September 1990

Editors' Notes

The articles of the Convention as they are excerpted here relate to the administration of criminal justice (see especially Article 40), the prohibition of the use of torture and protection against the use of capital punishment or life imprisonment (Article 37). Overall the Convention is extremely comprehensive, detailing civil, political, economic, psychological, social and cultural rights as they apply to children.[1]

PREAMBLE

The States Parties to the present Convention,

... *Bearing in mind* that, as indicated in the Declaration of the Rights of the Child, "the child, by reason of his physical and mental immaturity, needs special safeguards and care, including appropriate legal protection, before as well as after birth",
... *Have agreed* as follows:

PART I

Article 1

For the purposes of the present Convention, a child means every human being below the age of eighteen years unless under the law applicable to the child, majority is attained earlier.

---

[1] See also: International Covenant on Civil and Political Rights, Articles 10(2)(b) & 14(4), *supra*. See generally: Van Bueren, G. (1995). *The International Law on the Rights of the Child*. Netherlands, Martinus Nijhoff.

Article 2

1. States Parties shall respect and ensure the rights set forth in the present Convention to each child within their jurisdiction without discrimination of any kind, irrespective of the child's or his or her parent's or legal guardian's race, colour, sex, language, religion, political or other opinion, national, ethnic or social origin, property, disability, birth or other status.
2. States Parties shall take all appropriate measures to ensure that the child is protected against all forms of discrimination or punishment on the basis of the status, activities, expressed opinions, or beliefs of the child's parents, legal guardians, or family members.

Article 4

States Parties shall undertake all appropriate legislative, administrative, and other measures for the implementation of the rights recognized in the present Convention. With regard to economic, social and cultural rights, States Parties shall undertake such measures to the maximum extent of their available resources and, where needed, within the framework of international co-operation.

Article 9

1. States Parties shall ensure that a child shall not be separated from his or her parents against their will, except when competent authorities subject to judicial review determine, in accordance with applicable law and procedures, that such separation is necessary for the best interests of the child. Such determination may be necessary in a particular case such as one involving abuse or neglect of the child by the parents, or one where the parents are living separately and a decision must be made as to the child's place of residence.
2. In any proceedings pursuant to paragraph 1 of the present article, all interested parties shall be given an opportunity to participate in the proceedings and make their views known.
3. States Parties shall respect the right of the child who is separated from one or both parents to maintain personal relations and direct contact with both parents on a regular basis, except if it is contrary to the child's best interests.
4. Where such separation results from any action initiated by a State Party, such as the detention, imprisonment, exile, deportation or death (including death arising from any cause while the person is in the custody of the State) of one or both parents or of the child, that State Party shall, upon request, provide the parents, the child or, if appropriate, another member of the family with the essential information concerning the whereabouts of the absent member(s) of the family unless the provision of the information would be detrimental to the well-being of the child. States Parties shall further ensure that the submission of such a request shall of itself entail no adverse consequences for the person(s) concerned.

Article 12

1. States Parties shall assure to the child who is capable of forming his or her own views the right to express those views freely in all matters affecting the child, the views of the child being given due weight in accordance with the age and maturity of the child.

2. For this purpose, the child shall in particular be provided the opportunity to be heard in any judicial and administrative proceedings affecting the child, either directly, or through a representative or an appropriate body, in a manner consistent with the procedural rules of national law.

Article 16

1. No child shall be subjected to arbitrary or unlawful interference with his or her privacy, family, home or correspondence, nor to unlawful attacks on his or her honour and reputation.
2. The child has the right to the protection of the law against such interference or attacks.

Article 19

1. States Parties shall take all appropriate legislative, administrative, social and educational measures to protect the child from all forms of physical or mental violence, injury or abuse, neglect or negligent treatment, maltreatment or exploitation, including sexual abuse, while in the care of parent(s), legal guardian(s) or any other person who has the care of the child.
2. Such protective measures should, as appropriate, include effective procedures for the establishment of social programmes to provide necessary support for the child and for those who have the care of the child, as well as for other forms of prevention and for identification, reporting, referral, investigation, treatment and follow-up of instances of child maltreatment described heretofore, and, as appropriate, for judicial involvement.

Article 37

States Parties shall ensure that:

(a) No child shall be subjected to torture or other cruel, inhuman or degrading treatment or punishment. Neither capital punishment nor life imprisonment without possibility of release shall be imposed for offences committed by persons below eighteen years of age;

(b) No child shall be deprived of his or her liberty unlawfully or arbitrarily. The arrest, detention or imprisonment of a child shall be in conformity with the law and shall be used only as a measure of last resort and for the shortest appropriate period of time;

(c) Every child deprived of liberty shall be treated with humanity and respect for the inherent dignity of the human person, and in a manner which takes into account the needs of persons of his or her age. In particular, every child deprived of liberty shall be separated from adults unless it is considered in the child's best interest not to do so and shall have the right to maintain contact with his or her family through correspondence and visits, save in exceptional circumstances;

(d) Every child deprived of his or her liberty shall have the right to prompt access to legal and other appropriate assistance, as well as the right to challenge the legality of the deprivation of his or her liberty before a court or other competent, independent and impartial authority, and to a prompt decision on any such action.

Article 40

1. States Parties recognise the right of every child alleged as, accused of, or recognized as having infringed the penal law to be treated in a manner consistent with the promotion of the child's sense of dignity and worth, which reinforces the child's respect for the human rights and fundamental freedoms of others and which takes into account the child's age and the desirability of promoting the child's reintegration and the child's assuming a constructive role in society.

2. To this end, and having regard to the relevant provisions of international instruments, States Parties shall, in particular, ensure that:

    (a) No child shall be alleged as, be accused of, or recognized as having infringed the penal law by reason of acts or omissions that were not prohibited by national or international law at the time they were committed;

    (b) Every child alleged as or accused of having infringed the penal law has at least the following guarantees:

    (i) To be presumed innocent until proven guilty according to law;

    (ii) To be informed promptly and directly of the charges against him or her, and, if appropriate, through his or her parents or legal guardians, and to have legal or other appropriate assistance in the preparation and presentation of his or her defence;

    (iii) To have the matter determined without delay by a competent, independent and impartial authority or judicial body in a fair hearing according to law, in the presence of legal or other appropriate assistance and, unless it is considered not to be in the best interest of the child, in particular, taking into account his or her age or situation, his or her parents or legal guardians;

    (iv) Not to be compelled to give testimony or to confess guilt; to examine or have examined adverse witnesses and to obtain the participation and examination of witnesses on his or her behalf under conditions of equality;

    (v) If considered to have infringed the penal law, to have this decision and any measures imposed in consequence thereof reviewed by a higher competent, independent and impartial authority or judicial body according to law;

(vi) To have the free assistance of an interpreter if the child cannot understand or speak the language used;

(vii) To have his or her privacy fully respected at all stages of the proceedings.

3. States Parties shall seek to promote the establishment of laws, procedures, authorities and institutions specifically applicable to children alleged as, accused of, or recognized as having infringed the penal law, and, in particular:

    (a) The establishment of a minimum age below which children shall be presumed not to have the capacity to infringe the penal law;

    (b) Whenever appropriate and desirable, measures for dealing with such children without resorting to judicial proceedings, providing that human rights and legal safeguards are fully respected.

4. A variety of dispositions, such as care, guidance and supervision orders; counselling; probation; foster care; education and vocational training programmes and other alternatives to institutional care shall be available to ensure that children are dealt with in a manner appropriate to their well-being and proportionate both to their circumstances and the offence.

40. COUNCIL OF EUROPE: EUROPEAN CONVENTION ON THE EXERCISE OF CHILDREN'S RIGHTS

Opened for signature at Strasbourg: 25 January 1996

ETS 160

Not in force

Editors' Notes

As stated in the preamble to the Convention, a prime motivation behind the preparation of this agreement was the United Nations Convention on the Rights of the Child,[1] in particular Article 4 which calls for member states to undertake the necessary measures to implement children's rights. The Council of Europe Treaty is much more restricted in scope than the United Nations Treaty, in that it seeks to guarantee the procedural rights of children and enable them to participate fully in "proceedings affecting them before a judicial authority", which in this instance means "family proceedings, in particular those involving the exercise of parental responsibilities such as residence and access to children" (Article 1). It should be noted that other aspects of children's rights have been considered by both the European and the Inter-American Courts of Human Rights.[2]

Amongst the concerns of the Treaty are that a child should have a right to know of and participate in any proceedings concerning them (Article 3), and to be properly represented in those proceedings (Articles 4, 9 and 10). Parties are placed under an obligation to promote the exercise of children's rights (Article 12) and to encourage the use of mediation wherever possible so as to avoid recourse to judicial proceedings (Article 13).

PREAMBLE

The member States of the Council of Europe and the other States signatory hereto,

Considering that the aim of the Council of Europe is to achieve greater unity between its members;

Having regard to the United Nations Convention on the rights of the child and in particular Article 4 which requires States Parties to undertake all appropriate legislative, administrative and other measures for the implementation of the rights recognised in the said Convention;

Noting the contents of Recommendation 1121 (1990) of the Parliamentary Assembly on the rights of the child;

Convinced that the rights and best interests of children should be promoted and

---

[1] *Supra.*

[2] See: Van Bueren, G. (1996). "Protecting Children's Rights in Europe – A Test Case Strategy". EHRLR 171, and the cases cited therein.

to that end children should have the opportunity to exercise their rights, in particular in family proceedings affecting them;

Recognising that children should be provided with relevant information to enable such rights and best interests to be promoted and that due weight should be given to the views of children;

Recognising the importance of the parental role in protecting and promoting the rights and best interests of children and considering that, where necessary, states should also engage in such protection and promotion;

Considering, however, that in the event of conflict it is desirable for families to try to reach agreement before bringing the matter before a judicial authority;

Have agreed as follows:

CHAPTER I
SCOPE AND OBJECT OF THE CONVENTION AND DEFINITIONS

Article 1: Scope and object of the Convention

1   This Convention shall apply to children who have not reached the age of 18 years.
2   The object of the present Convention is, in the best interests of children, to promote their rights, to grant them procedural rights and to facilitate the exercise of these rights by ensuring that children are, themselves or through other persons or bodies, informed and allowed to participate in proceedings affecting them before a judicial authority.
3   For the purposes of this Convention proceedings before a judicial authority affecting children are family proceedings, in particular those involving the exercise of parental responsibilities such as residence and access to children.
4   Every State shall, at the time of signature or when depositing its instrument of ratification, acceptance, approval or accession, by a declaration addressed to the Secretary General of the Council of Europe, specify at least three categories of family cases before a judicial authority to which this Convention is to apply.
5   Any Party may, by further declaration, specify additional categories of family cases to which this Convention is to apply or provide information concerning the application of Article 5, paragraph 2 of Article 9, paragraph 2 of Article 10 and Article 11.
6   Nothing in this Convention shall prevent Parties from applying rules more favourable to the promotion and the exercise of children's rights.

Article 2: Definitions

For the purposes of this Convention:

a   the term "judicial authority" means a court or an administrative authority having equivalent powers;
b   the term "holders of parental responsibilities" means parents and other persons or bodies entitled to exercise some or all parental responsibilities;

c   the term "representative" means a person, such as a lawyer, or a body appointed to act before a judicial authority on behalf of a child;

d   the term "relevant information" means information which is appropriate to the age and understanding of the child, and which will be given to enable the child to exercise his or her rights fully unless the provision of such information were contrary to the welfare of the child.

CHAPTER II
PROCEDURAL MEASURES TO PROMOTE THE EXERCISE OF CHILDREN'S RIGHTS

A. Procedural rights of a child

Article 3: Right to be informed and to express his or her views in proceedings

A child considered by internal law as having sufficient understanding, in the case of proceedings before a judicial authority affecting him or her, shall be granted, and shall be entitled to request, the following rights:

a   to receive all relevant information;

b   to be consulted and express his or her views;

c   to be informed of the possible consequences of compliance with these views and the possible consequences of any decision.

Article 4: Right to apply for the appointment of a special representative

1   Subject to Article 9, the child shall have the right to apply, in person or through other persons or bodies, for a special representative in proceedings before a judicial authority affecting the child where internal law precludes the holders of parental responsibilities from representing the child as a result of a conflict of interest with the latter.

2   States are free to limit the right in paragraph 1 to children who are considered by internal law to have sufficient understanding.

Article 5: Other possible procedural rights

Parties shall consider granting children additional procedural rights in relation to proceedings before a judicial authority affecting them, in particular:

a.   the right to apply to be assisted by an appropriate person of their choice in order to help them express their views;

b.   the right to apply themselves, or through other persons or bodies, for the appointment of a separate representative, in appropriate cases a lawyer;

c.   the right to appoint their own representative;

d.   the right to exercise some or all of the rights of parties to such proceedings.

B. Role of judicial authorities

Article 6: Decision-making process

In proceedings affecting a child, the judicial authority, before taking a decision, shall:

a. consider whether it has sufficient information at its disposal in order to take a decision in the best interests of the child and, where necessary, it shall obtain further information, in particular from the holders of parental responsibilities;

b. in a case where the child is considered by internal law as having sufficient understanding:

 – ensure that the child has received all relevant information;

 – consult the child in person in appropriate cases, if necessary privately, itself or through other persons or bodies, in a manner appropriate to his or her understanding, unless this would be manifestly contrary to the best interests of the child;

 – allow the child to express his or her views;

c. give due weight to the views expressed by the child.

Article 7: Duty to act speedily

In proceedings affecting a child the judicial authority shall act speedily to avoid any unnecessary delay and procedures shall be available to ensure that its decisions are rapidly enforced. In urgent cases the judicial authority shall have the power, where appropriate, to take decisions which are immediately enforceable.

Article 8: Acting on own motion

In proceedings affecting a child the judicial authority shall have the power to act on its own motion in cases determined by internal law where the welfare of a child is in serious danger.

Article 9: Appointment of a representative

1 In proceedings affecting a child where, by internal law, the holders of parental responsibilities are precluded from representing the child as a result of a conflict of interest between them and the child, the judicial authority shall have the power to appoint a special representative for the child in those proceedings.

2 Parties shall consider providing that, in proceedings affecting a child, the judicial authority shall have the power to appoint a separate representative, in appropriate cases a lawyer, to represent the child.

C. Role of representatives

Article 10

1   In the case of proceedings before a judicial authority affecting a child the representative shall, unless this would be manifestly contrary to the best interests of the child:

    a.   provide all relevant information to the child, if the child is considered by internal law as having sufficient understanding;

    b.   provide explanations to the child if the child is considered by internal law as having sufficient understanding, concerning the possible consequences of compliance with his or her views and the possible consequences of any action by the representative;

    c.   determine the views of the child and present these views to the judicial authority.

2   Parties shall consider extending the provisions of paragraph 1 to the holders of parental responsibilities.

D. Extension of certain provisions

Article 11

Parties shall consider extending the provisions of Articles 3, 4 and 9 to proceedings affecting children before other bodies and to matters affecting children which are not the subject of proceedings.

E. National bodies

Article 12

1   Parties shall encourage, through bodies which perform, inter alia, the functions set out in paragraph 2, the promotion and the exercise of children's rights.

2   The functions are as follows:

    a.   to make proposals to strengthen the law relating to the exercise of children's rights;

    b.   to give opinions concerning draft legislation relating to the exercise of children's rights;

    c.   to provide general information concerning the exercise of children's rights to the media, the public and persons and bodies dealing with questions relating to children;

    d.   to seek the views of children and provide them with relevant information.

F. Other matters

Article 13: Mediation or other processes to resolve disputes

In order to prevent or resolve disputes or to avoid proceedings before a judicial authority affecting children, Parties shall encourage the provision of mediation or other processes to resolve disputes and the use of such processes to reach agreement in appropriate cases to be determined by Parties.

Article 14: Legal aid and advice

Where internal law provides for legal aid or advice for the representation of children in proceedings before a judicial authority affecting them, such provisions shall apply in relation to the matters covered by Articles 4 and 9.

Article 15: Relations with other international instruments

This Convention shall not restrict the application of any other international instrument which deals with specific issues arising in the context of the protection of children and families, and to which a Party to this Convention is, or becomes, a Party.

CHAPTER III
STANDING COMMITTEE

Article 16: Establishment and functions of the Standing Committee

1 A Standing Committee is set up for the purposes of this Convention.
2 The Standing Committee shall keep under review problems relating to this Convention. It may, in particular:

  a. consider any relevant questions concerning the interpretation or implementation of the Convention. The Standing Committee's conclusions concerning the implementation of the Convention may take the form of a recommendation; recommendations shall be adopted by a three-quarters majority of the votes cast;
  b. propose amendments to the Convention and examine those proposed in accordance with Article 20;
  c. provide advice and assistance to the national bodies having the functions under paragraph 2 of Article 12 and promote international co-operation between them.

Article 17: Composition

1 Each Party may be represented on the Standing Committee by one or more delegates. Each Party shall have one vote.
2 Any State referred to in Article 21, which is not a Party to this Convention,

may be represented in the Standing Committee by an observer. The same applies to any other State or to the European Community after having been invited to accede to the Convention in accordance with the provisions of Article 22.

3   Unless a Party has informed the Secretary General of its objection at least one month before the meeting, the Standing Committee may invite the following to attend as observers at all its meetings or at one meeting or part of a meeting:

- any State not referred to in paragraph 2 above;
- the United Nations Committee on the Rights of the Child;
- the European Community;
- any international governmental body;
- any international non-governmental body with one or more functions mentioned under paragraph 2 of Article 12;
- any national governmental or non-governmental body with one or more functions mentioned under paragraph 2 of Article 12.

4   The Standing Committee may exchange information with relevant organisations dealing with the exercise of children's rights.

Article 18: Meetings

1   At the end of the third year following the date of entry into force of this Convention and, on his or her own initiative, at any time after this date, the Secretary General of the Council of Europe shall invite the Standing Committee to meet.

2   Decisions may only be taken in the Standing Committee if at least one-half of the Parties are present.

3   Subject to Articles 16 and 20 the decisions of the Standing Committee shall be taken by a majority of the members present.

4   Subject to the provisions of this Convention the Standing Committee shall draw up its own rules of procedure and the rules of procedure of any working party it may set up to carry out all appropriate tasks under the Convention.

Article 19: Reports of the Standing Committee

After each meeting, the Standing Committee shall forward to the Parties and the Committee of Ministers of the Council of Europe a report on its discussions and any decisions taken.

CHAPTER IV
AMENDMENTS TO THE CONVENTION

Article 20

1   Any amendment to the articles of this Convention proposed by a Party or the Standing Committee shall be communicated to the Secretary General of the Council of Europe and forwarded by him or her, at least two months before the next meeting of the Standing Committee, to the member States of the Council of Europe, any signatory, any Party, any State invited to sign this Convention in accordance with the provisions of Article 21 and any State or the European Community invited to accede to it in accordance with the provisions of Article 22.

2   Any amendment proposed in accordance with the provisions of the preceding paragraph shall be examined by the Standing Committee which shall submit the text adopted by a three-quarters majority of the votes cast to the Committee of Ministers for approval. After its approval, this text shall be forwarded to the Parties for acceptance.

3   Any amendment shall enter into force on the first day of the month following the expiration of a period of one month after the date on which all Parties have informed the Secretary General that they have accepted it.

CHAPTER V
FINAL CLAUSES

Article 21: Signature, ratification and entry into force

1   This Convention shall be open for signature by the member States of the Council of Europe and the non-member States which have participated in its elaboration.

2   This Convention is subject to ratification, acceptance or approval. Instruments of ratification, acceptance or approval shall be deposited with the Secretary General of the Council of Europe.

3   This Convention shall enter into force on the first day of the month following the expiration of a period of three months after the date on which three States, including at least two member States of the Council of Europe, have expressed their consent to be bound by the Convention in accordance with the provisions of the preceding paragraph.

4   In respect of any signatory which subsequently expresses its consent to be bound by it, the Convention shall enter into force on the first day of the month following the expiration of a period of three months after the date of the deposit of its instrument of ratification, acceptance or approval.

Article 22: Non-member States and the European Community

1   After the entry into force of this Convention, the Committee of Ministers of the Council of Europe may, on its own initiative or following a proposal from the Standing Committee and after consultation of the Parties, invite any non-member State of the Council of Europe, which has not participated in the elaboration of the Convention, as well as the European Community to accede to this Convention by a decision taken by the majority provided for in Article 20, sub-paragraph d of the Statute of the Council of Europe, and by the unanimous vote of the representatives of the contracting States entitled to sit on the Committee of Ministers.

2   In respect of any acceding State or the European Community, the Convention shall enter into force on the first day of the month following the expiration of a period of three months after the date of deposit of the instrument of accession with the Secretary General of the Council of Europe.

Article 23: Territorial application

1   Any State may, at the time of signature or when depositing its instrument of ratification, acceptance, approval or accession, specify the territory or territories to which this Convention shall apply.

2   Any Party may, at any later date, by a declaration addressed to the Secretary General of the Council of Europe, extend the application of this Convention to any other territory specified in the declaration and for whose international relations it is responsible or on whose behalf it is authorised to give undertakings. In respect of such territory the Convention shall enter into force on the first day of the month following the expiration of a period of three months after the date of receipt of such declaration by the Secretary General.

3   Any declaration made under the two preceding paragraphs may, in respect of any territory specified in such declaration, be withdrawn by a notification addressed to the Secretary General. The withdrawal shall become effective on the first day of the month following the expiration of a period of three months after the date of receipt of such notification by the Secretary General.

Article 24: Reservations

No reservation may be made to the Convention.

Article 25: Denunciation

1   Any Party may at any time denounce this Convention by means of a notification addressed to the Secretary General of the Council of Europe.

2   Such denunciation shall become effective on the first day of the month following the expiration of a period of three months after the date of receipt of notification by the Secretary General.

Article 26: Notifications

The Secretary General of the Council of Europe shall notify the member States of the Council, any signatory, any Party and any other State or the European Community which has been invited to accede to this Convention of:

a. any signature;
b. the deposit of any instrument of ratification, acceptance, approval or accession;
c. any date of entry into force of this Convention in accordance with Articles 21 or 22;
d. any amendment adopted in accordance with Article 20 and the date on which such an amendment enters into force;
e. any declaration made under the provisions of Articles 1 and 23;
f. any denunciation made in pursuance of the provisions of Article 25;
g. any other act, notification or communication relating to this Convention.

41. UNITED NATIONS: STANDARD MINIMUM RULES FOR THE ADMINISTRATION OF JUVENILE JUSTICE ("THE BEIJING RULES")

Adopted by General Assembly resolution 40/33 (1985)

Editors' Notes

The work of the United Nations on specific instruments relating to the protection of juveniles within the criminal justice process has resulted in provisions within the Convention on the Rights of the Child and three sets of juvenile justice standards emerging within a six-year time period.[1] This work supplements those provisions set out within the International Covenant on Civil and Political Rights.[2] The Rules for the Administration of Juvenile Justice (the "Beijing Rules"), adopted by the Seventh United Nations Congress on the Prevention of Crime and the Treatment of Offenders in 1985, was the first of these measures. A proposal to have the Beijing Rules incorporated in their entirety into the Convention on the Rights of the Child was rejected during the negotiations to the Convention,[3] however their content is reflected within Article 40 of that Treaty.[4]

A central purpose of the Beijing rules is to divert the juvenile from the criminal justice process and in particular, to ensure that the juvenile is kept separate from adult proceedings (see Part 2 generally). The rules are designed to be capable of application to all legal systems (commentary to Rule 2), and include: that the age of criminal responsibility should not be set too low (Rule 4), that the sentencing of juveniles should not be out of proportion to the gravity of the offence (Rule 5.1), and that the basic rights of due process be applied to juvenile proceedings (Rule 7.1) including the presumption of innocence, the right to be notified of the charges, the right to remain silent and the right to counsel (Rule 7.1).

PART ONE
GENERAL PRINCIPLES

1. Fundamental perspectives

1.1 Member States shall seek, in conformity with their respective general interests, to further the well-being of the juvenile and her or his family.

---

[1] See also: UN Convention on the Rights of the Child, excerpted *supra*; UN Rules for the Protection of Juveniles Deprived of their Liberty, *Supra*; UN Guidelines for the Prevention of Juvenile Delinquency 1990.

[2] *Supra*. See Articles 10(2)(b) & 14(4).

[3] Cohen, C.P. (1989). "Juvenile Justice Provisions of the Draft Convention to the Rights of the Child". 7 N.Y.L. Sch. J. Hum. Rts. 1. See also: Levesque, J.R. (1996). "Future Visions of Juvenile Justice: Lessons from International and Comparative Law". 29 Creighton L.Rev. 1563.

[4] *Supra*.

1.2 Member States shall endeavour to develop conditions that will ensure for the juvenile a meaningful life when she or he is most susceptible to deviant behaviour, will foster a process of personal development and education that is as free from crime and delinquency as possible.

1.3 Sufficient attention shall be given to positive measures that involve the full mobilisation of all possible resources, including the family, volunteers and other community groups, as well as schools and other community institutions, for the purpose of promoting the well-being of the juvenile, with a view to reducing the need for intervention under the law, and of effectively, fairly and humanely dealing with the juvenile in conflict with the law.

1.4 Juvenile justice shall be conceived as an integral part of the national development process of each country, within a comprehensive framework of social justice for all juveniles, thus, at the same time, contributing to protection of the young and the maintenance of a peaceful order in society.

1.5 These Rules shall be implemented in the context of economic, social and cultural conditions prevailing in each Member State.

1.6 Juvenile justice services shall be systematically developed and co-ordinated with a view to improving and sustaining the competence of personnel involved in the services, including their methods, approaches and attitudes.

2. Scope of the Rules and definitions used

2.1 The following Standard Minimum Rules shall be applied to juvenile offenders impartially, without distinction of any kind, for example as to race, colour, sex, language, religion, political or other opinions, national or social origin, property, birth or other status.

2.2 For purposes of these Rules, the following definitions shall be applied by Member States in a manner which is compatible with their respective legal systems and concepts:

(a) A juvenile is a child or young person who, under the respective legal systems, may be dealt with for an offence in a manner which is different from an adult;

(b) An offence is any behaviour (act or omission) that is punishable by law under the respective legal systems;

(c) A juvenile offender is a child or young person who is alleged to have committed or who has been found to have committed an offence.

2.3 Efforts have been made to establish, in each national jurisdiction, a set of laws, rules and provisions specifically applicable to juvenile offenders and institutions and bodies entrusted with the functions of the administration of juvenile justice and designed:

(a) To meet the varying needs of juvenile offenders, while protecting their basic rights;

(b) To meet the needs of society;

(c) To implement the following rules thoroughly and fairly.

3. Extension of the Rules

3.1 The relevant provisions of the Rules shall be applied not only to juvenile offenders but also to juveniles who may be proceeded against for any specific behaviour that would not be punishable if committed by an adult.

3.2 Efforts shall be made to extend the principles embodied in the Rules of all juveniles who are dealt with in welfare and care proceedings.

3.3 Efforts shall also be made to extend the principles embodied in the Rules to young adult offenders.

5. Aims of juvenile justice

5.1 The juvenile justice system shall emphasise the well-being of the juvenile and shall ensure that any reaction to juvenile offenders shall always be in proportion to the circumstances of both the offenders and the offence.

6. Scope of discretion

6.1 In view of the varying special needs of juveniles as well as the variety of measures available, appropriate scope for discretion shall be allowed at all stages of proceedings and at the different levels of juvenile justice administration, including investigation, prosecution, adjudication and the follow-up of dispositions.

6.2 Efforts shall be made, however, to ensure sufficient accountability at all stages and levels in the exercise of any such discretion.

6.3 Those who exercise discretion shall be specifically qualified or trained to exercise it judiciously and in accordance with their functions and mandates.

7. Rights of juveniles

7.1 Basic procedural safeguards such as the presumption of innocence, the right to be notified of the charges, the right to remain silent, the right to counsel, the right to the presence of a parent or guardian, the right to confront and cross-examine witnesses and the right to appeal to a higher authority shall be guaranteed at all stages of proceedings.

8. Protection of privacy

8.1 The juvenile's right to privacy shall be respected at all stages in order to avoid harm being caused to her or him by undue publicity or by the process of labelling.

8.2 In principle, no information that may lead to the identification of a juvenile offender shall be published.

9. Saving clause

9.1 Nothing in these Rules shall be interpreted as precluding the application of the

Standard Minimum Rules for the Treatment of Prisoners adopted by the United Nations and other human rights instruments and standards recognized by the international community that relate to the care and protection of the young.

PART TWO
INVESTIGATION AND PROSECUTION

10. Initial contact

10.1 Upon the apprehension of a juvenile, her or his parents or guardian shall be immediately notified of such apprehension, and, where such immediate notification is not possible, the parents or guardian shall be notified within the shortest possible time thereafter.

10.2 A judge or other competent official or body shall, without delay, consider the issue of release.

10.3 Contacts between the law enforcement agencies and a juvenile offender shall be managed in such a way as to respect the legal status of the juvenile, promote the well-being of the juvenile and avoid harm to her or him, with due regard to the circumstances of the case.

11. Diversion

11.1 Consideration shall be given, wherever appropriate, to dealing with juvenile offenders without resorting to formal trial by the competent authority, referred to in rule 14.1 below.

11.2 The police, the prosecution and other agencies dealing with juvenile cases shall be empowered to dispose of such cases, at their discretion, without recourse to formal hearings, in accordance with the criteria laid down for that purpose in the respective legal system and also in accordance with the principles contained in these Rules.

11.3 Any diversion involving referral to appropriate community or other services shall require the consent of the juvenile, or her or his parents or guardian, provided that such decision to refer to case shall be subject to review by a competent authority, upon application.

11.4 In order to facilitate the discretionary disposition of juvenile cases, efforts shall be made to provide for community programmes, such as temporary supervision and guidance, restitution, and compensation of victims.

12. Specialisation within the police

12.1 In order to best fulfil their functions, police officers who frequently or exclusively deal with juveniles or who are primarily engaged in the prevention of juvenile crime shall be specially instructed and trained. In large cities, special police units should be established for that purpose.

13. Detention pending trial

13.1 Detention pending trial shall be used only as a measure of last resort and for the shortest possible period of time.

13.2 Whenever possible, detention pending trial shall be replaced by alternative measures, such as close supervision, intensive care or placement with a family or in an educational setting or home.

13.3 Juveniles under detention pending trial shall be entitled to all rights and guarantees of the Standard Minimum Rules for the Treatment of Prisoners adopted by the United Nations.

13.4 Juveniles under detention pending trial shall be kept separate from adults and shall be detained in a separate institution or in a separate part of an institution also holding adults.

13.5 While in custody, juveniles shall receive care, protection and all necessary individual assistance – social, educational, vocational, psychological, medical and physical – that they may require in view of their age, sex and personality.

PART THREE
ADJUDICATION AND DISPOSITION

14. Competent authority to adjudicate

14.1 Where the case of a juvenile offender has not been diverted (under rule 11), she or he shall be dealt with by the competent authority (court, tribunal, board, council, etc.) according to the principles of fair and just trial.

14.2 The proceedings shall be conducive to the best interests of the juvenile and shall be conducted in an atmosphere of understanding, which shall allow the juvenile to participate therein and to express herself or himself freely.

15. Legal counsel, parents and guardians

15.1 Throughout the proceedings the juvenile shall have the right to be represented by a legal adviser or to apply for free legal aid where there is provision for such aid in the country.

15.2 The parents or the guardian shall be entitled to participate in the proceedings and may be required by the competent authority to attend them in the interest of the juvenile. They may, however, be denied participation by the competent authority if there are reasons to assume that such exclusion is necessary in the interest of the juvenile.

16. Social inquiry reports

16.1 In all cases except those involving minor offences, before the competent authority renders a final disposition prior to sentencing, the background and circumstances in which the juvenile is living or the conditions under which the offence has been committed shall be properly investigated so as to facilitate judicious adjunction of the case by the competent authority.

17. Guiding principles in adjudication and disposition

17.1 The disposition of the competent authority shall be guided by the following principles:

    (a) The reaction taken shall always be in proportion not only to the circumstances and the gravity of the offence but also to the circumstances and the needs of the juvenile as well as to the needs of the society;

    (b) Restriction on the personal liberty of the juvenile shall be imposed only after careful consideration and shall be limited to the possible minimum;

    (c) Deprivation of personal liberty shall not be imposed unless the juvenile is adjudicated of a serious act involving violence against another person or of persistence in committing other serious offences and unless there is no other appropriate response;

    (d) The well-being of the juvenile shall be the guiding factor in the consideration of her of his case.

17.2 Capital punishment shall not be imposed for any crime committed by juveniles.

17.3 Juveniles shall not be subject to corporal punishment.

17.4 The competent authority shall have the power to discontinue the proceedings at any time.

18. Various disposition measures

18.1 A large variety of disposition measures shall be made available to the competent authority, following for flexibility so as to avoid institutionalisation to the greatest extent possible. Such measures, some of which may be combined, include:

    (a) Care, guidance and supervision orders;

    (b) Probation;

    (c) Community service orders;

    (d) Financial penalties, compensation and restitution;

    (e) Intermediate treatment and other treatment orders;

    (f) Order to participate in group counselling and similar activities;

    (g) Orders concerning foster care, living communities or other educational settings;

    (h) Other relevant orders.

18.2 No juvenile shall be removed from parental supervision, whether partly or entirely, unless the circumstances of her or his case make this necessary.

19. Least possible use of institutionalisation

19.1 The placement of a juvenile in an institution shall always be a disposition of last resort and for the minimum necessary period.

20. Avoidance of unnecessary delay

20.1 Each case shall from the outset be handled expeditiously, without any unnecessary delay.

21. Records

21.1 Records of juvenile offenders shall be kept strictly confidential and closed to third parties. Access to such records shall be limited to persons directly concerned with the disposition of the case at hand or other duly authorised persons.

21.2 Records of juvenile offenders shall not be used in adult proceedings in subsequent cases involving the same offender.

22. Need for professionalism and training

22.1 Professional education, in-service training, refresher courses and other appropriate modes of instruction shall be utilised to establish and maintain the necessary professional competence of all personnel dealing with juvenile cases.

22.2 Juvenile justice personnel shall reflect the diversity of juveniles who come into contact with the juvenile justice system. Efforts shall be made to ensure the fair representation of women and minorities in juvenile justice agencies.

PART FOUR
NON-INSTITUTIONAL TREATMENT

23. Effective implementation of disposition

23.1 Appropriate provisions shall be made for the implementation of orders of the competent authority, as referred to in rule 14.1 above, by that authority itself or by some other authority as circumstances may require.

23.2 Such provisions shall include the power to modify the orders as the competent authority may deem necessary from time to time, provided that such modification shall be determined in accordance with the principles contained in these Rules.

24. Provision of needed assistance

24.1 Efforts shall be made to provide juveniles, at all stages of the proceedings, with necessary assistance such as lodging, education or vocational training, employment or any other assistance, helpful and practical, in order to facilitate the rehabilitative process.

25. Mobilisation of volunteers and other community services

25.1 Volunteers, voluntary organisations, local institutions and other community resources shall be called upon to contribute effectively to the rehabilitation of the juvenile in a community setting and, as far as possible, within the family unit.

PART FIVE
INSTITUTIONAL TREATMENT

26. Objectives of institutional treatment

26.1 The objective of training and treatment of juveniles placed in institutions is to provide care, protection, education and vocational skills, with a view to assisting them to assume socially constructive and productive roles in society.

26.2 Juveniles in institutions shall receive care, protection and all necessary assistance — social, educational, vocational, psychological, medical and physical — that they may require because of their age, sex, and personality and in the interest of their wholesome development.

26.3 Juveniles in institutions shall be kept separate from adults and shall be detained in a separate institution or in a separate part of an institution also holding adults.

26.4 Young female offenders placed in an institution deserve special attention as to their personal needs and problems. They shall by no means receive less care, protection, assistance, treatment and training than young male offenders. Their fair treatment shall be ensured.

26.5 In the interest and well-being of the institutionalised juvenile, the parents or guardians shall have a right to access.

26.6 Inter-ministerial and inter-departmental co-operation shall be fostered for the purpose of providing adequate academic or, as appropriate, vocational training to institutionalised juveniles, with a view to ensuring that they do not leave the institution at an educational disadvantage.

27. Application of the Standard Minimum Rules for the Treatment of Prisoners adopted by the United Nations

27.1 The Standard Minimum Rules for the Treatment of Prisoners and related recommendations shall be applicable as far as relevant to the treatment of juvenile offenders in institutions, including those in detention pending adjudication.

27.2 Efforts shall be made to implement the relevant principles laid down in the Standard Minimum Rules for the Treatment of Prisoners to the largest possible extent so as to meet the varying needs of juveniles specific to their age, sex and personality.

28. Frequent and early recourse to conditional release

28.1 Conditional release from an institution shall be used by the appropriate authority to the greatest possible extent, and shall be granted at the earliest possible time.

28.2 Juveniles released conditionally from an institution shall be assisted and supervised by an appropriate authority and shall receive full support by the community.

29. Semi-institutional arrangements

29.1 Efforts shall be made to provide semi-institutional arrangements, such as half-way house, educational homes, day-time training centres and other such appropriate arrangements that may assist juveniles in their proper reintegration into society.

PART SIX
RESEARCH, PLANNING, POLICY FORMULATION AND EVALUATION

30. Research as a basis for planning, policy formulation and evaluation

30.1 Efforts shall be made to organise and promote necessary research as a basis for effective planning and policy formulation.

30.2 Efforts shall be made to review and appraise periodically the trends, problems and causes of juvenile delinquency and crime as well as the varying particular needs of juveniles in custody.

30.3 Efforts shall be made to establish a regular evaluative research mechanism built into the system of juvenile justice administration and to collect and analyse relevant data and information for appropriate assessment and future improvement and reform of the administration.

30.4 The delivery of services in juvenile justice administration shall be systematically planned and implemented as an integral part of national development efforts.

42. UNITED NATIONS: GENERAL ASSEMBLY RESOLUTION ON UN RULES FOR THE PROTECTION OF JUVENILES DEPRIVED OF THEIR LIBERTY

Adopted by the General Assembly resolution 45/113 (1990)

Editors' Notes

While a central aim of the Beijing Rules[1] is to divert juveniles from the criminal justice system where possible,[2] the Rules for the Protection of Juveniles Deprived of their Liberty were adopted in recognition of the reality that in many instances, juveniles around the world are placed in detention. Rule 2 emphasises the premise that juveniles should only lose their liberty as a measure of "last resort". Section C of the rules relating to "Classification and Placement" reiterate the principle of separating juvenile offenders from adults.[3] The standards set out elsewhere within the Rules are to some degree based on those within the Standard Minimum Rules for the Treatment of Prisoners.[4]

The General Assembly,

Bearing in mind the Universal Declaration of Human Rights, the International Covenant on Civil and Political Rights, the Convention against Torture and Other Cruel, Inhuman or Degrading Treatment or Punishment and the Convention on the Rights of the Child, as well as other international instruments relating to the protection of the rights and well-being of young persons,

Bearing in mind also the Standard Minimum Rules for the Treatment of Prisoners adopted by the First United Nations Congress on the Prevention of Crime and the Treatment of Offenders,

Bearing in mind further the Body of Principles for the Protection of All Persons under Any Form of Detention or Imprisonment, approved by the General Assembly by its resolution 43/173 of 9 December 1988 and contained in the annex thereto,

Recalling the United Nations Standard Minimum Rules for the Administration of Juvenile Justice (The Beijing Rules),

Recalling also resolution 21 of the Seventh United Nations Congress on the Prevention of Crime and the Treatment of Offenders, in which the Congress called for the development of rules for the protection of juveniles deprived of their liberty,

Recalling further that the Economic and Social Council, in section II of its

---

[1] UN Standard Minimum Rules for the Administration of Juvenile Justice, *supra.*

[2] See also the social policies set out in the United Nations Guidelines for the Prevention of Juvenile Delinquency 1990 (the "Riyadh Guidelines").

[3] See: UN Standard Minimum Rules for the Administration of Juvenile Justice, Part 2 generally, *supra.*

[4] *Supra.*

resolution 1986/10 of 21 May 1986, requested the Secretary-General to report on progress achieved in the development of the rules to the Committee on Crime Prevention and Control at its tenth session and requested the Eighth United Nations Congress on the Prevention of Crime and the Treatment of Offenders to consider the proposed rules with a view to their adoption,

Alarmed at the conditions and circumstances under which juveniles are being deprived of their liberty world wide,

Aware that juveniles deprived of their liberty are highly vulnerable to abuse, victimization and the violation of their rights,

Concerned that many systems do not differentiate between adults and juveniles at various stages of the administration of justice and that juveniles are therefore being held in gaols and facilities with adults,

1. Affirms that the placement of a juvenile in an institution should always be a disposition of last resort and for the minimum necessary period;
2. Recognises that, because of their high vulnerability, juveniles deprived of their liberty require special attention and protection and that their rights and well-being should be guaranteed during and after the period when they are deprived of their liberty;
3. Notes with appreciation the valuable work of the Secretariat and the collaboration which has been established between the Secretariat and experts, practitioners, intergovernmental organizations, the non-governmental community, particularly Amnesty International, Defence for Children International and Radda Barnen International (Swedish Save the Children Federation), and scientific institutions concerned with the rights of children and juvenile justice in the development of the United Nations draft Rules for the Protection of Juveniles Deprived of their Liberty;
4. Adopts the United Nations Rules for the Protection of Juveniles Deprived of their Liberty contained in the annex to the present resolution;
5. Calls upon the Committee on Crime Prevention and Control to formulate measures for the effective implementation of the Rules, with the assistance of the United Nations institutes on the prevention of crime and the treatment of offenders;
6. Invites Member States to adapt, wherever necessary, their national legislation, policies and practices, particularly in the training of all categories of juvenile justice personnel, to the spirit of the Rules, and to bring them to the attention of relevant authorities and the public in general;
7. Also invites Member States to inform the Secretary-General of their efforts to apply the Rules in law, policy and practice and to report regularly to the Committee on Crime Prevention and Control on the results achieved in their implementation;
8. Requests the Secretary-General and invites Member States to ensure the widest possible dissemination of the text of the Rules in all of the official languages of the United Nations;
9. Requests the Secretary-General to conduct comparative research, pursue the requisite collaboration and devise strategies to deal with the different categories of serious and persistent young offenders, and to prepare a policy-

oriented report thereon for submission to the Ninth United Nations Congress on the Prevention of Crime and the Treatment of Offenders;

10. Also requests the Secretary-General and urges Member States to allocate the necessary resources to ensure the successful application and implementation of the Rules, in particular in the areas of recruitment, training and exchange of all categories of juvenile justice personnel;

11. Urges all relevant bodies of the United Nations system, in particular the United Nations Children's Fund, the regional commissions and specialized agencies, the United Nations institutes for the prevention of crime and the treatment of offenders and all concerned intergovernmental and non-governmental organizations, to collaborate with the Secretary-General and to take the necessary measures to ensure a concerted and sustained effort within their respective fields of technical competence to promote the application of the Rules;

12. Invites the Sub-Commission on Prevention of Discrimination and Protection of Minorities of the Commission on Human Rights to consider this new international instrument, with a view to promoting the application of its provisions;

13. Requests the Ninth Congress to review the progress made on the promotion and application of the Rules and on the recommendations contained in the present resolution, under a separate agenda item on juvenile justice.

68TH PLENARY MEETING 14 DECEMBER 1990

ANNEX

UNITED NATIONS RULES FOR THE PROTECTION OF JUVENILES DEPRIVED OF THEIR LIBERTY

I FUNDAMENTAL PERSPECTIVES

1. The juvenile justice system should uphold the rights and safety and promote the physical and mental well-being of juveniles. Imprisonment should be used as a last resort.

2. Juveniles should only be deprived of their liberty in accordance with the principles and procedures set forth in these Rules and in the United Nations Standard Minimum Rules for the Administration of Juvenile Justice (The Beijing Rules). Deprivation of the liberty of a juvenile should be a disposition of last resort and for the minimum necessary period and should be limited to exceptional cases. The length of the sanction should be determined by the judicial authority, without precluding the possibility of his or her early release.

3. The Rules are intended to establish minimum standards accepted by the United Nations for the protection of juveniles deprived of their liberty in all forms, consistent with human rights and fundamental freedoms, with a view to

counteracting the detrimental effects of all types of detention and to fostering integration in society.

4. The Rules should be applied impartially, without discrimination of any kind as to race, colour, sex, age, language, religion, nationality, political or other opinion, cultural beliefs or practices, property, birth or family status, ethnic or social origin, and disability. The religious and cultural beliefs, practices and moral concepts of the juvenile should be respected.

5. The Rules are designed to serve as convenient standards of reference and to provide encouragement and guidance to professionals involved in the management of the juvenile justice system.

6. The Rules should be made readily available to juvenile justice personnel in their national languages. Juveniles who are not fluent in the language spoken by the personnel of the detention facility should have the right to the services of an interpreter free of charge whenever necessary, in particular during medical examinations and disciplinary proceedings.

7. Where appropriate, States should incorporate the Rules into their legislation or amend it accordingly and provide effective remedies for their breach, including compensation when injuries are inflicted on juveniles. States should also monitor the application of the Rules.

8. The competent authorities should constantly seek to increase the awareness of the public that the care of detained juveniles and preparation for their return to society is a social service of great importance, and to this end active steps should be taken to foster open contacts between the juveniles and the local community.

9. Nothing in the Rules should be interpreted as precluding the application of the relevant United Nations and human rights instruments and standards, recognized by the international community, that are more conducive to ensuring the rights, care and protection of juveniles, children and all young persons.

10. In the event that the practical application of particular Rules contained in sections II to V, inclusive, presents any conflict with the Rules contained in the present section, compliance with the latter shall be regarded as the predominant requirement.

II. SCOPE AND APPLICATION OF THE RULES

11. For the purposes of the Rules, the following definitions should apply:

    (a) A juvenile is every person under the age of 18. The age limit below which it should not be permitted to deprive a child of his or her liberty should be determined by law;

    (b) The deprivation of liberty means any form of detention or imprisonment or the placement of a person in a public or private custodial setting, from which this person is not permitted to leave at will, by order of any judicial, administrative or other public authority.

12. The deprivation of liberty should be effected in conditions and circumstances which ensure respect for the human rights of juveniles. Juveniles detained in facilities should be guaranteed the benefit of meaningful activities and programmes which would serve to promote and sustain their health and self-respect, to foster their sense of responsibility and encourage those attitudes and skills that will assist them in developing their potential as members of society.
13. Juveniles deprived of their liberty shall not for any reason related to their status be denied the civil, economic, political, social or cultural rights to which they are entitled under national or international law, and which are compatible with the deprivation of liberty.
14. The protection of the individual rights of juveniles with special regard to the legality of the execution of the detention measures shall be ensured by the competent authority, while the objectives of social integration should be secured by regular inspections and other means of control carried out, according to international standards, national laws and regulations, by a duly constituted body authorised to visit the juveniles and not belonging to the detention facility.
15. The Rules apply to all types and forms of detention facilities in which juveniles are deprived of their liberty. Sections I, II, IV and V of the Rules apply to all detention facilities and institutional settings in which juveniles are detained, and section III applies specifically to juveniles under arrest or awaiting trial.
16. The Rules shall be implemented in the context of the economic, social and cultural conditions prevailing in each Member State.

III. JUVENILES UNDER ARREST OR AWAITING TRIAL

17. Juveniles who are detained under arrest or awaiting trial ("untried") are presumed innocent and shall be treated as such. Detention before trial shall be avoided to the extent possible and limited to exceptional circumstances. Therefore, all efforts shall be made to apply alternative measures. When preventive detention is nevertheless used, juvenile courts and investigative bodies shall give the highest priority to the most expeditious processing of such cases to ensure the shortest possible duration of detention. Untried detainees should be separated from convicted juveniles.
18. The conditions under which an untried juvenile is detained should be consistent with the rules set out below, with additional specific provisions as are necessary and appropriate, given the requirements of the presumption of innocence, the duration of the detention and the legal status and circumstances of the juvenile. These provisions would include, but not necessarily be restricted to, the following:

    (a) Juveniles should have the right of legal counsel and be enabled to apply for free legal aid, where such aid is available, and to communicate regularly with their legal advisers. Privacy and confidentiality shall be ensured for such communications;

(b) Juveniles should be provided, where possible, with opportunities to pursue work, with remuneration, and continue education or training, but should not be required to do so. Work, education or training should not cause the continuation of the detention;

(c) Juveniles should receive and retain materials for their leisure and recreation as are compatible with the interests of the administration of justice.

IV. THE MANAGEMENT OF JUVENILE FACILITIES

A. Records

19. All reports, including legal records, medical records and records of disciplinary proceedings, and all other documents relating to the form, content and details of treatment, should be placed in a confidential individual file, which should be kept up to date, accessible only to authorised persons and classified in such a way as to be easily understood. Where possible, every juvenile should have the right to contest any fact or opinion contained in his or her file so as to permit rectification of inaccurate, unfounded or unfair statements. In order to exercise this right, there should be procedures that allow an appropriate third party to have access to and to consult the file on request. Upon release, the records of juveniles shall be sealed, and, at an appropriate time, expunged.

20. No juvenile should be received in any detention facility without a valid commitment order of a judicial, administrative or other public authority. The details of this order should be immediately entered in the register. No juvenile should be detained in any facility where there is no such register.

B. Admission, registration, movement and transfer

21. In every place where juveniles are detained, a complete and secure record of the following information should be kept concerning each juvenile received:

(a) Information on the identity of the juvenile;

(b) The fact of and reasons for commitment and the authority therefor;

(c) The day and hour of admission, transfer and release;

(d) Details of the notifications to parents and guardians on every admission, transfer or release of the juvenile in their care at the time of commitment;

(e) Details of known physical and mental health problems, including drug and alcohol abuse.

22. The information on admission, place, transfer and release should be provided without delay to the parents and guardians or closest relative of the juvenile concerned.

23. As soon as possible after reception, full reports and relevant information on the personal situation and circumstances of each juvenile should be drawn up and submitted to the administration.

24. On admission, all juveniles shall be given a copy of the rules governing the detention facility and a written description of their rights and obligations in a language they can understand, together with the address of the authorities competent to receive complaints, as well as the address of public or private agencies and organizations which provide legal assistance. For those juveniles who are illiterate or who cannot understand the language in the written form, the information should be conveyed in a manner enabling full comprehension.

25. All juveniles should be helped to understand the regulations governing the internal organization of the facility, the goals and methodology of the care provided, the disciplinary requirements and procedures, other authorised methods of seeking information and of making complaints, and all such other matters as are necessary to enable them to understand fully their rights and obligations during detention.

26. The transport of juveniles should be carried out at the expense of the administration in conveyances with adequate ventilation and light, in conditions that should in no way subject them to hardship or indignity. Juveniles should not be transferred from one facility to another arbitrarily.

C. Classification and placement

27. As soon as possible after the moment of admission, each juvenile should be interviewed, and a psychological and social report identifying any factors relevant to the specific type and level of care and programme required by the juvenile should be prepared. This report, together with the report prepared by a medical officer who has examined the juvenile upon admission, should be forwarded to the director for purposes of determining the most appropriate placement for the juvenile within the facility and the specific type and level of care and programme required and to be pursued. When special rehabilitative treatment is required, and the length of stay in the facility permits, trained personnel of the facility should prepare a written, individualized treatment plan specifying treatment objectives and time-frame and the means, stages and delays with which the objectives should be approached.

28. The detention of juveniles should only take place under conditions that take full account of their particular needs, status and special requirements according to their age, personality, sex and type of offence, as well as mental and physical health, and which ensure their protection from harmful influences and risk situations. The principal criterion for the separation of different categories of juveniles deprived of their liberty should be the provision of the type of care best suited to the particular needs of the individuals concerned and the protection of their physical, mental and moral integrity and well-being.

29. In all detention facilities juveniles should be separated from adults, unless they are members of the same family. Under controlled conditions, juveniles may be brought together with carefully selected adults as part of a special programme that has been shown to be beneficial for the juveniles concerned.

30. Open detention facilities for juveniles should be established. Open detention facilities are those with no or minimal security measures. The population in such detention facilities should be as small as possible. The number of

juveniles detained in closed facilities should be small enough to enable individualized treatment. Detention facilities for juveniles should be decentralised and of such size as to facilitate access and contact between the juveniles and their families. Small-scale detention facilities should be established and integrated into the social, economic and cultural environment of the community.

D. Physical environment and accommodation

31. Juveniles deprived of their liberty have the right to facilities and services that meet all the requirements of health and human dignity.
32. The design of detention facilities for juveniles and the physical environment should be in keeping with the rehabilitative aim of residential treatment, with due regard to the need of the juvenile for privacy, sensory stimuli, opportunities for association with peers and participation in sports, physical exercise and leisure-time activities. The design and structure of juvenile detention facilities should be such as to minimise the risk of fire and to ensure safe evacuation from the premises. There should be an effective alarm system in case of fire, as well as formal and drilled procedures to ensure the safety of the juveniles. Detention facilities should not be located in areas where there are known health or other hazards or risks.
33. Sleeping accommodation should normally consist of small group dormitories or individual bedrooms, account being taken of local standards. During sleeping hours there should be regular, unobtrusive supervision of all sleeping areas, including individual rooms and group dormitories, in order to ensure the protection of each juvenile. Every juvenile should, in accordance with local or national standards, be provided with separate and sufficient bedding, which should be clean when issued, kept in good order and changed often enough to ensure cleanliness.
34. Sanitary installations should be so located and of a sufficient standard to enable every juvenile to comply, as required, with their physical needs in privacy and in a clean and decent manner.
35. The possession of personal effects is a basic element of the right to privacy and essential to the psychological well-being of the juvenile. The right of every juvenile to possess personal effects and to have adequate storage facilities for them should be fully recognized and respected. Personal effects that the juvenile does not choose to retain or that are confiscated should be placed in safe custody. An inventory thereof should be signed by the juvenile. Steps should be taken to keep them in good condition. All such articles and money should be returned to the juvenile on release, except in so far as he or she has been authorised to spend money or send such property out of the facility. If a juvenile receives or is found in possession of any medicine, the medical officer should decide what use should be made of it.
36. To the extent possible juveniles should have the right to use their own clothing. Detention facilities should ensure that each juvenile has personal clothing suitable for the climate and adequate to ensure good health, and which should in no manner be degrading or humiliating. Juveniles removed

from or leaving a facility for any purpose should be allowed to wear their own clothing.

37. Every detention facility shall ensure that every juvenile receives food that is suitably prepared and presented at normal meal times and of a quality and quantity to satisfy the standards of dietetics, hygiene and health and, as far as possible, religious and cultural requirements. Clean drinking water should be available to every juvenile at any time.

E. Education, vocational training and work

38. Every juvenile of compulsory school age has the right to education suited to his or her needs and abilities and designed to prepare him or her for return to society. Such education should be provided outside the detention facility in community schools wherever possible and, in any case, by qualified teachers through programmes integrated with the education system of the country so that, after release, juveniles may continue their education without difficulty. Special attention should be given by the administration of the detention facilities to the education of juveniles of foreign origin or with particular cultural or ethnic needs. Juveniles who are illiterate or have cognitive or learning difficulties should have the right to special education.

39. Juveniles above compulsory school age who wish to continue their education should be permitted and encouraged to do so, and every effort should be made to provide them with access to appropriate educational programmes.

40. Diplomas or educational certificates awarded to juveniles while in detention should not indicate in any way that the juvenile has been institutionalized.

41. Every detention facility should provide access to a library that is adequately stocked with both instructional and recreational books and periodicals suitable for the juveniles, who should be encouraged and enabled to make full use of it.

42. Every juvenile should have the right to receive vocational training in occupations likely to prepare him or her for future employment.

43. With due regard to proper vocational selection and to the requirements of institutional administration, juveniles should be able to choose the type of work they wish to perform.

44. All protective national and international standards applicable to child labour and young workers should apply to juveniles deprived of their liberty.

45. Wherever possible, juveniles should be provided with the opportunity to perform remunerated labour, if possible within the local community, as a complement to the vocational training provided in order to enhance the possibility of finding suitable employment when they return to their communities. The type of work should be such as to provide appropriate training that will be of benefit to the juveniles following release. The organization and methods of work offered in detention facilities should resemble as closely as possible those of similar work in the community, so as to prepare juveniles for the conditions of normal occupational life.

46. Every juvenile who performs work should have the right to an equitable remuneration. The interests of the juveniles and of their vocational training should not be subordinated to the purpose of making a profit for the detention

facility or a third party. Part of the earnings of a juvenile should normally be set aside to constitute a savings fund to be handed over to the juvenile on release. The juvenile should have the right to use the remainder of those earnings to purchase articles for his or her own use or to indemnify the victim injured by his or her offence or to send it to his or her family or other persons outside the detention facility.

F. Recreation

47. Every juvenile should have the right to a suitable amount of time for daily free exercise, in the open air whenever weather permits, during which time appropriate recreational and physical training should normally be provided. Adequate space, installations and equipment should be provided for these activities. Every juvenile should have additional time for daily leisure activities, part of which should be devoted, if the juvenile so wishes, to arts and crafts skill development. The detention facility should ensure that each juvenile is physically able to participate in the available programmes of physical education. Remedial physical education and therapy should be offered, under medical supervision, to juveniles needing it.

G. Religion

48. Every juvenile should be allowed to satisfy the needs or his or her religious and spiritual life, in particular by attending the services or meetings provided in the detention facility or by conducting his or her own services and having possession of the necessary books or items of religious observance and instruction of his or her denomination. If a detention facility contains a sufficient number of juveniles of a given religion, one or more qualified representatives of that religion should be appointed or approved and allowed to hold regular services and to pay pastoral visits in private to juveniles at their request. Every juvenile should have the right to receive visits from a qualified representative of any religion of his or her choice, as well as the right not to participate in religious services and freely to decline religious education, counselling or indoctrination.

H. Medical care

49. Every juvenile shall receive adequate medical care, both preventive and remedial, including dental, ophthalmological and mental health care, as well as pharmaceutical products and special diets as medically indicated. All such medical care should, where possible, be provided to detained juveniles through the appropriate health facilities and services of the community in which the detention facility is located, in order to prevent stigmatization of the juvenile and promote self-respect and integration into the community.

50. Every juvenile has a right to be examined by a physician immediately upon admission to a detention facility, for the purpose of recording any evidence of

prior ill-treatment and identifying any physical or mental condition requiring medical attention.

51. The medical services provided to juveniles should seek to detect and should treat any physical or mental illness, substance abuse or other condition that may hinder the integration of the juvenile into society. Every detention facility for juveniles should have immediate access to adequate medical facilities and equipment appropriate to the number and requirements of its residents and staff trained in preventive health care and the handling of medical emergencies. Every juvenile who is ill, who complains of illness or who demonstrates symptoms of physical or mental difficulties, should be examined promptly by a medical officer.

52. Any medical officer who has reason to believe that the physical or mental health of a juvenile has been or will be injuriously affected by continued detention, a hunger strike or any condition of detention should report this fact immediately to the director of the detention facility in question and to the independent authority responsible for safeguarding the well-being of the juvenile.

53. A juvenile who is suffering from mental illness should be treated in a specialised institution under independent medical management. Steps should be taken, by arrangement with appropriate agencies, to ensure any necessary continuation of mental health care after release.

54. Juvenile detention facilities should adopt specialized drug abuse prevention and rehabilitation programmes administered by qualified personnel. These programmes should be adapted to the age, sex and other requirements of the juveniles concerned, and detoxification facilities and services staffed by trained personnel should be available to drug- or alcohol-dependent juveniles.

55. Medicines should be administered only for necessary treatment on medical grounds and, when possible, after having obtained the informed consent of the juvenile concerned. In particular, they must not be administered with a view to eliciting information or a confession, as a punishment or as a means of restraint. Juveniles shall never be testees in the experimental use of drugs and treatment. The administration of any drug should always be authorised and carried out by qualified medical personnel.

I. Notification of illness, injury and death

56. The family or guardian of a juvenile and any other person designated by the juvenile have the right to be informed of the state of health of the juvenile on request and in the event of any important changes in the health of the juvenile. The director of the detention facility should notify immediately the family or guardian of the juvenile concerned, or other designated person, in case of death, illness requiring transfer of the juvenile to an outside medical facility, or a condition requiring clinical care within the detention facility for more than 48 hours. Notification should also be given to the consular authorities of the State of which a foreign juvenile is a citizen.

57. Upon the death of a juvenile during the period of deprivation of liberty, the nearest relative should have the right to inspect the death certificate, see the

body and determine the method of disposal of the body. Upon the death of a juvenile in detention, there should be an independent inquiry into the causes of death, the report of which should be made accessible to the nearest relative. This inquiry should also be made when the death of a juvenile occurs within six months from the date of his or her release from the detention facility and there is reason to believe that the death is related to the period of detention.

58. A juvenile should be informed at the earliest possible time of the death, serious illness or injury of any immediate family member and should be provided with the opportunity to attend the funeral of the deceased or go to the bedside of a critically ill relative.

J. Contacts with the wider community

59. Every means should be provided to ensure that juveniles have adequate communication with the outside world, which is an integral part of the right to fair and humane treatment and is essential to the preparation of juveniles for their return to society. Juveniles should be allowed to communicate with their families, friends and other persons or representatives of reputable outside organizations, to leave detention facilities for a visit to their home and family and to receive special permission to leave the detention facility for educational, vocational or other important reasons. Should the juvenile be serving a sentence, the time spent outside a detention facility should be counted as part of the period of sentence.

60. Every juvenile should have the right to receive regular and frequent visits, in principle once a week and not less than once a month, in circumstances that respect the need of the juvenile for privacy, contact and unrestricted communication with the family and the defence counsel.

61. Every juvenile should have the right to communicate in writing or by telephone at least twice a week with the person of his or her choice, unless legally restricted, and should be assisted as necessary in order effectively to enjoy this right. Every juvenile should have the right to receive correspondence.

62. Juveniles should have the opportunity to keep themselves informed regularly of the news by reading newspapers, periodicals and other publications, through access to radio and television programmes and motion pictures, and through the visits of the representatives of any lawful club or organization in which the juvenile is interested.

K. Limitations of physical restraint and the use of force

63. Recourse to instruments of restraint and to force for any purpose should be prohibited, except as set forth in rule 64 below.

64. Instruments of restraint and force can only be used in exceptional cases, where all other control methods have been exhausted and failed, and only as explicitly authorised and specified by law and regulation. They should not cause humiliation or degradation, and should be used restrictively and only for the shortest possible period of time. By order of the director of the

administration, such instruments might be resorted to in order to prevent the juvenile from inflicting self-injury, injuries to others or serious destruction of property. In such instances, the director should at once consult medical and other relevant personnel and report to the higher administrative authority.

65. The carrying and use of weapons by personnel should be prohibited in any facility where juveniles are detained.

L. Disciplinary procedures

66. Any disciplinary measures and procedures should maintain the interest of safety and an ordered community life and should be consistent with the upholding of the inherent dignity of the juvenile and the fundamental objective of institutional care, namely, instilling a sense of justice, self-respect and respect for the basic rights of every person.

67. All disciplinary measures constituting cruel, inhuman or degrading treatment shall be strictly prohibited, including corporal punishment, placement in a dark cell, closed or solitary confinement or any other punishment that may compromise the physical or mental health of the juvenile concerned. The reduction of diet and the restriction or denial of contact with family members should be prohibited for any purpose. Labour should always be viewed as an educational tool and a means of promoting the self-respect of the juvenile in preparing him or her for return to the community and should not be imposed as a disciplinary sanction. No juvenile should be sanctioned more than once for the same disciplinary infraction. Collective sanctions should be prohibited.

68. Legislation or regulations adopted by the competent administrative authority should establish norms concerning the following, taking full account of the fundamental characteristics, needs and rights of juveniles:

   (a) Conduct constituting a disciplinary offence;
   (b) Type and duration of disciplinary sanctions that may be inflicted;
   (c) The authority competent to impose such sanctions;
   (d) The authority competent to consider appeals.

69. A report of misconduct should be presented promptly to the competent authority, which should decide on it without undue delay. The competent authority should conduct a thorough examination of the case.

70. No juvenile should be disciplinary sanctioned except in strict accordance with the terms of the law and regulations in force. No juvenile should be sanctioned unless he or she has been informed of the alleged infraction in a manner appropriate to the full understanding of the juvenile, and given a proper opportunity of presenting his or her defence, including the right of appeal to a competent impartial authority. Complete records should be kept of all disciplinary proceedings.

71. No juveniles should be responsible for disciplinary functions except in the supervision of specified social, educational or sports activities or in self-government programmes.

M. Inspection and complaints

72. Qualified inspectors or an equivalent duly constituted authority not belonging to the administration of the facility should be empowered to conduct inspections on a regular basis and to undertake unannounced inspections on their own initiative, and should enjoy full guarantees of independence in the exercise of this function. Inspectors should have unrestricted access to all persons employed by or working in any facility where juveniles are or may be deprived of their liberty, to all juveniles and to all records of such facilities.

73. Qualified medical officers attached to the inspecting authority or the public health service should participate in the inspections, evaluating compliance with the rules concerning the physical environment, hygiene, accommodation, food, exercise and medical services, as well as any other aspect or conditions of institutional life that affect the physical and mental health of juveniles. Every juvenile should have the right to talk in confidence to any inspecting officer.

74. After completing the inspection, the inspector should be required to submit a report on the findings. The report should include an evaluation of the compliance of the detention facilities with the present rules and relevant provisions of national law, and recommendations regarding any steps considered necessary to ensure compliance with them. Any facts discovered by an inspector that appear to indicate that a violation of legal provisions concerning the rights of juveniles or the operation of a juvenile detention facility has occurred should be communicated to the competent authorities for investigation and prosecution.

75. Every juvenile should have the opportunity of making requests or complaints to the director of the detention facility and to his or her authorised representative.

76. Every juvenile should have the right to make a request or complaint, without censorship as to substance, to the central administration, the judicial authority or other proper authorities through approved channels, and to be informed of the response without delay.

77. Efforts should be made to establish an independent office (ombudsman) to receive and investigate complaints made by juveniles deprived of their liberty and to assist in the achievement of equitable settlements.

78. Every juvenile should have the right to request assistance from family members, legal counsellors, humanitarian groups or others where possible, in order to make a complaint. Illiterate juveniles should be provided with assistance should they need to use the services of public or private agencies and organizations which provide legal counsel or which are competent to receive complaints.

N. Return to the community

79. All juveniles should benefit from arrangements designed to assist them in returning to society, family life, education or employment after release. Procedures, including early release, and special courses should be devised to this end.

80. Competent authorities should provide or ensure services to assist juveniles in re-establishing themselves in society and to lessen prejudice against such juveniles. These services should ensure, to the extent possible, that the juvenile is provided with suitable residence, employment, clothing, and sufficient means to maintain himself or herself upon release in order to facilitate successful reintegration. The representatives of agencies providing such services should be consulted and should have access to juveniles while detained, with a view to assisting them in their return to the community.

V. Personnel

81. Personnel should be qualified and include a sufficient number of specialists such as educators, vocational instructors, counsellors, social workers, psychiatrists and psychologists. These and other specialist staff should normally be employed on a permanent basis. This should not preclude part-time or volunteer workers when the level of support and training they can provide is appropriate and beneficial. Detention facilities should make use of all remedial, educational, moral, spiritual, and other resources and forms of assistance that are appropriate and available in the community, according to the individual needs and problems of detained juveniles.

82. The administration should provide for the careful selection and recruitment of every grade and type of personnel, since the proper management of detention facilities depends on their integrity, humanity, ability and professional capacity to deal with juveniles, as well as personal suitability for the work.

83. To secure the foregoing ends, personnel should be appointed as professional officers with adequate remuneration to attract and retain suitable women and men. The personnel of juvenile detention facilities should be continually encouraged to fulfil their duties and obligations in a humane, committed, professional, fair and efficient manner, to conduct themselves at all times in such a way as to deserve and gain the respect of the juveniles, and to provide juveniles with a positive role model and perspective.

84. The administration should introduce forms of organization and management that facilitate communications between different categories of staff in each detention facility so as to enhance co-operation between the various services engaged in the care of juveniles, as well as between staff and the administration, with a view to ensuring that staff directly in contact with juveniles are able to function in conditions favourable to the efficient fulfilment of their duties.

85. The personnel should receive such training as will enable them to carry out their responsibilities effectively, in particular training in child psychology, child welfare and international standards and norms of human rights and the rights of the child, including the present rules. The personnel should maintain and improve their knowledge and professional capacity by attending courses of in-service training, to be organised at suitable intervals throughout their career.

86. The director of a facility should be adequately qualified for his or her task, with administrative ability and suitable training and experience, and should carry out his or her duties on a full-time basis.

87. In the performance of their duties, personnel of detention facilities should respect and protect the human dignity and fundamental human rights of all juveniles, in particular, as follows:

    (a) No member of the detention facility or institutional personnel may inflict, instigate or tolerate any act of torture or any form of harsh, cruel, inhuman or degrading treatment, punishment, correction or discipline under any pretext or circumstance whatsoever;

    (b) All personnel should rigorously oppose and combat any act of corruption, reporting it without delay to the competent authorities;

    (c) All personnel should respect the present Rules. Personnel who have reason to believe that a serious violation of the present Rules has occurred or is about to occur should report the matter to their superior authorities or organs vested with reviewing or remedial power;

    (d) All personnel should ensure the full protection of the physical and mental health of juveniles, including protection from physical, sexual and emotional abuse and exploitation, and should take immediate action to secure medical attention whenever required;

    (e) All personnel should respect the right of the juvenile to privacy, and in particular should safeguard all confidential matters concerning juveniles or their families learned as a result of their professional capacity;

    (f) All personnel should seek to minimise any differences between life inside and outside the detention facility which tend to lessen due respect for the dignity of juveniles as human beings.

43. UNITED NATIONS: DECLARATION OF BASIC PRINCIPLES OF JUSTICE FOR VICTIMS OF CRIME AND ABUSE OF POWER

Adopted by United Nations General Assembly resolution 40/34 (1985)

Editors' Notes

The Declaration of Basic Principles of Justice for Victims of Crime and Abuse of Power was adopted by the United Nations General Assembly in 1985. The Declaration deals with victims of crime – those suffering harm through the transgression of domestic criminal laws (Principle 1), and with victims of the abuse of power – those suffering harm through acts which are not offences under their domestic criminal law but which are violations of international human rights norms (Principle 18). The principles allow for victims of crime to be treated with respect for their dignity (Principle 4), to be given representation and assistance throughout proceedings (Principle 6), and to be entitled to restitution and compensation where appropriate (Principles 8–13). Supplementary implementation principles call upon states to investigate death and serious injury caused by law enforcement agents, and to try or extradite those responsible, and to prohibit any immunity from prosecution for offences that violate non-derogable human right norms.[1]

A. VICTIMS OF CRIME

1. "Victims" means persons who, individually or collectively, have suffered harm, including physical or mental injury, emotional suffering, economic loss or substantial impairment of their fundamental rights, through acts or omissions that are in violation of criminal laws operative within Member States, including those laws proscribing criminal abuse of power.

2. A person may be considered a victim, under this Declaration, regardless of whether the perpetrator is identified, apprehended, prosecuted or convicted and regardless of the familial relationship between the perpetrator and the victim. The term "victim" also includes, where appropriate, the immediate family or dependants of the direct victim and persons who have suffered harm in intervening to assist victims in distress or to prevent victimization.

3. The provisions contained herein shall be applicable to all, without distinction of any kind, such as race, colour, sex, age, language, religion, nationality, political or other opinion, cultural beliefs or practices, property, birth or family status, ethnic or social origin, and disability.

---

[1] See: Implementation Principles R4(d).5, R4(d).6 and R4(d).8, reprinted in Bassiouni, M.C. (Ed.)(1988). *International Protection of Victims.* pp.31–32.

Access to justice and fair treatment

4.   Victims should be treated with compassion and respect for their dignity. They are entitled to access to the mechanisms of justice and to prompt redress, as provided for by national legislation, for the harm that they have suffered.

5.   Judicial and administrative mechanisms should be established and strengthened where necessary to enable victims to obtain redress through formal or informal procedures that are expeditious, fair, inexpensive and accessible. Victims should be informed of their rights in seeking redress through such mechanisms.

6.   The responsiveness of judicial and administrative process to the needs of victims should be facilitated by:

   (a) Informing victims of their role and the scope, timing and progress of the proceedings and of the disposition of their cases, especially where serious crimes are involved and where they have requested such information;

   (b) Allowing the views and concerns of victims to be presented and considered at appropriate stages of the proceedings where their personal interests are affected, without prejudice to the accused and consistent with the relevant national criminal justice system;

   (c) Providing proper assistance to victims throughout the legal process;

   (d) Taking measures to minimise inconvenience to victims, protect their privacy, when necessary, and ensure their safety, as well as that of their families and witnesses on their behalf, from intimidation and retaliation;

   (e) Avoiding unnecessary delay in the disposition of cases and the execution of orders or decrees granting awards to victims.

7.   Informal mechanisms for the resolution of disputes, including mediation, arbitration and customary justice or indigenous practices, should be utilised where appropriate to facilitate conciliation and regress for victims.

Restitution

8.   Offenders or third parties responsible for their behaviour should, where appropriate, make fair restitution to victims, their families or dependants. Such restitution should include the return of property or payment for the harm or loss suffered, reimbursement of expenses incurred as a result of the victimization, the provision of services and the restoration of rights.

9.   Governments should review their practices, regulations and laws to consider restitution as an available sentencing option in criminal cases, in addition to other criminal sanctions.

10. In cases of substantial harm to the environment, restitution, if ordered, should include, so far as possible, restoration of the environment, reconstruction of the infrastructure, replacement of community facilities and reimbursement of the expenses of relocation, wherever such harm results in the dislocation of a community.

11. Where public officials or other agents acting in an official or quasi-official capacity have violated national criminal laws, the victims should receive

restitution from the State whose officials or agents were responsible for the harm inflicted. In cases where the Government under whose authority the victimising act or omission occurred is no longer in existence, the State or Government successor in title should provide restitution to the victims.

Compensation

12. When compensation is not fully available from the offender or other sources, States should endeavour to provide financial compensation to:
    (a) Victims who have sustained significant bodily injury or impairment of physical or mental health as a result of serious crimes;
    (b) The family, in particular dependants of persons who have died or become physically or mentally incapacitated as a result of such victimization.

13. The establishment, strengthening and expansion of national funds for compensation to victims should be encouraged. Where appropriate, other funds may also be established for this purpose, including in those cases where the State of which the victim is a national is not in a position to compensate the victim for the harm.

Assistance

14. Victims should receive the necessary material, medical, psychological and social assistance through governmental, voluntary, community-based and indigenous means.

15. Victims should be informed of the availability of health and social services and other relevant assistance and be readily afforded access to them.

16. Police, justice, health, social service and other personnel concerned should receive training to sensitise them to the needs of victims, and guidelines to ensure proper and prompt aid.

17. In providing services and assistance to victims, attention should be given to those who have special needs because of the nature of the harm inflicted or because of factors such as those mentioned in paragraph 3 above.

B. VICTIMS OF ABUSE OF POWER

18. "Victims" means persons who, individually or collectively, have suffered harm, including physical or mental injury, emotional suffering, economic loss or substantial impairment of their fundamental rights, through acts or omissions that do not yet constitute violations of national criminal laws but of internationally recognized norms relating to human rights.

19. States should consider incorporating into the national law norms proscribing abuses of power and providing remedies to victims of such abuses. In particular, such remedies should include restitution and/or compensation, and necessary material, medical, psychological and social assistance and support.

20. States should consider negotiating multilateral international treaties relating to victims, as defined in paragraph 18.
21. States should periodically review existing legislation and practices to ensure their responsiveness to changing circumstances, should enact and enforce, if necessary, legislation proscribing acts that constitute serious abuses of political or economic power, as well as promoting policies and mechanisms for the prevention of such acts, and should develop and make readily available appropriate rights and remedies for victims of such acts.

44. COUNCIL OF EUROPE: EUROPEAN CONVENTION ON THE COMPENSATION OF VICTIMS OF VIOLENT CRIMES

Opened for signature at Strasbourg: 24 November 1983

ETS 116

Entry into force: 1 February 1988

Editors' Notes

The European Convention on the Compensation of Victims of Violent Crime was drawn up under the auspices of the Council of Europe's Committee on Crime Problems and opened for signature in 1983. The Treaty follows on from a Resolution by the Committee of Ministers in 1977[1] which had recommended that member states provide for the state compensation of victims of violence or their dependants, where compensation could not be obtained by other means, often because of the offenders non-apprehension or lack of means.

Under the terms of the Treaty, the member states undertake to ensure that current and future legislation makes adequate provision for the compensation for victims of crimes of violence (Article 1). The state pays compensation to the victim, only where compensation cannot be obtained from other sources such as the offender and this is only available where the offence is intentional, violent and the direct cause of serious bodily harm (Article 2). Article 3 recognises that non-nationals are entitled to compensation. Generally, such persons must be a national of a member state of the Council of Europe. Article 8 sets out circumstances when compensation may be reduced or withheld. Part II of the Convention requires the parties to co-operate fully in implementing the Treaty, in particular by way of mutual legal assistance.[2]

Since the completion of the Convention, the Committee of Ministers have added further recommendations relating to the position of the victims of crime.[3]

The member States of the Council of Europe, signatory hereto,

Considering that the aim of the Council of Europe is to achieve a greater unity between its members;

Considering that for reasons of equity and social solidarity it is necessary to deal with the situation of victims of intentional crimes of violence who have suffered

---

[1] Committee of Ministers of the Council of Europe Resolution (77) 27 on the Compensation of Victims of Crime.

[2] See: European Convention on Mutual Legal Assistance in Criminal Matters, *infra*.

[3] See: Recommendation No. R (85) 11 on the Position of the Victim in the framework of Criminal Law and Procedure, and; Recommendation No. R (87) 21 on Assistance to Victims and the Prevention of Victimisation.

bodily injury or impairment of health and of dependants of persons who have died as a result of such crimes;

Considering that it is necessary to introduce or develop schemes for the compensation of these victims by the State in whose territory such crimes were committed, in particular when the offender has not been identified or is without resources;

Considering that it is necessary to establish minimum provisions in this field;

Having regard to Resolution (77)27 of the Committee of Ministers of the Council of Europe on the compensation of victims of crime,

Have agreed as follows:

PART I
BASIC PRINCIPLES

Article 1

The Parties undertake to take the necessary steps to give effect to the principles set out in Part I of this Convention.

Article 2

When compensation is not fully available from other sources the State shall contribute to compensate:

    a.   those who have sustained serious bodily injury or impairment of health directly attributable to an intentional crime of violence;

    b.   the dependants of persons who have died as a result of such crime.

Compensation shall be awarded in the above cases even if the offender cannot be prosecuted or punished.

Article 3

Compensation shall be paid by the State on whose territory the crime was committed:

    a.   to nationals of the States party to this Convention;

    b.   to nationals of all member States of the Council of Europe who are permanent residents in the State on whose territory the crime was committed.

Article 4

Compensation shall cover, according to the case under consideration, at least the following items: loss of earnings, medical and hospitalisation expenses and funeral expenses, and, as regards dependants, loss of maintenance.

Article 5

The compensation scheme may, if necessary, set for any or all elements of compensation an upper limit above which and a minimum threshold below which such compensation shall not be granted.

Article 6

The compensation scheme may specify a period within which any application for compensation must be made.

Article 7

Compensation may be reduced or refused on account of the applicant's financial situation.

Article 8

Compensation may be reduced or refused on account of the victim's or the applicant's conduct before, during or after the crime, or in relation to the injury or death.

Compensation may also be reduced or refused on account of the victim's or the applicant's involvement in organised crime or his membership of an organisation which engages in crimes of violence.

Compensation may also be reduced or refused if an award or a full award would be contrary to a sense of justice or to public policy ("ordre public").

Article 9

With a view to avoiding double compensation, the State or the competent authority may deduct from the compensation awarded or reclaim from the person compensated any amount of money received, in consequence of the injury or death, from the offender, social security or insurance, or coming from any other source.

Article 10

The State or the competent authority may be subrogated to the rights of the person compensated for the amount of the compensation paid.

Article 11

Each Party shall take appropriate steps to ensure that information about the scheme is available to potential applicants.

PART II
INTERNATIONAL CO-OPERATION

Article 12

Subject to the application of bilateral or multilateral agreements on mutual assistance concluded between Contracting States, the competent authorities of each Party shall, at the request of the appropriate authorities of any other Party, give the maximum possible assistance in connection with the matters covered by this Convention. To this end, each Contracting State shall designate a central authority to receive, and to take action on, requests for such assistance, and shall inform thereof the Secretary General of the Council of Europe when depositing its instrument of ratification, acceptance, approval or accession.

Article 13

The European Committee on Crime Problems (CDPC) of the Council of Europe shall be kept informed regarding the application of the Convention.

To this end, each Party shall transmit to the Secretary General of the Council of Europe any relevant information about its legislative or regulatory provisions concerning the matters covered by the Convention.

PART III
FINAL CLAUSES

Article 14

This Convention shall be open for signature by the member States of the Council of Europe. It is subject to ratification, acceptance or approval. Instruments of ratification, acceptance or approval shall be deposited with the Secretary General of the Council of Europe.

Article 15

1. This Convention shall enter into force on the first day of the month following the expiration of a period of three months after the date on which three member States of the Council of Europe have expressed their consent to be bound by the Convention in accordance with the provisions of Article 14.
2. In respect of any member State which subsequently expresses its consent to be bound by it, the Convention shall enter into force on the first day of the month following the expiration of a period of three months after the date of the deposit of the instrument of ratification, acceptance or approval.

Article 16

1. After the entry into force of this Convention, the Committee of Ministers of the Council of Europe may invite any State not a member of the Council of Europe to accede to this Convention by a decision taken by the majority provided for in Article 20.d of the Statute of the Council of Europe and by the unanimous vote of the representatives of the Contracting States entitled to sit on the Committee.
2. In respect of any acceding State, the Convention shall enter into force on the first day of the month following the expiration of a period of three months after the date of deposit of the instrument of accession with the Secretary General of the Council of Europe.

Article 17

1. Any State may at the time of signature or when depositing its instrument of ratification, acceptance, approval or accession, specify the territory or territories to which this Convention shall apply.
2. Any State may at any later date, by a declaration addressed to the Secretary-General of the Council of Europe, extend the application of this Convention to any other territory specified in the declaration. In respect of such territory the Convention shall enter into force on the first day of the month following the expiration of a period of three months after the date of receipt of such declaration by the Secretary General.
3. Any declaration made under the two preceding paragraphs may, in respect of any territory specified in such declaration, be withdrawn by a notification addressed to the Secretary General. The withdrawal shall become effective on the first day of the month following the expiration of a period of six months after the date of receipt of such notification by the Secretary General.

Article 18

1. Any State may, at the time of signature or when depositing its instrument of ratification, acceptance, approval or accession, declare that it avails itself of one or more reservations.
2. Any Contracting State which has made a reservation under the preceding paragraph may wholly or partly withdraw it by means of a notification addressed to the Secretary General of the Council of Europe. The withdrawal shall take effect on the date of receipt of such notification by the Secretary General.
3. A Party which has made a reservation in respect of a provision of this Convention may not claim the application of that provision by any other Party; it may, however, if its reservation is partial or conditional, claim the application of that provision in so far as it has itself accepted it.

Article 19

1. Any Party may at any time denounce this Convention by means of a notification addressed to the Secretary General of the Council of Europe.
2. Such a denunciation shall become effective on the first day of the month following the expiration of a period of six months after the date of receipt of the notification by the Secretary General.

Article 20

The Secretary General of the Council of Europe shall notify the member States of the Council and any State which has acceded to this Convention, of

a. any signature;
b. the deposit of any instrument of ratification, acceptance, approval or accession
c. any date of entry into force of this Convention in accordance with Articles 15, 16 and 17
d. any other act, notification or communication relating to this Convention.

SECTION TWO

TORTURE AND ENFORCED DISAPPEARANCE

45. UNITED NATIONS: CONVENTION AGAINST TORTURE AND OTHER CRUEL, INHUMAN OR DEGRADING TREATMENT OR PUNISHMENT

Opened for signature: 10 December 1984 by
General Assembly Resolution 39/46 (1984)

Entry into force: 26 June 1987

Editors' Notes

With the atrocities of the second world war fresh in the mind of the international community, the United Nations immediately condemned the use of torture, cruel inhuman and degrading treatment or punishment in Article 5 of the Universal Declaration of Human Rights in 1948.[1] The wording of the provision has been included into many of the subsequent instruments condemning and outlawing the use of torture. Article 7 of the International Covenant on Civil and Political Rights adopts this exact wording, adding a prohibition on medical or scientific experimentation without free consent of the person.[2]

Prompted by pressure from both Governments and non-governmental organisations, the UN General Assembly adopted, without dissent, the Declaration on the Protection of All Persons from being Subjected to Torture and Other Cruel or Degrading Treatment or Punishment in 1975. Although none of these measures were binding, such were the number of international provisions on the prohibition of torture, and such was their unequivocal condemnation, that the United States Court of Appeals concluded in *Filartiga v Pena-Irala* that an unambiguous prohibition of torture exists under international law.[3] Following a proposal by Sweden in 1977, the UN Commission on Human Rights was given the task of drafting a treaty against torture, and this was concluded when the Convention was adopted by the General Assembly in 1984.

The central aim of the present Convention is to repress the use of torture by obliging states to prevent acts of torture within domestic law and policy (Article 2).[4] Additionally, all acts of torture (including attempts and complicity) must be offences under domestic law (Article 4), law enforcement officials should

---

[1] *Supra.*

[2] *Supra.*

[3] *Filartiga v Pena-Irala*, 630 F. 2d. 876 (1980). 19 ILM 966 (1980). US Court of Appeals, Second Circuit.

[4] See: Boulesbaa, A. (1990). The Nature of the Obligations Incurred by States under Article 2 of the UN Convention against Torture. 12 HRQ 52. See also the duty upon states under international law to prevent violations of human rights discussed in *Velasquez Rodriguez v Honduras*, Judgement of 29 July 1988, Inter-American Court of Human Rights, Series C: Decisions and Judgements no.4. Reported in HRLJ (1988) 212.

be educated and informed about the prohibition of torture (Article 10), rules of interrogation and custody must be kept under review so as to prevent practices constituting torture (Article 11) and allegations of torture must be promptly and impartially investigated (Articles 12 and 13). Any statement obtained as a result of the use of torture should not be admitted into any proceedings (Article 15). Articles 5 to 8 of the Convention provide for universal jurisdiction over the prosecution for acts of torture and includes the principle of try or extradite.

Further to these provisions, Part II of the Convention provides the basis for the establishment of the Committee against Torture (CAT). It is the job of the Committee to monitor the implementation of the Convention by way of reviewing and circulating the reports required from the parties on the their response to the obligations established under the Convention, to produce an annual report, to undertake inquiries into any reported systematic use of torture and to respond to inter-state and individual complaints established on an optional basis. When the CAT has completed its examination of a complaint, the findings of the Committee are forwarded to the state or individual concerned. These findings are not binding in law.

Given the continued reported incidence of torture around the world,[5] a more direct element for the prevention of torture was proposed within a Draft Optional Protocol to the Convention submitted by Costa Rica, involving a system for the inspection of places of detention similar to that subsequently established under the European Convention for the Prevention of Torture.[6] While the proposal was not accepted, a study as to its future introduction continues under the auspices of the UN Human Rights Committee.

The States Parties to this Convention,

Considering that, in accordance with the principles proclaimed in the Charter of the United Nations, recognition of the equal and inalienable rights of all members of the human family is the foundation of freedom, justice and peace in the world,

Recognising that those rights derive from the inherent dignity of the human person,

Considering the obligation of States under the Charter, in particular Article 55, to promote universal respect for, and observance of, human rights and fundamental freedoms,

Having regard to article 5 of the Universal Declaration of Human Rights and article 7 of the International Covenant on Civil and Political Rights, both of which provide that no one shall be subjected to torture or to cruel, inhuman or degrading treatment or punishment,

Having regard also to the Declaration on the Protection of All Persons from Being Subjected to Torture and Other Cruel, Inhuman or Degrading Treatment or Punishment, adopted by the General Assembly on 9 December 1975,

Desiring to make more effective the struggle against torture and other cruel, inhuman or degrading treatment or punishment throughout the world,

---

[5] See generally: The Annual Reports of Amnesty International, London, Amnesty International.
[6] *Infra.*

Have agreed as follows:

PART I

Article 1

1. For the purposes of this Convention, the term "torture" means any act by which severe pain or suffering, whether physical or mental, is intentionally inflicted on a person for such purposes as obtaining from him or a third person information or a confession, punishing him for an act he or a third person has committed or is suspected of having committed, or intimidating or coercing him or a third person, or for any reason based on discrimination of any kind, when such pain or suffering is inflicted by or at the instigation of or with the consent or acquiescence of a public official or other person acting in an official capacity. It does not include pain or suffering arising only from, inherent in or incidental to lawful sanctions.
2. This article is without prejudice to any international instrument or national legislation which does or may contain provisions of wider application.

Article 2

1. Each State Party shall take effective legislative, administrative, judicial or other measures to prevent acts of torture in any territory under its jurisdiction.
2. No exceptional circumstances whatsoever, whether a state of war or a threat of war, internal political in stability or any other public emergency, may be invoked as a justification of torture.
3. An order from a superior officer or a public authority may not be invoked as a justification of torture.

Article 3

1. No State Party shall expel, return ("refouler") or extradite a person to another State where there are substantial grounds for believing that he would be in danger of being subjected to torture.
2. For the purpose of determining whether there are such grounds, the competent authorities shall take into account all relevant considerations including, where applicable, the existence in the State concerned of a consistent pattern of gross, flagrant or mass violations of human rights.

Article 4

1. Each State Party shall ensure that all acts of torture are offences under its criminal law. The same shall apply to an attempt to commit torture and to an act by any person which constitutes complicity or participation in torture.
2. Each State Party shall make these offences punishable by appropriate penalties which take into account their grave nature.

Article 5

1. Each State Party shall take such measures as may be necessary to establish its jurisdiction over the offences referred to in article 4 in the following cases:

   (a) When the offences are committed in any territory under its jurisdiction or on board a ship or aircraft registered in that State;
   (b) When the alleged offender is a national of that State;
   (c) When the victim is a national of that State if that State considers it appropriate.

2. Each State Party shall likewise take such measures as may be necessary to establish its jurisdiction over such offences in cases where the alleged offender is present in any territory under its jurisdiction and it does not extradite him pursuant to article 8 to any of the States mentioned in paragraph I of this article.

3. This Convention does not exclude any criminal jurisdiction exercised in accordance with internal law.

Article 6

1. Upon being satisfied, after an examination of information available to it, that the circumstances so warrant, any State Party in whose territory a person alleged to have committed any offence referred to in article 4 is present shall take him into custody or take other legal measures to ensure his presence. The custody and other legal measures shall be as provided in the law of that State but may be continued only for such time as is necessary to enable any criminal or extradition proceedings to be instituted.

2. Such State shall immediately make a preliminary inquiry into the facts.

3. Any person in custody pursuant to paragraph 1 of this article shall be assisted in communicating immediately with the nearest appropriate representative of the State of which he is a national, or, if he is a stateless person, with the representative of the State where he usually resides.

4. When a State, pursuant to this article, has taken a person into custody, it shall immediately notify the States referred to in article 5, paragraph 1, of the fact that such person is in custody and of the circumstances which warrant his detention. The State which makes the preliminary inquiry contemplated in paragraph 2 of this article shall promptly report its findings to the said States and shall indicate whether it intends to exercise jurisdiction.

Article 7

1. The State Party in the territory under whose jurisdiction a person alleged to have committed any offence referred to in article 4 is found shall in the cases contemplated in article 5, if it does not extradite him, submit the case to its competent authorities for the purpose of prosecution.

2. These authorities shall take their decision in the same manner as in the case of any ordinary offence of a serious nature under the law of that State. In the

cases referred to in article 5, paragraph 2, the standards of evidence required for prosecution and conviction shall in no way be less stringent than those which apply in the cases referred to in article 5, paragraph 1.

3. Any person regarding whom proceedings are brought in connection with any of the offences referred to in article 4 shall be guaranteed fair treatment at all stages of the proceedings.

Article 8

1. The offences referred to in article 4 shall be deemed to be included as extraditable offences in any extradition treaty existing between States Parties. States Parties undertake to include such offences as extraditable offences in every extradition treaty to be concluded between them.

2. If a State Party which makes extradition conditional on the existence of a treaty receives a request for extradition from another. State Party with which it has no extradition treaty, it may consider this Convention as the legal basis for extradition in respect of such offences. Extradition shall be subject to the other conditions provided by the law of the requested State.

3. States Parties which do not make extradition conditional on the existence of a treaty shall recognize such offences as extraditable offences between themselves subject to the conditions provided by the law of the requested State.

4. Such offences shall be treated, for the purpose of extradition between States Parties, as if they had been committed not only in the place in which they occurred but also in the territories of the States required to establish their jurisdiction in accordance with article 5, paragraph 1.

Article 9

1. States Parties shall afford one another the greatest measure of assistance in connection with criminal proceedings brought in respect of any of the offences referred to in article 4, including the supply of all evidence at their disposal necessary for the proceedings.

2. States Parties shall carry out their obligations under paragraph 1 of this article in conformity with any treaties on mutual judicial assistance that may exist between them.

Article 10

1. Each State Party shall ensure that education and information regarding the prohibition against torture are fully included in the training of law enforcement personnel, civil or military, medical personnel, public officials and other persons who may be involved in the custody, interrogation or treatment of any individual subjected to any form of arrest, detention or imprisonment.

2. Each State Party shall include this prohibition in the rules or instructions issued in regard to the duties and functions of any such person.

Article 11

Each State Party shall keep under systematic review interrogation rules, instructions, methods and practices as well as arrangements for the custody and treatment of persons subjected to any form of arrest, detention or imprisonment in any territory under its jurisdiction, with a view to preventing any cases of torture.

Article 12

Each State Party shall ensure that its competent authorities proceed to a prompt and impartial investigation, wherever there is reasonable ground to believe that an act of torture has been committed in any territory under its jurisdiction.

Article 13

Each State Party shall ensure that any individual who alleges he has been subjected to torture in any territory under its jurisdiction has the right to complain to, and to have his case promptly and impartially examined by, its competent authorities. Steps shall be taken to ensure that the complainant and witnesses are protected against all ill-treatment or intimidation as a consequence of his complaint or any evidence given.

Article 14

1. Each State Party shall ensure in its legal system that the victim of an act of torture obtains redress and has an enforceable right to fair and adequate compensation, including the means for as full rehabilitation as possible. In the event of the death of the victim as a result of an act of torture, his dependants shall be entitled to compensation.
2. Nothing in this article shall affect any right of the victim or other persons to compensation which may exist under national law.

Article 15

Each State Party shall ensure that any statement which is established to have been made as a result of torture shall not be invoked as evidence in any proceedings, except against a person accused of torture as evidence that the statement was made.

Article 16

1. Each State Party shall undertake to prevent in any territory under its jurisdiction other acts of cruel, inhuman or degrading treatment or punishment which do not amount to torture as defined in article 1, when such acts are committed by or at the instigation of or with the consent or acquiescence of a public official or other person acting in an official capacity. In particular, the obligations contained in articles 10, 11, 12 and 13 shall apply with the

substitution for references to torture of references to other forms of cruel, inhuman or degrading treatment or punishment.

2. The provisions of this Convention are without prejudice to the provisions of any other international instrument or national law which prohibits cruel, inhuman or degrading treatment or punishment or which relates to extradition or expulsion.

PART II

Article 17

1. There shall be established a Committee against Torture (hereinafter referred to as the Committee) which shall carry out the functions hereinafter provided. The Committee shall consist of ten experts of high moral standing and recognized competence in the field of human rights, who shall serve in their personal capacity. The experts shall be elected by the States Parties, consideration being given to equitable geographical distribution and to the usefulness of the participation of some persons having legal experience.

2. The members of the Committee shall be elected by secret ballot from a list of persons nominated by States Parties. Each State Party may nominate one person from among its own nationals. States Parties shall bear in mind the usefulness of nominating persons who are also members of the Human Rights Committee established under the International Covenant on Civil and Political Rights and who are willing to serve on the Committee against Torture.

3. Elections of the members of the Committee shall be held at biennial meetings of States Parties convened by the Secretary-General of the United Nations. At those meetings, for which two thirds of the States Parties shall constitute a quorum, the persons elected to the Committee shall be those who obtain the largest number of votes and an absolute majority of the votes of the representatives of States Parties present and voting.

4. The initial election shall be held no later than six months after the date of the entry into force of this Convention. At least four months before the date of each election, the Secretary-General of the United Nations shall address a letter to the States Parties inviting them to submit their nominations within three months. The Secretary-General shall prepare a list in alphabetical order of all persons thus nominated, indicating the States Parties which have nominated them, and shall submit it to the States Parties.

5. The members of the Committee shall be elected for a term of four years. They shall be eligible for re-election if renominated. However, the term of five of the members elected at the first election shall expire at the end of two years; immediately after the first election the names of these five members shall be chosen by lot by the chairman of the meeting referred to in paragraph 3 of this article.

6. If a member of the Committee dies or resigns or for any other cause can no longer perform his Committee duties, the State Party which nominated him shall appoint another expert from among its nationals to serve for the

remainder of his term, subject to the approval of the majority of the States Parties. The approval shall be considered given unless half or more of the States Parties respond negatively within six weeks after having been informed by the Secretary-General of the United Nations of the proposed appointment.

7. States Parties shall be responsible for the expenses of the members of the Committee while they are in performance of Committee duties.

Article 18

1. The Committee shall elect its officers for a term of two years. They may be re-elected.
2. The Committee shall establish its own rules of procedure, but these rules shall provide, *inter alia*, that:

    (a) Six members shall constitute a quorum;
    (b) Decisions of the Committee shall be made by a majority vote of the members present.

3. The Secretary-General of the United Nations shall provide the necessary staff and facilities for the effective performance of the functions of the Committee under this Convention.
4. The Secretary-General of the United Nations shall convene the initial meeting of the Committee. After its initial meeting, the Committee shall meet at such times as shall be provided in its rules of procedure.
5. The States Parties shall be responsible for expenses incurred in connection with the holding of meetings of the States Parties and of the Committee, including reimbursement to the United Nations for any expenses, such as the cost of staff and facilities, incurred by the United Nations pursuant to paragraph 3 of this article.

Article 19

1. The States Parties shall submit to the Committee, through the Secretary-General of the United Nations, reports on the measures they have taken to give effect to their undertakings under this Convention, within one year after the entry into force of the Convention for the State Party concerned. Thereafter the States Parties shall submit supplementary reports every four years on any new measures taken and such other reports as the Committee may request.
2. The Secretary-General of the United Nations shall transmit the reports to all States Parties.
3. Each report shall be considered by the Committee which may make such general comments on the report as it may consider appropriate and shall forward these to the State Party concerned. That State Party may respond with any observations it chooses to the Committee.
4. The Committee may, at its discretion, decide to include any comments made by it in accordance with paragraph 3 of this article, together with the observations thereon received from the State Party concerned, in its annual

report made in accordance with article 24. If so requested by the State Party concerned, the Committee may also include a copy of the report submitted under paragraph 1 of this article.

Article 20

1. If the Committee receives reliable information which appears to it to contain well-founded indications that torture is being systematically practised in the territory of a State Party, the Committee shall invite that State Party to co-operate in the examination of the information and to this end to submit observations with regard to the information concerned.

2. Taking into account any observations which may have been submitted by the State Party concerned, as well as any other relevant information available to it, the Committee may, if it decides that this is warranted, designate one or more of its members to make a confidential inquiry and to report to the Committee urgently.

3. If an inquiry is made in accordance with paragraph 2 of this article, the Committee shall seek the co-operation of the State Party concerned. In agreement with that State Party, such an inquiry may include a visit to its territory.

4. After examining the findings of its member or members submitted in accordance with paragraph 2 of this article, the Commission shall transmit these findings to the State Party concerned together with any comments or suggestions which seem appropriate in view of the situation.

5. All the proceedings of the Committee referred to in paragraphs 1 to 4 of this article shall be confidential, and at all stages of the proceedings the co-operation of the State Party shall be sought. After such proceedings have been completed with regard to an inquiry made in accordance with paragraph 2, the Committee may, after consultations with the State Party concerned, decide to include a summary account of the results of the proceedings in its annual report made in accordance with article 24.

Article 21

1. A State Party to this Convention may at any time declare under this article that it recognises the competence of the Committee to receive and consider communications to the effect that a State Party claims that another State Party is not fulfilling its obligations under this Convention. Such communications may be received and considered according to the procedures laid down in this article only if submitted by a State Party which has made a declaration recognising in regard to itself the competence of the Committee. No communication shall be dealt with by the Committee under this article if it concerns a State Party which has not made such a declaration. Communications received under this article shall be dealt with in accordance with the following procedure:

   (a) If a State Party considers that another State Party is not giving effect to the provisions of this Convention, it may, by written communication, bring the matter to the attention of that State Party. Within three months after the receipt of the communication the receiving State shall afford the State which sent the communication an explanation or any other statement in writing clarifying the matter, which should include, to the extent possible and pertinent, reference to domestic procedures and remedies taken, pending or available in the matter;

(b) If the matter is not adjusted to the satisfaction of both States Parties concerned within six months after the receipt by the receiving State of the initial communication, either State shall have the right to refer the matter to the Committee, by notice given to the Committee and to the other State;

(c) The Committee shall deal with a matter referred to it under this article only after it has ascertained that all domestic remedies have been invoked and exhausted in the matter, in conformity with the generally recognized principles of international law. This shall not be the rule where the application of the remedies is unreasonably prolonged or is unlikely to bring effective relief to the person who is the victim of the violation of this Convention;

(d) The Committee shall hold closed meetings when examining communications under this article;

(e) Subject to the provisions of subparagraph (c), the Committee shall make available its good offices to the States Parties concerned with a view to a friendly solution of the matter on the basis of respect for the obligations provided for in this Convention. For this purpose, the Committee may, when appropriate, set up an ad hoc conciliation commission;

(f) In any matter referred to it under this article, the Committee may call upon the States Parties concerned, referred to in subparagraph (b), to supply any relevant information;

(g) The States Parties concerned, referred to in subparagraph (b), shall have the right to be represented when the matter is being considered by the Committee and to make submissions orally and/or in writing;

(h) The Committee shall, within twelve months after the date of receipt of notice under subparagraph (b), submit a report:

(i) If a solution within the terms of subparagraph (e) is reached, the Committee shall confine its report to a brief statement of the facts and of the solution reached;

(ii) If a solution within the terms of subparagraph (e) is not reached, the Committee shall confine its report to a brief statement of the facts; the written submissions and record of the oral submissions made by the States Parties concerned shall be attached to the report. In every matter, the report shall be communicated to the States Parties concerned.

2. The provisions of this article shall come into force when five States Parties to this Convention have made declarations under paragraph 1 of this article. Such declarations shall be deposited by the States Parties with the Secretary-

General of the United Nations, who shall transmit copies thereof to the other States Parties. A declaration may be withdrawn at any time by notification to the Secretary-General. Such a withdrawal shall not prejudice the consideration of any matter which is the subject of a communication already transmitted under this article; no further communication by any State Party shall be received under this article after the notification of withdrawal of the declaration has been received by the Secretary-General, unless the State Party concerned has made a new declaration.

Article 22

1. A State Party to this Convention may at any time declare under this article that it recognises the competence of the Committee to receive and consider communications from or on behalf of individuals subject to its jurisdiction who claim to be victims of a violation by a State Party of the provisions of the Convention. No communication shall be received by the Committee if it concerns a State Party which has not made such a declaration.
2. The Committee shall consider inadmissible any communication under this article which is anonymous or which it considers to be an abuse of the right of submission of such communications or to be incompatible with the provisions of this Convention.
3. Subject to the provisions of paragraph 2, the Committee shall bring any communications submitted to it under this article to the attention of the State Party to this Convention which has made a declaration under paragraph 1 and is alleged to be violating any provisions of the Convention. Within six months, the receiving State shall submit to the Committee written explanations or statements clarifying the matter and the remedy, if any, that may have been taken by that State.
4. The Committee shall consider communications received under this article in the light of all information made available to it by or on behalf of the individual and by the State Party concerned.
5. The Committee shall not consider any communications from an individual under this article unless it has ascertained that:
    (a) The same matter has not been, and is not being, examined under another procedure of international investigation or settlement;
    (b) The individual has exhausted all available domestic remedies; this shall not be the rule where the application of the remedies is unreasonably prolonged or is unlikely to bring effective relief to the person who is the victim of the violation of this Convention.
6. The Committee shall hold closed meetings when examining communications under this article.
7. The Committee shall forward its views to the State Party concerned and to the individual.
8. The provisions of this article shall come into force when five States Parties to this Convention have made declarations under paragraph 1 of this article. Such declarations shall be deposited by the States Parties with the Secretary-

General of the United Nations, who shall transmit copies thereof to the other States Parties. A declaration may be withdrawn at any time by notification to the Secretary-General. Such a withdrawal shall not prejudice the consideration of any matter which is the subject of a communication already transmitted under this article; no further communication by or on behalf of an individual shall be received under this article after the notification of withdrawal of the declaration has been received by the Secretary-General, unless the State Party has made a new declaration.

Article 23

The members of the Committee and of the ad hoc conciliation commissions which may be appointed under article 21, paragraph 1(e), shall be entitled to the facilities, privileges and immunities of experts on mission for the United Nations as laid down in the relevant sections of the Convention on the Privileges and Immunities of the United Nations.

Article 24

The Committee shall submit an annual report on its activities under this Convention to the States Parties and to the General Assembly of the United Nations.

PART III

Article 25

1. This Convention is open for signature by all States.
2. This Convention is subject to ratification. Instruments of ratification shall be deposited with the Secretary-General of the United Nations.

Article 26

This Convention is open to accession by all States. Accession shall be effected by the deposit of an instrument of accession with the Secretary-General of the United Nations.

Article 27

1. This Convention shall enter into force on the thirtieth day after the date of the deposit with the Secretary-General of the United Nations of the twentieth instrument of ratification or accession.
2. For each State ratifying this Convention or acceding to it after the deposit of the twentieth instrument of ratification or accession, the Convention shall enter into force on the thirtieth day after the date of the deposit of its own instrument of ratification or accession.

Article 28

1. Each State may, at the time of signature or ratification of this Convention or accession thereto, declare that it does not recognize the competence of the Committee provided for in article 20.
2. Any State Party having made a reservation in accordance with paragraph 1 of this article may, at any time, withdraw this reservation by notification to the Secretary-General of the United Nations.

Article 29

1. Any State Party to this Convention may propose an amendment and file it with the Secretary-General of the United Nations. The Secretary General shall thereupon communicate the proposed amendment to the States Parties with a request that they notify him whether they favour a conference of States Parties for the purpose of considering and voting upon the proposal. In the event that within four months from the date of such communication at least one third of the States Parties favours such a conference, the Secretary-General shall convene the conference under the auspices of the United Nations. Any amendment adopted by a majority of the States Parties present and voting at the conference shall be submitted by the Secretary-General to all the States Parties for acceptance.
2. An amendment adopted in accordance with paragraph 1 of this article shall enter into force when two thirds of the States Parties to this Convention have notified the Secretary-General of the United Nations that they have accepted it in accordance with their respective constitutional processes.
3. When amendments enter into force, they shall be binding on those States Parties which have accepted them, other States Parties still being bound by the provisions of this Convention and any earlier amendments which they have accepted.

Article 30

1. Any dispute between two or more States Parties concerning the interpretation or application of this Convention which cannot be settled through negotiation shall, at the request of one of them, be submitted to arbitration. If within six months from the date of the request for arbitration the Parties are unable to agree on the organization of the arbitration, any one of those Parties may refer the dispute to the International Court of Justice by request in conformity with the Statute of the Court.
2. Each State may, at the time of signature or ratification of this Convention or accession thereto, declare that it does not consider itself bound by paragraph 1 of this article. The other States Parties shall not be bound by paragraph 1 of this article with respect to any State Party having made such a reservation.
3. Any State Party having made a reservation in accordance with paragraph 2 of this article may at any time withdraw this reservation by notification to the Secretary-General of the United Nations.

Article 31

1. A State Party may denounce this Convention by written notification to the Secretary-General of the United Nations. Denunciation becomes effective one year after the date of receipt of the notification by the Secretary-General.
2. Such a denunciation shall not have the effect of releasing the State Party from its obligations under this Convention in regard to any act or omission which occurs prior to the date at which the denunciation becomes effective, nor shall denunciation prejudice in any way the continued consideration of any matter which is already under consideration by the Committee prior to the date at which the denunciation becomes effective.
3. Following the date at which the denunciation of a State Party becomes effective, the Committee shall not commence consideration of any new matter regarding that State.

Article 32

The Secretary-General of the United Nations shall inform all States Members of the United Nations and all States which have signed this Convention or acceded to it of the following:

    (a) Signatures, ratifications and accessions under articles 25 and 26;
    (b) The date of entry into force of this Convention under article 27 and the date of the entry into force of any amendments under article 29;
    (c) Denunciations under article 31.

Article 33

1. This Convention, of which the Arabic, Chinese, English, French, Russian and Spanish texts are equally authentic, shall be deposited with the Secretary-General of the United Nations.
2. The Secretary-General of the United Nations shall transmit certified copies of this Convention to all States.

46. ORGANIZATION OF AMERICAN STATES: INTER-AMERICAN CONVENTION TO PREVENT AND PUNISH TORTURE

Opened for signature at Cartagena de Indias: 9 December 1985

OAS TS 67

Entry into force: 28 February 1987

Editors' Notes
When the General Assembly of the Organization of American States adopted the Convention to Prevent and Punish Torture, the treaty expanded on the prohibition previously outlined within Article 5 of the American Convention on Human Rights.[1] The Treaty generally corresponds to the United Nations Torture Convention, although the Inter-American Convention does not provide for such an expansive role for the Commission on Human Rights, which is restricted to monitoring the measures taken by the parties in applying the Convention and producing an annual report, analysing the progress amongst the member states in eliminating torture. The definition of torture contained within Article 2 of the Inter-American Convention is broader than that contained within the UN Torture Treaty[2] in that it does not require that the pain or suffering inflicted to be "severe". Additionally under Article 2, torture is the infliction of pain or suffering for *any* purpose, whereas the UN definition contains a more restrictive list proscribing the use of torture "for such purposes as...". By way of further comparison, the prohibition of torture contained within Article 5 of the African Charter on Human and Peoples' Rights provides a radically different wording which reflects the historical experience of that continent.[3]

The American States signatory to the present Convention,

Aware of the provision of the American Convention on Human Rights that no one shall be subjected to torture or to cruel, inhuman, or degrading punishment or treatment;

Reaffirming that all acts of torture or any other cruel, inhuman, or degrading treatment or punishment constitute an offense against human dignity and a denial of the principles set forth in the Charter of the Organization of American States and in the Charter of the United Nations and are violations of the fundamental human rights and freedoms proclaimed in the American Declaration of the Rights and Duties of Man and the Universal Declaration of Human Rights;

---

[1] *Supra.* UN Convention against Torture and other Cruel, Inhuman or Degrading Treatment or Punishment,

[2] Article 1, *supra.*

[3] *Supra.*

Noting that, in order for the pertinent rules contained in the aforementioned global and regional instruments to take effect, it is necessary to draft an Inter-American Convention that prevents and punishes torture;

Reaffirming their purpose of consolidating in this hemisphere the conditions that make for recognition of and respect for the inherent dignity of man, and ensure the full exercise of his fundamental rights and freedoms,

Have agreed upon the following:

Article 1

The State Parties undertake to prevent and punish torture in accordance with the terms of this Convention.

Article 2

For the purposes of this Convention, torture shall be understood to be any act intentionally performed whereby physical or mental pain or suffering is inflicted on a person for purposes of criminal investigation, as a means of intimidation, as personal punishment, as a preventive measure, as a penalty, or for any other purpose. Torture shall also be understood to be the use of methods upon a person intended to obliterate the personality of the victim or to diminish his physical or mental capacities, even if they do not cause physical pain or mental anguish.

The concept of torture shall not include physical or mental pain or suffering that is inherent in or solely the consequence of lawful measures, provided that they do not include the performance of the acts or use of the methods referred to in this article.

Article 3

The following shall be held guilty of the crime of torture:

    a.   A public servant or employee who acting in that capacity orders, instigates or induces the use of torture, or who directly commits it or who, being able to prevent it, fails to do so.

    b.   A person who at the instigation of a public servant or employee mentioned in subparagraph (a) orders, instigates or induces the use of torture, directly commits it or is an accomplice thereto.

Article 4

The fact of having acted under orders of a superior shall not provide exemption from the corresponding criminal liability.

Article 5

The existence of circumstances such as a state of war, threat of war, state of siege or of emergency, domestic disturbance or strife, suspension of constitutional guarantees, domestic political instability, or other public emergencies or disasters shall not be invoked or admitted as justification for the crime of torture.

Neither the dangerous character of the detainee or prisoner, nor the lack of security of the prison establishment or penitentiary shall justify torture.

Article 6

In accordance with the terms of Article 1, the States Parties shall take effective measures to prevent and punish torture within their jurisdiction.

The States Parties shall ensure that all acts of torture and attempts to commit torture are offenses under their criminal law and shall make such acts punishable by severe penalties that take into account their serious nature.

The States Parties likewise shall take effective measures to prevent and punish other cruel, inhuman, or degrading treatment or punishment within their jurisdiction.

Article 7

The States Parties shall take measures so that, in the training of police officers and other public officials responsible for the custody of persons temporarily or definitively deprived of their freedom, special emphasis shall be put on the prohibition of the use of torture in interrogation, detention, or arrest.

The States Parties likewise shall take similar measures to prevent other cruel, inhuman, or degrading treatment or punishment.

Article 8

The States Parties shall guarantee that any person making an accusation of having been subjected to torture within their jurisdiction shall have the right to an impartial examination of his case.

Likewise, if there is an accusation or well-grounded reason to believe that an act of torture has been committed within their jurisdiction, the States Parties shall guarantee that their respective authorities will proceed properly and immediately to conduct an investigation into the case and to initiate, whenever appropriate, the corresponding criminal process.

After all the domestic legal procedures of the respective State and the corresponding appeals have been exhausted, the case may be submitted to the international for a whose competence has been recognized by that State.

Article 9

The States Parties undertake to incorporate into their national laws regulations guaranteeing suitable compensation for victims of torture.

None of the provisions of this article shall affect the right to receive compensation that the victim or other persons may have by virtue of existing national legislation.

Article 10

No statement that is verified as having been obtained through torture shall be admissible as evidence in a legal proceeding, except in a legal action taken against a person or persons accused of having elicited it through acts of torture, and only as evidence that the accused obtained such statement by such means.

Article 11

The States Parties shall take the necessary steps to extradite anyone accused of having committed the crime of torture or sentenced for commission of that crime, in accordance with their respective national laws on extradition and their international commitments on this matter.

Article 12

Every State Party shall take the necessary measures to establish its jurisdiction over the crime described in this Convention in the following cases:

    a.   When torture has been committed within its jurisdiction;
    b.   When the alleged criminal is a national of that State; or
    c.   When the victim is a national of that State and it so deems appropriate.

Every State Party shall also take the necessary measures to establish its jurisdiction over the crime described in this Convention when the alleged criminal is within the area under its jurisdiction and it is not appropriate to extradite him in accordance with Article 11.

This Convention does not exclude criminal jurisdiction exercised in accordance with domestic law.

Article 13

The crime referred to in Article 2 shall be deemed to be included among the extraditable crimes in every extradition treaty entered into between States Parties. The States Parties undertake to include the crime of torture as an extraditable offence in every extradition treaty to be concluded between them.

Every State Party that makes extradition conditional on the existence of a treaty may, if it receives a request for extradition from another State Party with which it has no extradition treaty, consider this Convention as the legal basis for extradition in respect of the crime of torture.

Extradition shall be subject to the other conditions that may be required by the law of the requested State.

States Parties which do not make extradition conditional on the existence of a treaty shall recognize such crimes as extraditable offences between themselves, subject to the conditions required by the law of the requested State.

Extradition shall not be granted nor shall the person sought be returned when there are grounds to believe that his life is in danger, that he will be subjected to torture or to cruel, inhuman or degrading treatment, or that he will be tried by special or ad hoc courts in the requesting State.

Article 14

When a State Party does not grant the extradition, the case shall be submitted to its competent authorities as if the crime had been committed within its jurisdiction, for the purposes of investigation, and when appropriate, for criminal action, in accordance with its national law. Any decision adopted by these authorities shall be communicated to the State that has requested the extradition.

Article 15

No provision of this Convention may be interpreted as limiting the right of asylum, when appropriate, nor as altering the obligations of the States Parties in the matter of extradition.

Article 16

This Convention shall not limit the provisions of the American Convention on Human Rights, other conventions on the subject, or the Statutes of the Inter-American Commission on Human Rights, with respect to the crime of torture.

Article 17

The States Parties undertake to inform the Inter-American Commission on Human Rights of any legislative, judicial, administrative, or other measures they adopt in application of this Convention. In keeping with its duties and responsibilities, the Inter-American Commission on Human Rights will endeavour in its annual report to analyse the existing situation in the member states of the Organization of American States in regard to the prevention and elimination of torture.

Article 18

This Convention is open to signature by the member states of the Organization of American States.

Article 19

This Convention is subject to ratification. The instruments of ratification shall be deposited with the General Secretariat of the Organization of American States.

Article 20

This Convention is open to accession by any other American state. The instruments of accession shall be deposited with the General Secretariat of the Organization of American States.

Article 21

The States Parties may, at the time of approval, signature, ratification, or accession, make reservations to this Convention, provided that such reservations are not incompatible with the object and purpose of the Convention and concern one or more specific provisions.

Article 22

This Convention shall enter into force on the thirtieth day following the date on which the second instrument of ratification is deposited. For each State ratifying or acceding to the Convention after the second instrument of ratification has been deposited, the Convention shall enter into force on the thirtieth day following the date on which that State deposits its instrument of ratification or accession.

Article 23

This Convention shall remain in force indefinitely, but may be denounced by any State Party. The instrument of denunciation shall be deposited with the General Secretariat of the Organization of American States. After one year from the date of deposit of the instrument of denunciation, this Convention shall cease to be in effect for the denouncing State but shall remain in force for the remaining States Parties.

Article 24

The original instrument of this Convention, the English, French, Portuguese, and Spanish texts of which are equally authentic, shall be deposited with the General Secretariat of the Organization of American States, which shall send a certified copy to the Secretariat of the United Nations for registration and publication, in accordance with the provisions of Article 102 of the United Nations Charter. The General Secretariat of the Organization of American States shall notify the member states of the Organization and the States that have acceded to the Convention of signatures and of deposits of instruments of ratification, accession, and denunciation, as well as reservations, if any.

47. COUNCIL OF EUROPE: EUROPEAN CONVENTION FOR THE PREVENTION OF TORTURE AND INHUMAN OR DEGRADING TREATMENT OR PUNISHMENT

Opened for signature at Strasbourg: 26 November 1987

ETS 126

Entry into force: 1 February 1989

Editors' Notes

The European Convention for the Prevention of Torture supplements the prohibition of torture established by the Council of Europe within Article 3 of the European Convention on Human Rights.[1] As with other treaties directly addressing the prohibition of the use of torture, this obligation under the ECHR cannot be derogated, even in time of war or public emergency (Article 15).[2] The protection under the Article 3 is couched in similar terms to other treaties prohibiting torture except that the word "cruel" is omitted.[3] No particular significance has been attached to this difference.

Discussion of Article 3 by the European Commission and Court has been copious.[4] Significant decisions include: *Ireland v UK*,[5] where the Court defined torture as "deliberate inhuman treatment causing very serious and cruel suffering" and distinguished between acts constituting torture and acts amounting to inhuman and degrading treatment; *Cyprus v Turkey*,[6] where the Commission found that a state is responsible for the actions of its servants, even if those acts are *ultra vires*; *Soering v UK*,[7] where the Court ruled that Article 3 restricts the use of the extradition process, thereby giving the Convention an "extraterritorial reach" and *Tyrer v UK*,[8] where the Court characterised degrading punishment as containing elements of humiliation and indignity.

---

[1] *Supra.*

[2] See: International Covenant on Civil and Political Rights, Article 4, *supra*; UN Convention against Torture, Article 2, *supra*; Inter-American Convention to Prevent and Punish Torture, Article 5, *supra*.

[3] See for example: Universal Declaration of Human Rights, Article 5, *supra*; International Covenant on Civil and Political Rights, Article 7, *supra*.

[4] See: Cassese, A. (1993). 'Prohibition of Torture and Inhuman or Degrading Treatment or Punishment', in Macdonald, R. St. J. et al (Eds). *The European System for the Protection of Human Rights*. Netherlands, Martinus Nijhoff; Harris, D.J., O'Boyle, M. & Warbrick, C. (1995). *Law of the European Convention on Human Rights*. London, Butterworths.

[5] *Ireland v UK*, ECtHRR A 25 (1978), 2 EHRR 25.

[6] *Cyprus v Turkey*, Nos 6780/74 and 6950/75 (First and Second Applications), 4 EHRR 482 (1976) Com Rep; CM Res DH (79) 1.

[7] *Soering v UK*, ECtHRR A 161 (1989), Eur Ct HR. See also notes on the European Convention on Extradition, *infra*.

[8] *Tyrer v UK*, ECtHRR A 26 (1978), Eur Ct HR.

While the European Convention on Human Rights provides a remedy for states or individuals when Article 3 is infringed, the Convention on the Prevention of Torture establishes a system for the inspection of the detention facilities of parties to the Convention, for the purposes of preventing practices amounting to torture, inhuman or degrading treatment (Article 1). The Committee for the Prevention of Torture produces national reports and an annual report detailing its findings and recommendations for improvement. Where a state refuses to make changes in response to the reports of the Committee, the Committee can issue a public statement (Article 10). It has done so only once.[9]

The member States of the Council of Europe, signatory hereto,

Having regard to the provisions of the Convention for the Protection of Human Rights and Fundamental Freedoms;

Recalling that, under Article 3 of the same Convention, "no one shall be subjected to torture or to inhuman or degrading treatment or punishment";

Noting that the machinery provided for in that Convention operates in relation to persons who allege that they are victims of violations of Article 3;

Convinced that the protection of persons deprived of their liberty against torture and inhuman or degrading treatment or punishment could be strengthened by non-judicial means of a preventive character based on visits;

Have agreed as follows:

CHAPTER I

Article 1

There shall be established a European Committee for the Prevention of Torture and Inhuman or Degrading Treatment or Punishment (hereinafter referred to as "the Committee"). The Committee shall, by means of visits, examine the treatment of persons deprived of their liberty with a view to strengthening, if necessary, the protection of such persons from torture and from inhuman or degrading treatment or punishment.

Article 2

Each Party shall permit visits, in accordance with this Convention, to any place within its jurisdiction where persons are deprived of their liberty by a public authority.

Article 3

In the application of this Convention, the Committee and the competent national authorities of the Party concerned shall cooperate with each other.

---

[9] See: *1992 Public Statement on Turkey*, 15 EHRR 309, at 315.

CHAPTER II

Article 4

1. The Committee shall consist of a number of members equal to that of the Parties.
2. The members of the Committee shall be chosen from among persons of high moral character, known for their competence in the field of human rights or having professional experience in the areas covered by this Convention.
3. No two members of the Committee may be nationals of the same State.
4. The members shall serve in their individual capacity, shall be independent and impartial, and shall be available to serve the Committee effectively.

Article 5

1. The members of the Committee shall be elected by the Committee of Ministers of the Council of Europe by an absolute majority of votes, from a list of names drawn up by the Bureau of the Consultative Assembly of the Council of Europe; each national delegation of the Parties in the Consultative Assembly shall put forward three candidates, of whom two at least shall be its nationals.
2. The same procedure shall be followed in filling casual vacancies.
3. The members of the Committee shall be elected for a period of four years. They may only be re-elected once. However, among the members elected at the first election, the terms of three members shall expire at the end of two years. The members whose terms are to expire at the end of the initial period of two years shall be chosen by lot by the Secretary General of the Council of Europe immediately after the first election has been completed.

Article 6

1. The Committee shall meet in camera. A quorum shall be equal to the majority of its members. The decisions of the Committee shall be taken by a majority of the members present, subject to the provisions of Article 10, paragraph 2.
2. The Committee shall draw up its own rules of procedure.
3. The Secretariat of the Committee shall be provided by the Secretary General of the Council of Europe.

CHAPTER III

Article 7

1. The Committee shall organise visits to places referred to in Article 2. Apart from periodic visits, the Committee may organise such other visits as appear to it to be required in the circumstances.
2. As a general rule, the visits shall be carried out by at least two members of the Committee. The Committee may, if it considers it necessary, be assisted by experts and interpreters.

Article 8

1. The Committee shall notify the Government of the Party concerned of its intention to carry out a visit. After such notification, it may at any time visit any place referred to in Article 2.
2. A Party shall provide the Committee with the following facilities to carry out its task:

   a. access to its territory and the right to travel without restriction;
   b. full information on the places where persons deprived of their liberty are being held;
   c. unlimited access to any place where persons are deprived of their liberty, including the right to move inside such places without restriction;
   d. other information available to the Party which is necessary for the Committee to carry out its task. In seeking such information, the Committee shall have regard to applicable rules of national law and professional ethics.

3. The Committee may interview in private persons deprived of their liberty.
4. The Committee may communicate freely with any person whom it believes can supply relevant information.
5. If necessary, the Committee may immediately communicate observations to the competent authorities of the Party concerned.

Article 9

1. In exceptional circumstances, the competent authorities of the Party concerned may make representations to the Committee against a visit at the time or to the particular place proposed by the Committee. Such representations may only be made on grounds of national defence, public safety, serious disorder in places where persons are deprived of their liberty, the medical condition of a person or that an urgent interrogation relating to a serious crime is in progress.
2. Following such representations, the Committee and the Party shall immediately enter into consultations in order to clarify the situation and seek agreement on arrangements to enable the Committee to exercise its functions expeditiously. Such arrangements may include the transfer to another place of any person whom the Committee proposed to visit. Until the visit takes place, the Party shall provide information to the Committee about any person concerned.

Article 10

1. After each visit, the Committee shall draw up a report on the facts found during the visit, taking account of any observations which may have been submitted by the Party concerned. It shall transmit to the latter its report containing any recommendations it considers necessary. The Committee may consult with the Party with a view to suggesting, if necessary, improvements

in the protection of persons deprived of their liberty.

2. If the Party fails to cooperate or refuses to improve the situation in the light of the Committee's recommendations, the Committee may decide, after the Party has had an opportunity to make known its views, by a majority of two-thirds of its members to make a public statement on the matter.

Article 11

1. The information gathered by the Committee in relation to a visit, its report and its consultations with the Party concerned shall be confidential.
2. The Committee shall publish its report, together with any comments of the Party concerned, whenever requested to do so by that Party.
3. However, no personal data shall be published without the express consent of the person concerned.

Article 12

Subject to the rules of confidentiality in Article 11, the Committee shall every year submit to the Committee of Ministers a general report on its activities which shall be transmitted to the Consultative Assembly and made public.

Article 13

The members of the Committee, experts and other persons assisting the Committee are required, during and after their terms of office, to maintain the confidentiality of the facts or information of which they have become aware during the discharge of their functions.

Article 14

1. The names of persons assisting the Committee shall be specified in the notification under Article 8, paragraph 1.
2. Experts shall act on the instructions and under the authority of the Committee. They shall have particular knowledge and experience in the areas covered by this Convention and shall be bound by the same duties of independence, impartiality and availability as the members of the Committee.
3. A Party may exceptionally declare that an expert or other person assisting the Committee may not be allowed to take part in a visit to a place within its jurisdiction.

CHAPTER IV

Article 15

Each Party shall inform the Committee of the name and address of the authority competent to receive notifications to its Government, and of any liaison officer it may appoint.

Article 16

The Committee, its members and experts referred to in Article 7, paragraph 2, shall enjoy the privileges and immunities set out in the annex to this Convention.

Article 17

1. This Convention shall not prejudice the provisions of domestic law or any international agreement which provide greater protection for persons deprived of their liberty.
2. Nothing in this Convention shall be construed as limiting or derogating from the competence of the organs of the European Convention on Human Rights or from the obligations assumed by the Parties under that Convention.
3. The Committee shall not visit places which representatives or delegates of protecting powers or the International Committee of the Red Cross effectively visit on a regular basis by virtue of the Geneva Conventions of 12 August 1949 and the Additional Protocols of 8 June 1977 thereto.

CHAPTER V

Article 18

This Convention shall be open for signature by the member States of the Council of Europe. It is subject to ratification, acceptance or approval. Instruments of ratification, acceptance or approval shall be deposited with the Secretary General of the Council of Europe.

Article 19

1. This Convention shall enter into force on the first day of the month following the expiration of a period of three months after the date on which seven member States of the Council of Europe have expressed their consent to be bound by the Convention in accordance with the provisions of Article 18.
2. In respect of any member State which subsequently expresses its consent to be bound by it, the Convention shall enter into force on the first day of the month following the expiration of a period of three months after the date of the deposit of the instrument of ratification, acceptance or approval.

Article 20

1. Any State may at the time of signature or when depositing its instrument of ratification, acceptance or approval, specify the territory or territories to which this Convention shall apply.
2. Any State may at any later date, by a declaration addressed to the Secretary General of the Council of Europe, extend the application of this Convention to any other territory specified in the declaration. In respect of such territory the Convention shall enter into force on the first day of the month following the

expiration of a period of three months after the date of receipt of such declaration by the Secretary General.

3. Any declaration made under the two preceding paragraphs may, in respect of any territory specified in such declaration, be withdrawn by a notification addressed to the Secretary General. The withdrawal shall become effective on the first day of the month following the expiration of a period of three months after the date of receipt of such notification by the Secretary General.

Article 21

No reservation may be made in respect of the provisions of this Convention.

Article 22

1. Any Party may, at any time, denounce this Convention by means of a notification addressed to the Secretary General of the Council of Europe.
2. Such denunciation shall become effective on the first day of the month following the expiration of a period of twelve months after the date of receipt of the notification by the Secretary General.

Article 23

The Secretary, General of the Council of Europe shall notify the member States of the Council of Europe of:

a. any signature;
b. the deposit of any instrument of ratification, acceptance or approval;
c. any date of entry into force of this Convention in accordance with Articles 19 and 20;
d. any other act, notification or communication relating to this Convention, except for action taken in pursuance of Articles 8 and 10.

In witness whereof, the undersigned, being duly authorised thereto, have signed this Convention.

Done at Strasbourg, this 26th day of November 1987, in English and French, both texts being equally authentic, in a single copy which shall be deposited in the archives of the Council of Europe. The Secretary General of the Council of Europe shall transmit certified copies to each member State of the Council of Europe.

ANNEX
PRIVILEGES AND IMMUNITIES

(Article 16)

1. For the purpose of this annex, references to members of the Committee shall be deemed to include references to experts mentioned in Article 7, paragraph 2.

2. The members of the Committee shall, while exercising their functions and during journeys made in the exercise of their functions, enjoy the following privileges and immunities:

    a. immunity from personal arrest or detention and from seizure of their personal baggage and, in respect of words spoken or written and all acts done by them in their official capacity, immunity from legal process of every kind;
    b. exemption from any restrictions on their freedom of movement: on exit from and return to their country of residence, and entry into and exit from the country in which they exercise their functions, and from alien registration in the country which they are visiting or through which they are passing in the exercise of their functions.

3. In the course of journeys undertaken in the exercise of their functions, the members of the Committee shall, in the matter of customs and exchange control, be accorded:

    a. by their own government, the same facilities as those accorded to senior officials travelling abroad on temporary official duty;
    b. by the governments of other Parties, the same facilities as those accorded to representatives of foreign governments on temporary official duty.

4. Documents and papers of the Committee, insofar as they relate to the business of the Committee, shall be inviolable.
    The official correspondence and other official communications of the Committee may not be held up or subjected to censorship.

5. In order to secure for the members of the Committee complete freedom of speech and complete independence in the discharge of heir duties, the immunity from legal process in respect of words spoken or written and all acts done by them in discharging their duties shall continue to be accorded, notwithstanding that the persons concerned are no longer engaged in the discharge of such duties.

6. Privileges and immunities are accorded to the members of the Committee, not for the personal benefit of the individuals themselves but in order to safeguard the independent exercise of their functions. The Committee alone shall be competent to waive the immunity, of its members; it has not only the right, but is under a duty, to waive the immunity of one of its members in any case where, in its opinion, the immunity would impede the course of justice, and where it can be waived without prejudice to the purpose for which the immunity is accorded.

FIRST PROTOCOL TO THE EUROPEAN CONVENTION FOR THE PREVENTION OF TORTURE AND INHUMAN OR DEGRADING TREATMENT OR PUNISHMENT (1993)

Opened for signature at Strasbourg: 4 November 1993

ETC 151

Not in force

The member States of the Council of Europe, signatories to this Protocol to the European Convention for the Prevention of Torture and Inhuman or degrading Treatment or Punishment, signed at Strasbourg on 26 November 1987 (hereinafter referred to as "the Convention"),

Considering that non-member States of the Council of Europe should be allowed to accede to the Convention at the invitation of the Committee of Ministers,
Have agreed as follows:

Article 1

A sub-paragraph shall be added to Article 5, paragraph I, of the Convention as follows:

"Where a member is to be elected to the Committee in respect of a non-member State of the Council of Europe, the Bureau of the Consultative Assembly shall invite the Parliament of that State to put forward three candidates, of whom two at least shall be its nationals. The election by the Committee of Ministers shall take place after consultation with the Party concerned."

Article 2

Article 12 of the Convention shall read as follows:

"Subject to the rules of confidentiality in Article 11, the committee shall every year submit to the Committee of Ministers a general report on its activities which shall be transmitted to the consultative Assembly and to any non-member State of the Council of Europe which is a party to the Convention, and made public."

Article 3

The text of Article 18 of the Convention shall become paragraph 1 of that article and shall be supplemented by the following second paragraph:

"2. 'The Committee of Ministers of the Council of Europe may invite any non-member State of the Council of Europe to accede to the Convention.'"

Article 8

This Protocol shall enter into force on the first day of the month following the expiration of a period of three months after the date on which all Parties to the Convention have expressed their consent to be bound by the Protocol, in accordance with the Provisions of Article 7.

SECOND PROTOCOL TO THE EUROPEAN CONVENTION FOR THE PREVENTION OF TORTURE AND INHUMAN OR DEGRADING TREATMENT OR PUNISHMENT(1993)

Opened for signature at Strasbourg: 4 November 1993

ETS 151

Not in force

The Member States of the Council of Europe, signatories to this Protocol to the European Convention for the Prevention of Torture and Inhuman or Degrading Treatment or Punishment, signed at Strasbourg on 26 November 1987 (hereinafter referred to as "the Convention"),

Convinced of the advisability of enabling members of the European Committee for the Prevention of Torture and Inhuman and Degrading Treatment (hereinafter referred to as "the Committee") to be re-elected twice;

Also considering the need to guarantee an orderly renewal of the membership of the Committee,

Have agreed as follows:

Article 1

1. In Article 5, paragraph 3, the second sentence shall read as follows:

    "They may be re-elected twice."

2. Article 5 of the Convention shall be supplemented by the following paragraphs 4 and 5:

    "4. In order to ensure that, as far as possible, one half of the membership of the Committee shall be renewed every two years, the Committee of Ministers may decide, before proceeding to any subsequent election, that the term or terms of office of one or more members to be elected shall be for a period other than four years but not more than six and not less than two years.

    5. In cases where more than one term of office is involved and the Committee of Ministers applies the preceding paragraph, the allocation of the terms of office shall be effected by the drawing of lots by the Secretary-General, immediately after the election."

Article 3

This Protocol shall enter into force on the first day of the month following the expiration of a period of three months after the date on which all Parties to the Convention have expressed their consent to be bound by the Protocol, in accordance with the provisions of Article 2.

48. UNITED NATIONS: DECLARATION ON THE PROTECTION OF ALL PERSONS FROM ENFORCED DISAPPEARANCE

Adopted by General Assembly resolution 47/133 (1992)

Editors' Notes

Since 1978, the United Nations has expressed concern about a number of states employing organised terror campaigns involving the systematic use of enforced disappearances as a form of suppression.[1] Following a report by the Human Rights Commission,[2] the United Nations General Assembly adopted The Declaration on the Protection of All Persons from Enforced Disappearance in 1992.[3]

The preamble links the provisions of the Declaration to a variety of other United Nations Treaties and measures adopted by the General Assembly, including those prohibiting torture and the treatment of prisoners. Article 1 of the Declaration denounces any act of disappearance as a "flagrant violation of human rights". The Declaration also establishes criminal and civil liability for the individual and the state (Articles 4–5), a duty on the state to prevent (Article 3) and investigate disappearances (Article 13), and allows for the compensation of victims and their families (Article 19). Article 18 specifically requires that the perpetrators of disappearances should not benefit from immunity or amnesty from prosecution.

The General Assembly,

Considering that, in accordance with the principles proclaimed in the Charter of the United Nations and other international instruments, recognition of the inherent dignity and of the equal and inalienable rights of all members of the human family is the foundation of freedom, justice and peace in the world,

Bearing in mind the obligation of States under the Charter, in particular Article 55, to promote universal respect for, and observance of, human rights and fundamental freedoms,

Deeply concerned that in many countries, often in a persistent manner, enforced disappearances occur, in the sense that persons are arrested, detained or abducted against their will or otherwise deprived of their liberty by officials of different

---

[1] See for example: Report prepared by the Special Rapporteur on the situation of human rights in Chile in accordance with paragraph 11 of the Commission on Human Rights. UN Doc. A/38/385 (1983); see also: Roht-Ariaza, N. (1995). *Impunity and Human Rights in International Law and Practice.* Oxford, Oxford University Press. Chap. 11.

[2] Report of the Working Group on Enforced or Involuntary Disappearances. UN Doc. E/CN.4/1991/20.

[3] See also: Principles on the Effective Prevention and Investigation of Extra-legal, Arbitary and Summary Executions, endorsed by G.A Res. 44/162 of Dec. 15, 1989, GAOR 44th Sess., Supp. No. 49, p.235 (1990).

branches or levels of Government, or by organized groups or private individuals acting on behalf of, or with the support, direct or indirect, consent or acquiescence of the Government, followed by a refusal to disclose the fate or whereabouts of the persons concerned or a refusal to acknowledge the deprivation of their liberty, which places such persons outside the protection of the law,

Considering that enforced disappearance undermines the deepest values of any society committed to respect for the rule of law, human rights and fundamental freedoms, and that the systematic practice of such acts is of the nature of a crime against humanity,

Recalling its resolution 33/173 of 20 December 1978, in which it expressed concern about the reports from various parts of the world relating to enforced or involuntary disappearances, as well as about the anguish and sorrow caused by those disappearances, and called upon Governments to hold law enforcement and security forces legally responsible for excesses which might lead to enforced or involuntary disappearances of persons,

Recalling also the protection afforded to victims of armed conflicts by the Geneva Conventions of 12 August 1949 and the Additional Protocols thereto, of 1977,

Having regard in particular to the relevant articles of the Universal Declaration of Human Rights and the International Covenant on Civil and Political Rights, which protect the right to life, the right to liberty and security of the person, the right not to be subjected to torture and the right to recognition as a person before the law,

Having regard also to the Convention against Torture and Other Cruel, Inhuman or Degrading Treatment or Punishment, which provides that States parties shall take effective measures to prevent and punish acts of torture,

Bearing in mind the Code of Conduct for Law Enforcement Officials, the Basic Principles on the Use of Force and Firearms by Law Enforcement Officials, the Declaration of Basic Principles of Justice for Victims of Crime and Abuse of Power and the Standard Minimum Rules for the Treatment of Prisoners,

Affirming that, in order to prevent enforced disappearances, it is necessary to ensure strict compliance with the Body of Principles for the Protection of All Persons under Any Form of Detention or Imprisonment contained in the annex to its resolution 43/173 of 9 December 1988, and with the Principles on the Effective Prevention and Investigation of Extra-legal, Arbitrary and Summary Executions, set forth in the annex to Economic and Social Council resolution 1989/65 of 24 May 1989 and endorsed by the General Assembly in its resolution 44/162 of 15 December 1989,

Bearing in mind that, while the acts which comprise enforced disappearance constitute a violation of the prohibitions found in the aforementioned international instruments, it is none the less important to devise an instrument which characterizes all acts of enforced disappearance of persons as very serious offences and sets forth standards designed to punish and prevent their commission,

1. Proclaims the present Declaration on the Protection of All Persons from Enforced Disappearance, as a body of principles for all States;
2. Urges that all efforts be made so that the Declaration becomes generally known and respected.

Article 1

1. Any act of enforced disappearance is an offence to human dignity. It is condemned as a denial of the purposes of the Charter of the United Nations and as a grave and flagrant violation of the human rights and fundamental freedoms proclaimed in the Universal Declaration of Human Rights and reaffirmed and developed in international instruments in this field.
2. Any act of enforced disappearance places the persons subjected thereto outside the protection of the law and inflicts severe suffering on them and their families. It constitutes a violation of the rules of international law guaranteeing, inter alia, the right to recognition as a person before the law, the right to liberty and security of the person and the right not to be subjected to torture and other cruel, inhuman or degrading treatment or punishment. It also violates or constitutes a grave threat to the right to life.

Article 2

1. No State shall practise, permit or tolerate enforced disappearances.
2. States shall act at the national and regional levels and in cooperation with the United Nations to contribute by all means to the prevention and eradication of enforced disappearance.

Article 3

Each State shall take effective legislative, administrative, judicial or other measures to prevent and terminate acts of enforced disappearance in any territory under its jurisdiction.

Article 4

1. All acts of enforced disappearance shall be offences under criminal law punishable by appropriate penalties which shall take into account their extreme seriousness.
2. Mitigating circumstances may be established in national legislation for persons who, having participated in enforced disappearances, are instrumental in bringing the victims forward alive or in providing voluntarily information which would contribute to clarifying cases of enforced disappearance.

Article 5

In addition to such criminal penalties as are applicable, enforced disappearances render their perpetrators and the State or State authorities which organize, acquiesce in or tolerate such disappearances liable under civil law, without prejudice to the international responsibility of the State concerned in accordance with the principles of international law.

Article 6

1. No order or instruction of any public authority, civilian, military or other, may be invoked to justify an enforced disappearance. Any person receiving such an order or instruction shall have the right and duty not to obey it.
2. Each State shall ensure that orders or instructions directing, authorizing or encouraging any enforced disappearance are prohibited.
3. Training of law enforcement officials shall emphasize the provisions in paragraphs 1 and 2 of the present article.

Article 7

No circumstances whatsoever, whether a threat of war, a state of war, internal political instability or any other public emergency, may be invoked to justify enforced disappearances.

Article 8

1. No State shall expel, return (refouler) or extradite a person to another State where there are substantial grounds to believe that he would be in danger of enforced disappearance.
2. For the purpose of determining whether there are such grounds, the competent authorities shall take into account all relevant considerations including, where applicable, the existence in the State concerned of a consistent pattern of gross, flagrant or mass violations of human rights.

Article 9

1. The right to a prompt and effective judicial remedy as a means of determining the whereabouts or state of health of persons deprived of their liberty and/or identifying the authority ordering or carrying out the deprivation of liberty is required to prevent enforced disappearances under all circumstances, including those referred to in article 7 above.
2. In such proceedings, competent national authorities shall have access to all places where persons deprived of their liberty are being held and to each part of those places, as well as to any place in which there are grounds to believe that such persons may be found.
3. Any other competent authority entitled under the law of the State or by any international legal instrument to which the State is a party may also have access to such places.

Article 10

1. Any person deprived of liberty shall be held in an officially recognized place of detention and, in conformity with national law, be brought before a judicial authority promptly after detention.
2. Accurate information on the detention of such persons and their place or

places of detention, including transfers, shall be made promptly available to their family members, their counsel or to any other persons having a legitimate interest in the information unless a wish to the contrary has been manifested by the persons concerned.

3. An official up-to-date register of all persons deprived of their liberty shall be maintained in every place of detention. Additionally, each State shall take steps to maintain similar centralized registers. The information contained in these registers shall be made available to the persons mentioned in the preceding paragraph, to any judicial or other competent and independent national authority and to any other competent authority entitled under the law of the State concerned or any international legal instrument to which a State concerned is a party, seeking to trace the whereabouts of a detained person.

Article 11

All persons deprived of liberty must be released in a manner permitting reliable verification that they have actually been released and, further, have been released in conditions in which their physical integrity and ability fully to exercise their rights are assured.

Article 12

1. Each State shall establish rules under its national law indicating those officials authorized to order deprivation of liberty, establishing the conditions under which such orders may be given, and stipulating penalties for officials who, without legal justification, refuse to provide information on any detention.
2. Each State shall likewise ensure strict supervision, including a clear chain of command, of all law enforcement officials responsible for apprehensions, arrests, detentions, custody, transfers and imprisonment, and of other officials authorized by law to use force and firearms.

Article 13

1. Each State shall ensure that any person having knowledge or a legitimate interest who alleges that a person has been subjected to enforced disappearance has the right to complain to a competent and independent State authority and to have that complaint promptly, thoroughly and impartially investigated by that authority. Whenever there are reasonable grounds to believe that an enforced disappearance has been committed, the State shall promptly refer the matter to that authority for such an investigation, even if there has been no formal complaint. No measure shall be taken to curtail or impede the investigation.
2. Each State shall ensure that the competent authority shall have the necessary powers and resources to conduct the investigation effectively, including powers to compel attendance of witnesses and production of relevant documents and to make immediate on-site visits.

3. Steps shall be taken to ensure that all involved in the investigation, including the complainant, counsel, witnesses and those conducting the investigation, are protected against ill-treatment, intimidation or reprisal.
4. The findings of such an investigation shall be made available upon request to all persons concerned, unless doing so would jeopardize an ongoing criminal investigation.
5. Steps shall be taken to ensure that any ill-treatment, intimidation or reprisal or any other form of interference on the occasion of the lodging of a complaint or during the investigation procedure is appropriately punished.
6. An investigation, in accordance with the procedures described above, should be able to be conducted for as long as the fate of the victim of enforced disappearance remains unclarified.

Article 14

Any person alleged to have perpetrated an act of enforced disappearance in a particular State shall, when the facts disclosed by an official investigation so warrant, be brought before the competent civil authorities of that State for the purpose of prosecution and trial unless he has been extradited to another State wishing to exercise jurisdiction in accordance with the relevant international agreements in force. All States should take any lawful and appropriate action available to them to bring to justice all persons presumed responsible for an act of enforced disappearance, who are found to be within their jurisdiction or under their control.

Article 15

The fact that there are grounds to believe that a person has participated in acts of an extremely serious nature such as those referred to in article 4, paragraph 1, above, regardless of the motives, shall be taken into account when the competent authorities of the State decide whether or not to grant asylum.

Article 16

1. Persons alleged to have committed any of the acts referred to in article 4, paragraph 1, above, shall be suspended from any official duties during the investigation referred to in article 13 above.
2. They shall be tried only by the competent ordinary courts in each State, and not by any other special tribunal, in particular military courts.
3. No privileges, immunities or special exemptions shall be admitted in such trials, without prejudice to the provisions contained in the Vienna Convention on Diplomatic Relations.
4. The persons presumed responsible for such acts shall be guaranteed fair treatment in accordance with the relevant provisions of the Universal Declaration of Human Rights and other relevant international agreements in force at all stages of the investigation and eventual prosecution and trial.

Article 17

1. Acts constituting enforced disappearance shall be considered a continuing offence as long as the perpetrators continue to conceal the fate and the whereabouts of persons who have disappeared and these facts remain unclarified.
2. When the remedies provided for in article 2 of the International Covenant on Civil and Political Rights are no longer effective, the statute of limitations relating to acts of enforced disappearance shall be suspended until these remedies are re-established.
3. Statutes of limitations, where they exist, relating to acts of enforced disappearance shall be substantial and commensurate with the extreme seriousness of the offence.

Article 18

1. Persons who have or are alleged to have committed offences referred to in article 4, paragraph 1, above, shall not benefit from any special amnesty law or similar measures that might have the effect of exempting them from any criminal proceedings or sanction.
2. In the exercise of the right of pardon, the extreme seriousness of acts of enforced disappearance shall be taken into account.

Article 19

The victims of acts of enforced disappearance and their family shall obtain redress and shall have the right to adequate compensation, including the means for as complete a rehabilitation as possible. In the event of the death of the victim as a result of an act of enforced disappearance, their dependants shall also be entitled to compensation.

Article 20

1. States shall prevent and suppress the abduction of children of parents subjected to enforced disappearance and of children born during their mother's enforced disappearance, and shall devote their efforts to the search for and identification of such children and to the restitution of the children to their families of origin.
2. Considering the need to protect the best interests of children referred to in the preceding paragraph, there shall be an opportunity, in States which recognize a system of adoption, for a review of the adoption of such children and, in particular, for annulment of any adoption which originated in enforced disappearance. Such adoption should, however, continue to be in force if consent is given, at the time of the review, by the child's closest relatives.
3. The abduction of children of parents subjected to enforced disappearance or of children born during their mother's enforced disappearance, and the act of

altering or suppressing documents attesting to their true identity, shall constitute an extremely serious offence, which shall be punished as such.

4. For these purposes, States shall, where appropriate, conclude bilateral and multilateral agreements.

Article 21

The provisions of the present Declaration are without prejudice to the provisions enunciated in the Universal Declaration of Human Rights or in any other international instrument, and shall not be construed as restricting or derogating from any of those provisions.

49. ORGANIZATION OF AMERICAN STATES: INTER-AMERICAN CONVENTION ON THE FORCED DISAPPEARANCE OF PERSONS

Adopted by the OAS General Assembly: 9 June 1994
OAE/ser.P, AG/doc.3 114/94 rev.1

Not in force

Editors' Notes

Prior to the Inter-American Convention on the Forced Disappearance of Persons, adopted in 1994, the Inter-American Court of Human Rights had previously characterised the nature of human rights violations occasioned by state involvement in disappearances in *Velasquez v Honduras*.[1] In its judgement the Court commented that:

> Disappearances are not new in the history of human rights violations. However, their systematic and repeated nature and their use not only for causing certain individuals to disappear, either briefly or permanently, but also as a means of creating a general state of anguish, insecurity and fear, is a recent phenomenon. Although this practice exists virtually worldwide, it has occurred with exceptional intensity in Latin America in the last few years. . . .[2]

The Court went on to hold that the disappearance in this instance violated Article 7 (the right to personal liberty), Article 5 (the right not to be subjected to torture) and Article 4 (the right to life) of the Inter-American Convention on Human Rights.

The use of "disappearances" as a method of intimidation and repression of the wider population by a number of other states in the region, including Uruguay, Paraguay, Bolivia, Guatemala and Argentina,[3] led the Organization of American States to adopt a specific treaty outlawing such actions. A "forced disappearance" is defined in Article II of the Treaty. The preamble to the Treaty reaffirms the systematic use of forced disappearance as a crime against humanity, requires states to criminalise acts of forced disappearance (Article I), to treat them as continuing offences (Article III), and to try or extradite the offender (Article IV). The accused cannot claim that such offences are political (Article V) or prosecution subject to statutes of limitation (Article VII – with exceptions). A defence of obedience to superior orders will not be admitted (Article VIII).

---

[1] Inter-American Court of Human Rights. Judgement of July 29, 1988. Reported at 28 ILM 294 (1989).

[2] *Ibid*, para. 149.

[3] See: Roht-Ariaza, N. (1995). *Impunity and Human Rights in International Law and Practice*. Oxford, Oxford University Press. Chap. 11.

PREAMBLE

The member states of the Organization of American States signatory to the present Convention,

Disturbed by the persistence of the forced disappearance of persons;

Reaffirming that the true meaning of American solidarity and good neighborliness can be none other than that of consolidating in this Hemisphere, in the framework of democratic institutions, a system of individual freedom and social justice based on respect for essential human rights;

Considering that the forced disappearance of persons is an affront to the conscience of the Hemisphere and a grave and abominable offense against the inherent dignity of the human being, and one that contradicts the principles and purposes enshrined in the Charter of the Organization of American States;

Considering that the forced disappearance of persons violates numerous non-derogable and essential human rights enshrined in the American Convention on Human Rights, in the American Declaration of the Rights and Duties of Man, and in the Universal Declaration of Human Rights;

Recalling that the international protection of human rights is in the form of a convention reinforcing or complementing the protection provided by domestic law and is based upon the attributes of the human personality;

Reaffirming that the systematic practice of the forced disappearance of persons constitutes a crime against humanity;

Hoping that this Convention may help to prevent, punish, and eliminate the forced disappearance of persons in the Hemisphere and make a decisive contribution to the protection of human rights and the rule of law;

Resolve to adopt the following Inter-American Convention on Forced Disappearance of Persons:

Article I

The States Parties to this Convention undertake:

    a. Not to practice, permit, or tolerate the forced disappearance of persons, even in states of emergency or suspension of individual guarantees;

    b. To punish within their jurisdictions, those persons who commit or attempt to commit the crime of forced disappearance of persons and their accomplices and accessories;

    c. To cooperate with one another in helping to prevent, punish, and eliminate the forced disappearance of persons;

    d. To take legislative, administrative, judicial, and any other measures necessary to comply with the commitments undertaken in this Convention.

Article II

For the purposes of this Convention, forced disappearance is considered to be the act of depriving a person or persons of his or their freedom, in whatever way, perpetrated by agents of the state or by persons or groups of persons acting with the authorization, support, or acquiescence of the state, followed by an absence of information or a refusal to acknowledge that deprivation of freedom or to give information on the whereabouts of that person, thereby impeding his or her recourse to the applicable legal remedies and procedural guarantees.

Article III

The States Parties undertake to adopt, in accordance with their constitutional procedures, the legislative measures that may be needed to define the forced disappearance of persons as an offense and to impose an appropriate punishment commensurate with its extreme gravity. This offense shall be deemed continuous or permanent as long as the fate or whereabouts of the victim has not been determined.

The States Parties may establish mitigating circumstances for persons who have participated in acts constituting forced disappearance when they help to cause the victim to reappear alive or provide information that sheds light on the forced disappearance of a person.

Article IV

The acts constituting the forced disappearance of persons shall be considered offenses in every State Party. Consequently, each State Party shall take measures to establish its jurisdiction over such cases in the following instances:

a. When the forced disappearance of persons or any act constituting such offense was committed within its jurisdiction;
b. When the accused is a national of that state;
c. When the victim is a national of that state and that state sees fit to do so.

Every State Party shall, moreover, take the necessary measures to establish its jurisdiction over the crime described in this Convention when the alleged criminal is within its territory and it does not proceed to extradite him.

This Convention does not authorize any State Party to undertake, in the territory of another State Party, the exercise of jurisdiction or the performance of functions that are placed within the exclusive purview of the authorities of that other Party by its domestic law.

Article V

The forced disappearance of persons shall not be considered a political offense for purposes of extradition.

The forced disappearance of persons shall be deemed to be included among the extraditable offenses in every extradition treaty entered into between States Parties.

The States Parties undertake to include the offense of forced disappearance as one which is extraditable in every extradition treaty to be concluded between them in the future.

Every State Party that makes extradition conditional on the existence of a treaty and receives a request for extradition from another State Party with which it has no extradition treaty may consider this Convention as the necessary legal basis for extradition with respect to the offense of forced disappearance.

States Parties which do not make extradition conditional on the existence of a treaty shall recognize such offense as extraditable, subject to the conditions imposed by the law of the requested state.

Extradition shall be subject to the provisions set forth in the constitution and other laws of the request state.

Article VI

When a State Party does not grant the extradition, the case shall be submitted to its competent authorities as if the offense had been committed within its jurisdiction, for the purposes of investigation and when appropriate, for criminal action, in accordance with its national law. Any decision adopted by these authorities shall be communicated to the state that has requested the extradition.

Article VII

Criminal prosecution for the forced disappearance of persons and the penalty judicially imposed on its perpetrator shall not be subject to statutes of limitations.

However, if there should be a norm of a fundamental character preventing application of the stipulation contained in the previous paragraph, the period of limitation shall be equal to that which applies to the gravest crime in the domestic laws of the corresponding State Party.

Article VII

The defense of due obedience to superior orders or instructions that stipulate, authorize, or encourage forced disappearance shall not be admitted. All persons who receive such orders have the right and duty not to obey them.

The States Parties shall ensure that the training of public law-enforcement personnel or officials includes the necessary education on the offense of forced disappearance of persons.

Article IX

Persons alleged to be responsible for the acts constituting the offense of forced disappearance of persons may be tried only in the competent jurisdictions of ordinary law in each state, to the exclusion of all other special jurisdictions, particularly military jurisdictions.

The acts constituting forced disappearance shall not be deemed to have been committed in the course of military duties.

Privileges, immunities, or special dispensations shall not be admitted in such trials, without prejudice to the provisions set forth in the Vienna Convention on Diplomatic Relations.

Article X

In no case may exceptional circumstances such as a state of war, the threat of war, internal political instability, or any other public emergency be invoked to justify the forced disappearance of persons. In such cases, the right to expeditious and effective judicial procedures and recourse shall be retained as a means of determining the whereabouts or state of health of a person who has been deprived of freedom, or of identifying the official who ordered or carried out such deprivation of freedom.

In pursuing such procedures or recourse, and in keeping with applicable domestic law, the competent judicial authorities shall have free and immediate access to all detention centers and to each of their units, and to all places where there is reason to believe the disappeared person might be found including places that are subject to military jurisdiction.

Article XI

Every person deprived of liberty shall be held in an officially recognized place of detention and be brought before a competent judicial authority without delay, in accordance with applicable domestic law.

The States Parties shall establish and maintain official up-to-date registries of their detainees and, in accordance with their domestic law, shall make them available to relatives, judges, attorneys, any other person having a legitimate interest, and other authorities.

Article XII

The States Parties shall give each other mutual assistance in the search for, identification, location, and return of minors who have been removed to another state or detained therein as a consequence of the forced disappearance of their parents or guardians.

Article XIII

For the purposes of this Convention, the processing of petitions or communications presented to the Inter-American Commission on Human Rights alleging the forced disappearance of persons shall be subject to the procedures established in the American Convention on Human Rights and to the Statue and Regulations of the Inter-American Commission on Human Rights and to the Statute and Rules of Procedure of the Inter-American Court of Human Rights, including the provisions on precautionary measures.

Article XIV

Without prejudice to the provisions of the preceding article, when the Inter-American Commission on Human Rights receives a petition or communication regarding an alleged forced disappearance, its Executive Secretariat shall urgently and confidentially address the respective government, and shall request that government to provide as soon as possible information as to the whereabouts of the allegedly disappeared person together with any other information it considers pertinent, and such request shall be without prejudice as to the admissibility of the petition.

Article XV

None of the provisions of this Convention shall be interpreted as limiting other bilateral or multilateral treaties or other agreements signed by the Parties.

This Convention shall not apply to the international conflicts governed by the 1949 Geneva Conventions and their Protocols, concerning protection of wounded, sick, and shipwrecked members of the armed forces; and prisoners of war and civilians in time of war.

Article XVI

This Convention is open to signature by the member states of the Organization of American States.

Article XVII

This Convention is subject to ratification. The instruments of ratification shall be deposited with the General Secretariat of the Organization of American States.

Article XVIII

This Convention shall be open to accession by any other state. The instruments of accession shall be deposited with the General Secretariat of the Organization of American States.

Article XIX

The states may express reservations with respect to this Convention when adopting, signing, ratifying or acceding to it, unless such reservations are incompatible with the object and purpose of the Convention and as long as they refer to one or more specific provisions.

Article XX

This Convention shall enter into force for the ratifying states on the thirtieth day from the date of deposit of the second instrument of ratification.

For each state ratifying or acceding to the Convention after the second instrument of ratification has been deposited, the Convention shall enter into force on the thirtieth day from the date on which that state deposited its instrument of ratification or accession.

Article XXI

This Convention shall remain in force indefinitely, but may be denounced by any state party. The instrument of denunciation shall be deposited with the General Secretariat of the Organization of American States. The Convention shall cease to be in effect for the denouncing state and shall be in force for the other parties one year from the date of deposit of the instrument of denunciation.

Article XXII

The original instrument of this Convention, the Spanish, English, Portugese, and French texts of which all are equally authentic, shall be deposited with the General Secretariat of the Organization of American States, which shall forward certified copies thereof to the United Nations Secretariat, for registration and publication, in accordance with Article 102 of the Charter of the United Nations. The General Secretariat of the Organization of American States shall notify member states of the Organization and states acceding to the Convention of the signatures and deposit of instruments of ratification, accession or denunciation, as well as of any reservations that may be expressed.

SECTION THREE

CRIMES AGAINST INTERNATIONAL LAW

50. UNITED NATIONS: CONVENTION ON THE PREVENTION AND PUNISHMENT OF THE CRIME OF GENOCIDE

Opened for signature: 9 December 1948

78 U.N.T.S. 277

Entry into force: 12 January 1951

Editors' Notes

The Genocide Convention unequivocally condemns genocide as a crime against international law which must be prevented and punished (Article 1). Genocide can be considered as one of a group of offences within the concept of "crimes against humanity" defined by the Charter of the International Military Tribunal at Nuremberg in 1945.[1] However, because the Tribunal had concerned itself with crimes committed in wartime or connected with the war, a loophole remained which omitted criminal liability for atrocities occurring in peacetime. The United Nations, mindful of the events in Germany prior to the war, clarified the position of genocide in the Genocide Convention, notably by defining the crime of genocide (Article 2), and prohibiting such acts "in time of peace or in time of war" (Article 1). A weakness in the drafting of the definition of genocide is that groups of people characterised by their political views fall outside of the meaning of Article 2, which it is argued, leaves the perpetrators of "ideological" slaughters untouched by the Convention.[2] In addition to direct acts of genocide, conspiracy, incitement, attempts and complicity to commit genocide are punishable under Article 3. Article 4 provides that no immunity as head of state or as a public official can be claimed.

The Convention provides that states must enact domestic laws to give effect to its provisions (Article 5) and that states shall try persons charged with offences in a competent court where the act was committed (Article 6). During discussions prior to the completion of the Convention, questions of international criminal jurisdiction and the establishment of a permanent international criminal court were mooted but not resolved.[3] Article 6 of the Convention reflects this discussion, however, by allowing for offences to be tried in an international penal tribunal with appropriate jurisdiction. While work to establish a permanent international criminal tribunal continues, the *ad hoc* tribunals established by the United Nations to try grave violations of human rights in the former Yugoslavia and Rwanda both have the

---

[1] Article 6(c).
[2] See: UN Report on the Study of the Question of the Prevention of the Crime of Genocide. UN Doc. E/CN.4/Sub.2/416 (1978); Fein, H. (1984). 'Scenarios of Genocide: Models of Genocide and Critical Responses', in Charney, I.W. (Ed.). *Toward the Understanding and Prevention of Genocide*.
[3] See: Draft Statute for a Permanent International Criminal Court, *infra*.

555

competence to try defendants for genocide.[4] This has already led to the indictment in 1995 of the President of the Bosnian Serb administration, Radovan Karadzic, and the General of the Bosnian Serb army, Ratko Mladic, on charges of genocide. Prior to the creation of the International Tribunal, Bosnia had brought two applications before the International Court of Justice, whose limited jurisdiction is given under Article 9 of the Genocide Convention, to request that the Court order provisional measures preventing Serbia and Montenegro from pursuing acts of genocide.[5]

Both the United Nations and the Council of Europe have established treaties to ensure that prosecutions for acts of genocide are not barred by time.[6]

PREAMBLE

The Contracting Parties,

Having considered the declaration made by the General Assembly of the United Nations in its resolution 96 (I) dated 11 December 1946 that genocide is a crime under international law, contrary to the spirit and aims of the United Nations and condemned by the civilized world,

Recognizing that at all periods of history genocide has inflicted great losses on humanity, and

Being convinced that, in order to liberate mankind from such an odious scourge, international co-operation is required,

Hereby agree as hereinafter provided:

Article 1

The Contracting Parties confirm that genocide, whether committed in time of peace or in time of war, is a crime under international law which they undertake to prevent and to punish.

Article 2

In the present Convention, genocide means any of the following acts committed with intent to destroy, in whole or in part, a national, ethnical, racial or religious group, as such:

(a) Killing members of the group;
(b) Causing serious bodily or mental harm to members of the group;
(c) Deliberately inflicting on the group conditions of life calculated to bring about its physical destruction in whole or in part;

---

[4] See: International Tribunal for the Prosecution of Persons Responsible for Serious Violations of International Humanitarian Law Committed in the Territory of the Former Yugoslavia since 1991, *infra.* esp. Article 4.

[5] See: Gray, C. (1994). 43 ICLQ 704.

[6] United Nations Convention on the Non-applicability of Statutory Limitations to War Crimes and Crimes against Humanity (1968); Council of Europe Convention on the Non-applicability of Statutory Limitations to Crimes against Humanity and War Crimes (1974).

(d) Imposing measures intended to prevent births within the group;

(e) Forcibly transferring children of the group to another group.

Article 3

The following acts shall be punishable:

(a) Genocide;

(b) Conspiracy to commit genocide;

(c) Direct and public incitement to commit genocide;

(d) Attempt to commit genocide;

(e) Complicity in genocide.

Article 4

Persons committing genocide or any of the other acts enumerated in article 3 shall be punished, whether they are constitutionally responsible rulers, public officials or private individuals.

Article 5

The Contracting Parties undertake to enact, in accordance with their respective Constitutions, the necessary legislation to give effect to the provisions of the present Convention and, in particular, to provide effective penalties for persons guilty of genocide or any of the other acts enumerated in article 3.

Article 6

Persons charged with genocide or any of the other acts enumerated in article 3 shall be tried by a competent tribunal of the State in the territory of which the act was committed, or by such international penal tribunal as may have jurisdiction with respect to those Contracting Parties which shall have accepted its jurisdiction.

Article 7

Genocide and the other acts enumerated in article 3 shall not be considered as political crimes for the purpose of extradition.

The Contracting Parties pledge themselves in such cases to grant extradition in accordance with their laws and treaties in force.

Article 8

Any Contracting Party may call upon the competent organs of the United Nations to take such action under the Charter of the United Nations as they consider appropriate for the prevention and suppression of acts of genocide or any of the other acts enumerated in article 3.

Article 9

Disputes between the Contracting Parties relating to the interpretation, application or fulfilment of the present Convention, including those relating to the responsibility of a State for genocide or for any of the other acts enumerated in article 3, shall be submitted to the International Court of Justice at the request of any of the parties to the dispute.

Article 10

The present Convention, of which the Chinese, English, French, Russian and Spanish texts are equally authentic, shall bear the date of 9 December 1948.

Article 11

The present Convention shall be open until 31 December 1949 for signature on behalf of any Member of the United Nations and of any non-member State to which an invitation to sign has been addressed by the General Assembly.

The present Convention shall be ratified, and the instruments of ratification shall be deposited with the Secretary-General of the United Nations.

After 1 January 1950, the present Convention may be acceded to on behalf of any Member of the United Nations and of any non-member State which has received an invitation as aforesaid.

Instruments of accession shall be deposited with the Secretary-General of the United Nations.

Article 12

Any Contracting Party may at any time, by notification addressed to the Secretary-General of the United Nations, extend the application of the present Convention to all or any of the territories for the conduct of whose foreign relations that Contracting Party is responsible.

Article 13

On the day when the first twenty instruments of ratification or accession have been deposited, the Secretary-General shall draw up a procès-verbal and transmit a copy thereof to each Member of the United Nations and to each of the non-member States contemplated in article 11.

The present Convention shall come into force on the ninetieth day following the date of deposit of the twentieth instrument of ratification or accession.

Any ratification or accession effected, subsequent to the latter date shall become effective on the ninetieth day following the deposit of the instrument of ratification or accession.

Article 14

The present Convention shall remain in effect for a period of ten years as from the date of its coming into force. It shall thereafter remain in force for successive periods of five years for such Contracting Parties as have not denounced it at least six months before the expiration of the current period. Denunciation shall be effected by a written notification addressed to the Secretary-General of the United Nations.

Article 15

If, as a result of denunciations, the number of Parties to the present Convention should become less than sixteen, the Convention shall cease to be in force as from the date on which the last of these denunciations shall become effective.

Article 16

A request for the revision of the present Convention may be made at any time by any Contracting Party by means of a notification in writing addressed to the Secretary-General. The General Assembly shall decide upon the steps, if any, to be taken in respect of such request.

Article 17

The Secretary-General of the United Nations shall notify all Members of the United Nations and the non-member States contemplated in article 11 of the following:

(a) Signatures, ratifications and accessions received in accordance with article 11;
(b) Notifications received in accordance with article 12;
(c) The date upon which the present Convention comes into force in accordance with article 13;
(d) Denunciations received in accordance with article 14;
(e) The abrogation of the Convention in accordance with article 15;
(f) Notifications received in accordance with article 16.

Article 18

The original of the present Convention shall be deposited in the archives of the United Nations. A certified copy of the Convention shall be transmitted to each Member of the United Nations and to each of the non-member States contemplated in article 11.

Article 19

The present Convention shall be registered by the Secretary-General of the United Nations on the date of its coming into force.

GRAVE VIOLATIONS OF THE GENEVA CONVENTIONS
(EXCERPTED PROVISIONS)

Editors' Notes

The four Geneva Conventions of 1949 and their two additional protocols of 1977 set out at length humanitarian standards in war. They deal with the wounded and sick in armed forces in the field, wounded, sick and ship-wrecked in the armed forces at sea, prisoners of war and civilians. Immediately following World War II, the International Committee of the Red Cross proposed measures to develop the international law applicable to armed conflicts and the present Conventions were adopted to revise and expand previous international frameworks.[1] While the Conventions include more than 600 articles, they cannot foresee all circumstances in the context or war, and Article 1 of Protocol I, makes it clear that parties should abide not only by the provisions of the Conventions but also to "generally recognised principles and rules of international law which are applicable to armed conflict".

The Conventions require parties to provide effective penal sanctions for those committing grave breaches of the provisions and to take steps to bring those alleged to have committed those breaches before their courts (Articles 49/50/129/146 of the respective Conventions). Alternatively, parties may if appropriate, transfer those persons for trial. Additionally, universal jurisdiction is afforded for the prosecution of offenders.

As well as supplementing the provisions of the four Conventions, Protocol I adds two measures to assist implementation. Article 90 allows for a Fact-finding Commission to undertake enquiries and gather evidence so as to monitor the occurrence and extent of breaches to the Conventions. Article 88 of the Protocol provides for mutual legal assistance in criminal prosecutions relating to breaches of the Conventions.[2]

---

[1] See: Sandoz, Y. (1986). "Penal Aspects of International Humanitarian Law", in, Bassiouni, M.C. *International Criminal Law − Crimes*. United States, Transnational Pubs. pp. 209–242.

[2] See generally: Best, G. (1994). *War and Law since 1945*. Oxford, Clarendon Press; Swinarski, C. (1984). *Studies and Essays on International Humanitarian Law and Red Cross Principles, in Honour of Jean Pictet*. Netherlands, Martinus Nijhoff and International Committee of the Red Cross.

51. GENEVA CONVENTION FOR THE AMELIORATION OF THE CONDITION OF THE WOUNDED AND SICK IN ARMED FORCES IN THE FIELD

(GENEVA CONVENTION I)

75 U.N.T.S. 31

Entry into force: 21 October 1950

CHAPTER I
GENERAL PROVISIONS

Article 1

The High Contracting Parties undertake to respect and to ensure respect for the present Convention in all circumstances.

Article 2

In addition to the provisions which shall be implemented in peacetime, the present Convention shall apply to all cases of declared war or of any other armed conflict which may arise between two or more of the High Contracting Parties, even if the state of war is not recognized by one of them.

The Convention shall also apply to all cases of partial or total occupation of the territory of a High Contracting Party, even if the said occupation meets with no armed resistance.

Although one of the Powers in conflict may not be a party to the present Convention, the Powers who are parties thereto shall remain bound by it in their mutual relations. They shall furthermore be bound by the Convention in relation to the said Power, if the latter accepts and applies the provisions thereof.

Article 3

In the case of armed conflict not of an international character occurring in the territory of one of the High Contracting Parties, each Party to the conflict shall be bound to apply, as a minimum, the following provisions:

1. Persons taking no active part in the hostilities, including members of armed forces who have laid down their arms and those placed hors de combat by sickness, wounds, detention, or any other cause, shall in all circumstances be treated humanely, without any adverse distinction founded on race, colour, religion or faith, sex, birth or wealth, or any other similar criteria.

   To this end, the following acts are and shall remain prohibited at any time and in any place whatsoever with respect to the above-mentioned persons:

(a) Violence to life and person. in particular murder of all kinds, mutilation, cruel treatment and torture;
(b) Taking of hostages;
(c) Outrages upon personal dignity, in particular humiliating and degrading treatment;
(d) The passing of sentences and the carrying out of executions without previous judgment pronounced by a regularly constituted court, affording all the judicial guarantees which are recognized as indispensable by civilised peoples.

2. The wounded and sick shall be collected and cared for. An impartial humanitarian body, such as the International Committee of the Red Cross, may offer its services to the Parties to the conflict.

The Parties to the conflict should further endeavour to bring into force, by means of special agreements, all or part of the other provisions of the present Convention.

The application of the preceding provisions shall not affect the legal status of the Parties to the conflict.

Article 4

Neutral Powers shall apply by analogy the provisions of the present Convention to the wounded and sick, and to members of the medical personnel and to chaplains of the armed forces of the Parties to the conflict, received or interned in their territory, as well as to dead persons found.

Article 5

For the protected persons who have fallen into the hands of the enemy, the present Convention shall apply until their final repatriation.

Article 6

In addition to the agreements expressly provided for in Articles 10, 15, 23, 28, 31, 36, 37 and 52, the High Contracting Parties may conclude other special agreements for all matters concerning which they may deem it suitable to make separate provision. No special agreement shall adversely affect the situation of the wounded and sick, of members of the medical personnel or of chaplains, as defined by the present Convention, nor restrict the rights which it confers upon them.

Wounded and sick, as well as medical personnel and chaplains, shall continue to have the benefit of such agreements as long as the Convention is applicable to them, except where express provisions to the contrary are contained in the aforesaid or in subsequent agreements, or where more favourable measures have been taken with regard to them by one or other of the Parties to the conflict.

Article 7

Wounded and sick, as well as members of the medical personnel and chaplains, may in no circumstances renounce in part or in entirety the rights secured to them by the present Convention, and by the special agreements referred to in the foregoing Article, if such there be.

Article 8

The present Convention shall be applied with the co-operation and under the scrutiny of the Protecting Powers whose duty it is to safeguard the interests of the Parties to the conflict. For this purpose, the Protecting Powers may appoint, apart from their diplomatic or consular staff, delegates from amongst their own nationals or the nationals of other neutral Powers. The said delegates shall be subject to the approval of the Power with which they are to carry out their duties.

The Parties to the conflict shall facilitate, to the greatest extent possible, the task of the representatives or delegates of the Protecting Powers.

The representatives or delegates of the Protecting Powers shall not in any case exceed their mission under the present Convention. They shall, in particular, take account of the imperative necessities of security of the State wherein they carry out their duties. Their activities shall only be restricted as an exceptional and temporary measure when this is rendered necessary by imperative military necessities...

CHAPTER IX
REPRESSION OF ABUSES AND INFRACTIONS

Article 49

The High Contracting Parties undertake to enact any legislation necessary to provide effective penal sanctions for persons committing, or ordering to be committed, any of the grave breaches of the present Convention defined in the following Article.

Each High Contracting Party shall be under the obligation to search for persons alleged to have committed, or to have ordered to be committed, such grave breaches, and shall bring such persons, regardless of their nationality, before its own courts. It may also, if it prefers, and in accordance with the provisions of its own legislation, hand such persons over for trial to another High Contracting Party concerned, provided such High Contracting Party has made out a prima facie case.

Each High Contracting Party shall take measures necessary for the suppression of all acts contrary to the provisions of the present Convention other than the grave breaches defined in the following Article.

In all circumstances, the accused persons shall benefit by safeguards of proper trial and defence, which shall not be less favourable than those provided by Article 105 and those following of the Geneva Convention relative to the Treatment of Prisoners of War of August 12, 1949.

Article 50

Grave breaches to which the preceding Article relates shall be those involving any of the following acts, if committed against persons or property protected by the Convention: wilful killing, torture or inhuman treatment, including biological experiments, wilfully causing great suffering or serious injury to body or health, and extensive destruction and appropriation of property, not justified by military necessity and carried out unlawfully and wantonly.

Article 51

No High Contracting Party shall be allowed to absolve itself or any other High Contracting Party of any liability incurred by itself or by another High Contracting Party in respect of breaches referred to in the preceding Article.

Article 52

At the request of a Party to the conflict, an enquiry shall be instituted, in a manner to be decided between the interested Parties, concerning any alleged violation of the Convention.

If agreement has not been reached concerning the procedure for the enquiry, the Parties should agree on the choice of an umpire who will decide upon the procedure to be followed.

Once the violation has been established, the Parties to the conflict shall put an end to it and shall repress it with the least possible delay.

Article 53

The use by individuals, societies, firms or companies either public or private, other than those entitled thereto under the present Convention, of the emblem or the designation "Red Cross" or "Geneva Cross", or any sign or designation constituting an imitation there of, whatever the object of such use, and irrespective of the date of its adoption, shall be prohibited at all times.

By reason of the tribute paid to Switzerland by the adoption of the reversed Federal colours, and of the confusion which may arise between the arms of Switzerland and the distinctive emblem of the Convention, the use by private individuals, societies or firms, of the arms of the Swiss Confederation, or of marks constituting an imitation thereof, whether as trademarks or commercial marks, or as parts of such marks, or for a purpose contrary to commercial honesty, or in circumstances capable of wounding Swiss national sentiment, shall be prohibited at all times.

Nevertheless, such High Contracting Parties as were not party to the Geneva Convention of July 27, 1929, may grant to prior users of the emblems, designations, signs or marks designated in the first paragraph, a time limit not to exceed three years from the coming into force of the present Convention to discontinue such use, provided that the said use shall not be such as would appear, in time of war, to confer the protection of the Convention.

The prohibition laid down in the first paragraph of the present Article shall also apply, without effect on any rights acquired through prior use, to the emblems and marks mentioned in the second paragraph of Article 38.

Article 54

The High Contracting Parties shall, if their legislation is not already adequate, take measures necessary for the prevention and repression, at all times, of the abuses referred to under Article 53.

52. GENEVA CONVENTION FOR THE AMELIORATION OF THE CONDITION OF WOUNDED, SICK AND SHIPWRECKED MEMBERS OF ARMED FORCES AT SEA

(GENEVA CONVENTION II)

75 U.N.T.S. 85

Entry into force: 21 October, 1950

CHAPTER VIII
REPRESSION OF ABUSES AND INFRACTIONS

Article 50

The High Contracting Parties undertake to enact any legislation necessary to provide effective penal sanctions for persons committing, or ordering to be committed, any of the grave breaches of the present Convention defined in the following Article.

Each High Contracting Party shall be under the obligation to search for persons alleged to have committed, or to have ordered to be committed, such grave breaches, and shall bring such persons, regardless of their nationality, before its own courts. It may also, if it prefers, and in accordance with the provisions of its own legislation, hand such persons over for trial to another High Contracting Party concerned, provided such High Contracting Party has made out a prima facie case.

Each High Contracting Party shall take measures necessary for the suppression of all acts contrary to the provisions of the present Convention other than the grave breaches defined in the following Article.

In all circumstances, the accused persons shall benefit by safeguards of proper trial and defence, which shall not be less favourable than those provided by Article 105 and those following of the Geneva Convention relative to the Treatment of Prisoners of War of August 12, 1949.

Article 51

Grave breaches to which the preceding Article relates shall be those involving any of the following acts, if committed against persons or property protected by the Convention: wilful killing, torture or inhuman treatment, including biological experiments, wilfully causing great suffering or serious injury to body or health, and extensive destruction and appropriation of property, not justified by military necessity and carried out unlawfully and wantonly.

Article 52

No High Contracting Party shall be allowed to absolve itself or any other High Contracting Party of any liability incurred by itself or by another High

Contracting Party in respect of breaches referred to in the preceding Article.

Article 53

At the request of a Party to the conflict, an enquiry shall be instituted, in a manner to be decided between the interested Parties, concerning any alleged violation of the Convention.

If agreement has not been reached concerning the procedure for the enquiry, the Parties should agree on the choice of an umpire, who will decide upon the procedure to be followed.

Once the violation has been established, the Parties to the conflict shall put an end to it and shall repress it with the least possible delay.

53. GENEVA CONVENTION RELATIVE TO THE TREATMENT OF PRISONERS OF WAR

(GENEVA CONVENTION III)

75 U.N.T.S. 135

Entry into force: 21 October 1950

CHAPTER III
PENAL AND DISCIPLINARY SANCTIONS

I. General provisions

Article 82

A prisoner of war shall be subject to the laws, regulations and orders in force in the armed forces of the Detaining Power; the Detaining Power shall be justified in taking judicial or disciplinary measures in respect of any offence committed by a prisoner of war against such laws, regulations or orders. However, no proceedings or punishments contrary to the provisions of this Chapter shall be allowed. If any law, regulation or order of the Detaining Power shall declare acts committed by a prisoner of war to be punishable, whereas the same acts would not be punishable if committed by a member of the forces of the Detaining Power, such acts shall entail disciplinary punishments only.

Article 83

In deciding whether proceedings in respect of an offence alleged to have been committed by a prisoner of war shall be judicial or disciplinary, the Detaining Power shall ensure that the competent authorities exercise the greatest leniency and adopt, wherever possible, disciplinary rather than judicial measures.

Article 84

A prisoner of war shall be tried only by a military court, unless the existing laws of the Detaining Power expressly permit the civil courts to try a member of the armed forces of the Detaining Power in respect of the particular offence alleged to have been committed by the prisoner of war.

In no circumstances whatever shall a prisoner of war be tried by a court of any kind which does not offer the essential guarantees of independence and impartiality as generally recognized, and, in particular, the procedure of which does not afford the accused the rights and means of defence provided for in Article 105.

Article 85

Prisoners of war prosecuted under the laws of the Detaining Power for acts committed prior to capture shall retain, even if convicted, the benefits of the present Convention.

Article 86

No prisoner of war may be punished more than once for the same act, or on the same charge.

Article 87

Prisoners of war may not be sentenced by the military authorities and courts of the Detaining Power to any penalties except those provided for in respect of members of the armed forces of the said Power who have committed the same acts.

When fixing the penalty, the courts or authorities of the Detaining Power shall take into consideration, to the widest extent possible, the fact that the accused, not being a national of the Detaining Power, is not bound to it by any duty of allegiance, and that he is in its power as the result of circumstances independent of his own will. The said courts or authorities shall be at liberty to reduce the penalty provided for the violation of which the prisoner of war is accused, and shall therefore not be bound to apply the minimum penalty prescribed.

Collective punishment for individual acts, corporal punishments, imprisonment in premises without daylight and, in general, any form of torture or cruelty, are forbidden.

No prisoner of war may be deprived of his rank by the Detaining Power, or prevented from wearing his badges.

Article 88

Officers, non-commissioned officers and men who are prisoners of war undergoing a disciplinary or judicial punishment, shall not be subjected to more severe treatment than that applied in respect of the same punishment to members of the armed forces of the Detaining Power of equivalent rank.

A woman prisoner of war shall not be awarded or sentenced to a punishment more severe, or treated whilst undergoing punishment more severely, than a woman member of the armed forces of the Detaining Power dealt with for a similar offence.

In no case may a woman prisoner of war be awarded or sentenced to a punishment more severe, or treated whilst undergoing punishment more severely, than a male member of the armed forces of the Detaining Power dealt with for a similar offence.

Prisoners of war who have served disciplinary or judicial sentences may not be treated differently from other prisoners of war.

II. Disciplinary sanctions

Article 89

The disciplinary punishments applicable to prisoners of war are the following:

1. A fine which shall not exceed 50 per cent of the advances of pay and working pay which the prisoner of war would otherwise receive under the provisions of Articles 60 and 62 during a period of not more than thirty days.
2. Discontinuance of privileges granted over and above the treatment provided for by the present Convention.
3. Fatigue duties not exceeding two hours daily.
4. Confinement.

The punishment referred to under (3) shall not be applied to officers.

In no case shall disciplinary punishments be inhuman, brutal or dangerous to the health of prisoners of war.

Article 90

The duration of any single punishment shall in no case exceed thirty days. Any period of confinement awaiting the hearing of a disciplinary offence or the award of disciplinary punishment shall be deducted from an award pronounced against a prisoner of war.

The maximum of thirty days provided above may not be exceeded, even if the prisoner of war is answerable for several acts at the same time when he is awarded punishment, whether such acts are related or not.

The period between the pronouncing of an award of disciplinary punishment and its execution shall not exceed one month.

When a prisoner of war is awarded a further disciplinary punishment, a period of at least three days shall elapse between the execution of any two of the punishments, if the duration of one of these is ten days or more.

Article 91

The escape of a prisoner of war shall be deemed to have succeeded when:

1. He has joined the armed forces of the Power on which he depends, or those of an allied Power;
2. He has left the territory under the control of the Detaining Power, or of an ally of the said Power;
3. He has joined a ship flying the flag of the Power on which he depends, or of an allied Power, in the territorial waters of the Detaining Power, the said ship not being under the control of the last named Power.

Prisoners of war who have made good their escape in the sense of this Article and who are recaptured, shall not be liable to any punishment in respect of their previous escape.

Article 92

A prisoner of war who attempts to escape and is recaptured before having made good his escape in the sense of Article 91 shall be liable only to a disciplinary punishment in respect of this act, even if it is a repeated offence.

A prisoner of war who is recaptured shall be handed over without delay to the competent military authority.

Article 88, fourth paragraph, notwithstanding, prisoners of war punished as a result of an unsuccessful escape may be subjected to special surveillance. Such surveillance must not affect the state of their health, must be undergone in a prisoner of war camp, and must not entail the suppression of any of the safeguards granted them by the present Convention.

Article 93

Escape or attempt to escape, even if it is a repeated offence, shall not be deemed an aggravating circumstance if the prisoner of war is subjected to trial by judicial proceedings in respect of an offence committed during his escape or attempt to escape.

In conformity with the principle stated in Article 83, offences committed by prisoners of war with the sole intention of facilitating their escape and which do not entail any violence against life or limb, such as offences against public property, theft without intention of self-enrichment, the drawing up or use of false papers, the wearing of civilian clothing, shall occasion disciplinary punishment only.

Prisoners of war who aid or abet an escape or an attempt to escape shall be liable on this count to disciplinary punishment only.

Article 94

If an escaped prisoner of war is recaptured, the Power on which he depends shall be notified thereof in the manner defined in Article 122, provided notification of his escape has been made.

Article 95

A prisoner of war accused of an offence against discipline shall not be kept in confinement pending the hearing unless a member of the armed forces of the Detaining Power would be so kept if he were accused of a similar offence , or if it is essential in the interests of camp order and discipline.

Any period spent by a prisoner of war in confinement awaiting the disposal of an offence against discipline shall be reduced to an absolute minimum and shall not exceed fourteen days.

The provisions of Articles 97 and 98 of this Chapter shall apply to prisoners of war who are in confinement awaiting the disposal of offences against discipline.

Article 96

Acts which constitute offences against discipline shall be investigated immediately.

Without prejudice to the competence of courts and superior military authorities, disciplinary punishment may be ordered only by an officer having disciplinary powers in his capacity as camp commander, or by a responsible officer who replaces him or to whom he has delegated his disciplinary powers.

In no case may such powers be delegated to a prisoner of war or be exercised by a prisoner of war.

Before any disciplinary award is pronounced, the accused shall be given precise information regarding the offences of which he is accused, and given an opportunity of explaining his conduct and of defending himself. He shall be permitted, in particular, to call witnesses and to have recourse, if necessary, to the services of a qualified interpreter. The decision shall be announced to the accused prisoner of war and to the prisoners' representative.

A record of disciplinary punishments shall be maintained by the camp commander and shall be open to inspection by representatives of the Protecting Power.

Article 97

Prisoners of war shall not in any case be transferred to penitentiary establishments (prisons, penitentiaries, convict prisons, etc.) to undergo disciplinary punishment therein.

All premises in which disciplinary punishments are undergone shall conform to the sanitary requirements set forth in Article 25. A prisoner of war undergoing punishment shall be enabled to keep himself in a state of cleanliness, in conformity with Article 29.

Officers and persons of equivalent status shall not be lodged in the same quarters as non-commissioned officers or men.

Women prisoners of war undergoing disciplinary punishment shall be confined in separate quarters from male prisoners of war and shall be under the immediate supervision of women.

Article 98

A prisoner of war undergoing confinement as a disciplinary punishment, shall continue to enjoy the benefits of the provisions of this Convention except in so far as these are necessarily rendered inapplicable by the mere fact that he is confined. In no case may he be deprived of the benefits of the provisions of Articles 78 and 126.

A prisoner of war awarded disciplinary punishment may not be deprived of the prerogatives attached to his rank.

Prisoners of war awarded disciplinary punishment shall be allowed to exercise and to stay in the open air at least two hours daily.

They shall be allowed, on their request, to be present at the daily medical inspections. They shall receive the attention which their state of health requires and, if necessary, shall be removed to the camp infirmary or to a hospital.

They shall have permission to read and write, likewise to send and receive letters. Parcels and remittances of money, however, may be withheld from them until the completion of the punishment; they shall meanwhile be entrusted to the prisoners' representative, who will hand over to the infirmary the perishable goods contained in such parcels.

III. Judicial proceedings

Article 99

No prisoner of war may be tried or sentenced for an act which is not forbidden by the law of the Detaining Power or by international law, in force at the time the said act was committed.

No moral or physical coercion may be exerted on a prisoner of war in order to induce him to admit himself guilty of the act of which he is accused.

No prisoner of war may be convicted without having had an opportunity to present his defence and the assistance of a qualified advocate or counsel.

Article 100

Prisoners of war and the Protecting Powers shall be informed as soon as possible of the offences which are punishable by the death sentence under the laws of the Detaining Power.

Other offences shall not thereafter be made punishable by the death penalty without the concurrence of the Power upon which the prisoners of war depend.

The death sentence cannot be pronounced on a prisoner of war unless the attention of the court has, in accordance with Article 87, second paragraph, been particularly called to the fact that since the accused is not a national of the Detaining Power, he is not bound to it by any duty of allegiance, and that he is in its power as the result of circumstances independent of his own will.

Article 101

If the death penalty is pronounced on a prisoner of war, the sentence shall not be executed before the expiration of a period of at least six months from the date when the Protecting Power receives, at an indicated address, the detailed communication provided for in Article 107.

Article 102

A prisoner of war can be validly sentenced only if the sentence has been pronounced by the same courts according to the same procedure as in the case of members of the armed forces of the Detaining Power, and if, furthermore, the provisions of the present Chapter have been observed.

Article 103

Judicial investigations relating to a prisoner of war shall be conducted as rapidly as circumstances permit and so that his trial shall take place as soon as possible. A prisoner of war shall not be confined while awaiting trial unless a member of the armed forces of the Detaining Power would be so confined if he were accused of a similar offence, or if it is essential to do so in the interests of national security. In no circumstances shall this confinement exceed three months.

Any period spent by a prisoner of war in confinement awaiting trial shall be deducted from any sentence of imprisonment passed upon him and taken into account in fixing any penalty.

The provisions of Articles 97 and 98 of this Chapter shall apply to a prisoner of war whilst in confinement awaiting trial.

Article 104

In any case in which the Detaining Power has decided to institute judicial proceedings against a prisoner of war, it shall notify the Protecting Power as soon as possible and at least three weeks before the opening of the trial. This period of three weeks shall run as from the day on which such notification reaches the Protecting Power at the address previously indicated by the latter to the Detaining Power.

The said notification shall contain the following information:

1. Surname and first names of the prisoner of war, his rank, his army, regimental, personal or serial number, his date of birth, and his profession or trade, if any;
2. Place of internment or confinement;
3. Specification of the charge or charges on which the prisoner of war is to be arraigned, giving the legal provisions applicable;
4. Designation of the court which will try the case, like wise the date and place fixed for the opening of the trial.

The same communication shall be made by the Detaining Power to the prisoners' representative. If no evidence is submitted, at the opening of a trial, that the notification referred to above was received by the Protecting Power, by the prisoner of war and by the prisoners' representative concerned, at least three weeks before the opening of the trial, then the latter cannot take place and must be adjourned.

Article 105

The prisoner of war shall be entitled to assistance by one of his prisoner comrades, to defence by a qualified advocate or counsel of his own choice, to the calling of witnesses and, if he deems necessary, to the services of a competent interpreter. He shall be advised of these rights by the Detaining Power in due time before the trial.

Failing a choice by the prisoner of war, the Protecting Power shall find him an advocate or counsel, and shall have at least one week at its disposal for the purpose. The Detaining Power shall deliver to the said Power, on request, a list of persons qualified to present the defence. Failing a choice of an advocate or counsel by the prisoner of war or the Protecting Power, the Detaining Power shall appoint a competent advocate or counsel to conduct the defence.

The advocate or counsel conducting the defence on behalf of the prisoner of war shall have at his disposal a period of two weeks at least before the opening of the trial, as well as the necessary facilities to prepare the defence of the accused. He may, in particular, freely visit the accused and interview him in private. He may also confer with any witnesses for the defence, including prisoners of war. He shall have the benefit of these facilities until the term of appeal or petition has expired.

Particulars of the charge or charges on which the prisoner of war is to be arraigned, as well as the documents which are generally communicated to the accused by virtue of the laws in force in the armed forces of the Detaining Power, shall be communicated to the accused prisoner of war in a language which he understands, and in good time before the opening of the trial. The same communication in the same circumstances shall be made to the advocate or counsel conducting the defence on behalf of the prisoner of war.

The representatives of the Protecting Power shall be entitled to attend the trial of the case, unless, exceptionally, this is held in camera in the interest of State security. In such a case the Detaining Power shall advise the Protecting Power accordingly.

Article 106

Every prisoner of war shall have, in the same manner as the members of the armed forces of the Detaining Power, the right of appeal or petition from any sentence pronounced upon him, with a view to the quashing or revising of the sentence or the reopening of the trial. He shall be fully informed of his right to appeal or petition and of the time limit within which he may do so.

Article 107

Any judgment and sentence pronounced upon a prisoner of war shall be immediately reported to the Protecting Power in the form of a summary communication, which shall also indicate whether he has the right of appeal with a view to the quashing of the sentence or the reopening of the trial. This communication shall likewise be sent to the prisoners' representative concerned. It shall also be sent to the accused prisoner of war in a language he understands, if the sentence was not pronounced in his presence. The Detaining Power shall also immediately communicate to the Protecting Power the decision of the prisoner of war to use or to waive his right of appeal.

Furthermore, if a prisoner of war is finally convicted or if a sentence pronounced on a prisoner of war in the first instance is a death sentence, the Detaining Power shall as soon as possible address to the Protecting Power a detailed communication containing:

1. The precise wording of the finding and sentence;

2. A summarised report of any preliminary investigation and of the trial, emphasising in particular the elements of the prosecution and the defence;
3. Notification, where applicable, of the establishment where the sentence will be served. The communications provided for in the foregoing subparagraphs shall be sent to the Protecting Power at the address previously made known to the Detaining Power.

Article 108

Sentences pronounced on prisoners of war after a conviction has become duly enforceable, shall be served in the same establishments and under the same conditions as in the case of members of the armed forces of the Detaining Power. These conditions shall in all cases conform to the requirements of health and humanity.

A woman prisoner of war on whom such a sentence has been pronounced shall be confined in separate quarters and shall be under the supervision of women.

In any case, prisoners of war sentenced to a penalty depriving them of their liberty shall retain the benefit of the provisions of Articles 78 and 126 of the present Convention. Furthermore, they shall be entitled to receive and despatch correspondence, to receive at least one relief parcel monthly, to take regular exercise in the open air, to have the medical care required by their state of health, and the spiritual assistance they may desire. Penalties to which they may be subjected shall be in accordance with the provisions of Article 87, third paragraph.

PART VI EXECUTION OF THE CONVENTION

SECTION I GENERAL PROVISIONS

Article 126

Representatives or delegates of the Protecting Powers shall have permission to go to all places where prisoners of war may be, particularly to places of internment, imprisonment and labour, and shall have access to all premises occupied by prisoners of war; they shall also be allowed to go to the places of departure, passage and arrival of prisoners who are being transferred. They shall be able to interview the prisoners, and in particular the prisoners' representatives, without witnesses, either personally or through an interpreter.

Representatives and delegates of the Protecting Powers shall have full liberty to select the places they wish to visit. The duration and frequency of these visits shall not be restricted. Visits may not be prohibited except for reasons of imperative military necessity, and then only as an exceptional and temporary measure.

The Detaining Power and the Power on which the said prisoners of war depend may agree, if necessary, that compatriots of these prisoners of war be permitted to participate in the visits.

The delegates of the International Committee of the Red Cross shall enjoy the same prerogatives. The appointment of such delegates shall be submitted to the approval of the Power detaining the prisoners of war to be visited.

Article 127

The High Contracting Parties undertake, in time of peace as in time of war, to disseminate the text of the present Convention as widely as possible in their respective countries, and, in particular, to include the study thereof in their programmes of military and, if possible, civil instruction, so that the principles thereof may become known to all their armed forces and to the entire population.

Any military or other authorities, who in time of war assume responsibilities in respect of prisoners of war, must possess the text of the Convention and be specially instructed as to its provisions.

Article 128

The High Contracting Parties shall communicate to one another through the Swiss Federal Council and, during hostilities, through the Protecting Powers, the official translations of the present Convention, as well as the laws and regulations which they may adopt to ensure the application thereof.

Article 129

The High Contracting Parties undertake to enact any legislation necessary to provide effective penal sanctions for persons committing, or ordering to be committed, any of the grave breaches of the present Convention defined in the following Article.

Each High Contracting Party shall be under the obligation to search for persons alleged to have committed, or to have ordered to be committed, such grave breaches, and shall bring such persons, regardless of their nationality, before its own courts. It may also, if it prefers, and in accordance with the provisions of its own legislation, hand such persons over for trial to another High Contracting Party concerned, provided such High Contracting Party has made out a *prima facie* case.

Each High Contracting Party shall take measures necessary for the suppression of all acts contrary to the provisions of the present Convention other than the grave breaches defined in the following Article. In all circumstances, the accused persons shall benefit by safeguards of proper trial and defence, which shall not be less favourable than those provided by Article 105 and those following of the present Convention.

Article 130

Grave breaches to which the preceding Article relates shall be those involving any of the following acts, if committed against persons or property protected by the Convention: wilful killing, torture or inhuman treatment, including biological experiments, wilfully causing great suffering or serious injury to body or health, compelling a prisoner of war to serve in the forces of the hostile Power, or wilfully depriving a prisoner of war of the rights of fair and regular trial prescribed in this Convention.

Article 131

No High Contracting Party shall be allowed to absolve itself or any other High Contracting Party of any liability incurred by itself or by another High Contracting Party in respect of breaches referred to in the preceding Article.

Article 132

At the request of a Party to the conflict, an enquiry shall be instituted, in a manner to be decided between the interested Parties, concerning any alleged violation of the Convention.

If agreement has not been reached concerning the procedure for the enquiry, the Parties should agree on the choice of an umpire who will decide upon the procedure to be followed.

Once the violation has been established, the Parties to the conflict shall put an end to it and shall repress it with the least possible delay.

54. GENEVA CONVENTION RELATIVE TO THE PROTECTION OF CIVILIAN PERSONS IN TIME OF WAR

(GENEVA CONVENTION IV)

75 U.N.T.S. 287

Signed at Geneva: 12 August 1949

Entry into force: 21 October 1950

PART IV
EXECUTION OF THE CONVENTION

SECTION I GENERAL PROVISIONS

Article 142

Subject to the measures which the Detaining Powers may consider essential to ensure their security or to meet any other reasonable need, the representatives of religious organizations, relief societies, or any other organizations assisting the protected persons, shall receive from these Powers, for themselves or their duly accredited agents, all facilities for visiting the protected persons, for distributing relief supplies and material from any source, intended for educational, recreational or religious purposes, or for assisting them in organizing their leisure time within the places of internment. Such societies or organizations may be constituted in the territory of the Detaining Power, or in any other country, or they may have an international character.

The Detaining Power may limit the number of societies and organizations whose delegates are allowed to carry out their activities in its territory and under its supervision, on condition, however, that such limitation shall not hinder the supply of effective and adequate relief to all protected persons.

The special position of the International Committee of the Red Cross in this field shall be recognized and respected at all times.

Article 143

Representatives or delegates of the Protecting Powers shall have permission to go to all places where protected persons are, particularly to places of internment, detention and work.

They shall have access to all premises occupied by protected persons and shall be able to interview the latter without witnesses, personally or through an interpreter.

Such visits may not be prohibited except for reasons of imperative military necessity, and then only as an exceptional and temporary measure Their duration and frequency shall not be restricted.

Such representatives and delegates shall have full liberty to select the places they wish to visit. The Detaining or Occupying Power, the Protecting Power and when occasion arises the Power of origin of the persons to be visited, may agree that compatriots of the internees shall be permitted to participate in the visits.

The delegates of the International Committee of the Red Cross shall also enjoy the above prerogatives. The appointment of such delegates shall be submitted to the approval of the Power governing the territories where they will carry out their duties.

Article 144

The High Contracting Parties undertake, in time of peace as in time of war, to disseminate the text of the present Convention as widely as possible in their respective countries, and, in particular, to include the study thereof in their programmes of military and, if possible, civil instruction, so that the principles thereof may become known to the entire population.

Any civilian, military, police or other authorities, who in time of war assume responsibilities in respect of protected persons, must possess the text of the Convention and be specially instructed as to its provisions.

Article 145

The High Contracting Parties shall communicate to one another through the Swiss Federal Council and, during hostilities, through the Protecting Powers, the official translations of the present Convention, as well as the laws and regulations which they may adopt to ensure the application thereof.

Article 146

The High Contracting Parties undertake to enact any legislation necessary to provide effective penal sanctions for persons committing, or ordering to be committed, any of the grave breaches of the present Convention defined in the following Article.

Each High Contracting Party shall be under the obligation to search for persons alleged to have committed, or to have ordered to be committed, such grave breaches, and shall bring such persons, regardless of their nationality, before its own courts. It may also, if it prefers, and in accordance with the provisions of its own legislation, hand such persons over for trial to another High Contracting Party concerned, provided such High Contracting Party has made out a *prima facie* case.

Each High Contracting Party shall take measures necessary for the suppression of all acts contrary to the provisions of the present Convention other than the grave breaches defined in the following Article.

In all circumstances, the accused persons shall benefit by safeguards of proper trial and defence, which shall not be less favourable than those provided by Article

105 and those following of the Geneva Convention relative to the Treatment of Prisoners of War of August 12, 1949.

Article 147

Grave breaches to which the preceding Article relates shall be those involving any of the following acts, if committed against persons or property protected by the present Convention: wilful killing, torture or inhuman treatment, including biological experiments, wilfully causing great suffering or serious injury to body or health, unlawful deportation or transfer or unlawful confinement of a protected person, compelling a protected person to serve in the forces of a hostile Power, or wilfully depriving a protected person of the rights of fair and regular trial prescribed in the present Convention, taking of hostages and extensive destruction and appropriation of property, not justified by military necessity and carried out unlawfully and wantonly.

Article 148

No High Contracting Party shall be allowed to absolve itself or any other High Contracting Party of any liability incurred by itself or by another High Contracting Party in respect of breaches referred to in the preceding Article.

Article 149

At the request of a Party to the conflict, an enquiry shall be instituted, in a manner to be decided between the interested Parties, concerning any alleged violation of the Convention. If agreement has not been reached concerning the procedure for the enquiry, the Parties should agree on the choice of an umpire who will decide upon the procedure to be followed. Once the violation has been established, the Parties to the conflict shall put an end to it and shall repress it with the least possible delay.

55. PROTOCOL ADDITIONAL TO THE GENEVA CONVENTIONS OF 12 AUGUST 1949, AND RELATING TO THE PROTECTION OF VICTIMS OF INTERNATIONAL ARMED CONFLICTS (PROTOCOL I)

1125 U.N.T.S. 3

Entry into force: 7 December 1978

PART I
GENERAL PROVISIONS

Article 1. – General principles and scope of application

1. The High Contracting Parties undertake to respect and to ensure respect for this Protocol in all circumstances.
2. In cases not covered by this Protocol or by other international agreements, civilians and combatants remain under the protection and authority of the principles of international law derived from established custom, from the principles of humanity and from the dictates of public conscience.
3. This Protocol, which supplements the Geneva Conventions of 12 August 1949 for the protection of war victims, shall apply in the situations referred to in Article 2 common to those Conventions.
4. The situations referred to in the preceding paragraph include armed conflicts in which peoples are fighting against colonial domination and alien occupation and against racist regimes in the exercise of their right of self-determination, as enshrined in the Charter of the United Nations and the Declaration on Principles of International Law concerning Friendly Relations and Co-operation among States in accordance with the Charter of the United Nations.

PART II
WOUNDED, SICK AND SHIPWRECKED

SECTION I GENERAL PROTECTION

Article 10. – Protection and care

1. All the wounded, sick and shipwrecked, to whichever Party they belong, shall be respected and protected.
2. In all circumstances they shall be treated humanely and shall receive, to the fullest extent practicable and with the least possible delay, the medical care

and attention required by their condition. There shall be no distinction among them founded on any grounds other than medical ones.

Article 11. – Protection of persons

1. The physical or mental health and integrity of persons who are in the power of the adverse Party or who are interned, detained or otherwise deprived of liberty as a result of a situation referred to in Article 1 shall not be endangered by any unjustified act or omission. Accordingly, it is prohibited to subject the persons described in this Article to any medical procedure which is not indicated by the state of health of the person concerned and which is not consistent with generally accepted medical standards which would be applied under similar medical circumstances to persons who are nationals of the Party conducting the procedure and who are in no way deprived of liberty.

2. It is, in particular, prohibited to carry out on such persons, even with their consent:

    (a) Physical mutilations;
    (b) Medical or scientific experiments;
    (c) Removal of tissue or organs for transplantation, except where these acts are justified in conformity with the conditions provided for in paragraph 1.

3. Exceptions to the prohibition in paragraph 2 (c) may be made only in the case of donations of blood for transfusion or of skin for grafting, provided that they are given voluntarily and without any coercion or inducement, and then only for therapeutic purposes, under conditions consistent with generally accepted medical standards and controls designed for the benefit of both the donor and the recipient.

4. Any wilful act or omission which seriously endangers the physical or mental health or integrity of any person who is in the power of a Party other than the one on which he depends and which either violates any of the prohibitions in paragraphs 1 and 2 or fails to comply with the requirements of paragraph 3 shall be a grave breach of this Protocol.

5. The persons described in paragraph 1 have the right to refuse any surgical operation. In case of refusal, medical personnel shall endeavour to obtain a written statement to that effect, signed or acknowledged by the patient.

6. Each Party to the conflict shall keep a medical record for every donation of blood for transfusion or skin for grafting by persons referred to in paragraph 1, if that donation is made under the responsibility of that Party. In addition, each Party to the conflict shall endeavour to keep a record of all medical procedures undertaken with respect to any person who is interned, detained or otherwise deprived of liberty as a result of a situation referred to in Article 1. These records shall be available at all times for inspection by the Protecting Power.

Article 75. – Fundamental guarantees

1. In so far as they are affected by a situation referred to in Article 1 of this Protocol, persons who are in the power of a Party to the conflict and who do

not benefit from more favourable treatment under the Conventions or under this Protocol shall be treated humanely in all circumstances and shall enjoy, as a minimum, the protection provided by this Article without any adverse distinction based upon race, colour, sex, language, religion or belief, political or other opinion, national or social origin, wealth, birth or other status, or on any other similar criteria. Each Party shall respect the person, honour, convictions and religious practices of all such persons.

2. The following acts are and shall remain prohibited at any time and in any place whatsoever, whether committed by civilian or by military agents:

   (a) Violence to the life, health, or physical or mental well-being of persons, in particular:

       (i)   Murder;
       (ii) Torture of all kinds, whether physical or mental;
       (iii) Corporal punishment ; and
       (iv) Mutilation;

   (b) Outrages upon personal dignity, in particular humiliating and degrading treatment, enforced prostitution and any form of indecent assault;
   (c) The taking of hostages;
   (d) Collective punishments; and
   (e) Threats to commit any of the foregoing acts.

3. Any person arrested, detained or interned for actions related to the armed conflict shall be informed promptly, in a language he understands, of the reasons why these measures have been taken. Except in cases of arrest or detention for penal offences, such persons shall be released with the minimum delay possible and in any event as soon as the circumstances justifying the arrest, detention or internment have ceased to exist.

4. No sentence may be passed and no penalty may be executed on a person found guilty of a penal offence related to the armed conflict except pursuant to a conviction pronounced by an impartial and regularly constituted court respecting the generally recognized principles of regular judicial procedure, which include the following:

   (a) The procedure shall provide for an accused to be informed without delay of the particulars of the offence alleged against him and shall afford the accused before and during his trial all necessary rights and means of defence;
   (b) No one shall be convicted of an offence except on the basis of individual penal responsibility;
   (c) No one shall be accused or convicted of a criminal offence on account of any act or omission which did not constitute a criminal offence under the national or international law to which he was subject at the time when it was committed; nor shall a heavier penalty be imposed than that which was applicable at the time when the criminal offence was committed; if, after the commission of the offence, provision is made by law for the imposition of a lighter penalty, the offender shall benefit thereby;

(d) Anyone charged with an offence is presumed innocent until proved guilt according to law;

(e) Anyone charged with an offence shall have the right to be tried in his presence;

(f) No one shall be compelled to testify against himself or to confess guilt;

(g) Anyone charged with an offence shall have the right to examine, or have examined, the witnesses against him and to obtain the attendance and examination of witnesses on his behalf under the same conditions as witnesses against him;

(h) No one shall be prosecuted or punished by the same Party for an offence in respect of which a final judgement acquitting or convicting that person has been previously pronounced under the same law and judicial procedure;

(i) Anyone prosecuted for an offence shall have the right to have the judgement pronounced publicly; and

(j) A convicted person shall be advised on conviction of his judicial and other remedies and of the time-limits within which they may be exercised.

5. Women whose liberty has been restricted for reasons related to the armed conflict shall be held in quarters separated from men's quarters. They shall be under the immediate supervision of women. Nevertheless, in cases where families are detained or interned, they shall, whenever possible, be held in the same place and accommodated as family units.

6. Persons who are arrested, detained or interned for reasons related to the armed conflict shall enjoy the protection provided by this Article until their final release, repatriation or re-establishment, even after the end of the armed conflict.

7. In order to avoid any doubt concerning the prosecution and trial of persons accused of war crimes or crimes against humanity, the following principles shall apply:

(a) Persons who are accused of such crimes should be submitted for the purpose of prosecution and trial in accordance with the applicable rules of international law; and

(b) Any such persons who do not benefit from more favourable treatment under the Conventions or this Protocol shall be accorded the treatment provided by this Article, whether or not the crimes of which they are accused constitute grave breaches of the Conventions or of this Protocol.

8. No provision of this Article may be construed as limiting or infringing any other more favourable provision granting greater protection, under any applicable rules of international law, to persons covered by paragraph 1.

PART V
EXECUTION OF THE CONVENTIONS AND OF THIS PROTOCOL

SECTION II REPRESSION OF BREACHES OF THE CONVENTIONS AND OF THIS PROTOCOL

Article 85. – Repression of breaches of this Protocol

1. The provisions of the Conventions relating to the repression of breaches and grave breaches, supplemented by this Section, shall apply to the repression of breaches and grave breaches of this Protocol.
2. Acts described as grave breaches in the Conventions are grave breaches of this Protocol if committed against persons in the power of an adverse Party protected by Articles 44, 45 and 73 of this Protocol, or against the wounded, sick and shipwrecked of the adverse Party who are protected by this Protocol, or against those medical or religious personnel, medical units or medical transports which are under the control of the adverse Party and are protected by this Protocol.
3. In addition to the grave breaches defined in Article 11, the following acts shall be regarded as grave breaches of this Protocol, when committed wilfully, in violation of the relevant provisions of this Protocol, and causing death or serious injury to body or health:

    (a) Making the civilian population or individual civilians the object of attack;
    (b) Launching an indiscriminate attack affecting the civilian population or civilian objects in the knowledge that such attack will cause excessive loss of life, injury to civilians or damage to civilian objects, as defined in Article 57, paragraph 2 (a) (iii);
    (c) Launching an attack against works or installations containing dangerous forces in the knowledge that such attack will cause excessive loss of life, injury to civilians or damage to civilian objects, as defined in Article 57, paragraph 2 (a) (iii);
    (d) Making non-defended localities and demilitarized zones the object of attack;
    (e) Making a person the object of attack in the knowledge that he is hors de combat;
    (f) The perfidious use, in violation of Article 37, of the distinctive emblem of the red cross, red crescent or red lion and sun or of other protective signs recognized by the Conventions or this Protocol.

4. In addition to the grave breaches defined in the preceding paragraphs and in the Conventions, the following shall be regarded as grave breaches of this Protocol, when committed wilfully and in violation of the Conventions of the Protocol;

    (a) The transfer by the Occupying Power of parts of its own civilian population into the territory it occupies, or the deportation or transfer of

586

all or parts of the population of the occupied territory within or outside this territory, in violation of Article 49 of the Fourth Convention;
(b) Unjustifiable delay in the repatriation of prisoners of war or civilians;
(c) Practices of apartheid and other inhuman and degrading practices involving outrages upon personal dignity, based on racial discrimination;
(d) Making the clearly-recognized historic monuments, works of art or places of worship which constitute the cultural or spiritual heritage of peoples and to which special protection has been given by special arrangement, for example, within the framework of a competent international organization, the object of attack, causing as a result extensive destruction thereof, where there is no evidence of the violation by the adverse Party of Article 53, sub-paragraph (b), and when such historic monuments, works of art and places of worship are not located in the immediate proximity of military objectives;
(e) Depriving a person protected by the Conventions or referred to in paragraph 2 of this Article of the rights of fair and regular trial.

5. Without prejudice to the application of the Conventions and of this Protocol, grave breaches of these instruments shall be regarded as war crimes.

Article 86. – Failure to act

1. The High Contracting Parties and the Parties to the conflict shall repress grave breaches, and take measures necessary to suppress all other breaches, of the Conventions or of this Protocol which result from a failure to act when under a duty to do so.
2. The fact that a breach of the Conventions or of this Protocol was committed by a subordinate does not absolve his superiors from penal or disciplinary responsibility, as the case may be, if they knew, or had information which should have enabled them to conclude in the circumstances at the time, that he was committing or was going to commit such a breach and if they did not take all feasible measures within their power to prevent or repress the breach.

Article 87. – Duty of commanders

1. The High Contracting Parties and the Parties to the conflict shall require military commanders, with respect to members of the armed forces under their command and other persons under their control, to prevent and, where necessary, to suppress and to report to competent authorities breaches of the Conventions and of this Protocol.
2. In order to prevent and suppress breaches, High Contracting Parties and Parties to the conflict shall require that, commensurate with their level of responsibility, commanders ensure that members of the armed forces under their command are aware of their obligations under the Conventions and this Protocol.
3. The High Contracting Parties and Parties to the conflict shall require any commander who is aware that subordinates or other persons under his control

are going to commit or have committed a breach of the Conventions or of this Protocol, to initiate such steps as are necessary to prevent such violations of the Conventions or this Protocol, and, where appropriate, to initiate disciplinary or penal action against violators thereof.

Article 88. – Mutual assistance in criminal matters

1. The High Contracting Parties shall afford one another the greatest measure of assistance in connexion with criminal proceedings brought in respect of grave breaches of the Conventions or of this Protocol.
2. Subject to the rights and obligations established in the Conventions and in Article 85, paragraph 1, of this Protocol, and when circumstances permit, the High Contracting Parties shall co-operate in the matter of extradition. They shall give due consideration to the request of the State in whose territory the alleged offence has occurred.
3. The law of the High Contracting Party requested shall apply in all cases.
   The provisions of the preceding paragraphs shall not, however, affect the obligations arising from the provisions of any other treaty of a bilateral or multilateral nature which governs or will govern the whole or part of the subject of mutual assistance in criminal matters.

Article 89. – Co-operation

In situations of serious violations of the Conventions or of this Protocol, the High Contracting Parties undertake to act, jointly or individually, in co-operation with the United Nations and in conformity with the United Nations Charter.

Article 90. – International Fact-Finding Commission

1. (a) An International Fact-Finding Commission (hereinafter referred to as "the Commission") consisting of fifteen members of high moral standing and acknowledged impartiality shall be established.
   (b) When not less than twenty High Contracting Parties have agreed to accept the competence of the Commission pursuant to paragraph 2, the depositary shall then, and at intervals of five years thereafter, convene a meeting of representatives of those High Contracting Parties for the purpose of electing the members of the Commission. At the meeting, the representatives shall elect the members of the Commission by secret ballot from a list of persons to which each of those High Contracting Parties may nominate one person.
   (c) The members of the Commission shall serve in their personal capacity and shall hold office until the election of new members at the ensuing meeting.
   (d) At the election, the High Contracting Parties shall ensure that the persons to be elected to the Commission individually possess the qualifications required and that, in the Commission as a whole, equitable geographical representation is assured.

(e) In the case of a casual vacancy, the Commission itself shall fill the vacancy, having due regard to the provisions of the preceding sub-paragraphs.

(f) The depositary shall make available to the Commission the necessary administrative facilities for the performance of its functions.

2. (a) The High Contracting Parties may at the time of signing, ratifying or acceding to the Protocol, or at any other subsequent time, declare that they recognize *ipso facto* and without special agreement, in relation to any other High Contracting Party accepting the same obligation, the competence of the Commission to enquire into allegations by such other Party, as authorized by this Article.

(b) The declarations referred to above shall be deposited with the depositary, which shall transmit copies thereof to the High Contracting Parties.

(c) The Commission shall be competent to:

(i) Enquire into any facts alleged to be a grave breach as defined in the Conventions and this Protocol or other serious violation of the Conventions or of this Protocol;

(ii) Facilitate, through its good offices, the restoration of an attitude of respect for the Conventions and this Protocol.

(d) In other situations, the Commission shall institute an enquiry at the request of a Party to the conflict only with the consent of the other Party or Parties concerned.

(e) Subject to the foregoing provisions of this paragraph, the provisions of Article 52 of the First Convention, Article 53 of the Second Convention, Article 132 of the Third Convention and Article 149 of the Fourth Convention shall continue to apply to any alleged violation of the Conventions and shall extend to any alleged violation of this Protocol.

3. (a) Unless otherwise agreed by the Parties concerned, all enquiries shall be undertaken by a Chamber consisting of seven members appointed as follows:

(i) Five members of the Commission, not nationals of any Party to the conflict, appointed by the President of the Commission on the basis of equitable representation of the geographical areas, after consultation with the Parties to the conflict;

(ii) Two *ad hoc* members, not nationals of any Party to the conflict, one to be appointed by each side.

(b) Upon receipt of the request for an enquiry, the President of the Commission shall specify an appropriate time limit for setting up a Chamber. If any *ad hoc* member has not been appointed within the time limit, the President shall immediately appoint such additional member or members of the Commission as may be necessary to complete the membership of the Chamber.

4. (a) The Chamber set up under paragraph 3 to undertake an enquiry shall

invite the Parties to the conflict to assist it and to present evidence. The Chamber may also seek such other evidence as it deems appropriate and may carry out an investigation of the situation in loco.

(b) All evidence shall be fully disclosed to the Parties, which shall have the right to comment on it to the Commission.

(c) Each Party shall have the right to challenge such evidence.

5. (a) The Commission shall submit to the Parties a report on the findings of fact of the Chamber, with such recommendations as it may deem appropriate.

(b) If the Chamber is unable to secure sufficient evidence for factual and impartial findings, the Commission shall state the reasons for that inability.

(c) The Commission shall not report its findings publicly, unless all the Parties to the conflict have requested the Commission to do so.

6. The Commission shall establish its own rules, including rules for the presidency of the Commission and the presidency of the Chamber. Those rules shall ensure that the functions of the President of the Commission are exercised at all times and that, in the case of an enquiry, they are exercised by a person who is not a national of a Party to the conflict.

7. The administrative expenses of the Commission shall be met by contributions from the High Contracting Parties which made declarations under paragraph 2, and by voluntary contributions. The Party or Parties to the conflict requesting an enquiry shall advance the necessary funds for expenses incurred by a Chamber and shall be reimbursed by the Party or Parties against which the allegations are made to the extent of fifty per cent of the costs of the Chamber. Where there are counter-allegations before the Chamber each side shall advance fifty per cent of the necessary funds.

Article 91. – Responsibility

A Party to the conflict which violates the provisions of the Conventions or of this Protocol shall, if the case demands, be liable to pay compensation. It shall be responsible for all acts committed by persons forming part of its armed forces.

56. PROTOCOL ADDITIONAL TO THE GENEVA CONVENTIONS OF 12 AUGUST 1949, AND RELATING TO THE PROTECTION OF VICTIMS OF NON-INTERNATIONAL ARMED CONFLICTS (PROTOCOL II)

1125 U.N.T.S 609

PART I
SCOPE OF THIS PROTOCOL

Article 1 – Material field of application

1. This Protocol, which develops and supplements Article 3 common to the Geneva Conventions of 12 August 1949 without modifying its existing conditions or application, shall apply to all armed conflicts which are not covered by Article 1 of the Protocol Additional to the Geneva Conventions of 12 August 1949, and relating to the Protection of Victims of International Armed Conflicts (Protocol I) and which take place in the territory of a High Contracting Party between its armed forces and dissident armed forces or other organized armed groups which, under responsible command, exercise such control over a part of its territory as to enable them to carry out sustained and concerted military operations and to implement this Protocol.

2. This Protocol shall not apply to situations of internal disturbances and tensions, such as riots, isolated and sporadic acts of violence and other acts of a similar nature, as not being armed conflicts.

Article 2 – Personal field of application

1. This Protocol shall be applied without any adverse distinction founded on race, colour, sex, language, religion or belief, political or other opinion, national or social origin, wealth, birth or other status, or on any other similar criteria (hereinafter referred to as "adverse distinction") to all persons affected by an armed conflict as defined in Article 1.

2. At the end of the armed conflict, all the persons who have been deprived of their liberty or whose liberty has been restricted for reasons related to such conflict, as well as those deprived of their liberty or whose liberty is restricted after the conflict for the same reasons, shall enjoy the protection of Articles 5 and 6 until the end of such deprivation or restriction of liberty.

PART II
HUMANE TREATMENT

Article 4 – Fundamental guarantees

1. All persons who do not take a direct part or who have ceased to take part in hostilities, whether or not their liberty has been restricted, are entitled to respect for their person, honour and convictions and religious practices. They shall in all circumstances be treated humanely, without any adverse distinction. It is prohibited to order that there shall be no survivors.

2. Without prejudice to the generality of the foregoing, the following acts against the persons referred to in paragraph 1 are and shall remain prohibited at any time and in any place whatsoever:

    (a) violence to the life, health and physical or mental well-being of persons, in particular murder as well as cruel treatment such as torture, mutilation or any form of corporal punishment;
    (b) collective punishments;
    (c) taking of hostages;
    (d) acts of terrorism;
    (e) outrages upon personal dignity, in particular humiliating and degrading treatment, rape, enforced prostitution and any form or indecent assault;
    (f) slavery and the slave trade in all their forms;
    (g) pillage;
    (h) threats to commit any or all of the foregoing acts.

3. Children shall be provided with the care and aid they require, and in particular:

    (a) they shall receive an education, including religious and moral education, in keeping with the wishes of their parents, or in the absence of parents, of those responsible for their care;
    (b) all appropriate steps shall be taken to facilitate the reunion of families temporarily separated;
    (c) children who have not attained the age of fifteen years shall neither be recruited in the armed forces or groups nor allowed to take part in hostilities;
    (d) the special protection provided by this Article to children who have not attained the age of fifteen years shall remain applicable to them if they take a direct part in hostilities despite the provisions of subparagraph (c) and are captured;
    (e) measures shall be taken, if necessary, and whenever possible with the consent of their parents or persons who by law or custom are primarily responsible for their care, to remove children temporarily from the area in which hostilities are taking place to a safer area within the country and ensure that they are accompanied by persons responsible for their safety and well-being.

Article 5 – Persons whose liberty has been restricted

1. In addition to the provisions of Article 4 the following provisions shall be respected as a minimum with regard to persons deprived of their liberty for reasons related to the armed conflict, whether they are interned or detained:

    (a) the wounded and the sick shall be treated in accordance with Article 7;
    (b) the persons referred to in this paragraph shall, to the same extent as the local civilian population, be provided with food and drinking water and be afforded safeguards as regards health and hygiene and protection against the rigours of the climate and the dangers of the armed conflict;
    (c) they shall be allowed to receive individual or collective relief;
    (d) they shall be allowed to practise their religion and, if requested and appropriate, to receive spiritual assistance from persons, such as chaplains, performing religious functions;
    (e) they shall, if made to work, have the benefit of working conditions and safeguards similar to those enjoyed by the local civilian population.

2. Those who are responsible for the internment or detention of the persons referred to in paragraph 1 shall also, within the limits of their capabilities, respect the following provisions relating to such persons:

    (a) except when men and women of a family are accommodated together, women shall be held in quarters separated from those of men and shall be under the immediate supervision of women;
    (b) they shall be allowed to send and receive letters and cards, the number of which may be limited by competent authority if it deems necessary;
    (c) places of internment and detention shall not be located close to the combat zone. The persons referred to in paragraph 1 shall be evacuated when the places where they are interned or detained become particularly exposed to danger arising out of the armed conflict, if their evacuation can be carried out under adequate conditions of safety;
    (d) they shall have the benefit of medical examinations;
    (e) their physical or mental health and integrity shall not be endangered by any unjustified act or omission. Accordingly, it is prohibited to subject the persons described in this Article to any medical procedure which is not indicated by the state of health of the person concerned, and which is not consistent with the generally accepted medical standards applied to free persons under similar medical circumstances.

3. Persons who are not covered by paragraph 1 but whose liberty has been restricted in any way whatsoever for reasons related to the armed conflict shall be treated humanely in accordance with Article 4 and with paragraphs 1 (a), (c) and (d), and 2 (b) of this Article.

4. If it is decided to release persons deprived of their liberty, necessary measures to ensure their safety shall be taken by those so deciding.

Article 6 – Penal prosecutions

1. This Article applies to the prosecution and punishment of criminal offences related to the armed conflict.
2. No sentence shall be passed and no penalty shall be executed on a person found guilty of an offence except pursuant to a conviction pronounced by a court offering the essential guarantees of independence and impartiality. In particular:

    (a) the procedure shall provide for an accused to be informed without delay of the particulars of the offence alleged against him and shall afford the accused before and during his trial all necessary rights and means of defence;

    (b) no one shall be convicted of an offence except on the basis of individual penal responsibility;

    (c) no one shall be held guilty of any criminal offence on account of any act or omission which did not constitute a criminal offence, under the law, at the time when it was committed; nor shall a heavier penalty be imposed than that which was applicable at the time when the criminal offence was committed; if, after the commission of the offence, provision is made by law for the imposition of a lighter penalty, the offender shall benefit thereby;

    (d) anyone charged with an offence is presumed innocent until proved guilty according to law;

    (e) anyone charged with an offence shall have the right to be tried in his presence;

    (f) no one shall be compelled to testify against himself or to confess guilt.

3. A convicted person shall be advised on conviction of his judicial and other remedies and of the time-limits within which they may be exercised.
4. The death penalty shall not be pronounced on persons who were under the age of eighteen years at the time of the offence and shall not be carried out on pregnant women or mothers of young children.
5. At the end of hostilities, the authorities in power shall endeavour to grant the broadest possible amnesty to persons who have participated in the armed conflict, or those deprived of their liberty for reasons related to the armed conflict, whether they are interned or detained.

57. UNITED NATIONS: INTERNATIONAL CONVENTION ON THE SUPPRESSION AND PUNISHMENT OF THE CRIME OF *APARTHEID*

Opened for signature: 30 November 1973

1015 U.N.T.S. 243

Entry into force: 18 July 1976

Editors' Notes

The Apartheid Convention adopted by the United Nations General Assembly in 1973 is a product of the international condemnation of the South African domestic policy of racial domination finally ended by elections in that country in 1994.[1] The preamble to the Convention links apartheid with the crime of genocide and indicates that some acts may be common to both. The preamble also reiterates that apartheid is a crime against humanity,[2] and this is declared in Article I of the Convention. Apartheid is defined at length in Article II and includes some aspects of genocide. Article III stipulates that individual responsibility shall apply regardless of motive to "members of organisations and institutions and representatives of the state". Article IV obligates states to adopt legislative measures to ensure as wide a jurisdiction as possible to enable prosecution. Article V allows for any State party to bring a prosecution against persons accused of acts of apartheid should they acquire jurisdiction over them and provision for trial by an international penal tribunal is also included in common with the Genocide Convention.[3]

Under Article IX, the Convention allows for a monitoring committee to be established to study the periodic reports of the parties on the measures taken to implement the provisions of the Convention. The UN Commission on Human Rights ended its monitoring of apartheid in South Africa in 1995, concluding that apartheid "no longer exists anywhere".[4]

The States Parties to the present Convention,

Recalling the provisions of the Charter of the United Nations, in which all Members pledged themselves to take joint and separate action in co-operation with the Organization for the achievement of universal respect for, and observance

---

[1] See also: The International Convention on the Elimination of All Forms of Racial Discrimination 1965.

[2] See: United Nations General Assembly Resolutions 2545, 11 December. 1969 and 2438, dated 19 December 1968.

[3] See generally: Clark, R.S. (1986). "The Crime of Apartheid", in: Bassiouni, M.C. *International Criminal Law – Crimes*. New York, Transnational.

[4] Crook, J.R. (1996). "The Fifty-First Session of the UN Commission on Human Rights". 90 AJIL 126. p.128.

of, human rights and fundamental freedoms for all without distinction as to race, sex, language or religion,

Considering the Universal Declaration of Human Rights, which states that all human beings are born free and equal in dignity and rights and that everyone is entitled to all the rights and freedoms set forth in the Declaration, without distinction of any kind, such as race, colour or national origin,

Considering the Declaration on the Granting of Independence to Colonial Countries and Peoples, in which the General Assembly stated that the process of liberation is irresistible and irreversible and that, in the interests of human dignity, progress and justice, an end must be put to colonialism and all practices of segregation and discrimination associated therewith,

Observing that, in accordance with the International Convention on the Elimination of All Forms of Racial Discrimination, States particularly condemn racial segregation and *apartheid* and undertake to prevent, prohibit and eradicate all practices of this nature in territories under their jurisdiction,

Observing that, in the Convention on the Prevention and Punishment of the Crime of Genocide, certain acts which may also be qualified as acts of *apartheid* constitute a crime under international law,

Observing that, in the Convention on the Non-Applicability of Statutory Limitations to War Crimes and Crimes Against Humanity, "inhuman acts resulting from the policy *of apartheid*" are qualified as crimes against humanity.

Observing that the General Assembly of the United Nations has adopted a number of resolutions in which the policies and practices of *apartheid* are condemned as a crime against humanity,

Observing that the Security Council has emphasised that *apartheid, its* continued intensification and expansion, seriously disturbs and threatens international peace and security,

Convinced that an International Convention on the Suppression and Punishment of the Crime of *Apartheid* would make it possible to take more effective measures at the international and national levels with a view to the suppression and punishment of the crime of *apartheid,*

Have agreed as follows:

Article I

1. The States Parties to the present Convention declare that *apartheid is* a crime against humanity and that inhuman acts resulting from the policies and practices of *apartheid* and similar policies and practices of racial segregation and discrimination, as defined in article II of the Convention, are crimes violating the principles of international law, in particular the purposes and principles of the Charter of the United Nations, and constituting a serious threat to international peace and security.
2. The States Parties to the present Convention declare criminal those organizations institutions and individuals committing the crime of *apartheid.*

Article II

For the purpose of the present Convention, the term "the crime of *apartheid*", which shall include similar policies and practices of racial segregation and discrimination as practised in southern Africa, shall apply to the following inhuman acts committed for the purpose of establishing and maintaining domination by one racial group of persons over any other racial group of persons and systematically oppressing them:

(a) denial to a member or members of a racial group or groups of the right to life and liberty of person:

    (i) by murder of members of a racial group or groups;

    (ii) by the infliction upon the members of a racial group or groups of serious bodily or mental harm by the infringement of their freedom or dignity, or by subjecting them to torture or to cruel, inhuman or degrading treatment or punishment;

    (iii) by arbitrary arrest and illegal imprisonment of the members of a racial group or groups;

(b) deliberate imposition on a racial group or groups of living conditions calculated to cause its or their physical destruction in whole or in part;

(c) any legislative measures and other measures calculated to prevent a racial group or groups from participation in the political, social, economic and cultural life of the country and the deliberate creation of conditions preventing the full development of such a group or groups, in particular by denying to members of a racial group or groups basic human rights and freedoms, including the right to work, the right to form recognized trade unions, the right to education, the right to leave and to return to their country, the right to a nationality, the right to freedom of movement and residence, the right to freedom of opinion and expression, and the right to freedom of peaceful assembly and association;

(d) any measures, including legislative measures, designed to divide the population along racial lines by the creation of separate reserves and ghettos for the members of a racial group or groups, the prohibition of mixed marriages among members of various racial groups, the expropriation of landed property belonging to a racial group or groups or to members thereof;

(e) exploitation of the labour of the members of a racial group or groups, in particular by submitting them to forced labour;

(f) persecution of organizations and persons, by depriving them of fundamental rights and freedoms, because they oppose *apartheid*.

Article III

International criminal responsibility shall apply, irrespective of the motive involved, to individuals, members of organizations and institutions and representatives of the State, whether residing in the territory of the State in which the acts are perpetrated or in some other State, whenever they:

(a) commit, participate in, directly incite or conspire in the commission of the acts mentioned in article II of the present Convention;

(b) directly abet, encourage or co-operate in the commission of the crime of *apartheid*.

Article IV

The States Parties to the present Convention undertake:

(a) to adopt any legislative or other measures necessary to suppress as well as to prevent any encouragement of the crime of *apartheid* and similar segregationist policies or their manifestations and to punish persons guilty of that crime;

(b) to adopt legislative, judicial and administrative measures to prosecute, bring to trial and punish in accordance with their jurisdiction persons responsible for, or accused of, the acts defined in article II of the present Convention, whether or not such persons reside in the territory of the State in which the acts are committed or are nationals of that State or of some other State or are stateless persons.

Article V

Persons charged with the acts enumerated in article II of the present Convention may be tried by a competent tribunal of any State Party to the Convention which may acquire jurisdiction over the person of the accused or by an international penal tribunal having jurisdiction with respect to those States Parties which shall have accepted its jurisdiction.

Article VI

The States Parties to the present Convention undertake to accept and carry out in accordance with the Charter of the United Nations the decisions taken by the Security Council aimed at the prevention, suppression and punishment of the crime of *apartheid*, and to co-operate in the implementation of decisions adopted by other competent organs of the United Nations with a view to achieving the purposes of the Convention.

Article VII

1. The States Parties to the present Convention undertake to submit periodic reports to the group established under article IX on the legislative, judicial, administrative or other measures that they have adopted and that give effect to the provisions of the Convention.
2. Copies of the reports shall be transmitted through the Secretary-General of the United Nations to the Special Committee on *Apartheid*.

Article VIII

Any State Party to the present Convention may call upon any competent organ of the United Nations to take such action under the Charter of the United Nations as it considers appropriate for the prevention and suppression of the crime of *apartheid*.

Article IX

1. The Chairman of the Commission on Human Rights shall appoint a group consisting of three members of the Commission on Human Rights, who are also representatives of States Parties to the present Convention, to consider reports submitted by States Parties in accordance with article VII.
2. If, among the members of the Commission on Human Rights, there are no representatives of States Parties to the present Convention or if there are fewer than three such representatives, the Secretary-General of the United Nations shall, after consulting all States Parties to the Convention, designate a representative of the State Party or representatives of the States Parties which are not members of the Commission on Human Rights to take part in the work of the group established in accordance with paragraph 1 of this article, until such time as representatives of the States Parties to the Convention are elected to the Commission on Human Rights.
3. The group may meet for a period of not more than five days, either before the opening or after the closing of the session of the Commission on Human Rights, to consider the reports submitted in accordance with article VII.

Article X

1. The States Parties to the present Convention empower the Commission on Human Rights:

    (a) to request United Nations organs, when transmitting copies of petitions under article 15 of the International Convention on the Elimination of All Forms of Racial Discrimination, to draw its attention to complaints concerning acts which are enumerated in article II of the present Convention;

    (b) to prepare, on the basis of reports from competent organs of the United Nations and periodic reports from States Parties to the present Convention, a list of individuals, organizations, institutions and representatives of States which are alleged to be responsible for the crimes enumerated in article II of the Convention, as well as those against whom legal proceedings have been undertaken by States Parties to the Convention;

    (c) to request information from the competent United Nations organs concerning measures taken by the authorities responsible for the administration of Trust and Non-Self-Governing Territories, and all other Territories to which General Assembly resolution 1514 (XV) of 14

December 1960 applies, with regard to such individuals alleged to be responsible for crimes under article II of the Convention who are believed to be under their territorial and administrative jurisdiction.

2. Pending the achievement of the objectives of the Declaration on the Granting of Independence to Colonial Countries and Peoples, contained in General Assembly resolution 1514 (XV), the provisions of the present Convention shall in no way limit the right of petition granted to those peoples by other international instruments or by the United Nations and its specialized agencies.

Article XI

1. Acts enumerated in article II of the present Convention shall not be considered political crimes for the purpose of extradition.
2. The States Parties to the present Convention undertake in such cases to grant extradition in accordance with their legislation and with the treaties in force.

Article XII

Disputes between States Parties arising out of the interpretation, application or implementation of the present Convention which have not been settled by negotiation shall, at the request of the States Parties to the dispute, be brought before the International Court of Justice, save where the parties to the dispute have agreed on some other form of settlement.

Article XIII

The present Convention is open for signature by all States. Any State which does not sign the Convention before its entry into force may accede to it.

Article XIV

1. The present Convention is subject to ratification. Instruments of ratification shall be deposited with the Secretary-General of the United Nations.
2. Accession shall be effected by the deposit of an instrument of accession with the Secretary-General of the United Nations.

Article XV

1. The present Convention shall enter into force on the thirtieth day after the date of the deposit with the Secretary-General of the United Nations of the twentieth instrument of ratification or accession.
2. For each State ratifying the present Convention or acceding to it after the deposit of the twentieth instrument of ratification or instrument of accession the Convention shall enter into force on the thirtieth day after the date of the deposit of its own instrument of ratification or instrument of accession.

Article XVI

A State Party may denounce the present Convention by written notification to the Secretary-General of the United Nations. Denunciation shall take effect one year after the date of receipt of the notification by the Secretary-General.

Article XVII

1. A request for the revision of this Convention may be made at any time by any State Party by means of a notification in writing addressed to the Secretary-General of the United Nations.
2. The General Assembly of the United Nations shall decide upon the steps, if any, to be taken in respect of such request.

Article XVIII

The Secretary-General of the United Nations shall inform all States of the following particulars:

(a) signatures, ratifications and accessions under articles XIII and XIV;
(b) the date of entry into force of the present Convention under article XV;
(c) denunciations under article XVI;
(d) notifications under article XVII.

1. The present Convention, of which the Chinese, English, French, Russian and Spanish texts are equally authentic, shall be deposited in the archives of the United Nations.
2. The Secretary-General of the United Nations shall transmit certified copies of the present Convention to all States.

58. UNITED NATIONS: CONVENTION ON THE NON-APPLICABILITY OF STATUTORY LIMITATIONS TO WAR CRIMES AND CRIMES AGAINST HUMANITY

Adopted by resolution 2391 (XXIII) of the United Nations General Assembly: 26 November 1968

Entry into force: 11 November 1970

Article 1

No statutory limitation shall apply to the following crimes, irrespective of the date of their commission:

(a) War crimes as they are defined in the Charter of the International Military Tribunal, Nuremberg, of 8 August 1945 and confirmed by resolutions 3(1) of 13 February 1946 and 95(1) of 11 December 1946 of the General Assembly of the United Nations, particularly the "grave breaches" enumerated in the Geneva Conventions of 12 August 1949 for the protection of war victims;

(b) Crimes against humanity whether committed in time of war or in time of peace as they are defined in the Charter of the International Military Tribunal, Nuremberg, of 8 August 1945 and confirmed by resolutions 3(1) of 13 February 1946 and 95(1) of 11 December 1946 of the General Assembly of the United Nations, eviction by armed attack or occupation and inhuman acts resulting from the policy of apartheid and the crime of genocide as defused in the 1948 Convention on the Prevention and Punishment of the Crime of Genocide even if such acts do not constitute a violation of the domestic law of the country in which they were committed.

Article 2

If any of the crimes mentioned in Article 1 is committed, the provisions of this Convention shall apply to representatives of the State authority and private individuals who, as principals or accomplices, participate in or who directly incite others to the commission of any of those crimes, or who conspire to commit them, irrespective of the degree of completion, and to representatives of the State authority who tolerate their commission.

Article 3

The States Parties to the present Convention undertake to adopt all necessary domestic measures, legislative or otherwise, with a view to making possible the extradition in accordance with international law, of the persons referred to in Article 2 of this Convention.

Article 4

The States Parties to the present Convention undertake to adopt, in accordance with their respective constitutional processes, any legislative or other measures necessary to ensure that statutory or other limitations shall not apply to the prosecution and punishment of the crimes referred to in Articles 1 and 2 of this Convention and that, where they exist, such limitations shall be abolished.

Article 5

This Convention shall, until 31 December 1969, be open for signature by any State member of the United Nations or member of any of its specialized agencies or of the International Atomic Energy Agency, by any State Party to the Statute of the International Court of Justice, and by any other State which has been invited by the General Assembly of the United Nations to become a Party to this Convention.

Article 6

This Convention is subject to ratification. Instruments of ratification shall be deposited with the Secretary-General of the United Nations.

Article 7

This Convention shall be open to accession by any State referred to in Article 5. Instruments of accession shall be deposited with the Secretary-General of the United Nations.

Article 8

1. This Convention shall enter into force on the ninetieth day after the date of the deposit with the Secretary-General of the United Nations of the tenth instrument of ratification or accession.
2. For each State ratifying this Convention or acceding to it after the deposit of the tenth instrument of ratification or accession, the Convention shall enter into force upon the ninetieth day after the date of the deposit of its own instrument of ratification or accession.

Article 9

1. After the expiry of a period of ten years from the date on which this Convention enters into force, a request for the revision of the Convention may be made at any time by any Contracting Party by means of a notification in writing addressed to the Secretary-General of the United Nations.

2. The General Assembly of the United Nations shall decide upon the steps, if any, to be taken in respect of such a request.

Article 10

1. This Convention shall be deposited with the Secretary-General of the United Nations.
2. The Secretary-General of the United Nations shall transmit certified copies of this Convention to all States referred to in Article 5.
3. The Secretary-General of the United Nations shall inform all States referred to in Article 5 of the following particulars:

    (a) Signatures of this Convention, and instruments of ratification and accession deposited under Articles 5, 6 and 7;
    (b) The date of entry into force of this Convention in accordance with Article 8;
    (c) Communications received under Article 9.

Article 11

This Convention, of which the Chinese, English, French, Russian and Spanish texts are equally authentic, shall bear the date of 26 November 1968.

59. COUNCIL OF EUROPE: EUROPEAN CONVENTION ON THE NON-APPLICABILITY OF STATUTORY LIMITATION TO CRIMES AGAINST HUMANITY AND WAR CRIMES

Opened for signature at Strasbourg: 25 January 1974

ETS 82

Not in force

The member States of the Council of Europe, signatory hereto,

Considering the necessity to safeguard human dignity in time of war and in time of peace;

Considering that crimes against humanity and the most serious violations of the laws and customs of war constitute a serious infraction of human dignity;

Concerned in consequence to ensure that the punishment of those crimes is not prevented by statutory limitations whether in relation to prosecution or to the enforcement of the punishment;

Considering the essential interest in promoting a common criminal policy in the field, the aim of the Council of Europe being to achieve greater unity between her members;

Have agreed as follows:

Article 1

Each Contracting State undertakes to adopt any necessary measures to secure that statutory limitation shall not apply to the prosecution of the following offences, and to the enforcement of the sentences imposed for such offences, in so far as they are punishable under its domestic law:

1. the crimes against humanity specified in the Convention on the Prevention and Punishment of the Crime of Genocide adopted on 9 December 1948 by the General Assembly of the United Nations:

    (a) the violations specified in Article 50 of the 1949 Geneva Convention for the Amelioration of the Condition of the Wounded and sick in Armed Forces in the Field, Article 51 of the 1949 Geneva Convention for the Amelioration of the Condition of Wounded, Sick and Shipwrecked Members of Armed Forces at Sea, Article 130 of the 1949 Geneva Convention relative to the Treatment of Prisoners of War and Article 147 of the 1949 Geneva Convention relative to the Protection of Civilian Persons in Time of War,

    (b) any comparable violations of the laws of war having effect at the time when this Convention enters into force and of customs of war existing at that time, which are not already provided for in the above-mentioned provisions of the Geneva Conventions,

2. when the specific violation under consideration is of a particularly grave character by reason either of its factual and intentional elements or of the extent of its foreseeable consequences;

3. any other violation of a rule or custom of international law which may hereafter be established and which the Contracting State concerned considers according to a declaration under Article 6 as being of a comparable nature to those referred to in paragraph 1 or 2 of this Article.

Article 2

1. The present Convention applies to offences committed after its entry into force in respect of the Contracting State concerned.

2. It applies also to offences committed before such entry into force in those cases where the statutory limitation period had not expired at that time.

Article 3

1. This Convention shall be open to signature by the member States of the Council of Europe. It shall be subject to ratification or acceptance. Instruments of ratification or acceptance shall be deposited with the Secretary General of the Council of Europe.

2. The Convention shall enter into force three months after the date of deposit of the third instrument of ratification or acceptance.

3. In respect of a signatory State ratifying or accepting subsequently, the Convention shall come into force three months after the date of the deposit of its instrument of ratification or acceptance.

Article 4

1. After the entry into force of this Convention, the Committee of Ministers of the Council of Europe may invite any non-member State to accede thereto, provided that the resolution containing such invitation receives the unanimous agreement of the Members of the Council who have ratified the Convention.

2. Such accession shall be effected by depositing with the Secretary General of the Council of Europe an instrument of accession which shall take effect three months after the date of its deposit.

Article 5

1. Any State may, at the time of signature or when depositing its instrument of ratification, acceptance or accession, specify the territory or territories to which this Convention shall apply.

2. Any State may, when depositing its instrument of ratification, acceptance or accession or at any later date, by declaration addressed to the Secretary General of the Council of Europe, extend this Convention to any other territory or territories specified in the declaration and for whose international relations it is responsible or on whose behalf it is authorised to give undertakings.

3. Any declaration made in pursuance of the preceding paragraph may, in respect of any territory mentioned in such declaration, be withdrawn according to the procedure laid down in Article 7 of this Convention.

Article 6

1. Any Contracting State may, at any time, by declaration addressed to the Secretary General of the Council of Europe, extend this Convention to any violations provided for in Article 1, paragraph 3 of this Convention.
2. Any declaration made in pursuance of the preceding paragraph may be withdrawn according to the procedure laid down in Article 7 of this Convention.

Article 7

1. This Convention shall remain in force indefinitely.
2. Any Contracting State may, insofar as it is concerned, denounce this Convention by means of a notification addressed to the Secretary General of the Council of Europe.
3. Such denunciation shall take effect six months after the date of receipt by the Secretary General of such notification.

Article 8

The Secretary General of the Council of Europe shall notify the member States of the Council and any State which has acceded to this Convention of:

(a) any signature;
(b) any deposit of an instrument of ratification, acceptance or accession;
(c) any date of entry into force of this Convention in accordance with Article 3 thereof;
(d) any declaration received in pursuance of the provisions of Article 5 or Article 6;
(e) any notification received in pursuance of the provisions of Article 7 and the date on which the denunciation takes effect.

SECTION FOUR

INTERNATIONAL CO-OPERATION IN CRIMINAL MATTERS

60. UNITED NATIONS: GENERAL ASSEMBLY RESOLUTION ON A MODEL TREATY ON EXTRADITION

Adopted by General Assembly resolution 45/116 (1990)

Editors' Notes

The Model Treaty was adopted by the General Assembly of the United Nations, following its recommendation by the Eighth Congress on the Prevention of Crime and the Treatment of Offenders, held in Havana. The Model Treaty is part of an initiative by the UN to help and encourage states to enter into treaties for both extradition and mutual legal assistance so as to improve international co-operation against organised crime.[1]

The Model Treaty sets out a broadly similar approach to that taken under the European Convention on Extradition.[2] Thus, states are obligated to extradite in respect of offences identified in Article 2, subject to mandatory and optional grounds for refusal. The text allows for the states implementing an agreement according to the Model to modify the text according to various options.[3]

Whilst the international community is undoubtedly responding to the increase in transnational crime by way of multilateral agreements,[4] some countries, most notably the United States, have resisted joining such initiatives in favour of negotiating their own bilateral treaties. This approach has been ascribed to multilateral agreements adopting "minimum common denominators of coopera-tion" whereas their bilateral counterparts allow "each negotiating partner to include the provisions that are of greatest interest and advantage to the United States".[5] Such a policy, it is submitted, has seen a trend of United States extradition agreements become broader in ambit and more aggressive in approach.[6]

Unfortunately this "aggressiveness" in seeking the rendition of fugitives from abroad has seen the United States become one of a number of countries resorting, on occasion, to unacceptable measures of obtaining jurisdiction over the suspect including kidnapping and the use of forced deportation.[7] An important product of

---

[1] See: Seventh UN Congress on the Prevention of Crime and the Treatment of Offenders, Milan, 1985; report prepared by the Secretariat, Chap. I, Sect. E.

[2] *Supra.*

[3] See for example the text of Article 2.

[4] See for example: European Convention on Extradition, *supra*, Benelux Extradition Convention 1962, Arab League Extradition Agreement 1952, Inter-American Convention on Extradition 1981, The Scheme Relating to the Rendition of Fugitive Offenders Within the Commonwealth 1966.

[5] Nadelmann, E.A. (1993). *Cops Across Borders – The Internationalization of U.S. Law Enforcement.* United States, Pennsylvania State University Press. pp.409–410.

[6] *Ibid.* See Chapter 7 generally.

[7] See: Abbell, M. "The Need for US Legislation to Curb State-sponsored Kidnapping", and Woltring, H.F. & Grieg, J. "State-sponsored Kidnapping of Fugitives: An Alternative to Extradition?", in: Atkins, R.D. (Ed.) (1995). *The Alleged Transnational Criminal.* Netherlands, Martinus Nijhoff and the

the UN initiative to encourage the negotiation of formal arrangements for extradition is that such exchange takes place under a regulated procedure which includes appropriate protections for the accused.

The General Assembly,

Bearing in mind the Milan Plan of Action, adopted by the Seventh United Nations Congress on the Prevention of Crime and the Treatment of Offenders and approved by the General Assembly in its resolution 40/32 of 29 November 1985,

Bearing in mind also the Guiding Principles for Crime Prevention and Criminal Justice in the Context of Development and a New International Economic Order, principle 37 of which stipulates that the United Nations should prepare model instruments suitable for use as international and regional conventions and as guides for national implementing legislation,

Recalling resolution 1 of the Seventh Congress, on organised crime, in which Member States were urged, inter alia, to increase their activity at the international level in order to combat organised crime, including, as appropriate, entering into bilateral treaties on extradition and mutual legal assistance,

Recalling also resolution 23 of the Seventh Congress, on criminal acts of a terrorist character, in which all States were called upon to take steps to strengthen co-operation, inter alia, in the area of extradition,

Calling attention to the United Nations Convention against Illicit Traffic in Narcotic Drugs and Psychotropic Substances,

Acknowledging the valuable contributions of Governments, non-governmental organizations and individual experts, in particular the Government of Australia and the International Association of Penal Law,

Gravely concerned by the escalation of crime, both national and transnational,

Convinced that the establishment of bilateral and multilateral arrangements for extradition will greatly contribute to the development of more effective international co-operation for the control of crime,

Conscious of the need to respect human dignity and recalling the rights conferred upon every person involved in criminal proceedings, as embodied in the Universal Declaration of Human Rights and the International Covenant on Civil and Political Rights,

Conscious that in many cases existing bilateral extradition arrangements are outdated and should be replaced by modern arrangements which take into account recent developments in international criminal law,

Recognising the importance of a model treaty on extradition as an effective way of dealing with the complex aspects and serious consequences of crime, especially in its new forms and dimensions,

1.   Adopts the Model Treaty on Extradition contained in the annex to the present resolution as a useful framework that could be of assistance to States

cont.
International Bar Association; Gane, C. & Nash, S. (1996). "Illegal Extradition: The Irregular Return of Fugitive Offenders". 1 SLPQ 277.

interested in negotiating and concluding bilateral agreements aimed at improving co-operation in matters of crime prevention and criminal justice;

2. Invites Member States, if they have not yet established treaty relations with other States in the area of extradition, or if they wish to revise existing treaty relations, to take into account, whenever doing so, the Model Treaty on Extradition;

3. Urges all States to strengthen further international co-operation in criminal justice;

4. Requests the Secretary-General to bring the present resolution, with the Model Treaty, to the attention of Member States;

5. Urges Member States to inform the Secretary-General periodically of efforts undertaken to establish extradition arrangements;

6. Requests the Committee on Crime Prevention and Control to review periodically the progress attained in this field;

7. Also requests the Committee on Crime Prevention and Control, where requested, to provide guidance and assistance to Member States in the development of legislation that would enable giving effect to the obligations in such treaties as are to be negotiated on the basis of the Model Treaty on Extradition;

8. Invites Member States, on request, to make available to the Secretary-General the provisions of their extradition legislation so that these may be made available to those Member States desiring to enact or further develop legislation in this field.

ANNEX
MODEL TREATY ON EXTRADITION

Desirous of making more effective the co-operation of the two countries in the control of crime by concluding a treaty on extradition,

Have agreed as follows:

Article 1 Obligation to extradite

Each Party agrees to extradite to the other, upon request and subject to the provisions of the present Treaty, any person who is wanted in the requesting State for prosecution for an extraditable offence or for the imposition or enforcement of a sentence in respect of such an offence.

Article 2 Extraditable offences

1. For the purposes of the present Treaty, extraditable offences are offences that are punishable under the laws of both Parties by imprisonment or other deprivation of liberty for a maximum period of at least [one/two] year(s), or by a more severe penalty. Where the request for extradition relates to a person who is wanted for the enforcement of a sentence of imprisonment or other deprivation of liberty imposed for such an offence, extradition shall be

granted only if a period of at least [four/six] months of such sentence remains to be served.

2. In determining whether an offence is an offence punishable under the laws of both Parties, it shall not matter whether:

   (a) The laws of the Parties place the acts or omissions constituting the offence within the same category of offence or denominate the offence by the same terminology;

   (b) Under the laws of the Parties the constituent elements of the offence differ, it being understood that the totality of the acts or omissions as presented by the requesting State shall be taken into account.

3. Where extradition of a person is sought for an offence against a law relating to taxation, customs duties, exchange control or other revenue matters, extradition may not be refused on the ground that the law of the requested State does not impose the same kind of tax or duty or does not contain a tax, customs duty or exchange regulation of the same kind as the law of the requesting State.

4. If the request for extradition includes several separate offences each of which is punishable under the laws of both Parties, but some of which do not fulfil the other conditions set out in paragraph 1 of the present article, the requested Party may grant extradition for the latter offences provided that the person is to be extradited for at least one extraditable offence.

Article 3 Mandatory grounds for refusal

Extradition shall not be granted in any of the following circumstances:

   (a) If the offence for which extradition is requested is regarded by the requested State as an offence of a political nature;

   (b) If the requested State has substantial grounds for believing that the request for extradition has been made for the purpose of prosecuting or punishing a person on account of that person's race, religion, nationality, ethnic origin, political opinions, sex or status, or that that person's position may be prejudiced for any of those reasons;

   (c) If the offence for which extradition is requested is an offence under military law, which is not also an offence under ordinary criminal law;

   (d) If there has been a final judgement rendered against the person in the requested State in respect of the offence for which the person's extradition is requested;

   (e) If the person whose extradition is requested has, under the law of either Party, become immune from prosecution or punishment for any reason, including lapse of time or amnesty;

   (f) If the person whose extradition is requested has been or would be subjected in the requesting State to torture or cruel, inhuman or degrading treatment or punishment or if that person has not received or would not receive the minimum guarantees in criminal proceedings, as contained in the International Covenant on Civil and Political Rights, article 14;

(g) If the judgement of the requesting State has been rendered in absentia, the convicted person has not had sufficient notice of the trial or the opportunity to arrange for his or her defence and he has not had or will not have the opportunity to have the case retried in his or her presence.

Article 4 Optional grounds for refusal

Extradition may be refused in any of the following circumstances:

(a) If the person whose extradition is requested is a national of the requested State. Where extradition is refused on this ground, the requested State shall, if the other State so requests, submit the case to its competent authorities with a view to taking appropriate action against the person in respect of the offence for which extradition is requested;

(b) If the competent authorities of the requested State have decided either not to institute or to terminate proceedings against the person for the offence in respect of which extradition is requested;

(c) If a prosecution in respect of the offence for which extradition is requested is pending in the requested State against the person whose extradition is requested;

(d) If the offence for which extradition is requested carries the death penalty under the law of the requesting State, unless that State gives such assurance as the requested State considers sufficient that the death penalty will not be imposed or, if imposed, will not be carried out;

(e) If the offence for which extradition is requested has been committed outside the territory of either Party and the law of the requested State does not provide for jurisdiction over such an offence committed outside its territory in comparable circumstances;

(f) If the offence for which extradition is requested is regarded under the law of the requested State as having been committed in whole or in part within that State. Where extradition is refused on this ground, the requested State shall, if the other State so requests, submit the case to its competent authorities with a view to taking appropriate action against the person for the offence for which extradition had been requested;

(g) If the person whose extradition is requested has been sentenced or would be liable to be tried or sentenced in the requesting State by an extraordinary or ad hoc court or tribunal;

(h) If the requested State, while also taking into account the nature of the offence and the interests of the requesting State, considers that, in the circumstances of the case, the extradition of that person would be incompatible with humanitarian considerations in view of age, health or other personal circumstances of that person.

Article 5 Channels of communication and required documents

1. A request for extradition shall be made in writing. The request, supporting documents and subsequent communications shall be transmitted through the

diplomatic channel, directly between the ministries of justice or any other authorities designated by the Parties.

2. A request for extradition shall be accompanied by the following:

   (a) In all cases,

      (i) As accurate a description as possible of the person sought, together with any other information that may help to establish that person's identity, nationality and location;

      (ii) The text of the relevant provision of the law creating the offence or, where necessary, a statement of the law relevant to the offence and a statement of the penalty that can be imposed for the offence;

   (b) If the person is accused of an offence, by a warrant issued by a court or other competent judicial authority for the arrest of the person or a certified copy of that warrant, a statement of the offence for which extradition is requested and a description of the acts or omissions constituting the alleged offence, including an indication of the time and place of its commission;

   (c) If the person has been convicted of an offence, by a statement of the offence for which extradition is requested and a description of the acts or omissions constituting the offence and by the original or certified copy of the judgement or any other document setting out the conviction and the sentence imposed, the fact that the sentence is enforceable, and the extent to which the sentence remains to be served;

   (d) If the person has been convicted of an offence in his or her absence, in addition to the documents set out in paragraph 2 (c) of the present article, by a statement as to the legal means available to the person to prepare his or her to defence to have the case retried in his or her presence;

   (e) If the person has been convicted of an offence but no sentence has been imposed, by a statement of the offence for which extradition is requested and a description of the acts or omissions constituting the offence and by a document setting out the conviction and a statement affirming that there is an intention to impose a sentence.

3. The documents submitted in support of a request for extradition shall be accompanied by a translation into the language of the requested State or in another language acceptable to that State.

Article 6 Simplified extradition procedure

The requested State, if not precluded by its law, may grant extradition after receipt of a request for provisional arrest, provided that the person sought explicitly consents before a competent authority.

Article 7 Certification and authentication

Except as provided by the present Treaty, a request for extradition and the documents in support thereof, as well as documents or other material supplied in response to such a request, shall not require certification or authentication.

Article 8 Additional information

If the requested State considers that the information provided in support of a request for extradition is not sufficient, it may request that additional information be furnished within such reasonable time as it specifies.

Article 9 Provisional arrest

1. In case of urgency the requesting State may apply for the provisional arrest of the person sought pending the presentation of the request for extradition. The application shall be transmitted by means of the facilities of the International Criminal Police Organization, by post or telegraph or by any other means affording a record in writing.
2. The application shall contain a description of the person sought, a statement that extradition is to be requested, a statement of the existence of one of the documents mentioned in paragraph 2 of article 5 of the present Treaty, authorising the apprehension of the person, a statement of the punishment that can be or has been imposed for the offence, including the time left to be served and a concise statement of the facts of the case, and a statement of the location, where known, of the person.
3. The requested State shall decide on the application in accordance with its law and communicate its decision to the requesting State without delay.
4   The person arrested upon such an application shall be set at liberty upon the expiration of [40] days from the date of arrest if a request for extradition, supported by the relevant documents specified in paragraph 2 of article 5 of the present Treaty, has not been received. The present paragraph does not preclude the possibility of conditional release of the person prior to the expiration of the [40] days.
5. The release of the person pursuant to paragraph 4 of the present article shall not prevent re-arrest and institution of proceedings with a view to extraditing the person sought if the request and supporting documents are subsequently received.

Article 10 Decision on the request

1. The requested State shall deal with the request for extradition pursuant to procedures provided by its own law, and shall promptly communicate its decision to the requesting State.
2. Reasons shall be given for any complete or partial refusal of the request.

Article 11 Surrender of the person

1. Upon being informed that extradition has been granted, the Parties shall, without undue delay, arrange for the surrender of the person sought and the

requested State shall inform the requesting State of the length of time for which the person sought was detained with a view to surrender.

2. The person shall be removed from the territory of the requested State within such reasonable period as the requested State specifies and, if the person is not removed within that period, the requested State may release the person and may refuse to extradite that person for the same offence.

3. If circumstances beyond its control prevent a Party from surrendering or removing the person to be extradited, it shall notify the other Party. The two Parties shall mutually decide upon a new date of surrender, and the provisions of paragraph 2 of the present article shall apply.

Article 12 Postponed or conditional surrender

1. The requested State may, after making its decision on the request for extradition, postpone the surrender of a person sought, in order to proceed against that person, or, if that person has already been convicted, in order to enforce a sentence imposed for an offence other than that for which extradition is sought. In such a case the requested State shall advise the requesting State accordingly.

2. The requested State may, instead of postponing surrender, temporarily surrender the person sought to the requesting State in accordance with conditions to be determined between the Parties.

Article 13 Surrender of property

1. To the extent permitted under the law of the requested State and subject to the rights of third parties, which shall be duly respected, all property found in the requested State that has been acquired as a result of the offence or that may be required as evidence shall, if the requesting State so requests, be surrendered if extradition is granted.

2. The said property may, if the requesting State so requests, be surrendered to the requesting State even if the extradition agreed to cannot be carried out.

3. When the said property is liable to seizure or confiscation in the requested State, it may retain it or temporarily hand it over.

4. Where the law of the requested State or the protection of the rights of third parties so require, any property so surrendered shall be returned to the requested State free of charge after the completion of the proceedings, if that State so requests.

Article 14 Rule of speciality

1. A person extradited under the present Treaty shall not be proceeded against, sentenced, detained, re-extradited to a third State, or subjected to any other restriction of personal liberty in the territory of the requesting State for any offence committed before surrender other than:

   (a) An offence for which extradition was granted;

(b) Any other offence in respect of which the requested State consents. Consent shall be given if the offence for which it is requested is itself subject to extradition in accordance with the present Treaty.

2. A request for the consent of the requested State under the present article shall be accompanied by the documents mentioned in paragraph 2 of article 5 of the present Treaty and a legal record of any statement made by the extradited person with respect to the offence.

3. Paragraph 1 of the present article shall not apply if the person has had an opportunity to leave the requesting State and has not done so within [30/45] days of final discharge in respect of the offence for which that person was extradited or if the person has voluntarily returned to the territory of the requesting State after leaving it.

Article 15 Transit

1. Where a person is to be extradited to a Party from a third State through the territory of the other Party, the Party to which the person is to be extradited shall request the other Party to permit the transit of that person through its territory. This does not apply where air transport is used and no landing in the territory of the other Party is scheduled.

2. Upon receipt of such a request, which shall contain relevant information, the requested State shall deal with this request pursuant to procedures provided by its own law. The requested State shall grant the request expeditiously unless its essential interests would be prejudiced thereby.

3. The State of transit shall ensure that legal provisions exist that would enable detaining the person in custody during transit.

4. In the event of an unscheduled landing, the Party to be requested to permit transit may, at the request of the escorting officer, hold the person in custody for [48] hours, pending receipt of the transit request to be made in accordance with paragraph 1 of the present article.

Article 16 Concurrent requests

If a Party receives requests for extradition for the same person from both the other Party and a third State it shall, at its discretion, determine to which of those States the person is to be extradited.

Article 17 Costs

1. The requested State shall meet the cost of any proceedings in its jurisdiction arising out of a request for extradition.

2. The requested State shall also bear the costs incurred in its territory in connection with the seizure and handing over of property, or the arrest and detention of the person whose extradition is sought.

3. The requesting State shall bear the costs incurred in conveying the person from the territory of the requested State, including transit costs.

Article 18 Final provisions

1. The present Treaty is subject to [ratification, acceptance or approval]. The instruments of [ratification, acceptance or approval] shall be exchanged as soon as possible.
2. The present Treaty shall enter into force on the thirtieth day after the day on which the instruments of [ratification, acceptance or approval] are exchanged.
3. The present Treaty shall apply to requests made after its entry into force, even if the relevant acts or omissions occurred prior to that date.
4. Either Contracting Party may denounce the present Treaty by giving notice in writing to the other Party. Such denunciation shall take effect six months following the date on which such notice is received by the other Party.

61. COUNCIL OF EUROPE: EUROPEAN CONVENTION ON EXTRADITION

Opened for signature at Paris: 13 December 1957

ETS 24

Entry into force: 18 April 1960

Editors' Notes

The Council of Europe's Convention on Extradition is the product of a sustained study of extradition procedure by a Committee of Government Experts instructed by the Committee of Ministers during the 1950s.[1] During the drafting of the Convention, disagreement existed within the Committee of Experts as to whether the Convention should take the form of a bilateral model agreement, allowing states to tailor such a model to the pragmatic requirements of obtaining jurisdiction to facilitate the prosecution of the accused, or whether the treaty should be multilateral, introducing a standard regional practice with humanitarian protections.[2] The present multilateral option was proceeded with on the basis that as many states as possible would accede to the procedures and protections therein. It should be noted, however, that many of the parties to the Treaty have entered reservations as to its provisions.[3]

Under the Convention, the parties are placed under an obligation to extradite in respect of relevant offences (Article 2). This obligation is qualified however, by the requirements of double criminality (Article 2), the political offence exception (Article 3), the non-return of fugitives for purely military or fiscal offences (Articles 4–5), the rule of specialty (Article 14), restrictions in circumstances where the death penalty may be imposed by the requesting state (Article 11) and by the provisions of the "discrimination clause" (Article 3).

The Convention is now supplemented by an Additional Protocol which further defines political offences (Article 1) and the interpretation of the principle of *non bis in idem* (Article 2), and a Second Additional Protocol deals with accessory extradition (Article 1), judgements *in absentia* (Article 2) and allows parties to extradite for fiscal offences (Article 2). The Treaty is also supplemented by three Recommendations by the Committee of Ministers.[4]

---

[1] See: Explanatory Report to the European Convention on Extradition, in: Muller-Rappard, E. & Bassiouni, M.C. (1987). *European Inter-state Co-operation in Criminal Matters*. Netherlands, Martinus Nijhoff. Vol. 1, Chap. 2, p15.

[2] *Ibid*, pp.17–19.

[3] *Ibid*, pp. 41–62.

[4] Recommendation No. R (80) 7 Concerning the Practical Application of the European Convention on Extradition; Recommendation No. R (80) 9 Concerning Extradition to States not Party to the European Convention on Human Rights; Recommendation No. R. (86) 13 Concerning the Practical Application of the European Convention on Extradition in respect of Detention pending Extradition.

The extent to which the accused may enjoy human rights protection beyond the safeguards included within the Convention has been the subject of widespread academic discussion[5] following the decision of the European Court of Human Rights in the *Soering* case,[6] and by the Supreme Court of the Netherlands in the case of *Short*.[7] In *Soering*, it was held that the United Kingdom could not extradite the fugitive to the United States to face trials for capital murder, since to do so would violate Article 3 of the European Convention of Human Rights[8] prohibiting inhuman or degrading treatment or punishment. The Court held that while the death penalty as such did not violate the Convention as it applied to the United Kingdom, the so-called "death-row syndrome" attending capital cases in the United States would amount to inhumane treatment of the fugitive. In *Short*, the Court held that the accused could not be extradited to the United States so as to face charges of capital murder, since to do so would amount to the Netherlands breaching their obligations under the 6th Protocol to the European Convention on Human Rights, not to use the death penalty.[9]

The Governments signatory hereto, being Members of the Council of Europe,

Considering that the aim of the Council of Europe is to achieve a greater unity between its Members;

Considering that this purpose can be attained by the conclusion of agreements and by common action in legal matters;

Have agreed as follows:

Article 1: Obligation to extradite

The Contracting Parties undertake to surrender to each other, subject to the provisions and conditions laid down in this Convention, all persons against whom the competent authorities of the requesting Party are proceeding for an offence or who are wanted by the said authorities for the carrying out of a sentence or detention order.

Article 2: Extraditable offences

1. Extradition shall be granted in respect of offences punishable under the laws of the requesting Party and of the requested Party by deprivation of liberty or under a detention order for a maximum period of at least one year or by a more severe penalty. Where a conviction and prison sentence have occurred

---

[5] See for example: Van Den Wyngaert, C. (1990). "Applying the European Convention on Human Rights to Extradition: Opening Pandora's Box?" 39 ICLQ 757; Williams, S. (1992). "Human Rights Safeguards and International Cooperation in Extradition – Striking the Balance", in Eser, A & Lagodny, O. (Eds). *Principles and Procedures for a New Transnational Criminal Law.* Germany, Max-Planck-Institut. p.535.

[6] *Soering v United Kingdom* (1989), ECHR Ser.A. Vol. 161.

[7] *Netherlands v Short* (1990), reported at 29 ILM 1375.

[8] *Supra.*

[9] *Supra.*

or a detention order has been made in the territory of the requested Party, the punishment awarded must have been for a period of at least four months.

2. If the request for extradition includes several separate offences each of which is punishable under the laws of the requesting Party and the requested party by deprivation of liberty or under a detention order, but of which some do not fulfil the condition with regard to the count of punishment which may be awarded, the requested Party shall also have the right to grant extradition for the latter offences.

3. Any Contracting Party whose law does not allow extradition for certain of the offences referred to in paragraph 1 of this article may, in so far as it is concerned, exclude such offences from the application of this Convention.

4. Any Contracting Party which wishes to avail itself of the right provided for in paragraph 3 of this article shall, at the time of the deposit of its instrument of ratification or accession, transmit to the Secretary General of the Council of Europe either a list of the offences for which extradition is allowed or a list of those for which it is excluded and shall at the same time indicate the legal provisions which allow or exclude extradition. The Secretary General of the Council shall forward these lists to the other Signatories.

5. If extradition is subsequently excluded in respect of other offences by the law of a Contracting party, that Party shall notify the Secretary General. The Secretary General shall inform the other Signatories. Such notification shall not take effect until three months from the date of its receipt by the Secretary General.

6. Any Party which avails itself of the right provided for in paragraphs 4 or 5 of this article may at any time apply this Convention to offences which have been excluded from it. It shall inform the Secretary General of the Council of such changes, and the Secretary General shall inform the other Signatories.

7. Any Party may apply reciprocity in respect of any offences excluded from the application of the Convention under this article.

Article 3: Political offences

1. Extradition shall not be granted if the offence in respect of which it is requested is regarded by the requested Party as a political offence or as an offence connected with a political offence.

2. The same rule shall apply if the requested Party has substantial grounds for believing that a request for extradition for an ordinary criminal offence has been made for the purpose of prosecuting or punishing a person on account of his race, religion, nationality or political opinion, or that that person's position may be prejudiced for any of these reasons.

3. The taking or attempted taking of the life of a Head of State or a member of his family shall not be deemed to be a political offence for the purposes of this Convention.

4. This article shall not affect any obligations which the Contracting Parties may have undertaken or may undertake under any other international convention of a multilateral character.

623

Article 4: Military offences

Extradition for offences under military law which are not offences under ordinary criminal law is excluded from the application of this Convention.

Article 5: Fiscal offences

Extradition shall be granted, in accordance with the provisions of this Convention, for offences in connection with taxes, duties, customs and exchange only if the Contracting Parties have so decided in respect of any such offence or category of offences.

Article 6: Extradition of nationals

1. (a) A Contracting Party shall have the right to refuse extradition of its nationals.
    (b) Each Contracting Party may, by a declaration made at the time of signature or of deposit of its instrument of ratification or accession, define as far as it is concerned the term "nationals" within the meaning of this Convention.
    (c) Nationality shall be determined as at the time of the decision concerning extradition. If, however, the person claimed is first recognised as a national of the requested Party during the period between the time of the decision and the time contemplated for the surrender, the requested Party may avail itself of the provision contained in sub-paragraph (a) of this article.

2. If the requested Party does not extradite its national, it shall at the request of the requesting Party submit the case to its competent authorities in order that proceedings may be taken if they are considered appropriate. For this purpose, the files, information and exhibits relating to the offence shall be transmitted without charge by the means provided for in Article 12, paragraph 1. The requesting Party shall be informed of the result of its request.

Article 7: Place of Commission

1. The requested Party may refuse to extradite a person claimed for an offence which is regarded by its law as having been committed in whole or in part in its territory or in a place treated as its territory.
2. When the offence for which extradition is requested has been committed outside the territory of the requested Party, extradition may only be refused if the law of the requested Party does not allow prosecution for the same category of offence when committed outside the latter Party's territory or does not allow extradition for the offence concerned.

Article 8: Pending proceedings for the same offences

The requested Party may refuse to extradite the person claimed if the competent authorities of such Party are proceeding against him in respect of the offence or offences for which extradition is requested.

Article 9: Non bis in idem

Extradition shall not be granted if final judgment has been passed by the competent authorities of the requested Party upon the person claimed in respect of the offence or offences for which extradition is requested. Extradition may be refused if the competent authorities of the requested Party have decided either not to institute or to terminate proceedings in respect of the same offence or offences.

Article 10: Lapse of time

Extradition shall not be granted when the person claimed has, according to the law of either the requesting or the requested Party, become immune by reason of lapse of time from prosecution or punishment.

Article 11: Capital punishment

If the offence for which extradition is requested is punishable by death under the law of the requested Party, and if in respect of such offence the death-penalty is not proved for by the law of the requested Party or is not normally carried out, extradition may be refused unless the requesting Party gives such assurance as the requested Party considers sufficient that the death-penalty will not be carried out.

Article 12: The request and supporting documents

1. The request shall be in writing and shall be communicated through the diplomatic channel. Other means of communication may be arranged by direct agreement between two or more Parties.
2. The request shall be supported by:

    (a) the original or an authenticated copy of the convention and sentence or detention order immediately enforceable or of the warrant of arrest or other order having the same effect and issued in accordance with the procedure laid down in the law of the requesting Party;

    (b) a statement of the offences for which extradition is requested. The time and place of their commission, their legal descriptions and a reference to the relevant legal provisions shall be set out as accurately as possible; and

    (c) a copy of the relevant enactments or, where this is not possible, a statement of the relevant law and as accurate a description as possible of the person claimed, together with any other information which will help to establish his identity and nationality.

Article 13: Supplementary information

If the information communicated by the requested party is found to be insufficient to allow the requested Party to make a decision in pursuance of this Convention, the latter Party shall request the necessary supplementary information and may fix a time-limit for the receipt thereof.

Article 14: Rule of speciality

1. A person who has been extradited shall not be proceeded against, sentenced or detained with a view to the carrying out of a sentence or detention order for any offence committed prior to his surrender other than that for which he was extradited, nor shall he be for any other reason restricted in his personal freedom, except in the following cases:

    (a) when the Party which surrendered him consents. A request for consent shall be submitted, accompanied by the documents mentioned in Article 12 and a legal record of any statement made by the extradited person in respect of the offence concerned. Consent shall be given when the offence for which it is requested is itself subject to extradition in accordance with the provisions of this Convention;
    (b) when that person, having had an opportunity to leave the territory of the Party to which he has been surrendered, has not done so within 45 days of his final discharge, or has returned to that territory after leaving it.

2. The requesting Party may, however, take any measures necessary to remove the person from its territory, or any measures necessary under its law, including proceedings by default, to prevent any legal effects of lapse of time.
3. When the description of the offence charged is altered in the course of proceedings, the extradited person shall only be proceeded against or sentenced in so far as the offence under its new description is shown by its constituent elements to be an offence which would allow extradition.

Article 15: Re-extradition to a third State

Except as provided for in Article 14, paragraph 1(b), the requesting Party shall not, without the consent of the requested Party, surrender to another Party or to a third State a person surrendered to the requesting Party and sought by the said other Party or third State in respect of offences committed before his surrender. The requested Party may request the production of the documents mentioned in Article 12, paragraph 2.

Article 16: Provisional arrest

1. In case of urgency the competent authorities of the requesting Party may request the provisional arrest of the person sought. The competent authorities of the requested Party shall decide the matter in accordance with its law.
2. The request for provisional arrest shall state that one of the documents

mentioned in Article 12, paragraph 2(a), exists and that it is intended to send a request for extradition. It shall also state for what offence extradition will be requested and when and where such offence was committed and shall so far as possible give a description of the person sought.

3. A request for provisional arrest shall be sent to the competent authorities of the requested Party either through the diplomatic channel or direct by post or telegraph or through the International Criminal Police Organisation (Interpol) or by any other means affording evidence in writing or accepted by the requested Party. The requesting authority shall be informed without delay of the result of its request.

4. Provisional arrest may be terminated if, within a period of 18 days after arrest, the requested Party has not received the request for extradition of the documents mentioned in Article 12. It shall not, in any event, exceed 40 days from the date of such arrest. The possibility of provisional release at any time is not excluded, but the requested Party shall take any measures which it considers necessary to prevent the escape of the person sought.

5. Release shall not prejudice re-arrest and extradition if a request for extradition is received subsequently.

Article 17: Conflicting requests

If extradition is requested concurrently by more than one State, either for the same offence or for different offences, the requested Party shall make its decision having regard to all the circumstances and especially the relative seriousness and place of commission of the offences, the respective dates of the requests, the nationality of the person claimed and the possibility of subsequent extradition to another State.

Article 18: Surrender of the person to be extradited

1. The requested Party shall inform the requesting Party by the means mentioned in Article 12, paragraph 1, of its decision with regard to the extradition.

2. Reasons shall be given for any complete or partial rejection.

3. If the request is agreed to, the requesting Party shall be informed of the place and date of surrender and of the length of time for which the person claimed was detained with a view to surrender.

4. Subject to the provisions of paragraph 5 of this article, if the person claimed has not been taken over on the appointed date, he may be released after the expiry of 15 days and shall in any case be released after the expiry of 30 days. The requested party may refuse to extradite him for the same offence.

5. If circumstances beyond its control prevent a Party from surrendering or taking over the person to be extradited, it shall notify the other Party. The two Parties shall agree a new date for surrender and the provisions of paragraph 4 of this article shall apply.

Article 19: Postponed or conditional surrender

1. The requested Party may, after making its decision on the request for extradition, postpone the surrender of the person claimed in order that he may be proceeded against by that Party or, if he has already been convicted, in order that he may serve his sentence in the territory of that Party for an offence other than that for which extradition is requested.

2. The requested Party may, instead of postponing surrender, temporarily surrender the person claimed to be the requested Party in accordance with conditions to be determined by mutual agreement between the Parties.

Article 20: Handing over of property

1. The requested Party shall, in so far as its law permits and at the request of the requesting Party, seize and hand over property;

    (a) which may be required as evidence or
    (b) which has been acquired as a result of the offence and which, at the time of the arrest, is found in the possession of the person claimed or is discovered subsequently.

2. The property mentioned in paragraph 1 of this article shall be handed over even if extradition, having been agreed to, cannot be carried out owing to the death or escape of the person claimed.

3. When the said property is liable to seizure or confiscation in the territory of the requested Party, the latter may, in connection with pending criminal proceedings, temporarily retain it or hand it over on condition that it is returned.

4. Any rights which the requested Party or third parties may have acquired in the said property shall be preserved. Where these rights exist, the property shall be returned without charge to the requested Party as soon as possible after the trial.

Article 21: Transit

1. Transit through the territory of one of the Contracting Parties shall be granted on submission of a request by the means mentioned in Article 12, paragraph 1, provided that the offence concerned is not considered by the Party requested to grant transit as an offence of a political or purely military character having regard to Article 3 and 4 of this Convention.

2. Transit of a national, within the meaning of Article 6, of a country requested to grant transit may be refused.

3. Subject to the provisions of paragraph 4 of this article, it shall be necessary to produce the documents mentioned in Article 12, paragraph 2.

4. If air transport is used, the following provisions shall apply:

    (a) when it is not intended to land, the requesting Party shall notify the Party over whose territory the flight is to be made and shall certify that one of

628

the documents mentioned in Article 12, paragraph 2(a) exists. In the case of an unscheduled landing, such notification shall have the effect of a request for provisional arrest as provided for in Article 16, and the requesting Party shall submit a formal request for transit;

(b) when it is intended to land, the requesting Party shall submit a formal request for transit.

5. A Party may, however, at the time of signature or of the deposit of its instrument of ratification of, or accession to, this Convention, declare that it will only grant transit of a person on some or all of the conditions on which it grants extradition. In that event, reciprocity may be applied.

6. The transit of the extradited person shall not be carried out through any territory where there is reason to believe that his life or his freedom may be threatened by reason of his race, religion, nationality or political opinion.

Article 22: Procedure

Except where this Convention otherwise provides, the procedure with regard to extradition and provisional arrest shall be governed solely by the law of the requested party.

Article 23: Language to be used

The documents to be produced shall be in the language of the requesting or requested Party. The requested Party may require a translation into one of the official languages of the Council of Europe to be chosen by it.

Article 24: Expense

1. Expenses incurred in the territory of the requested Party by reason of extradition shall be borne by that Party.

2. Expenses incurred by reason of transit through the territory of a Party requested to grant transit shall be borne by the requesting Party.

3. In the event of extradition from a non-metropolitan territory of the requested Party, the expenses occasioned by travel between that territory and the metropolitan territory of the requesting Party shall be borne by the latter. The same rule shall apply to expenses occasioned by travel between the non-metropolitan territory of the requested Party and its metropolitan territory.

Article 25: Definition of "detention order"

For the purposes of this Convention, the expression "detention order" means any order involving deprivation of liberty which has been made by a criminal court in addition to or instead of a prison sentence.

Article 26: Reservations

1. Any Contracting Party may, when signing this Convention or when depositing its instrument of ratification or accession, make a reservation in respect of any provision or provisions of the Convention.
2. Any Contracting Party which has made a reservation shall withdraw it as soon as circumstances permit. Such withdrawal shall be made by notification to the Secretary General of the Council of Europe.
3. A Contracting Party which has made a reservation in respect of a provision of the Convention may not claim application of the said provision by another Party save in so far as it has itself accepted the provision.

Article 27: Territorial application

1. This Convention shall apply to the metropolitan territories of the Contracting Parties.
2. In respect of France, it shall also apply to Algeria and to the overseas Departments and, in respect of the United Kingdom of Great Britain and Northern Ireland, to the Channel Islands and to the Isle of Man.
3. The Federal Republic of Germany may extend the application of this Convention to the Land of Berlin by notice addressed to the Secretary General of the Council of Europe, who shall notify the other Parties of such declaration.
4. By direct arrangement between two or more Contracting Parties, the application of this Convention may be extended, subject to the conditions laid down in the arrangement, to any territory of such Parties, other than the territories mentioned in paragraphs 1, 2 and 3 of this article, for whose international relations any such Party is responsible.

Article 28: Relations between this Convention and bilateral Agreements

1. This Convention shall, in respect of those countries to which it applies, supersede the provisions of any bilateral treaties, conventions or agreements governing extradition between any two Contracting Parties.
2. The Contracting Parties may conclude between themselves bilateral or multilateral agreements only in order to supplement the provisions of this Convention or to facilitate the application of the principles contained therein.
3. Where, as between two or more Contracting Parties, extradition takes place on the basis of a uniform law, the Parties shall be free to regulate their mutual relations in respect of extradition exclusively in accordance with such a system notwithstanding the provisions of this Convention. The same principle shall apply as between two or more Contracting Parties each of which has in force a law providing for the execution in its territory of warrants of arrest issued in the territory of the other Party or Parties. Contracting Parties which exclude or may in the future exclude the application of this Convention as between themselves in accordance with this paragraph shall notify the Secretary General of the Council of Europe accordingly. The Secretary

General shall inform the other Contracting Parties of any notification received in accordance with this paragraph.

Article 29: Signature, ratification and entry into force

1. This Convention shall be open to signature by the Members of the Council of Europe. It shall be ratified. The instruments of ratification shall be deposited with the Secretary General of the Council.
2. The Convention shall come into force 90 days after the date of deposit of the third instrument of ratification.
3. As regards any signatory ratifying subsequently, the Convention shall come into force 90 days after the date of the deposit of its instrument of ratification.

Article 30: Accession

1. The Committee of Ministers of the Council of Europe may invite any State not a Member of the Council to accede to this Convention, provided that the resolution containing such invitation receives the unanimous agreement of the Members of the Council who have ratified the Convention.
2. Accession shall be by deposit with the Secretary General of the Council of an instrument of accession, which shall take effect 90 days after the date of its deposit.

Article 31: Denunciation

Any Contracting Party may denounce this Convention in so far as it is concerned by giving notice to the Secretary General of the Council of Europe. Denunciation shall take effect six months after the date when the Secretary General of the Council received such notification.

Article 32: Notifications

The Secretary General of the Council of Europe shall notify the Members of the Council and the government of any State which has acceded to this Convention to:
  (a) the deposit of any instrument of ratification or accession;
  (b) the date of entry into force of this Convention;
  (c) any declaration made in accordance with the provisions of Article 6, paragraph 1, and of Article 21, paragraph 5;
  (d) any reservation made in accordance with Article 26, paragraph 1;
  (e) the withdrawal of any reservation in accordance with Article 26, paragraph 2;
  (f) any notification of denunciation received in accordance with the provisions of Article 31 and by the date on which such denunciation will take effect.

62. COUNCIL OF EUROPE: ADDITIONAL PROTOCOL TO THE EUROPEAN CONVENTION ON EXTRADITION

Opened for signature at Strasbourg: 15 October 1975

ETS 86

Entry into force: 20 August 1979

The member States of the Council of Europe, signatory to this Protocol,

Having regard to the provisions of the European Convention on Extradition opened for signature in Paris on 13 December 1957 (hereinafter referred to as "the Convention") and in particular Articles 3 and 9 thereof;

Considering that it is desirable to supplement these Articles with a view to strengthening the protection of humanity and of individuals,

Have agreed as follows:

CHAPTER I

Article 1

For the application of Article 3 of the Convention, political offences shall not be considered to include the following:

(a) the crimes against humanity specified in the Convention on the Prevention and Punishment of the Crime of Genocide adopted on 9 December 1948 by the General Assembly of the United Nations;

(b) the violations specified in Article 50 of the 1949 Geneva Convention for the Amelioration of the Condition of the Wounded and Sick in Armed Forces in the Field, Article 51 of the 1949 Geneva Convention for the Amelioration of the Condition of Wounded, Sick and Shipwrecked Members of Armed Forces at Sea, Article 130 of the 1949 Geneva Convention relative to the Treatment of Prisoners of War and Article 147 of the 1949 Geneva Convention relative to the Protection of Civilian Persons in Time of War;

(c) any comparable violations of the laws of war having effect at the time when this Protocol enters into force and of customs of war existing at that time, which are not already provided for in the above-mentioned provisions of the Geneva Conventions.

CHAPTER II

Article 2

Article 9 of the Convention shall be supplemented by the following text, the original Article 9 of the Convention becoming paragraph 1 and the under-mentioned provisions becoming paragraphs 2, 3, and 4:

"2. The extradition of a person against whom a final judgment has been rendered in a third State, Contacting Party to the Convention, for the offence or offences in respect of which the claim was made, shall not be granted:

(a) if the afore-mentioned judgment resulted in his acquittal;
(b) if the term of imprisonment or other measure to which he was sentenced:

(i) has been completely enforced;
(ii) has been wholly, or with respect to the part not enforced, the subject of a pardon or any amnesty;

(c) if the court convicted the offender without imposing a sanction.

3. However, in the cases referred to in paragraph 2, extradition may be granted:

(a) if the offence in respect of which judgment has been rendered was committed against a person, an institution or any thing having public status in the requesting State;
(b) if the person on whom judgment was passed had himself a public status in the requesting State;
(c) if the offence in respect of which judgment was passed was committed completely or partly in the territory of the requesting State or in a place treated as its territory.

4. The provisions of paragraph 2 and 3 shall not prevent the application of wider domestic provisions relating to the effect of *ne bis in idem* attached to foreign criminal judgments."

CHAPTER III

Article 3

1. This Protocol shall be open to signature by the member States of the Council of Europe which have signed the Convention. It shall be subject to ratification, acceptance or approval. Instruments of ratification, acceptance or approval shall be deposited with the Secretary General of the Council of Europe.
2. The Protocol shall enter into force 90 days after the date of the deposit of the third instrument of ratification, acceptance or approval.
3. In respect of a signatory State ratifying, accepting or approving subsequently, the Protocol shall enter into force 90 days after the date of the deposit of its instrument of ratification, acceptance or approval.
4. A member State of the Council of Europe may not ratify, accept or approve

this Protocol without having, simultaneously or previously, ratified the Convention.

Article 4

1. Any State which has acceded to the Convention may accede to this Protocol after the Protocol has entered into force.
2. Such accession shall be effected by depositing with the Secretary General of the Council of Europe an instrument of accession which shall take effect 90 days after the date of its deposit.

Article 5

1. Any State may, at the time of signature or when depositing its instrument of ratification, acceptance, approval or accession, specify the territory or territories to which this Protocol shall apply.
2. Any State may, when depositing its instruments of ratification, acceptance, approval or accession or at any later date, by declaration addressed to the Secretary General of the Council of Europe, extend this Protocol to any other territory or territories specified in the declaration and for whose international relations it is responsible or on whose behalf it is authorised to give undertakings.
3. Any declaration made in pursuance of the preceding paragraph may, in respect of any territory mentioned in such declaration, be withdrawn according to the procedure laid down in Article 8 of this Protocol.

Article 6

1. Any State may, at the time of signature or when depositing its instrument of ratification, acceptance, approval or accession, declare that it does not accept one or the other of Chapter I or II.
2. Any Contracting Party may withdraw a declaration it has made in accordance with the foregoing paragraph by means of a declaration addressed to the Secretary General of the Council of Europe which shall become effective as from the date of its receipt.
3. No reservation may be made to the provisions of this Protocol.

Article 7

The European Committee on Crime Problems of the Council of Europe shall be kept informed regarding the application of this Protocol and shall do whatever is needful to facilitate a friendly settlement of any difficulty which may arise out of its execution.

Article 8

1. Any Contracting Party may, in so far as it is concerned, denounce this Protocol by means of a notification addressed to the Secretary General of the Council of Europe.
2. Such denunciation shall take effect six months after the date of receipt by the Secretary General of such notification.
3. Denunciation of the Convention entails automatically denunciation of this Protocol.

Article 9

The Secretary General of the Council of Europe shall notify the member States of the Council and any State which has acceded to the Convention of:

(a) any signature;
(b) any deposit of an instrument of ratification, acceptance, approval or accession;
(c) any date of entry into force of this Protocol in accordance with Article 3 thereof;
(d) any declaration received in pursuance of the provisions of Article 5 and any withdrawal of such a declaration;
(e) any declaration made in pursuance of the provisions of Article 6, paragraph 1;
(f) the withdrawal of any declaration carried out in pursuance of the provisions of Article 6, paragraph 2;
(g) any notification received in pursuance of the provisions of Article 8 and the date on which denunciation takes effect.

63. COUNCIL OF EUROPE: SECOND ADDITIONAL PROTOCOL TO THE EUROPEAN CONVENTION ON EXTRADITION

Opened for signature at Strasbourg: 17 March 1978

ETS 98

Entry into force: 5 May 1983

The member States of the Council of Europe, signatory to this Protocol,

Desirous of facilitating the application of the European Convention on Extradition opened for signature in Paris on 13 December 1957 (hereinafter referred to as "the Convention") in the field of fiscal offences;

Considering it also desirable to supplement the Convention in certain other respect,

Have agreed as follows:

CHAPTER I

Article 1

Paragraph 2 of Article 2 of the Convention shall be supplemented by the following provision:

"This right shall also apply to offences which are subject only to pecuniary sanctions."

CHAPTER II

Article 2

Article 5 of the Convention shall be replaced by the following provisions:

"Fiscal offences

1. For offences in connection with taxes, duties, customs and exchange extradition shall take place between the Contracting Parties in accordance with the provisions of the Convention if the offence, under the law of the requested Party, corresponded to an offence of the same nature.
2. Extradition may not be refused on the ground that the law of the requested Party does not impose the same kind of tax or duty or does not contain a tax, duty, customs or exchange regulation of the same kind as the law of the requesting Party."

CHAPTER III

Article 3

The Convention shall be supplemented by the following provisions:

"Judgments in absentia

1. When a Contracting Party requests from another Contracting Party the extradition of a person for the purpose of carrying out a sentence or detention order imposed by a decision rendered against him in absentia, the requested Party may refuse to extradite for this purpose if, in its opinion, the proceedings leading to the judgment did not satisfy the minimum rights of defence recognised as due to everyone charged with criminal offence. However, extradition shall be granted if the requesting Party gives an assurance considered sufficient to guarantee to the person claimed the right to a retrial which safeguards the rights of defence. This decision will authorise the requesting Party either to enforce the judgment in question if the convicted person does not make an opposition or, if he does, to take proceedings against the person extradited.
2. When the requested Party informs the person whose extradition has been requested of the judgment rendered against him in absentia, the requesting Party shall not regard this communication as a formal notification for the purpose of the criminal procedure in that State."

CHAPTER IV

Article 4

The Convention shall be supplemented by the following provisions:

"Amnesty

Extradition shall not be granted for an offence in respect of which an amnesty has been declared in the requested State and which that State had competence to prosecute under its own law."

CHAPTER V

Article 5

Paragraph 1 of Article 12 of the Convention shall be replaced by the following provisions:

> "The request shall be in writing and shall be addressed by the Ministry of Justice of the requesting Party to the Ministry of Justice of the requested Party; however, use of the diplomatic channel is not excluded. Other means of communication may be arranged by direct agreement between two or more Parties."

CHAPTER VI

Article 6

1. This Protocol shall be open to signature by the member States of the Council of Europe which have signed the Convention. It shall be subject to ratification, acceptance or approval. Instruments of ratification, acceptance or approval shall be deposited with the Secretary General of the Council of Europe.
2. The Protocol shall enter into force 90 days after the date of the deposit of the third instrument of ratification, acceptance or approval.
3. In respect of a signatory State ratifying, accepting or approving subsequently, the Protocol shall enter into force 90 days after the date of the deposit of its instrument of ratification, acceptance or approval.
4. A member State of the Council of Europe may not ratify, accept or approve this Protocol without having, simultaneously or previously, ratified the Convention.

Article 7

1. Any State which has acceded to the Convention may accede to this Protocol after the Protocol has entered into force.
2. Such accession shall be effected by depositing with the Secretary General of the Council of Europe an instrument of accession which shall take effect 90 days after the date of its deposit.

Article 8

1. Any State may, at the time of signature or when depositing its instrument of ratification, acceptance, approval or accession, specify the territory or territories to which this Protocol shall apply.
2. Any State may, when depositing its instrument of ratification, acceptance, approval or accession or at any later date, by declaration addressed to the Secretary General of the Council of Europe, extend this Protocol to any other territory or territories specified in the declaration and for whose international relations it is responsible or on whose behalf it is authorised to give undertakings.
3. Any declaration made in pursuance of the preceding paragraph may, in respect of any territory mentioned in such declaration, be withdrawn by means of a notification addressed to the Secretary General of the Council of Europe. Such withdrawal shall take effect six months after the date of receipt by the Secretary General of the Council of Europe of the notification.

Article 9

1. Reservations made by a State to a provision of the Convention shall be applicable also to this Protocol, unless that State otherwise declares at the time of signature or when depositing its instrument of ratification, acceptance, approval or accession.

2. Any State may, at the time of signature or when depositing its instrument of ratification, acceptance, approval or accession, declare that it reserves the right:

   (a) not to accept Chapter I;
   (b) not to accept Chapter II, or to accept it only in respect of certain offences or certain categories of the offences referred to in Article 2;
   (c) not to accept Chapter III, or to accept only paragraph 1 of Article 3;
   (d) not to accept Chapter IV:
   (e) not to accept Chapter V.

3. Any Contracting Party may withdraw a reservation it has made in accordance with the foregoing paragraph by means of a declaration addressed to the Secretary General of the Council of Europe which shall become effective as from the date of its receipt.

4. A Contracting Party which has applied to this Protocol a reservation made in respect of a provision of the Convention or which has made a reservation in respect of a provision of this Protocol may not claim the application of that provision by another Contracting Party; it may, however, if its reservation is partial or conditional, claim the application of that provision in so far as it has itself accepted it.

5. No other reservation may be made to the provisions of this Protocol.

Article 10

The European Committee on Crime Problems of the Council of Europe shall be kept informed regarding the application of this Protocol and shall do whatever is needful to facilitate a friendly settlement of any difficulty which may arise out of its execution.

Article 11

1. Any Contracting Party may, in so far as it is concerned, denounce this Protocol by means of a notification addressed to the Secretary General of the Council of Europe.

2. Such denunciation shall take effect six months after the date of receipt by the Secretary General of such notification.

3. Denunciation of the Convention entails automatically denunciation of this Protocol.

Article 12

The Secretary General of the Council of Europe shall notify the member States of the Council and any State which has acceded to the Convention of:

   (a) any signature of this Protocol;
   (b) any deposit of an instrument of ratification, acceptance, approval or accession;

(c) any date of entry into force of this Protocol in accordance with Articles 6 and 7;

(d) any declaration received in pursuance of the provisions of paragraphs 2 and 3 of Article 8;

(e) any declaration received in pursuance of the provisions of paragraph 1 of article 9;

(f) any reservation made in pursuance of the provisions of paragraph 2 of Article 9;

(g) the withdrawal of any reservation carried out in pursuance of the provisions of paragraph 3 of Article 9;

(h) any notification received in pursuance of the provisions of Article 11 and the date on which denunciation takes effect.

64. UNITED NATIONS: GENERAL ASSEMBLY RESOLUTION ON A MODEL TREATY ON MUTUAL ASSISTANCE IN CRIMINAL MATTERS

Adopted by General Assembly resolution 45/117 (1990)

Editors' Notes

The Model Treaty on Mutual Assistance stems from the preparatory meetings and discussions undertaken at the United Nations Eighth Congress on the Prevention of Crime and the Treatment of Offenders which met in Havana in 1990.

The Model Treaty reflects the development of mutual legal assistance treaties (MLAT's) since the 1970s and has taken the central features of these agreements which are increasingly being entered into on a bilateral basis[1] and welded them into a simple framework. Bilateral MLATs appear to offer certain advantages to states when compared with their multilateral counterparts. In the first place, they can be adopted (and abandoned) with relative ease, and states can tailor a bilateral agreement to focus on particular criminal problems or nuances in the other party's legal system. It should be recognised that the influence of United States' policy – which favours bilateral treaties – in these matters has been considerable.[2]

A pioneering example of the bilateral MLAT on criminal matters is that established between the United States and Switzerland,[3] an agreement formed in recognition of the fact that financial gains secured from crime in the United States were often seen to be deposited in Switzerland. Another example of a needs-based arrangement can be seen in the treaty between the United Kingdom and the United States Treaty concerning the Cayman Islands,[4] where drug-trafficking and related money laundering have been a particular problem.

Although MLATs necessarily vary in detail from case to case, there is a fairly well-established pattern to such treaties which is reflected in the Model Treaty, and as such the Model Treaty is an illustrative example by which to consider the workings of MLATs in general. Thus, each party is required to establish a "competent authority" through which assistance should be directed (Article 3), and the parties undertake to provide mutual assistance with regard to taking evidence from witnesses, carrying out searches and seizures, serving documents and supplying

---

[1] This is particularly the case with common law states including the United States, Canada, Australia and the United Kingdom.

[2] For commentary and instruments on mutual assistance in criminal and financial matters see: Gilmore, W.C. (1995). *Mutual Assistance in Criminal and Business Regulatory Matters*. Cambridge, Cambridge University Press.

[3] United States–Switzerland Treaty on Mutual Legal Assistance in Criminal Matters, 12 I.L.M. (1973) 916.

[4] United Kingdom–United States Treaty concerning the Cayman Islands and Mutual Legal Assistance in Criminal Matters, 26 I.L.M. (1987) 536.

documents and records (Article 1). A feature of the Model Treaty which is unusual, but not unique, is the inclusion of co-operation in fiscal cases and the related provision of bank documents and papers (Article 1(2)(g)).

As with extradition, there are grounds on which a requested state may refuse to comply with the request. Thus a request for assistance may be refused, if the offence under investigation is considered political in nature, if the request has been made in order to pursue a prosecution on grounds of race, sex, religion, nationality or political opinions, or if the request offends the requested state's rules on double jeopardy (Article 4). In contrast to extradition treaties there is no stipulation of double criminality attending the offences for which the information is requested. However there is the extradition equivalent of specialty, in that the evidence provided by the requested state should only be used in connection to matters for which the request was made, unless consent is granted otherwise by the requested state (Article 7). As to the procedures used in the taking of evidence, the Model Treaty accords with standard MLAT practice in that this is done under the law of the requested state (Article 11). A similar standard is set for search and seizure (Article 17). The Optional Protocol to the Model Treaty sets out provisions for assistance in searching for, freezing and seizing the proceeds of crime.

Whilst state parties appear to enjoy the increased speed, efficiency and flexibility offered by MLAT's, some criticism has been levelled at the position of the accused in relation to obtaining or challenging evidence under the arrangements.[5]

The General Assembly,

Bearing in mind the Milan Plan of Action, adopted by the Seventh United Nations Congress on the Prevention of Crime and the Treatment of Offenders and approved by the General Assembly in its resolution 40/32 of 29 November 1985;

Bearing in mind also the Guiding Principles for Crime Prevention and Criminal Justice in the Context of Development and a New International Economic Order, principle 37 of which stipulates that the United Nations should prepare model instruments suitable for use as international and regional conventions and as guides for national implementing legislation;

Recalling resolution 1 of the Seventh Congress, on organised crime, in which Member States were urged, inter alia, to increase their activity at the international level in order to combat organised crime, including, as appropriate, entering into bilateral treaties on extradition and mutual legal assistance;

Recalling also resolution 23 of the Seventh Congress, on criminal acts of a terrorist character, in which all States were called upon to take steps to strengthen co-operation particularly, *inter alia*, in the area of mutual legal assistance;

Recalling further the United Nations Convention against Illicit Traffic in Narcotic Drugs and Psychotropic Substances;

Acknowledging the valuable contributions to the development of a model treaty on mutual assistance in criminal matters that Governments, non-

---

[5] Gane, C. & Mackarel, M. (1996). "The Admissibility of Evidence obtained from abroad into Criminal Proceedings – The Interpretation of Mutual Legal Assistance Treaties and use of Evidence irregularly obtained". 4 Eur.J.Crime Cr.L.Cr.J. 98.

governmental organizations and individual experts have made, in particular the Government of Australia and the International Association of Penal Law;

Gravely concerned about the escalation of crime, both national and transnational;

Convinced that the establishment of bilateral and multilateral arrangements for mutual assistance in criminal matters will greatly contribute to the development of more effective international co-operation for the control of criminality;

Conscious of the need to respect human dignity and recalling the rights conferred upon every person involved in criminal proceedings, as embodied in the Universal Declaration of Human Rights and the International Covenant on Civil and Political Rights;

Recognising the importance of a model treaty on mutual assistance in criminal matters as an effective way of dealing with the complex aspects and serious consequences of crime, especially in its new forms and dimensions;

1. Adopts the Model Treaty on Mutual Assistance in Criminal Matters together with the Optional Protocol thereto, contained in the annex to the present resolution, as a useful framework that could be of assistance to States interested in negotiating and concluding bilateral agreements aimed at improving co-operation in matters of crime prevention and criminal justice;
2. Invites Member States, if they have not yet established treaty relations with other States in the matter of mutual assistance in criminal matters, or if they wish to revise existing treaty relations, to take into account, whenever doing so, the Model Treaty;
3. Urges all States to strengthen further international co-operation and mutual assistance in criminal justice;
4. Requests the Secretary-General to bring the present resolution, with the Model Treaty and the Optional Protocol thereto, to the attention of Governments;
5. Urges Member States to inform the Secretary-General periodically of efforts undertaken to establish mutual assistance arrangements in criminal matters;
6. Requests the Committee on Crime Prevention and Control to review periodically the progress attained in this field;
7. Also requests the Committee on Crime Prevention and Control, where requested, to provide guidance and assistance to Member States in the development of legislation which would enable giving effect to the obligations which will be contained in such treaties as are to be negotiated on the basis of the Model Treaty;
8. Invites Member States, on request, to make available to the Secretary-General the provisions of their legislation on mutual assistance in criminal matters so that these may be made available to those Member States desiring to enact or further develop legislation in this field.

ANNEX
MODEL TREATY ON MUTUAL ASSISTANCE IN CRIMINAL MATTERS

Desirous of extending to each other the widest measure of co-operation to combat crime,

Have agreed as follows:

Article 1: Scope of application[6]

1. The Parties shall, in accordance with the present Treaty, afford to each other the widest possible measure of mutual assistance in investigations or court proceedings in respect of offences the punishment of which at the time of the request for assistance, falls within the jurisdiction of the judicial authorities of the requesting State.

2. Mutual assistance to be afforded in accordance with the present Treaty may include:

   (a) Taking evidence or statements from persons;
   (b) Assisting in the availability of detained persons or others to give evidence or assist in investigations;
   (c) Effecting service of judicial documents;
   (d) Executing searches and seizures;
   (e) Examining objects and sites;
   (f) Providing information and evidentiary items;
   (g) Providing originals or certified copies of relevant documents and records, including bank, financial, corporate or business records.

3. The present Treaty does not apply to:

   (a) The arrest or detention of any person with a view to the extradition of that person;
   (b) The enforcement in the requested State of criminal judgements imposed in the requesting State except to the extent permitted by the law of the requested State and the Optional Protocol to the present Treaty;
   (c) The transfer of persons in custody to serve sentences;
   (d) The transfer of proceedings in criminal matters.

Article 2: Other arrangements[7]

Unless the Parties decide otherwise, the present Treaty shall not affect obligations subsisting between them whether pursuant to other treaties or arrangements or otherwise.

---

[6] Additions to the scope of assistance to be provided, such as provisions covering information on sentences passed on nationals of the Parties, can be considered bilaterally. Obviously, such assistance must be compatible with the law of the requested State.

[7] Article 2 recognises the continuing role of informal assistance between law enforcement agencies and associated agencies in different countries.

Article 3: Designation of competent authorities

Each Party shall designate and indicate to the other Party an authority or authorities by or through which requests for the purpose of the present Treaty should be made or received.

Article 4: Refusal of assistance[8]

1. Assistance may be refused if:[9]

    (a) The requested State is of the opinion that the request, if granted, would prejudice its sovereignty, security, public order (*ordre public*) or other essential public interests;

    (b) The offence is regarded by the requested State as being of a political nature;

    (c) There are substantial grounds for believing that the request for assistance has been made for the purpose of prosecuting a person on account of that person's race, sex, religion, nationality, ethnic origin or political opinions or that that person's position may be prejudiced for any of those reasons;

    (d) The request relates to an offence that is subject to investigation or prosecution in the requested State or the prosecution of which in the requesting State would be incompatible with the requested State's law on double jeopardy (*ne bis in idem*);

    (e) The assistance requested requires the requested State to carry out compulsory measures that would be inconsistent with its law and practice had the offence been the subject of investigation or prosecution under its own jurisdiction;

    (f) The act is an offence under military law, which is not also an offence under ordinary criminal law.

2. Assistance shall not be refused solely on the ground of secrecy of banks and similar financial institutions.

3. The requested State may postpone the execution of the request if its immediate execution would interfere with an ongoing investigation or prosecution in the requested State.

4. Before refusing a request or postponing its execution, the requested State shall consider whether assistance may be granted subject to certain conditions. If the requesting State accepts assistance subject to these conditions, it shall comply with them.

5. Reasons shall be given for any refusal or postponement of mutual assistance.

---

[8] Article 4 provides an illustrative list of the grounds for refusal.

[9] Some countries may wish to delete or modify some of the provisions or include other grounds for refusal, such as those related to the nature of the offence (e.g. fiscal), the nature of the applicable penalty (e.g. capital punishment), requirements of shared concepts (e.g. double jurisdiction, no lapse of time) or specific kinds of assistance (e.g. interception of telecommunications, performing deoxyribonucleic-acid (DNA) tests). In particular, some countries may wish to include as grounds for refusal the fact that the act on which the request is based would not be an offence if committed in the territory of the requested State (dual criminality).

Article 5: Contents of requests[10]

1. Requests for assistance shall include:

    (a) The name of the requesting office and the competent authority conducting the investigation or court proceedings to which the request relates;

    (b) The purpose of the request and a brief description of the assistance sought;

    (c) A description of the facts alleged to constitute the offence and a statement or text of the relevant laws, except in cases of a request for service of documents;

    (d) The name and address of the person to be served, where necessary;

    (e) The reasons for and details of any particular procedure or requirement that the requesting State wishes to be followed, including a statement as to whether sworn or affirmed evidence or statements are required;

    (f) Specification of any time-limit within which compliance with the request is desired;

    (g) Such other information as is necessary for the proper execution of the request.

2. Requests, supporting documents and other communications made pursuant to the present Treaty shall be accompanied by a translation into the language of the requested State or another language acceptable to that State.

3. If the requested State considers that the information contained in the request is not sufficient to enable the request to be dealt with, it may request additional information.

Article 6: Execution of requests[11]

Subject to article 19 of the present Treaty, requests for assistance shall be carried out promptly, in the manner provided for by the law and practice of the requested State. To the extent consistent with its law and practice, the requested State shall carry out the request in the manner specified by the requesting State.

Article 7: Return of material to the requested State

Any property, as well as original records or documents, handed over to the requesting State under the present Treaty shall be returned to the requested State as soon as possible unless the latter waives its right of return thereof.

---

[10] This list can be reduced or expanded in bilateral negotiations.

[11] More detailed provisions may be included concerning the provision of information on the time and place of execution of the request and requiring the requested State to inform promptly the requesting State in cases where significant delay is likely to occur or where a decision is made not to comply with the request and the reasons for refusal.

Article 8: Limitation on use[12]

The requesting State shall not, without the consent of the requested State, use or transfer information or evidence provided by the requested State for investigations or proceedings other than those stated in the request. However, in cases where the charge is altered, the material provided may be used in so far as the offence, as charged, is an offence in respect of which mutual assistance could be provided under the present Treaty.

Article 9: Protection of confidentiality[13]

Upon request:

(a) The requested State shall use its best endeavours to keep confidential the request for assistance, its contents and its supporting documents as well as the fact of granting of such assistance. If the request cannot be executed without breaching confidentiality, the requested State shall so inform the requesting State, which shall then determine whether the request should nevertheless be executed;

(b) The requesting State shall keep confidential evidence and information provided by the requested State, except to the extent that the evidence and information is needed for the investigation and proceedings described in the request.

Article 10: Service of documents[14]

1. The requested State shall effect service of documents that are transmitted to it for this purpose by the requesting State.
2. A request to effect service of summonses shall be made to a requested State not less than [. . .][15] days before the date on which the appearance of a person is required. In urgent cases, the requested State may waive the time requirement.

---

[12] Some countries may wish to omit article 8 or modify it, e.g. restrict it to fiscal offences.

[13] Provisions relating to confidentiality will be important for many countries but may present problems to others. The nature of the provisions in individual treaties can be determined in bilateral negotiations.

[14] More detailed provisions relating to the service of documents, such as writs and judicial verdicts, can be determined bilaterally. Provisions may be desired for the service of documents by mail or other manner and for the forwarding of proof of service of the documents. For example, proof of service could be given by means of a receipt dated and signed by the person served or by means of a declaration made by the requested State that service has been effected, with an indication of the form and date of such service. One or other of these documents could be sent promptly to the requesting State. The requested State could, if the requesting State so requests, state whether service has been effected in accordance with the law of the requested State. If service could not be effected, the reasons could be communicated promptly by the requested State to the requesting State.

[15] Depending on travel distance and related arrangements.

Article 11: Obtaining of evidence[16]

1. The requested State shall, in conformity with its law and upon request, take the sworn or affirmed testimony, or otherwise obtain statements of persons or require them to produce items of evidence for transmission to the requesting State.
2. Upon the request of the requesting State, the parties to the relevant proceedings in the requesting State, their legal representatives and representatives of the requesting State may, subject to the laws and procedures of the requested State, be present at the proceedings.

Article 12: Right or obligation to decline to give evidence

1. A person who is required to give evidence in the requested or requesting State may decline to give evidence where either:

    (a) The law of the requested State permits or requires that person to decline to give evidence in similar circumstances in proceedings originating in the requested State; or
    (b) The law of the requesting State permits or requires that person to decline to give evidence in similar circumstances in proceedings originating in the requesting State.

2. If a person claims that there is a right or obligation to decline to give evidence under the law of the other State, the State where that person is present shall, with respect thereto, rely on a certificate of the competent authority of the other State as evidence of the existence or non-existence of that right or obligation.

Article 13: Availability of persons in custody to give evidence or to assist in investigations[17]

1. Upon the request of the requesting State, and if the requested State agrees and its law so permits, a person in custody in the latter State may, subject to his or her consent, be temporarily transferred to the requesting State to give evidence or to assist in the investigations.
2. While the person transferred is required to be held in custody under the law of the requested State, the requesting State shall hold that person in custody and shall return that person in custody to the requested State at the conclusion of the matter in relation to which transfer was sought or at such earlier time as the person's presence is no longer required.
3. Where the requested State advises the requesting State that the transferred

---

[16] Article 11 is concerned with the obtaining of evidence in judicial proceedings, the taking of a person's statement by a less formal process and the production of items of evidence.

[17] In bilateral negotiations, provisions may also be introduced to deal with such matters as the modalities and time of restitution of evidence and the setting of a time-limit for the presence of the person in custody in the requesting State.

person is no longer required to be held in custody, that person shall be set at liberty and be treated as a person referred to in article 14 of the present Treaty.

Article 14: Availability of other persons to give evidence or assist in investigations[18]

1. The requesting State may request the assistance of the requested State in inviting a person:

    (a) To appear in proceedings in relation to a criminal matter in the requesting State unless that person is the person charged; or
    (b) To assist in the investigations in relation to a criminal matter in the requesting State.

2. The requested State shall invite the person to appear as a witness or expert in proceedings or to assist in the investigations. Where appropriate, the requested State shall satisfy itself that satisfactory arrangements have been made for the person's safety.
3. The request or the summons shall indicate the approximate allowances and the travel and subsistence expenses payable by the requesting State.

Upon request, the requested State may grant the person an advance, which shall be refunded by the requesting State.

Article 15: Safe conduct[19]

1. Subject to paragraph 2 of the present article, where a person is in the requesting State pursuant to a request made under article 13 or 14 of the present Treaty:

    (a) That person shall not be detained, prosecuted, punished or subjected to any other restrictions of personal liberty in the requesting State in respect of any acts or omissions or convictions that preceded the person's departure from the requested State;
    (b) That person shall not, without that person's consent, be required to give evidence in any proceeding or to assist in any investigation other than the proceeding or investigation to which the request relates.

2. Paragraph 1 of the present article shall cease to apply if that person, being free to leave, has not left the requesting State within a period of [15] consecutive days, or any longer period otherwise agreed on by the Parties, after that

---

[18] Provisions relating to the payment of the expenses of the person providing assistance are contained in paragraph 3 of article 14. Additional details, such as provision for the payment of costs in advance, can be the subject of bilateral negotiations.

[19] The provisions in article 15 may be required as the only way of securing important evidence in proceedings involving serious national and transnational crime. However, as they may raise difficulties for some countries, the precise content of the article, including any additions or modifications, can be determined in bilateral negotiations.

person has been officially told or notified that his or her presence is no longer required or, having left, has voluntarily returned.

3. A person who does not consent to a request pursuant to article 13 or accept an invitation pursuant to article 14 shall not, by reason thereof, be liable to any penalty or be subjected to any coercive measure, notwithstanding any contrary statement in the request or summons.

Article 16: Provision of publicly available documents and other records[20]

1. The requested State shall provide copies of documents and records in so far as they are open to public access as part of a public register or otherwise, or in so far as they are available for purchase or inspection by the public.
2. The requested State may provide copies of any other document or record under the same conditions as such document or record may be provided to its own law enforcement and judicial authorities.

Article 17: Search and seizure[21]

The requested State shall, in so far as its law permits, carry out requests for search and seizure and delivery of any material to the requesting State for evidentiary purposes, provided that the rights of *bona fide* third parties are protected.

Article 18: Certification and authentication[22]

A request for assistance and the documents in support thereof, as well as documents or other material supplied in response to such a request, shall not require certification or authentication.

Article 19: Costs[23]

The ordinary costs of executing a request shall be borne by the requested State, unless otherwise determined by the Parties. If expenses of a substantial or extraordinary nature are or will be required to execute the request, the Parties shall

---

[20] The question may arise as to whether this should be discretionary. This provision can be the subject of bilateral negotiations.

[21] Bilateral arrangements may cover the provision of information on the results of search and seizure and the observance of conditions imposed in relation to the delivery of seized property.

[22] The laws of some countries require authentication before documents transmitted from other countries can be admitted in their courts, and, therefore, would require a clause setting out the authentication required.

[23] More detailed provisions may be included, for example, the requested State would meet the ordinary cost of fulfilling the request for assistance except that the requesting State would bear (a) the exceptional or extraordinary expenses required to fulfil the request, where required by the requested State and subject to previous consultations; (b) the expenses associated with conveying any person to or from the territory of the requested State, and any fees, allowances or expenses payable to that person while in the requesting State pursuant to a request under article 11, 13 or 14; (c) the expenses associated with conveying custodial or escorting officers; and (d) the expenses involved in obtaining reports of experts.

consult in advance to determine the terms and conditions under which the request shall be executed as well as the manner in which the costs shall be borne.

Article 20: Consultation

The Parties shall consult promptly, at the request of either, concerning the interpretation, the application or the carrying out of the present Treaty either generally or in relation to a particular case.

Article 21: Final provisions

1. The present Treaty is subject to [ratification, acceptance or approval]. The instruments of [ratification, acceptance or approval] shall be exchanged as soon as possible.
2. The present Treaty shall enter into force on the thirtieth day after the day on which the instruments of [ratification, acceptance or approval] are exchanged.
3. The present Treaty shall apply to requests made after its entry into force, even if the relevant acts or omissions occurred prior to that date.
4. Either Contracting Party may denounce the present Treaty by giving notice in writing to the other Party. Such denunciation shall take effect six months following the date on which it is received by the other Party.

IN WITNESS WHEREOF the undersigned, being duly authorised thereto by their respective Governments, have signed the present Treaty.

DONE at ———— on ———— in ———— the ———— and ————
languages, [both/all] texts being equally authentic.

OPTIONAL PROTOCOL TO THE MODEL TREATY ON MUTUAL ASSISTANCE IN CRIMINAL MATTERS CONCERNING THE PROCEEDS OF CRIME[24]

1. In the present Protocol "proceeds of crime" means any property suspected, or found by a court, to be property directly or indirectly derived or realised as a result of the commission of an offence or to represent the value of property and other benefits derived from the commission of an offence.

2. The requested State shall, upon request, endeavour to ascertain whether any proceeds of the alleged crime are located within its jurisdiction and shall notify the requesting State of the results of its inquiries. In making the request, the requesting State shall notify the requested State of the basis of its belief that such proceeds may be located within its jurisdiction.

3. In pursuance of a request made under paragraph 2 of the present Protocol, the requested State shall endeavour to trace assets, investigate financial dealings, and obtain other information or evidence that may help to secure the recovery of proceeds of crime.

4. Where, pursuant to paragraph 2 of the present Protocol, suspected proceeds of crime are found, the requested State shall upon request take such measures as are permitted by its law to prevent any dealing in, transfer or disposal of, those suspected proceeds of crime, pending a final determination in respect of those proceeds by a court of the requesting State.

5. The requested State shall, to the extent permitted by its law, give effect to or permit enforcement of a final order forfeiting or confiscating the proceeds of crime made by a court of the requesting State or take other appropriate action to secure the proceeds following a request by the requesting State.[25]

6. The Parties shall ensure that the rights of bona fide third parties shall be respected in the application of the present Protocol.

---

[24] The present Optional Protocol is included on the ground that questions of forfeiture are conceptually different from, although closely related to, matters generally accepted as falling within the description of mutual assistance. However, States may wish to include these provisions in the text because of their importance in dealing with organised crime. Moreover, assistance in forfeiting the proceeds of crime has now emerged as a new instrument in international co-operation. Provisions similar to those outlined in the present Protocol appear in many bilateral assistance treaties. Further details can be provided in bilateral arrangements. One matter that could be considered is the need for other provisions dealing with issues related to bank secrecy. An addition could, for example, be made to paragraph 4 of the present Protocol providing that the requested State shall, upon request, take such measures as are permitted by its law to require compliance with monitoring orders by financial institutions. Provision could be made for the sharing of the proceeds of crime between the Contracting States or for consideration of the disposal of the proceeds on a case-by-case basis.

[25] The Parties might consider widening the scope of the present Protocol by the inclusion of references to victims' restitution and the recovery of fines imposed as a sentence in a criminal prosecution.

65. COUNCIL OF EUROPE: EUROPEAN CONVENTION ON MUTUAL ASSISTANCE IN CRIMINAL MATTERS

Opened for signature at Strasbourg: 20 April 1959

ETS 30

Entry into force: 12 June 1962

Editors' Notes

The European Convention represents one of the earliest treaties embodying a formal framework for the provision of mutual assistance in criminal matters. Preparations for drawing up the Treaty stemmed from the work of the Committee of Ministers of the Council of Europe who, during their work on the European Convention on Extradition,[1] realised that the provision of mutual assistance facilitating the exchange of evidence, testimony, judicial records and the service of documents abroad, would naturally supplement their work on extradition. Thus the Convention outlines in Articles 3–6 the procedure for the exchange of "letters rogatory" and includes a number of restrictions and safeguards on this process, presumably to ensure the accuracy of the evidence obtained, prevent infringements on the rights of citizens of the requested state and to protect the accused. For example, assistance may be refused if the relevant offence is considered political or fiscal (Article 1(2)(a)), or if the requested state considers that its "sovereignty, security, *ordre public* or other essential interests" would be prejudiced by the execution of such a request (Article 1(2)(b)). Other restrictions include that the offence be punishable in both the requesting and requested state, that the offence be extraditable in the requested state and that the execution of the request in the requested country be consistent with its domestic law (Article 5).

The Additional Protocol to the Convention was formulated as a response to what were perceived as problems implementing the Convention, and to facilitate the application of the Convention to the changing needs of the parties to the Convention.[2] The Protocol contains provisions on the extension of the Convention to fiscal offences (Chapter 1), mutual assistance relating to the enforcement of sentences (Chapter 2) and the communication of information from judicial records (Chapter 3). The Council of Europe have sought to maintain the practical operation of mutual assistance by formulating additional specific Recommendations relating to the safe conduct of witnesses and the interception of communications.[3]

---

[1] European Convention on Extradition, *supra.*

[2] See: Muller-Rappard, E. & Bassiouni, M.C. (1987). *European Inter-State Co-operation in Criminal Matters*. Martinus Nijhoff, Netherlands. Vol. 1, Chap. 1, p. 5.

[3] Recommendation No. R (83) 12 concerning safe conduct for witnesses in application of Article 12.1 of the European Convention on Mutual Assistance in Criminal Matters; Recommendation No R (85) 10 concerning the practical application of the European Convention on Mutual Assistance in Criminal Matters in respect of letters rogatory for the interception of telecommunications.

Whilst bringing some uniformity to the nature of mutual assistance in Europe, the procedures established under the Convention have been regularly criticised for being slow and inefficient.[4] It is perhaps for this reason the greatest activity in concluding agreements for mutual assistance has centred on bilateral treaties, which have allowed countries more flexibility in establishing procedural co-operation on a favourable basis to their own domestic interests (see UN Model Treaty on Mutual Assistance in Criminal Matters and notes). However, other regional agreements have been concluded[5] and international measures for mutual assistance in relation to the investigation of drug trafficking are included in the United Nations' Vienna Convention 1988.[6]

PREAMBLE

The Governments signatory hereto, being Members of the Council of Europe,

Considering that the aim of the Council of Europe is to achieve greater unity among its Members;

Believing that the adoption of common rules in the field of mutual assistance in criminal matters will contribute to the attainment of this aim:

Considering that such mutual assistance is related to the question of extradition, which has already formed the subject of a Convention signed on 13th December 1957,

Have agreed as follows:

CHAPTER I
GENERAL PROVISIONS

Article 1

1. The Contracting Parties undertake to afford each other, in accordance with the provisions of this Convention, the widest measure of mutual assistance in proceedings in respect of offences the punishment of which, at the time of the request for assistance, falls within the jurisdiction of the judicial authorities of the requesting Party.

2. This Convention does not apply to arrests, the enforcement of verdicts or offences under military law which are not offences under ordinary criminal law.

---

[4] See: Dussaix, R. (1971) Some Problems Arising from the Practical Application, from the Judicial Point of View, of the European Convention on Mutual Assistance in Criminal Matters, in European Committee on Crime Problems, Problems Arising from the Practical Application of the European Convention on Mutual Assistance in Criminal Matters. pp.51–52.

[5] See for example: Scheme Relating to Mutual Assistance in Criminal Matters within the Commonwealth 1986; Inter-American Convention on Mutual Assistance in Criminal Matters 1992; Economic Community of West African States Convention on Mutual Assistance in Criminal Matters 1992.

[6] United Nations Convention Against Illicit Traffic in Narcotic Drugs and Psychotropic Substances 1988. See Article 7.

Article 2

Assistance may be refused

- (a) if the request concerns an offence which the requested party considers a political offence, an offence connected with a political offence, or a fiscal offence;
- (b) if the requested Party considers that execution of the request is likely to prejudice the sovereignty, security, *ordre public* or other essential interests of its country.

CHAPTER II

LETTERS ROGATORY

Article 3

1. The requested Party shall execute in the manner provided for by its law any letters rogatory relating to a criminal matter and addressed to it by the judicial authorities of the requesting Party for the purpose of procuring evidence or transmitting articles to be produced in evidence, records or documents.
2. If the requesting Party desires witnesses or experts to give evidence on oath, it shall expressly so request, and the requested Party shall comply with the request if the law of its country does not prohibit it.
3. The requested Party may transmit certified copies or certified photostat copies of records or documents requested, unless the requesting Party expressly requests the transmission of originals, in which case the requested Party shall make every effort to comply with the request.

Article 4

On the express request of the requesting Party the requested Party shall state the date and place of execution of the letters rogatory. Officials and interested persons may be present if the requested Party consents.

Article 5

1. Any Contracting Party may, by a declaration addressed to the Secretary-General of the Council of Europe, when signing this Convention or depositing its instrument of ratification or accession, reserve the right to make the execution of letters rogatory for search or seizure of property dependent on one or more of the following conditions:

   - (a) that the offence motivating the letters rogatory is punishable under both the law of the requesting Party and the law of the requested Party;
   - (b) that the offence motivating the letters rogatory is an extraditable offence in the requested country;
   - (c) that execution of the letters rogatory is consistent with the law of the requested Party.

2. Where a Contracting Party makes a declaration in accordance with paragraph 1 of this Article, any other Party may apply reciprocity.

Article 6

1. The requested Party may delay the handing over of any property, records or documents requested, if it requires the said property, records or documents in connection with pending criminal proceedings.
2. Any property, as well as original records or documents, handed over in execution of letters rogatory shall be returned by the requesting Party to the requested Party as soon as possible unless the latter Party waives the return thereof.

CHAPTER III

SERVICE OF WRITS AND RECORDS OF JUDICIAL VERDICTS – APPEARANCE OF WITNESSES, EXPERTS AND PROSECUTED PERSONS

Article 7

1. The requested Party shall effect service of writs and records of judicial verdicts which are transmitted to it for this purpose by the requesting Party.

   Service may be effected by simple transmission of the writ or record to the person to be served. If the requesting Party expressly so requests, service shall be effected by the requested Party in the manner provided for the service of analogous documents under its own law or in a special manner consistent with such law.
2. Proof of service shall be given by means of a receipt dated and signed by the person served or by means of a declaration made by the requested Party that service has been effected and stating the form and date of such service. One or other of these documents shall be sent immediately to the requesting Party. The requested Party shall, if the requesting Party so requests, state whether service has been effected in accordance with the law of the requested Party. If service cannot be effected, the reasons shall be communicated immediately by the requested Party to the requesting Party.
3. Any Contracting Party may, by a declaration addressed to the Secretary-General of the Council of Europe, when signing this Convention or depositing its instrument of ratification or accession, request that service of a summons on an accused person who is in its territory be transmitted to its authorities by a certain time before the date set for appearance. This time shall be specified in the aforesaid declaration and shall not exceed 50 days.

   This time shall be taken into account when the date of appearance is being fixed and when the summons is being transmitted.

Article 8

A witness or expert who has failed to answer a summons to appear, service of which has been requested, shall not, even if the summons contains a notice of penalty, be subjected to any punishment or measure of restraint, unless subsequently he voluntarily enters the territory of the requesting Party and is there again duly summoned.

Article 9

The allowances, including subsistence, to be paid and the travelling expenses to be refunded to a witness or expert by the requesting Party shall be calculated as from his place of residence and shall be at rates at least equal to those provided for in the scales and rules in force in the country where the hearing is intended to take place.

Article 10

1. If the requesting Party considers the personal appearance of a witness or expert before its judicial authorities especially necessary, it shall so mention in its request for service of the summons and the requested Party shall invite the witness or expert to appear.

    The requested Party shall inform the requesting Party of the reply of the witness or expert.
2. In the case provided for under paragraph 1 of this Article the request or the summons shall indicate the approximate allowances payable and the travelling and subsistence expenses refundable.
3. If a specific request is made, the requested Party may grant the witness or expert an advance. The amount of the advance shall be endorsed on the summons and shall be refunded by the requesting Party.

Article 11

1. A person in custody whose personal appearance as a witness or for purposes of confrontation is applied for by the requesting Party, shall be temporarily transferred to the territory where the hearing is intended to take place, provided that he shall be sent back within the period stipulated by the requested Party and subject to the provisions of Article 12 in so far as these are applicable.

    Transfer may be refused:

    (a) if the person in custody does not consent,
    (b) if his presence is necessary at criminal proceedings pending in the territory of the requested Party,
    (c) if transfer is liable to prolong his detention, or
    (d) if there are other overriding grounds for not transferring him to the territory of the requesting Party.

2. Subject to the provisions of Article 2, in a case coming within the immediately preceding paragraph, transit of the person in custody through the territory of a third State, Party to this Convention, shall be granted on application, accompanied by all necessary documents, addressed by the Ministry of Justice of the requesting Party to the Ministry of Justice of the Party through whose territory transit is requested.

    A Contracting Party may refuse to grant transit to its own nationals.

3. The transferred person shall remain in custody in the territory of the requesting Party and, where applicable, in the territory of the Party through which transit is requested, unless the Party from whom transfer is requested applies for his release.

Article 12

1. A witness or expert, whatever his nationality, appearing on a summons before the judicial authorities of the requesting Party shall not be prosecuted or detained or subjected to any other restriction of his personal liberty in the territory of that Party in respect of acts or convictions anterior to his departure from the territory of the requested Party.

2. A person, whatever his nationality, summoned before the judicial authorities of the requesting Party to answer for acts forming the subject of proceedings against him, shall not be prosecuted or detained or subjected to any other restriction of his personal liberty for acts or convictions anterior to his departure from the territory of the requested Party and not specified in the summons.

3. The immunity provided for in this article shall cease when the witness or expert or prosecuted person, having had for a period of fifteen consecutive days from the date when his presence is no longer required by the judicial authorities an opportunity of leaving has nevertheless remained in the territory, or having left it, has returned.

CHAPTER IV
JUDICIAL RECORDS

Article 13

1. A requested Party shall communicate extracts from and information relating to judicial records, requested from it by the judicial authorities of a Contracting Party and needed in a criminal matter, to the same extent that these may be made available to its own judicial authorities in like cases.

2. In any case other than that provided for in paragraph 1 of this Article the request shall be complied with in accordance with the conditions provided for by the law, regulations or practice of the requested Party.

CHAPTER V
PROCEDURE

Article 14

1. Requests for mutual assistance shall indicate as follows:

    (a) the authority making the request,
    (b) the object of and the reason for the request,
    (c) where possible, the identity and the nationality of the person concerned, and
    (d) where necessary, the name and address of the person to be served.

2. Letters rogatory referred to in Articles 3, 4 and 5 shall, in addition, state the offence and contain a summary of the facts.

Article 15

1. Letters rogatory referred to in Articles 3, 4 and 5 as well as the applications referred to in Article 11 shall be addressed by the Ministry of Justice of the requesting Party to the Ministry of Justice of the requested Party and shall be returned through the same channels.
2. In case of urgency, letters rogatory may be addressed directly by the judicial authorities of the requesting Party to the judicial authorities of the requested Party. They shall be returned together with the relevant documents through the channels stipulated in paragraph 1 of this article.
3. Requests provided for in paragraph 1 of Article 13 may be addressed directly by the judicial authorities concerned to the appropriate authorities of the requested Party, and the replies may be returned directly by those authorities. Requests provided for in paragraph 2 of Article 13 shall be addressed by the Ministry of Justice of the requesting Party to the Ministry of Justice of the requested Party.
4. Requests for mutual assistance, other than those provided for in paragraphs 1 and 3 of this article and, in particular, requests for investigation preliminary to prosecution, may be communicated directly between the judicial authorities.
5. In cases where direct transmission is permitted under this Convention, it may take place through the International Criminal Police Organisation (Interpol).
6. A Contracting Party may, when signing this Convention or depositing its instrument of ratification or accession, by a declaration addressed to the Secretary-General of the Council of Europe, give notice that some or all requests for assistance shall be sent to it through channels other than those provided for in this article, or require that, in a case provided for in paragraph 2 of this article, a copy of the letters rogatory shall be transmitted at the same time to its Ministry of Justice.
7. The provisions of this article are without prejudice to those of bilateral agreements or arrangements in force between Contracting Parties which provide for the direct transmission of requests for assistance between their respective authorities.

Article 16

1. Subject to paragraph 2 of this article, translations of requests and annexed documents shall not be required.
2. Each Contracting Party may, when signing or depositing its instrument of ratification or accession, by means of a declaration addressed to the Secretary-General of the Council of Europe, reserve the right to stipulate that requests and annexed documents shall be addressed to it accompanied by a translation into its own language or into either of the official languages of the Council of Europe or into one of the latter languages, specified by it. The other Contracting Parties may apply reciprocity.
3. This article is without prejudice to the provisions concerning the translation of requests or annexed documents contained in the agreements or arrangements in force or to be made, between two or more Contracting Parties.

Article 17

Evidence or documents transmitted pursuant to this Convention shall not require any form of authentication.

Article 18

Where the authority which receives a request for mutual assistance has no jurisdiction to comply therewith, it shall, *ex officio*, transmit the request to the competent authority of its country and shall so inform the requesting Party through the direct channels, if the request has been addressed through such channels.

Article 19

Reasons shall be given for any refusal of mutual assistance.

Article 20

Subject to the provisions of Article 10, paragraph 3, execution of requests for mutual assistance shall not entail refunding of expenses except those incurred by the attendance of experts in the territory of the requested Party or the transfer of a person in custody carried out under Article 11.

CHAPTER VI
LAYING OF INFORMATION IN CONNECTION WITH PROCEEDINGS

Article 21

1. Information laid by one Contracting Party with a view to proceedings in the courts of another Party shall be transmitted between the Ministries of Justice

concerned unless a Contracting Party avails itself of the option provided for in paragraph 6 of Article 15.

2. The requested Party shall notify the requesting Party of any action taken on such information and shall forward a copy of the record of any verdict pronounced.
3. The provisions of Article 16 shall apply to information laid under paragraph 1 of this article.

CHAPTER VII
EXCHANGE OF INFORMATION FROM JUDICIAL RECORDS

Article 22

Each Contracting Party shall inform any other Party of all criminal convictions and subsequent measures in respect of nationals of the latter Party, entered in the judicial records. Ministries of Justice shall communicate such information to one another at least once a year. Where the person concerned is considered a national of two or more other Contracting Parties, the information shall be given to each of these Parties, unless the person convicted is a national of the Party in the territory of which he was convicted.

CHAPTER VIII
FINAL PROVISIONS

Article 23

1. Any Contracting Party may, when signing this Convention or when depositing its instrument of ratification or accession, make a reservation in respect of any provision or provisions of the Convention.
2. Any Contracting Party which has made a reservation shall withdraw it as soon as circumstances permit. Such withdrawal shall be made by notification to the Secretary-General of the Council of Europe.
3. A Contracting Party which has made a reservation in respect of a provision of the Convention may not claim application of the said provision by another Party save in so far as it has itself accepted the provision.

Article 24

A Contracting Party may, when signing the Convention or depositing its instrument of ratification or accession, by a declaration addressed to the Secretary-General of the Council of Europe, define what authorities it will, for the purposes of the Convention, deem judicial authorities.

Article 25

1. This Convention shall apply to the metropolitan territories of the Contracting Parties.

2. In respect of France, it shall also apply to Algeria and to the overseas Departments, and, in respect of Italy, it shall also apply to the territory of Somaliland under Italian administration.
3. The Federal Republic of Germany may extend the application of this Convention to the Land of Berlin by notice addressed to the Secretary-General of the Council of Europe.
4. In respect of the Kingdom of the Netherlands, the Convention shall apply to its European territory. The Netherlands may extend the application of this Convention to the Netherlands Antilles, Surinam and Netherlands New Guinea by notice addressed to the Secretary-General of the Council of Europe.
5. By direct arrangement between two or more Contracting Parties and subject to the conditions laid down in the arrangement, the application of this Convention may be extended to any territory, other than the territories mentioned in paragraphs 1, 2, 3 and 4 of this article, of one of these Parties, for the international relations of which any such Party is responsible.

Article 26

1. Subject to the provisions of Article 15, paragraph 7, and Article 16, paragraph 3, this Convention shall, in respect of those countries to which it applies, supersede the provisions of any treaties, conventions or bilateral agreements governing mutual assistance in criminal matters between any two Contracting Parties.
2. This Convention shall not affect obligations incurred under the terms of any other bilateral or multilateral international convention which contains or may contain clauses governing specific aspects of mutual assistance in a given field.
3. The Contracting Parties may conclude between themselves bilateral or multilateral agreements on mutual assistance in criminal matters only in order to supplement the provisions of this Convention or to facilitate the application of the principles contained therein.
4. Where, as between two or more Contracting Parties, mutual assistance in criminal matters is practised on the basis of uniform legislation or of a special system providing for the reciprocal application in their respective territories of measures of mutual assistance, these Parties shall, notwithstanding the provisions of this Convention, be free to regulate their mutual relations in this field exclusively in accordance with such legislation or system. Contracting Parties which, in accordance with this paragraph, exclude as between themselves the application of this Convention shall notify the Secretary-General of the Council of Europe accordingly.

Article 27

1. This Convention shall be open to signature by the Members of the Council of Europe. It shall be ratified. The instruments of ratification shall be deposited with the Secretary-General of the Council.
2. The Convention shall come into force 90 days after the date of deposit of the third instrument of ratification.

3. As regards any signatory ratifying subsequently the Convention shall come into force 90 days after the date of the deposit of its instrument of ratification.

Article 28

1. The Committee of Ministers of the Council of Europe may invite any State not a Member of the Council to accede to this Convention, provided that the resolution containing such invitation obtains the unanimous agreement of the Members of the Council who have ratified the convention.
2. Accession shall be by deposit with the Secretary-General of the Council of an instrument of accession which shall take effect 90 days after the date of its deposit.

Article 29

Any Contracting Party may denounce this Convention in so far as it is concerned by giving notice to the Secretary-General of the Council of Europe. Denunciation shall take effect six months after the date when the Secretary-General of the Council received such notification.

Article 30

The Secretary-General of the Council of Europe shall notify the Members of the Council and the Government of any State which has acceded to this Convention of:

(a) the names of the Signatories and the deposit of any instrument of ratification or accession;
(b) the date of entry into force of this Convention;
(c) any notification received in accordance with the provisions of Article 5, paragraph 1, Article 7, paragraph 3, Article 15, paragraph 6, Article 16, paragraph 2, Article 24, Article 25, paragraphs 3 and 4, or Article 26, paragraph 4;
(d) any reservation made in accordance with Article 23, paragraph 1;
(e) the withdrawal of any reservation in accordance with Article 23, paragraph 2;
(f) any notification of denunciation received in accordance with the provisions of Article 29 and the date on which such denunciation will take effect.

66. COUNCIL OF EUROPE: ADDITIONAL PROTOCOL OF 1978 TO THE EUROPEAN CONVENTION ON MUTUAL ASSISTANCE IN CRIMINAL MATTERS, 1959

Opened for signature at Strasbourg: 17 March 1973

ETS 99

Entry into force: 12 April 1982

The member States of the Council of Europe, signatory to this Protocol,

Desirous of facilitating the application of the European Convention on Mutual Assistance in Criminal Matters opened for signature in Strasbourg on 20 April 1959 (hereinafter referred to as "the Convention") in the field of fiscal offences;

Considering it also desirable to supplement the Convention in certain other respects,

Have agreed as follows:

CHAPTER I

Article 1

The Contracting Parties shall not exercise the right provided for in Article 2.a of the Convention to refuse assistance solely on the ground that the request concerns an offence which the requested Party considers a fiscal offence.

Article 2

1. In the case where a Contracting Party has made the execution of letters rogatory for search or seizure of property dependent on the condition that the offence motivating the letters rogatory is punishable under both the law of the requesting Party and the law of the requested Party, this condition shall be fulfilled, as regards fiscal offences, if the offence is punishable under the law of the requesting Party and corresponds to an offence of the same nature under the law of the requested Party.

2. The request may not be refused on the ground that the law of the requested Party does not impose the same kind of tax or duty or does not contain a tax, duty, customs and exchange regulation of the same kind as the law of the requesting Party.

Article 3

The Convention shall also apply to:

    a.   the service of documents concerning the enforcement of a sentence the recover of a fine or the payment of costs of proceedings;

    b.   measures relating to the suspension of pronouncement of a sentence or of its enforcement, to conditional release, to deferment of the commencement of the enforcement of a sentence or to the interruption of such enforcement.

CHAPTER II

Article 4

Article 22 of the Convention shall be supplemented by the following text, the original Article 22 of the Convention becoming paragraph 1 and the below-mentioned provisions becoming paragraph 2:

"2. Furthermore, any Contracting Party which has supplied the above-mentioned information shall communicate to the Party concerned, on the latter's request in individual cases, a copy of the convictions and measures in question as well as any other information relevant thereto in order to enable it to consider whether they necessitate any measures at national level. This communication shall take place between the Ministries of Justice concerned."

CHAPTER III

Article 5

1.   This Protocol shall be open to signature by the member States of the Council of Europe which have signed the Convention. It shall be subject to ratification, acceptance or approval. Instruments of ratification, acceptance or approval shall be deposited with the Secretary General of the Council of Europe.

2.   The Protocol shall enter into force 90 days after the date of the deposit of the third instrument of ratification, acceptance or approval.

3.   In respect of a signatory State ratifying, accepting or approving subsequently, the Protocol shall enter into force 90 days after the date of the deposit of its instrument of ratification, acceptance or approval.

4.   A member State of the Council of Europe may not ratify, accept or approve this Protocol without having, simultaneously or previously, ratified the Convention.

Article 6

1.   Any State which has acceded to the Convention may accede to this Protocol after the Protocol has entered into force.

2.   Such accession shall be effected by depositing with the Secretary General of

the Council of Europe an instrument of accession which shall take effect 90 days after the date of its deposit.

Article 7

1. Any State may, at the time of signature or when depositing its instrument of ratification, acceptance, approval or accession, specify the territory or territories to which this Protocol shall apply.
2. Any State may, when depositing its instrument of ratification, acceptance, approval or accession or at any later date, by declaration addressed to the Secretary General of the Council of Europe. extend this Protocol to any other territory or territories specified in the declaration and for whose international relations it is responsible or on whose behalf it is authorized to give undertakings.
3. Any declaration made in pursuance of the preceding paragraph may, in respect of any territory mentioned in such declaration, be withdrawn by means of a notification addressed to the Secretary General of the Council of Europe. Such withdrawal shall take effect six months after the date of receipt by the Secretary General of the Council of Europe of the notification.

Article 8

1. Reservations made by a Contracting Party to a provision of the Convention shall be applicable also to this Protocol, unless that Party otherwise declares at the time of signature or when depositing its instrument of ratification, acceptance, approval or accession. The same shall apply to the declarations made by virtue of Article 24 of the Convention.
2. Any State may, at the time of signature or when depositing its instrument of ratification, acceptance, approval or accession, declare that it reserves the right:
   a. not to accept Chapter I, or to accept it only in respect of certain offences or certain categories of the offences referred to in Article 1, or not to comply with letters rogatory for search or seizure of property in respect of fiscal offences;
   b. not to accept Chapter II;
   c. not to accept Chapter III.
3. Any Contracting Party may withdraw a declaration it has made in accordance with the foregoing paragraph by means of a declaration addressed to the Secretary General of the Council of Europe which shall become effective as from the date of its receipt.
4. A Contracting Party which has applied to this Protocol a reservation made in respect of a provision of the Convention or which has made a reservation in respect of a provision of this Protocol may not claim the application of that provision by another Contracting Party. It may, however if its reservation is partial or conditional claim the application of that provision in so far as it has itself accepted it.

5. No other reservation may be made to the provisions of this Protocol.

Article 9

The provisions of this Protocol are without prejudice to more extensive regulations in bilateral or multilateral agreements concluded between Contracting Parties in application of Article 25, paragraph 3, of the Convention.

Article 10

The European Committee on Crime Problems of the Council of Europe shall be kept informed regarding the application of this Protocol and shall do whatever is needful to facilitate a friendly settlement of any difficulty which may arise out of its execution.

Article 11

1. Any Contracting Party may, in so far as it is concerned, denounce this Protocol by means of a notification addressed to the Secretary General of the Council of Europe.
2. Such denunciation shall take effect six months after the date of receipt by the Secretary General of such notification.
3. Denunciation of the Convention entails automatically denunciation of this Protocol.

Article 12

The Secretary General of the Council of Europe shall notify the member States of the Council and any State which has acceded to the Convention of:

a. any signature of this Protocol;
b. any deposit of an instrument of ratification, acceptance, approval or accession;
c. any date of entry into force of this Protocol in accordance with Articles 5 and 6;
d. any declaration received in pursuance of the provisions of paragraphs 2 and 3 of Article 7;
e. any declaration received in pursuance of the provisions of paragraph 1 of Article 8;
f. any reservation made in pursuance of the provisions of paragraph 2 of Article 8;
g. the withdrawal of any reservation carried out in pursuance of the provisions of paragraph 3 of Article 8;
h. any notification received in pursuance of the provisions of Article 11 and the date on which denunciation takes effect.

67. UNITED NATIONS: GENERAL ASSEMBLY RESOLUTION ON A MODEL TREATY ON THE TRANSFER OF PROCEEDINGS IN CRIMINAL MATTERS

Adopted by General Assembly resolution 45/118 (1990)

Editors' Notes

The Model Treaty on the Transfer of Proceedings is a product of the United Nations Eighth Congress on the Prevention of Crime and the Treatment of Offenders 1990. The central purpose of the Model is that "[w]here a person is suspected of having committed an offence, the state whose laws were violated may, if the proper interests of justice so require, request that another state take proceedings in respect of that offence...."[1] The parties to the Treaty would be required to enact domestic legislation to ensure that valid jurisdiction may be taken over what would otherwise often be a purely extra-territorial matter.

The provisions of the Model Treaty are basic and designed as a starting point for countries wishing to negotiate their own arrangements. Article 6 provides that the offence must be criminal in both the requesting and requested states. Article 7 sets out grounds on which a request may be refused. Article 8 allows for the suspect to express a view on the proposed proceedings and their transfer; however it has been observed that the Model Treaty makes no obligation for these views to be communicated to the state requested to undertake those proceedings.[2] The victim's rights, for example those to compensation, are not affected by any transfer of proceedings under Article 9.

The General Assembly,

Recalling the Milan Plan of Action, adopted by the Seventh United Nations Congress on the Prevention of Crime and the Treatment of Offenders and approved by the General Assembly in its resolution 40/32 of 29 November 1985,

Recalling also the Guiding Principles for Crime Prevention and Criminal Justice in the Context of Development and a New International Economic Order, principle 37 of which stipulates that the United Nations should prepare model instruments suitable for use as international and regional conventions and as guides for national implementing legislation,

Recalling further resolution 12 of the Seventh Congress, on the transfer of proceedings in criminal matters, in which the Committee on Crime Prevention and Control was requested to study the question and to consider the possibility of formulating a model agreement in this area,

---

[1] McClean, D. (1992). *International Judicial Assistance*. Oxford, Clarendon Press. p.169.
[2] *Ibid.* p.170.

Acknowledging the valuable contributions made by Governments, non-governmental organizations and individual experts to the drafting of a model treaty on the transfer of proceedings in criminal matters, in particular the International Expert Meeting on the United Nations and Law Enforcement, held under the auspices of the United Nations at Baden, Austria, from 16 to 19 November 1987, the Interregional Preparatory Meeting for the Eighth United Nations Congress on the Prevention of Crime and the Treatment of Offenders on topic V, "United Nations norms and guidelines in crime prevention and criminal justice: implementation and priorities for further standard setting" and the regional preparatory meetings for the Eighth Congress,

Convinced that the establishment of bilateral and multilateral arrangements for the transfer of proceedings in criminal matters will greatly contribute to the development of more effective international co-operation aimed at controlling crime,

Conscious of the need to respect human dignity and recalling the rights conferred upon every person involved in criminal proceedings, as embodied in the Universal Declaration of Human Rights and the International Covenant on Civil and Political Rights,

Recognising the importance of a model treaty on the transfer of proceedings in criminal matters as an effective way of dealing with the complex aspects, consequences and modern evolution of transnational crime,

1. Adopts the Model Treaty on the Transfer of Proceedings in Criminal Matters, contained in the annex to the present resolution, as a useful framework that could be of assistance to States interested in negotiating and concluding bilateral or multilateral treaties aimed at improving co-operation in matters of crime prevention and criminal justice;

2. Invites Member States, if they have not yet established treaty relations with other States in regard to transfer of proceedings in criminal matters, or if they wish to revise existing treaty relations, to take the Model Treaty into account whenever doing so;

3. Urges Member States to strengthen international co-operation in criminal justice;

4. Also urges Member States to inform the Secretary-General periodically of efforts undertaken to establish arrangements for the transfer of proceedings in criminal matters;

5. Requests the Committee on Crime Prevention and Control to conduct periodic reviews of the progress attained in this field;

6. Requests the Secretary-General to assist Member States, at their request, in the development of treaties on the transfer of proceedings in criminal matters and to report regularly thereon to the Committee.

ANNEX
MODEL TREATY ON THE TRANSFER OF PROCEEDINGS IN CRIMINAL MATTERS

Desirous of further strengthening international co-operation and mutual assistance in criminal justice, on the basis of the principles of respect for national sovereignty and jurisdiction and of non-interference in the internal affairs of States,

Believing that such co-operation should further the ends of justice, the social resettlement of offenders and the interests of the victims of crime,

Bearing in mind that the transfer of proceedings in criminal matters contributes to effective administration of justice and to reducing conflicts of competence,

Aware that the transfer of proceedings in criminal matters can help to avoid pre-trial detention and thus reduce the prison population,

Convinced, therefore, that the transfer of proceedings in criminal matters should be promoted,

Have agreed as follows:

Article 1 Scope of application

1. When a person is suspected of having committed an offence under the law of a State which is a Contracting Party, that State may, if the interests of the proper administration of justice so require, request another State which is a Contracting Party to take proceedings in respect of this offence.
2. For the purpose of applying the present Treaty, the Contracting Parties shall take the necessary legislative measures to ensure that a request of the requesting State to take proceedings shall allow the requested State to exercise the necessary jurisdiction.

Article 2 Channels of communication

A request to take proceedings shall be made in writing. The request, supporting documents and subsequent communication shall be transmitted through diplomatic channels, directly between the Ministries of Justice or any other authorities designated by the Parties.

Article 3 Required documents

1. The request to take proceedings shall contain or be accompanied by the following information:

   (a) The authority presenting the request;
   (b) A description of the act for which transfer of proceedings is being requested, including the specific time and place of the offence;
   (c) A statement on the results of investigations which substantiate the suspicion of an offence;
   (d) The legal provisions of the requesting State on the basis of which the act is considered to be an offence;

(e) A reasonably exact statement on the identity, nationality and residence of the suspected person.

2. The documents submitted in support of a request to take proceedings shall be accompanied by a translation into the language of the requested State or into another language acceptable to that State.

Article 4 Certification and authentication

Subject to national law and unless the Parties decide otherwise, a request to take proceedings and the documents in support thereof, as well as the documents and other material supplied in response to such a request, shall not require certification or authentication.

Article 5 Decision on the request

The competent authorities of the requested State shall examine what action to take on the request to take proceedings in order to comply, as fully as possible, with the request under their own law, and shall promptly communicate their decision to the requesting State.

Article 6 Dual criminality

A request to take proceedings can be complied with only if the act on which the request is based would be an offence if committed in the territory of the requested State.

Article 7 Grounds for refusal

If the requested State refuses acceptance of a request for transfer of proceedings, it shall communicate the reasons for refusal to the requesting State. Acceptance may be refused if:

(a) The suspected person is not a national of or ordinary resident in the requested State;

(b) The act is an offence under military law, which is not also an offence under ordinary criminal law;

(c) The offence is in connection with taxes, duties, customs or exchange;

(d) The offence is regarded by the requested State as being of a political nature.

Article 8 The position of the suspected person

1. The suspected person may express to either State his or her interest in the transfer of the proceedings. Similarly, such interest may be expressed by the legal representative or close relatives of the suspected person.

2. Before a request for transfer of proceedings is made, the requesting State shall, if practicable, allow the suspected person to present his or her views on the

alleged offence and the intended transfer, unless that person has absconded or otherwise obstructed the course of justice.

Article 9 The rights of the victim

The requesting and requested States shall ensure in the transfer of proceedings that the rights of the victim of the offence, in particular his or her right to restitution or compensation, shall not be affected as a result of the transfer. If a settlement of the claim of the victim has not been reached before the transfer, the requested State shall permit the representation of the claim in the transferred proceedings, if its law provides for such a possibility. In the event of the death of the victim, these provisions shall apply to his or her dependants accordingly.

Article 10 Effects of the transfer of proceedings on the requesting State (*ne bis in idem*)

Upon acceptance by the requested State of the request to take proceedings against the suspected person, the requesting State shall provisionally discontinue prosecution, except necessary investigation, including judicial assistance to the requested State, until the requested State informs the requesting State that the case has been finally disposed of. From that date on, the requesting State shall definitely refrain from further prosecution of the same offence.

Article 11 Effects of the transfer of proceedings on the requested State

1. The proceedings transferred upon agreement shall be governed by the law of the requested State. When charging the suspected person under its law, the requested State shall make the necessary adjustment with respect to particular elements in the legal description of the offence. Where the competence of the requested State is based on the provision set forth in paragraph 2 of article 1 of the present Treaty, the sanction pronounced in that State shall not be more severe than that provided by the law of the requesting State.
2. As far as compatible with the law of the requested State, any act with a view to proceedings or procedural requirements performed in the requesting State in accordance with its law shall have the same validity in the requested State as if the act had been performed in or by the authorities of that State.
3. The requested State shall inform the requesting State of the decision taken as a result of the proceedings. To this end a copy of any final decision shall be transmitted to the requesting State upon request.

Article 12 Provisional measures

When the requesting State announces its intention to transmit a request for transfer of proceedings, the requested State may, upon a specific request made for this purpose by the requesting State, apply all such provisional measures, including provisional detention and seizure, as could be applied under its own law if the offence in respect of which transfer of proceedings is requested had been committed in its territory.

Article 13 The plurality of criminal proceeding

When criminal proceedings are pending in two or more States against the same suspected person in respect of the same offence, the States concerned shall conduct consultations to decide which of them alone should continue the proceedings. An agreement reached thereupon shall have the consequences of a request for transfer of proceedings.

Article 14 Costs

Any costs incurred by a Contracting Party because of a transfer of proceedings shall not be refunded, unless otherwise agreed by both the requesting and requested States.

Article 15 Final provisions

1. The present Treaty is subject to [ratification, acceptance or approval]. The instruments of [ratification, acceptance or approval] shall be exchanged as soon as possible.
2. The present Treaty shall enter into force on the thirtieth day after the day on which the instruments of [ratification, acceptance or approval] are exchanged.
3. The present Treaty shall apply to requests made after its entry into force, even if the relevant acts or omissions occurred prior to that date.
4. Either Contracting Party may denounce the present Treaty by giving notice in writing to the other Party. Such denunciation shall take effect six months following the date on which it is received by the other Party.

68. COUNCIL OF EUROPE: EUROPEAN CONVENTION ON THE TRANSFER OF PROCEEDINGS IN CRIMINAL MATTERS

Opened for signature at Strasbourg: 15 May 1972

ETS 73

Entry into force: 30 March 1978

Editors' Notes

The Council of Europe's Treaty on the transfer of proceedings in criminal matters is a product of the work of the European Committee on Crime Problems (ECCP) in the late 1960s. The Committee had undertaken a study examining problems of conflicting criminal jurisdiction between member states. From this study, and in particular, their scrutiny of the problems connected with the recognition of foreign judgements, the ECCP found that "[i]t was highly desirable to extend European co-operation to the equally complex problems of determining competence between several states to prosecute, and of arranging for the transfer of proceedings from one state to another before judgement was rendered".[1]

The transfer of proceedings can take place when a country has waived its right to prosecute the accused, and permits another country to undertake that prosecution. It can be regarded as a complementary process to extradition, in particular, in circumstances where the principle of non-extradition of nationals is invoked. Under these circumstances, the prosecution of the accused can still be achieved where a state denies extradition on such grounds. There are a number of other reasons why a country may favour a transfer of proceedings. It may facilitate the accused being tried in his own country, in his own language and if convicted, serving sentence in a domestic gaol. Time and money can be saved in avoiding the extradition of the accused, which may anyway be precluded on grounds of nationality. The country to which the proceedings are being transferred may be able to prosecute for other offences, thereby allowing a number of offences to be tried simultaneously.[2]

The circumstances in which a request for a transfer of proceedings can be made are set out under Article 8 of the Treaty. If a request is made, parties are bound to accept the request unless it can invoke a mandatory ground for refusal (Article 10) or optional refusal (Article 11). The courts of the requested state receive jurisdiction

---

[1] See: Explanatory Report on the European Convention on the Transfer of Proceedings in Criminal Matters, in: Muller-Rappard, E. & Bassiouni, M.C. (1987). *European Inter-state Co-operation in Criminal Matters*. Netherlands, Martinus Nijhoff. Vol. 2, Chap, 4 pp.16–17.

[2] See: Schutte, J. (1986). "Transfer of Criminal Proceedings The European System", in Bassiouni, M.C. (Ed.). *International Criminal Law – Volume 2, Procedure*. United States, Transnational Pubs. p.319; Gardocki, L. (1992). "Transfer of Proceedings and Transfer of Prisoners as New Forms of International Co-operation", in Eser, A. & Lagodny, O. (Eds). *Principles and Procedures for a New Transnational Criminal Law*. Germany, Max-Planck-Institut. p.317.

over proceedings (outside any it may otherwise possess) by way of the request of the requesting state (Article 2). A requirement of double criminality is imposed (Article 7). Having made a request, the requesting state loses the power to prosecute the accused for the offences specified (Article 21), it may however continue investigations in relation to those offences. The right of prosecution only reverts to the requesting state, once the request has been refused (Article 21).

The member States of the Council of Europe, signatory hereto,

Considering that the aim of the Council of Europe is the achievement of greater unity between its Members;

Desiring to supplement the work which they have already accomplished in the field of criminal law with a view to arriving at more just and efficient sanctions;

Considering it useful to this end to ensure, in a spirit of mutual confidence, the organisation of criminal proceedings on the international level, in particular, by avoiding the disadvantages resulting from conflicts of competence,

Have agreed as follows:

PART I
DEFINITIONS

Article 1

For the purposes of this Convention

(a) "offence" comprises acts dealt with under the criminal law and those dealt with under the legal provisions listed in Appendix III to this Convention on condition that where an administrative authority is competent to deal with the offence it must be possible for the person concerned to have the case tried by a court;

(b) "sanction" means any punishment or other measure incurred or pronounced in respect of an offence or in respect of a violation of the legal provisions listed in Appendix 111.

PART II
COMPETENCE

Article 2

1. For the purposes of applying this Convention, any Contracting State shall have competence to prosecute under its own criminal law any offence to which the law of another Contracting State is applicable.

2. The competence conferred on a Contracting State exclusively by virtue of paragraph 1 of this Article may be exercised only pursuant to a request for proceedings presented by another Contracting State.

Article 3

Any Contracting State having competence under its own law to prosecute an offence may, for the purposes of applying this Convention, waive or desist from proceedings against a suspected person who is being or will be prosecuted for the same offence by another Contracting State. Having regard to Article 21, paragraph 2, any such decision to waive or to desist from proceedings shall be provisional pending a final decision in the other contracting State.

Article 4

The requested State shall discontinue proceedings exclusively grounded on Article 2 when to its knowledge the right of punishment is extinguished under the law of the requesting State for a reason other than time-limitation, to which Articles 10(c), 11(f) and (9), 22, 23 and 26 in particular apply.

Article 5

The provisions of Part III of this Convention do not limit the competence given to a requested State by its municipal law in regard to prosecutions.

PART III
TRANSFER OF PROCEEDINGS

SECTION 1: REQUEST FOR PROCEEDINGS

Article 6

1. When a person is suspected of having committed an offence under the law of a Contracting State, that State may request another Contracting State to take proceedings in the cases and under the conditions provided for in this Convention.
2. If under the provisions of this Convention a Contracting State may request another Contracting State to take proceedings, the competent authorities of the first State shall take that possibility into consideration.

Article 7

1. Proceedings may not be taken in the requested State unless the offence in respect of which the proceedings are requested would be an offence if committed in its territory and when, under these circumstances, the offender would be liable to sanction under its own law also.
2. If the offence was committed by a person of public status or against a person, an institution or any thing of public status in the requesting State, it shall be considered in the requested State as having been committed by a person of

public status or against such a person, an institution or any thing corresponding, in the latter State, to that against which it was actually committed:

(a) if the request does not comply with the provisions of Articles 6, paragraph 1, and 7, paragraph 1;

(b) if the institution of proceedings is contrary to the provisions of Article 35;

(c) if, at the date on the request, the time-limit for criminal proceedings has already expired in the requesting State under the legislation of that State.

Article 8

1. A Contracting State may request another Contracting State to take proceedings in any one of the following cases:

(a) if the suspected person is ordinarily resident in the requested State;

(b) if the suspected person is a national of the requested State or if that State is his State of origin;

(c) if the suspected person is undergoing or is to undergo a sentence involving deprivation of liberty in the requested State;

(d) if proceedings for the same or other offences are being taken against the suspected person in the requested State;

(e) if it considers that transfer of proceedings is warranted in the interests of arriving at the truth and in particular that the most important items of evidence are located in the requested State;

(f) if it considers that the enforcement in the requested State of a sentence if one were passed is likely to improve the prospects for the social rehabilitation of the person sentenced;

(g) if it considers that the presence of the suspected person cannot be ensured at the hearing of proceedings in the requesting State and that his presence in person at the hearing of proceedings in the requested State can be ensured;

(h) if it considers that it could itself enforce a sentence if one were passed, even by having recourse to extradition, and that the requested State could do so.

(2) Where the suspected person has been finally sentenced in a Contracting State, that State may request the transfer of proceedings in one or more of the cases referred to in paragraph 1 of this Article only if it cannot enforce the sentence, even by having recourse to extradition, and if the other Contracting State does not accept enforcement of a foreign judgment as a matter of principle or refuses to enforce such sentence.

Article 9

1. The competent authorities in the requested State shall examine the request for proceedings made in pursuance of the preceding Articles. They shall decide, in accordance with their own law, what action to take thereon.

2. Where the law of the requested State provides for the punishment of the offence by an administrative authority, that State shall, as soon as possible, so inform the requesting State unless the requested State has made a declaration under paragraph 3 of this Article.

3. Any Contracting State may at the time of signature, or when depositing its instrument of ratification, acceptance or accession, or at any later date indicate, by declaration addressed to the Secretary-General of the Council of Europe, the conditions under which its domestic law permits the punishment of certain offences by an administrative authority. Such declaration shall replace the notification envisaged in paragraph 2 of this Article.

Article 10

The requested State shall not take action on the request:

(a) if the request does not comply with the provisions of Articles 6, paragraph 1, and 7, paragraph 1;

(b) if the institution of proceedings is contrary to the provisions of Article 35;

(c) if, at the date on the request, the time-limit for criminal proceedings has already expired in the requesting State under the legislation of that State.

Article 11

Save as provided for in Article 10 the requested State may not refuse acceptance of the request in whole or in part, except in any one or more of the following cases:

(a) if it considers that the grounds on which the request is based under Article 8 are not justified;

(b) if the suspected person is not ordinarily resident in the requested State;

(c) if the suspected person is not a national of the requested State and was not ordinarily resident in the territory of that State at the time of the offence;

(d) if it considers that the offence for which proceedings are requested is an offence of a political nature or a purely military or fiscal one;

(e) if it considers that there are substantial grounds for believing that the request for proceedings was motivated by considerations of race, religion, nationality or political opinion;

(f) if its own law is already applicable to the offence and if at the time of the receipt of the request proceedings were precluded by lapse of time according to that law; Article 26, paragraph 2, shall not apply in such a case;

(g) if its competence is exclusively grounded on Article 2 and if at the time of the receipt of the request proceedings would be precluded by lapse of time according to its law, the prolongation of the time-limit by six months under the terms of Article 23 being taken into consideration;

(h) if the offence was committed outside the territory of the requesting State;

(i) if proceedings would be contrary to the intentional undertakings of the requested State;
(j) if proceedings would be contrary to the fundamental principles of the legal system of the requested State;
(k) if the requesting State has violated a rule of procedure laid down in this Convention.

Article 12

1. The requested State shall withdraw its acceptance of the request if, subsequent to this acceptance, a ground mentioned in Article 10 of this Convention for not taking action on the request becomes apparent.
2. The requested State may withdraw its acceptance of the request:

    (a) if it becomes apparent that the presence in person of the suspected person cannot be ensured at the hearing of proceedings in that State or that any sentence, which might be passed, could not be enforced in that State;
    (b) if one of the grounds for refusal mentioned in Article 11 becomes apparent before the case is brought before a court; or
    (c) in other cases, if the requesting State agrees.

SECTION 2: TRANSFER PROCEDURE

Article 13

1. All requests specified in this Convention shall be made in writing. They, and all communications necessary for the application of this Convention, shall be sent either by the Ministry of Justice of the requesting State to the Ministry of Justice of the requested State or, by virtue of special mutual arrangement, direct by the authorities of the requesting State to those of the requested State; they shall be returned by the same channel.
2. In urgent cases, requests and communications may be sent through the International Criminal Police Organization (INTERPOL).
3. Any Contracting State may, by declaration addressed to the Secretary General of the Council of Europe, give notice of its intention to adopt insofar as it itself is concerned rules of transmission other than those laid down in paragraph 1 of this Article.

Article 14

If a Contracting State considers that the information supplied by another Contracting State is not adequate to enable it to apply this Convention, it shall ask for the necessary additional information. It may prescribe a date for the receipt of such information.

Article 15

1. A request for proceedings shall be accompanied by the original, or a certified copy, of the criminal file and all other necessary documents. However, if the suspected person is remanded in custody in accordance with the provisions of Section 5 and if the requesting State is unable to transmit these documents at the same time as the request for proceedings, the documents may be sent subsequently.
2. The requesting State shall also inform the requested State in writing of any procedural acts performed or measures taken in the requesting State after the transmission of the request which have a bearing on the proceedings. This communication shall be accompanied by any relevant documents.

Article 16

1. The requested State shall promptly communicate its decision on the request for proceedings to the requesting State.
2. The requested State shall also inform the requesting State of a waiver of proceedings or of the decision taken as a result of proceedings. A certified copy of any written decision shall be transmitted to the requesting State.

Article 17

If the competence of the requested State is exclusively grounded on Article 2 that State shall inform the suspected person of the request for proceedings with a view to allowing him to present his views on the matter before that State has taken a decision on the request.

Article 18

1. Subject to paragraph 2 of this Article, no translation of the documents relating to the application of this Convention shall be required.
2. Any Contracting State may, at the time of signature or when depositing its instrument of ratification, acceptance or accession, by declaration addressed to the Secretary General of the Council of Europe, reserve the right to require that, with the exception of the copy of the written decision referred to in Article 16, paragraph 2, the said documents be accompanied by a translation. The other Contracting States shall send the translations in either the national language of the receiving State or such one of the official languages of the Council of Europe as the receiving State shall indicate. However, such an indication is not obligatory. The other Contracting States may claim reciprocity.
3. This Article shall be without prejudice to any provisions concerning translation of requests and supporting documents that may be contained in agreements or arrangements now in force or that may be concluded between two or more Contracting States.

Article 19

Documents transmitted in application of this convention need not be authenticated.

Article 20

Contracting Parties shall not claim from each other the refund of any expenses resulting from the application of this Convention.

SECTION 3: EFFECTS IN THE REQUESTING STATE OF A REQUEST FOR PROCEEDINGS

Article 21

1. When the requesting State has requested proceedings, it can no longer prosecute the suspected person for the offence in respect of which the proceedings have been requested or enforce a judgment which has been pronounced previously in that State against him for that offence. Until the requested State's decision on the request for proceedings has been received, the requesting State shall, however, retain its right to take all steps in respect of prosecution, short of bringing the case to trial, or, as the case may be, allowing the competent administrative authority to decide on the case.
2. The right of prosecution and of enforcement shall revert to the requesting State:

    (a) if the requested State informs it of a decision in accordance with Article 10 not to take action on the request;
    (b) if the requested State informs it of a decision in accordance with Article 11 to refuse acceptance of the request;
    (c) if the requested State informs it of a decision in accordance with Article 12 to withdraw acceptance of the request;
    (d) if the requested State informs it of a decision not to institute proceedings or discontinue them;
    (e) if it withdraws its request before the requested State has informed it of a decision to take action on the request.

Article 22

A request for proceedings, made in accordance with the provisions of this Part, shall have the effect in the requesting State of prolonging the time-limit for proceedings by six months.

SECTION 4: EFFECTS IN THE REQUESTED STATE OF A REQUEST FOR PROCEEDINGS

Article 23

If the competence of the requested State is exclusively grounded on Article 2 the time-limit for proceedings in that State shall be prolonged by six months.

Article 24

1. If proceedings are dependent on a complaint in both States the complaint brought in the requesting State shall have equal validity with that brought in the requested State
2. If a complaint is necessary only in the requested State, that State may take proceedings even in the absence of a complaint if the person who is empowered to bring the complaint has not objected within a period of one month from the date of receipt by him of notice from the competent authority informing him of his right to object.

Article 25

In the requested State the sanction applicable to the offence shall be that prescribed by its own law unless that law provides otherwise Where the competence of the requested State is exclusively grounded on Article 2, the sanction pronounced in that State shall not be more severe than that provided for in the law of the requesting State.

Article 26

1. Any act with a view to proceedings, taken in the requesting State in accordance with its law and regulations, shall have the same validity in the requested State as if it had been taken by the authorities of that State, provided that assimilation does not give such act a greater evidential weight than it has in the requesting State.
2. Any act which interrupts time-limitation and which has been validly performed in the requesting State shall have the same effects in the requested State and vice versa.

SECTION 5: PROVISIONAL MEASURES IN THE REQUESTED STATE

Article 27

1. When the requesting State announces its intention to transmit a request for proceedings, and if the competence of the requested State would be exclusively grounded on Article 2, the requested State may, on application by the

requesting State and by virtue of this Convention, provisionally arrest the suspected person:

    (a) if the law of the requested State authorizes remand in custody for the offence, and

    (b) if there are reasons to fear that the suspected person will abscond or that he will cause evidence to be suppressed.

2.   The application for provisional arrest shall state that there exists a warrant of arrest or other order having the same effect, issued in accordance with the procedure laid down in the law of the requesting State; it shall also state for what offence proceedings will be requested and when and where such offence was committed and it shall contain as accurate a description of the suspected person as possible. It shall also contain a brief statement of the circumstances of the case.

3.   An application for provisional arrest shall be sent direct by the authorities in the requesting State mentioned in Article 13 to the corresponding authorities in the requested State, by post or telegram or by any other means affording evidence in writing or accepted by the requested State. The requesting State shall be informed without delay of the result of its application.

Article 28

Upon receipt of a request for proceedings accompanied by the documents referred to in Article 15, paragraph 1, the requested State shall have jurisdiction to apply all such provisional measures, including remand in custody of the suspected person and seizure of property, as could be applied under its own law if the offence in respect of which proceedings are requested had been committed in its territory.

Article 29

1.   The provisional measures provided in Articles 27 and 28 shall be governed by the provisions of this Convention and the law of the requested State. The law of that State, or the Convention shall also determine the conditions on which the measures may lapse.

2.   These measures shall lapse in the cases referred to in Article 21, paragraph 2.

3.   A person in custody shall in any event be released if he is arrested in pursuance of Article 27 and the requested State does not receive the request for proceedings within 18 days from the date of the arrest.

4.   A person in custody shall in any event be released if he is arrested in pursuance of Article 27 and the documents which should accompany the request for proceedings have not been received by the requested State within 15 days from the receipt of the request for proceedings.

5.   The period of custody applied exclusively by virtue of Article 27 shall not in any event exceed 40 days.

PART IV
PLURALITY OF CRIMINAL PROCEEDINGS

Article 30

1. Any Contracting State which, before the institution or in the course of proceedings for an offence which it considers to be neither of a political nature nor a purely military one, is aware of proceedings pending in another Contracting State against the same person in respect of the same offence shall consider whether it can either waive or suspend its own proceedings or transfer them to the other State.
2. If it deems it advisable in the circumstances not to waive or suspend its own proceedings it shall so notify the other State in good time and in any event before judgment is given on the merits.

Article 31

1. In the eventuality referred to in Article 30, paragraph 2, the States concerned shall endeavour as far as possible to determine, after evaluation in each case of the circumstances mentioned in Article 8, which of them alone shall continue to conduct proceedings. During this consultative procedure the States concerned shall postpone judgment on the merits without however being obliged to prolong such postponement beyond a period of 30 days as from the despatch of the notification provided for in Article 30, paragraph 2.
2. The provisions of paragraph 1 shall not be binding:
   (a) on the State despatching the notification provided for in Article 30, paragraph 9, if the main trial has been declared open there in the presence of the accused before despatch of the notification;
   (b) on the State to which the notification is addressed, if the main trial has been declared open there in the presence of the accused before receipt of the notification.

Article 32

In the interests of arriving at the truth and with a view to the application of an appropriate sanction, the States concerned shall examine whether it is expedient that one of them alone shall conduct proceedings and, if so, endeavour to determine which one, when:
   (a) several offences which are materially distinct and which fall under the criminal law of each of those states are ascribed either to a single person to several persons having acted in unison;
   (b) a single offence which falls under the criminal law of each of those States is ascribed to several persons having acted in unison.

Article 33

All decisions reached in accordance with Articles 31 paragraph 1, and 32 shall entail, as between the States concerned, all the consequences of a transfer of proceedings as provided for in this Convention. The State which waives its own proceedings shall be deemed to have transferred them to the other State.

Article 34

The transfer procedure provided for in Section 2 of Part III shall apply in so far as its provisions are compatible with those contained in the present Part.

PART V
NE BIS IN IDEM

Article 35

1. A person in respect of whom a final and enforceable criminal judgment has been rendered may for the same act neither be prosecuted nor sentenced nor subjected to enforcement of a sanction in another Contracting State:

   (a) if he was acquitted;
   (b) if the sanction imposed:

      (i) has been completely enforced or is being enforced, or
      (ii) has been wholly, or with respect to the part not enforced, the subject of a pardon or an amnesty, or
      (iii) can no longer be enforced because of lapse of time;

   (c) if the court convicted the offender without imposing a sanction.

2. Nevertheless, a Contracting State shall not, unless it has itself requested the proceedings, be obliged to recognise the effect of *ne bis in idem* if the act which gave rise to the judgment was directed against either a person or an institution or any thing having public status in that State, or if the subject of the judgment had himself a public status in that State.
3. Furthermore, a Contracting State where the act was committed or considered as such according to the law of that State shall not be obliged to recognise the effect of *ne bis in idem* unless that State has itself requested the proceedings.

Article 36

If new proceedings are instituted against a person who in another Contracting State has been sentenced for the same act, then any period of deprivation of liberty arising from the sentence enforced shall be deducted from the sanction which may be imposed.

Article 37

This Part shall not prevent the application of wider domestic provisions relating to the effect of *ne bis in idem* attached to foreign criminal judgments.

PART VI
FINAL CLAUSES

Article 38

1. This Convention shall be open to signature by the member States of the Council of Europe. It shall be subject to ratification or acceptance. Instruments of ratification or acceptance shall be deposited with the Secretary General of the Council of Europe.
2. This Convention shall enter into force three months after the date of the deposit of the third instrument of ratification or acceptance.
3. In respect of a signatory State ratifying or accepting subsequently, the Convention shall come into force three months after the date of the deposit of its instrument of ratification or acceptance.

Article 39

1. After the entry into force of this Convention, the Committee of Ministers of the Council of Europe may invite any non-member State to accede thereto provided that the resolution containing such invitation receives the unanimous agreement of the Members of the Council who have ratified the Convention.
2. Such accession shall be effected by depositing with the Secretary General of the Council of Europe an instrument of accession which shall take effect three months after the date of its deposit.

Article 40

1. Any Contracting State may, at the time of signature or when depositing its instrument of ratification, acceptance or accession, specify the territory or territories to which this Convention shall apply.
2. Any Contracting State may, when depositing its instrument of ratification, acceptance or accession or at any later date, by declaration addressed to the Secretary General of the Council of Europe, extend this Convention to any other territory or territories specified in the declaration and for whose intentional relations it is responsible or on whose behalf it is authorised to give undertakings.
3. Any declaration made in pursuance of the preceding paragraph may, in respect of any territory mentioned in such declaration, be withdrawn according to the procedure laid down in Article 45 of this Convention.

Article 41

1. Any Contracting State may, at the time of signature or when depositing its instrument of ratification, acceptance or accession, declare that it avails itself of one or more of the reservations provided for in Appendix I or make a declaration provided for in Appendix II to this Convention.
2. Any Contracting State may wholly or partly withdraw a reservation or declaration it has made in accordance with the foregoing paragraph by means of a declaration addressed to the Secretary General of the Council of Europe which shall become effective as from the date of its receipt.
3. A Contracting State which has made a reservation in respect of any provision of this Convention may not claim the application of that provision by any other Contracting State; it may, however, if its reservation is partial or conditional, claim the application of that provision insofar as it has itself accepted it.

Article 42

1. Any Contracting State may at any time, by declaration addressed to the Secretary General of the Council of Europe, set out the legal provisions to be included in Appendix III to this Convention.
2. Any change of the national provisions listed in Appendix III shall be notified to the Secretary General of the Council of Europe if such a change renders the information in this Appendix incorrect.
3. Any changes made in Appendix III in application of the preceding paragraphs shall take effect in each Contracting State one month after the date of their notification by the Secretary General of the Council of Europe.

Article 43

1. This Convention affects neither the rights and the undertakings derived from extradition treaties and intentional multilateral conventions concerning special matters, nor provisions concerning matters which are dealt with in the present Convention and which are contained in other existing conventions between Contracting States.
2. The Contracting States may not conclude bilateral or multilateral agreements with one another on the matters dealt with in this Convention, except in order to supplement its Provisions or facilitate application of the principles embodied in it.
3. Should two or more Contracting States, however, have already established their relations in this matter on the basis of uniform legislation, or instituted a special system of their own, or should they in future do so, they shall be entitled to regulate those relations accordingly, notwithstanding the terms of this Convention.
4. Contracting States ceasing to apply the terms of this Convention to their mutual relations in this matter in accordance with the provisions of the preceding paragraph shall notify the Secretary General of the Council of Europe to that effect.

Article 44

The European Committee on Crime Problems of the Council of Europe shall be kept informed regarding the application of this Convention and shall do whatever is needful to facilitate a friendly settlement of any difficulty which may arise out of its execution.

Article 45

1. This Convention shall remain in force indefinitely.
2. Any Contracting State may, insofar as it is concerned, denounce this Convention by means of a notification addressed to the Secretary General of the Council of Europe.
3. Such denunciation shall take effect six months after the date of receipt by the Secretary General of such notification.

Article 46

The Secretary General of the Council of Europe shall notify the member States of the Council and any State which has acceded to this Convention of:

(a) any signature;
(b) any deposit of an instrument of ratification, acceptance or accession;
(c) any date of entry into force of this Convention in accordance with Article 38 thereof;
(d) any declaration received in pursuance of the provisions of Article 9, paragraph 3;
(e) any declaration received in pursuance of the provisions of Article 13, paragraph 3;
(f) any declaration received in pursuance of the provisions of Article 18, paragraph 2;
(g) any declaration received in pursuance of the provisions of Article 40, paragraphs 2 and 3;
(h) any reservation or declaration made in pursuance of the provisions of Article 41, paragraph 1;
(i) the withdrawal of any reservation or declaration carried out in pursuance of the provisions of Article 41, paragraph 2;
(j) any declaration received in pursuance of Article 42, paragraph 1, and any subsequent notification received in pursuance of paragraph 2 of that Article;
(k) any notification received in pursuance of the provisions of Article 43, paragraph 4;
(l) any notification received in pursuance of the provisions of Article 45 and the, date on which denunciation takes effect.

Article 47

This Convention and the notifications and declarations authorised thereunder shall apply only to offences committed after the Convention comes into effect for the Contracting States involved.

69. UNITED NATIONS: MODEL AGREEMENT ON THE TRANSFER OF FOREIGN PRISONERS

Adopted by General Assembly resolution 40/146 (1985)

I. GENERAL PRINCIPLES

1. The social resettlement of offenders should be promoted by facilitating the return of persons convicted of crime abroad to their country of nationality or of residence to serve their sentence at the earliest possible stage. In accordance with the above, States should afford each other the widest measure of co-operation.

2. A transfer of prisoners should be effected on the basis of mutual respect for national sovereignty and jurisdiction.

3. A transfer of prisoners should be effected in cases where the offence giving rise to conviction is punishable by deprivation of liberty by the judicial authorities of both the sending (sentencing) State and the State to which the transfer is to be effected (administering State) according to their national laws.

4. A transfer may be requested by either the sentencing or the administering State. The prisoner, as well as close relatives, may express to either State their interest in the transfer. To that end, the contracting State shall inform the prisoner of their competent authorities.

5. A transfer shall be dependent on the agreement of both the sentencing and the administering State, and should also be based on the consent of the prisoner.

6. The prisoner shall be fully informed of the possibility and of the legal consequences of a transfer, in particular whether or not he might be prosecuted because of other offences committed before his transfer.

7. The administering State should be given the opportunity to verify the free consent of the prisoner.

8. Any regulation concerning the transfer of prisoners shall be applicable to sentences of imprisonment as well as to sentences imposing measures involving deprivation of liberty because of the commission of a criminal act.

9. In cases of the person's incapability of freely determining his will, his legal representative shall be competent to consent to the transfer.

II. OTHER REQUIREMENTS

10. A transfer shall be made only on the basis of a final and definitive sentence having executive force.

11. At the time of the request for a transfer, the prisoner shall, as a general rule, still have to serve at least six months of the sentence, a transfer should, however, be granted also in cases of indeterminate sentences.

12. The decision whether to transfer a prisoner shall be taken without any delay.
13. The person transferred for the enforcement of a sentence passed in the sentencing State may not be tried again in the administering State for the same act upon which the sentence to be executed is based.

III. PROCEDURAL REGULATIONS

14. The competent authorities of the administering State shall:

    (a) continue the enforcement of the sentence immediately or through a court or administrative order; or
    (b) convert the sentence, thereby substituting for the sanction imposed in the sentencing State a sanction prescribed by the law of the administering State for a corresponding offence.

15. In the case of continued enforcement, the administering State shall be bound by the legal nature and duration of the sentence as determined by the sentencing State. If, however, this sentence is by its nature or duration incompatible with the law of the administering State, this State may adapt the sanction to the punishment or measure prescribed by its own law for a corresponding offence.
16. In the case of conversion of sentence, the administering State shall be entitled to adapt the sanction as to its nature or duration according to its national law, taking into due consideration the sentence passed in the sentencing State. A sanction involving deprivation of liberty shall, however, not be converted to a pecuniary sanction.
17. The administering state shall be bound by the findings as to the facts in so far as they appear from the judgement imposed in the sentencing State. Thus the sentencing State has the sole competence for a review of the sentence.
18. The period of deprivation of liberty already served by the sentenced person in either State shall be fully deducted from the final sentence.
19. A transfer shall in no case lead to an aggravation of the situation of the prisoner.
20. Any costs incurred because of a transfer and related to transportation should be borne by the administering State, unless otherwise decided by both the sentencing and administering States.

IV. ENFORCEMENT AND PARDON

21. The enforcement of the sentence shall be governed by the law of the administering State.
22. Both the sentencing and the administering State shall be competent to grant pardon and amnesty.

V. FINAL CLAUSES

23. This agreement shall be applicable to the enforcement of sentences imposed either before or after its entry into force.
24. This agreement is subject to ratification. The instruments of ratification shall be deposited as soon as possible in ─────────
25. This agreement shall enter into force on the thirtieth day after the day on which the instruments of ratification are exchanged.
26. Either Contracting Party may denounce this agreement in writing to the... Denunciation shall take effect six months following the date on which the notification is received by the ─────────

70. COUNCIL OF EUROPE: CONVENTION ON THE TRANSFER OF SENTENCED PERSONS

Opened for signature at Strasbourg: 21 March 1983

ETS 112

Entry into force: 1 July 1985

Editors' Notes

The dramatic increase in the numbers of people being incarcerated in foreign countries as a result of the growing internationalisation of crime, combined with the admitted failings of the European Convention on the International Validity of Criminal Judgements,[1] saw the Council of Europe respond with the preparation of a new treaty to address both problems. The Transfer of Sentenced Persons Treaty is specifically differentiated from the International Validity of Criminal Judgements agreement, in that it is designed to complement the earlier convention and addresses the repatriation of sentenced prisoners by providing a simplified framework under which either the "convicting state" or the prisoners domestic state may apply for transfer.[2] The sentenced person must consent to the transfer (Article 3). The Convention does not obligate states to comply with the request – a state need not give grounds for refusal (Article 2). In contrast to other Council of Europe Conventions on international criminal co-operation, this treaty does not carry the label "European", the hope being that "outside" states would contract to the arrangements. Canada, Finland and the United States are parties to the agreement.

So as to promote use of the arrangements under the Treaty, Recommendation (84)11 was adopted by the Committee of Ministers.[3] Article 4(1) of the Transfer of Sentenced Persons Treaty provides that any sentenced person eligible for transfer should be informed of the arrangements, and the Recommendation sets out a standard text setting out the relevant information for prisoners.

Whilst the number of multilateral and bilateral prisoner transfer agreements[4] and

---

[1] Signed at The Hague, 28 May 1970, ETS 70. Entered into force 26 July 1974.

[2] See: Explanatory Report to the Convention on the Transfer of Sentenced Persons, in: Muller-Rappard, E. & Bassiouni, M.C. (1987). *European Inter-state Co-operation in Criminal Matters*. Netherlands, Martinus Nijhoff. Vol. 2, Chap. 3, p.9.

[3] Recommendation No.R (84)11 Concerning Information about the Convention on the Transfer of Sentenced Persons.

[4] See for example: Arab Agreement on Judicial Co-operation 1983, Benelux Convention on the Enforcement of Judicial Judgements in Criminal Matters 1968, Commonwealth Scheme for the Transfer of Convicted Offenders 1986, Inter-American Convention on Serving Criminal Sentences Abroad 1993. UN Model Treaty on the Transfer of Foreign Prisoners 1985. See also bilateral agreements concluded by the United States, Canada, Thailand, France, Poland and Spain. For a comprehensive review of prisoner transfer agreements see: Plachta, M. (1993). *The Transfer of Prisoners under International Instruments and Domestic Legislation: A Comparative Study*. Germany, Max-Planck-Institut.

the use of those arrangements appears to be increasing over time, commentators still feel that the prisoner transfer mechanism remains underused.[5]

The member States of the Council of Europe and the other States, signatory hereto,

Considering that the aim of the Council of Europe is to achieve a greater unity between its Members;

Desirous of further developing international co-operation in the field of criminal law;

Considering that such co-operation should further the ends of justice and the social rehabilitation of sentenced persons;

Considering that these objectives require that foreigners who are deprived of their liberty as a result of their commission of a criminal offence should be given the opportunity to serve their sentences within their own society; and

Considering that this aim can best be achieved by having them transferred to their own countries.

Have agreed as follows:

Article 1 Definitions

For the purposes of this Convention:

    a.   "sentence" means any punishment or measure involving deprivation of liberty ordered by a court for a limited or unlimited period of time on account of a criminal offence;

    b.   "judgment" means a decision or order of a court imposing a sentence;

    c.   "sentencing State" means the State in which the sentence was imposed on the person who may be, or has been transferred;

    d.   "administering State" means the State to which the sentenced person may be, or has been, transferred in order to serve his sentence.

Article 2 General principles

1.   The Parties undertake to afford each other the widest measure of co-operation in respect of the transfer of sentenced persons in accordance with the provisions of this Convention.

2.   A person sentenced in the territory of a Party may be transferred to the territory of another Party, in accordance with the provisions of this Convention, in order to serve the sentence imposed on him. To that end, he may express his interest to the sentencing State or to the administering State in being transferred under this Convention.

---

[5] See: Orie, A. "Problems with the Effective Use of Prisoner Transfer Treaties", and, Simon, T. & Atkins, R.D. "Prisoner Transfer Treaties: Crucial Times Ahead", both in: Atkins: R.D. (1995). *The Alleged Transnational Criminal*. The Netherlands, Martinus Nijhoff and International Bar Association.

3. Transfer may be requested by either the sentencing State or the administering State.

Article 3 Conditions for transfer

1. A sentenced person may be transferred under this Convention only on the following conditions:

    a. if that person is a national of the administering State;
    b. if the judgment is final;
    c. if, at the time of receipt of the request for transfer, the sentenced person still has at least six months of the sentence to serve or if the sentence is indeterminate;
    d. if the transfer is consented to by the sentenced person or, where in view of his age or his physical or mental condition one of the two States considers it necessary, by the sentenced person's legal representative;
    e. if the acts or omissions on account of which the sentence has been imposed constitute a criminal offence according to the law of the administering State or would constitute a criminal offence if committed on its territory; and
    f. if the sentencing and administering States agree to the transfer.

2. In exceptional cases, Parties may agree to a transfer even if the time to be served by the sentenced Person is less than that specified in paragraph l.c.
3. Any State may, at the time of signature or when depositing its instrument of ratification, acceptance, approval or accession, by a declaration addressed to the Secretary General of the Council of Europe, indicate that it intends to exclude the application of one of the procedures provided in Article 9.1.a and b in its relations with other Parties.
4. Any State may, at any time, by a declaration addressed to the Secretary General of the Council of Europe, define, as far as it is concerned, the term "national" for the purposes of this Convention.

Article 4 Obligation to furnish information

1. Any sentenced person to whom this Convention may apply shall be informed by the sentencing State of the substance of this Convention.
2. If the sentenced person has expressed an interest to the sentencing State in being transferred under this Convention, that State shall so inform the administering State as soon as practicable after the judgment becomes final.
3. The information shall include:

    a. the name, date and place of birth of the sentenced person;
    b. his address, if any, in the administering State;
    c. a statement of the facts upon which the sentence was based;
    d. the nature, duration and date of commencement of the sentence.

4. If the sentenced person has expressed his interest to the administering State,

the sentencing State shall, on request, communicate to that State the information referred to in paragraph 3 above.

5. The sentenced person shall be informed, in writing, of any action taken by the sentencing State or the administering State under the preceding paragraphs, as well as of any decision taken by either State on a request for transfer.

Article 5 Requests and replies

1. Requests for transfer and replies shall be made in writing.
2. Requests shall be addressed by the Ministry of Justice of the requesting State to the Ministry of Justice of the requested State. Replies shall be communicated through the same channels.
3. Any Party may, by a declaration addressed to the Secretary General of the Council of Europe, indicate that it will use other channels of communication.
4. The requested State shall promptly inform the requesting State of its decision whether or not to agree to the requested transfer.

Article 6 Supporting documents

1. The administering State, if requested by the sentencing State, shall furnish it with:

   a. a document or statement indicating that the sentenced person is a national of that State;
   b. a copy of the relevant law of the administering State which provides that the acts or omissions on account of which the sentence has been imposed in the sentencing State constitute a criminal offence according to the law of the administering State, or would constitute a criminal offence it committed on its territory;
   c. a statement containing the information mentioned in Article 9.2.

2. If a transfer is requested, the sentencing State shall provide the following documents to the administering State unless either State has already indicated that it will not agree to the transfer:

   a. a certified copy of the judgment and the law on which it is based;
   b. a statement indicating how much of the sentence has already been served, including information on any pre-trial detention, remission, and any other factor relevant to the enforcement of the sentence;
   c. a declaration containing the consent to the transfer as referred to in Article 3.1.d; and
   d. whenever appropriate, any medical or social reports on the sentenced person, information about his treatment in the sentencing State, and any recommendation for his further treatment in the administering State.

3. Either State may ask to be provided with any of the documents or statements referred to in paragraphs 1 or 2 above before making a request for transfer or taking a decision on whether or not to agree to the transfer.

Article 7 Consent and its verification

1. The sentencing State shall ensure that the person required to give consent to the transfer in accordance with Article 3.1.d does so voluntarily and with full knowledge of the legal consequences thereof. The procedure for giving such consent shall be governed by the law of the sentencing State.
2. The sentencing State shall afford an opportunity to the administering State to verify, through a consul or other official agreed upon with the administering State, that the consent is given in accordance with the conditions set out in paragraph 1 above.

Article 8 Effect of transfer for sentencing State

1. The taking into charge of the sentenced person by the authorities of the administering State shall have the effect of suspending the enforcement of the sentence in the sentencing State.
2. The sentencing State may no longer enforce the sentence if the administering State considers enforcement of the sentence to have been completed.

Article 9 Effect of transfer for administering State

1. The competent authorities of the administering State shall:

    a. continue the enforcement of the sentence immediately or through a court or administrative order, under the conditions set out in Article 10, or
    b. convert the sentence, through a judicial or administrative procedure, into a decision of that State, thereby substituting for the sanction imposed in the sentencing State a sanction prescribed by the law of the administering State for the same offence, under the conditions set out in Article 11.

2. The administering State, if requested, shall inform the sentencing State before the transfer of the sentenced person as to which of these procedures it will follow.
3. The enforcement of the sentence shall be governed by the law of the administering State and that State alone shall be competent to take all appropriate decisions.
4. Any State which, according to its national law, cannot avail itself of one of the procedures referred to in paragraph 1 to enforce measures imposed in the territory of another Party on persons who by reasons of mental condition have been held not criminally responsible for the commission of the offence, and which is prepared to receive such persons for further treatment may, by way of a declaration addressed to the Secretary General of the Council of Europe, indicate the procedures it will follow in such cases.

Article 10 Continued enforcement

1. In the case of continued enforcement, the administering State shall be bound by the legal nature and duration of the sentence as determined by the sentencing State.

2. If, however, this sentence is by its nature or duration incompatible with the law of the administering State, or its law so requires, that State may, by a court or administrative order, adapt the sanction to the punishment or measure prescribed by its own law for a similar offence. As to its nature, the punishment or measure shall, as far as possible, correspond with that imposed by the sentence to be enforced. It shall not aggravate, by its nature or duration, the sanction imposed in the sentencing State, nor exceed the maximum prescribed by the law of the administering State.

Article 11 Conversion of sentence

1. In the case of conversion of sentence, the procedures provided for by the law of the administering State apply. When converting the sentence, the competent authority:

    a. shall be bound by the findings as to the facts insofar as they appear explicitly or implicitly from the judgment imposed in the sentencing State:
    b. may not convert a sanction involving deprivation of liberty to a pecuniary sanction;
    c. shall deduct the full period of deprivation of liberty served by the sentenced person; and
    d. shall not aggravate the penal position of the sentenced person, and shall not be bound by any minimum which the law of the administering State may provide for the offence or offences committed.

2. If the conversion procedure takes place after the transfer of the sentenced person, the administering State shall keep that person in custody or otherwise ensure his presence in the administering State pending the outcome of that procedure.

Article 12 Pardon, amnesty, commutation

Each Party may grant pardon, amnesty or commutation of the sentence in accordance with its Constitution and other laws.

Article 13 Review of judgment

The sentencing State alone shall have the right to decide on any application for review of the judgment.

Article 14 Termination of enforcement

The administering State shall terminate enforcement of the sentence as soon as it is informed by the sentencing State of any decision or measure as a result of which the sentence ceases to be enforceable.

Article 15 Information on enforcement

The administering State shall provide information to the sentencing State concerning the enforcement of the sentence:

    a.   when it considers enforcement of the sentence to have been completed;

    b.   if the sentenced person has escaped from custody before enforcement of the sentence has been completed; or

    c.   if the sentencing State requests a special report.

Article 16 Transit

1.   A Party shall, in accordance with its law, grant a request for transit of a sentenced person through its territory if such a request is made by another Party and that State has agreed with another Party or with a third State to the transfer of that person to or from its territory.

2.   A Party may refuse to grant transit:

    a.   if the sentenced person is one of its nationals, or

    b.   if the offence for which the sentence was imposed is not an offence under its own law.

3.   Requests for transit and replies shall be communicated through the channels referred to in the provisions of Article 5.2 and 3.

4.   A Party may grant a request for transit of a sentenced person through its territory made by a third State if that State has agreed with another Party to the transfer to or from its territory.

5.   The Party requested to grant transit may hold the sentenced person in custody only for such time as transit through its territory requires.

6.   The Party requested to grant transit may be asked to give an assurance that the sentenced person will not be prosecuted, or, except as provided in the preceding paragraph, detained, or otherwise subjected to any restriction on his liberty in the territory of the transit State for any offence committed or sentence imposed prior to his departure from the territory of the sentencing State.

7.   No request for transit shall be required if transport is by air over the territory of a Party and no landing there is scheduled. However, each State may, by a declaration addressed to the Secretary General of the Council of Europe at the time of signature or of deposit of its instrument of ratification, acceptance, approval or accession, require that it be notified of any such transit over its territory.

Article 17 Language and costs

1.   Information under Article 4, paragraphs 2 to 4, shall be furnished in the language of the Party to which it is addressed or in one of the official languages of the Council of Europe.

2.   Subject to paragraph 3 below, no translation of requests for transfer or of supporting documents shall be required.

3. Any State may, at the time of signature or when depositing its instrument of ratification, acceptance, approval or accession, by a declaration addressed to the Secretary General of the Council of Europe, require that requests for transfer and supporting documents be accompanied by a translation into its own language or into one of the official languages of the Council of Europe or into such one of these languages as it shall indicate. It may on that occasion declare its readiness to accept translations in any other language in addition to the official language or languages of the Council of Europe.
4. Except as provided in Article 6.2.a, documents transmitted in application of this Convention need not he certified.
5. Any costs incurred in the application of this Convention shall be borne by the administering State, except costs incurred exclusively in the territory of the sentencing State.

Article 18 Signature and entry into force

1. This Convention shall be open for signature by the member States of the Council of Europe and non-member States which have participated in its elaboration. It is subject to ratification, acceptance or approval. Instruments of ratification, acceptance or approval shall be deposited with the Secretary General of the Council of Europe.
2. This Convention shall enter into force on the first day of the month following the expiration of a period of three months after the date on which three member States of the Council of Europe have expressed their consent to be bound by the Convention in accordance with the provisions of paragraph 1.
3. In respect of any signatory State which subsequently expresses its consent to be bound by it, the Convention shall enter into force on the first day of the month following the expiration of a period of three months after the date of the deposit of the instrument of ratification, acceptance or approval.

Article 19 Accession by non-member States

1. After the entry into force of this Convention, the Committee of Ministers of the Council of Europe, after consulting the Contracting States, may invite any State not a member of the Council and not mentioned in Article 18.1 to accede to this Convention, by a decision taken by the majority provided for in Article 20.d of the Statute of the Council of Europe and by the unanimous vote of the representatives of the Contracting States entitled to sit on the Committee.
2. In respect of any acceding State, the Convention shall enter into force on the first day of the month following the expiration of a period of three months after the date of deposit of the instrument of accession with the Secretary General of the Council of Europe.

Article 20 Territorial application

1. Any State may at the time of signature or when depositing its instrument of

ratification, acceptance, approval or accession, specify the territory or territories to which this Convention shall apply.

2. Any State may at any later date, by a declaration addressed to the Secretary General of the Council of Europe, extend the application of this Convention to any other territory specified in the declaration. In respect of such territory the Convention shall enter into force on the first day of the month following the expiration of a period of three months after the date of receipt of such declaration by the Secretary General.

3. Any declaration made under the two preceding paragraphs may, in respect of any territory specified in such declaration, be withdrawn by a notification addressed to the Secretary General. The withdrawal shall become effective on the first day of the month following the expiration of a period of three months after the date of receipt of such notification by the Secretary General.

Article 21 Temporal application

This Convention shall be applicable to the enforcement of sentences imposed either before or after its entry into force.

Article 22 Relationship to other Conventions and Agreements

1. This Convention does not affect the rights and undertakings derived from extradition treaties and other treaties on international co-operation in criminal matters providing for the transfer of detained persons for purposes of confrontation or testimony.

2. If two or more Parties have already concluded an agreement or treaty on the transfer of sentenced persons or otherwise have established their relations in this matter, or should they in future do so, they shall be entitled to apply that agreement or treaty or to regulate those relations accordingly, in lieu of the present Convention.

3. The present Convention does not affect the right of States party to the European Convention on the International Validity of Criminal Judgments to conclude bilateral or multilateral agreements with one another on matters dealt with in that Convention in order to supplement its provisions or facilitate the application of the principles embodied in it.

4. If a request for transfer falls within the scope of both the present Convention and the European Convention on the International Validity of Criminal Judgments or another agreement or treaty on the transfer of sentenced persons, the requesting State shall, when making the request, indicate on the basis of which instrument it is made.

Article 23 Friendly settlement

The European Committee on Crime Problems of the Council of Europe shall be kept informed regarding the application of this Convention and shall do whatever is necessary to facilitate a friendly settlement of any difficulty which may arise out of its application.

Article 24 Denunciation

1. Any Party may at any time denounce this Convention by means of a notification addressed to the Secretary General of the Council of Europe.
2. Such denunciation shall become effective on the first day of the month following the expiration of a period of three months after the date of receipt of the notification by the Secretary General.
3. The present Convention shall, however, continue to apply to the enforcement of sentences of persons who have been transferred in conformity with the provisions of the Convention before the date on which such a denunciation takes effect.

Article 25 Notifications

The Secretary General of the Council of Europe shall notify the member States of the Council of Europe, the non-member States which have participated in the elaboration of this Convention and any State which has acceded to this Convention of:

   a. any signature;
   b. the deposit of any instrument of ratification, acceptance, approval or accession;
   c. any date of entry into force of this Convention in accordance with Articles 18.2 and 3, 19.2 and 20.2 and 3;
   d. any other act, declaration, notification or communication relating to this Convention.

In witness whereof the undersigned, being duly authorised thereto, have signed this Convention.

Done at Strasbourg this 21st day of March 1983 in English and French both to texts being equally authentic, in a single copy which shall be deposited in the archives of the Council of Europe.

The Secretary General of the Council of Europe shall transmit certified copies to each member State of the Council of Europe, to the non-member States which have participated in the elaboration of this Convention and to any State invited to accede to it.

71. UNITED NATIONS: GENERAL ASSEMBLY RESOLUTION ON A MODEL TREATY ON THE TRANSFER OF SUPERVISION OF OFFENDERS CONDITIONALLY SENTENCED OR CONDITIONALLY RELEASED

Adopted by the General Assembly resolution 45/119 (1990)

Editors' Notes

The Model Treaty is a product of the Milan Plan of Action, adopted by the Seventh United Nations Congress on the Prevention of Crime and the Treatment of Offenders, 1985. The Model allows for the transfer of persons where they have been placed on probation pending sentence, given a suspended sentence which would entail imprisonment or given a sentence which has been modified or conditionally suspended (Article 1).[1] Following such a transfer the requested state would be responsible for administering the terms of the sentencing states decision. Curiously, given the arguments for requiring a persons consent under the Model Agreement for the Transfer of Foreign Prisoners,[2] the Supervision Model only provides that the person subject to transfer may express their interest in the transfer, with no requirement that those views will be taken into account (Article 8). The Model Treaty on the Transfer of Supervision explicitly includes provision that the rights of the victim, especially those to compensation or restitution, are not affected by any transfer (Article 9).

The General Assembly,

Bearing in mind the Milan Plan of Action, adopted by the Seventh United Nations Congress on the Prevention of Crime and the Treatment of Offenders and approved by the General Assembly in its resolution 40/32 of 29 November 1985,

Bearing in mind also the Guiding Principles for Crime Prevention and Criminal Justice in the Context of Development and a New International Economic Order, principle 37 of which stipulates that the United Nations should prepare model instruments suitable for use as international and regional conventions and as guides for national implementing legislation,

Recalling resolution 13 of the Seventh Congress, on the transfer of supervision of foreign offenders who have been conditionally sentenced or conditionally released, in which the Committee on Crime Prevention and Control was requested to study this subject and to consider the possibility of formulating a model treaty in this area,

Acknowledging the valuable contributions made by Governments, non-governmental organizations and individual experts to the drafting of a model treaty on

---

[1] See also: European Convention on the Supervision of Conditionally Sentenced or Conditionally Released Offenders, 1964.

[2] United Nations Model Agreement on the Transfer of Foreign Prisoners 1985.

the transfer of supervision of offenders conditionally sentenced or conditionally released, in particular the International Expert Meeting on the United Nations and Law Enforcement, held under the auspices of the United Nations at Baden, Austria, from 16 to 19 November 1987, the Interregional Preparatory Meeting for the Eighth United Nations Congress on the Prevention of Crime and the Treatment of Offenders on topic V, "United Nations norms and guidelines in crime prevention and criminal justice: implementation and priorities for further standard setting" and the regional preparatory meetings for the Eighth Congress,

Convinced that the establishment of bilateral and multilateral arrangements for transfer of supervision of offenders conditionally sentenced or conditionally released will greatly contribute to the development of more effective international co-operation in penal matters,

Conscious of the need to respect human dignity and recalling the rights conferred upon every person involved in criminal proceedings, as embodied in the Universal Declaration of Human Rights and the International Covenant on Civil and Political Rights:

1. Adopts the Model Treaty on the Transfer of Supervision of Offenders Conditionally Sentenced or Conditionally Released, contained in the annex to the present resolution, as a useful framework that could be of assistance to States interested in negotiating and concluding bilateral or multilateral treaties aimed at improving co-operation in matters of crime prevention and criminal justice;

2. Invites Member States, if they have not yet established treaty relations with other States in the area of the transfer of supervision of offenders conditionally sentenced or conditionally released, or if they wish to revise existing treaty relations, to take into account the Model Treaty whenever doing so;

3. Urges all Member States to strengthen international co-operation in criminal justice;

4. Also urges Member States to inform the Secretary-General periodically of efforts undertaken to establish arrangements on the transfer of supervision of offenders conditionally sentenced or conditionally released;

5. Requests the Committee on Crime Prevention and Control to conduct periodic reviews of the progress attained in this field;

6. Requests the Secretary-General to assist Member States, at their request, in the development of treaties on the transfer of supervision of offenders conditionally sentenced or conditionally released and to report regularly thereon to the Committee.

ANNEX
MODEL TREATY ON THE TRANSFER OF SUPERVISION OF OFFENDERS CONDITIONALLY SENTENCED OR CONDITIONALLY RELEASED

The ——————— and the ———————

Desirous of further strengthening international co-operation and mutual assistance in criminal justice, on the basis of the principles of respect for national sovereignty and jurisdiction and of non-interference in the internal affairs of States,

Believing that such co-operation should further the ends of justice, the social resettlement of sentenced persons and the interests of the victims of crime,

Bearing in mind that the transfer of supervision of offenders conditionally sentenced or conditionally released can contribute to an increase in the use of alternatives to imprisonment,

Aware that supervision in the home country of the offender rather than enforcement of the sentence in a country where the offender has no roots also contributes to an earlier and more effective reintegration into society,

Convinced, therefore, that the social rehabilitation of offenders and the increased application of alternatives to imprisonment would be promoted by facilitating the supervision of conditionally sentenced or conditionally released offenders in their State of ordinary residence,

Have agreed as follows:

Article 1 Scope of application

1. The present Treaty shall be applicable, if, according to a final court decision, a person has been found guilty of an offence and has been:

    (a) Placed on probation without sentence having been pronounced;
    (b) Given a suspended sentence involving deprivation of liberty;
    (c) Given a sentence, the enforcement of which has been modified (parole) or conditionally suspended, in whole or in part, either at the time of the sentence or subsequently.

2. The State where the decision was taken (sentencing State) may request another State (administering State) to take responsibility for applying the terms of the decision (transfer of supervision).

Article 2 Channels of communications

A request for the transfer of supervision shall be made in writing. The request, supporting documents and subsequent communication shall be transmitted through diplomatic channels, directly between the Ministries of Justice or any other authorities designated by the Parties.

705

Article 3 Required documents

1. A request for the transfer of supervision shall contain all necessary information on the identity, nationality and residence of the sentenced person. The request shall be accompanied by the original or a copy of any court decision referred to in article 1 of the present Treaty and a certificate that this decision is final.
2. The documents submitted in support of a request for transfer of supervision shall be accompanied by a translation into the language of the requested State or into another language acceptable to that State.

Article 4 Certification and authentication

Subject to national law and unless the Parties decide otherwise, a request for transfer of supervision and the documents in support thereof, as well as the documents and other material supplied in response to such a request, shall not require certification or authentication.

Article 5 Decision on the request

The competent authorities of the administering State shall examine what action to take on the request for supervision in order to comply, as fully as possible, with the request under their own law, and shall promptly communicate their decision to the sentencing State.

Article 6 Dual criminality

A request for transfer of supervision can be complied with only if the act on which the request is based would constitute an offence if committed in the territory of the administering State.

Article 7 Grounds for refusal

If the administering State refuses acceptance of a request for transfer of supervision, it shall communicate the reasons for refusal to the sentencing State. Acceptance may be refused where:

(a) The sentenced person is not an ordinary resident in the administering State;
(b) The act is an offence under military law, which is not also an offence under ordinary criminal law;
(c) The offence is in connection with taxes, duties, customs or exchange;
(d) The offence is regarded by the administering State as being of a political nature;
(e) The administering State, under its own law, can no longer carry out the supervision or enforce the sanction in the event of revocation because of lapse of time.

Article 8 The position of the sentenced person

Whether sentenced or standing trial, a person may express to the sentencing State his or her interest in a transfer of supervision and his or her willingness to fulfil any conditions to be imposed. Similarly, such interest may be expressed by his or her legal representative or close relatives. Where appropriate, the Contracting States shall inform the offender or his or her close relatives of the possibilities under the present Treaty.

Article 9 The rights of the victim

The sentencing State and the administering State shall ensure in the transfer of supervision that the rights of the victims of the offence, in particular his or her rights to restitution or compensation, shall not be affected as a result of the transfer. In the event of the death of the victim, this provision shall apply to his or her dependants accordingly.

Article 10 The effects of the transfer of supervision on the sentencing State

The acceptance by the administering State of the responsibility for applying the terms of the decision rendered in the sentencing State shall extinguish the competence of the latter State to enforce the sentence.

Article 11 The effects of the transfer of supervision on the administering State

1. The supervision transferred upon agreement and the subsequent procedure shall be carried out in accordance with the law of the administering State. That State alone shall have the right of revocation. That State may, to the extent necessary, adapt to its own law the conditions or measures prescribed, provided that such conditions or measures are, in terms of their nature or duration, not more severe than those pronounced in the sentencing State.
2. If the administering State revokes the conditional sentence or conditional release, it shall enforce the sentence in accordance with its own law without, however, going beyond the limits imposed by the sentencing State.

Article 12 Review, pardon and amnesty

1. The sentencing State alone shall have the right to decide on any application to reopen the case.
2. Each Party may grant pardon, amnesty or commutation of the sentence in accordance with the provisions of its Constitution or other laws.

Article 13 Information

1. The Contracting Parties shall keep each other informed, in so far as it is necessary, of all circumstances likely to affect measures of supervision or

enforcement in the administering State. To this end they shall transmit to each other copies of any relevant decisions in this respect.

2. After expiration of the period of supervision, the administering State shall provide to the sentencing State, at its request, a final report concerning the supervised person's conduct and compliance with the measures imposed.

Article 14 Costs

Supervision and enforcement costs incurred in the administering State shall not be refunded, unless otherwise agreed by both the sentencing State and the administering State.

Article 15 Final provisions

1. The present Treaty is subject to [ratification, acceptance or approval]. The instruments of [ratification, acceptance or approval] shall be exchanged as soon as possible.
2. The present Treaty shall enter into force on the thirtieth day after the day on which the instruments of [ratification, acceptance or approval] are exchanged.
3. The present Treaty shall apply to requests made after its entry into force, even if the relevant acts or omissions occurred prior to that date.
4. Either Contracting Party may denounce the present Treaty by giving notice in writing to the other Party. Such denunciation shall take effect six months following the date on which it is received by the other Party.

SECTION FIVE

INTERNATIONAL TRIBUNALS

72. INTERNATIONAL TRIBUNAL FOR THE PROSECUTION OF PERSONS RESPONSIBLE FOR SERIOUS VIOLATIONS OF INTERNATIONAL HUMANITARIAN LAW COMMITTED IN THE TERRITORY OF THE FORMER YUGOSLAVIA SINCE 1991

Editors' Notes

After persistent media coverage of the civil war in Yugoslavia, the United Nations Security Council was moved to gather reports of atrocities taking place in the territory[1] and subsequently established a Commission of Experts to investigate "grave breaches of the Geneva Conventions and other violations of international humanitarian law".[2] The report by the Commission led to Security Council Resolution 808 which called for the creation of an *ad hoc* war crimes tribunal for the former Yugoslavia.[3] There followed the process of drafting the Statute for the Tribunal, which was accomplished in a matter of months[4] and the Security Council adopted the Secretary-General's draft of the Statute without amendment.[5] The use of Security Council Resolutions to establish an international criminal tribunal should certainly be regarded as an evolutionary step in international law, and was formally justified by dynamically interpreting powers given to the Security Council under Chapter VII of the United Nations Charter allowing action to be taken against "threats to peace, breaches of the peace and acts of aggression".[6] From a pragmatic point of view, this method of establishing the Tribunal circumvented the delays made likely in attempting to create such a body by international treaty.

Perhaps due to the haste in which the Statute to the Tribunal was completed, various "flaws" have been identified in its contents, which were not amended for fear of delaying the adoption of the Statute and the work of the Tribunal. For example, the Additional Protocols to the 1949 Geneva Conventions were omitted from Article 2 of the Statute. It will be for the Tribunal to clarify those various legal issues, a process that has already begun with the Appeals Chamber affirming the competence and jurisdiction of the Tribunal.[7]

The Tribunal has jurisdiction over individuals (Article 6) and has primacy over national courts (Article 9). An independent prosecutor is responsible for the investigation and prosecution of offences (Article 16 and 18), and submits an

---

[1] See: Security Council Resolution 771, UN SCOR, 3106th Meeting, UN Doc. S/RES/771 (1992).
[2] See: Security Council Resolution 780, UN SCOR, 3119th Meeting, UN Doc. S/RES/780 (1992).
[3] See: Security Council Resolution 808, UN SCOR, 3175th Meeting, UN Doc. S/RES/808 (1993).
[4] Secretary-General, Report Pursuant to Paragraph 2 of Security Council Resolution 808, UN Doc. S/25704/Add.1/Corr.1 (1993).
[5] Security Council Resolution 827, UN SCOR, 3217th Meeting, UN Doc. S/RES/827 (1993).
[6] UN Charter, Ch. VII, part I, ss. C.
[7] See: Case No.IT-94-1-AR72, Decision on the Defence Motion for Interlocutory Appeal on the Jurisdiction, 2 Oct. 1995, Appeals Chamber. Reported at (1996) ILM 32.

indictment to the Tribunal for review. If the Tribunal is satisfied that a *prima facie* case has been established against the accused, the indictment is confirmed and a warrant of arrest may be issued or transfer for trial can be requested (Article 19). The rights of the accused are set out in Article 21 and have been supplemented by separate standards of treatment of detainees of the Tribunal[8] and for the provision of defence counsel.[9] The Statute of the Tribunal is supplemented by detailed Rules of Procedure and Evidence.[10] Despite obstacles including the obtaining of evidence and the translation of large quantities of documents with limited resources, indictments have now been issued against a range of defendants from "ordinary" military personnel to political leaders and trials are now under way.[11]

STATUTE OF THE INTERNATIONAL TRIBUNAL

Having been established by the Security Council acting under Chapter VII of the Charter of the United Nations, the International Tribunal for the Prosecution of Persons Responsible for Serious Violations of International Humanitarian Law Committed in the Territory of the Former Yugoslavia since 1991 (hereinafter referred to as "the International Tribunal") shall function in accordance with the provisions of the present Statute.

Article 1: Competence of the International Tribunal

The International Tribunal shall have the power to prosecute persons responsible for serious violations of international humanitarian law committed in the territory of the former Yugoslavia since 1991 in accordance with the provisions of the present Statute.

Article 2: Grave breaches of the Geneva Conventions of 1949

The International Tribunal shall have the power to prosecute persons committing or ordering to be committed grave breaches of the Geneva Conventions of 12 August 1949, namely the following acts against persons or property protected under the provisions of the relevant Geneva Convention:

(a) wilful killing;

---

[8] Rules governing the detention of persons awaiting trial or appeal or otherwise detained on the authority of the Tribunal, 5 May 1994, reprinted at (1994) 33 ILM 1590.

[9] Directive on the assignment of Defence Counsel (Directive No.1/94), IT/73/Rev.1, reprinted at (1994) 33 ILM 1581.

[10] The Rules of procedure and Evidence for the International Tribunal for the Former Yugoslavia, reported at (1994) 33 ILM 484.

[11] See further: McGoldrick, D. & Warbrick, C. (1995). "Current Developments – International Criminal Law". 44 ICLQ 466; Levie, H.S. (1995). "The Statute of the International Tribunal for the Former Yugoslavia: A Comparison with the Past and a look at the Future". 21 Syracuse J. Int'l L. & Com. 1; Aldrich, G.H. (1996). "Jurisdiction of the International Criminal Tribunal for the Former Yugoslavia". 90 AJIL 64.

(b) torture or inhuman treatment, including biological experiments;

(c) wilfully causing great suffering or serious injury to body or health;

(d) extensive destruction and appropriation of property, not justified by military necessity and carried out unlawfully and wantonly;

(e) compelling a prisoner of war or a civilian to serve in the forces of a hostile power;

(f) wilfully depriving a prisoner of war or a civilian of the rights of fair and regular trial;

(g) unlawful deportation or transfer or unlawful confinement of a civilian;

(h) taking civilians as hostages.

Article 3: Violations of the laws or customs of war

The International Tribunal shall have the power to prosecute persons violating the laws or customs of war. Such violations shall include, but not be limited to:

(a) employment of poisonous weapons or other weapons calculated to cause unnecessary suffering;

(b) wanton destruction of cities, towns or villages, or devastation not justified by military necessity;

(c) attack, or bombardment, by whatever means, of undefended towns, villages, dwellings, or buildings;

(d) seizure of, destruction or wilful damage done to institutions dedicated to religion, charity and education, the arts and sciences, historic monuments and works of art and science;

(e) plunder of public or private property.

Article 4: Genocide

1. The International Tribunal shall have the power to prosecute persons committing genocide as defined in paragraph 2 of this article or of committing any of the other acts enumerated in paragraph 3 of this article.

2. Genocide means any of the following acts committed with intent to destroy, in whole or in part, a national, ethnical, racial or religious group, as such:

(a) killing members of the group;

(b) causing serious bodily or mental harm to members of the group;

(c) deliberately inflicting on the group conditions of life calculated to bring about its physical destruction in whole or in part;

(d) imposing measures intended to prevent births within the group;

(e) forcibly transferring children of the group to another group.

3. The following acts shall be punishable:

(a) genocide;

(b) conspiracy to commit genocide;

(c) direct and public incitement to commit genocide;

(d) attempt to commit genocide;

(e) complicity in genocide.

Article 5: Crimes against humanity

The International Tribunal shall have the power to prosecute persons responsible for the following crimes when committed in armed conflict, whether international or internal in character, and directed against any civilian population:

    (a) murder;
    (b) extermination;
    (c) enslavement;
    (d) deportation;
    (e) imprisonment;
    (f) torture;
    (g) rape;
    (h) persecutions on political, racial and religious grounds;
    (i) other inhumane acts.

Article 6: Personal jurisdiction

The International Tribunal shall have jurisdiction over natural persons pursuant to the provisions of the present Statute.

Article 7: Individual criminal responsibility

1. A person who planned, instigated, ordered, committed or otherwise aided and abetted in the planning, preparation or execution of a crime referred to in articles 2 to 5 of the present Statute, shall be individually responsible for the crime.
2. The official position of any accused person, whether as Head of State or Government or as a responsible Government official, shall not relieve such person of criminal responsibility nor mitigate punishment.
3. The fact that any of the acts referred to in articles 2 to 5 of the present Statute was committed by a subordinate does not relieve his superior of criminal responsibility if he knew or had reason to know that the subordinate was about to commit such acts or had done so and the superior failed to take the necessary and reasonable measures to prevent such acts or to punish the perpetrators thereof.
4. The fact that an accused person acted pursuant to an order of a Government or of a superior shall not relieve him of criminal responsibility, but may be considered in mitigation of punishment if the International Tribunal determines that justice so requires.

Article 8: Territorial and temporal jurisdiction

The territorial jurisdiction of the International Tribunal shall extend to the territory of the former Socialist Federal Republic of Yugoslavia, including its land surface, airspace and territorial waters. The temporal jurisdiction of the International Tribunal shall extend to a period beginning on 1 January 1991.

Article 9: Concurrent jurisdiction

1. The International Tribunal and national courts shall have concurrent jurisdiction to prosecute persons for serious violations of international humanitarian law committed in the territory of the former Yugoslavia since 1 January 1991.
2. The International Tribunal shall have primacy over national courts. At any stage of the procedure, the International Tribunal may formally request national courts to defer to the competence of the International Tribunal in accordance with the present Statute and the Rules of Procedure and Evidence of the International Tribunal.

Article 10: *Non-bis-in-idem*

1. No person shall be tried before a national court for acts constituting serious violations of international humanitarian law under the present Statute, for which he or she has already been tried by the International Tribunal.
2. A person who has been tried by a national court for acts constituting serious violations of international humanitarian law may be subsequently tried by the International Tribunal only if:

   (a) the act for which he or she was tried was characterised as an ordinary crime; or
   (b) the national court proceedings were not impartial or independent, were designed to shield the accused from international criminal responsibility, or the case was not diligently prosecuted.

3. In considering the penalty to be imposed on a person convicted of a crime under the present Statute, the International Tribunal shall take into account the extent to which any penalty imposed by a national court on the same person for the same act has already been served.

Article 11: Organisation of the International Tribunal

The International Tribunal shall consist of the following organs:

   (a) The Chambers, comprising two Trial Chambers and an Appeals Chamber;
   (b) The Prosecutor, and
   (c) A Registry, servicing both the Chambers and the Prosecutor.

Article 12: Composition of the Chambers

The Chambers shall be composed of eleven independent judges, no two of whom may be nationals of the same State, who shall serve as follows:

   (a) Three judges shall serve in each of the Trial Chambers;
   (b) Five judges shall serve in the Appeals Chamber.

Article 13: Qualifications and election of judges

1. The judges shall be persons of high moral character, impartiality and integrity who possess the qualifications required in their respective countries for appointment to the highest judicial offices. In the overall composition of the Chambers due account shall be taken of the experience of the judges in criminal law, international law, including international humanitarian law and human rights law.

2. The judges of the International Tribunal shall be elected by the General Assembly from a list submitted by the Security Council, in the following manner:

   (a) The Secretary-General shall invite nominations for judges of the International Tribunal from States Members of the United Nations and non-member States maintaining permanent observer missions at United Nations Headquarters;

   (b) Within sixty days of the date of the invitation of the Secretary-General, each State may nominate up to two candidates meeting the qualifications set out in paragraph 1 above, no two of whom shall be of the same nationality;

   (c) The Secretary-General shall forward the nominations received to the Security Council. From the nominations received the Security Council shall establish a list of not less than twenty-two and not more than thirty-three candidates, taking due account of the adequate representation of the principal legal systems of the world;

   (d) The President of the Security Council shall transmit the list of candidates to the President of the General Assembly. From that list the General Assembly shall elect the eleven judges of the International Tribunal. The candidates who receive an absolute majority of the votes of the States Members of the United Nations and of the non-Member States maintaining permanent observer missions at United Nations Head-quarters, shall be declared elected. Should two candidates of the same nationality obtain the required majority vote, the one who received the higher number of votes shall be considered elected.

3. In the event of a vacancy in the Chambers, after consultation with the Presidents of the Security Council and of the General Assembly, the Secretary-General shall appoint a person meeting the qualifications of paragraph 1 above, for the remainder of the term of office concerned.

4. The judges shall be elected for a term of four years. The terms and conditions of service shall be those of the judges of the International Court of Justice. They shall be eligible for re-election.

Article 14: Officers and members of the Chambers

1. The judges of the International Tribunal shall elect a President.

2. The President of the International Tribunal shall be a member of the Appeals Chamber and shall preside over its proceedings.

3. After consultation with the judges of the International Tribunal, the President shall assign the judges to the Appeals Chamber and to the Trial Chambers. A judge shall serve only in the Chamber to which he or she was assigned.
4. The judges of each Trial Chamber shall elect a Presiding Judge, who shall conduct all of the proceedings of the Trial Chamber as a whole.

Article 15: Rules of procedure and evidence

The judges of the International Tribunal shall adopt rules of procedure and evidence for the conduct of the pre-trial phase of the proceedings, trials and appeals, the admission of evidence, the protection of victims and witnesses and other appropriate matters.

Article 16: The Prosecutor

1. The Prosecutor shall be responsible for the investigation and prosecution of persons responsible for serious violations of international humanitarian law committed in the territory of the former Yugoslavia since 1 January 1991.
2. The Prosecutor shall act independently as a separate organ of the International Tribunal. He or she shall not seek or receive instructions from any Government or from any other source.
3. The Office of the Prosecutor shall be composed of a Prosecutor and such other qualified staff as may be required.
4. The Prosecutor shall be appointed by the Security Council on nomination by the Secretary-General. He or she shall be of high moral character and possess the highest level of competence and experience in the conduct of investigations and prosecutions of criminal cases. The Prosecutor shall serve for a four-year term and be eligible for reappointment. The terms and conditions of service of the Prosecutor shall be those of an Under-Secretary-General of the United Nations.
5. The staff of the Office of the Prosecutor shall be appointed by the Secretary-General on the recommendation of the Prosecutor.

Article 17: The Registry

1. The Registry shall be responsible for the administration and servicing of the International Tribunal.
2. The Registry shall consist of a Registrar and such other staff as may be required.
3. The Registrar shall be appointed by the Secretary-General after consultation with the President of the International Tribunal. He or she shall serve for a four-year term and be eligible for reappointment. The terms and conditions of service of the Registrar shall be those of an Assistant Secretary-General of the United Nations.
4. The staff of the Registry shall be appointed by the Secretary-General on the recommendation of the Registrar.

Article 18: Investigation and preparation of indictment

1. The Prosecutor shall initiate investigations ex-officio or on the basis of information obtained from any source, particularly from Governments, United Nations organs, intergovernmental and non-governmental organisations. The Prosecutor shall assess the information received or obtained and decide whether there is sufficient basis to proceed.

2. The Prosecutor shall have the power to question suspects, victims and witnesses, to collect evidence and to conduct on-site investigations. In carrying out these tasks, the Prosecutor may, as appropriate, seek the assistance of the State authorities concerned.

3. If questioned, the suspect shall be entitled to be assisted by counsel of his own choice, including the right to have legal assistance assigned to him without payment by him in any such case if he does not have sufficient means to pay for it, as well as to necessary translation into and from a language he speaks and understands.

4. Upon a determination that a prima facie case exists, the Prosecutor shall prepare an indictment containing a concise statement of the facts and the crime or crimes with which the accused is charged under the Statute. The indictment shall be transmitted to a judge of the Trial Chamber.

Article 19: Review of the indictment

1. The judge of the Trial Chamber to whom the indictment has been transmitted shall review it. If satisfied that a prima facie case has been established by the Prosecutor, he shall confirm the indictment. If not so satisfied, the indictment shall be dismissed.

2. Upon confirmation of an indictment, the judge may, at the request of the Prosecutor, issue such orders and warrants for the arrest, detention, surrender or transfer of persons, and any other orders as may be required for the conduct of the trial.

Article 20: Commencement and conduct of trial proceedings

1. The Trial Chambers shall ensure that a trial is fair and expeditious and that proceedings are conducted in accordance with the rules of procedure and evidence, with full respect for the rights of the accused and due regard for the protection of victims and witnesses.

2. A person against whom an indictment has been confirmed shall, pursuant to an order or an arrest warrant of the International Tribunal, be taken into custody, immediately informed of the charges against him and transferred to the International Tribunal.

3. The Trial Chamber shall read the indictment, satisfy itself that the rights of the accused are respected, confirm that the accused understands the indictment, and instruct the accused to enter a plea. The Trial Chamber shall then set the date for trial.

4. The hearings shall be public unless the Trial Chamber decides to close the proceedings in accordance with its rules of procedure and evidence.

Article 21: Rights of the accused

1. All persons shall be equal before the International Tribunal.
2. In the determination of charges against him, the accused shall be entitled to a fair and public hearing, subject to article 22 of the Statute.
3. The accused shall be presumed innocent until proved guilty according to the provisions of the present Statute.
4. In the determination of any charge against the accused pursuant to the present Statute, the accused shall be entitled to the following minimum guarantees, in full equality:

   (a) to be informed promptly and in detail in a language which he understands of the nature and cause of the charge against him;
   (b) to have adequate time and facilities for the preparation of his defence and to communicate with counsel of his own choosing;
   (c) to be tried without undue delay;
   (d) to be tried in his presence, and to defend himself in person or through legal assistance of his own choosing; to be informed, if he does not have legal assistance, of this right; and to have legal assistance assigned to him, in any case where the interests of justice so require, and without payment by him in any such case if he does not have sufficient means to pay for it;
   (e) to examine, or have examined, the witnesses against him and to obtain the attendance and examination of witnesses on his behalf under the same conditions as witnesses against him;
   (f) to have the free assistance of an interpreter if he cannot understand or speak the language used in the International Tribunal;
   (g) not to be compelled to testify against himself or to confess guilt.

Article 22: Protection of victims and witnesses

The International Tribunal shall provide in its rules of procedure and evidence for the protection of victims and witnesses. Such protection measures shall include, but shall not be limited to, the conduct of in camera proceedings and the protection of the victim's identity.

Article 23: Judgement

1. The Trial Chambers shall pronounce judgements and impose sentences and penalties on persons convicted of serious violations of international humanitarian law.
2. The judgement shall be rendered by a majority of the judges of the Trial Chamber, and shall be delivered by the Trial Chamber in public. It shall be accompanied by a reasoned opinion in writing, to which separate or dissenting opinions may be appended.

Article 24: Penalties

1. The penalty imposed by the Trial Chamber shall be limited to imprisonment.

In determining the terms of imprisonment, the Trial Chambers shall have recourse to the general practice regarding prison sentences in the courts of the former Yugoslavia.

2. In imposing the sentences, the Trial Chambers should take into account such factors as the gravity of the offence and the individual circumstances of the convicted person.

3. In addition to imprisonment, the Trial Chambers may order the return of any property and proceeds acquired by criminal conduct, including by means of duress, to their rightful owners.

Article 25: Appellate proceedings

1. The Appeals Chamber shall hear appeals from persons convicted by the Trial Chambers or from the Prosecutor on the following grounds:

   (a) an error on a question of law invalidating the decision; or
   (b) an error of fact which has occasioned a miscarriage of justice.

2. The Appeals Chamber may affirm, reverse or revise the decisions taken by the Trial Chambers.

Article 26: Review proceedings

Where a new fact has been discovered which was not known at the time of the proceedings before the Trial Chambers or the Appeals Chamber and which could have been a decisive factor in reaching the decision, the convicted person or the Prosecutor may submit to the International Tribunal an application for review of the judgement.

Article 27: Enforcement of sentences

Imprisonment shall be served in a State designated by the International Tribunal from a list of States which have indicated to the Security Council their willingness to accept convicted persons. Such imprisonment shall be in accordance with the applicable law of the State concerned, subject to the supervision of the International Tribunal.

Article 28: Pardon or commutation of sentences

If, pursuant to the applicable law of the State in which the convicted person is imprisoned, he or she is eligible for pardon or commutation of sentence, the State concerned shall notify the International Tribunal accordingly. The President of the International Tribunal, in consultation with the judges, shall decide the matter on the basis of the interests of justice and the general principles of law.

Article 29: Co-operation and judicial assistance

1. States shall cooperate with the International Tribunal in the investigation and

prosecution of persons accused of committing serious violations of international humanitarian law.

2. States shall comply without undue delay with any request for assistance or an order issued by a Trial Chamber, including, but not limited to:

   (a) the identification and location of persons;
   (b) the taking of testimony and the production of evidence;
   (c) the service of documents;
   (d) the arrest or detention of persons;
   (e) the surrender or the transfer of the accused to the International Tribunal.

Article 30: The status, privileges and immunities of the International Tribunal

1. The Convention on the Privileges and Immunities of the United Nations of 13 February 1946 shall apply to the International Tribunal, the judges, the Prosecutor and his staff, and the Registrar and his staff.
2. The judges, the Prosecutor and the Registrar shall enjoy the privileges and immunities, exemptions and facilities accorded to diplomatic envoys, in accordance with international law.
3. The staff of the Prosecutor and of the Registrar shall enjoy the privileges and immunities accorded to officials of the United Nations under articles V and VII of the Convention referred to in paragraph 1 of this article.
4. Other persons, including the accused, required at the seat of the International Tribunal shall be accorded such treatment as is necessary for the proper functioning of the International Tribunal.

Article 31: Seat of the International Tribunal

The International Tribunal shall have its seat at The Hague.

Article 32: Expenses of the International Tribunal

The expenses of the International Tribunal shall be borne by the regular budget of the United Nations in accordance with Article 17 of the Charter of the United Nations.

Article 33: Working languages

The working languages of the International Tribunal shall be English and French.

Article 34: Annual report

The President of the International Tribunal shall submit an annual report of the International Tribunal to the Security Council and to the General Assembly.

73. RULES OF PROCEDURE AND EVIDENCE FOR THE INTERNATIONAL TRIBUNAL FOR THE FORMER YUGOSLAVIA

UN Document IT/32 of 14 March 1994

Adopted: 11 February 1994

Operative from 14 March 1994

Editors' Notes

The Rules of Procedure and Evidence for the International Tribunal for the Former Yugoslavia complement the Statute establishing the Tribunal[1] and set out its manner of operation. These Rules have also been adopted for use by the Tribunal for Rwanda.[2] The Rules contain nine sections. They are: general provisions; primacy of the tribunal; organisation of the Tribunal; investigations and the rights of suspects; pre-trial proceedings; proceedings before trial chambers; appellate proceedings; review proceedings; and pardon and commutation of sentence. Separate rules have been established concerning the detention of those awaiting trial.[3]

Under Rule 6, the Rules can be amended on the unanimous approval of the judges. Such a power has been included so as to allow unforeseen problems within proceedings before the Tribunal to be addressed and a number of amendments have been made since the original rules entered into force in 1994. Under Part Two of the Rules, the Tribunal is given substantial powers to ensure that a national court defers trial in favour of the Tribunal. Failure of a national state to co-operate with such a request can be referred to the Security Council for suitable action (Rules 11 and 13).

The trial chamber of the Tribunal has already been called to consider a request by the Chief Prosecutors that certain measures be taken to protect the identities of victims and witnesses and has accepted that trial may proceed including unidentified and anonymous witnesses.[4]

The use of the Rules of Procedure and Evidence will be carefully observed for their potential future application to operation of a permanent international criminal court.

---

[1] *Supra.*

[2] See: Statute of the International Tribunal for Rwanda, Article 14.

[3] Rules covering the detention of persons awaiting trial or appeal before the Tribunal or otherwise detained on the authority of the Tribunal. UN Doc. IT/38/Rev.4 (1995).

[4] *Prosecutor v Tadic*, Case IT-94-1-T, (Aug. 10 1995). See also: Leigh, M. (1996). "The Yugoslav Tribunal: Use of unnamed Witnesses against the Accused". 90 AJIL 234.

PART ONE
GENERAL PROVISIONS

Rule 1: Entry into Force

These Rules of Procedure and Evidence, adopted pursuant to Article 15 of the Statute of the Tribunal, shall come into force on 14 March 1994.

Rule 2: Definitions

(A) In the Rules, unless the context otherwise requires, the following terms shall mean:

Rules: The Rules referred to in Rule 1;

Statute: The Statute of the Tribunal adopted by Security Council resolution 827 of 25 May 1993;

Tribunal: The International Tribunal for the Prosecution of Persons Responsible for Serious Violations of International Humanitarian Law Committed in the Territory of the Former Yugoslavia since 1991, established by Security Council resolution 827 of 25 May 1993.

Accused: A person against whom an indictment has been submitted in accordance with Rule 47;

Arrest: The act of taking a suspect or an accused into custody by a national authority;

Bureau: A body composed of the President, the Vice-President and the Presiding Judges of the Trial Chambers;

Investigation: All activities undertaken by the Prosecutor under the Statute and the Rules for the collection of information and evidence;

Party: The Prosecutor or the accused;

President: The President of the Tribunal;

Prosecutor: The Prosecutor appointed pursuant to Article 16 of the Statute;

Suspect: A person concerning whom the Prosecutor possesses information which tends to show that he may have committed a crime over which the Tribunal has jurisdiction;

Victim: A person against whom a crime over which the Tribunal has jurisdiction has allegedly been committed.

(B) In the Rules, the masculine shall include the feminine and the singular the plural, and vice-versa.

Rule 3: Languages

(A)   The working languages of the Tribunal shall be English and French.

(B)   An accused shall have the right to use his own language.

(C)   Any other person appearing before the Tribunal may, subject to Sub-rule (D), use his own language if he does not have sufficient knowledge of either of the two working languages.

(D)   Counsel for an accused may apply to the Presiding Judge of a Chamber for leave to use a language other than the two working ones or the language of the accused. If such leave is granted, the expenses of interpretation and translation shall be borne by the Tribunal to the extent, if any, determined by the President, taking into account the rights of the defence and the interests of justice.

(E)   The Registrar shall make any necessary arrangements for interpretation and translation into and from the working languages.

Rule 4: Meetings away from the Seat of the Tribunal

A Chamber may exercise its functions at a place other than the seat of the Tribunal, if so authorised by the President in the interests of justice.

Rule 5: Non-compliance with Rules

Any objection by a party to an act of another party on the ground of non-compliance with the Rules shall be raised at the earliest opportunity; it shall be upheld, and the act declared null, only if the act was inconsistent with the fundamental principles of fairness and has occasioned a miscarriage of justice.

Rule 6: Amendment of the Rules

(A)   Proposals for amendment of the Rules may be made by a Judge, the Prosecutor or the Registrar and shall be adopted if agreed to by not less than seven Judges at a plenary meeting of the Tribunal convened with notice of the proposal addressed to all Judges.

(B)   An amendment to the Rules may be otherwise adopted, provided it is unanimously approved by the Judges.

(C)   An amendment shall enter into force immediately, but shall not operate to prejudice the rights of the accused in any pending case.

Rule 7: Authentic Texts

The English and French texts of the Rules shall be equally authentic. In case of discrepancy, the version which is more consonant with the spirit of the Statute and the Rules shall prevail.

PART TWO
PRIMACY OF THE TRIBUNAL

Rule 8: Request for Information

Where it appears to the Prosecutor that a crime within the jurisdiction of the Tribunal is or has been the subject of investigations or criminal proceedings instituted in the national courts of any State, he may request the State to forward to him all relevant information in that respect, and the State shall transmit to him such information forthwith in accordance with Article 29(1) of the Statute.

Rule 9: Prosecutor's Request for Deferral

Where it appears to the Prosecutor that in any such investigations or criminal proceedings instituted in the national courts of any State:

(i) the act being investigated or which is the subject of those proceedings is characterised as an ordinary crime;

(ii) there is a lack of impartiality or independence, or the investigations or proceedings are designed to shield the accused from international criminal responsibility, or the case is not diligently prosecuted; or

(iii) what is in issue is closely related to, or otherwise involves, significant factual or legal questions which may have implications for investigations or prosecutions before the Tribunal,

the Prosecutor may propose to the Trial Chamber designated by the President that a formal request be made that the national court defer to the competence of the Tribunal.

Rule 10: Formal Request for Deferral

(A) If it appears to the Trial Chamber seised of a proposal for deferral that, on any of the grounds specified in Rule 9, deferral is appropriate, the Trial Chamber may issue a formal request to the State concerned that its national court defer to the competence of the Tribunal.

(B) A request for deferral shall include a request that the results of the investigation and a copy of the court's records and the judgement, if already delivered, be forwarded to the Tribunal.

(C) Where deferral to the Tribunal has been requested by a Trial Chamber, any subsequent proceedings shall be held before the other Trial Chamber.

Rule 11: Non-compliance with a Request for Deferral

If, within sixty days after a request for deferral has been notified by the Registrar to the State under whose jurisdiction the investigations or criminal proceedings have been instituted, the State fails to file a response which satisfies the Trial Chamber that the State has taken or is taking adequate steps to comply with the order, the Trial Chamber may request the President to report the matter to the Security Council.

Rule 12: Determinations of National Courts

Subject to Article 10(2) of the Statute, determinations of national courts are not binding on the Tribunal.

Rule 13: *Non Bis in Idem*

When the President receives reliable information to show that criminal proceedings have been instituted against a person before a national court for a crime for which that person has already been tried by the Tribunal, a Trial Chamber shall, following mutatis mutandis the procedure provided in Rule 10, issue a reasoned order requesting the national court permanently to discontinue its proceedings. If the national court fails to do so, the President may report the matter to the Security Council.

PART THREE
ORGANISATION OF THE TRIBUNAL

SECTION 1: THE JUDGES

Rule 14: Solemn Declaration

(A) Before taking up his duties each Judge shall make the following solemn declaration:

"I solemnly declare that I will perform my duties and exercise my powers as a Judge of the International Tribunal for the Prosecution of Persons Responsible for Serious Violations of International Humanitarian Law Committed in the Territory of the Former Yugoslavia since 1991 honourably, faithfully, impartially and conscientiously".

(B) The declaration, signed by the Judge and witnessed by the Secretary-General of the United Nations or his representative, shall be kept in the records of the Tribunal.

Rule 15: Disqualification of Judges

(A) A Judge may not sit on a trial or appeal in any case in which he has a personal interest or concerning which he has or has had any association which might affect his impartiality. He shall in any such circumstance withdraw, and the President shall assign another Judge to sit in his place.

(B) Any party may apply to the Presiding Judge of a Chamber for the disqualification and withdrawal of a Judge of that Chamber from a trial upon the above grounds. The Presiding Judge shall confer with the Judge in question, and if necessary the Bureau shall determine the matter. If the Bureau upholds the application, the President shall assign another Judge to sit in place of the disqualified Judge.

(C)   The Judge of the Trial Chamber who reviews an indictment against an accused, pursuant to Article 19 of the Statute and Rule 47, shall not sit as a member of the Trial Chamber for the trial of that accused.

(D)   No member of the Appeals Chamber shall sit on any appeal in a case in which he sat as a member of the Trial Chamber.

(E)   If a Judge is, for any reason, unable to continue sitting in a part-heard case, the Presiding Judge may, if that inability seems likely to be of short duration, adjourn the proceedings; otherwise he shall report to the President who may assign another Judge to the case and order either a rehearing or, with the consent of the accused, continuation of the proceedings from that point.

Rule 16: Resignation

A Judge who decides to resign shall communicate his resignation in writing to the President who shall transmit it to the Secretary-General of the United Nations.

Rule 17: Precedence

(A)   All Judges are equal in the exercise of their judicial functions, regardless of dates of election, appointment, age or period of service.

(B)   The Presiding Judges of the Trial Chambers shall take precedence according to age after the President and the Vice-President.

(C)   Judges elected or appointed on different dates shall take precedence according to the dates of their election or appointment; Judges elected or appointed on the same date shall take precedence according to age.

(D)   In case of re-election, the total period of service as a Judge of the Tribunal shall be taken into account.

SECTION 2: THE PRESIDENCY

Rule 18: Election of the President

(A)   The President shall be elected for a term of two years, or such shorter term as shall coincide with the duration of his term of office as a Judge. He may be re-elected once.

(B)   If the President ceases to be a member of the Tribunal or resigns his office before the expiration of his term, the Judges shall elect from among their number a successor for the remainder of the term.

(C)   The President shall be elected by a majority of the votes of the Judges composing the Tribunal. If no Judge obtains such a majority, the second ballot shall be limited to the two Judges who obtained the greatest number of votes on the first ballot. In the case of equality of votes on the second ballot, the Judge who takes precedence in accordance with Rule 17 shall be declared elected.

Rule 19: Functions of the President

The President shall preside at all plenary meetings of the Tribunal; he shall co-ordinate the work of the Chambers and supervise the activities of the Registry as well as exercise all the other functions conferred on him by the Statute and the Rules.

Rule 20: The Vice-President

(A)   The Vice-President shall be elected for a term of two years, or such short-term as shall coincide with the duration of his term of office as a Judge. He may be re-elected once.
(B)   The Vice-President may sit as a member of a Trial Chamber or of the Appeals Chamber.
(C)   Sub-rules 18(B) and (C) shall apply mutatis mutandis to the Vice-President.

Rule 21: Functions of the Vice-President

Subject to Sub-rule 22(B), the Vice-President shall exercise the functions of the President in case of his absence or inability to act.

Rule 22: Replacements

(A)   If neither the President nor the Vice-President can carry out the functions of the President, these shall be assumed by the senior Judge, determined in accordance with Rule 17.
(B)   If the President is unable to exercise his functions as Presiding Judge of the Appeals Chamber, that Chamber shall elect a Presiding Judge from among its number.

SECTION 3: INTERNAL FUNCTIONING OF THE TRIBUNAL

Rule 23: The Bureau

(A)   The Bureau shall be composed of the President, the Vice-President and the Presiding Judges of the Trial Chambers.
(B)   The President shall consult the other members of the Bureau on all major questions relating to the functioning of the Tribunal.
(C)   A Judge may draw the attention of any member of the Bureau to issues that in his opinion ought to be discussed by the Bureau or submitted to a plenary meeting of the Tribunal.

Rule 24: Plenary Meetings of the Tribunal

The Judges shall meet in plenary to:

(i)   elect the President and Vice-President;
(ii) adopt and amend the Rules;
(iii) adopt the Annual Report provided for in Article 34 of the Statute;
(iv) decide upon matters relating to the internal functioning of the Chambers and the Tribunal;
(v)   determine or supervise the conditions of detention;
(vi) exercise any other functions provided for in the Statute or in the Rules.

Rule 25: Dates of Plenary Sessions

(A)   The dates of the plenary sessions of the Tribunal shall normally be agreed upon in July of each year for the following calendar year.
(B)   Other plenary meetings shall be convened by the President if so requested by at least six Judges, and may be convened whenever the exercise of his functions under the Statute or the Rules so requires.

Rule 26: Quorum and Vote

(A)   The quorum for each plenary meeting of the Tribunal shall be seven Judges.
(B)   Subject to Sub-rules 6(A) and (B) and Sub-rule 18(C), the decisions of the plenary meetings of the Tribunal shall be taken by the majority of the Judges present. In the event of an equality of votes, the President or the Judge who acts in his place shall have a casting vote.

SECTION 4: THE CHAMBERS

Rule 27: Rotation

(A)   Judges shall rotate on a regular basis between the Trial Chambers and the Appeals Chamber. Rotation shall take into account the efficient disposal of cases.
(B)   The Judges shall take their places in their new Chamber as soon as the President thinks it convenient, having regard to the disposal of part-heard cases.
(C)   The President may at any time temporarily assign a member of a Trial Chamber or of the Appeals Chamber to another Chamber.

Rule 28: Assignment to Review Indictments

The President shall, in July of each year and after consultation with the Judges, assign for each month of the next calendar year a Judge of a Trial Chamber as the Judge to whom indictments shall be transmitted for review under Rule 47, and shall publish the list of assignments.

Rule 29: Deliberations

The deliberations of the Chambers shall take place in private and remain secret.

SECTION 5: THE REGISTRY

Rule 30: Appointment of the Registrar

The President shall seek the opinion of the Judges on the candidates for the post of Registrar, before consulting with the Secretary-General of the United Nations pursuant to Article 17(3) of the Statute.

Rule 31: Appointment of the Deputy Registrar and Registry Staff

The Registrar, after consultation with the Bureau, shall make his recommendations to the Secretary-General of the United Nations for the appointment of the Deputy Registrar and other Registry staff.

Rule 32: Solemn Declaration

(A) Before taking up his duties, the Registrar shall make the following declaration before the President:

"I solemnly declare that I will perform the duties incumbent upon me as Registrar of the International Tribunal for the Prosecution of Persons Responsible for Serious Violations of International Humanitarian Law Committed in the Territory of the Former Yugoslavia since 1991 in all loyalty, discretion and good conscience and that I will faithfully observe all the provisions of the Statute and the Rules of Procedure and Evidence of the Tribunal".

(B) Before taking up his duties, the Deputy Registrar shall make a similar declaration before the President.

(C) Every staff member of the Registry shall make a similar declaration before the Registrar.

Rule 33: Functions of the Registrar

The Registrar shall assist the Chambers, the plenary meetings of the Tribunal, the Judges and the Prosecutor in the performance of their functions. Under the authority of the President, he shall be responsible for the administration and servicing of the Tribunal and shall serve as its channel of communication.

Rule 34: Victims and Witnesses Unit

(A) There shall be set up under the authority of the Registrar a Victims and Witnesses Unit consisting of qualified staff to:

(i) recommend protective measures for victims and witnesses in accordance with Article 22 of the Statute; and
(ii) provide counselling and support for them, in particular in cases of rape and sexual assault.

(B) Due consideration shall be given, in the appointment of staff, to the employment of qualified women.

Rule 35: Minutes

Except where a full record is made under Rule 81, the Registrar, or Registry staff designated by him, shall take minutes of the plenary meetings of the Tribunal and of the sittings of the Chambers, other than private deliberations.

Rule 36: Record Book

The Registrar shall keep a Record Book which shall list all the particulars of each case brought before the Tribunal. The Record Book shall be open to the public.

SECTION 6: THE PROSECUTOR

Rule 37: Functions

(A) The Prosecutor shall exercise all the functions provided by the Statute in accordance with the Rules and such Regulations as may be framed by him.
(B) His powers under Parts Four to Eight of the Rules may be exercised by staff members of the Office of the Prosecutor authorised by him, or by any person acting under his direction.

Rule 38: Deputy Prosecutor

(A) The Prosecutor shall make his recommendations to the Secretary-General of the United Nations for the appointment of a Deputy Prosecutor.
(B) The Deputy Prosecutor shall exercise the functions of the Prosecutor in the event of his absence or inability to act or upon the Prosecutor's express instructions.

PART FOUR
INVESTIGATIONS AND RIGHTS OF SUSPECTS

SECTION 1: INVESTIGATIONS

Rule 39: Conduct of Investigations

In the conduct of an investigation, the Prosecutor may:

(i)   summon and question suspects, victims and witnesses and record their statements, collect evidence and conduct on-site investigations;

(ii) undertake such other matters as may appear necessary for completing the investigation and the preparation and conduct of the prosecution at the trial;

(iii) seek, to that end, the assistance of any State authority concerned, as well as of any relevant international body including the International Criminal Police Organisation (INTERPOL); and

(iv) request such orders as may be necessary from a Trial Chamber or a Judge.

Rule 40: Provisional Measures

In case of urgency, the Prosecutor may request any State:

(i)   to arrest a suspect provisionally;

(ii) to seize physical evidence;

(iii) to take all necessary measures to prevent the escape of a suspect or an accused, injury to or intimidation of a victim or witness, or the destruction of evidence.

Rule 41: Retention of Information

The Prosecutor shall be responsible for the retention, storage and security of information and physical evidence obtained in the course of his investigations.

Rule 42: Rights of Suspects during Investigation

(A)   A suspect who is to be questioned by the Prosecutor shall have the following rights, of which he shall be informed by the Prosecutor prior to questioning, in a language he speaks and understands:

(i) the right to be assisted by counsel of his choice or to have legal assistance assigned to him without payment if he does not have sufficient means to pay for it; and

(ii) the right to have the free assistance of an interpreter if he cannot understand or speak the language to be used for questioning.

(B)   Questioning of a suspect shall not proceed without the presence of counsel unless the suspect has voluntarily waived his right to counsel. In case of waiver, if the suspect subsequently expresses a desire to have counsel, questioning shall thereupon cease, and shall only resume when the suspect has obtained or has been assigned counsel.

Rule 43: Recording Questioning of Suspects

Whenever the Prosecutor questions a suspect, the questioning shall be tape-recorded or video-recorded, in accordance with the following procedure:

(i)   the suspect shall be informed in a language he speaks and understands that the questioning is being tape-recorded or video-recorded;

(ii) in the event of a break in the course of the questioning, the fact and the time of the break shall be recorded before tape-recording or video-recording ends and the time of resumption of the questioning shall also be recorded;

(iii) at the conclusion of the questioning the suspect shall be offered the opportunity to clarify anything he has said, and to add anything he may wish, and the time of conclusion shall be recorded;

(iv) the tape shall then be transcribed and a copy of the transcript supplied to the suspect, together with a copy of the recorded tape or, if multiple recording apparatus was used, one of the original recorded tapes; and

(v)   after a copy has been made, if necessary, of the recorded tape for purposes of transcription, the original recorded tape or one of the original tapes shall be sealed in the presence of the suspect under the signature of the Prosecutor and the suspect.

SECTION 2: OF COUNSEL

Rule 44: Appointment and Qualifications of Counsel

Counsel engaged by a suspect or an accused shall file his power of attorney with the Registrar at the earliest opportunity. A counsel shall be considered qualified to represent a suspect or accused if he satisfies the Registrar that he is admitted to the practice of law in a State, or is a University professor of law.

Rule 45: Assignment of Counsel

(A)   A list of counsel who speak one or both of the working languages of the Tribunal, meet the requirements of Rule 44 and have indicated their willingness to be assigned by the Tribunal to indigent suspects or accused, shall be kept by the Registrar.

(B)   The criteria for determination of indigency shall be established by the Registrar and approved by the Judges.

(C)   In assigning counsel to an indigent suspect or accused, the following procedure shall be observed:

(i)   a request for assignment of counsel shall be made to the Registrar;

(ii) the Registrar shall enquire into the means of the suspect or accused and determine whether the criteria of indigency are met;

(iii) if he decides that the criteria are met, he shall assign counsel from the list; if he decides to the contrary, he shall inform the suspect or accused that the request is refused.

(D)   If a request is refused, a further request may be made by a suspect or an accused to the Registrar upon showing a change in circumstances.

(E)   The Registrar shall assign counsel to a suspect or an accused who fails to obtain counsel or to request assignment of counsel, unless the suspect or the accused elects in writing to conduct his own defence.

(F)   The Registrar shall, in consultation with the Judges, establish the criteria for the payment of fees to assigned counsel.

Rule 46: Misconduct of Counsel

(A)   A Chamber may, after a warning, refuse audience to counsel if, in its opinion, his conduct is offensive, abusive or otherwise obstructs the proper conduct of the proceedings.

(B)   A Judge or a Chamber may also, with the approval of the President, communicate any misconduct of counsel to the professional body regulating the conduct of counsel in his State of admission or, if a professor and not otherwise admitted to the profession, to the governing body of his University.

PART FIVE
PRE-TRIAL PROCEEDINGS

SECTION 1: INDICTMENTS

Rule 47 Submission of Indictment by the Prosecutor

(A)   If in the course of an investigation the Prosecutor is satisfied that there is sufficient evidence to provide reasonable grounds for believing that a suspect has committed a crime within the jurisdiction of the Tribunal, he shall prepare and forward to the Registrar an indictment for confirmation by a Judge, together with supporting material.

(B)   The indictment shall set forth the name and particulars of the suspect, and a concise statement of the facts of the case and of the crime with which the suspect is charged.

(C)   The Registrar shall forward the indictment and accompanying material to the Judge currently assigned under Rule 28, who will inform the Prosecutor of the date fixed for review of the indictment.

(D)   On reviewing the indictment, the Judge shall hear the Prosecutor, who may present additional material in support of any count. The Judge may confirm or dismiss each count or may adjourn the review.

(E)   The dismissal of a count in an indictment shall not preclude the Prosecutor from subsequently bringing a new indictment based on the acts underlying that count if supported by additional evidence.

Rule 48: Joinder of Accused

Persons accused of the same or different crimes committed in the course of the same transaction may be jointly charged and tried.

Rule 49: Joinder of Crimes

Two or more crimes may be joined in one indictment if the series of acts committed together form the same transaction, and the said crimes were committed by the same accused.

Rule 50: Amendment of Indictment

The Prosecutor may amend an indictment, without leave, at any time before its confirmation, but thereafter only with leave of the Judge who confirmed it or, if at trial, with leave of the Trial Chamber. If leave to amend is granted, the amended indictment shall be transmitted to the accused and to his counsel and where necessary the date for trial shall be postponed to ensure adequate time for the preparation of the defence.

Rule 51: Withdrawal of Indictment

(A)   The Prosecutor may withdraw an indictment, without leave, at any time before its confirmation, but thereafter only with leave of the Judge who confirmed it or, if at trial, only with leave of the Trial Chamber.
(B)   The withdrawal of the indictment shall be promptly notified to the suspect or the accused and to his counsel.

Rule 52: Public Character of Indictment

Subject to Rule 53, upon confirmation by a Judge of a Trial Chamber, the indictment shall be made public.

Rule 53: Non-disclosure of Indictment

(A)   When confirming an indictment the Judge may, in consultation with the Prosecutor, order that there be no public disclosure of the indictment until it is served on the accused, or, in the case of joint accused, on all the accused.
(B)   A Judge or Trial Chamber may, in consultation with the Prosecutor, also order that there be no public disclosure of an indictment, or part thereof, or of any particular document or information, if satisfied that the making of such an order is in the interests of justice.

SECTION 2: ORDERS AND WARRANTS

Rule 54: General Rule

At the request of either party or *proprio motu*, a Judge or a Trial Chamber may issue such orders, summonses and warrants as may be necessary for the purposes of an investigation or for the preparation or conduct of the trial.

Rule 55: Execution of Arrest Warrants

(A)   A warrant of arrest shall be signed by a Judge and shall bear the seal of the Tribunal. It shall be accompanied by a copy of the indictment, and a statement of the rights of the accused. These rights include those set forth in Article 21 of the Statute, and in Rules 42 and 43 *mutatis mutandis*, together with the right of the accused to remain silent, and to be cautioned that any statement he makes shall be recorded and may be used in evidence.

(B)   A warrant for the arrest of the accused and his surrender to the Tribunal shall be transmitted by the Registrar to the national authorities of the State in whose territory or under whose jurisdiction or control the accused resides, or was last known to be, together with instructions that at the time of arrest the indictment and the statement of the rights of the accused be read to him in a language he understands and that he be cautioned in that language.

(C)   When an arrest warrant issued by the Tribunal is executed, a member of the Prosecutor's Office may be present as from the time of arrest.

Rule 56: Co-operation of States

The State to which a warrant of arrest is transmitted shall act promptly and with all due diligence to ensure proper and effective execution thereof, in accordance with Article 29 of the Statute.

Rule 57: Procedure after Arrest

Upon the arrest of the accused, the State concerned shall detain him, and shall promptly notify the Registrar. The transfer of the accused to the seat of the Tribunal shall be arranged between the State authorities concerned and the Registrar.

Rule 58: National Extradition Provisions

The obligations laid down in Article 29 of the Statute shall prevail over any legal impediment to the surrender or transfer of the accused to the Tribunal which may exist under the national law or extradition treaties of the State concerned.

Rule 59: Failure to Execute a Warrant

(A)   Where the State to which a warrant of arrest has been transmitted has been unable to execute the warrant, it shall report forthwith its inability to the Registrar, and the reasons therefor.

(B)   If, within a reasonable time after the warrant of arrest has been transmitted to the State, no report is made on action taken, this shall be deemed a failure to execute the warrant of arrest and the Tribunal, through the President, may notify the Security Council accordingly.

Rule 60: Advertisement of Indictment

At the request of the Prosecutor, a form of advertisement shall be transmitted by the Registrar to the national authorities of any State or States in whose territory the Prosecutor has reason to believe that the accused may be found, for publication in newspapers having wide circulation in that territory, intimating to the accused that service of an indictment against him is sought.

Rule 61: Procedure in Case of Failure to Execute a Warrant

(A)   If a warrant of arrest has not been executed, and personal service of the indictment has consequently not been effected, and the Prosecutor satisfies a Judge of a Trial Chamber that:

   (i)   he has taken all reasonable steps to effect personal service, including recourse to the appropriate authorities of the State in whose territory or under whose jurisdiction and control the person to be served resides or was last known to him to be; and

   (ii) he has otherwise tried to inform the accused of the existence of the indictment by seeking publication of newspaper advertisements pursuant to the Judge shall order that the indictment be submitted by the Prosecutor to the Trial Chamber.

(B)   Upon obtaining such an order the Prosecutor shall submit the indictment to the Trial Chamber in open court, together with all the evidence that was before the Judge who initially confirmed the indictment.

(C)   If the Trial Chamber is satisfied on that evidence, together with such additional evidence as the Prosecutor may tender, that there are reasonable grounds for believing that the accused has committed all or any of the crimes charged in the indictment, it shall so determine. The Trial Chamber shall have the relevant parts of the indictment read out by the Prosecutor together with an account of the efforts to effect service referred to in Sub-rule (A) above.

(D)   The Trial Chamber shall also issue an international arrest warrant in respect of the accused which shall be transmitted to all States.

(E)   If the Prosecutor satisfies the Trial Chamber that the failure to effect personal service was due in whole or in part to a failure or refusal of a State to cooperate with the Tribunal in accordance with Article 29 of the Statute, the Trial Chamber shall so certify, in which event the President shall notify the Security Council.

Rule 62: Initial Appearance of Accused

Upon his transfer to the seat of the Tribunal, the accused shall be brought before a Trial Chamber without delay, and shall be formally charged. The Trial Chamber shall:

   (i)   satisfy itself that the right of the accused to counsel is respected;

   (ii) read or have the indictment read to the accused in a language he speaks and understands, and satisfy itself that the accused understands the indictment;

(iii) call upon the accused to enter a plea of guilty or not guilty; should the accused fail to do so, enter a plea of not guilty on his behalf;

(iv) instruct the Registrar to set a date for trial.

Rule 63: Questioning of Accused

After the initial appearance of the accused the Prosecutor shall not question him unless his counsel is present and the questioning is tape-recorded or video-recorded in accordance with the procedure provided for in Rule 43. The Prosecutor shall at the beginning of the questioning caution the accused that he is not obliged to say anything unless he wishes to do so but that whatever he says may be given in evidence.

Rule 64: Detention on Remand

Upon his transfer to the seat of the Tribunal, the accused shall be detained in facilities provided by the host country, or by another country. The President may, on the application of a party, request modification of the conditions of detention of an accused.

Rule 65: Provisional Release

(A) Once detained, an accused may not be released except upon an order of a Trial Chamber.

(B) Release may be ordered by a Trial Chamber only in exceptional circumstances, and only if it is satisfied that the accused will appear for trial and, if released, will not pose a danger to any victim, witness or other person.

(C) The Trial Chamber may impose such conditions upon the release of the accused as it may determine appropriate, including the execution of a bail bond and the observance of such conditions as are necessary to ensure his presence for trial and the protection of others.

(D) If necessary, the Trial Chamber may issue a warrant of arrest to secure the presence of an accused who has been released or is for any other reason at liberty.

SECTION 3: PRODUCTION OF EVIDENCE

Rule 66: Disclosure by the Prosecutor

(A) The Prosecutor shall make available to the defence, as soon as practicable after the initial appearance of the accused, copies of the supporting material which accompanied the indictment when confirmation was sought.

(B) The Prosecutor shall on request permit the defence to inspect any books, documents, photographs and tangible objects in his custody or control, which are material to the preparation of the defence, or are intended for use by the Prosecutor as evidence at trial or were obtained from or belonged to the accused.

Rule 67: Reciprocal Disclosure

(A) As early as reasonably practicable and in any event prior to the commencement of the trial:

    (i) the Prosecutor shall notify the defence of the names of the witnesses that he intends to call in proof of the guilt of the accused and in rebuttal of any defence plea of which the Prosecutor has received notice in accordance with Sub-rule (ii) below;

    (ii) the defence shall notify the Prosecutor of its intent to offer:

        (a) the defence of alibi; in which case the notification shall specify the place or places at which the accused claims to have been present at the time of the alleged crime and the names and addresses of witnesses and any other evidence upon which the accused intends to rely to establish the alibi;

        (b) any special defence, including that of diminished or lack of mental responsibility; in which case the notification shall specify the names and addresses of witnesses and any other evidence upon which the accused intends to rely to establish the special defence.

(B) Failure of the defence to provide notice under this Rule shall not limit the right of the accused to testify on the above defences.

(C) If the defence makes a request pursuant to Sub-rule 66(B), the Prosecutor shall be entitled to inspect any books, documents, photographs and tangible objects, which are within the custody or control of the defence and which it intends to use as evidence at the trial.

(D) If either party discovers additional evidence or material which should have been produced earlier pursuant to the Rules, that party shall promptly notify the other party and the Trial Chamber of the existence of the additional evidence or material.

Rule 68: Disclosure of Exculpatory Evidence

The Prosecutor shall, as soon as practicable, disclose to the defence the existence of evidence known to the Prosecutor which in any way tends to suggest the innocence or mitigate the guilt of the accused of a crime charged in the indictment.

Rule 69: Protection of Victims and Witnesses

(A) In exceptional circumstances, the Prosecutor may apply to a Trial Chamber to order the non-disclosure of the identity of a victim or witness who may be in danger or at risk until such person is brought under the protection of the Tribunal.

(B) Subject to Rule 75, the identity of the victim or witness shall be disclosed in sufficient time prior to the trial to allow adequate time for preparation of the defence.

Rule 70: Matters not Subject to Disclosure

(A) Notwithstanding the provisions of Rules 66 and 67, reports, memoranda, or other internal documents prepared by a party, its assistants or representatives in connection with the investigation or preparation of the case, are not subject to disclosure or notification under those Rules.

(B) If the Prosecutor is in possession of information which has been provided to him on a confidential basis and which has been used solely for the purpose of generating new evidence, that initial information and its origin shall not be disclosed by the Prosecutor without the consent of the person or entity providing the initial information.[5]

SECTION 4: DEPOSITIONS

Rule 71: Depositions

(A) At the request of either party, a Trial Chamber may, in exceptional circumstances and in the interests of justice, order that a deposition be taken for use at trial, and appoint, for that purpose, a Presiding Officer.

(B) The motion for the taking of a deposition shall be in writing and shall indicate the name and whereabouts of the person whose deposition is sought, the date and place at which the deposition is to be taken, a statement of the matters on which the person is to be examined, and of the exceptional circumstances justifying the taking of the deposition.

(C) If the motion is granted, the party at whose request the deposition is to betaken shall give reasonable notice to the other party, who shall have the right to attend the taking of the deposition and cross-examine the person whose deposition is being taken.

(D) Deposition evidence may also be given by means of a video-conference.

(E) The Presiding Officer shall ensure that the deposition is taken in accordance with the Rules and that a record is made of the deposition, including cross-examination and objections raised by either party for decision by the Trial Chamber. He shall transmit the record to the Trial Chamber.

---

[5] Amended Rule 70, adopted by the Tribunal on October 4 1994.

SECTION 5 PRELIMINARY MOTIONS

Rule 72: General Provisions

(A) After the initial appearance of the accused, either party may move before a Trial Chamber for appropriate relief or ruling. Such motions may be written or oral, at the discretion of the Trial Chamber.

(B) The Trial Chamber shall dispose of preliminary motions in *limine litis*.

Rule 73: Preliminary Motions by Accused

(A) Preliminary motions by the accused shall include:

  (i)   objections based on lack of jurisdiction;
  (ii) objections based on defects in the form of the indictment;
  (iii) applications for the exclusion of evidence obtained from the accused or having belonged to him;
  (iv) applications for severance of crimes joined in one indictment under Rule 49, or for separate trials under Sub-rule 82(B);
  (v)   objections based on the denial of request for assignment of counsel.

(B) Any of the motions by the accused referred to in Sub-rule (A) shall be brought within sixty days after his initial appearance, and in any case before the hearing on the merits.

(C) Failure to apply within the time-limit prescribed shall constitute a waiver of the right. Upon a showing of good cause, the Trial Chamber may grant relief from the waiver.

PART SIX
PROCEEDINGS BEFORE TRIAL CHAMBERS

SECTION 1 GENERAL PROVISIONS

Rule 74: Amicus Curiae

A Chamber may, if it considers it desirable for the proper determination of the case, invite or grant leave to a State, organisation or person to appear before it and make submissions on any issue specified by the Chamber.

Rule 75: Protection of Victims and Witnesses

(A) A Judge or a Chamber may, *proprio motu* or at the request of either party, or of the victim or witness concerned, order appropriate measures for the privacy and protection of victims and witnesses, provided that the measures are consistent with the rights of the accused.

(B)   A Chamber may hold an *ex parte* (*non-contradictoire*) proceeding to determine whether to order:

   (i)   measures to prevent disclosure to the public or the media of the identity or whereabouts of a victim or a witness, or of persons related to or associated with him by such means as:

      (a) expunging names and identifying information from the Chamber's public records;
      (b) non-disclosure to the public of any records identifying the victim;
      (c) giving of testimony through image- or voice-altering devices or closed circuit television; and
      (d) assignment of a pseudonym;

   (ii) closed sessions, in accordance with Rule 79;
   (iii) appropriate measures to facilitate the testimony of vulnerable victims and witnesses, such as one-way closed circuit television.

(C)   A Chamber shall, whenever necessary, control the manner of questioning to avoid any harassment or intimidation.

Rule 76: Solemn Declaration by Interpreters and Translators

Before performing any duties, an interpreter or a translator shall solemnly declare to do so faithfully, independently, impartially and with full respect for the duty of confidentiality.

Rule 77: Contempt of Court

(A)   Subject to the provisions of Sub-rule 90(D), a witness who refuses or fails contumaciously to answer a question relevant to the issue before a Chamber may be found in contempt of the Tribunal. The Chamber may impose a fine not exceeding US $10,000 or a term of imprisonment not exceeding six months.
(B)   The Chamber may, however, relieve the witness of the duty to answer, for reasons which it deems appropriate.
(C)   Payment of a fine shall be made to the Registrar to be held in a separate account.

Rule 78: Open Sessions

All proceedings before a Trial Chamber, other than deliberations of the Chamber, shall be held in public, unless otherwise provided.

Rule 79: Closed Sessions

(A)   The Trial Chamber may order that the press and the public be excluded from all or part of the proceedings for reasons of:

   (i)   public order or morality;
   (ii) safety, security or non-disclosure of the identity of a victim or witness as provided in Rule 75; or
   (iii) the protection of the interests of justice.

(B)   The Trial Chamber shall make public the reasons for its order.

Rule 80: Control of Proceedings

(A)   The Trial Chamber may exclude a person from the courtroom in order to protect the right of the accused to a fair and public trial, or to maintain the dignity and decorum of the proceedings.
(B)   The Trial Chamber may order the removal of an accused from the courtroom and continue the proceedings in his absence if he has persisted in disruptive conduct following a warning that he may be removed.

Rule 81: Records of Proceedings and Evidence

(A)   The Registrar shall cause to be made and preserve a full and accurate record of all proceedings, including audio recordings, transcripts and, when deemed necessary by the Trial Chamber, video recordings.
(B)   The Trial Chamber may order the disclosure of all or part of the record of closed proceedings when the reasons for ordering its non-disclosure no longer exist.
(C)   The Registrar shall retain and preserve all physical evidence offered during the proceedings.
(D)   Photography, video-recording or audio-recording of the trial, otherwise than by the Registry, may be authorised at the discretion of the Trial Chamber.

SECTION 2 CASE PRESENTATION

Rule 82: Joint and Separate Trials

(A)   In joint trials, each accused shall be accorded the same rights as if he were being tried separately.
(B)   The Trial Chamber may order that persons accused jointly under Rule 48 be tried separately if it considers it necessary in order to avoid a conflict of interests that might cause serious prejudice to an accused, or to protect the interests of justice.

Rule 83: Instruments of Restraint

Instruments of restraint, such as handcuffs, shall not be used except as a precaution against escape during transfer or for security reasons, and shall be removed when the accused appears before a Chamber.

Rule 84: Opening Statements

Before presentation of evidence by the Prosecutor, each party may make an opening statement. The defence may however elect to make its statement after the Prosecutor has concluded his presentation of evidence and before the presentation of evidence for the defence.

Rule 85: Presentation of Evidence

(A)   Each party is entitled to call witnesses and present evidence. Unless otherwise directed by the Trial Chamber in the interests of justice, evidence at the trial shall be presented in the following sequence:

    (i)   evidence for the prosecution;
    (ii)   evidence for the defence;
    (iii) prosecution evidence in rebuttal;
    (iv)   defence evidence in rejoinder;
    (v)   evidence ordered by the Trial Chamber pursuant to Rule 98.

(B)   Examination-in-chief, cross-examination and re-examination shall be allowed in each case. It shall be for the party calling a witness to examine him in chief, but a Judge may at any stage put any question to the witness.

(C)   The accused may, if he so desires, appear as a witness in his own defence.

Rule 86: Closing Arguments

After the presentation of all the evidence, the Prosecutor may present an initial argument, to which the defence may reply. The Prosecutor may, if he wishes, present a rebuttal argument, to which the defence may present a rejoinder.

Rule 87: Deliberations

(A)   When both parties have completed their presentation of the case, the Presiding Judge shall declare the hearing closed, and the Trial Chamber shall deliberate in private. A finding of guilt may be reached only when a majority of the Trial Chamber is satisfied that guilt has been proved beyond reasonable doubt.

(B)   The Trial Chamber shall vote separately on each charge contained in the indictment. If two or more accused are tried together under Rule 48, separate findings shall be made as to each accused.

Rule 88: Judgement

(A)   The judgement shall be pronounced in public and in the presence of the accused, on a date of which notice shall have been given to the parties and counsel.

(B)   If the Trial Chamber finds the accused guilty of a crime and concludes from the evidence that unlawful taking of property by the accused was associated with it, it shall make a specific finding to that effect in its judgement. The Trial Chamber may order restitution as provided in Rule 105.

(C)   A Judge of the Trial Chamber may append a separate or dissenting opinion to the judgement.

SECTION 3 RULES OF EVIDENCE

Rule 89: General Provisions

(A) The rules of evidence set forth in this Section shall govern the proceedings before the Chambers. The Chambers shall not be bound by national rules of evidence.

(B) In cases not otherwise provided for in this Section, a Chamber shall apply rules of evidence which will best favour a fair determination of the matter before it and are consonant with the spirit of the Statute and the general principles of law.

(C) A Chamber may admit any relevant evidence which it deems to have probative value.

(D) A Chamber may exclude evidence if its probative value is substantially outweighed by the need to ensure a fair trial.

(E) A Chamber may request verification of the authenticity of evidence obtained out of court.

Rule 90: Testimony of Witnesses

(A) Witnesses shall, in principle, be heard directly by the Chambers. In cases, however, where it is not possible to secure the presence of a witness, a Chamber may order that the witness be heard by means of a deposition as provided for in Rule 71.

(B) Every witness shall, before giving evidence, make the following solemn declaration:

"I solemnly declare that I will speak the truth, the whole truth and nothing but the truth".

(C) A witness, other than an expert, who has not yet testified shall not be present when the testimony of another witness is given. However, a witness who has heard the testimony of another witness shall not for that reason alone be disqualified from testifying.

(D) A witness may decline to make any statement which might tend to incriminate him.

Rule 91: False Testimony under Solemn Declaration

(A) A Chamber, on its own initiative or at the request of a party, may warn a witness of the duty to tell the truth and the consequences that may result from a failure to do so.

(B) If a Chamber has strong grounds for believing that a witness has knowingly and wilfully given false testimony, it may direct the Prosecutor to investigate the matter with a view to the preparation and submission of an indictment for false testimony.

(C) The rules of procedure and evidence in Parts Four to Eight shall apply mutatis mutandis to proceedings under this Rule.

(D) No Judge who sat as a member of the Trial Chamber before which the witness appeared shall sit for the trial of the witness for false testimony.

(E) The maximum penalty for false testimony under solemn declaration shall be a fine of US$ 10,000 or a term of imprisonment of twelve months, or both. The payment of any fine imposed shall be made to the Registrar to be held in the account referred to in Sub-rule 77(C).

Rule 92: Confessions

A confession by the accused given during questioning by the Prosecutor shall, provided the requirements of Rule 63 were strictly complied with, be presumed to have been free and voluntary unless the contrary is proved.

Rule 93: Evidence of Consistent Pattern of Conduct

Evidence of a consistent pattern of conduct may be admissible in the interests of justice.

Rule 94: Judicial Notice

A Trial Chamber shall not require proof of facts of common knowledge but shall take judicial notice thereof.

Rule 95: Evidence Obtained by Means Contrary to Internationally Protected Human Rights

Evidence obtained directly or indirectly by means which constitute a serious violation of internationally protected human rights shall not be admissible.

Rule 96: Evidence in Cases of Sexual Assault

In cases of sexual assault:

(i)   no corroboration of the victim's testimony shall be required;

(ii) consent shall not be allowed as a defence if the victim:

- has been subjected to or threatened with or has had reason to fear violence, duress, detention or psychological oppression, or
- has reasonably believed that if she did not submit, another might be so subjected, threatened or put in fear;

(iii) prior sexual conduct of the victim shall not be admitted in evidence.

Rule 97: Lawyer-Client Privilege

All communications between lawyer and client shall be regarded as privileged, and consequently not subject to disclosure at trial, unless:

(i)   the client consents to such disclosure; or

(ii) the client has voluntarily disclosed the content of the communication to a third party, and that third party then gives evidence of that disclosure.

Rule 98: Power of Chambers to Order Production of Additional Evidence

A Trial Chamber may order either party to produce additional evidence. It may itself summon witnesses and order their attendance.

SECTION 4 SENTENCING PROCEDURE

Rule 99: Status of the Acquitted Person

(A) In case of acquittal, the accused shall be released immediately.
(B) If, at the time the judgement is pronounced, the Prosecutor advises the Trial Chamber in open court of his intention to file notice of appeal pursuant to Rule 108, the Trial Chamber may, at the request of the Prosecutor, issue a warrant for the arrest of the accused to take effect immediately.

Rule 100: Pre-sentencing Procedure

If a Trial Chamber finds the accused guilty of a crime, the Prosecutor and the defence may submit any relevant information that may assist the Trial Chamber in determining an appropriate sentence.

Rule 101: Penalties

(A) A convicted person may be sentenced to imprisonment for a term up to and including the remainder of his life.
(B) In determining the sentence, the Trial Chamber shall take into account the factors mentioned in Article 24(2) of the Statute, as well as such factors as:

(i) any aggravating circumstances;
(ii) any mitigating circumstances including the substantial co-operation with the Prosecutor by the convicted person before or after conviction;
(iii) the general practice regarding prison sentences in the courts of the former Yugoslavia;
(iv) the period, if any, during which the convicted person was detained in custody pending his surrender to the Tribunal or pending trial;
(v) the extent to which any penalty imposed by a national court on the convicted person for the same act has already been served, as referred to in Article 10(3) of the Statute.

(C) The Trial Chamber shall indicate whether multiple sentences shall be served consecutively or concurrently.
(D) The sentence shall be pronounced in public and in the presence of the convicted person, subject to Sub-rule 102(B).

Rule 102: Status of the Convicted Person

(A)   The sentence shall begin to run from the day it is pronounced under sub-rule 101(D). However, as soon as notice of appeal is given, the enforcement of the judgement shall thereupon be stayed until the decision on the appeal has been delivered, the convicted person meanwhile remaining in detention, as provided Rule 64.

(B)   If, by a previous decision of the Trial Chamber, the convicted person has been released, or is for any other reason at liberty, and he is not present when the judgement is pronounced, the Trial Chamber shall issue a warrant for his arrest. On arrest, he shall be notified of the conviction and sentence, and the procedure provided in Rule 103 shall be followed.

Rule 103: Place of Imprisonment

(A)   Imprisonment shall be served in a State designated by the Tribunal from a list of States which have indicated their willingness to accept convicted persons.

(B)   Transfer of the convicted person to that State shall be effected as soon as possible after the time-limit for appeal has elapsed.

Rule 104: Supervision of Imprisonment

All sentences of imprisonment shall be supervised by the Tribunal or a body designated by it.

Rule 105: Restitution of Property

(A)   After a judgement of conviction containing a specific finding as provided in Sub-rule 88(B), the Trial Chamber shall, at the request of the Prosecutor, or may, at its own initiative, hold a special hearing to determine the matter of the restitution of the property or the proceeds thereof, and may in the meantime order such provisional measures for the preservation and protection of the property or proceeds as it considers appropriate.

(B)   The determination may extend to such property or its proceeds, even in the hands of third parties not otherwise connected with the crime of which the convicted person has been found guilty.

(C)   Such third parties shall be summoned before the Trial Chamber and be given an opportunity to justify their claim to the property or its proceeds.

(D)   Should the Trial Chamber be able to determine the rightful owner on the balance of probabilities, it shall order the restitution either of the property or the proceeds as appropriate.

(E)   Should the Trial Chamber not be able to determine ownership, it shall notify the competent national authorities and request them so to determine.

(F)   The Registrar shall transmit to the competent national authorities any summonses, orders and requests issued by a Trial Chamber pursuant to Sub-rules (C), (D) and (E).

Rule 106: compensation to victims

(A) The registrar shall transmit to the competent authorities of the states concerned the judgement finding the accused guilty of a crime which has caused injury to a victim.

(B) Pursuant to the relevant national legislation, a victim or persons claiming through him may bring an action in a national court or other competent body to obtain compensation.

(C) For the purposes of a claim made under sub-rule (b) the judgement of the tribunal shall be final and binding as to the criminal responsibility of the convicted person for such injury.

PART SEVEN
APPELLATE PROCEEDINGS

Rule 107: General Provision

The rules of procedure and evidence that govern proceedings in the Trial Chambers shall apply *mutatis mutandis* to proceedings in the Appeals Chamber.

Rule 108: Notice of Appeal

A party seeking to appeal a judgement shall, not more than thirty days from the date on which the judgement was pronounced, file with the Registrar and serve upon the other party a written notice of appeal, setting forth the grounds.

Rule 109: Record on Appeal

(A) The record on appeal shall consist of the parts of the trial record, as certified by the Registrar, designated by the parties.

(B) The parties, within thirty days of the certification of the trial record by the Registrar, may by agreement designate the parts of that record which, in their opinion, are necessary for the decision on the appeal.

(C) Should the parties fail so to agree within that time, the Appellant and the Respondent shall each designate to the Registrar, within sixty days of the certification, the parts of the trial record which he considers necessary for the decision on the appeal.

(D) The Appeals Chamber shall remain free to call for the whole of the trial record.

Rule 110: Copies of Record

The Registrar shall make a sufficient number of copies of the record on appeal for the use of the Judges of the Appeals Chamber and of the parties.

Rule 111: Appellant's Brief

An Appellant's brief of argument and authorities shall be served on the other party and filed with the Registrar within ninety days of the certification of the record.

Rule 112: Respondent's Brief

A Respondent's brief of argument and authorities shall be served on the other party and filed with the Registrar within thirty days of the filing of the Appellant's brief.

Rule 113: Brief in Reply

An Appellant may file a brief in reply within fifteen days after the filing of the Respondent's brief.

Rule 114: Date of Hearing

After the expiry of the time-limits for filing the briefs provided for in Rules 111, 112 and 113, the Appeals Chamber shall set the date for the hearing and the Registrar shall notify the parties.

Rule 115: Additional Evidence

(A)   A party may apply by motion to present before the Appeals Chamber additional evidence which was not available to it at the trial. Such motion must be served on the other party and filed with the Registrar not less than fifteen days before the date of the hearing.

(B)   The Appeals Chamber shall authorise the presentation of such evidence if it considers that the interests of justice so require.

Rule 116: Extension of Time-limits

The Appeals Chamber may grant a motion to extend a time-limit upon a showing of good cause.

Rule 117: Judgement

(A)   The Appeals Chamber shall pronounce judgement on the basis of the record on appeal together with such additional evidence as has been presented to it.

(B)   The judgement shall be pronounced in public, and in the presence of the accused, on a date of which notice shall have been given to the parties and counsel.

Rule 118: Status of the Accused Following Appeal

(A)   A sentence pronounced by the Appeals Chamber shall be enforced immediately.

(B)   Where the accused is not present when the judgement is due to be delivered, either as having been acquitted on all charges or as a result of an order issued pursuant to Rule 65, or for any other reason, the Appeals Chamber may deliver its judgement in the absence of the accused and shall, unless it pronounces his acquittal, order his arrest or surrender to the Tribunal.

PART EIGHT
REVIEW PROCEEDINGS

Rule 119 Request for Review

Where a new fact has been discovered which was not known to the moving party at the time of the proceedings before a Trial Chamber or the Appeals Chamber, and could not have been discovered through the exercise of due diligence, the defence or, within one year after the final judgement has been pronounced, the Prosecutor, may make a motion to that Chamber for review of the judgement.

Rule 120: Preliminary Examination

If a majority of Judges of the Chamber that pronounced the judgement agree that the new fact, if proved, could have been a decisive factor in reaching a decision, the Chamber shall review the judgement, and pronounce a further judgement after hearing the parties.

Rule 121: Appeals

The judgement of a Trial Chamber on review may be appealed in accordance with the provisions of Part Seven.

Rule 122: Return of Case to Trial Chamber

If the judgement to be reviewed is under appeal at the time the motion for review is filed, the Appeals Chamber may return the case to the Trial Chamber for disposition of the motion.

PART NINE
PARDON AND COMMUTATION OF SENTENCE

Rule 123: Notification by States

If, according to the law of the State in which a convicted person is imprisoned, he is eligible for pardon or commutation of sentence, the State shall, in accordance with Article 28 of the Statute, notify the Tribunal of such eligibility.

Rule 124: Determination by the President

The President shall, upon such notice, determine, in consultation with the Judges, whether pardon or commutation is appropriate.

Rule 125: General Standards for Granting Pardon or Commutation

In determining whether pardon or commutation is appropriate, the President shall take into account, inter alia, the gravity of the crime or crimes for which the prisoner was convicted, the treatment of similarly-situated prisoners, the prisoner's demonstration of rehabilitation, as well as any substantial co-operation of the prisoner with the Prosecutor.

74. STATUTE OF THE INTERNATIONAL TRIBUNAL FOR RWANDA

Editors' Notes

The creation of the International Criminal Tribunal for Rwanda by the UN Security Council in 1994[1] drew heavily on the experience and principles of the Tribunal for the Former Yugoslavia. Prior to the establishment of the Tribunal, the United Nations Security Council had established a Commission of Experts[2] to report on evidence of individual criminal responsibility for the atrocities reported in Rwanda. The Tribunal was established on the basis of the findings of the Committee of Experts, and while it is a separate entity to the Yugoslav Tribunal, the Security Council recognised that it would have "a similar legal approach" and "certain organisational and institutional links" so as to ensure "unity of legal approach, as well as economy and efficiency of resources".[3] Thus, the Statute for the Tribunal in Rwanda provides that the appeals chamber and prosecutor for the Yugoslav Tribunal will also serve the Rwandan Tribunal (Articles 12 and 15). The Tribunal for Rwanda will also utilise the Rules of Procedure and Evidence drawn up for the Yugoslav Tribunal (Article 14).

A significant difference between the Rwanda and Yugoslav Tribunals lies in the jurisdiction of the two courts. The Rwandan Tribunal is concerned with serious violations of international humanitarian law committed in the territory of Rwanda committed in 1994 (Article 1), in particular genocide (Article 2), crimes against humanity (Article 2) and violations of the common Article 3 of the Geneva Conventions (Article 4). While the Yugoslav and Rwandan Tribunals reproduce provisions of the Genocide Convention verbatim, the definition of crimes against humanity within the Rwandan Statute does not require any connection with war. The inclusion of the common Article 3 of the Geneva Conventions and Additional Protocol II into the Statute for the Rwandan Tribunal, which deals with an internal rather than international conflict "reflects a more expansive approach to the choice of the applicable law than the one underlying the statute of the Yugoslav Tribunal".[4]

Indictments are currently being issued for inhumane acts committed against the civilian population of Rwanda.[5]

Having been established by the Security Council acting under Chapter VII of the Charter of the United Nations, the International Criminal Tribunal for the Prosecution of Persons Responsible for Genocide and Other Serious Violations of

---

[1] See: Security Council Resolution 955, 8 Nov. 1994. Reprinted at (1994) 33 ILM 1602.

[2] Security Council Resolution 935, 1 July 1994.

[3] See: Report of the Secretary-General pursuant to paragraph 5 of Security Council Resolution 955 (1994), UN Doc. S/1995/134, para. 9.

[4] Ibid. para. 12. See also: Meron, T. (1995). "International Criminalization of Internal Atrocities". 89 AJIL 554.

[5] See: Akhavan, P. (1996). "The International Criminal Tribunal for Rwanda: The Politics and Pragmatics of Punishment". 90 AJIL 501.

International Humanitarian Law Committed in the Territory of Rwanda and Rwandan citizens responsible for genocide and other such violations committed in the territory of neighbouring States, between 1 January 1994 and 31 December 1994 (hereinafter referred to as "the International Tribunal for Rwanda") shall function in accordance with the provisions of the present Statute.

Article 1: Competence of the International Tribunal for Rwanda

The International Tribunal for Rwanda shall have the power to prosecute persons responsible for serious violations of international humanitarian law committed in the territory of Rwanda and Rwandan citizens responsible for such violations committed in the territory of neighbouring States, between 1 January 1994 and 31 December 1994, in accordance with the provisions of the present Statute.

Article 2: Genocide

1. The International Tribunal for Rwanda shall have the power to prosecute persons committing genocide as defined in paragraph 2 of this article or of committing any of the other acts enumerated in paragraph 3 of this article.
2. Genocide means any of the following acts committed with intent to destroy, in whole or in part, a national, ethnical, racial or religious group, as such:

    (a) Killing members of the group;
    (b) Causing serious bodily or mental harm to members of the group;
    (c) Deliberately inflicting on the group conditions of life calculated to bring about its physical destruction in whole or in part;
    (d) Imposing measures intended to prevent births within the group;
    (e) Forcibly transferring children of the group to another group.

3. The following acts shall be punishable:

    (a) Genocide;
    (b) Conspiracy to commit genocide;
    (c) Direct and public incitement to commit genocide;
    (d) Attempt to commit genocide;
    (e) Complicity in genocide.

Article 3: Crimes against humanity

The International Tribunal for Rwanda shall have the power to prosecute persons responsible for the following crimes when committed as part of a widespread or systematic attack against any civilian population on national, political, ethnic, racial or religious grounds:

    (a) Murder;
    (b) Extermination;
    (c) Enslavement;
    (d) Deportation;
    (e) Imprisonment;

(f)   Torture;

(g)   Rape;

(h)   Persecutions on political, racial and religious grounds;

(i)   Other inhumane acts.

Article 4: Violations of Article 3 common to the Geneva Conventions and of Additional Protocol II

The International Tribunal for Rwanda shall have the power to prosecute persons committing or ordering to be committed serious violations of Article 3 common to the Geneva Conventions of 12 August 1949 for the Protection of War Victims, and of Additional Protocol II thereto of 8 June 1977. These violations shall include, but shall not be limited to:

(a)   Violence to life, health and physical or mental well-being of persons, in particular murder as well as cruel treatment such as torture, mutilation or any form of corporal punishment;

(b)   Collective punishments;

(c)   Taking of hostages;

(d)   Acts of terrorism;

(e)   Outrages upon personal dignity, in particular humiliating and degrading treatment, rape, enforced prostitution and any form of indecent assault;

(f)   Pillage;

(g)   The passing of sentences and the carrying out of executions without previous judgment pronounced by a regularly constituted court, affording all the judicial guarantees which are recognized as indispensable by civilized peoples;

(h)   Threats to commit any of the foregoing acts.

Article 5: Personal jurisdiction

The International Tribunal for Rwanda shall have jurisdiction over natural persons pursuant to the provisions of the present Statute.

Article 6: Individual criminal responsibility

1.   A person who planned, instigated, ordered, committed or otherwise aided and abetted in the planning, preparation or execution of a crime referred to in articles 2 to 4 of the present Statute, shall be individually responsible for the crime.

2.   The official position of any accused person, whether as Head of State or government or as a responsible Government official, shall not relieve such person of criminal responsibility nor mitigate punishment.

3.   The fact that any of the acts referred to in articles 2 to 4 of the present Statute was committed by a subordinate does not relieve his or her superior of criminal responsibility if he or she knew or had reason to know that the subordinate was about to commit such acts or had done so and the superior

failed to take the necessary and reasonable measures to prevent such acts or to punish the perpetrators thereof.

4. The fact that an accused person acted pursuant to an order of a Government or of a superior shall not relieve him or her of criminal responsibility, but may be considered in mitigation of punishment if the International Tribunal for Rwanda determines that justice so requires.

Article 7: Territorial and temporal jurisdiction

The territorial jurisdiction of the International Tribunal for Rwanda shall extend to the territory of Rwanda including its land surface and airspace as well as to the territory of neighbouring States in respect of serious violations of international humanitarian law committed by Rwandan citizens. The temporal jurisdiction of the International Tribunal for Rwanda shall extend to a period beginning on 1 January 1994 and ending on 31 December 1994.

Article 8: Concurrent jurisdiction

1. The International Tribunal for Rwanda and national courts shall have concurrent jurisdiction to prosecute persons for serious violations of international humanitarian law committed in the territory of Rwanda and Rwandan citizens for such violations committed in the territory of neighbouring States, between 1 January 1994 and 31 December 1994.
2. The International Tribunal for Rwanda shall have primacy over the national courts of all States. At any stage of the procedure, the International Tribunal for Rwanda may formally request national courts to defer to its competence in accordance with the present Statute and the Rules of Procedure and Evidence of the International Tribunal for Rwanda.

Article 9: *Non bis in idem*

1. No person shall be tried before a national court for acts constituting serious violations of international humanitarian law under the present Statute, for which he or she has already been tried by the International Tribunal for Rwanda.
2. A person who has been tried by a national court for acts constituting serious violations of international humanitarian law may be subsequently tried by the International Tribunal for Rwanda only if:

    (a) The act for which he or she was tried was characterized as an ordinary crime; or
    (b) The national court proceedings were not impartial or independent, were designed to shield the accused from international criminal responsibility, or the case was not diligently prosecuted.

3. In considering the penalty to be imposed on a person convicted of a crime under the present Statute, the International Tribunal for Rwanda shall take into account the extent to which any penalty imposed by a national court on the same person for the same act has already been served.

Article 10: Organization of the International Tribunal for Rwanda

The International Tribunal for Rwanda shall consist of the following organs:

   (a) The Chambers, comprising two Trial Chambers and an Appeals Chamber;

   (b) The Prosecutor; and

   (c) A Registry.

Article 11: Composition of the Chambers

The Chambers shall be composed of eleven independent judges, no two of whom may be nationals of the same State, who shall serve as follows:

   (a) Three judges shall serve in each of the Trial Chambers;

   (b) Five judges shall serve in the Appeals Chamber.

Article 12: Qualification and election of judges

1. The judges shall be persons of high moral character, impartiality and integrity who possess the qualifications required in their respective countries for appointment to the highest judicial offices. In the overall composition of the Chambers due account shall be taken of the experience of the judges in criminal law, international law, including international humanitarian law and human rights law.

2. The members of the Appeals Chamber of the International Tribunal for the Prosecution of Persons Responsible for Serious Violations of International Law Committed in the Territory of the Former Yugoslavia since 1991 (hereinafter referred to as "the International Tribunal for the Former Yugoslavia") shall also serve as the members of the Appeals Chamber of the International Tribunal for Rwanda.

3. The judges of the Trial Chambers of the International Tribunal for Rwanda shall be elected by the General Assembly from a list submitted by the Security Council, in the following manner:

   (a) The Secretary-General shall invite nominations for judges of the Trial Chambers from States Members of the United Nations and non-member States maintaining permanent observer missions at United Nations Headquarters;

   (b) Within thirty days of the date of the invitation of the Secretary-General, each State may nominate up to two candidates meeting the qualifications set out in paragraph 1 above, no two of whom shall be of the same nationality and neither of whom shall be of the same nationality as any judge on the Appeals Chamber;

   (c) The Secretary-General shall forward the nominations received to the Security Council. From the nominations received the Security Council shall establish a list of not less than twelve and not more than eighteen candidates, taking due account of adequate representation on the International Tribunal for Rwanda of the principal legal systems of the world;

(d) The President of the Security Council shall transmit the list of candidates to the President of the General Assembly. From that list the General Assembly shall elect the six judges of the Trial Chambers. The candidates who receive an absolute majority of the votes of the States Members of the United Nations and of the non-Member States maintaining permanent observer missions at United Nations Headquarters, shall be declared elected. Should two candidates of the same nationality obtain the required majority vote, the one who received the higher number of votes shall be considered elected.

4. In the event of a vacancy in the Trial Chambers, after consultation with the Presidents of the Security Council and of the General Assembly, the Secretary-General shall appoint a person meeting the qualifications of paragraph 1 above, for the remainder of the term of office concerned.

5. The judges of the Trial Chambers shall be elected for a term of four years. The terms and conditions of service shall be those of the judges of the International Tribunal for the Former Yugoslavia. They shall be eligible for re-election.

Article 13: Officers and members of the Chambers

1. The judges of the International Tribunal for Rwanda shall elect a President.
2. After consultation with the judges of the International Tribunal for Rwanda, the President shall assign the judges to the Trial Chambers. A judge shall serve only in the Chamber to which he or she was assigned.
3. The judges of each Trial Chamber shall elect a Presiding Judge, who shall conduct all of the proceedings of that Trial Chamber as a whole.

Article 14: Rules of procedure and evidence

The judges of the International Tribunal for Rwanda shall adopt, for the purpose of proceedings before the International Tribunal for Rwanda, the rules of procedure and evidence for the conduct of the pre-trial phase of the proceedings, trials and appeals, the admission of evidence, the protection of victims and witnesses and other appropriate matters of the International Tribunal for the Former Yugoslavia with such changes as they deem necessary.

Article 15: The Prosecutor

1. The Prosecutor shall be responsible for the investigation and prosecution of persons responsible for serious violations of international humanitarian law committed in the territory of Rwanda and Rwandan citizens responsible for such violations committed in the territory of neighbouring States, between 1 January 1994 and 31 December 1994.
2. The Prosecutor shall act independently as a separate organ of the International Tribunal for Rwanda. He or she shall not seek or receive instructions from any Government or from any other source.

3. The Prosecutor of the International Tribunal for the Former Yugoslavia shall also serve as the Prosecutor of the International Tribunal for Rwanda. He or she shall have additional staff, including an additional Deputy Prosecutor, to assist with prosecutions before the International Tribunal for Rwanda. Such staff shall be appointed by the Secretary-General on the recommendation of the Prosecutor.

Article 16: The Registry

1. The Registry shall be responsible for the administration and servicing of the international Tribunal for Rwanda.
2. The Registry shall consist of a Registrar and such other staff as may be required.
3. The Registrar shall be appointed by the Secretary-General after consultation with the President of the International Tribunal for Rwanda. He or she shall serve for a four-year term and be eligible for reappointment. The terms and conditions of service of the Registrar shall be those of an Assistant Secretary-General of the United Nations.
4. The staff of the Registry shall be appointed by the Secretary-General on the recommendation of the Registrar.

Article 17: Investigation and preparation of indictment

1. The Prosecutor shall initiate investigations ex-officio or on the basis of information obtained from any source, particularly from Governments, United Nations organs, intergovernmental and non-governmental organizations. The Prosecutor shall assess the information received or obtained and decide whether there is sufficient basis to proceed.
2. The Prosecutor shall have the power to question suspects, victims and witnesses, to collect evidence and to conduct on-site investigations. In carrying out these tasks, the Prosecutor may, as appropriate, seek the assistance of the State authorities concerned.
3. If questioned, the suspect shall be entitled to be assisted by counsel of his or her own choice, including the right to have legal assistance assigned to the suspect without payment by him or her in any such case if he or she does not have sufficient means to pay for it, as well as to necessary translation into and from a language he or she speaks and understands.
4. Upon a determination that a prima facie case exists, the Prosecutor shall prepare an indictment containing a concise statement of the facts and the crime or crimes with which the accused is charged under the Statute. The indictment shall be transmitted to a judge of the Trial Chamber.

Article 18: Review of the indictment

1. The judge of the Trial Chamber to whom the indictment has been transmitted shall review it. If satisfied that a prima facie case has been established by the Prosecutor, he or she shall confirm the indictment. If not so satisfied, the indictment shall be dismissed.

2. Upon confirmation of an indictment, the judge may, at the request of the prosecutor, issue such orders and warrants for the arrest, detention, surrender or transfer of persons, and any other orders as may be required for the conduct of the trial.

Article 19: Commencement and conduct of trial proceedings

1. The Trial Chambers shall ensure that a trial is fair and expeditious and that proceedings are conducted in accordance with the rules of procedure and evidence, with full respect for the rights of the accused and due regard for the protection of victims and witnesses.
2. A person against whom an indictment has been confirmed shall, pursuant to an order or an arrest warrant of the International Tribunal for Rwanda, be taken into custody, immediately informed of the charges against him or her and transferred to the International Tribunal for Rwanda.
3. The Trial Chamber shall read the indictment, satisfy itself that the rights of the accused are respected, confirm that the accused understands the indictment, and instruct the accused to enter a plea. The Trial Chamber shall then set the date for trial.
4. The hearings shall be public unless the Trial Chamber decides to close the proceedings in accordance with its rules of procedure and evidence.

Article 20: Rights of the accused

1. All persons shall be equal before the International Tribunal for Rwanda.
2. In the determination of charges against him or her, the accused shall be entitled to a fair and public hearing, subject to article 21 of the Statute.
3. The accused shall be presumed innocent until proved guilty according to the provisions of the present Statute.
4. In the determination of any charge against the accused pursuant to the present Statute, the accused shall be entitled to the following minimum guarantees, in full equality:

    (a) To be informed promptly and in detail in a language which he or she understands of the nature and cause of the charge against him or her;
    (b) To have adequate time and facilities for the preparation of his or her defence and to communicate with counsel of his or her own choosing;
    (c) To be tried without undue delay;
    (d) To be tried in his or her presence, and to defend himself or herself in person or through legal assistance of his or her own choosing; to be informed, if he or she does not have legal assistance, of this right; and to have legal assistance assigned to him or her, in any case where the interests of justice so require, and without payment by him or her in any such case if he or she does not have sufficient means to pay for it;
    (e) To examine, or have examined, the witnesses against him or her and to obtain the attendance and examination of witnesses on his or her behalf under the same conditions as witnesses against him or her;

(f) To have the free assistance of an interpreter if he or she cannot understand or speak the language used in the International Tribunal for Rwanda;

(g) Not to be compelled to testify against himself or herself or to confess guilt.

Article 21: Protection of victims and witnesses

The International Tribunal for Rwanda shall provide in its rules of procedure and evidence for the protection of victims and witnesses. Such protection measures shall include, but shall not be limited to, the conduct of in camera proceedings and the protection of the victim's identity.

Article 22: Judgment

1. The Trial Chambers shall pronounce judgments and impose sentences and penalties on persons convicted of serious violations of international humanitarian law.

2. The judgment shall be rendered by a majority of the judges of the Trial Chamber, and shall be delivered by the Trial Chamber in public. It shall be accompanied by a reasoned opinion in writing, to which separate or dissenting opinions may be appended.

Article 23: Penalties

1. The penalty imposed by the Trial Chamber shall be limited to imprisonment. In determining the terms of imprisonment, the Trial Chambers shall have recourse to the general practice regarding prison sentences in the courts of Rwanda.

2. In imposing the sentences, the Trial Chambers should take into account such factors as the gravity of the offence and the individual circumstances of the convicted person.

3. In addition to imprisonment, the Trial Chambers may order the return of any property and proceeds acquired by criminal conduct, including by means of duress, to their rightful owners.

Article 24: Appellate proceedings

1. The Appeals Chamber shall hear appeals from persons convicted by the Trial Chambers or from the Prosecutor on the following grounds:

   (a) An error on a question of law invalidating the decision; or
   (b) An error of fact which has occasioned a miscarriage of justice.

2. The Appeals Chamber may affirm, reverse or revise the decisions taken by the Trial Chambers.

Article 25: Review proceedings

Where a new fact has been discovered which was not known at the time of the proceedings before the Trial Chambers or the Appeals Chamber and which could have been a decisive factor in reaching the decision, the convicted person or the Prosecutor may submit to the International Tribunal for Rwanda an application for review of the judgment.

Article 26: Enforcement of sentences

Imprisonment shall be served in Rwanda or any of the States on a list of States which have indicated to the Security Council their willingness to accept convicted persons, as designated by the International Tribunal for Rwanda.

Such imprisonment shall be in accordance with the applicable law of the State concerned, subject to the supervision of the International Tribunal for Rwanda.

Article 27: Pardon or commutation of sentences

If, pursuant to the applicable law of the State in which the convicted person is imprisoned, he or she is eligible for pardon or commutation of sentence, the State concerned shall notify the International Tribunal for Rwanda accordingly. There shall only be pardon or commutation of sentence if the President of the International Tribunal for Rwanda, in consultation with the judges, so decides on the basis of the interests of justice and the general principles of law.

Article 28: Cooperation and judicial assistance

1. States shall cooperate with the International Tribunal for Rwanda in the investigation and prosecution of persons accused of committing serious violations of international humanitarian law.
2. States shall comply without undue delay with any request for assistance or an order issued by a Trial Chamber, including, but not limited to:

   (a) The identification and location of persons;
   (b) The taking of testimony and the production of evidence;
   (c) The service of documents;
   (d) The arrest or detention of persons;
   (e) The surrender or the transfer of the accused to the International Tribunal for Rwanda.

Article 29: The status, privileges and immunities of the International Tribunal for Rwanda

1. The Convention on the Privileges and Immunities of the United Nations of 13 February 1946 shall apply to the International Tribunal for Rwanda, the judges, the Prosecutor and his or her staff, and the Registrar and his or her staff.

762

2. The judges, the Prosecutor and the Registrar shall enjoy the privileges and immunities, exemptions and facilities accorded to diplomatic envoys, in accordance with international law.
3. The staff of the Prosecutor and of the Registrar shall enjoy the privileges and immunities accorded to officials of the United Nations under articles V and VII of the Convention referred to in paragraph 1 of this article.
4. Other persons, including the accused, required at the seat or meeting place of the International Tribunal for Rwanda shall be accorded such treatment as is necessary for the proper functioning of the International Tribunal for Rwanda.

Article 30: Expenses of the International Tribunal for Rwanda

The expenses of the International Tribunal for Rwanda shall be expenses of the Organization in accordance with Article 17 of the Charter of the United Nations.

Article 31: Working languages

The working languages of the International Tribunal shall be English and French.

Article 32: Annual report

The President of the International Tribunal for Rwanda shall submit an annual report of the International Tribunal for Rwanda to the Security Council and to the General Assembly.

75. UNITED NATIONS: INTERNATIONAL LAW COMMISSION: DRAFT STATUTE FOR AN INTERNATIONAL CRIMINAL COURT

Editors' Notes

Efforts to establish an international criminal code and a permanent criminal court have been underway almost since the conception of the United Nations. In 1949 the International Law Commission (ILC) undertook work on the *Formulation of the Nuremberg Principles and Preparation of a Draft Code of Offences Against the Peace and Security of Mankind*[1] and research into the feasibility of establishing an international criminal court started almost in parallel to this. In the first report of the study it was concluded that an international court was required to supplement a substantive criminal code.[2]

The interim development of a Draft Statute for an International Criminal Court has been slow,[3] with a steady expansion of jurisdiction and refinement of procedure often reflecting the work taking place on the Draft International Criminal Code.[4] Aside from the work of the ILC, the creation of a permanent international criminal tribunal is also foreseen within the provisions of the United Nation's Genocide and the Apartheid Conventions which provide that persons accused of the crimes in question may in certain circumstances be tried by such a court.[5] The current text of the Draft Statute for an International Criminal Code, reproduced here, is that adopted by the ILC in 1994.[6]

The principles underlying the 1994 Draft are those set out by the ILC's working group in 1992.[7] They include that an international criminal court should be established by treaty rather than United Nations Resolution (as was the case with the Tribunals for the Former Yugoslavia and Rwanda), that the court should exercise jurisdiction over individuals rather than states (Article 21), that the jurisdiction of the court should extend to gross violations of human rights and crimes set out in the Annex to the Statute (Article 20) and that such jurisdiction is

---

[1] See: UN G.A. Res. 177(II), 21 November 1947.

[2] Report of the International Law Commissions on questions of International Criminal Jurisdiction, UN Doc. A/CN.4/15, 3 March 1950.

[3] See: Bassiouni, M.C. (1987). *A Draft International Criminal Code and Draft Statute for an International Criminal Tribunal.* Netherlands, Martinus Nijhoff. pp. 1–11.

[4] Recent appraisal of the progress on the Draft Code can be found in: Twelfth Report on the Draft Code of Crimes against the Peace and Security of Mankind, submitted by Doudou Thiam, UN Doc. A/CN.4/460 (1994).

[5] See: Convention on the Prevention and Punishment of the Crime of Genocide, Article VI, *supra;* International Convention on the Suppression and Punishment of the Crime of Apartheid (1973), Article V.

[6] See also the report of the working group, UN Doc. A/CN.4/L.491/Rev.2/Adds. 1 & 2 (1994).

[7] Report of the International Law Commission on the Work of its forty-fourth Session, UN GAOR, 47th Sess., Supp. No.10, UN Doc. A/47/10 (1992).

conditional on the consent of a state party who may limit that jurisdiction by way of declaration (Article 22).[8] The relationship between the proposed court and the Draft Code of Crimes Against the Peace and Security of Mankind is not an automatic one – it is envisaged that states would become a party to the Statute for the Court independently to the Code of Crimes, which if concluded, would in turn be added to the jurisdiction of the Court.[9]

Although the establishment of a permanent international court has been described as the "missing link of international law",[10] a significant increase in the political will of the world's states is needed before the Court can become a reality.

The States parties to this Statute,

Desiring to further international co-operation to enhance the effective suppression and prosecution of crimes of international concern, and for that purpose to establish an international criminal court;

Emphasising that such a court is intended to exercise jurisdiction only over the most serious crimes of concern to the international community as a whole;

Emphasising further that such a court is intended to be complementary to national criminal justice systems in cases where such trial procedures may not be available or may be ineffective;

Have agreed as follows:

PART 1
ESTABLISHMENT OF THE COURT

Article 1: The Court

There is established an International Criminal Court ("the Court"), whose jurisdiction and functioning shall be governed by the provisions of this Statute.

Article 2: Relationship of the Court to the United Nations

The President, with the approval of the States parties to this Statute ("States parties"), may conclude an agreement establishing an appropriate relationship between the Court and the United Nations.

---

[8] For further commentary on the provisions of the 1994 Draft Statute see: Crawford, J. (1995). "The ILC Adopts a Statute for an International Criminal Court". 89 AJIL 404; Gilmore, W.C. (1995). "The Proposed International Criminal Court: Recent Developments". 5 Transnat'l. Law & Contem. Probs. 264.

[9] Crawford, *supra*, p.408.

[10] See: Comments Received Pursuant to Paragraph 4 of General Assembly Resolution 49/53 on the Establishment of an International Criminal Court, Report of the Secretary General, UN Doc. A/AC.244/1 (1995), p.32.

Article 3: Seat of the Court

1. The seat of the Court shall be established at ————— in ————— ("the host State").
2. The President, with the approval of the States parties, may conclude an agreement with the host State establishing the relationship between that State and the Court.
3. The Court may exercise its powers and functions on the territory of any State party and, by special agreement, on the territory of any other State.

Article 4: Status and legal capacity

1. The Court is a permanent institution open to States parties in accordance with this Statute. It shall act when required to consider a case submitted to it.
2. The Court shall enjoy in the territory of each State party such legal capacity as may be necessary for the exercise of its functions and the fulfilment of its purposes.

PART 2
COMPOSITION AND ADMINISTRATION OF THE COURT

Article 5: Organs of the Court

The Court consists of the following organs:

   (a) a Presidency, as provided in article 8;
   (b) an Appeals Chamber, Trial Chambers and other chambers, as provided in article 9;
   (c) a Procuracy, as provided in article 12; and
   (d) a Registry, as provided in article 13.

Article 6: Qualification and election of judges

1. The judges of the Court shall be persons of high moral character, impartiality and integrity who possess the qualifications required in their respective countries for appointment to the highest judicial offices, and have, in addition:

   (a) criminal trial experience;
   (b) recognized competence in international law.

2. Each State party may nominate for election not more than two persons, of different nationality, who possess the qualification referred to in paragraph 1(a) or that referred to in paragraph 1(b), and who are willing to serve as may be required on the Court.
3. Eighteen judges shall be elected, by an absolute majority vote of the States parties by secret ballot. Ten judges shall first be elected, from among the persons nominated as having the qualification referred to in paragraph 1(a).

766

Eight judges shall then be elected, from among the persons nominated as having the qualification referred to in paragraph 1(b).

4. No two judges may be nationals of the same State.
5. States parties should bear in mind in the election of the judges that the representation of the principal legal systems of the world should be assured.
6. Judges hold office for a term of nine years and, subject to paragraph 7 and article 7(2), are not eligible for reelection. A judge shall, however, continue in office in order to complete any case the hearing of which has commenced.
7. At the first election, six judges chosen by lot shall serve for a term of three years and are eligible for reelection; six judges chosen by lot shall serve for a term of six years; and the remainder shall serve for a term of nine years.
8. Judges nominated as having the qualification referred to in paragraph 1(a) or 1(b), as the case may be, shall be replaced by persons nominated as having the same qualification.

Article 7: Judicial vacancie

1. In the event of a vacancy, a replacement judge shall be elected in accordance with article 6.
2. A judge elected to fill a vacancy shall serve for the remainder of the predecessor's term, and if that period is less than five years is eligible for reelection for a further term.

Article 8: The Presidency

1. The President, the first and second Vice-presidents and two alternate Vice-presidents shall be elected by an absolute majority of the judges. They shall serve for a term of three years or until the end of their term of office as judges, whichever is earlier.
2. The first or second Vice-president, as the case may be, may act in place of the President in the event that the President is unavailable or disqualified. An alternate Vice-president may act in place of either Vice-president as required.
3. The President and the Vice-presidents shall constitute the Presidency which shall be responsible for:

    (a) the due administration of the Court; and
    (b) the other functions conferred on it by this Statute.

4. Unless otherwise indicated, pre-trial and other procedural functions conferred under this Statute on the Court may be exercised by the Presidency in any case where a chamber of the Court is not seized of the matter.
5. The Presidency may, in accordance with the Rules, delegate to one or more judges the exercise of a power vested in it under articles 26 (3), 27 (5), 28, 29 or 30 (3) in relation to a case, during the period before a Trial Chamber is established for that case.

Article 9: Chambers

1. As soon as possible after each election of judges to the Court, the Presidency shall in accordance with the Rules constitute an Appeals Chamber consisting of the President and six other judges, of whom at least three shall be judges elected from among the persons nominated as having the qualification referred to in article 6 (1) (b). The President shall preside over the Appeals Chamber.
2. The Appeals Chamber shall be constituted for a term of three years. Members of the Appeals Chamber shall, however, continue to sit on the Chamber in order to complete any case the hearing of which has commenced.
3. Judges may be renewed as members of the Appeals Chamber for a second or subsequent term.
4. Judges not members of the Appeals Chamber shall be available to serve on Trial Chambers and other chambers required by this Statute, and to act as substitute members of the Appeals Chamber, in the event that a member of that Chamber is unavailable or disqualified.
5. The Presidency shall nominate in accordance with the Rules five such judges to be members of the Trial Chamber for a given case. A Trial Chamber shall include at least three judges elected from among the persons nominated as having the qualification referred to in article 6(1)(a).
6. The Rules may provide for alternate judges to be nominated to attend a trial and to act as members of the Trial Chamber in the event that a judge dies or becomes unavailable during the course of the trial.
7. No judge who is a national of a complainant State or of a State of which the accused is a national shall be a member of a chamber dealing with the case.

Article 10: Independence of the judges

1. In performing their functions, the judges shall be independent.
2. Judges shall not engage in any activity which is likely to interfere with their judicial functions or to affect confidence in their independence. In particular, they shall not while holding the office of judge be a member of the legislative or executive branches of the Government of a State, or of a body responsible for the investigation or prosecution of crimes.
3. Any question as to the application of paragraph 2 shall be decided by the Presidency.
4. On the recommendation of the Presidency, the States parties may by a two-thirds majority decide that the work-load of the Court requires that the judges should serve on a full-time basis. In that case:

    (a) existing judges who elect to serve on a full-time basis shall not hold any other office or employment; and
    (b) judges subsequently elected shall not hold any other office or employment.

Article 11: Excusing and disqualification of judges

1. The Presidency at the request of a judge may excuse that judge from the exercise of a function under this Statute.
2. Judges shall not participate in any case in which they have previously been involved in any capacity or in which their impartiality might reasonably be doubted on any ground, including an actual, apparent or potential conflict of interest.
3. The Prosecutor or the accused may request the disqualification of a judge under paragraph 2.
4. Any question as to the disqualification of a judge shall be decided by an absolute majority of the members of the Chamber concerned. The challenged judge shall not take part in the decision.

Article 12: The Procuracy

1. The Procuracy is an independent organ of the Court responsible for the investigation of complaints brought in accordance with this Statute and for the conduct of prosecutions. A member of the Procuracy shall not seek or act on instructions from any external source.
2. The Procuracy shall be headed by the Prosecutor, assisted by one or more Deputy Prosecutors, who may act in place of the Prosecutor in the event that the Prosecutor is unavailable. The Prosecutor and the Deputy Prosecutors shall be of different nationalities. The Prosecutor may appoint such other qualified staff as may be required.
3. The Prosecutor and Deputy Prosecutors shall be persons of high moral character and have high competence and experience in the prosecution of criminal cases. They shall be elected by secret ballot by an absolute majority of the States parties, from among candidates nominated by States parties. Unless a shorter term is otherwise decided on at the time of their election, they shall hold office for a term of five years and are eligible for reelection.
4. The States parties may elect the Prosecutor and a Deputy Prosecutor on the basis that they will be available to serve as required.
5. The Prosecutor and Deputy Prosecutors shall not act in relation to a complaint involving a person of their own nationality.
6. The Presidency may excuse the Prosecutor or a Deputy Prosecutor at their request from acting in a particular case, and shall decide any question raised in a particular case as to the disqualification of the Prosecutor or a Deputy Prosecutor.
7. The staff of the Procuracy shall be subject to Staff Regulations drawn up by the Prosecutor so far as possible in conformity with the United Nations Staff Regulations and Staff Rules and approved by the Presidency.

Article 13: The Registry

1. On the proposal of the Presidency, the judges by an absolute majority by secret ballot shall elect a Registrar, who shall be the principal administrative

officer of the Court. They may in the same manner elect a Deputy Registrar.

2. The Registrar shall hold office for a term of five years, is eligible for reelection and shall be available on a full-time basis. The Deputy Registrar shall hold office for a term of five years or such shorter term as may be decided on, and may be elected on the basis that the Deputy Registrar will be available to serve as required.

3. The Presidency may appoint or authorize the Registrar to appoint such other staff of the Registry as may be necessary.

4. The staff of the Registry shall be subject to Staff Regulations drawn up by the Registrar so far as possible in conformity with the United Nations Staff Regulations and Staff Rules, and approved by the Presidency.

Article 14: Solemn undertaking

Before first exercising their functions under this Statute, judges and other officers of the Court shall make a public and solemn undertaking to do so impartially and conscientiously.

Article 15: Loss of office

1. A judge, the Prosecutor or other officer of the Court who is found to have committed misconduct or a serious breach of this Statue, or to be unable to exercise the functions required by this Statute because of long-term illness or disability, shall cease to hold office.

2. A decision as to the loss of office under paragraph 1 shall be made by secret ballot:

   (a) in the case of the Prosecutor or a Deputy Prosecutor, by an absolute majority of the States parties;
   (b) in any other case, by a two-thirds majority of the judges.

4. The judge, the Prosecutor or other officer whose conduct or fitness for office is impugned shall have full opportunity to present evidence and to make submissions but shall not otherwise participate in the discussion of the question.

Article 16: Privileges and immunities

1. The judges, the Prosecutor, the Deputy Prosecutors and the staff of the Procuracy, the Registrar and the Deputy Registrar shall enjoy the privileges, immunities and facilities of a diplomatic agent within the meaning of the Vienna Convention on Diplomatic Relations of 16 April 1961.

2. The staff of the Registry shall enjoy the privileges, immunities and facilities necessary to the performance of their functions.

3. Counsel, experts and witnesses before the Court shall enjoy the privileges and immunities necessary to the independent exercise of their duties.

4. The judges may by an absolute majority decide to revoke a privilege or waive an immunity conferred by this article, other than an immunity of a judge, the

Prosecutor or Registrar as such. In the case of other officers and staff of the Procuracy or Registry, they may do so only on the recommendation of the Prosecutor or Registrar, as the case may be.

Article 17: Allowances and expenses

1. The President shall receive an annual allowance.
2. The Vice-presidents shall receive a special allowance for each day they exercise the functions of the President.
3. Subject to paragraph 4, the judges shall receive a daily allowance during the period in which they exercise their functions. They may continue to receive a salary payable in respect of another position occupied by them consistently with article 10.
4. If it is decided under article 10 (4) that judges shall thereafter serve on a full-time basis, existing judges who elect to serve on a full-time basis, and all judges subsequently elected, shall be paid a salary.

Article 18: Working languages

The working languages of the Court shall be English and French.

Article 19: Rules of the Court

1. Subject to paragraphs 2 and 3, the judges may by an absolute majority make rules for the functioning of the Court in accordance with this Statute, including rules regulating:

    (a) the conduct of investigations;
    (b) the procedure to be followed and the rules of evidence to be applied;
    (c) any other matter which is necessary for the implementation of this Statute.

2. The initial Rules of the Court shall be drafted by the judges within six months of the first elections for the Court, and submitted to a conference of States parties for approval. The judges may decide that a rule subsequently made under paragraph 1 should also be submitted to a conference of States parties for approval.
3. In any case to which paragraph 2 does not apply, rules made under paragraph 1 shall be transmitted to States parties and may be confirmed by the Presidency unless, within six months after transmission, a majority of States parties have communicated in writing their objections.
4. A rule may provide for its provisional application in the period prior to its approval or confirmation. A rule not approved or confirmed shall lapse.

PART 3
JURISDICTION OF THE COURT

Article 20 Crimes within the jurisdiction of the Court

The Court has jurisdiction in accordance with this Statute with respect to the following crimes:

(a) the crime of genocide;
(b) the crime of aggression;
(c) serious violations of the laws and customs applicable in armed conflict;
(d) crimes against humanity;
(e) crimes, established under or pursuant to the treaty provisions listed in the Annex;

which, having regard to the conduct alleged, constitute exceptionally serious crimes of international concern.

Article 21 Preconditions to the exercise of jurisdiction

1. The Court may exercise its jurisdiction over a person with respect to a crime referred to in article 20 if:

(a) in a case of genocide, a complaint is brought under article 25(1);
(b) in any other case, a complaint is brought under article 25(2) and the jurisdiction of the Court with respect to the crime is accepted under article 22:

(i) by the State which has custody of the suspect with respect to the crime ("the custodial State"); and
(ii) by the State on the territory of which the act or omission in question occurred.

2. If, with respect to a crime to which paragraph 1(b) applies, the custodial State has received, under an international agreement, a request from another State to surrender a suspect for the purposes of prosecution, then, unless the request is rejected, the acceptance by the requesting State of the Court's jurisdiction with respect to the crime is also required.

Article 22: Acceptance of the jurisdiction of the Court for the purposes of article 21

1. A State party to this Statute may:

(a) at the time it expresses its consent to be bound by the Statute, by declaration lodged with the depository; or
(b) at a later time, by declaration lodged with the Registrar;

accept the jurisdiction of the Court with respect to such of the crimes referred to in article 20 as it specifies in the declaration.

2. A declaration may be of general application, or may be limited to particular conduct or to conduct committed during a particular period of time.

3. A declaration may be made for a specified period, in which case it may not be withdrawn before the end of that period, or for an unspecified period, in which case it may be withdrawn only upon giving six months' notice of withdrawal to the Registrar. Withdrawal does not affect proceedings already commenced under this Statute.

4. If under article 21 the acceptance of a State which is not a party to this Statute is required, that State may, by declaration lodged with the Registrar, consent to the Court exercising jurisdiction with respect to the crime.

Article 23: Action by the Security Council

1. Notwithstanding article 21, the Court has jurisdiction in accordance with this Statute with respect to crimes referred to in article 20 as a consequence of the referral of a matter to the Court by the Security Council acting under Chapter VII of the Charter of the United Nations.

2. A complaint of or directly related to an act of aggression may not be brought under this Statute unless the Security Council has first determined that a State has committed the act of aggression which is the subject of the complaint.

3. No prosecution may be commenced under this Statute arising from a situation which is being dealt with by the Security Council as a threat to or breach of the peace or an act of aggression under Chapter VII of the Charter, unless the Security Council otherwise decides.

Article 24: Duty of the Court as to jurisdictio

The Court shall satisfy itself that it has jurisdiction in any case brought before it.

PART 4
INVESTIGATION AND PROSECUTION

Article 25: Complaint

1. A State party which is also a Contracting Party to the Convention on the Prevention and Punishment of the Crime of Genocide of 9 December 1948 may lodge a complaint with the Prosecutor alleging that a crime of genocide appears to have been committed.

2. A State party which accepts the jurisdiction of the Court under article 22 with respect to a crime may lodge a complaint with the Prosecutor alleging that such a crime appears to have been committed.

3. As far as possible a complaint shall specify the circumstances of the alleged crime and the identity and whereabouts of any suspect, and be accompanied by such supporting documentation as is available to the complainant State.

4. In a case to which article 23 (1) applies, a complaint is not required for the initiation of an investigation.

Article 26: Investigation of alleged crimes

1. On receiving a complaint or upon notification of a decision of the Security Council referred to in article 23 (1), the Prosecutor shall initiate an investigation unless the Prosecutor concludes that there is no possible basis for a prosecution under this Statute and decides not to initiate an investigation, in which case the Prosecutor shall so inform the Presidency.

2. The Prosecutor may:

   (a) request the presence of and question suspects, victims and witnesses;
   (b) collect documentary and other evidence;
   (c) conduct on site investigations;
   (d) take necessary measures to ensure the confidentiality of information or the protection of any person;
   (e) as appropriate, seek the co-operation of any State or of the United Nations.

3. The Presidency may, at the request of the Prosecutor, issue such subpoenas and warrants as may be required for the purposes of an investigation, including a warrant under article 28(1) for the provisional arrest of a suspect.

4. If, upon investigation and having regard, inter alia, to the matters referred to in article 35, the Prosecutor concludes that there is no sufficient basis for a prosecution under this Statute and decides not to file an indictment, the Prosecutor shall so inform the Presidency giving details of the nature and basis of the complaint and of the reasons for not filing an indictment.

5. At the request of a complainant State or, in a case to which article 23(1) applies, at the request of the Security Council, the Presidency shall review a decision of the Prosecutor not to initiate an investigation or not to file an indictment, and may request the Prosecutor to reconsider the decision.

6. A person suspected of a crime under this Statute shall:

   (a) prior to being questioned, be informed that the person is a suspect and of the rights:

      (i) to remain silent, without such silence being a consideration in the determination of guilt or innocence; and
      (ii) to have the assistance of counsel of the suspect's choice or, if the suspect lacks the means to retain counsel, to have legal assistance assigned by the Court;

   (b) not be compelled to testify or to confess guilt; and
   (c) if questioned in a language other than a language the suspect understands and speaks, be provided with competent interpretation services and with a translation of any document on which the suspect is to be questioned.

Article 27: Commencement of prosecution

1. If upon investigation the Prosecutor concludes that there is a *prima facie* case, the Prosecutor shall file with the Registrar an indictment containing a concise

statement of the allegations of fact and of the crime or crimes with which the suspect is charged.

2. The Presidency shall examine the indictment and any supporting material and determine:

   (a) whether a prima facie case exists with respect to a crime within the jurisdiction of the Court; and
   (b) whether, having regard, inter alia, to the matters referred to in article 35, the case could on the information available be heard by the Court.

   If so, it shall confirm the indictment and establish a trial chamber in accordance with article 9.

3. If, after any adjournment that may be necessary to allow additional material to be produced, the Presidency decides not to confirm the indictment, it shall so inform the complainant State or, in a case to which article 23(1) applies, the Security Council.

4. The Presidency may at the request of the Prosecutor amend the indictment, in which case it shall make any necessary orders to ensure that the accused is notified of the amendment and has adequate time to prepare a defence.

5. The Presidency may make any further orders required for the conduct of the trial, including an order:

   (a) determining the language or languages to be used during the trial;
   (b) requiring the disclosure to the defence, within a sufficient time before the trial to enable the preparation of the defence, of documentary or other evidence available to the Prosecutor, whether or not the Prosecutor intends to rely on that evidence;
   (c) providing for the exchange of information between the Prosecutor and the defence, so that both parties are sufficiently aware of the issues to be decided at the trial;
   (d) providing for the protection of the accused, victims and witnesses and of confidential information.

Article 28: Arrest

1. At any time after an investigation has been initiated, the Presidency may at the request of the Prosecutor issue a warrant for the provisional arrest of a suspect if:

   (a) there is probable cause to believe that the suspect may have committed a crime within the jurisdiction of the Court; and
   (b) the suspect may not be available to stand trial unless provisionally arrested.

2. A suspect who has been provisionally arrested is entitled to release from arrest if the indictment has not been confirmed within 90 days of the arrest, or such longer time as the Presidency may allow.

3. As soon as practicable after the confirmation of the indictment, the Prosecutor shall seek from the Presidency a warrant for the arrest and transfer of the

accused. The Presidency shall issue such a warrant unless it is satisfied that:

(a) the accused will voluntarily appear for trial; or
(b) there are special circumstances making it unnecessary for the time being to issue the warrant.

4. A person arrested shall be informed at the time of arrest of the reasons for the arrest and shall be promptly informed of any charges.

Article 29: Pre-Trial detention or release

1. A person arrested shall be brought promptly before a judicial officer of the State where the arrest occurred. The judicial officer shall determine, in accordance with the procedures applicable in that State, that the warrant has been duly served and that the rights of the accused have been respected.
2. A person arrested may apply to the Presidency for release pending trial. The Presidency may release the person unconditionally or on bail if it is satisfied that the accused will appear at the trial.
3. A person arrested may apply to the Presidency for a determination of the lawfulness under this Statute of the arrest or detention. If the Presidency decides that the arrest or detention was unlawful, it shall order the release of the accused, and may award compensation.
4. A person arrested shall be held, pending trial or release on bail, in an appropriate place of detention in the arresting State, in the State in which the trial is to be held or if necessary, in the host State.

Article 30: Notification of the indictment

1. The Prosecutor shall ensure that a person who has been arrested is personally served, as soon as possible after being taken into custody, with certified copies of the following documents, in a language understood by that person:

(a) in the case of a suspect provisionally arrested, a statement of the grounds for the arrest;
(b) in any other case, the confirmed indictment;
(c) a statement of the accused's rights under this Statute.

2. In any case to which paragraph (1)(a) applies, the indictment shall be served on the accused as soon as possible after it has been confirmed.
3. If, 60 days after the indictment has been confirmed, the accused is not in custody pursuant to a warrant issued under article 28(3), or for some reason the requirements of paragraph 1 cannot be complied with, the Presidency may on the application of the Prosecutor prescribe some other manner of bringing the indictment to the attention of the accused.

Article 31: Designation of persons to assist in a prosecution

1. A State party may, at the request of the Prosecutor, designate persons to assist in a prosecution.

2. Such persons should be available for the duration of the prosecution, unless otherwise agreed. They shall serve at the direction of the Prosecutor, and shall not seek or receive instructions from any Government or source other than the Prosecutor in relation to their exercise of functions under this article.
3. The terms and conditions on which persons may be designated under this article shall be approved by the Presidency on the recommendation of the Prosecutor.

PART 5
THE TRIAL

Article 32: Place of trial

1. Unless otherwise decided by the Presidency, the place of the trial will be the seat of the Court.

Article 33: Applicable law

The Court shall apply:

(a) this Statute;
(b) applicable treaties and the principles and rules of general international law; and
(c) to the extent applicable, any rule of national law.

Article 34: Challenges to jurisdiction

Challenges to the jurisdiction of the Court may be made, in accordance with the Rules:

(a) prior to or at the commencement of the hearing, by an accused or any interested State; and
(b) at any later stage of the trial, by an accused.

Article 35: Issues of admissibility

The Court may, on application by the accused or at the request of an interested State at any time prior to the commencement of the trial, or of its own motion, decide, having regard to the purposes of this Statute set out in the preamble, that a case before it is inadmissible on the ground that the crime in question:

(a) has been duly investigated by a State with jurisdiction over it, and the decision of that State not to proceed to a prosecution is apparently well-founded;
(b) is under investigation by a State which has or may have jurisdiction over it, and there is no reason for the Court to take any further action for the time being with respect to the crime; or

(c) is not of such gravity to justify further action by the Court.

Article 36: Procedure under articles 34 and 35

1. In proceedings under articles 34 and 35, the accused and the complainant State have the right to be heard.
2. Proceedings under articles 34 and 35 shall be decided by the Trial Chamber, unless it considers, having regard to the importance of the issues involved, that the matter should be referred to the Appeals Chamber.

Article 37: Trial in the presence of the accused

1. As a general rule, the accused should be present during the trial.
2. The Trial Chamber may order that the trial proceed in the absence of the accused if:

   (a) the accused is in custody, or has been released pending trial, and for reasons of security or the ill health of the accused it is undesirable for the accused to be present;
   (b) the accused is continuing to disrupt the trial; or
   (c) the accused has escaped from lawful custody under this Statute or has broken bail.

3. The Chamber shall, if it makes an order under paragraph 2, ensure that the rights of the accused under this Statute are respected, and in particular:

   (a) that all reasonable steps have been taken to inform the accused of the charge; and
   (b) that the accused is legally represented, if necessary by a lawyer appointed by the Court.

4. In cases where a trial cannot be held because of the deliberate absence of an accused, the Court may establish, in accordance with the Rules, an Indictment Chamber for the purpose of:

   (a) recording the evidence;
   (b) considering whether the evidence establishes a prima facie case of a crime within the jurisdiction of the Court; and
   (c) issuing and publishing a warrant of arrest in respect of an accused against whom a prima facie case is established.

5. If the accused is subsequently tried under this Statute:

   (a) the record of evidence before the Indictment Chamber shall be admissible;
   (b) any judge who was a member of the Indictment Chamber may not be a member of the Trial Chamber.

Article 38: Functions and powers of the Trial Chamber

1. At the commencement of the trial, the Trial Chamber shall:

    (a) have the indictment read;
    (b) ensure that articles 27(5)(b) and 30 have been complied with sufficiently in advance of the trial to enable adequate preparation of the defence;
    (c) satisfy itself that the other rights of the accused under this Statute have been respected; and
    (d) allow the accused to enter a plea of guilty or not guilty.

2.   The Chamber shall ensure that a trial is fair and expeditious, and is conducted in accordance with this Statute and the Rules, with full respect for the rights of the accused and due regard for the protection of victims and witnesses.

3.   The Chamber may, subject to the Rules, hear charges against more than one accused arising out of the same factual situation.

4.   The trial shall be held in public, unless the Chamber determines that certain proceedings be in closed session in accordance with article 43, or for the purpose of protecting confidential or sensitive information which is to be given in evidence.

5.   The Chamber shall, subject to this Statute and the Rules have, inter alia, the power on the application of a party or of its own motion, to:

    (a) issue a warrant for the arrest and transfer of an accused who is not already in the custody of the Court;
    (b) require the attendance and testimony of witnesses;
    (c) require the production of documentary and other evidentiary materials;
    (d) rule on the admissibility or relevance of evidence;
    (e) protect confidential information; and
    (f) maintain order in the course of a hearing.

7.   The Chamber shall ensure that a complete record of the trial, which accurately reflects the proceedings, is maintained and preserved by the Registrar.

Article 39: Principle of legality (*nullum crimen sine lege*)

An accused shall not be held guilty:

    (a) in the case of a prosecution with respect to a crime referred to in article 20(a) to (d), unless the act or omission in question constituted a crime under international law;
    (b) in the case of a prosecution with respect to a crime referred to in article 20(e), unless the treaty in question was applicable to the conduct of the accused;

at the time the act or omission occurred.

Article 40: Presumption of innocence

An accused shall be presumed innocent until proved guilty in accordance with law. The onus is on the Prosecutor to establish the guilt of the accused beyond reasonable doubt.

Article 41: Rights of the accused

1. In the determination of any charge under this Statute, the accused is entitled to a fair and public hearing, subject to article 43, and to the following minimum guarantees:

   (a) to be informed promptly and in detail, in a language which the accused understands, of the nature and cause of the charge;

   (b) to have adequate time and facilities for the preparation of the defence, and to communicate with counsel of the accused's choosing;

   (c) to be tried without undue delay;

   (d) subject to article 37(2), to be present at the trial, to conduct the defence in person or through legal assistance of the accused's choosing, to be informed, if the accused does not have legal assistance, of this right and to have legal assistance assigned by the Court, without payment if the accused lacks sufficient means to pay for such assistance;

   (e) to examine or have examined, the prosecution witnesses and to obtain the attendance and examination of witnesses for the defence under the same conditions as witnesses for the prosecution;

   (f) if any of the proceedings of or documents presented to the Court are not in a language the accused understands and speaks, to have, free of any cost, the assistance of: a competent interpreter and such translations as are necessary to meet the requirements of fairness;

   (g) not to be compelled to testify or to confess guilt.

2. Exculpatory evidence that becomes available to the Procuracy prior to the conclusion of the trial shall be made available to the defence. In case of doubt as to the application of this paragraph or as to the admissibility of the evidence, the Trial Chamber shall decide.

Article 42: *Non bis in idem*

1. No person shall be tried before any other court for acts constituting a crime of the kind referred to in article 20 for which that person has already been tried by the Court.

2. A person who has been tried by another court for acts constituting a crime of the kind referred to in article 20 may be tried under this Statute only if:

   (a) the acts in question were characterised by that court as an ordinary crime and not as a crime which is within the jurisdiction of the Court; or

   (b) the proceedings in the other court were not impartial or independent or were designed to shield the accused from international criminal responsibility or the case was not diligently prosecuted.

3. In considering the penalty to be imposed on a person convicted under this Statute, the Court shall take into account the extent to which a penalty imposed by another court on the same person for the same act has already been served.

Article 43: Protection of the accused, victims and witnesses

The Court shall take necessary measures available to it to protect the accused, victims and witnesses and may to that end conduct closed proceedings or allow the presentation of evidence by electronic or other special means.

Article 44: Evidence

1. Before testifying, each witness shall, in accordance with the Rules, give an undertaking as to the truthfulness of the evidence to be given by that witness.
2. States parties shall extend their laws of perjury to cover evidence given under this Statute by their nationals, and shall cooperate with the Court in investigating and where appropriate prosecuting any case of suspected perjury.
3. The Court may require to be informed of the nature of any evidence before it is offered so that it may rule on its relevance or admissibility.
4. The Court shall not require proof of facts of common knowledge but may take judicial notice of them.
5. Evidence obtained by means of a serious violation of this Statute or of other rules of international law shall not be admissible.

Article 45: Quorum and judgment

1. At least four members of the Trial Chamber must be present at each stage of the trial.
2. The decisions of the Trial Chamber shall be taken by a majority of the judges. At least three judges must concur in a decision as to conviction or acquittal and as to the sentence to be imposed.
3. If after sufficient time for deliberation a Chamber which has been reduced to four judges is unable to agree on a decision, it may order a new trial.
4. The deliberations of the Court shall be and remain secret.
5. The judgment shall be in writing and shall contain a full and reasoned statement of the findings and conclusions. It shall be the sole judgment issued, and shall be delivered in open court.

Article 46: Sentencing

1. In the event of a conviction, the Trial Chamber shall hold a further hearing to hear any evidence relevant to sentence, to allow the Prosecutor and the defence to make submissions and to consider the appropriate sentence to be imposed.
2. In imposing sentence, the Trial Chamber should take into account such factors as the gravity of the crime and the individual circumstances of the convicted person.

Article 47: Applicable Penalties

1. The Court may impose on a person convicted of a crime under this Statute one or more of the following penalties:

    (a) a term of life imprisonment, or of imprisonment for a specified number of years;
    (b) a fine.

2. In determining the length of a term of imprisonment or the amount of a fine to be imposed, the Court may have regard to the penalties provided for by the law of:

    (a) the State of which the convicted person is a national;
    (b) the State where the crime was committed; and
    (c) the State which had custody of and jurisdiction over the accused.

3. Fines paid may be transferred, by order of the Court, to one or more of the following:

    (a) the Registrar, to defray the costs of the trial;
    (b) a State the nationals of which were the victims of the crime;
    (c) a trust fund established by the Secretary-General of the United Nations for the benefit of victims of crime.

PART 6
APPEAL AND REVIEW

Article 48: Appeal against judgement or sentence

1. The Prosecutor and the convicted person may, in accordance with the Rules, appeal against a decision under articles 45 or 47 on grounds of procedural unfairness, error of fact or of law, or disproportion between the crime and the sentence.
2. Unless the Trial Chamber otherwise orders, a convicted person shall remain in custody pending an appeal.

Article 49: Proceedings on appeal

1. The Appeals Chamber has all the powers of the Trial Chamber.
2. If the Appeals Chamber finds that the proceedings appealed from were unfair or that the decision is vitiated by error of fact or law, it may:

    (a) if the appeal is brought by the convicted person, reverse or amend the decision, or, if necessary, order a new trial;
    (b) if the appeal is brought by the Prosecutor against an acquittal, order a new trial.

3. If in an appeal against sentence the Chamber finds that the sentence is manifestly disproportionate to the crime, it may vary the sentence in accordance with article 47.
4. The decision of the Chamber shall be taken by a majority of the judges, and shall be delivered in open court. Six judges constitute a quorum.
5. Subject to article 50, the decision of the Chamber shall be final.

Article 50: Revision

1. The convicted person or the Prosecutor may, in accordance with the Rules, apply to the Presidency for revision of a conviction on the ground that evidence has been discovered which was not available to the applicant at the time the conviction was pronounced or affirmed and which could have been a decisive factor in the conviction.
2. The Presidency shall request the Prosecutor or the convicted person, as the case may be, to present written observations on whether the application should be accepted.
3. If the Presidency is of the view that the new evidence could lead to the revision of the conviction, it may:

   (a) reconvene the Trial Chamber;
   (b) constitute a new Trial Chamber; or
   (c) refer the matter to the Appeals Chamber;
      with a view to the Chamber determining, after hearing the parties, whether the new evidence should lead to a revision of the conviction.

PART 7
INTERNATIONAL CO-OPERATION AND JUDICIAL ASSISTANCE

Article 51: Co-operation and judicial assistance

1. States parties shall cooperate with the Court in connection with criminal investigations and proceedings under this Statute.
2. The Registrar may transmit to any State a request for co-operation and judicial assistance with respect to a crime, including, but not limited to:

   (a) the identification and location of persons;
   (b) the taking of testimony and the production of evidence;
   (c) the service of documents;
   (d) the arrest or detention of persons; and
   (e) any other request which may facilitate the administration of justice, including provisional measures as required.

3. Upon receipt of a request under paragraph 2:

   (a) in a case covered by article 21(1)(a), all States parties;
   (b) in any other case, States parties which have accepted the jurisdiction of the Court with respect to the crime in question;

shall respond without undue delay to the request.

Article 52: Provisional measures

1. In case of need, the Court may request a State to take necessary provisional measures, including the following:

    (a) to provisionally arrest a suspect;
    (b) to seize documents or other evidence; or
    (c) to prevent injury to or the intimidation of a witness or the destruction of evidence.

2. The Court shall follow up a request under paragraph 1 by providing, as soon as possible and in any case within 28 days, a formal request for assistance complying with article 57.

Article 53: Transfer of an accused to the Court

1. The Registrar shall transmit to any State on the territory of which the accused may be found a warrant for the arrest and transfer of an accused issued under article 28, and shall request the co-operation of that State in the arrest and transfer of the accused.

2. Upon receipt of a request under paragraph 1:

    (a) all States parties:

        (i) in a case covered by article 21(1)(a), or
        (ii) which have accepted the jurisdiction of the Court with respect to the crime in question;

    shall, subject to paragraphs 5 and 6, take immediate steps to arrest and transfer the accused to the Court;

    (b) in the case of a crime to which article 20(e) applies, a State party which is a party to the treaty in question but which has not accepted the Court's jurisdiction with respect to that crime shall, if it decides not to transfer the accused to the Court, forthwith take all necessary steps to extradite the accused to a requesting State or refer the case to its competent authorities for the purpose of prosecution;
    (c) in any other case, a State party shall consider whether it can, in accordance with its legal procedures, take steps to arrest and transfer the accused to the Court, or whether it should take steps to extradite the accused to a requesting State or refer the case to its competent authorities for the purpose of prosecution.

3. The transfer of an accused to the Court constitutes, as between States parties which accept the jurisdiction of the Court with respect to the crime, sufficient compliance with a provision of any treaty requiring that a suspect be extradited or the case referred to the competent authorities of the requested State for the purpose of prosecution.

4. A State party which accepts the jurisdiction of the Court with respect to the crime shall, as far as possible, give priority to a request under paragraph 1 over requests for extradition from other States.

5. A State party may delay complying with paragraph 2 if the accused is in its custody or control and is being proceeded against for a serious crime, or serving a sentence imposed by a court for a crime. It shall within 45 days of receiving the request inform the Registrar of the reasons for the delay. In such cases, the requested State:

   (a) may agree to the temporary transfer of the accused for the purpose of standing trial under this Statute; or
   (b) shall comply with paragraph 2 after the prosecution has been completed or abandoned or the sentence has been served, as the case may be.

6. A State party may, within 45 days of receiving a request under paragraph 1, file a written application with the Registrar requesting the Court to set aside the request on specified grounds. Pending a decision of the Court on the application, the State concerned may delay complying with paragraph 2, but shall take any provisional measures requested by the Court.

Article 54: Obligation to extradite or prosecute

In a case of a crime referred to in article 20(e), a custodial State party to this Statute which is a party to the treaty in question but which has not accepted the Court's jurisdiction with respect to the crime for the purposes of article 21(1)(b)(i) shall either take all necessary steps to extradite the suspect to a requesting State for the purpose of prosecution or refer the case to its competent authorities for that purpose.

Article 55: Rule of speciality

1. A person transferred to the Court under article 53 shall not be subject to prosecution or punishment for any crime other than that for which the person was transferred.

2. Evidence provided under this Part shall not, if the State when providing it 80 requests, be used as evidence for any purpose other than that for which it was provided, unless this is necessary to preserve the right of an accused under article 41(2).

3. The Court may request the State concerned to waive the requirements of paragraphs 1 or 2, for the reasons and purposes specified in the request.

Article 56: Co-operation with States not parties to this Statute

States not parties to this Statute may assist in relation to the matters, referred to in this Part on the basis of comity, a unilateral declaration, an ad hoc arrangement or other agreement with the Court.

Article 57: Communications and documentation

1. Requests under this Part shall be in writing, or be forthwith reduced to writing, and shall be between the competent national authority and the Registrar. States parties shall inform the Registrar of the name and address of their national authority for this purpose.
2. When appropriate, communications may also be made through the International Criminal Police Organization.
3. A request under this Part shall include the following, as applicable:

   (a) a brief statement of the purpose of the request and of the assistance sought, including the legal basis and grounds for the request;
   (b) information concerning the person who is the subject of the request on the evidence sought, in sufficient detail to enable identification;
   (c) a brief description of the essential facts underlying the request; and
   (d) information concerning the complaint or charge to which the request relates and of the basis for the Court's jurisdiction.

4. A requested State which considers the information provided insufficient to enable the request to be complied with may seek further particulars.

PART 8
ENFORCEMENT

Article 58: Recognition of judgments

States parties undertake to recognize the judgments of the Court.

Article 59: Enforcement of sentences

1. A sentence of imprisonment shall be served in a State designated by the Court from a list of States which have indicated to the Court their willingness to accept convicted persons.
2. If no State is designated under paragraph 1, the sentence of imprisonment shall be served in a prison facility made available by the host State.
3. A sentence of imprisonment shall be subject to the supervision of the Court in accordance with the Rules.

Article 60: Pardon, parole and commutation of sentences

1. If, under a generally applicable law of the State of imprisonment, a person in the same circumstances who had been convicted for the same conduct by a court of that State would be eligible for pardon, parole or commutation of sentence, the State shall so notify the Court.
2. If a notification has been given under paragraph 1, the prisoner may apply to the Court in accordance with the Rules, seeking an order for pardon, parole or commutation of the sentence.

3. If the Presidency decides that an application under paragraph 2 is apparently well-founded, it shall convene a Chamber of five judges to consider and decide whether in the interests of justice the person convicted should be pardoned or paroled or the sentence commuted, and on what basis.

4. When imposing a sentence of imprisonment, a Chamber may stipulate that the sentence is to be served in accordance with specified laws as to pardon, parole or commutation of sentence of the State of imprisonment. The consent of the Court is not required to subsequent action by that State in conformity with those laws, but the Court shall be given at least 45 days' notice of any decision which might materially affect the terms or extent of the imprisonment.

5. Except as provided in paragraphs 3 and 4, a person serving a sentence imposed by the Court is not to be released before the expiry of the sentence.

ANNEX

Crimes pursuant to Treaties (see art. 20(e))

1. Grave breaches of:

    (i)   the Geneva Convention for the Amelioration of the Condition of the Wounded and Sick in Armed Forces in the Field of 12 August 1949, as defined by Article 50 of that Convention;

    (ii)   the Geneva Convention for the Amelioration of the Condition of Wounded, Sick and Shipwrecked Members of Armed Forces at Sea of 12 August 1949, as defined by Article 51 of that Convention;

    (iii) the Geneva Convention relative to the Treatment of Prisoners of War of 12 August 1949, as defined by Article 130 of that Convention;

    (iv)   the Geneva Convention relative to the Protection of Civilian Persons in Time of War of 12 August 1949, as defined by Article 147 of that Convention;

    (v)   Protocol I Additional to the Geneva Conventions of 12 August 1949 and relating to the Protection of Victims of International Armed Conflicts of June 1977, as defined by Article 85 of that Protocol.

2. The unlawful seizure of aircraft as defined by Article 1 of the Hague Convention for the Suppression of Unlawful Seizure of Aircraft of 16 December 1970.

3. The crimes defined by Article 1 of the Montreal Convention for the Suppression of Unlawful Acts against the Safety of Civil Aviation of 23 September 1971.

4. Apartheid and related crimes as defined by Article II of the International Convention on the Suppression and Punishment of the Crime of Apartheid of 30 November 1973.

5. The crimes defined by Article 2 of the Convention on the Prevention and Punishment of Crimes against Internationally Protected Persons, including Diplomatic Agents of 14 December 1973.

6. Hostage-taking and related crimes as defined by Article 1 of the International Convention against the Taking of Hostages of 17 December 1979.

7. The crime of torture made punishable pursuant to Article 4 of the Convention against Torture and Other Cruel, Inhuman or Degrading Treatment or Punishment of 10 December 1984.

8. The crimes defined by Article 3 of the Convention for the Suppression of Unlawful Acts against the Safety of Maritime Navigation of 10 March 1988 and by Article 2 of the Protocol for the Suppression of Unlawful Acts against the Safety of Fixed Platforms Located on the Continental Shelf of 10 March 1988.

9. Crimes involving illicit traffic in narcotic drugs and psychotropic substances as envisaged by Article 3(1) of the United Nations Convention against Illicit Traffic in Narcotic Drugs and Psychotropic Substances of 20 December 1988 which, having regard to Article 2 of the Convention, are crimes with an international dimension.